BR115.P7 R93 2009

God in the corridors of power
:Christian conservatives, the media,
and

33663004444598

DATE DUE

SEP 3 0 2013	

God in the Corridors of Power

God in the Corridors of Power

Christian Conservatives, the Media, and Politics in America

MICHAEL RYAN AND LES SWITZER

PRAEGER
An Imprint of ABC-CLIO, LLC

Santa Barbara, California • Denver, Colorado • Oxford, England

Library of Congress Cataloging-in-Publication Data

Ryan, Michael, 1951–
   God in the corridors of power : Christian conservatives, the media, and politics in America / Michael Ryan and Les Switzer.
      p. cm.
   Includes bibliographical references and index.
   ISBN 978–0–313–35610–0 (alk. paper) – ISBN 978–0–313–35611–7 (ebk.)
1. Conservatism—Religious aspects—Christianity. 2. Religious right—United States. 3. United States—Politics and government—2001– I. Switzer, Les. II. Title.
BR115.P7.R93   2009
322´.10973—dc22   2009015779

13 12 11 10 9   1 2 3 4 5

This book is also available on the World Wide Web as an eBook.
Visit www.abc-clio.com for details.

ABC-CLIO, LLC
130 Cremona Drive, P.O. Box 1911
Santa Barbara, California 93116-1911

This book is printed on acid-free paper (∞)

Manufactured in the United States of America

To Mike's grandson, Zachary James Ryan,
To Les's 12 grandchildren, and
To the memory of Vincent Creek

Contents

Preface

In a recent *New York Times* review of a memoir by contemporary American composer John Adams, the reviewer quoted a passage about the creative process in a section on collaboration in music: "Next to double murder-suicide, it might be the most painful thing two people can do together."[1] We can certainly identify with this statement.

Our partnership on this book project has been a long journey that at times did result in disagreements that seemed to be irresolvable. We were like two architects who had drawn up plans to build a multistory house: we found that not only did the plans not match, but also neither plan alone could do the job. Each room in the house, moreover, required special attention to detail. A comprehensive design would gradually emerge only when our plans were merged and we began to discern what we really wanted to build.

We are from different American Christian traditions—Mike Ryan from the Roman Catholic tradition and Les Switzer from the Protestant tradition. While we tried our best to describe the complexities of the Christian conservative response to the modern world, we recognize only too well that even our treatment of Protestant conservatives —especially denominations such as the Mormons, which are nurtured largely in the United States—is inadequate. Our treatment of the conservative Roman Catholic response is incomplete, and we have essentially ignored the Eastern Orthodox response. Our coverage of conservative themes in other faith traditions is also virtually absent: we have referenced only some Jewish responses to specific issues detailed in the book.

Nevertheless, we are convinced that our understanding of Christian conservatives in America's political culture in the past and at present offers a unique perspective. We examine the origins of Protestant conservatism at the beginning of the twentieth century—with its own peculiarly American brand of theological orthodoxy—and its impact on conservative politics, especially in the last 40 years or so. We frame contemporary Protestant conservative political activism as part of a larger conservative coalition that includes (a) a broad range of religious groups (other Protestant faith groups, Roman Catholics, and non-Christian groups, especially Orthodox Jews) and (b) secular conservatives associated with the Republican Party, categorized as traditionalist conservatives and neoconservatives.

We argue that the astonishing electoral successes of Christian conservatives at all levels of national, state, and local governments were made possible not only because of this coalition of political interests, but also because of an emerging consensus about what constitutes a conservative mindset in America today. And we also argue that religious conservatives would not have succeeded as well as they have without their ownership of and/or influence over commercial and noncommercial media to disseminate their ideas and attitudes. The power of the mass media, in particular, was instrumental in delivering conservative religious messages to a larger audience.

We explore the limits of Christian conservative power in America's political culture and suggest that no consensus has emerged about what role, if any, religion should play in civil society. The conservative coalition began to fracture as a political force even before the invasion of Iraq in 2003, and we offer some thoughts about what impact this might have on the Christian conservative voice in politics in the future.

We wanted to produce a book that would be a work of scholarship and that also would be easily accessible and of interest to a general audience. We have sought to provide a fair and balanced perspective, and we have tried to simplify complex issues and debates without being simplistic.

To this end, we have avoided academic jargon and most acronyms, and we have kept the number of tables and figures to a minimum. We have also defined key concepts employed in discussing specific issues, such as "homosexual," sex and sexuality, gender and the social construction of gendering, and premodern, modern, and postmodern cultures. We have tried to adhere to contemporary standards in avoiding perceived bias in our use of language. Hence we avoid personal pronouns such as "he" or "she" when referring to a generic noun. We use "humanity" or "humankind" instead of "mankind," and CE (Common Era) and BCE (Before the Common Era) instead of AD and BC.

We have standardized all biblical references. All references to the Hebrew Bible (Old Testament), for example, are based on the latest edition (1999) of *The Jewish Study Bible*, the standard English-language translation for the Jewish community.[2] All references to the Christian Bible (New Testament) are based on the 1989 edition of the New Revised Standard Version.[3]

Some of our sources are available only online. This is problematic because some URLs (uniform resource locators) may not work in the months and years after we have cited them. In most cases, however, an interested reader can visit the Web site that published the material and track it down from there. We have not provided URLs for the many court cases cited, but the original decisions are easy to find: simply type the reference—for example, *Roe v. Wade*, 410 U.S. 113 (1973) —into your Internet browser, and you should find many routes to the decision.

We leave it to the reader to decide if we succeeded with this analysis.

NOTES

1. David Hajdu, "Music Lessons," *New York Times*, October 24, 2008, Opinion-15. Hajdu was citing a passage in John Adams's memoir, *Hallelujah Junction: Composing an American Life* (New York: Farrar, Straus and Giroux, 2008).

2. The "Hebrew Masoretic Text" is the only "official Bible" for Jews, which has never been substituted for official translations in other languages as they have with some Christian denominations. "For contemporary English-speaking Jews," however, *The Jewish Study Bible* (JSB) is "the best and most widely read Jewish translation" in English. For all Jews, the TANAKH is their Bible, so they will use the two terms interchangeably. The TANAKH translation rendered by the JSB is based on the standard Hebrew Masoretic Text. The term "Hebrew Bible" is redundant for Jews, since Jews have no Bible other than the TANAKH. Translations, moreover, were less an issue "in Jewish communal life than in Christian communities" before the modern era, "because public liturgical readings from the Bible have always been in Hebrew." Since many Jewish communities in the past few centuries no longer read or understand Hebrew, the TANAKH was translated into various languages, including English. Adele Berlin and Marc

Zvi Brettler, eds., and Michael Fishbane, cons. ed., "Introduction," *The Jewish Study Bible* (Oxford, UK: Oxford University Press, 1999 edition, published in 2003), x.

3. The New Revised Standard Version (NRSV), sponsored by the Society of Biblical Literature, is the most popular English translation used both in church liturgy and in personal use for mainstream Protestant denominations (such as United Methodist, American Baptist, Presbyterian, Evangelical Lutheran Church in America, Episcopalian, Disciples of Christ, United Church of Christ, and Reformed Church of America) and for many smaller denominations. Indeed, the NRSV is "officially authorized for use by all major Christian churches: Protestant, Anglican, Roman Catholic, and Eastern Orthodox." Wayne A. Meeks, gen. ed., *New Revised Standard Version* (New York: HarperCollins, 1989 edition, published in 1993), xxv. Popularly referred to as the *HarperCollins Study Bible*, it includes the so-called Apocryphal/Deuterocanonical texts—cited in one reference in Chapter 5 (2 Maccabees).

Acknowledgments

We received considerable help along the way. We want to extend our heartfelt thanks to Michael Jost, Bill Hawes, Rabbi Samuel Karff, John Lienhard, Rabbi Shaul and Bobbie Osadchey, and Ted Stanton, who read drafts of some of these chapters; to Daniel Harmon, acquisitions editor, popular culture, Praeger Publishers, who made our project possible; and to Diana Marsan, project manager for BeaconPMG publishing services, whose editing was superb. We also want to thank those attending various adult Sunday school classes Les Switzer taught in Houston churches, who provided valuable feedback on various topics explored in the book.

We have published together or separately three book chapters and five journal articles on various themes that eventually found a home in *God in the Corridors of Power*. We have expanded considerably on these themes, and we are grateful to the book publishers and journals that printed our early efforts. These are the following:

- Michael Ryan and Les Switzer, "Propaganda and the Subversion of Objectivity: Media Coverage of the War on Terrorism in Iraq," *Critical Studies on Terrorism* 2, no. 1 (2009): 45–64.
- Michael Ryan, "Science Literacy and Risk Analysis: Relationship to the Postmodernist Critique, Conservative Christian Activists, and Professional Obfuscators," in *Handbook of Risk and Crisis Communication*, ed. Robert L. Heath and H. Dan O'Hair (New York: Routledge, 2009), 247–267.
- Michael Ryan and Les Switzer, "Mirror on a War Agenda: Conservative Christian Activists and Media Coverage of the Invasion of Iraq," in

Terrorism: Communication and Rhetorical Perspective, ed. H. Dan O'Hair, Robert L. Heath, Kevin J. Ayotte, and Gerald R. Ledlow (Cresskill, NJ: Hampton, 2008), 299–335.

- Michael Ryan, "Mainstream News Media, an Objective Approach, and the March to War in Iraq," *Journal of Mass Media Ethics* 21, no. 1 (2006): 4–29.

- Michael Ryan and Les Switzer, "Using Binary Language to Sell the War in Afghanistan," in *Community Preparedness and Response to Terrorism: Vol. 3. Communication and the Media*, series ed. James A. Johnson, Gerald R. Ledlow, and Mark A. Cwiek, and vol. ed. H. Dan O'Hair, Robert L. Heath, and Gerald R. Ledlow (Westport, CT: Praeger, 2005), 97–124.

- Les Switzer and Michael Ryan, "Reflections on Religion, Media and the Marketing of America's Wars," *International Journal of Media and Cultural Politics* 1, no. 1 (2005): 41–46.

- Michael Ryan, "Framing the War against Terrorism: US Newspaper Editorials and Military Action in Afghanistan," Gazette 66, no. 4 (2004): 363–382.

- Les Switzer, "Mediating Religion in the War on Terrorism," *Equid Novi: South African Journal for Journalism Research* 25, no. 2 (2004): 338–346.

Introduction

Christian values would be far easier to define and to live by if Jesus had simply been made to say somewhere in the gospels that scripture is (or is not) God's Word and it should (or should not) be taken literally; that a Christian is obligated (or not) to impose Christian ideology on non-Christians—to convert (or not) non-Christians to the "true" faith so they might enter the Kingdom of Heaven. It would also be helpful if Christians could know how Jesus felt about abortion and gay marriage, intelligent design and science, public funding for religious schools, and other "theological" issues that seem to plague so many Christians today.

Jesus, however, did not render judgments on these issues—issues that have ignited the ire of religious conservatives and sometimes have been molded into a powerful force in American politics. They cut across individual Christian churches and denominations, across synagogues and other places of worship, and across laity and clergy. Conservative religious language pervades not only a broad spectrum of Christianity but also significant voting constituencies of non-Christian and even nonreligious Americans. *God in the Corridors of Power* seeks to identify and to clarify these multiple, and sometimes contradictory, Christian voices and to situate them in contexts that reflect the complexities of American Christianity in the past and at present.

Before the 1960s, the views of Christian conservatives about what it meant to be a Christian in America were typically based on denominational differences. Protestants and Catholics, for example, were perceived at the time as cool or even antagonistic toward one another. Harold John Ockenga (1905–1985)—a founder with

Charles E. Fuller (1887–1968) and others of Fuller Theological Seminary, which would become a leading Protestant training school for evangelical fundamentalist clergy—"identified Catholicism as one of the chief threats to America, along with communism and secularism" in a speech before the National Association of Evangelicals in 1942.[1] Anti-Catholic prejudices among Protestant conservatives would reach a high point with the exploitation of the anti-Catholic vote during the 1960 Kennedy/Nixon presidential election.

Protestants and Catholics in reality, however, held similar economic, political, and even religious values. American Christianity began to fragment along *political* lines essentially in response to social changes that first surfaced in public discourse in the extraordinary decade of the 1960s. Ecclesiastical divisions became less distinct, while other divisions—rooted in America's changing cultural landscape—became more visible *within* these faith communities.

Roman Catholicism reflects the ideological rifts that permeated many Christian communities. Various religious and social issues in the wake of the reforms mandated by the Second Ecumenical Council of the Vatican (1962–1965), popularly known as Vatican II, had a decisive impact on American Catholicism. Reformers stepped up their challenge to official church policies on a wide range of ecclesiastical practices, including the liturgy and the status of women in religious appointments and activities, in church discipline, and in the role of the pope and the Roman Curia in church governance. They urged more robust participation in interdenominational discussions of theology and the meaning of spirituality, seminary education, and the sharing of fundamental liturgical rites such as Holy Communion. They urged a greater commitment to the Christian ecumenical movement, and they urged a more determined response to the plight of the world's poor and powerless.[2]

Vatican II was intended to liberalize the church and to make it more transparent, but these religious and social changes prompted many Catholic conservatives to seek a return to the pre-Vatican II church. The activities of Catholic reformers provoked a backlash that mirrored in some respects the experiences of their Protestant counterparts. Catholic conservatives would become the second largest religious grouping, after Protestant conservatives, in the Republican Party in the waning decades of the twentieth century.[3]

The influence of Protestant and Catholic conservatives in American politics has seldom been stronger than it has been in the past generation. These Christians are part of a political coalition—linked largely to the Republican Party—that is even broader and stronger than they are. Christian conservatives have been extremely skilled at getting their messages across, and one of their own held for eight years the most powerful political office in the United States. Though frequently misunderstood and misinterpreted, Christian conservative activism is one of the hottest continuing news topics in the mass media and the subject of numerous books, articles, and essays. In the view of many critics and admirers, these Christians have had a commanding presence in public affairs, and they have imposed, or attempted to impose, their ideological values at all levels of government.[4]

ORTHODOX CHRISTIANITY IN AMERICA

Christian conservatives differ from other Christians on a host of issues, but one overarching issue sets most apart from their more moderate or progressive Christian counterparts: their religious agenda is anchored in a very specific theological framework, which they define as Christian orthodoxy. This orthodoxy drives their political, economic, and social agendas, and they fully intend for it to drive America's political, economic, and social agendas.

Orthodox believers subscribe to several basic beliefs. They believe in God as a "Holy Trinity" (God as Father, God as Son, and God as Holy Spirit), in Jesus as The Christ (as being fully human and fully divine), and in the concept of original sin (a pollution that they believe has corrupted all of humanity from the origins of humanity). And they believe that original sin necessitated Christ's death and bodily resurrection for the salvation of humanity. The orthodox Christian knows these beliefs are the Truth, because they are proclaimed in the Word of God as foretold in what Christians call the Old Testament (Hebrew Bible) and declared in the New Testament (Christian Bible). They also believe scripture—together with reason, church tradition, and the experiences of the Christian believer—teaches them that these beliefs (a) are rooted in the beginnings of the Christian faith and (b) provide the guidelines for Christian living today.

This orthodoxy is the theological and ecclesiastical lynchpin that is supposed to bind all Christians together. Christianity must be interpreted through the lens of orthodox (meaning the "right belief") Christian doctrine, which also "implies both originality and majority opinion."[5] But the right belief was not hammered out until about 400 years after the death of Jesus. Orthodox Christianity was codified in seven so-called ecumenical councils, of which four—Nicea (325), Constantinople (381), Ephesus (431), and Chalcedon (451–452)— defined and described the boundaries of traditional Christianity, whereby orthodoxy triumphed over heresy (meaning "wrong belief").[6]

Christianity for the next 1,500 years or so adhered to an orthodox set of doctrines, creed-based ritual and liturgical practices, and a prescribed scriptural canon. For the most part, male members of a church hierarchy in Protestant, Catholic, and Eastern Orthodox congregations controlled the ecclesiastical structure until well into the twentieth century.

Some or all aspects of orthodoxy are still communicated by most Christian churches in America, and this orthodoxy is rarely questioned either in Christian media outlets or in the mass media's coverage of Christianity. Many Christian conservatives yearn for an orthodox Christian past that they believe is in harmony with their most deeply held religious and social convictions. As we shall see in Chapter 3, the essence of conservatism is continuity—continuity with established institutions and religious, ethical, and moral traditions based on a real or an imagined past.

Nevertheless, Christians in America, and America is hardly alone, have witnessed a quiet revolution in religious scholarship and ecclesiastical practice in the past 40 years or so. More and more Christians of all denominations are questioning and challenging the conditions that gave rise to an orthodox mindset, and the cumulative impact of this inquiry amounts to a crisis in the meaning of Christianity for many Christians in America.

While the church affiliations of a majority of Christians suggest that their religious perspectives are probably close to traditional orthodoxy, we argue that most Christians do not base their lives on adherence to doctrines and creeds. Orthodox Christianity, moreover, means different things to individual Christians. Above all, their religious agenda does not inevitably drive their political and social agendas—as so many contemporary political, religious, and media observers seem to think.

A DIVERSE CHRISTIAN COMMUNITY

It is not hard to imagine that someone from another planet attending almost any Sunday service in the United States might well conclude that Christianity in this country is monolithic. Members in church that day would all seem to believe in the same religious doctrines (anchored in the Bible and interpreted by the local priest or minister for believers) and worship similar religious symbols (such as the cross or the veneration of saints). The congregants would almost certainly represent a narrow range of demographics based primarily on race or ethnicity and socioeconomic status.

Beneath the surface, however, Christian perspectives across denominations and within many congregations seem to be increasingly diverse—just as the religious landscape as a whole across America is becoming more diverse. We explore differing Christian perspectives in this section by focusing on (a) the diversity of Christianity in American life, primarily by examining surveys by the polling agency Pew Forum on Religion & Public Life,[7] and (b) three distinct Christian perspectives identified as progressive, moderate, and conservative.

Diversity by the Numbers

The United States may or may not be a "Christian country," but 78.4 percent of American adults identify themselves as Christians, according to the Pew Forum's 2008 survey. Another 4.7 percent are members of other faith groups and 16.1 percent are unaffiliated. Pew surveyed 35,000 randomly selected adults 18 and over and conducted many interviews in Spanish, thereby including many Americans who often are excluded from polls.[8] An earlier Pew study conducted in 2001, moreover, suggested that many Americans take their religion seriously.[9] Sixty-four percent said religion was "very important" in their lives, 46 percent attended church at least once a week, and 60 percent attended at least once a month, as shown in Table 1. These respondents represent the core of the Christian conservative community.[10]

The 2008 survey shows that 51.3 percent of all adult Americans now say they identify with Protestant denominations, whereas 60–65 percent of respondents in surveys in the 1970s and 1980s claimed they were Protestants. The Protestant community "is characterized by significant internal diversity and fragmentation, encompassing hundreds of different denominations," but most can be categorized into one of three traditions—evangelical faith groups

Table 1. Religious and Political Attitudes and Behaviors in the United States, in Percent (2008)

Religion is "very important" in daily lives (all Americans)	56
Evangelical Churches	79
Mainline Churches	52
Black Churches	85
Catholic Churches	56
Attend church at least once a week	39
Evangelical Churches	58
Mainline Churches	34
Black Churches	59
Catholic Churches	42
Attend church at least once a month	15
Evangelical Churches	14
Mainline Churches	19
Black Churches	16
Catholic Churches	19
Bible is the Word of God to be taken literally	33
Evangelical Churches	59
Mainline Churches	2
Black Churches	62
Catholic Churches	23
There is only one way to interpret "teachings of my religion"	27
Evangelical Churches	41
Mainline Churches	14
Black Churches	39
Catholic Churches	19
"My religion is the one true faith leading to eternal life"	24
Evangelical Churches	36
Mainline Churches	12
Black Churches	34
Catholic Churches	16
Self-described political ideology is conservative	37
Evangelical Churches	52
Mainline Churches	36

Black Churches	35
Catholic Churches	36
Self-described political ideology is moderate	36
Evangelical Churches	30
Mainline Churches	41
Black Churches	36
Catholic Churches	38
Self-described political ideology is liberal	20
Evangelical Churches	11
Mainline Churches	18
Black Churches	21
Catholic Churches	18

Source: Pew Forum on Religion & Public Life, "Religion in America: Non-Dogmatic, Diverse and Politically Relevant," Pew Research Center, Washington, DC, June 23, 2008, http://pewresearch.org/pubs/876/religion-america-part-two.

(26.3 percent), mainline faith groups (18.1 percent), and historically black churches (6.9 percent).[11]

The Catholic Church has recorded, among major denominations, the largest net loss of members as many Catholics have changed their affiliations, the 2008 survey shows. While 31 percent of Americans were raised as Catholics, only 23.9 percent identified themselves as Catholic in the study. Many Catholics have opted for other faith groups—especially Protestant evangelical groups—or are no longer affiliated with any faith group. This loss is offset mainly by an influx of immigrants and partly by individuals who left another faith group for Catholicism. Catholics outnumber Protestants among foreign-born adults by 46 percent to 24 percent, but among native-born Americans, Protestants outnumber Catholics by 55 percent to 21 percent.[12]

Other denominations within the Christian community include Mormon, 1.7 percent; Jehovah's Witness, .7 percent; and Eastern Orthodox, .6 percent, according to the 2008 Pew survey. The Eastern Orthodox tradition is comprised primarily of Greek and Russian churches, but respondents mentioned roughly 12 other Orthodox churches (including Syrian, Armenian, Ukrainian, and Ethiopian Orthodox churches) of which they are members. Religious diversity and change is reflected also in the growth of the "religious unaffiliated" group, a category with which 5.8 percent of all adults identify. But even these respondents claimed that "religion," not necessarily a

Christian religion, is "somewhat important" or "very important." More than 10 percent of all adults claimed they were not religious; 4 percent identified themselves as "atheist" or "agnostic" and 6.3 percent as "secular unaffiliated."[13]

Christians in the United States are marked by variations in some demographic characteristics across denominations. Members of Protestant mainline churches, for example, seem to have higher incomes and education levels than members of Catholic and evangelical Protestant churches, as shown in Table 2.

These communities have substantially higher incomes and education levels than members of historically black churches. The percentage of people 50 and older in mainline and evangelical Protestant congregations is also somewhat higher than those of historically black and Catholic congregations.

The four Christian communities depicted in Table 2 are not diverse with regard to race. Mainline Protestant churches are overwhelmingly white, and historically black Protestant churches are overwhelmingly black. Evangelical Protestant churches also are overwhelmingly white, but they do have larger percentages of black and Latino members. The Catholic Church is more diverse than the Protestant churches with its large Hispanic population, but it has few black members.

Progressive, Moderate, and Conservative Perspectives

The Christian response to the shifts in American culture that accelerated in the 1960s has been the topic of considerable discussion in religious, academic, and political circles. Three distinct, though not mutually exclusive, strains were discernible by the 1980s. These progressive, moderate, and conservative perspectives are represented in Protestant, Catholic, and Eastern Orthodox denominations across America today.

Christian Progressives

Christian progressives are in the minority, and they represent the sharpest break with the orthodox belief system. "Orthodoxy," as retired Episcopal Bishop John Shelby Spong says, "does not mean that this point of view is true; it only means that this point of view won!"[14] They question (a) orthodox concepts of the Trinitarian Godhead, of Jesus and his ministry, (b) orthodox responses to

Table 2.   Demographics of Four Christian Communities, in Percent (2008)

Demographic Variable	Evangelical Protestant	Mainline Protestant	Historically Black Protestant	Catholic
Age				
18–29	17	14	24	18
30–49	39	36	36	41
50–64	26	28	24	24
65 and over	19	23	15	16
Race				
White	81	91	2	65
Black	6	2	92	2
Latino	7	3	4	29
Asian	2	1	0	0
Education				
Less than high school	16	8	19	17
High school graduate	40	34	40	36
Some college	24	24	25	21
College graduate	13	20	11	16
Postgraduate	7	14	5	10
Income				
Less than $30,000	34	25	47	31
$30,000–>$50,000	24	21	26	20
$50,000–>$100,000	29	33	19	30
$100,000 plus	13	21	8	19

Source: Pew Forum on Religion & Public Life, "U.S. Religious Landscape Survey," Pew Research Center, Washington, DC, June 23, 2008, http://religions.pewforum.org, 39, 44, 56, 60.

scriptural authority, (c) orthodox interpretations of the early history of Christianity, and (d) orthodox perspectives on politics and patriotism in America.

They argue that the meaning of who Jesus was and what he said and did was contested for centuries, and remains contested to this day. Scholars have shown that scribes inserted orthodox statements into many biblical texts in the centuries before the New Testament was

codified, beginning with the gospel texts themselves. Indeed, there are
so many variations in ancient manuscripts that it is impossible to
recreate the original text for any book in the New Testament.
In essence, Christian orthodoxy as we know it today is the product of
the early church fathers.[15]

Christian progressives see the Bible as a human document and the
New Testament as the human witness in words to Jesus's understanding of God. Both the Hebrew Bible and the Christian Bible consist of
literary and historical texts, whose authors are unknown, and these
texts must be examined critically using strategies and techniques
developed over the past 200 years or so. While most biblical scholars
agree that Jesus was a real human being who died about 30 CE, the
quest to reconstruct the Jesus of history has proved futile. Progressives
believe there was never an original biblical text and there was never an
original Christianity. The Bible may be *an* authority for guidance—
although many progressives would deny that the Bible is an authority—but not for specific direction in living the Christian life. The
Bible alone cannot be a template for living in today's world.

These theologians have constructed a more nuanced appreciation
of the origins and early history of Christianity that they argue forms
part of the context for the debate about the meaning of Christianity.
The development of orthodox doctrines and an established canon
has a distinct historical, linguistic, and etiological or causal trajectory
that has influenced our understanding of how and why the orthodox
Christian message came to be.

Several contemporary biblical scholars, for example, have demonstrated that the life and message of Jesus were framed in both oral
and written tradition through the sacred writings, liturgies, and
expectations of first-century Judaism. The memory of Jesus as
depicted in the gospels is not a historical narrative of his life but an
interpretive reconstruction shaped largely by the biblical traditions
of the Jewish faith. Jesus was a Jew. This Christian stance fully privileges the Judeo in the Judeo-Christian tradition, which has some profound implications for later Christian doctrine.[16]

They also challenge the mindset that gives rise to the dichotomous
language that is characteristic of Christian orthodoxy. Such language
includes opposites such as heaven versus hell, good versus bad, and
saved versus unsaved. This language inevitably privileges the orthodox
and condemns heresy. This mindset, which progressives say misinter-
prets the Jesus Way, leads to banishment from the Christian community and consignment after death to what conservatives define as hell.

They are sensitive to the reality that all of us bring a host of perspectives to bear on such terms as faith and sin and even God, perspectives that help determine how we understand these terms.

Christian progressives are generally inclusive in responding to America's contemporary culture. They do not believe Christianity is the only path to God's grace. They believe that Jews, Muslims, Buddhists, Hindus, and other faith traditions; Christians who do not believe as Christian conservatives do; and even persons of no religious faith can experience the Kingdom of God.

They subscribe to what Deepak Chopra, the celebrated writer and metaphysician of spirituality, calls the "third Jesus" that "we cannot ignore"—the Jesus beyond the mythical Jesus of history and the Jesus of Christian dogma.[17] This Jesus, as Bishop Spong puts it, is beyond "creeds, doctrines and dogmas," and beyond the "tribal boundaries" of human "theistic" definitions of God. Spong cites the words of the Christian martyr, Dietrich Bonhoeoffer (1906–1945), who said that to be a Christian "is not to be a religious human being: it is to be a whole human being. Jesus is the portrait of that wholeness."[18] This is not what the media sometimes refer to as liberal Christians or the religious Left but a religious stance that locates God's image in all of humanity—and beyond.

Christian progressives reacted much earlier and more strenuously than mainstream Christianity to the role of Christian conservatives in American political culture. They saw more clearly perhaps than other Christians how strict adherence to orthodox Christian doctrine helped generate a Christian conservative mindset that they perceive has had a devastating impact on American political, social, economic, scientific, and religious life for at least a generation. Progressive perspectives have played at best a marginal role in public debates about the role of religion in American political life, but that is the subject for another book.

Christian Moderates

Christian moderates constitute the mainstream Protestant, Eastern Orthodox, and Roman Catholic (post-Vatican II) churches in America. They may recite the Nicene Creed, for example, on a given Sunday, but individual members may also interpret the Bible through Enlightenment lenses and doubt or even reject aspects of orthodox theology, such as Jesus's virgin birth or the sinfulness of humanity as the fundamental human condition. Most accept, however, the authority of orthodox doctrine.

Many moderates are as saddened as heartened by the recorded Christian tradition—by what they see has been done and is being done in the name of Christianity. They accept that biblical authors were human, but they see the Bible as God's Word to humanity. They also accept the Bible as *an* authority for personal guidance but not necessarily for specific direction in living the Christian life. They embrace the progressive quest to find the earliest versions of biblical texts in the belief that these writings will be closer to the authors' original intent.

Moderates, often conflated with progressives in the liberal pantheon by religious conservatives, probably exhibit the widest range of theological perspectives. The varieties of religious experience within this community are reflected in a survey conducted in 2005 by Baylor University in Waco, Texas, an institution affiliated to the Southern Baptists. Demonstrating that "under the surface" American Christianity is "startlingly complex and diverse," the survey among other measures provided a revealing snapshot of how Americans conceive of God. While most Americans do agree that God exists, they do not agree about "what God is like, what God wants in the world, or how God feels about politics."[19]

Most of the 1,721 respondents who participated in the survey held a view of God that fit one of four basic types. Slightly more than 31 percent had what the researchers called a Type A view of God, who is authoritarian, angry, and punishing, but who helps them in decision making, and was active both in individual lives and in the wider world. About 23 percent held what they called a Type B view of God, who is benevolent and more forgiving, an active and positive influence in individual lives and in the wider world. About 16 percent held what they called a Type C view of God, who is critical and not pleased with what is happening in the world, but who is nevertheless not actively engaged in the world (divine justice will be meted out in another life). Slightly more than 24 percent held what they called a Type D view of God, who is distant and indifferent, neither benevolent nor judgmental nor active in human affairs, but who is a kind of transcendental force that sets the laws of nature in motion.

Members of the same churches often held different concepts of God, which suggests at least a partial explanation for enduring tensions over orthodox doctrine within all three categories of Christians. The four-type God model was also somewhat predictive of political and social attitudes. Evangelical Protestants (about 35 percent of the respondents were white) and African-American Protestants (evangelicals constituted 72 percent of this population) were most inclined to see God as authoritarian and to find abortion and gay marriage, for example, as "always wrong."

Christian moderates wrestle with contemporary social issues because, above all, the religious perspectives of their denominational affiliations do not necessarily drive their personal political, economic, and social perspectives. They are more open to an inclusive, egalitarian society than their counterparts were in previous generations, but responses to specific social issues are often diverse and even contradictory, both within and among specific denominations.

Most moderates accept scientific evolution—finally established as official Catholic Church doctrine in 1996, for example, by the late Pope John Paul II (1920–2005)—but some sympathize with the teaching of intelligent design alongside scientific evolution in the classroom. Some distinguish between gay civil rights, which they support, and gay marriage rights, which they oppose. While some moderates believe early-stage embryos are human and must be protected against stem cell research and cloning, others join Orthodox Jews, who accept "the moral status of the pre-embryo as less than fully human" and "endorse a range of stem-cell research that involves therapeutic cloning."[20] While the mass media seldom have provided the kind of coverage that reflects these ambiguities, the majority of Christians in America today are Christian moderates. In America's present political culture, they could with justification be called swing voters.

Christian Conservatives

Christian conservatives, the focus of this book, demonstrate the most rigid support of the orthodox belief system. Indeed, they adhere to an interpretation of orthodox doctrine that in some ways is distinctly American in origin. They insist that God intervened in the human story once and for all time in the person of Jesus The Christ, the personal savior of humankind. Eternal salvation for these Christians is possible only for those who accept The Word as expressed in biblical texts (such as John 1:1–4).[21] This perspective frames all other expressions of Christian belief and behavior.

Christian conservatives generally believe the Bible is inspired directly by God, biblical writings are inerrant and infallible (free of error), and the believer must read the Bible literally (using acceptable translations such as the Authorized King James Version or the New International Version). Orthodox doctrine is accepted without question, because they believe these creeds are centered in the Bible. The Bible was *the* authority for living the Christian life in the past, and it remains *the* authority for living the Christian life today.

Orthodox theology as interpreted by many Christian conservatives, moreover, is tied inextricably to a range of political, social, and economic values that they define as components of an orthodox Christian perspective. Conservative theology and political philosophy, church-state relations, heterosexual domestic marriage and family life, the capitalist free-enterprise system, and the meaning of patriotism are among the components of a distinctly American form of Christian conservative orthodoxy.

As we shall outline in subsequent chapters, the portrait of American life that emerges from this worldview constitutes the key religious component of the conservative coalition in Republican Party (GOP) politics. Christian conservatives have wielded enormous power within the coalition because they help determine (a) which issues will be emphasized and which will not, (b) the positions other conservative coalition members take on these issues, and (c) who will be the GOP standard-bearers in national, state, and local elections.

Christian conservative orthodoxy has also generated and continues to generate tensions *within* conservative coalition politics. Tensions may be heightened, for example, when Christian conservatives use their elected or appointed positions to impose their religious values on the larger society (as when a school board votes to have sex abstinence or intelligent design taught in health and biology classes), or when Christian leaders try to blackmail public officials to vote in particular ways (as when a Catholic bishop urges congregants to vote against abortion candidates or orders a local priest to withhold Holy Communion from a public servant who will not use his position to oppose abortion). These tensions are important for understanding today's Christian conservative challenge.

Christian conservatives are the counterparts in many ways to Christian progressives. Both perspectives represent minority views within the American Christian population as a whole, but Christian conservatives are generally narrow in their vision of how God is revealed in the world and narrow in their response to contemporary cultural politics. Although the Christian conservative community is not a monolithic force, many Christian conservatives do demonstrate the habit of mind, as religion scholar Martin E. Marty and historian R. Scott Appleby once put it, of "beleaguered believers." While this is a reference to the evangelical fundamentalist core of this religious community, it also manifests a conservative state of mind that is broader than the need "to preserve their distinctive identity as a people or group."[22]

The cliché that the most segregated time of the week is in church on a Sunday morning remains a reality for all so-called racial or ethnic groups in America.[23] But white Christians in monoracial churches, especially Protestant conservatives, constitute the religious bedrock of Christian conservatism today. They conform in many respects to an expanded WASP label (White, Anglo-Saxon, Protestant-Catholic-Eastern Orthodox). Mass media's coverage of the role of religion in contemporary politics, moreover, has focused overwhelmingly on these Christian conservative perspectives.

CHRISTIAN POLITICAL ACTIVISM

Christians and non-Christians have long argued about the extent to which organized religion should be involved in politics—some suggesting that religious groups and individuals have an *obligation* to participate in politics and some maintaining that *any* participation is inappropriate. One finds a myriad of attitudes between these dichotomous positions, as shown in Table 3, which reports results from a 2004 national survey by the Pew Forum on Religion & Public Life.

Members of several religious traditions were represented in this survey, but three major Christian communities in America—evangelical Protestants, mainline Protestants, and Roman Catholics—were identified. Christians within these three communities (all white adults) were further subdivided into traditionalist, centrist, or modernist—a political distinction that parallels the theological distinction we have made among Christian conservatives (traditionalists), moderates (centrists), and progressives (modernists). Traditionalists identified with the highest levels, modernists with the lowest levels, and centrists with medium levels of religious engagement (based on a range of variables such as church attendance). Traditionalists are characterized by more orthodox beliefs, modernists by more heterodox beliefs, and centrists by a combination of orthodox and heterodox beliefs.[24]

The divisions among the three main white religious communities were most prominent in response to the question, "Organized religious groups should stay out of politics." A mean of 67.3 percent of the traditionalists within each of these groups *disagreed* that organized religion should stay out of politics, as shown in Table 3. The major ethnic Christian minority communities—black Protestants, Latino Protestants, and Latino Catholics—also supported religious participation in politics. The modernists in these communities *agreed* by a mean of 59.3 percent that religious groups should *not* be involved in politics. Other religious constituencies also agreed by a majority in all cases that religious groups should stay out of politics. The centrists were more or less evenly divided.

The volatility of Christian views about the acceptability of mixing religion and politics is reflected in the latest survey results by the Pew Center. While 28 percent of *all* white, evangelical Protestants said churches should keep out of politics in 2004, 39 percent expressed that view in 2008. Sixty percent of white, non-Hispanic Catholics said churches should stay out of politics in 2004, compared to 59 percent in 2008. Twenty-four percent of *Republicans* who attend church weekly said in 2004 that churches should keep out of politics (compared to 48 percent who attend less frequently), and 43 percent who attend weekly said in 2008 that churches should keep out of politics (compared to 59 percent who attend less often).[25]

Christian views about the religion-politics relationship, however, apparently are more complex than these survey data suggest. A study by the Pew Research Center in 2007 shows 90 percent of evangelical Protestants "completely agree" or "mostly agree" that it is important for a president to have strong religious beliefs, compared to 66 percent for mainline Protestants, and 70 percent for Catholics. Nevertheless, 53 percent of evangelical Protestants, 68 percent of mainline Protestants, and 68 percent of white, non-Hispanic Catholics *disagreed* that churches should endorse political candidates. These opinions may have been influenced by the fact that federal law prohibits tax-exempt groups from opposing or supporting political candidates.[26]

Some who agree that it is appropriate for religious groups to participate in politics are activists, and it seems reasonable to assume that the ranks of Christian conservative activists are filled primarily by traditionalists in evangelical Protestant, mainline Protestant, and Roman Catholic denominations. If this assumption is accurate, the 2004 survey suggests that perhaps 15 percent (based on the percentage of those traditionalist respondents who agreed that religious groups should *be* in politics) are potential political activists. This excludes centrists and modernists within these communities, individuals within other

Table 3.   American Views of Political Activism by Religious Affiliation (2004)

Religion	Percentage of Population	Question: Organized religious groups should stay out of politics, in percent	
		Agree	Disagree
Evangelical Protestant	26.3	35	65
Traditionalist	12.6	25	75
Centrist	10.8	43	57
Modernist	2.9	53	47
Mainline Protestant	16.0	48	52
Traditionalist	4.3	35	65
Centrist	7.0	49	51
Modernist	4.7	61	39
Latino Protestant	2.8	40	60
Black Protestant	9.6	35	65
Catholic	17.5	52	48
Traditionalist	4.4	38	62
Centrist	8.1	53	47
Modernist	5.0	64	36
Latino Catholic	4.5	40	60
Other Christians	2.7	57	43
Other Faiths	2.7	60	40
Jewish	1.9	57	43
Unaffiliated	16.0	64	36
Unaffiliated Believer	5.3	53	47
Secular	7.5	68	32
Atheist, Agnostic	3.2	74	26

Source: John C. Green, *The American Religious Landscape and Political Attitudes: A Baseline for 2004* (Akron, OH: University of Akron's Ray C. Bliss Institute of Applied Politics, 2004). Survey cosponsored by Pew Forum on Religion & Public Life, http://pewforum.org/docs/index.php?DocID=55.

religious groups, and nonreligious respondents who might also be political activists.

Christian traditionalists—what we are referring to as Christian conservatives—are most likely to be political activists: these Christians are most likely to campaign and to vote for conservative candidates and issues. They serve conservative political causes by writing letters to editors and officials, marching in demonstrations, making speeches, filing lawsuits, posting photographs of women entering abortion clinics, and working in political campaigns.

Most Christian conservatives, however, are not political activists. They support and oppose causes primarily by voting, and like all Americans, they are subjected to a sometimes-bewildering array of choices. These choices generate a variety of diverse and sometimes unpredictable responses, as suggested by their attitudes toward social issues.

Diverse Views of Social Issues

Evangelical Protestants and other Christian conservatives often are referred to as social conservatives, in part because many do take a high-profile conservative stance on issues such as abortion, the death penalty, prayer in schools, and using fetal stem cells in medical research. The only statement a majority in the religious community could agree on in the 2004 Pew Forum survey (Table 4) was one supporting government aid for the disadvantaged—57 percent of all respondents agreed on this issue. There was also wide support for the death penalty. Fifty-nine percent of white evangelical Protestants, however, disagreed with the statement, "The death penalty for convicted murderers should be replaced with life in prison without parole." Only 34 percent of black Protestants disagreed and 53 percent of Catholics disagreed.[27]

There were important differences between Protestant and Catholic traditionalists and centrists on most of the remaining issues. Protestants and Catholic traditionalists stood out in rejecting same-sex marriage. Evangelical Protestants and Catholics also stood out for supporting bans on fetal stem cell research, and they had the highest percentages of respondents (along with "other Christians," mainly Mormons) who believed that abortions should always be illegal. Modernists in each of the three dominant white Christian communities

Table 4. Religious Responses to Six Social Issues, in Percent (2004)

Faith Group	Agree Abortion Always Illegal	Agree to Ban Fetal Stem Cell Research	Replace Death Penalty with Life Sentence	Support Same-Sex Marriage	Support Gay Rights	Government Must Help Disadvantaged
Traditionalist						
Evangelical Protestant	32	50	25	3	36	52
Mainline Protestant	8	33	36	10	44	56
Catholic	26	51	33	11	51	52
Centrist						
Evangelical Protestant	19	34	26	17	50	57
Mainline Protestant	7	28	27	27	62	47
Catholic	12	32	27	29	59	59
Modernist						
Evangelical Protestant	7	22	32	34	63	62
Mainline Protestant	2	12	39	38	73	55
Catholic	3	15	34	51	83	53
Latino Protestant	22	35	49	20	47	65

Table 4 (continued)

Faith Group	Agree Abortion Always Illegal	Agree to Ban Fetal Stem Cell Research	Replace Death Penalty with Life Sentence	Support Same-Sex Marriage	Support Gay Rights	Government Must Help Disadvantaged
Black Protestant	21	47	34	18	40	60
Latino Catholic	18	33	44	34	61	60
Other Christian	35	34	32	15	41	52
Other Faiths	3	18	41	50	68	67
Jewish	0	9	49	55	82	72
Unaffiliated Believers	13	33	30	32	57	62
Secular	5	14	31	53	79	62
Atheist, Agnostic	0	5	39	72	89	64

Source: John C. Green, *The American Religious Landscape and Political Attitudes: A Baseline for 2004* (Akron, OH: University of Akron's Ray C. Bliss Institute of Applied Politics, 2004), 28, 40, 43, 45. Survey cosponsored by Pew Forum on Religion & Public Life, http://pewforum.org/docs/index.php?DocID=55.

were at variance with traditionalists in all social categories except for the death penalty and government aid to the disadvantaged.

Pew's 2007 survey suggests the view of social issues by Christians who attend church at least once a week is somewhat different from those who attend less frequently. Eighty-eight percent of white evangelical Protestants who attend church weekly, for example, opposed gay marriage, compared to 69 percent of those who attend less frequently. Fifty-nine percent of Catholics (and 58 percent of white mainline Protestants) who attend at least weekly opposed gay marriage, compared to 42 percent (and 44 percent) who attend less frequently. Results are similar for using fetal stem cells in medical research. Sixty-eight percent of white evangelicals who attend church at least weekly opted to save the stem cells, compared to 37 percent who attend less often. Forty-six percent of white, non-Hispanic Catholics who attend Mass at least weekly opted for preserving stem cells, compared to 22 percent for those attending less often.[28]

Attitude Changes over Time

Two contentious social issues, abortion and gay rights, illustrate the unpredictability of Christian voting patterns between the 1992 and 2004 national elections. Opposition to abortion rights has steadily increased within the religious community, the Pew Forum surveys suggest. Anti-abortion positions for the evangelical Protestant community, which stood at 56 percent in the 1992 survey, had increased to 69 percent by the 2004 survey, and similar increases occurred among black Protestants (to 54 percent from 46 percent), white Catholics (to 48 percent from 40 percent), and Latino Catholics (to 57 percent from 47 percent).

Only Christian modernists and the Jewish community became less enamored with anti-abortion positions during this period. Jewish responses to this issue declined to 16 percent from 20 percent— reflecting the 2004 survey, in which none of the Jewish respondents (along with atheists and agnostics) agreed that abortions should always be illegal. Anti-abortion advocates among religious communities overall rose to 48 percent in 2004 from 40 percent in 1992, a net increase of 8 percentage points.[29]

Attitudes toward gay rights showed the opposite trend in the Pew Forum surveys. Given the question that "homosexuals should have the same rights as other Americans," even evangelical Protestants as a whole recorded an increase of 10 percentage points between 1992 (35 percent) and 2004 (45 percent). Mainline Protestant support increased by 5 percentage points (to 60 percent), Roman Catholic support by 7 percentage points (to 64 percent), Latino Catholic support by 5 percentage points (to 61 percent), and Jewish support by 14 percentage points (to 82 percent). Support by the religiously "unaffiliated" increased by 16 percentage points (to 73 percent) in 2004. The only negative view on gay rights was in the black Protestant category, in which support decreased by a remarkable 19 percentage points between the 1992 (59 percent) and 2004 (40 percent) surveys.[30]

Personal views, of course, change as new issues and problems emerge. Polling just prior to the 2008 election suggests that the economy was the number one concern for white, non-Hispanic Catholic voters who attend Mass weekly, and the number two concern for white evangelical Protestants who attend church weekly. Terrorism was the number two concern for these Catholic voters, and moral values was the number one concern for white evangelical Protestants who attend church weekly. Abortion was number 10, and gay marriage was number 12 for evangelicals; abortion was number 10 for Catholic voters, and gay marriage was number 12.[31]

Religious Affiliation and Party Membership

Forty-two percent of Americans who claimed religious affiliations in 2004 were self-described Democrats and 38 percent were self-described Republicans—a ratio that had not changed since 1992.[32] Nevertheless, the figures had changed dramatically among some Christian conservative groups, which were indeed partially responsible for a rightward drift in U.S. politics in the 2004 national elections, as suggested in Table 5.

Evangelical Protestants made the most dramatic shift regardless of their level of religious engagement: while they favored Republicans (48 percent) over Democrats (32 percent) in 1992, the ratio had widened considerably by 2004 with 56 percent favoring Republicans and 27 percent Democrats. Roman Catholic voting patterns, once a majority Democratic constituency, have also been shifting toward the Republicans. Democratic loyalties (44 percent) were nearly on a par with Republican loyalties (41 percent) in 2004.

Table 5. Religious Preference and Party Affiliations, in Percent (2004)*

	2004		1992–2004 Net Change	
	Republican	**Democrat**	**Republican**	**Democrat**
Evangelical Protestant	56	27	+8	−5
Mainline Protestant	44	39	−6	+7
Black Protestant	11	71	+1	−6
Roman Catholic	41	44	+3	+1
Latino Catholic	15	61	−7	+12
Jewish	21	68	+3	+23
Unaffiliated	27	43	−3	+2

*Independents were omitted from this presentation.
Source: John C. Green, *The American Religious Landscape and Political Attitudes: A Baseline for 2004* (Akron, OH: University of Akron's Ray C. Bliss Institute of Applied Politics, 2004), 9. Survey cosponsored by The Pew Forum on Religion & Public Life, http://pewforum.org/docs/index.php?DocID=55.

Democratic gains have been most noticeable, according to these surveys, among mainline Protestants (narrowing the Republican majority, which stood at 50 percent in 1992 to 44 percent in 2004), Latino Catholics, Jewish, and religious "unaffiliated" voters. The traditionalists in the three major faith communities—evangelical Protestant (70 percent), mainline Protestant (59 percent), and Catholic (57 percent) Christians—stood out as the leaders in terms of Republican partisanship in 2004.[33]

Democrats had scored some gains at the Republicans' expense by late 2007. Thirty-four percent of Protestant evangelicals said they were Democrats or leaned toward the Democratic Party (as opposed to 50 percent for the Republicans), compared to 43 percent of mainline church members (41 percent for the Republicans), 78 percent of black church members (10 percent for the Republicans), and 48 percent of Catholics (33 percent for the Republicans). Republicans lost strength, and Democrats gained support among all religious groups except evangelicals.[34]

The Democratic Party was perceived to be far less friendly toward religion in general than the Republican Party—a precipitous drop to 29 percent in 2005, for example, from 40 percent in 2004 and 42 percent in 2003. The majority of respondents (55 percent) felt the Republican Party was friendlier toward religion. Respondents overall said Republicans were most concerned about protecting religious values—the margin was 51 percent Republican and 28 percent Democratic in 2005. But respondents also said Democrats were most concerned about "protecting the freedom of citizens to make personal choices"—the margin being almost identically reversed with 52 percent Democratic and 30 percent Republican in 2005.[35]

THE CONSERVATIVE COALITION

The seeds of the conservative coalition, as we define the term, were planted even before the 1960s, but the coalition emerged as a potent political force essentially during the 1970s and 1980s and consolidated its gains in the 1990s. It began losing some of this force during the first decade of the twenty-first century. The coalition developed in three steps, beginning with Christian conservatives, who formed the largest segment of this coalition. A driving force behind the Christian conservative movement was Protestant evangelical fundamentalism–a force that has a distinct historical and ecclesiastical trajectory in the United States.

The second step was the effort by Protestant conservative activists to forge alliances with like-minded conservatives in nonconformist Protestant communities (especially the Mormons), in non-Protestant Christian communities (especially the Roman Catholics), and in some non-Christian communities (especially Orthodox Jews), as struggles over various religious-cum-social issues, the so-called culture wars, intensified.

The third step was the attempt by secular conservatives—politicians whose understanding of conservatism is not driven by perceptions of divine intent—to tap into these alienated religious communities. These conservatives—composed initially of traditionalists with a later infusion of so-called neoconservatives—have been associated with the Republican Party for at least 50 years.

Some traditionalist conservatives adhered to the historic themes of political conservatism—limited government, free markets, and a balanced budget—but the neoconservatives in positions of influence during and after the Reagan era were more concerned about issues relating to the economy, the military establishment, and America's post-Cold War role in international affairs. While they might have had few if any religious convictions, these secular fundamentalists recognized much earlier than their Democratic counterparts that religious groups constituted a vast, alienated, and largely underutilized source of new recruits for the Republican Party.[36]

GOD IN THE CORRIDORS OF POWER

Christian conservatives comprise the core of a coalition of religious and secular interest groups determined to shape public policy, and in the process they have left an indelible mark on America's political culture. Protestant conservatives are the dominant religious force in the conservative coalition, and this study begins by framing the history of this movement in the context of changes in America's economy, knowledge industry, and society over the past century or so. Protestant conservatives—however diverse members were in terms of motives and interests—were unquestionably the most significant constituency in the Republican Party by the last decades of the twentieth century (Chapter 1).

Second, we describe some of the ways in which Christian conservatives use various media of communication to promote the gospel of Christian conservatism. They exercise power within Christian communities, for example, by using church-controlled media, influencing seminary curricula, and disseminating religious materials with orthodox interpretations of scripture and church history. Nevertheless, these activists would not have succeeded as well as they did without their ownership of and/or influence over commercial as well as noncommercial media to disseminate their ideas to broader audiences.

Mainstream media coverage of religion became more critical with the emergence of a conservative religious coalition during the latter part of the twentieth century, but the kind of skepticism journalists typically brought to their interactions with politicians and other partisan sources remained relatively rare in their coverage of religion news. The emergence of an independent conservative media establishment in America in the past 35 years or so—and Christian conservatives have been in the forefront of these developments—had an enormous impact on the framing of a conservative mindset in America's political culture (Chapter 2).

Third, we explore the meaning of political conservatism and profile the conservative mindset in America today. Conservatives tend to resist change, yearn for an imagined state of affairs that they believe once constituted the *status quo* in America, and accept the view that societies are invariably hierarchical. The last point suggests for conservatives that freedom takes precedence over equality, because they are convinced wealth and power cannot be shared equally. The conservative mindset is also characterized by certain psychological tendencies—tendencies toward authoritarianism and intolerance of ambiguity, and the need to seek closure (Chapter 3).

Fourth, we examine the limits of religious power in America's political culture today. Though formidable, Christian conservatives are still constrained by constitutional and federal case law—even though the activities of the George W. Bush White House may seem to blur traditional distinctions between church and state. No consensus has emerged within the Christian majority about what role if any religion should play in civil society (Chapter 4).

Fifth, we demonstrate, using five contemporary issues, the ways in which Christian conservative activists gain and exercise political power through elective and appointive positions. We decided to focus on predominately national, rather than international, issues and on issues that provoke conflict within conservative religious communities. Each issue exhibits a broader context and generates enduring tensions that are explored in the chapter.

Chapter 5 first describes the power of patriarchy and religion in the construction and maintenance of sex and gender models and then explores the controversies about abortion and contraception. Chapter 6 focuses on gay marriage and family rights. Chapter 7 probes the battle over the teaching of scientific evolution and intelligent design in the context of the campaign to transform public school education. Chapter 8 considers the response to terrorism just before the invasion of Afghanistan, and Chapter 9 examines the run-up to the war in Iraq in the context of what has now been stereotyped as the war against terrorism.

We conclude this book by revisiting the cumulative impact of the conservative religious voice on public policies today. The conservative political coalition began to fracture even before George W. Bush started his second term in 2004 and accelerated after the election. We end with some thoughts about what a Christian stance in American politics might look like now and in the future (Chapter 10).

NOTES

1. D. G. Hart, "Conservatism, the Protestant Right, and the Failure of Religious History," *The Journal of the Historical Society* 4, no. 4 (2004): 447–493, p. 465.

2. The Second Ecumenical Council of the Vatican was opened in 1962 by Pope John XXIII and was closed in 1965 by Pope Paul VI. "Cover Story: Vatican II; 40 Years Later," *National Catholic Reporter Online*, undated, www.natcath.org/NCR_Online/archives/100402/vaticanII.htm.

3. An estimated 31 million Catholics, for example, voted in the 2004 presidential election: 16 million Catholics (52 percent of the total Catholic vote and 56 percent of the white Catholic vote) voted for George W. Bush. An estimated 21 million Protestant evangelicals (78 percent of the white evangelical vote) voted for this candidate. Richard N. Ostling, "The 2004 Election Reinforced America's Religious and Moral Divide," *Standard Times*, November 4, 2004, at http://archive.southcoasttoday.com/daily/11-04/11-05-04/a02wn865.htm. Ostling is the Associated Press's religion writer.

4. The critique of the conservative religious presence in America's contemporary political culture has become virtually a cottage industry. Three recent books suggest the range of responses to this challenge. Michelle Goldberg, *Kingdom Coming: The Rise of Christian Nationalism* (New York: W. W. Norton, 2006); Chris Hedges, *American Fascists: The Christian Right and the War on America* (New York: Free Press, 2006); Kevin Phillips, *American Theocracy: The Peril and Politics of Radical Religion, Oil, and Borrowed Money in the 21st Century* (New York: Viking, 2006). For an uncritical but scholarly reading in support of the new religious establishment, see D. Michael Lindsay, *Faith in the Halls of Power: How Evangelicals Joined the American Elite* (Oxford, UK: Oxford University Press, 2007).

5. Bart D. Ehrman, *Lost Christianities: The Battles for Scripture and the Faiths We Never Knew* (Oxford, UK: Oxford University Press, 2003), 164.

6. See Henry Bettenson and Chris Maunder, eds., *Documents of the Christian Church*, 3rd ed. (Oxford, UK: Oxford University Press, 1999), especially 27–28 (on the Nicene Creed).

7. The U.S. census does not include a religious profile of the American population, so surveys on religion in America are conducted by nongovernmental agencies.

8. Pew Forum on Religion & Public Life, "U.S. Religious Landscape Survey," Pew Research Center, Washington, DC, 2008, http://religions.pewforum.org. The telephone survey (including 500 respondents who had cell phones only) was conducted by Princeton Survey Research Associates from May 8 to August 13, 2007. The survey was not bilingual in that most interviewers could not speak Spanish. Households identified in an initial call as non-English speaking were contacted later by an interviewer who could speak Spanish.

9. The Pew Research Center conducted random-digit, nationwide telephone interviews with 2,041 adults, including an over-sample of 197 African Americans, in March 5–18, 2001. The margin of error was plus or minus 2.5 percentage points. Pew Research Center for the People & the Press, "Faith-Based Funding Backed, But Church-State Doubts Abound," Pew Research Center, Washington, DC, April 10, 2001, http://people-press. org/report/15/faith-based-funding-backed-but-church-state-doubts-abound (introduction and summary) and http://people-press.org/report/? pageid=117 (survey methodology).

10. America's religious stance is relatively strong, however, only in relation to other nations deemed to be developed. In a 2002 survey, 59 percent of U.S. respondents claimed religion was "very important" in their lives. The combined average of selected countries in Europe, Canada, South Korea, and Japan was 23 percent—Poland being closest to the United States in the "developed" group with 36 percent. Religion, however, would seem to be a dominant factor in the lives of the vast majority of the world's population living in the so-called emerging or developing nations. Respondents in selected countries of Africa (average of 87 percent), Asia (77 percent), and Latin America (65 percent) reacted even more positively to this question than U.S. respondents. The Pew Research Center interviewed 38,263 people in the 44-nation survey, and the questionnaire was translated into 46 languages and dialects. The religion component was part of a Pew Global Attitudes Project entitled, "What The World Thinks in 2002." Respondents were asked the following religion question: "How important is religion in your life—very important, somewhat important, not too important, or not at all important?" The data were collected in July–October 2002. The margins of error, depending on the nation, ranged from 1.8 to 4.4 percentage points. "Among Wealthy Nations, U.S. Stands Alone in Its Embrace of Religion," Pew Research Center for the People & the Press, Washington, DC, December 19, 2002, http://people-press.org/report/15/faith-based-funding-backed-but-church-state-doubts-abound (introduction and summary).

11. "U.S. Religious Landscape," 5. For a list of Protestant denominations by family and tradition, see pp. 103–107.

12. Ibid., 5–6.

13. Ibid, 5. For figures in other surveys on respondents declaring they were not affiliated to any religion, see fn. 19 below and Chapter 1, fn. 30.

14. John Shelby Spong, "The Rise of Fundamentalism, Part I: Fundamentalism's Roots," March 7, 2007, unpublished article, https://secure .agoramedia.com/manage_spong.asp (requires registration and fee). Spong and numerous other religious scholars have been arguing for many years for a new paradigm—see, for example, Spong's, *A New Christianity for a New World: Why Traditional Faith Is Dying and How a New Faith Is Being Born* (San Francisco: HarperSanFrancisco, 2001)—that in part calls for a non-theistic God, a God freed of much that has been traditionally defined as the

doctrinal content of the Christian faith. Methodist Bishop of Chicago C. Joseph Sprague—to take another example—has said much the same thing in claiming, "Jesus the Messiah, the Christ of God, Was Fully Human," *United Methodist Reporter*, November 8, 2002.

15. See, for example, Bart D. Ehrman, *The Orthodox Corruption of Scripture: The Effect of Early Christological Controversies on the Text of the New Testament* (New York: Oxford University Press, 1993). As Ehrman puts it, "[T]here are more differences among our [biblical] manuscripts than there are words in the New Testament." Bart D. Ehrman, *Misquoting Jesus: The Story Behind Who Changed the Bible and Why* (San Francisco: HarperSanFrancisco, 2005), 10.

16. The literature on Jesus in the context of the Judaism of his day has also become a cottage industry for Jewish as well as Christian scholars. Geza Vermes is one of the early interpreters, and his book, *Jesus the Jew: A Historian's Reading of the Gospels* (Minneapolis: Fortress Press 1973), is a classic text in the field. See also Amy-Jill Levine, *The Misunderstood Jew: The Church and the Scandal of the Jewish Jesus* (New York: HarperCollins, 2006); and John Shelby Spong, *Jesus for the Non-Religious: Recovering the Divine at the Heart of the Human* (New York: HarperSanFrancisco, 2007), Part 2 (chapters 12–18).

17. Chopra describes the "third" Jesus as a man whose spiritual teachings guide and inspire men and women, not just Christians, to experience God personally. The first Jesus is the historical Jesus, the "rabbi who wandered the shores of northern Galilee many centuries ago," who "intended to save the world by showing others the path to God-consciousness," and who has been "swept away by history." Millions worship the second Jesus, but he never existed and he "doesn't even lay claim to the fleeting substance of the first Jesus. This is the Jesus built up over thousands of years by theologians and other scholars. . . . This second Jesus cannot be embraced without embracing theology first." Chopra argues that Christianity should embrace the third Jesus; it should be inclusive, not exclusive, and it should strive to encourage individual spiritual growth and insight. See Deepak Chopra, *The Third Jesus: The Christ We Cannot Ignore* (New York: Harmony, 2008), 8–10.

18. Spong, *Jesus for the Non-Religious*, 137, 204, 213–214, 263, 275. As Spong says, "I am elated to discern that theism is nothing more than a human definition of God and that atheism is simply the denial of that human definition" (133).

19. Baylor Institute for Studies of Religion, "American Piety in the 21st Century: New Insights to the Depth and Complexity of Religion in the U.S.," unpublished report, September 6, 2006, www.baylor.edu/content/services/document.php/33304.pdf. And 10.8 percent of the respondents claimed they were "truly unaffiliated"—having no interest in or ties to religion. The survey utilized a mixed-mode sampling design (telephone and self-administered mailed surveys) and demographic measures as well as religion measures. It was administered by the Gallup organization. The questionnaire (with 77 questions and almost 400 possible responses) was the

most nuanced and most detailed of any religious survey the authors have seen. The Baylor study offered 16 words to characterize God and provided 10 descriptions relating to God's involvement in the world. The margin of error was plus or minus 4 percentage points.

20. William A. Galston, "Catholics, Jews & Stem Cells: When Believers Beg to Differ," *Commonweal*, May 20, 2005, 13–17, p. 16.

21. John 1:1–4: "In the beginning was the Word, and the Word was with God, and the Word was God. He was in the beginning with God. All things came into being through him, and without him not one thing came into being. What has come into being in him was life, and the life was the light of all people."

22. Martin E. Marty and R. Scott Appleby, *Fundamentalism and the State: Remaking Polities, Economies, and Militance*, Vol. 3, The Fundamentalism Project (Chicago: University of Chicago Press, 1993), 3.

23. Most Protestants—indeed, most Christians—reside in segregated congregations. About 7 percent of America's congregations—and less than 5 percent of Protestant congregations—are multiracial (no ethnic group is 80 percent or more of the total congregation). Tara Dooley, "A Mix in Faith: Fort Bend Church Eschews Ethnicity in Favor of Outreach to Community," *Houston Chronicle*, May 22, 2004, E1, E4.

24. Progressive (modernist) and moderate (centrist) Christians, of course, are also actively engaged in political as well as religious activities, but they are a minority within these constituencies. Green and his colleagues surveyed 4,000 randomly selected adults representing 18 Christian communities (with a margin of error plus or minus 2 percentage points). The questions used in developing these subcategories (questions relating to religious belief and behavior) were combined in a single religious scale—from the lowest to the highest levels of religious engagement. The pollsters decided that the Jewish faith should be identified independently of other, non-Christian faiths.

25. The Pew Research Center for the People & the Press, *More Americans Question Religion's Role in Politics*, Pew Research Center, Washington, DC, August 21, 2008, http://pewforum.org/docs/?DocID=337. Thirty-seven percent of Republicans said in 2004 that churches should stay out of politics, compared to 51 percent in 2008. Results, based on a nationwide sample of 2,905 adults, were gathered July 31–August 10, 2008. The margin of error was plus or minus 2 percentage points.

26. The Pew Research Center for the People & the Press, "Religion in Campaign '08: Clinton and Giuliani Seen as Not Highly Religious; Romney's Religion Raises Concerns," Pew Research Center, Washington, DC, September 6, 2007, http://pewforum.org/surveys/campaign08. Pew surveyed 3,002 adults in this random sample during the period August 1–18, 2007. The margin of error was plus or minus 2 percentage points.

27. John C. Green, *The American Religious Landscape and Political Attitudes: A Baseline for 2004* (Akron, OH: University of Akron's Ray C. Bliss Institute of Applied Politics, 2004), 43, 44. Survey cosponsored by the Pew Research Center, Washington, DC.

28. The 2007 Pew Research Center survey cited 57 percent of white evangelical Protestant respondents, who said it was more important to preserve the potential lives of human embryos than to use those embryos to find medical cures. Only 28 percent of mainline Protestants and 32 percent of Catholics, however, said it was more important to save the embryos. "Religion in Campaign '08," 14.

29. Green, *American Religious Landscape*, 42 (Table 21).

30. Ibid., 47 (Table 24).

31. Pew Research Center, *More Americans Question*.

32. Green, *American Religious Landscape*, 9 (Table 3).

33. Ibid., 8–9 (Tables 1–3 for Republican-Democratic ratios in 1992 and 2004, and traditionalist Christians in GOP in 2004).

34. Pew Forum on Religion & Public Life, "Religion in America: Non-Dogmatic, Diverse and Politically Relevant," Pew Research Center, Washington, DC, June 23, 2008, http://pewresearch.org/pubs/876/religion-america-part-two. The Pew Center surveyed more than 35,000 Americans for this research.

35. Pew Research Center for the People & the Press, "Religion a Strength and Weakness for Both Parties: Public Divided on Origins of Life," Pew Research Center, Washington, DC, August 30, 2005, 1, 3–4, http://people-press.org/report/254/religion-a-strength-and-weakness-for-both-parties. Both parties were criticized "for being too beholden to ideological constituencies." Respondents were split evenly between those who thought secular or nonreligious liberals had too much control over the Democratic Party (44 percent), and religious conservatives had too much control over the Republican Party (45 percent). The survey, conducted July 7–17, 2005, was based on telephone interviews with a nationwide, randomly selected sample of 2,000 adults (with a margin of error of plus or minus 2.5 percentage points).

36. Hart, "Conservatism, the Protestant Right"; and Jerome L. Himmelstein, *To The Right: The Transformation of American Conservatism* (Berkeley: University of California Press, 1990), 80–94.

CHAPTER 1

Christian Conservatives: Past and Present

The Reverend John Hagee, senior pastor of Cornerstone Church in San Antonio, does not want you as part of his flock if you do not believe the Bible is literally God's Word and that biblical miracles, such as Jesus walking on the water or turning water into wine, are real. He expects members "to believe in the absolute authority of the scripture to govern the affairs of men." His ministry, he says, is "absolutely committed to changing America and the world by being obedient to the Great Commission, to win the lost to Christ, to take America and the world back to the God of our fathers."[1]

Catholic Bishop Michael Sheridan of Colorado Springs, Colorado, does not want you either if you are an elected official, or have voted for an elected official, who supports gay marriage or abortion rights. "Any Catholic politicians who advocate for abortion, for illicit stem-cell research or for any form of euthanasia ipso facto place themselves outside full Communion with the church and so jeopardise their salvation," Sheridan wrote. "These Catholics, whether candidates for office or those who would vote for them, may not receive Holy Communion until they have recanted their positions." St. Louis Archbishop Raymond Burke went further down this slippery slope when he said he would not allow John Kerry, the 2004 Democratic presidential candidate, to take Holy Communion.[2]

Hagee, Sheridan, and Burke are high-profile members of the conservative religious community—a community that is also referred to as the Religious Right or the Christian Right—in America. They insist (a) that their followers adhere to this interpretation of the Christian Gospel and (b) that this interpretation guide their political actions.

Christian conservative activists have formed the nucleus of the conservative coalition that has dominated the Republican Party for at least a generation. The ideals and values of three distinct groups were unified under one political umbrella with (a) Christian conservatives, (b) conservatives of other faith groups, and (c) secular conservatives—individuals not necessarily influenced by a religious agenda.

Christian conservatives, as we noted in the Introduction, retain an exclusivist vision of how God is revealed in the world. This is the vision of an insider group that values less highly the experiences of outsiders who, in their view, are not members of their group. They can say comfortably that Jews "don't know how I really feel about what they are doing to this country. And I have no power, no way to handle them," as Southern Baptist evangelist Billy Graham did in 1972 in the Oval Office, or that Islam is a "very evil and wicked religion," as Graham's son Franklin did nearly three decades later.[3]

The Roman Catholic Church historically targeted Jews for conversion to Christianity. The official view did not begin to change until Vatican II (1962–1965), and the Church did not alter its one official prayer for Jews (calling for their conversion) until 1970. A committee of the United States Conference of Catholic Bishops finally declared in 2002 that Jews did not need to be converted to Christianity to earn eternal salvation.[4] Jewish and Catholic groups, however, expressed concern when Pope Benedict XVI announced his intention to revive the Tridentine (Latin) Mass in 2008, because it *does* include the prayer for the conversion of Jews. Roman Catholic overtures toward Jews, moreover, have not been extended to any other non-Christian faith group.

Christian conservatives certainly have become a more distinct and influential political force in the past three decades in the United States than they have been in previous decades, perhaps in our entire history as a nation.[5] Christian conservatives were a dominant force at the federal level during George W. Bush's administration, but for many years their voices had already been heard in many state governments, and in a range of local government activities—from city councils and managers to the makeup of school boards and committees, the appointment of teachers, the content of curricula, and the topics covered in the schools. The Christian conservative religious and social agenda has become in critical areas the regional and national political agenda.[6]

This chapter provides a framework for understanding the interaction between Christian conservatives and conservative politics in America. Section 1 offers a snapshot of the roots of Christian conservatism.

Section 2 outlines Christian conservatism between the 1920s and the 1960s, when the evangelical fundamentalist movement retreated to rural and small-town America, especially in the South. Section 3 explores the impact of Christian conservatism on contemporary political culture. Section 4 examines the role of Christian conservative organizations in national politics, and Section 5 reflects on the plurality of voices in Christian conservative politics and religion today.

ROOTS OF CHRISTIAN CONSERVATISM

A driving force behind the Christian conservative movement in America has been a deep and abiding disenchantment with aspects of the modern and postmodern condition. Many long to return to some aspects of a premodern, prescientific, pre-Enlightenment condition anchored in biblically based religious and moral values.

The term culture embraces the ideas, images, symbols, narratives, objects, and practices that make life meaningful, but the classification of three distinct cultural conditions in human history—scholars refer to them as premodern, modern, and postmodern cultural conditions— is arbitrary. The boundaries between these cultural categories cannot be fixed; the chronological sequence of these cultures is subject to fierce debate; and not all their accompanying political, economic, and social practices have been identified. The cultural categories outlined here are conditioned by our understanding of the Western cultural model.

The Dynamics of Premodern, Modern, and Postmodern Cultures

Individuals rarely define what they mean by culture, which might be described as a way of looking at, and experiencing, the social world. We live with a particular cultural mentality and occupy a particular status within society, so our perception of a cultural practice, such as religion, may appear to be reality itself—what we might call "human nature"—without critically examining our perception in terms of its conditions and consequences. We cannot escape, moreover, the preju- dicial assumption that human beings *progress* from one state of being to the next: hence, humans in premodern cultures are somehow inferior to those in modern cultures, and modernity is somehow inferior to the emerging postmodern condition.

Premodern cultures were anchored in hunting-gathering and herding-horticultural societies, and later in ever-expanding agrarian economies characterized by extreme disparities in wealth, privilege, and power. Relatively low technologies were employed to drive these economies, and initially the marketing of goods and services occurred on a small scale. Social organization, especially in farming communities, was hierarchical and patriarchal for the most part and was based primarily on kinship systems. The emphasis was on the rights and duties of the communal group, rather than on the individual, who did not have control over his or her own life.

The divine was an active and controlling presence in all aspects of human life, and premoderns did not distinguish between secular and sacred activities, as most contemporary men and women do. They had a holistic view of the body, mind, and spirit and a reverence for life in all its forms that was conditioned by their vulnerability to the vicissitudes of life. A peculiar form of premodern agrarian society was created with the rise of feudal Europe in the centuries following the demise of the Roman Empire, but premodern cultural practices were present thousands of years ago and in some respects are as important today as they were then.

The modern conception of culture emerged with the breakdown of the feudal system and the rise of mercantile capitalism in Western Europe, the formation of nation-states, and the colonial expansion of Europe throughout the world. The new culture was conceptualized during the Enlightenment in the eighteenth century and materialized in the nineteenth-century world of industrial capitalism.

The culture of modernity was characterized by rapid developments in science, technology, urbanization, and industrialization, along with the increasing orderliness of education and social life. Modern culture in Western Europe benefited a specific social class—then referred to as the "middling classes"—who became the arbiters of their own destiny. They experienced their world initially through language, and the language of the middle class gradually came to occupy what German philosopher and social theorist Jürgen Habermas has called a *bourgeois* public sphere—a mode for communicating knowledge for moderns in public life.[7]

The middle class intervened in and transformed everyday life as the culture of modernity adopted the new economic system. It was important to observe the language of the public sphere, because it presumed a world of individuals—unified, centered subjects—who were of a certain social class. When the standards of linguistic correctness were ritualized, society had an "objective" measure to verify a person's membership in the public sphere. Standards of good speech, manners, and tastes in things such as clothes, art, music, and even architecture—in other words, the social norms for appropriate conduct in the public sphere—were gradually established.

The middle class learned how to learn—from financial and business practices to science—with empirically derived evidence for its theories and with standardized measurements to evaluate results. A middle-class-driven history celebrated human progress, and Europe represented the most advanced stage in this progress. Therefore, Europe and its cultural progeny such as the United States assumed they were entitled to establish for the rest of the world the norms for "civilized" society—an assumption that was sustained through most of the twentieth century.

A postmodernist mindset points to a fundamental shift away from the culture of modernity. The postmodern critique begins with the idea that language and therefore meaning is unstable and without boundaries. Language—the language of the natural world and the human world—is continually eluding *all* efforts to make it stand still. The opening up of language to seemingly endless levels of meaning—a hallmark of the postmodern condition—inevitably destabilizes all meanings that might once have been regarded as sacrosanct.

"Reality" or "truth" is found not in bipolar oppositions—as in the binary religious lexicon of God versus Satan, of good versus evil, of sin versus grace, of heaven versus hell—but in the semantic space individuals negotiate between these signs. Postmodernists argue that anyone who hopes to understand another's meaning must abandon language that seeks to fix meaning. In the postmodern world, meaning is forever partial, situational, and localized.

Conceptualizing the self, the idea of personhood, becomes much more problematic in the postmodern condition. The self is understood by the postmodernist as being more like an orchestra of voices than a single voice, because the self does not possess its own fixed language, its own center of meaning. This perspective potentially undermines for many Christians the concept of personal salvation, which requires an individual, speaking with a singular voice, to make a total, permanent commitment to Jesus Christ as his or her personal savior. In postmodern culture, no condition is permanent: all conditions of being are uncertain in an uncertain world.

Postmodern culture from this perspective has no fixed maps of meaning. There are no master narratives—no orthodox histories, no universally accepted religious narratives, no eternal boundaries—in the postmodern condition. There are no authoritative discourses, no everlasting Truths. The quest for authenticity requires the continual deconstruction of the very conditions that Christian conservatives have traditionally relied on to prescribe and regulate meaning in their everyday lives.

The tensions of postmodern culture place enormous pressures on Christian conservatives—a theme we shall take up again and again in *God in the Corridors of Power*. While many Christians see postmodernism as an opportunity to redefine their understanding of God's Kingdom in *this* world, Christian conservatives are at war with these postmodern mentalities. They are fighting back on a wide range of fronts to impose their views on America's cultural order. Religion scholars Martin E. Marty and R. Scott Appleby describe this mindset quite succinctly: "Boundaries are set, the enemy identified, converts sought, and institutions created and sustained in pursuit of a comprehensive reconstruction of society."[8]

Reactions to Modernity: Mainstream Christian Perspectives

Protestant Christianity was the faith tradition of the overwhelming majority of Americans in the nineteenth century, and the conservative-liberal religious debate at the time was essentially a debate among Protestant clergy and within Protestant congregations about the meaning of modernity. Protestant conservatives are associated in American church history with what is called the Third Great Awakening, and they began to organize late in the nineteenth century as a distinctly American religious reaction to certain trends in an emerging modernist mindset—a mindset that (a) provoked powerful intellectual challenges to the existing religious order and (b) generated widespread social, technological, and economic upheavals.[9]

Many members of the Protestant establishment elite endorsed the intellectual challenges—emanating essentially from Europe—that gave rise to the modern mindset. They included biblical criticism (a pattern in religious scholarship that stemmed from at least the late eighteenth century), Darwinism (following the publication of Charles Darwin's *On the Origin of Species by Means of Natural Selection* in 1859), and a transformation in what we might call the knowledge industry (providing intellectual support for the general belief that modern science could explain the natural world better than scripture).

The faculties of many (if not most) of the church-related northern universities had embraced biblical criticism and modern science by the 1890s. The major Protestant theological seminaries—such as Union Theological Seminary in New York, Harvard Divinity School in Cambridge, Yale Divinity School in New Haven, and the University of Chicago's Divinity School—regarded themselves and were regarded by others as "religious liberals who were no longer bound by core Christian principles."[10] Protestant institutions in New England and the Midwest were especially affected by the intellectual ferment caused by these challenges to Christian beliefs.

The development of a modern culture, however, also generated economic, technological, and social upheavals that were changing the landscape of much of America—especially in the decades between roughly the Civil War and World War I. A new urban culture was emerging in the revolution wrought by industrial capitalism. The changes in transportation and communication generated by new technologies—from the dramatic expansion of railroads and telegraph lines to photography, electricity, and the telephone—were among the forces transforming the economy and society.

Waves of non-Anglo-Saxon European immigrants were entering the country, especially between the 1880s and 1920s, with their exotic languages, customs, and religious traditions. Literacy rates soared and a mass, popular press came of age in the generation or so before World War I, but poor housing and health, unemployment, crime, and a generalized culture of violence dramatically highlighted the plight of those who lived in poverty in the overcrowded cities in America's industrializing Northeast and Midwest.

Members of the Protestant establishment elite were in the forefront of campaigns to provide better living and working conditions for the poor and promote the civil rights of the powerless. They were leading exponents, for example, of the social gospel movement, which encouraged Christians to help construct the Kingdom of God in this world by addressing unfair labor practices, advocating decent health-care and other social services for the at-risk population, and generally trying to alleviate the plight of the impoverished—especially in the cities.

The movement was championed initially by people such as Charles Monroe Sheldon (1857–1946), a Congregational minister and writer, whose ideas (his perennial question: "What would Jesus do?") influenced people such as Walter Rauschenbusch (1861–1918), a Baptist minister who worked in a New York slum called Hell's Kitchen and first articulated the theology of a social gospel. The movement in the next generation featured people such as Jane Addams (1860–1935), a pioneer social worker and feminist and the first woman to receive the Nobel Peace Prize (1931), and Harry Hopkins (1890–1946), the chief architect of Franklin Delano Roosevelt's (FDR) federal relief programs.

African-American Protestants had a long tradition of advocacy within their own communities—beginning in the eighteenth century, when black churches began breaking away from white churches, and in the antislavery movement, as we shall see in Chapter 4, before the Civil War. Sojourner Truth (1797–1883), Harriet Tubman (1820–1913), and Frederick Douglass (1818–1895), for example, were prominent leaders in the fight against slavery.[11] Others continued to fight for black civil rights—especially in higher education and especially in the South— after the Civil War.[12] In the twentieth century, educators such as Mary McLeod Bethune (1875–1955) would eventually play a role in the social reforms embodied in FDR's New Deal, and black clergy were in the forefront of the civil rights movement led by Martin Luther King Jr. (1929–1968) during the 1950s and 1960s.

When immigrants from Southern Europe began demanding social assistance, they got help from, among others, Roman Catholics, many of whom placed considerable emphasis on the plight of the poor. John A. Ryan (1869–1945), for example, was one of the foremost spokespersons for social justice in the American Catholic Church in the first half of the twentieth century. The National Catholic Welfare Conference meeting in Milwaukee in 1938 demanded that industry provide stable employment "at not less than a family living income," that hours of labor be restricted "in keeping with human need for rest and relaxation," that a minimum wage and collective bargaining be assured, and that monopolies be controlled.[13] Dorothy Day (1897–1980)— a journalist (and editor of *The Catholic Worker*), a writer (she produced eight books of fiction and a memoir), and a political activist—was co-founder (with Peter Maurin) of the Catholic Worker Movement— arguably the most significant of the poverty organizations launched by faith groups during the Depression Era and still very active today.

Reactions to Modernity: The Fundamentalist Challenge

The shock troops of the Christian conservative movement were and are Protestant conservatives. They rejected the evolutionary themes in Darwinism and the new sciences and deplored the undermining by critical theologians of what they believed to be biblical truths. They also felt threatened by various other issues in America at the time—from the rising tide of Roman Catholic immigrants to new Protestant religious groups (such as the Mormons, Christian Scientists, and Jehovah's Witnesses) outside mainstream Protestantism.

Working within the System

The initial response of many Protestants who would later identify themselves as evangelical fundamentalists was to work within the Protestant establishment to restore what they saw as the purity of the orthodox Trinitarian faith. Fundamentalism in the early twentieth century was largely a product of dissent in northern Protestant denominations: it was a conscious attempt to construct a rational, orthodox, Christian response to modernity in opposition to those antiorthodox rationalists who would remake Christianity to fit their own version of the modern image.

The "fundamentals" were essentially a restatement of orthodox Christian doctrine. They emphasized a commonsense understanding of the essentials of the Christian faith designed to appeal to all American Christians. The fundamentals began with five truths: the Bible is God's inerrant, infallible word; Jesus was born of a virgin; his death is the sacrifice made by Jesus The Christ for the sins of humanity (the idea of "substitutionary atonement"); Jesus rose physically from the dead and will eventually return (the second coming); and God actively intervenes in the natural world through what human beings call miracles (beginning and ending the Christian calendar with Jesus's virgin birth and resurrection).

The fundamentals were first published in the early 1900s in a series of tracts or pamphlets funded by conservative oil executives under the leadership of Lyman Stewart (1840–1923), founder of Union Oil Company of California (now Unocal), and mailed to about 300,000 Christian workers worldwide each year for several years. Conservative Princeton University academics associated with the Presbyterian Church then turned the pamphlets into a series of 12 paperback books between 1910 and 1915.[14]

Seminarians, pastors, YMCA (Young Men's Christian Association) workers, and agents in religious bookstores marketed the paperbacks, giving fundamentalists both academic and congregational credibility. The Scofield Reference Bible, based on the Authorized King James

Version and first published by Oxford University Press in 1909, for example, provided many conservative Protestants with a standard fundamentalist reference text for much of the twentieth century.[15]

Other Protestant dissenters broke away from established Protestant institutions and launched new movements that would reinterpret the signs of the times and provide alternative responses to the Kingdom of God in this world and the next. The Seventh Day Adventists, the Mormons (who began to explore the religious terrain outside Utah toward the end of the nineteenth century), and even the Jehovah's Witnesses are examples of homegrown American faith traditions that eventually found homes in at least some conservative religious, political, and social activities. All these groups emphasized the literal inerrancy of scripture and a moral lifestyle that was in harmony with (selected) biblical injunctions, but they also claimed new revelatory truths that challenged traditional Christian beliefs.

The Pentecostal Response

Perhaps the most significant religious innovation that would resonate with fundamentalism was the Pentecostal movement with its focus on the power of the Holy Spirit to reshape the believer's world. William Joseph Seymour (1870–1922), the son of former slaves, is generally regarded as the founder of modern Pentecostalism. Seymour's message was first communicated in a small, dilapidated nondenominational church on Azusa Street in Los Angeles in 1906. The Azusa Street Revival, as it was called, lasted three years and stamped the face of Pentecostalism forever as an interracial, egalitarian, charismatic, nondenominational movement that preached a personal encounter with God manifested primarily through *glossolalia* (speaking in tongues).

The Pentecostal movement became one of the most powerful forces in evangelical fundamentalist Christianity. Contemporary adherents may belong to specific Pentecostal churches, the largest being the Church of God in Christ (now essentially an African-American denomination) and the Assemblies of God (a mixed white, African-American, and Latino denomination). But Pentecostalism also became a fixture in mainstream churches—most noticeably in more liturgical-based, high-church denominations such as the Episcopalians (called Anglicans outside the United States), Lutherans, and Roman Catholics—and in the burgeoning, nondenominational Protestant church movement.[16]

CHRISTIAN CONSERVATIVES BETWEEN THE 1920s AND THE 1960s

Christian conservatives after World War I tried to place their own stamp on orthodoxy by a cautious expansion of orthodox Christian interpretations, always with religious timelines and biblical proof texts, on an expanding range of theological and social issues. While these activities included a renewed and more exclusivist emphasis on evangelism and a reemphasis on the sinful nature of humanity, two issues galvanized Christian conservatives before the 1960s.

Premillennialism and Cultural Exclusivity

The first was the trend toward a premillennial eschatology (which deals with issues such as the meaning of death, judgment, and immortality) in theology. Premillennialism is the belief that this hopelessly evil and corrupt world will be destroyed on Armageddon Day, when Christ will return physically to redeem resurrected and living believers and to restore the Kingdom of God, ushering in a millennium of peace.

A premillennial eschatology, among other things, provided Christian conservatives with a theological rationale for conservative political rhetoric framing end-time scenarios for an America and a world anchored in sin. Premillennialism also provided a theological rationale for providing political and monetary support for the Holy Land, Israel, the site of Christ's return on Armageddon Day. Conservative support for the Jewish state, and the active rejection of any Muslim presence in this territory, has been a constant theme since Israel was created (or recreated, as Christian conservatives would say) in 1948.

The second was the trend toward exclusivity on such matters as the role of women in the family, in the congregation, and in leisure-time activities. Christian conservatives remained patriarchal within the family and within the church, and they were not out of step with most Protestant denominations, which accepted the ordination of women, for example, only in the last decades of the twentieth century. Indeed, some (such as the Southern Baptist Convention, Lutheran Church-Missouri Synod, and Seventh Day Adventists) still reject the ordination of women (along with the Roman Catholics and the Eastern Orthodox).

The trend also meant exclusivity in a wide range of cultural activities, from graduation exercises to sporting events, where even today in different parts of the country the program will sometimes feature an orthodox

Christian prayer that is inextricably linked to the American flag or
to other symbols representing America. It meant exclusivity in a
conservative ecumenical movement that is still confined to Christians
or Jews who have been "born again" as Christians. And it meant that
topics deemed inappropriate for Christians (like evolution, sex education, noncapitalist economics, or American history and politics
perceived to be unpatriotic) should not be taught in the public schools.

Protestant evangelical fundamentalists created their own distinct
identity beginning in the 1920s and 1930s. Revivals, holiness groups,
a resurgence of evangelical missions, and the prophetic millenarianism
that had long characterized the religious experiences of many pious
Protestants furnished the first generation of leaders. Protestant conservatives, led by the fundamentalists, began holding their own conferences, producing and distributing their own devotional tracts, and
creating their own networks of church-related schools and mission
outreach programs.

Protestant conservatives in the 1920s were involved in a range of
religious and social issues—from the alcohol prohibition movement[17]
to anti-Catholicism (sparked by the landslide defeat of Catholic
Democratic candidate Al Smith [1873–1944] in the 1928 presidential
election)—but the first significant political crusade was against the
teaching of scientific evolution in the public schools. This crusade
eventually sparked a nationwide debate over religion and science with
the Scopes trial in 1925. John Scopes (1900–1970), a public school
teacher, was convicted of teaching evolution, but "in the trial by public opinion and the press," as historian George M. Marsden puts it, "it
was clear that the twentieth century, the cities, and the universities had
won a resounding victory, and that the country, the South, and the
fundamentalists were guilty as charged."[18] Science had triumphed
over religion, and the fundamentalist vision had failed in its initial
bid to win the support of Christian America.

A Retreat to the South

Protestant liberals essentially won these cultural wars with conservatives within the Protestant establishment. In the aftermath of the
Scopes trial, most scholars suggest, the conservatives turned inward
for the next 40 years or so—retreating into rural and small-town
America, where a new religious base would be established effectively
insulated from national public scrutiny before the 1960s.

The evangelical fundamentalist movement as a whole shifted from the North to the South. Some congregations remained as a marginalized presence in northern Protestant denominations. Some congregations joined the powerful Southern Baptist Convention, virtually the state church in the South at the time. Some congregations broke away to form new conservative denominations, while some congregations became independent—they were forerunners of today's non-denominational (often called "community" or "Christian") churches.

White Protestant churches in the South at the time were not particularly influenced by the theological turmoil in the universities or by the social and economic stress brought on by industrialization and urbanization. Conservative religious leaders no longer rallied their followers against modernism as a perversion that had to be purged from their lives. Instead, they began a multipronged attack against what they were calling secular humanism by the 1960s, an assault ultimately directed against an emerging postmodern culture.

Protestant conservatives focused initially on mass evangelism and personal witnessing for Christ, which transcended denomination. Religious perspectives also were marketed by evangelists using nonreligious and religious media—a strategy that can be traced to Protestant preachers such as Charles Finney (1792–1875), Dwight L. Moody (1837–1899), William A. "Billy" Sunday (1862–1935), and Aimee Semple McPherson (1890–1944) and continued after World War II with Protestant preachers like William F. "Billy" Graham, Jerry Lamon Falwell Sr. (1933–2007), Marion G. "Pat" Robertson, James Clayton "Jim" Dobson, and a seemingly endless stream of evangelists communicating conservative religious values in print, radio, and later television.

The South would remain the heartland of the movement, and white, evangelical fundamentalist Protestants drove the political, social, and religious agendas. The foremost support base continued to be the Southern Baptists, which grew to become America's largest Protestant denomination.

Conservative Protestant Networking

Networks between northern and southern Protestant conservatives were gradually set up between roughly 1930 and 1960 in such cooperative ventures as the Independent Fundamental Churches of America (1930), Baptist Bible Fellowship International (1950), and especially the American Council of Christian Churches (1941), which was a direct response to the first ecumenical organization in the United States, the Federal Council of Churches (1908, but absorbed in 1950 by the National Council of Churches USA).

The American Council became a partner in a broader conservative church movement, the International Council of Christian Churches (ICCC), which provided an evangelical fundamentalist counterpart to the World Council of Churches (WCC). The WCC held its inaugural meeting in Amsterdam (The Netherlands) in 1948, and the ICCC held its inaugural meeting in the same year in Charlotte, North Carolina. Under the leadership of Carl McIntire (1906–2002), a media-savvy evangelist, the International Council created regional councils in parallel with the WCC in North America, South America, Asia, and Africa.[19] Conservative Protestant church organizations also created dozens of independent missionary agencies around the world— especially after World War II—in another response to mainstream Protestant missionary agencies that had deemphasized evangelism in favor of teacher training, health, and public welfare.

The National Association of Evangelicals (NAE), launched in 1942, is a good example of an umbrella organization for conservatives that would prosper in the 1950s and 1960s and establish an autonomous power base independent of the mainstream Protestant and Roman Catholic establishments. These early years of the postwar baby-boomer generation were characterized by rapid economic growth, expanding suburbia in the larger towns and cities, and new homes and churches dotting the landscape. The NAE's focus was on these suburban population groups. One of its members was Billy Graham, who was just beginning to establish a national reputation, and an NAE delegation was actually welcomed to the White House during Dwight D. Eisenhower's presidency.

NAE membership had doubled to 32 denominations with nearly 1.5 million members by 1960. *Life* magazine in 1958 had already cited an emerging "Third Force" in Christianity, the Christian conservative movement, which, alongside mainstream Protestantism and Catholicism, was "the most extraordinary religious phenomenon of our time." Although the NAE was not mentioned in the story, according to the NAE Web site, "it [*Life*] identified among the new force five denominations that comprised nearly two-thirds of NAE's membership. All of them were associated with Pentecostal churches— Assemblies of God, Church of God (Cleveland), International Church of the Foursquare Gospel, Pentecostal Church of God, and the Pentecostal Holiness Church."[20]

Virtually every Protestant denomination in America was influenced by national and regional youth organizations created or sponsored by conservative religious groups—although not all of them were overtly fundamentalist—in the postwar era. These included Youth for Christ, InterVarsity Christian Fellowship, and Campus Crusade for Christ and smaller groups such as Young Life and Word of Life—along with the introduction of Christian day schools, Christian summer camps, and summer Bible conferences in various parts of the country.

Conservative Protestant Higher Education

Protestant conservatives had created some religious colleges even in the nineteenth century, such as Wheaton College (1860) and Moody Bible Institute (1886). Others were created in the early twentieth century—such as the Bible Institute of Los Angeles (BIOLA-1908) in the West, Westminster Theological Seminary (1929) in the East, and Dallas Theological Seminary (1924) in the South. Thereafter, new Bible colleges, institutes, and seminaries mushroomed all over the United States. Some had become four-year institutions with graduate programs by the 1970s. They would remain politically, socially, and religiously conservative.[21]

Conservative Protestant seminaries and colleges today retain a relatively exclusive religious stance, and several are partisan political institutions. Some were founded by evangelists—such as Oral Roberts University (1963), founded by Granville Oral Roberts; Lynchburg Baptist College (1971), founded by Jerry Falwell and later renamed Liberty Baptist College and then Liberty University; and CBN University (1977–1978), founded by Pat Robertson and later renamed Regent University. Others were founded by political activists. Michael P. Farris, a constitutional lawyer and leader in the contemporary Christian home-school movement, launched Patrick Henry College in 2000 as an overt attempt to combine "fundamentalist faith and political action." Dubbed "God's Harvard" in a recent study of the college, Patrick Henry seeks to train mainly home-schooled evangelicals "to rescue secular America from fallen grace."[22]

Conservative religious colleges and universities have their own accrediting agency—the Council for Christian Colleges & Universities (CCCU)—and more than 170 around the world (105 in the

United States) are now affiliated with the CCCU. These schools tend to be nondenominational—as opposed to church-affiliated institutions such as Southern Methodist University or the Roman Catholic universities[23]—and they represent only 1.5 percent of the nation's total college population. But they are the fastest growing segment—an increase in enrollment of 67 percent in the past decade as compared to 2 percent for America's mainstream religious and secular institutions.

The curriculum in many colleges tried to respond to modern professional academic standards, and the conservative Protestant academy now has its own journals, scholarly presses, and advanced degrees. It has become a power broker on issues such as school textbooks, the censorship of material acquired by school and local libraries, and the teaching of certain subjects (such as sex education, evolutionary science, and history/social studies) in the public schools.[24]

The theology of Christian conservatives, a topic usually ignored by the media, also remains pervasive even in mainstream Christian religious institutions. Most American seminaries and Bible colleges—regardless of whether they are Protestant, Roman Catholic, or Eastern Orthodox, are deemed to be liberal or conservative, and are academically accredited or not by mainstream accrediting agencies—communicate orthodox Christological and Trinitarian perspectives. The curriculum is also overwhelmingly Eurocentric. When students do explore other regions or religions of the world, it is usually from Christian perspectives. The conservative stance is reflected especially in required courses and in orthodox statements of belief generally expected of individuals who are about to become clergy even in mainstream churches.

CHRISTIAN CONSERVATISM AND CONTEMPORARY POLITICAL CULTURE

The Christian conservative movement, the umbrella term we employ in this book, did not exist as a significant *political* force at the national level before the 1970s, although, as we have seen, the seeds for such a movement were planted much earlier. There were many conservative adherents within the Protestant establishment (in denominations such as the Methodists, Presbyterians, Lutherans, Episcopalians, and Congregationalists), but they were essentially a marginal force in the political arena (other than the Southern Baptists in the South) until Protestant conservatives began to shed extremist views and to expand their cultural agenda in reaching out to like-minded conservatives in mainstream Christian denominations and in other religious communities. The war against secular humanism took on a whole new meaning in the so-called cultural wars of the next generation.

Some Protestant evangelicals sought to distance themselves from fundamentalist tests of faith, but they retained (a) the tenants of an orthodox theology, (b) the belief that salvation was dependent on a personal acceptance of Jesus Christ as Lord and Savior, and (c) the commitment of these born-again Christians to proselytize this exclusive gospel throughout the world by word and deed. Above all, most Protestant evangelicals identified with Protestant fundamentalists on core cultural (especially social) values. "Evangelical" and "fundamentalist" were interchangeable terms when Christian conservatives became a dominant force in America's political culture.

The power to confer meaning on religious language in the public arena was mediated by Christian conservatives in the waning decades of the twentieth century. Conservative norms and values cut across churches and denominations, across synagogues and other places of worship, and across laity and clergy.[25] The contemporary Christian conservative message, as we shall see in Chapter 2, was conveyed by commercial and noncommercial media, including sermons, Sunday school sessions and other religious activity groups meeting during the week, catechisms, specialized religious magazines and journals, religious music and religious films and videos, religious radio and cable-satellite television stations, religious Internet sites, and religious fictional and nonfictional literature. As a political movement, Christian conservative language pervaded not only a broad spectrum of Christianity, but also significant voting constituencies of non-Christian and even nonreligious Americans.

Biblical law remained natural law for Christian conservatives of all denominations. Many Protestant conservatives agreed with many Catholic conservatives in asserting that this was a *rational* response to modernity. Catholic conservative "assumptions about an inherently imperfect human nature, an objective moral order, and an indispensable tradition," as Mary Jo Weaver, a specialist in religious studies, puts it, "clustered around a set of 'family values' and natural law principles." And their "political convictions" were drawn "from their religious beliefs."[26]

The "God-given mission" of these religious conservatives, according to Linda Kintz, a specialist in literature and religious studies, "depends on the reconstruction of U.S. culture so that it is in tune with the natural law of the Ten Commandments and Judeo-Christian values, as natural law and biblical law are conflated."[27] Contemporary crusades reflect this understanding of modernity. For many if not most Christian conservatives in America, the heterosexual nuclear family, heterosexual behavior based on monogamy and procreation, the primary role of the woman as wife and mother/caregiver, and the capitalist free market system have remained components of "natural law."

Forces of Change

The Christian conservative stance today is a response in part to new forces of change sweeping America and the rest of the world in the last generation of so before the end of the twentieth century. They are similar in their impact to the upheavals that changed the landscape of America in the post–Civil War era. The collapse of the Soviet Union, for example, brought to the surface the inherent fragility of numerous artificially constructed, postcolonial states. The factionalism and disorder—and the reemergence of narrow nationalisms in many parts of the world following the end of the Cold War—seemed to undermine positions Protestant organizations, such as the National Council of Churches, had fostered in the quest for ecumenism and cultural competency in a pluralistic society. Christian conservatives tried to fill this vacuum with their own visions of God's Kingdom.

Economic and Social Changes

America's economy and society were undergoing a transformation from an industrial to a postindustrial, information-based culture that was characterized in part by a vast outsourcing of the traditional underpinnings of industrial culture, especially mining and manufacturing, and a growing dependence on skilled manual and mental labor living in foreign countries. While economic sectors in some regions, such as the South and the West, flourished in a new era of global capitalism, economic sectors in other regions, especially in the Northeast and the Midwest, did not.

A dramatic shift in immigration policy in 1965 unintentionally opened the floodgates to millions of legal and illegal immigrants. Most came from Latin America, especially Mexico and Central America, but hundreds of thousands also came from various parts of

Asia, the Middle East, and Africa. For the first time the United States was admitting huge numbers of immigrants (other than slaves or indentured labor) from outside Europe—nonwhites with different languages and social and religious values. The United States by the end of the twentieth century was deemed "the most religiously diverse nation in the world."[28]

These changes effectively undermined the dominant Anglo-Saxon Protestant order of the South—a culture that for decades had offered Protestant conservatives an environment to develop relatively independently of the rest of society. The New South, however, adapted remarkably well to the new era. It became an urbanized Mecca for northern manufacturing, service, and computerized information industries seeking lower-wage workers and a more attractive financial environment. The New South offered a range of incentives that few other regions of the country could match. Migrants from the North—including returning generations of African Americans—trekked to the South in large numbers, and a flood of relatively low-wage, unskilled foreign immigrants joined them.

The Protestant Political Divide

Protestant conservatives were the torchbearers in grassroots conservative religious politics at local and state levels, but we cannot really talk about a *political* divide between liberal and conservative Protestants before the 1960s. Up to this point, "conservative Protestant politics were virtually indistinguishable from those of mainline Protestants," as church historian Darryl G. Hart says, because "the Right wing of Anglo-American Protestantism benefited from the cultural hegemony of their liberal Protestant rivals." The dominant Protestant Anglo-American culture—in its religious and educational assumptions, in its political and social values, and in its understanding of the righteousness of America's free-enterprise system—was relatively homogeneous.[29]

Political attitudes began to change—and Protestant conservatives emerged from decades of self-imposed isolation—when the culture itself was perceived to be in trouble. A new generation of Republican conservatives, many of them with ties to the Christian conservative movement, gained influence within the party in the mid-1960s, and religious conservatism thereafter was more closely linked to Republican politics.

Christian conservatives felt they were in a position to provide a distinct ideological alternative to what they saw as the atrophied religious leadership of the past. Much of what mainstream Protestants and Catholics had pioneered—such as hospitals, orphanages, adoption bureaus, employment services, housing agencies, meal deliveries to the poor and otherwise disadvantaged—was now standard practice and under the control of governmental and nongovernmental agencies. Social values previously attributed mainly to Christian liberals—such as pluralism, tolerance, civil rights, intellectual freedom of inquiry, and personal autonomy—now seemed to their conservative counterparts to be undermining the stability of America's social order.

The Protestant majority in the United States was also in jeopardy by the last decade of the twentieth century. As noted in the Introduction, the percentage of Americans who identified with Protestant churches, which had not changed significantly between 1972 and 1993, had dropped to 51.3 percent in 2008. The percentage indicating they were Roman Catholic during this period remained more or less stable—declining slightly to 23.9 percent in 2008—largely due to new immigrants from Latin America.[30]

The Protestant establishment was losing its dominance in the public sphere as church membership in denominations such as the Methodists, Presbyterians, Lutherans, Episcopalians, and the United Church of Christ (Congregationalists) declined. American Protestants were joining conservative congregations in ever-greater numbers, and conservative Protestant activists knew it. "Protestant churches once may have 'delivered the votes,'" as religion scholar Phillip E. Hammond put it in the early 1990s, "but clearly they do not now. Quite the contrary, those parishioners most inclined to vote in accord with their liberal leaders are the parishioners most inclined to cease being parishioners."[31]

From the perspective of religious conservatives, feminism and the so-called sexual revolution, the hitherto underground GLBT (gay, lesbian, bisexual, transgender) communities, and abortion advocates were threatening the sanctity of the heterosexual nuclear family. One of the first contemporary antifeminist crusades, for example, was in the 1960s against having sex education in public schools. The civil rights movement and the demand to recognize America's growing cultural diversity threatened the social order in the schools (from racial and ethnic quotas, to school busing, to banning prayer and bible reading). The anti-Vietnam war movement—along with urban violence and rising crime rates, the threat of inflation, and the imagined threat of campus radicals in universities and colleges—posed challenges to all patriotic Americans as far as the Christian Right was concerned.

Christian conservatives became a force in national politics, at least in the popular imagination, with the election of Jimmy Carter, a born-again Southern Baptist, as president in 1976. In America's bicentennial year, *Newsweek* magazine even declared 1976 the "Year of the Evangelicals," but Carter maintained a strict separation between church and state. Evangelicals were not given high posts in the administration, and his presidency did not provide support for conservative religious positions on domestic and foreign issues. Nevertheless, his election did focus the nation's attention for the first time on religious conservatives in politics and in a real sense privileged their moral-reform agenda.

Alliances and Divisions in Religion and Politics

The lynchpin holding Christian conservatives together was and is a conservative theology and a conservative perspective on cultural issues, especially issues affecting the heterosexual family. Activists were able to surmount very different ecclesiastical differences and to establish political links with conservatives in other Christian communities by appealing to these common standards of belief and conduct.

First, they broadened the meaning of Christian conservatism beyond its evangelical fundamentalist base, as we noted in the Introduction. They reached out to conservative, mainstream Protestants, non-traditional Protestants (especially the Mormons), and non-Protestant Christians (especially the Roman Catholics).[32] Second, they reached out to conservative non-Christians—especially Orthodox Jews. Third, they began to forge alliances with secular politicians, those who did not have a religious agenda, within the Republican Party. This conservative coalition had emerged as a force in national politics by the latter 1970s.

Conservative Protestant political activism outside the South had been fractured by numerous schisms in the past over the actions of extremist elements challenging the social order. Many Protestants were embarrassed by the Scopes trial and the fact that believers in the South were often associated with the Ku Klux Klan or in the Midwest with fanatical antisemitic groups such as Defenders of the Christian Faith. Some also disassociated themselves from politics because of the tendency of fringe groups (such as the John Birch Society and other militant anti-communist crusaders of the 1950s and

1960s) toward intolerance—persecuting those who did not support fundamentalist ideologies.

As the Christian conservative movement grew beyond its evangelical fundamentalist Protestant roots in seeking popular political support, the image of evangelical fundamentalism became more and more diffuse. Stereotyped terms, such as fundamentalist and evangelical, were increasingly regarded as too narrow and pejorative as Protestant conservatives sought political alliances with Christian conservatives of all denominations.[33]

Billy Graham himself broke with the fundamentalists because he did not agree with their rejection of nonfundamentalist churches. Graham retained conservative religious credentials, but he wanted those who were "converted" in his crusades to return to their home churches, if they had them, or to join whatever churches they felt most comfortable attending, whether fundamentalist or not. Even Jerry Falwell (1933–2007) faced censure when he encouraged his political organization, the Moral Majority, to seek common moral ground with conservative "unbelievers"—infuriating zealots such as Christian educator Bob Jones Jr. (son of the founder of ultraconservative Bob Jones University), who once called Falwell "the most dangerous man in America."[34]

Protestants struggling to gain political credence for an ever-expanding national agenda soon found that other Christian groups had their own religious agendas. Many Catholic conservatives, for example, were dismayed by the liberalizing tendencies of Vatican II (1962–1965). They emphasized "church teachings against same-sex marriage, euthanasia, and embryonic stem-cell research," while liberal Catholic counterparts emphasized "church teachings against the death penalty, racism, and environmental degradation." Conservative Catholics focused mainly on abortion, whereas liberal Catholics focused primarily on poverty.[35]

Conservative Catholics and Protestants joined forces to lobby against such domestic issues as abortion rights, gay marriage, fetal stem-cell research, euthanasia, and pornography and to lobby for such domestic and foreign issues as limited social welfare programs, religious school vouchers (state funding for religious education), and increased funding for military defense. They also promoted films such as Mel Gibson's *The Passion of The Christ* as a valid representation of the passion story—a film that became "one of the most profitable films ever produced."[36]

Political relations between Christian conservatives and Jewish conservatives were always ambiguous—especially from the Jewish perspective. Jews would retain a special place in the Protestant conservative pantheon as the "Chosen People"—a remnant of whom would be "saved" at the second coming of Christ. Protestant conservatives continued to provide enormous material and symbolic support for Israel and for the privileged status of the Jewish people (even though they were more likely than mainstream Protestants or Roman Catholics to urge them to convert to Christianity).[37]

CONSERVATIVE RELIGIOUS ORGANIZATIONS IN NATIONAL POLITICS

The Christian conservative political constituency broadened especially from the 1980s with the emergence to national prominence of several key organizations, three of which were led by evangelical figures linked closely to the conservative political and social values espoused by the Republican Party. Jerry Falwell and his Moral Majority played a major role in Republican politics during the early- to mid-1980s, and Pat Robertson and his Christian Coalition was its evangelical successor during the early- to mid-1990s. James Dobson and his Focus on the Family and Family Research Council (together with various affiliated groups) provided the main thrust of Christian conservatism in Republican Party politics in the decade between roughly 1998 and the end of the George W. Bush presidency in 2009.[38]

These three organizations enjoyed high profiles during the past 30 years or so, but other Protestant conservatives created a plethora of new groups, including the male-bonding Promise Keepers (1990), and parallel women's groups such as the Promise Reapers, Praise Keepers, and Women of Faith (all launched in the mid-1990s). While the Promise Keepers and the women's groups were not involved overtly in partisan politics, their theological, political, and social beliefs were "congenial to conservative American Protestantism."[39]

Similar efforts were made to form alliances with nontraditional Protestant denominations such as the Mormons. The Church of Jesus Christ of Latter-Day Saints (LDS)—the official name of the Mormon Church—was now the fourth largest Christian denomination in America. The LDS made great efforts to demonstrate that this denomination was similar to other Christian conservative denominations on all political and social issues (especially its pro-family stance), and even on most fundamentalist theological issues.[40]

These groups injected unanticipated energy into American politics. "What was new and unexpected," sociologist José Casanova noted in 1994, was "the revitalization and the assumption of public roles by precisely those religious traditions which both theories of secularization and cyclical theories of religious revival had assumed were becoming ever more marginal and irrelevant in the modern world."[41]

The Moral Majority

Jerry Falwell will forever be associated with the Moral Majority, which he co-founded in 1979 with Paul Weyrich (1942–2008), the doyen of conservative political strategists inside the Washington Beltway.[42] A variety of religious-cum-political groups were formed at the time, but no group drew as much media and public attention as the Moral Majority during the 1980s, according to religious scholar Nancy T. Ammerman.[43]

Falwell was already an established national leader in the Protestant evangelical movement. He had branched out into higher education with the founding of Liberty University, which became one of the biggest (at more than 11,000 on-campus students on a 4,400-acre campus) evangelical-fundamentalist undergraduate institutions in the nation. He was also a leader among Protestant conservatives in campaigns to allow prayer and the teaching of creationism in public schools and to allow parents to avoid secular schools if they wished in favor of funding religious private schools (such as his own Liberty Christian Academy) through the school-voucher system. He condemned gays and lesbians—initially linking the AIDS epidemic, for example, solely to homosexual lifestyles. He took a "Christian Zionist" stand in support of Israel while condemning all religions, especially Islam, not in the Jewish and Christian traditions in the United States and the Holy Land. Falwell retained his status as a political spokesman for a conservative religious voice against the increasingly inclusive and culturally diverse society America was becoming in the closing decades of the twentieth century.

The Moral Majority was the major national forum for religious conservatives in Republican politics. Falwell worked closely with partisan-political and so-called pro-family groups such as the Religious Roundtable (1978) and the Christian Voice (1978),[44] James Dobson's Focus on the Family (1977), the Traditional Values Coalition (1980),[45] Citizens for Community Values (1983),[46] and Concerned

Women for America (founded in 1979 by Beverly LaHaye, wife of leading evangelical author and political activist Tim LaHaye).

One of the early attempts by religious conservatives to stake a place for themselves inside Washington Beltway politics was the secretive Council for National Policy (CNP), which LaHaye, Weyrich, and others established in Washington, D.C., in 1981.[47] The CNP, the Moral Majority, and numerous family-issues activist groups set up political action committees for Ronald Reagan, the Republican Party (GOP) presidential candidate, and other conservative GOP members of Congress during the election cycles of the 1980s. They held rallies, initiated mass petitions, and launched direct-mail campaigns through newsletters, radio, and especially cable television on political and social issues of concern to religious conservatives. These activists received widespread attention for promoting conservative religious values, and they are credited with rallying religious voters to join the Republican Party in the 1980 and 1984 elections.

But they did not enjoy the personal access to the White House that they had anticipated as potential power brokers in Reagan's administration. Conservative religious activists were not placed in important positions, and several appointments were a disappointment—such as the appointment of centrist Sandra Day O'Connor to the U.S. Supreme Court. *Roe v. Wade* (1973) was not overturned, and other elements of the Christian conservative agenda were downplayed. Falwell's Moral Majority was already a spent force in national politics by 1986. Falwell resigned as director a year later, and the organization was dissolved in 1989.

Christian Coalition of America

The Christian Coalition of America—founded in 1989 by Pat Robertson and Ralph Reed, an activist initially at the University of Georgia and a prominent leader among college Republicans—succeeded the Moral Majority as the principal national political forum for religious conservatives in the early-mid 1990s.[48] Robertson was an established figure in evangelical politics. Like Falwell, he had founded a university—originally called CBN University (after his media conglomerate, the Christian Broadcasting Network) and renamed Regent University in 1989.

Unlike Falwell, he was much more involved in day-to-day conservative politics. Robertson's Freedom Council (founded in

1981) was an early example of a nonprofit organization seeking to educate evangelicals in grassroots political organizing.[49] Above all, Robertson had been a candidate for the highest office in the land. The Christian Coalition actually was created after Robertson's unsuccessful bid to become the Republican Party's nominee in the 1988 presidential election. Under Reed's leadership as executive director, the Coalition became a powerful machine of the Republican Party.

Robertson initially appealed to a much broader base of Christian conservatives than Falwell—especially disillusioned suburbanites with children, middle-aged empty nesters, white-collar professionals, and business entrepreneurs who had traditional pro-family values or were otherwise cultural conservatives. While organizations affiliated with the Moral Majority, such as the Christian Voice, had supplied voters' guides to church congregations during congressional elections, the Coalition, with its broader fund-raising base, generated voters' guides to a much larger audience outside the evangelical core.

The Christian Coalition was a major promoter of so-called Christian family values and a thorn in the side of the Democratic administration under Bill Clinton in the 1990s. The pro-family agenda was gradually widened beyond contentious issues such as abortion, gay rights, sex education, and prayer in the schools. Christian Coalition director Reed tried to expand family-related issues "to attract a majority of voters" by proposing tax law changes that would "ease the time and work burdens on stressed families" and promote welfare and "school choice" to benefit families.[50] The Coalition played a significant role in defeating Clinton's health-care plan in 1993–1994 and in the campaign that swept Republicans to a majority in Congress in the 1994 midterm elections (the first time in 40 years). The Coalition signed on to the GOP's Contract with America and joined the crusade that led to impeachment charges against President Clinton in 1998.

Christian conservatives, however, were seriously questioning Reed's leadership of the Coalition by the late 1990s. The Contract with America had not included social issues of concern to religious conservatives; the Coalition's own Contract with the American Family in 1995 downplayed the Christian Right's homosexuality and abortion agenda; and the Coalition supported Robert Dole over Patrick Buchanan, the preferred candidate for religious conservatives, as the GOP nominee in the 1996 presidential election. Reed's resignation in 1997,[51] the lackluster performance of Republican candidates in the 1998 midterm elections, and the loss of the Coalition's nonprofit, tax-exempt status at the end of Clinton's administration in 1999 signaled its decline in influence. The Bush administration restored the Coalition's tax-exempt status in 2005, but by then the organization was truly a spent force in GOP politics.[52]

Focus on the Family

James Dobson assumed the mantle of leadership in conservative religious politics at the national level from the late 1990s. He was raised in the Church of the Nazarene, another conservative Protestant denomination born in America,[53] and three generations of male for-bearers (beginning with his great grandfather) had been Nazarene evangelists.

Dobson established the nonprofit Focus on the Family and a radio program of the same name in 1977 (it was a 30-minute daily broadcast by 1981), but he was already known in Christian conservative circles far beyond the Nazarene community as a public speaker and author of self-help books on traditional marriage, family life, and parenting.[54] Dobson moved the Focus on the Family organization from California to Colorado Springs, Colorado, in 1992, where it continued to expand. Dobson's publications, along with tapes, films, and videocassettes of his speeches and seminars, the radio program, and various cable-television specials would make Dobson a household name for most Christian conservatives in America by the 1990s.

Dobson was not one to seek the media limelight even in conservative religious circles, but he was already a spokesperson on public morals as a member of the Commission on Pornography, which had been established in 1985 during the Reagan administration. He had become the trusted voice on any issue that related to what conservatives referred to as family values by the 1990s—on private school vouchers and tax credits for religious schools, on school prayer and corporal punishment for children, on the value of intelligent design as opposed to evolution in the teaching of science in schools, on anti-abortion issues, and on the sanctity of the heterosexual marriage and family.

Dobson's influence inside the Washington Beltway began when he founded the Family Research Council (FRC) in 1983—initially as a vehicle for conservative scholars to provide briefings to legislators on family-oriented issues. FRC struggled financially and was taken over by the Focus group in 1989, but Gary Bauer, a former Reagan adviser, had been selected to head the organization a year earlier, and its autonomy was restored in 1992. Under Bauer's guidance, the FRC became an advocacy group that rivaled Robertson's Christian Coalition as a representative of religious conservatism in the Capitol in the latter 1990s.[55]

Focus on the Family was also instrumental in changing the dynamics of the relationship between the Republican Party and the Christian Right in national politics. Once in power, evangelicals had been denied key posts in Republican administrations—critics would point most often to the Reagan and George H. W. Bush administrations—and their interests were downplayed. Even out of power, issues of concern to conservative religious activists had not been given the priority they felt they deserved in the Republican Party. While Christian conservatives constituted at least one-third of the party's voters, the biggest single component, they were still a minority within the conservative coalition.

Dobson wanted to place family-values issues at the center of Republican priorities, and he had been doing just that at the grassroots level for at least a decade. Focus established what it called Family Policy Councils in several states beginning in the late 1980s to get conservative state legislators involved in promoting legislation upholding traditional family values. Focus launched a magazine entitled the *Citizen* as a vehicle for public policy on family matters, and a radio feature separate from Dobson's radio show called *Family News in Focus* reported on political news concerning family life. A Focus on the Family Institute was set up in 1995 in Colorado Springs specifically to train young evangelicals in the politics of defending and promoting a traditional family-values agenda.

Family Planning Councils displaced the Christian Coalition's chapters by the beginning of the new century as the main family-values groups in local and state politics. They were decentralized, autonomous state bodies, and they had spent years lobbying to get individual states to erect barriers against gay marriage.

Dobson enhanced these efforts by helping to establish a secretive committee of political and evangelical leaders in Washington, D.C., called the Arlington Group; it was set up in 2002 by close associates Paul Weyrich and Don Wildmon, head of the American Family Association (1977), and chaired by Dobson. It had been 21 years since another secretive political committee created by Protestant conservatives, the Council for National Policy, was launched inside the Washington Beltway. The Arlington Group, along with Focus on the Family Action groups created by Dobson for the 2004 elections, would raise funds and lobby for legislators who supported a gay marriage ban.[56] A meeting in 1998 between a group of GOP and evangelical leaders led by Dobson resulted in the creation of so-called Values Action Teams that set up committees in both houses of Congress to discuss pragmatic ways to shape legislation of concern to pro-family conservatives.

The Catholic Alliance

Catholic conservatives also played a much more active role in the political arena during this decade.[57] The Christian Coalition made progress in broadening its alliance by reaching out to like-minded Catholics—launching an autonomous organization called the Catholic Alliance in 1995. Conservative Catholic publications like *Crisis* and *First Things* sought to give voice to conservative Catholic political and social views in opposition to liberal groups such as the Catholic-sponsored Interfaith Alliance.

The Christian Coalition initially hoped that a conservative Protestant-Catholic bloc might focus the attention of the wider Catholic community on issues such as abortion and euthanasia, and trump longtime Catholic concerns over economic justice and opposition to the death penalty. Conservative Catholic activists now focused on practicing rather than nonpracticing Catholics, and these efforts brought some success as Catholics were estimated to comprise 16 percent of the Coalition membership in the mid-1990s.

The Catholic Alliance did not have a real impact on the wider Catholic community, but it did lay the groundwork for a new conservative Catholic organization within the Republican Party, the National Catholic Leadership Forum (2002). Numerous other Catholic interest groups—such as the Catholic League for Religious and Civil Rights, Priests for Life, Opus Dei, and the Legionnaires of Christ, a Mexican-based order that publishes the conservative *National Catholic Register*—were also providing strong support for Republican politicians and policies by the end of the century.[58]

The Catholic Alliance, however, broke away from Robertson's Christian Coalition in 1997 following disputes over health care and the death penalty. Two years later Democrat Raymond Flynn, a former mayor of Boston and ambassador to the Vatican in the Clinton administration, was head of the organization. The Alliance encouraged Catholics to vote for "working-class" issues, such as social welfare and economic parity, while opposing abortion and euthanasia.

Seeking a higher ground than "left-" or "right-wing" politics, the Alliance became the Catholics in Alliance for the Common Good in 2004—finding alliances with other Catholic organizations in focusing on "the unifying moral priority to care for all humanity." The Alliance also associated itself with progressive interfaith groups such as Faith in Public Life in fighting the "go-it-alone culture of excessive greed." They lobbied for a number of progressive causes, including compassionate immigration reform in Congress.[59]

Contemporary Conservative Religious Politics

Focus on the Family, the Focus Research Council, the Arlington Group, and the Values Action Teams, along with the Christian Coalition and other conservative religious groups, such as Concerned Women for America, would play a major role in conservative religious politics during the Clinton and George W. Bush administrations. The Clinton administration was pressured to take a more conservative stance on some social issues in the late 1990s. Clauses, for example, were inserted into the Balanced Budget Act of 1997 that among other things provided families with a $500 tax credit per child, and Clinton was forced to abandon efforts to allow gays to join the military officially. Above all, these groups were instrumental in helping to broker the Defense of Marriage Act of 1996, the first salvo in the looming battle over gay marriage and family rights.

The victory of the Republican Party in the 2000 elections established a new framework for religious conservatives in politics, and the GOP understood it had to deliver on at least some demands. Programs supported under the president's Faith-Based and Community Initiatives, for example, were established in 10 cabinet-level departments to fund conservative religious projects. A key provision of the Initiatives was that federal funding to "religious groups ... would not be required to comply with certain civil rights statutes, and could discriminate by hiring employees of specific religious faiths." While hundreds of financially strapped, abstinence-only, sex-education programs, anti-abortion groups, and crisis pregnancy clinics received funding, the bulk of the money went to charities generated by conservative faith- and community-based groups that actively worked for the Republican Party in the 2000 elections.[60]

Public opinion polls suggested that "moral values" were by far the most important issues for white evangelical voters in the 2004 election—more important "than the combined percentages of those who cited Iraq, terrorism, or the economy," according to journalist Dan Gilgoff in his study of Dobson and Focus on the Family. The key moral issues for these voters were abortion and gay marriage rights, and these issues helped give the White House to George W. Bush and the Republicans for another four years.[61] While respondents generally cited the economy and terrorism as their major concerns prior to the 2008 elections, as we noted in the Introduction, white evangelical Protestants who claimed they attended church weekly constituted the one faith group represented who still cited moral values as their top priority.[62]

The conservative religious impact on American politics was also apparent in congressional battles over Bush's judicial nominees. Activists had long recognized that the federal courts, and especially the Supreme Court, were the final arbitrators in key pro-family legislative decisions. They "worked to popularize judicial activism," as Gilgoff puts it, "as a political issue among rank-and-file conservative voters."[63] Dobson and his allies played a key role in pressuring Republican members of Congress to adopt a strategy for evaluating Supreme Court nominees based almost solely on conservative religious pro-family issues.

John G. Roberts Jr.—a lawyer in the Reagan and George H. W. Bush administrations, a strict constructionist on constitutional issues, and a traditionalist Roman Catholic—was approved to replace William Rehnquist (1924–2005) as chief justice of the Supreme Court after Rehnquist's death. A tumultuous campaign backed by Dobson to replace the retired Sandra Day O'Connor with Harriet Miers, a woman with strong evangelical credentials but no judicial record, ended in failure. Dobson then backed Samuel Anthony Alito Jr.—another traditionalist Roman Catholic with impeccable conservative, pro-family judicial credentials—to replace the centrist O'Connor. He was confirmed in 2006. Religious conservatives believed the Supreme Court would tilt in a direction most favorable to their interests and concerns—an act of "divine intervention," as the head of the Texas Family Policy Council said.[64]

The president's personal beliefs were in harmony with the Christian conservative cultural agenda—engendering a relationship that had an enormous impact on public policy.[65] Many Americans, whether religious or not, became more and more fearful that civil

liberties were being undermined as the relationship between church
and state became ever more blurred during the Bush administration.
The real question for those who were fearful of the Bush political
agenda, however, was not how to reestablish boundaries between
church and state. This was not a fight over religion in politics but a
fight over the politics of religion. It was a battle, as Protestant
evangelical Jim Wallis put it, to recover a "stolen" faith: in the politics
of religion, "an enormous public misrepresentation of Christianity has
taken place."[66]

A PLURALITY OF VOICES IN CONSERVATIVE POLITICS AND RELIGION

Christian conservatives have been at the core of the conservative
coalition since the beginning, and the power of these activists has long
been expressed in the language of religion, social life, and politics.
A plurality of voices, however, has emerged in recent years to compromise both the unity of the conservative coalition and its base in the
Christian conservative movement.

These voices are apparent on a range of political and social issues, as
we shall see in subsequent chapters. The religious community, in particular, is sharply divided over such issues as church-state relations and
American civil religion (Chapter 4), contraception and abortion rights
(Chapter 5), gay marriage and family rights (Chapter 6), the teaching
of science in schools and the broader question of engagement with
the environment (Chapter 7), the war against terrorism (Chapter 8),
and militarism and the war in Iraq (Chapter 9).

We outline briefly in this section three issues that illustrate the
range of voices one finds within the Christian community today:

- First, we describe the fragility of the political alliance between religious
  and secular conservatives.
- Second, we offer examples of dissension within the conservative Protestant community over matters of politics, faith, and worship. While dissension within other conservative religious groups was also apparent, it
  seemed less disruptive within these faith traditions. Catholic dissension,
  for example, centered primarily on life issues (abortion, fetal stem-cell
  research, and homosexuality), rather than on political or theological
  issues, although attitudes and actions could and did intersect. Many
  Catholics felt a disconnect between themselves and their leaders—
  Vatican officials, local bishops, and even parish priests—but dissension

did not lead to more breakaways from the Catholic Church as seemed to be the case within Protestant denominations. Dissident Catholics simply left the church or joined evangelical churches.

- Third, we focus on two corollaries of human rights—international human rights and torture—in which Christians and believers in other faith traditions are working together to bring about a change in political attitudes.

A Fragmenting Political Alliance

The alliance between religious and secular conservatives was always a marriage of convenience. Secular conservatives endorsed parts of the conservative religious program in the belief that their political agenda would be supported—especially at election time. Scholarly forbearers of the neoconservative movement such as Leo Strauss (1899–1973) claimed that religion was a useful tool to generate support for public policy, but he was not wedded to a particular religion. As Strauss suggested, "almost any religion would succeed in accomplishing the political task at hand."[67]

The conservative coalition began to fragment even before the 2004 elections. It was rocked by a series of scandals involving Republican operatives such as the lobbyist Jack Abramoff and congressmen such as Mark Foley (R-Florida), the uproar over bribes paid to members of Congress to secure Department of Defense contracts (the so-called Cunningham Scandal), congressional interference in the Terri Schiavo right-to-life saga, growing public unrest over events that led to the war in Iraq, and a worsening economy—these and other issues had a cumulative and negative impact for Republicans in the 2006 midterm elections.

While religious conservatives continued to wield disproportional power in Bush's second term, public dissatisfaction with the performance both of the president and what Democrats called a "do-nothing" Congress turned many religious voters against the Republican Party. The Democrats regained control over both houses of Congress, for the first time since 1994, and a majority of the state legislatures. A majority of the state governors were also now Democrats.

The impact of a generation and more of religious conservatives on Republican politics, however, was also having an impact on Democratic politics. Congressional leaders were more public in stating their religious beliefs and Nancy Pelosi (D-California), a Roman Catholic mother of five and the speaker of the House, trumpeted the

values of American family life in launching what she called a Faith
Working Group for House Democrats.

Democrats had been working with various activists even before the
2004 elections to alter their "secular image" with religious conservatives. They adopted what the Republicans had adopted decades earlier
and constructed a moral foundation of their own for progressive public
policy. Anticipating the 2008 elections, the Democratic National Committee hired its first full-time religious outreach director in 2005 and
began working with a political consulting firm called Common Good
Strategies (headed by the person responsible for faith outreach in the
2004 Kerry-Edwards presidential campaign), whose mission was "to
help Democrats build relationships with Christian communities, most
importantly, the evangelical subculture."[68] It was a beginning.

Dissenting Protestant Voices

Christian conservatives, even with Protestant evangelical fundamentalists at the core, were never the singular voice that is often
assumed. Evangelicals "lack a center," as John Wilson, editor of the
magazine published by the conservative flagship company Christianity
Today International, put it. Critics of the contemporary evangelical
political movement "give a false impression of evangelical unity . . .
[and] underestimate the fluidity of religious identities."[69]

If Protestant conservatives ever did speak with one voice, there is
little evidence of this today. Sociologist Christian Smith, who has documented several misconceptions about Protestant evangelicalism,
noted more than a decade ago: "A most common error that observers
of evangelicals make is to presume that evangelical leaders speak as
representatives of ordinary evangelicals."[70]

The credibility of evangelical fundamentalist leaders such as Jerry
Falwell, Pat Robertson, John Agee, Ted Haggard (former head of the
National Association of Evangelicals), and numerous other national
and regional figures—it is a long list—is being severely tested in America's
present political climate. Terry Fox, the former pastor of a megachurch
in Wichita, Kansas, is a good example of what has happened to several
of these religious firebrands. Fox now preaches in a Best Western hotel,
and he told journalist David D. Kirkpatrick of the *New York Times* that
he paid a price for the stands he took. "The pendulum in the Christian
world has swung back to the moderate point of view. The real battle
now is among evangelicals."[71]

The mainstream media, moreover, no longer can be counted on to cite Protestant conservatives as a litmus test for Christian values. *New York Times* columnist Frank Rich asserts these "self-promoting values hacks don't speak for the American mainstream. They don't speak for the Republican Party. They no longer speak for many evangelical ministers and their flocks. The emperors of morality have in fact had no clothes for some time."[72]

Older leaders, such as Dobson (who was 70 years old in 2006), want Christian conservatives to adhere to the fixed family-values political agenda that they had promoted for more than 30 years. Dobson has been either neutral (as in his attitude toward human rights legislation) or negative (as in his response to climate initiatives) to current cultural concerns. Younger evangelicals, however, are turning away from this insistence on partisan politics to concentrate on "the ethic of Jesus" in a wide range of foreign and domestic social and environmental issues—from UN efforts to combat poverty and HIV/AIDS (especially in sub-Saharan Africa) to "climate change" and "working with poor, academically troubled inner-city schools ... [and] against human trafficking."[73]

The Dominion/Reconstructionist Movement

As religious conservatives expanded their public agenda and membership became more diverse, there were increasing signs of stress. Some Protestant conservatives sought to replace liberal elements within their church organizations with leaders who had remained faithful to what they regarded as a purer form of evangelical fundamentalism. An early but classic case was the rebirth of the Southern Baptist Convention in 1979 as a more strictly defined fundamentalist faith tradition with a more rigid social and political agenda—an agenda that no longer advocated strict separation between church and state.[74]

Other Protestant conservatives were joining extremist groups associated with the Dominion/Reconstructionist movement—a term for those who were essentially determined to turn America into an Old Testament–style, Christian theocratic state. The label "Dominion Theology" is often used today as the preferred term for the movement, because it suggests that the "true" Christian believer should have dominion over every area of life. "He" (women are relegated to a subordinate status) does not, because "Satan" has usurped man's dominion over the earth. Christ will not return until man reasserts his dominance.

The Dominion groups are postmillennialist in their eschatology—
the belief that Christ will not return to earth until after the millennium or after the entire world has been converted to this form of
Christianity. Even some conservative religious leaders have condemned the Dominionists for their extremism—which includes death
for offenses such as adultery, homosexuality, and blasphemy, an anti-
Israel stance, and a genocidal solution for "unbelievers." Dominion
groups launched their own political-action committee called Coalition on Revival, active in some GOP precincts, which was deemed to
be a purer form of political fundamentalism.[75]

The Evangelical "Emergent" Church

Still other Protestant conservatives moved in the opposite direction
as they began to explore new religious conversations within—or outside—their congregations. In essence, they were emulating other kinds
of conversations going on in moderate and progressive Protestant and
Catholic congregations on similar issues. The inspiration for many
conservative women's groups in the 1990s, for example, stemmed from
the Women's Aglow Fellowship International, founded in 1967.
Aglow today constitutes the largest Protestant women's mission
organization in the world (in more than 164 countries as of 2006).
But it has emerged from American Pentecostalism to become an interdenominational movement challenging stereotypical images of wom-
en's spirituality and female submission to male authority.[76]

Some evangelicals at the turn of the twenty-first century were calling themselves members of an *emergent* church, which they claimed
was a quest "to deconstruct and reconstruct Christianity," as Brian
D. McLaren, one of the leaders in the movement, put it, "in a postmodern culture." They were a diverse group of young (the rank and
file are mainly in their 20s and 30s), white, English-speaking members
of evangelical Protestant churches in North America, Britain, and
Australia. McLaren called this conversation "an as-yet ill-defined
borderland in which central modern values like objectivity, analysis,
and control will become less compelling. They are superseded by
postmodern values like mystery and wonder."[77]

Members of the emergent church are a localized, decentralized, and
unstructured phenomenon at the moment: while some churches openly
declare themselves as emerging, most emerging Protestant evangelicals
are members of churches in established denominations—from

Episcopalians to Southern Baptists. They employ a variety of techniques in the visual and performing arts in developing the worship service. There is no uniformity of beliefs or practices in this conversation, no confessional creeds or doctrines, no acceptable method, or even a goal in evangelizing the world, which pleases adherents and angers detractors.[78]

The "emerging church conversation" offers a hopeful rather than a despairing or defensive reading of Christian evangelicals, and they have been favorably compared to other alternative expressions of Christianity such as the Roman Catholic Taizé Community and the Religious Society of Friends (the Quakers). Eileen W. Lindner, editor of the *Yearbook of American & Canadian Churches 2006*, cites the emerging churches and the new technologies they are using to communicate their ideas (primarily through blogs and Web sites) as the twin twenty-first century trends in American Protestantism.[79]

Christianity and Human Rights

The Christian stance on human rights begins with consideration of the human person, for one cannot decide how a human being should interact with the natural and human worlds without first determining what a human being is or should be. Personhood, the term frequently used in discussions of ethics and morality, encompasses "the idea that human beings are members of a moral community, that they have moral rights and privileges as a result, and that there is an inherent value to this status."[80]

There is considerable disagreement among Christians, however, about what constitutes a human rights violation. Some argue that imposing the death penalty is a violation of the condemned person's human rights, while others do not. Some argue that civil laws making it illegal for a church to marry gay couples is a violation, while some do not. Some Christians even argue that torture is morally acceptable to achieve a larger moral goal, to keep the population safe. Other Christians argue that torture is *never* morally acceptable.

Some Christians suggest that debates about human rights and other moral issues are insufficiently grounded in Christian literature, particularly the Bible, and "the notion of collective good has been progressively overwhelmed by the conjunction of capitalist ideology and human autonomy," as Anthony Dancer, social justice commissioner for the Anglican Church in Aotearoa, New Zealand, and Polynesia puts it.[81] The idea of a moral community has been replaced with moti-vations based largely on self-interest—the focus being on individual rights. In a liberal democracy, "conversation about virtue has largely given way to this language about rights, and the state, as a conse-quence, has become the means through which rights are protected without the benefit of a shared common narrative, or 'common good,' other than a belief in human autonomy and freedom." Christians have too often submitted to state authority and have not held the state "accountable to the (just) reign of God."[82]

Nevertheless, Christians have for millennia believed that human beings have "transcendent worth," because they were made in God's image, and therefore human rights are universal and unconditional. Many Christians argue that because they are part of a moral commu-nity, they must be responsible for their own actions and the actions of their communities. Religious conservatives in recent years have joined their liberal counterparts in addressing two recent problems that are of concern to the moral community—international human rights and torture.

International Human Rights

Religious conservatives have formed loose alliances with main-stream religious and secular groups—including the National Associa-tion of Evangelicals in alliance with the National Council of Churches, the United States Conference of Catholic Bishops, the Anti-Defamation League, and Human Rights Watch—to fight for international human rights.

The evangelical stance on international human rights grew out of long-standing concerns about Christian minorities in non-Christian countries. The National Association of Evangelicals had actually spon-sored an international religious persecution conference in 1996—it was initiated by GOP operative Michael Horowitz, who is a Jew, and Richard Cizik, the prominent spokesperson and chief lobbyist for the National Association of Evangelicals in Washington, D.C. The conference issued what its members called a "Statement of Conscience" that provided specific guidelines about religious persecution for government policy makers. They joined Catholics and various other Christian and non-Christian groups to campaign for the International Religious Freedom Act, which President Bill Clinton signed into law in 1998 (and strengthened with further amendments in 1999).

The Department of State, with its own roving ambassador-at-large, was required to produce yearly reports on religious freedom in almost every country in the world. An independent United States Commission on International Religious Freedom, which was responsible to Congress, was also created to identify discrimination where it occurred. Like the Department of State, the Religious Freedom Commission was required to produce yearly reports targeting countries that "engaged in or tolerated violations of religious freedom," and both bodies made "non-binding policy recommendations" to the White House and Congress.[83]

Mainstream religious human rights groups joined forces with evangelicals when they saw that they were genuinely committed to religious freedom for all faiths. A loosely knit religious coalition was formed that proved to be instrumental in passing numerous pieces of legislation during the Bush administration—including the Trafficking Victims Protection Act (2000), Sudan Peace Act (2002), Prison Rape Elimination Act (2003), and the North Korea Human Rights Act (2004). They extended the meaning of human rights into areas that had "received scant attention," as Gilgoff puts it, "from secular human rights organizations" or from news media.[84]

Torture

Defining torture is not particularly easy. The International Committee of the Red Cross "uses the broad term 'ill-treatment' to cover both torture and other methods of abuse prohibited by international law, including inhuman, cruel, humiliating, and degrading treatment, outrages upon personal dignity and physical or moral coercion."[85] Heated debates often center on the definitions of these individual terms. Some define waterboarding (which induces extreme fear but no long-term physical injury) as torture, while others do not. Sleep deprivation constitutes torture for some but not for others. Keeping detainees in harsh conditions or uncomfortable positions is defined as torture by some but not others. Christians can find little help in the Bible, for torture is not mentioned.[86]

Whether they can define torture or not, the U.S. government's approval of torture to extract information from detainees—particularly those at Guantanamo Bay Naval Base in Cuba—has often dominated discussions of human rights issues in recent years. Many Christians agree with *The Christian Century*, flagship publication of progressive Christians, that "it is deeply troubling that officials continue to invoke the misleading scenario of the 'ticking time bomb' to justify coercive physical interrogation." These Christians are concerned primarily about the degradation of the individual human person, of course, but they also fear that the approval of torture by one government agency will encourage another agency to use the same technique. "Ordinary police officers begin to think: why engage in the hard work of an investigation if we can do what the elite forces do—use force to get results."[87]

Torture is officially condemned by the Roman Catholic church, and Evangelicals for Human Rights, a group of 17 activists, spent roughly six months in 2007 writing "An Evangelical Declaration against Torture: Protecting Human Rights in an Age of Terror." The declaration argues "every human life is sacred. As evangelical Christians, recognition of this transcendent moral dignity is non-negotiable in every area of life, including our assessment of public policies." The declaration states that Christians must act in behalf of those whose rights are violated. "[W]e renounce the resort to torture and cruel, inhuman, and degrading treatment of detainees," the declaration says, ". . . and urge the reversal of any U.S. government law, policy, or practice that violates the moral standards outlined in this declaration."[88]

The "Declaration of Principles for a Presidential Executive Order on Prisoner Treatment, Torture and Cruelty"—sponsored by the interfaith National Religious Campaign Against Torture, Evangelicals for Human Rights, and the nonpartisan Center for Victims of Torture—calls on the president, in essence, to reject the use of torture against prisoners. The petition has been signed by prominent leaders around the country, including Bishop Thomas Wenski of Orlando, Florida, chairman of the international justice and peace committee of the United States Conference of Catholic Bishops.[89] Former President George W. Bush did not sign the proposed executive order, but President Barack Obama expressed opposition to torture and will be asked to sign the order.

Conclusion

The conservative religion-cum-political agenda in America for more than a generation has been securely grounded in a boundary-laden understanding of Christian orthodoxy in the modern world. A broad range of religious and nonreligious conservatives were attracted to this agenda in their efforts to reconstruct America's political order.

Some conservative religious beliefs and evangelical priorities, moreover, continue to resonate with many other Christians, who do not perceive themselves to be politically conservative. Most mainstream Christians of all denominations (whether Protestant, Catholic, or Eastern Orthodox), for example, can claim a common biblical heritage, an orthodox Christology, and a Trinitarian credo that is deeply engrained in American Christian culture.

The Christian Right's outrage over the seemingly amoral behavior of so many Americans in public life has also resonated with other Christians and other religious communities unable to cope with the sheer banality of American materialism and its culture of greed. Christian conservatives do offer a distinct sacred narrative that provides emotional comfort and perhaps a sociopolitical haven for those seeking religious guidelines in the past that seem more stable and secure, and more value-laden, than the religious guidelines of the present.

Many contemporary Christian conservatives in politics are no longer necessarily biblical literalists or stereotypically uneducated rednecks. Conflating biblical law with natural law in a conservative mold, they believe they are apostles of modernity, and their ranks are filled with some of the nation's most educated and prosperous citizens. They have become masters at exploiting the technologies and organizational acumen of the postmodern world without buying into its cultural implications.

While most observers still regard the white evangelical Protestant South as the heartland of Christian conservatism,[90] this religious mindset is now a truly interdenominational, cross-cultural, national, and international phenomenon. The focus of all Christian conservatives remains the heterosexual family, and the one political link that binds them together is their social conservatism.[91]

"Religious fundamentalist movements are popular as well as conservative," and they all have "the potential for mass appeal," as Catholic law professor John H. Garvey wrote 15 years ago. This is because they offer a model of political faith that is drawn from their model of religious faith: God is active in their world, and God has a plan for the future of humanity. They offer a belief system that is short and concrete in its simplicity: scripture provides the only sacred text for daily living. They are "practical" in stressing a moral code based on conduct or *right* behavior. And they deliver their moral and ethical messages in a nonhierarchical style that is nonthreatening.[92]

Many Christian conservative activists have provided a coherent, visible, and seemingly viable political vision for their audiences, a vision that is thoroughly grounded in what we have described as a peculiarly Christian conservative vision of modernity. The cumulative impact of this vision on America's contemporary political culture has been enormous, as we shall argue in subsequent chapters. It is an especially compelling vision for many Americans in times of crisis, as in the postmodern world of America since 9/11.

NOTES

1. From "John Hagee Ministries: All the Gospel to All the World," www.jhm.org/beliefs.asp and www.jhm.org/partnership.asp (requires registration for access).

2. "The Politics of Communion," *Christianity Today*, June 2004, 24–25; and Gerard Wright, "Kerry Needs Miracle to Part Holy See from the State," *USA Today*, May 22, 2004, A20.

3. David Firestone, "Billy Graham Responds to Lingering Anger over 1972 Remarks on Jews," *New York Times*, March 17, 2002, A29; Matthew Engel, "War in the Gulf: Bringing Aid and the Bible; The Man Who Called Islam Wicked," *Guardian* (Manchester), April 4, 2003, 6.

4. Alan Cooperman, "Catholics No Longer Out to Convert Jews," *Houston Chronicle*, August 18, 2002, A4.

5. Glenn H. Utter and John W. Storey, *The Religious Right. A Reference Handbook*, 3rd ed. (Millerton, NY: Grey House, 2007). Utter and Storey provide a reliable chronology of key events and issues in the history of Christian conservatism in America.

6. Religious scholars have documented the rise of Christian conservative activism at all levels of government. On religion and politics, see John C. Green, Mark J. Rozell, and Clyde Wilcox, eds., *The Christian Right in American Politics: Marching to the Millennium* (Washington, DC: Georgetown University Press, 2003). Rozell and Wilcox also analyzed the Christian Right's role in specific congressional and presidential elections beginning with the 1994 elections. See Rozell and Wilcox, eds., *God at the Grass Roots: The Christian Right in the 1994 Elections* (Lanham, MD: Rowman & Littlefield, 1995); Rozell and Wilcox, eds., *God at the Grass Roots, 1996: The Christian Right in the American Elections* (Lanham, MD: Rowman & Littlefield, 1997). See also M. V. Hood III and Mark Caleb Smith, "On the Prospect of Linking Religious-Right Identification with Political Behavior: Panacea or Snipe Hunt?" *Journal for the Scientific Study of Religion* 41, no. 4 (2002): 697–710; Kraig Beyerlein and Mark Chaves, "The Political Activities of Religious Congregations in the United States," *Journal for the Scientific Study of Religion* 42, no. 2 (2003): 229–246. *The Journal for the Scientific Study of*

Religion (JSSR) devoted its entire December 2003 issue to American clergy as political activists. JSSR is one of the few journals we have found that provides consistent empirical evidence of the link between religious belief and political outlook.

7. Habermas set out his ideas in *The Structural Transformation of the Public Sphere: An Inquiry into a Category of Bourgeois Society*, trans. Thomas Burger with Frederick Lawrence (Cambridge, MA: MIT, 1989, first published in German in 1962). The best interpretation we have found is by Steven Seidman, ed., *Jürgen Habermas on Society and Politics: A Reader* (Boston: Beacon Press, 1989). While the notion of a *bourgeois* public sphere is not without its feminist, postcolonial, and postmodern critics, we believe it provides a revealing outline of the social contours of modernity as it emerged and later declined in Western culture.

8. Martin E. Marty and R. Scott Appleby, eds., *Fundamentalisms and the State: Remaking Polities, Economies, and Militance*, Vol. 3, *The Fundamentalism Project* (Chicago: University of Chicago Press, 1993), 3.

9. The periodic resurgence of massive religious revivals is a common theme in American church history. The First Great Awakening occurred essentially in the New England colonies between the 1730s and 1740s. The Second Great Awakening stretched to America's frontier at the time—in places such as the Appalachian region, in western New York, and in Ohio and adjacent districts—between the 1820s and 1830s. The Third Great Awakening focused mainly on urban revivals, and it occurred roughly between the 1880s and the 1910s.

10. John Shelby Spong, "The Rise of Fundamentalism, Part III: The Five Fundamentals," March 21, 2007, unpublished article, http://secure .agoramedia.com/manage_spong.asp (requires paid subscription for access).

11. Mary R. Sawyer, "The Black Church and Black Politics: Models of Ministerial Activism," *Journal of Religious Thought* 52/53, nos. 2/1 (1995–1996): 45–62.

12. Protestant educators such as Booker T. Washington (1856–1915), the founder of Tuskegee Normal and Industrial Institute (now Tuskegee University), and its most famous instructor, the scientist George Washington Carver (1864–1943), helped spearhead the drive to create independent black colleges in the decades before World War I. Hampton in Virginia (1868), Morehouse in Georgia (1867), Fisk in Tennessee (1866), Shaw in North Carolina (1865), and dozens of others would provide the educational foundation for several generations of African-American middle-class elites in the South.

13. Anson Phelps Stokes, *Church and State in the United States*, Vol. III (New York: Harper, 1950), 13–14.

14. Union Oil also financed the publication and marketing of the 12 books produced by the Presbyterians at Princeton. Spong, "The Rise of Fundamentalism."

15. Cyrus I. Scofield (1843–1921) was actually a lawyer and later a preacher, who was pastor of the First Congregational Church in Dallas, Texas, from 1882 to 1895 and again from 1902 to 1907. His commentaries on scripture were regarded as sacrosanct in Protestant working-class households—such as the one Les Switzer grew up in during the 1940s and early 1950s.

16. The Pentecostal-Charismatic movement today claims 400–600 million adherents worldwide and 10–12 million in the United States (depending on the source). Three independent groups are credited with being the pioneers of contemporary Pentecostalism. One was formed at a Bible school in Kansas in 1899 under the leadership of Charles Parham (1873–1929). This group eventually established its headquarters in Houston, Texas, in 1905, where Parham founded the Houston Bible College and named his group the Apostolic Faith Mission. One was also formed initially in Mississippi in 1897 as the Church of God in Christ under Charles Mason before migrating to Arkansas and then to Tennessee. Both men were strictly segregationist in the beginning, but Seymour's ministry—he had been Parham's student in Houston—quickly eclipsed those of Mason and Parham. The Azusa Street Revival is regarded as the birthplace of the Pentecostal-Charismatic movement (as it is now called). Seymour's ministry transformed Mason and his followers, but Parham could not accept racial and gender comingling. He was disgraced by a sodomy charge (even though it was later dropped) and eventually ended up joining the Ku Klux Klan. See Jack W. Hayford and S. David Moore, *The Charismatic Century: The Enduring Impact of the Azusa Street Revival* (New York: Warner Faith, 2006); Richard Vara, "Birth of Pentecostalism: The Houston Connection," *Houston Chronicle*, April 22, 2006, F1, F4; Benjamin Anastas, "The Pentecostal Promise," *New York Times Magazine*, April 23, 2006, 32, 34; history of Elder Charles Harrison Mason, Holy Trinity Lutheran Church, New Rochelle, New York, undated, www.holytrinitynewrochelle.org/CHMason.html.

17. The precise role of Protestant conservatives in the prohibition movement is not clear. What is clear is that anti-immigrant and anti-Catholic sentiments among the dominant white Protestant middle classes fueled the temperance movement. A number of states had antialcohol laws by the end of the nineteenth century. The National Prohibition Party (1869) won its first seat in Congress in 1890, and the Anti-Saloon League— perhaps the most powerful lobby group in the prohibition struggle—was formed in 1893. The 18th Amendment was ratified in 1919 along with the Volstead Act, which provided the mechanism to enforce the ban on alcohol. Prohibition lasted 13 years before it was repealed with the 21st Amendment in 1933.

18. George M. Marsden, *Fundamentalism and American Culture: The Shaping of Twentieth-Century Evangelicalism: 1870–1925* (New York: Oxford University Press, 1980), 186.

19. The National Council of Churches is affiliated to the WCC just as the American Council of Christian Churches is affiliated to the ICCC. Carl McIntire helped launch the American Council and the ICCC. See International Council of Christian Churches Web site, www.iccc.org.sg/iccc.htm.

20. National Association of Evangelicals, www.nae.net/index.cfm? FUSEACTION=nae.history.

21. BIOLA, for example, is now a full-fledged university offering 145 academic programs at undergraduate and graduate levels. It was the only school affiliated to the Council for Christian Colleges and Universities to be ranked by *US News & World Report* in the "major leagues" of American universities in 2005. See BIOLA University, www.biola.edu. Westminster in 2006 had campuses in Philadelphia and Dallas, and three "programs" in New York, London, and Seoul, South Korea. See Westminster Theology Seminary, www.wts.edu.

22. Nina Easton, "Political Fundamentals: Patrick Henry College Trains Religious Students for the Secular Fight," *New York Times*, September 9, 2007, Book Review-12, reviewing Hanna Rosin, *God's Harvard. A Christian College on a Mission to Save America* (Orlando, FL: Harcourt, 2007).

23. Most Catholic institutions of higher learning were created in the late nineteenth and early–mid twentieth centuries, and they are located in every region of the United States. Essentially nonsectarian today, they include such highly regarded universities as Notre Dame (Indiana), Boston College (Massachusetts), La Salle (Pennsylvania), Georgetown (District of Columbia), Fordham (New York), Gonzaga (Washington), University of San Diego (California), and, at one time, Trinity University (Texas).

24. Council for Christian Colleges and Universities, www.cccu.org; Samantha M. Shapiro, "All God's Children," *New York Times Magazine*, September 5, 2004, 46–51; Melissa Deckman, "Religion Makes the Difference: Why Christian Right Candidates Run for the School Board," *Review of Religious Research* 42, no. 4 (2001): 349–371.

25. Very few critical studies have been done on conservative theological and social practices in mainstream, so-called liberal Protestant or Roman Catholic congregations in the United States. Les Switzer examined a single congregation in the mainstream United Methodist Church—President George W. Bush's denomination—in 2000. The church is in Houston, Texas, and it was at the time one of the flagship churches in America's second-largest Protestant denomination (after the Southern Baptists). He found that the congregation's political, social, and economic networks were staunchly representative of the conservative social order. One of the more interesting exercises was to examine the titles and descriptions of the 33 adult Sunday school classes then in operation each week. "The overwhelming emphasis is on bible studies and bible-centered 'faith-in-life-issues,' and it

is essentially devotional in terms of content. Only one or two classes have had more than a marginal interest in examining the bible as an historical or literary text, and there is virtually no effort to offer critical perspectives on biblical content. A few classes in the past tried to focus on contemporary social concerns, but interest was limited and even the generally moderate approach to issues raised [even when they were based on the Methodist Church's own Book of Resolutions] often met with resistance." Les Switzer, "A Profile of St. Luke's United Methodist Church (Houston, Texas): Religion, Power & Society in Contemporary America" (unpublished report, 2001).

26. Mary Jo Weaver, "Catholics on the Right," *Commonweal*, February 11, 1994, 24–25. See also William D. Dinges and James Hitchcock, "Roman Catholic Traditionalism and Activist Conservatism in the United States," in *Fundamentalisms Observed*, Vol. 1, ed. Martin E. Marty and R. Scott Appleby (Chicago: University of Chicago Press, 1991), 66–141, p. 82: "The [Catholic] fundamentalist orientation therefore is not an emotional one but a strongly rationalistic one where religion is based on a standardized, objective knowledge of God." Orthodox doctrine is "correct belief" for the "traditionalist Catholic," which is in harmony with natural law and the only path to "salvation." See also Patrick Allitt, *Catholic Intellectuals and Conservative Politics in America, 1950–1985* (Ithaca, NY: Cornell University Press, 1993).

27. Linda Kintz, "Culture and the Religious Right," in *Media, Culture, and the Religious Right*, ed. Linda Kintz and Julia Lesage (Minneapolis: University of Minnesota Press, 1998), 3–20, p. 7.

28. Gregg Easterbrook, "The New Ecumenicalism: Believers of Many Faiths Embrace in America," *United Methodist Reporter*, February 8, 2002, 2–3 (citing a study published in 2001). See also Tom W. Smith, "Religious Diversity in America: The Emergence of Muslims, Buddhists, Hindus, and Others," *Journal for the Scientific Study of Religion* 41, no. 3 (2002): 577–585.

29. This is rarely acknowledged in the literature, but see Darryl G. Hart, "Mainstream Protestantism, 'Conservative' Religion, and Civil Society," in *Religion Returns to the Public Square: Faith and Policy in America*, ed. Hugh Heclo and Wilfred M. McClay (Washington, DC: Woodrow Wilson Center, 2003), 199, 202.

30. See Tom W. Smith and Seokho Kim, "The Vanishing Protestant Majority," National Opinion Research Center/University of Chicago, July 2004, www.news.uchicago.edu/releases/04/040720.protestant.pdf, Table 2. While a majority of non-Christians were Jewish in 1972 (3 percent Jewish and 1.9 percent other religions), for example, as a percentage of the total population most non-Christians were non-Jews in 2002 (1.5 percent Jewish and 6.9 percent other religions). The nonreligious population today will vary according to the survey. More than 14 percent of respondents, for example, did not identify with any religion and more than 5 percent "refused to reply to the question about their religious preference" in one nationwide religious survey in 2001. This study—a religious identification survey first conducted

in 1990—was "a random digit-dialed telephone survey of 50,281 American residential households" residing in the lower-48 states. Barry A. Kosmin, Egon Mayer, and Ariela Keysar, "American Religious Identification Survey 2001," The Graduate Center of the City University of New York, New York City, December 19, 2001, www.gc.cuny.edu/faculty/research_briefs/aris.pdf.

31. Phillip E. Hammond, *The Protestant Presence in Twentieth-Century America: Religion and Political Culture* (Albany, NY: State University of New York Press, 1992), 171. See also Michael Hout, Andrew Greeley, and Melissa J. Wilde, "The Demographic Imperative in Religious Change in the United States," *American Journal of Sociology* 107, no. 2 (2001): 468–500.

32. The Roman Catholics (with 67.8 million adherents) are by far the largest Christian denomination in America followed by the Southern Baptists (with 16.3 million) and the United Methodist Church (with 8.2 million). The fastest-growing denominations between 2001 and 2004, however, were the Assemblies of God (Pentecostal) followed by the Mormons and Roman Catholics. Eileen W. Lindner, ed., *Yearbook of American & Canadian Churches 2006* (Nashville: Abingdon Press, 2006), 11 (Table 2), 12 (Table 3). The *Yearbook* is prepared and edited for the National Council of Churches of Christ in the U.S.A.

33. "Political involvement may alter the original exclusivist, dogmatic, and confrontational mode of the fundamentalist to such a degree," Marty and Appleby have argued, "that the word 'fundamentalist' no longer applies." David Neff, editor of *Christianity Today*, cited discussions among evangelical power brokers, who thought the term "evangelical"—like the term "fundamentalist"—should be dropped in favor of "classic Christians or historic orthodox Christians," Marty and Appleby, *Fundamentalism and the State*, 6; Michael Luo, "Big Tent Religion: Evangelicals Debate the Meaning of 'Evangelical,'" *New York Times*, April 16, 2006, Week in Review-5.

34. As quoted by Nancy T. Ammerman, "North American Protestant Fundamentalism," in Kintz and Lesage, *Media, Culture*, 55–113, pp. 98–99. Ammerman cites Bob Jones Sr. as the source of the quote, but it must have been Bob Jones Jr. since his father died decades before the Moral Majority was created in 1979. Bob Jones Sr. (1883–1968) founded the university as a "whites only" Bible college in 1927, and it was eventually moved to its permanent home in Greenville, South Carolina, in 1947 and renamed Bob Jones University. Bob Jones Jr. followed his father as president (1947–1971), and Bob Jones III followed him (1971–2005). George W. Bush addressed students at the university during the presidential election primaries in 2000.

35. John J. Dilulio, "The Catholic Voter: A Description with Recommendations," *Commonweal*, March 24, 2006, 10–12, p. 11.

36. Laurie Goodstein, "The 'Hypermodern' Foe; How the Evangelicals and Catholics Joined Forces," *New York Times*, May 30, 2004, Week in Review-4.

37. Tom W. Smith, "The Religious Right and Anti-Semitism," *Review of Religious Research* 40, no. 3 (1999): 244–258.

38. Clyde Wilcox wrote two engaging books that have informed our understanding of the role played by the Moral Majority and the Christian Coalition in the context of conservative religious politics during this era: *God's Warriors: The Christian Right in Twentieth-Century America* (Baltimore: Johns Hopkins University Press, 1992), and a sequel, *Onward Christian Soldiers? The Religious Right in American Politics*, 2nd ed. (Boulder, CO: Westview, 2000). We also consulted Sara Diamond, *Not by Politics Alone: The Enduring Influence of the Christian Right* (New York: Guilford Press, 1998); and William Martin, *With God on Our Side: The Rise of the Religious Right in America* (New York: Broadway, 1996). For the James Dobson era, we relied mainly on Dan Gilgoff, *The Jesus Machine: How James Dobson, Focus on the Family, and Evangelical America Are Winning the Culture War* (New York: St. Martin's, 2007).

39. Sean F. Everton, "The Promise Keepers: Religious Revival or Third Way of the Religious Right?" *Review of Religious Research* 43, no. 1 (2001): 51–69, p. 52. Everton concludes that while the Promise Keepers were basically apolitical, their theological and social agendas were conservative.

40. LDS had just under 6 million adherents (and just under 13 million worldwide) in 2007. Just under 100 Mormon fundamentalist splinter groups exist, but they have relatively few adherents. See "Mormon Splinter Groups: Sects That Broke Away from the Church of Jesus Christ of Latter-Day Saints," Latter-Day Saints (Mormons), undated, www.4mormon.org/mormon-splinter-groups.php.

41. José Casanova, *Public Religions in the Modern World* (Chicago: University of Chicago Press, 1994), 5. See also Talal Asad, "Religion, Nation-State, Secularism," in *Nation and Religion: Perspectives on Europe and Asia*, ed. Peter van der Veer and Hartmut Lehmann (Princeton, NJ: Princeton University Press, 1999), 178–196.

42. For useful overviews of Christian conservatives in politics before and during the 1980s other than those cited in footnotes 6 and 38, see David G. Bromley and Anson D. Shupe, eds., *New Christian Politics* (Macom, GA: Mercer University Press, 1984); and Mark A. Shibley, *Resurgent Evangelicalism in the United States: Mapping Cultural Change Since 1970* (Columbia: University of South Carolina Press, 1996).

43. Ammerman, "North American Protestant," 95–100.

44. Wilcox, *God's Warriors*, 156. The Religious Roundtable and Christian Voice were Moral Majority sister organizations in the 1980s. The Religious Roundtable Council of 56 (its formal name, which was changed to American Policy Roundtable in 2004) was launched by Ed McAteer, a retired executive for Colgate-Palmolive, as a coalition of conservative business, military, political, and religious leaders seeking to "restore Judeo-Christian principles," according to its Web site, www.aproundtable.org. The Christian

Voice, founded by Baptist minister Richard Grant, was one of the earliest of the values-based political action groups to have a national impact on voters. The organization had dubious "morality scorecard" ratings for members of Congress that were used in voters' guides for churches. These guides were "precursors" to "more sophisticated" guides used by the Christian Coalition to galvanize conservative religious voters from the 1990s. See The Christian Voice, www.christianvoice.org.uk.

45. The Traditional Values Coalition today claims it is a nondenominational church lobby that speaks to Congress and the White House about "pro-family" issues on behalf of more than 43,000 churches. The chair is Louis P. "Lou" Sheldon, a Presbyterian minister (his mother was Jewish) and another representative of the anti-gay wing of Christian Right leaders in the Republican Party. See The Traditional Values Coalition, www .traditionalvalues.org/about.php.

46. The Citizens for Community Values was started by yet another group of clergy and laymen. The founder and head is a Presbyterian minister from Cincinnati, Ohio. The group is based in the Cincinnati metropolitan area and focuses on pornography. Espousing "traditional Judeo-Christian values," it is a good example of pro-family grassroots organizing at the local and state level. It also coordinates several other antipornography groups located in the Midwest (Indiana, Kentucky, and Ohio). See Citizens for Community Values, www.ccv.org/aboutus.aspx.

47. See the Council for National Policy Web site, www.policycounsel .org/24508.html; and David D. Kirkpatrick, "Club of the Most Powerful Gathers in Strictest Privacy," *New York Times*, August 28, 2004, A10.

48. For useful overviews of Christian conservatives in politics during the 1990s other than those cited in footnote 38, see Justin Watson, *Christian Coalition: Dreams of Restoration, Demands for Recognition* (New York: St. Martin's, 1997); and evangelical scholar Mark Noll's "Evangelicals Past and Present," in *Religion, Politics, and the American Experience: Reflections on Religion and American Public Life*, ed, Edith L. Blumhofer (Tuscaloosa: University of Alabama Press, 2002), 103–122.

49. The Freedom Council would come under IRS scrutiny because it was funded illegally by Robertson's nonprofit Christian Broadcasting Network, and it was forced to close down in 1986.

50. Nina J. Easton, *Gang of Five: Leaders at the Center of the Conservative Crusade* (New York: Simon & Schuster, 2000), 257–258.

51. Reed became much more active in Republican politics after he left the Coalition—as chair of the Georgia Republican Party and a key adviser in the 2000 and 2004 Bush-Cheney election campaigns. He entered politics himself as a candidate for lieutenant governor in the 2006 Georgia primary election. Like other evangelicals in the past generation who have become embedded in America's political culture, however, Reed was linked to scandal—in this case, to the notorious Washington, D.C., lobbyist

Jack Abramoff—and he was defeated by a Republican opponent in the primaries.

52. The Coalition's budget gradually shrank from $26 million to $1 million. Robertson also resigned from the organization—now heavily in debt—in 2001. Pressure from creditors and the unwanted publicity over the Coalition's tax-exempt status as a nonprofit organization "sapped its strength." Forced to pay back taxes by the IRS, the Coalition lost thousands of members and "never fully recovered." Alan Cooperman and Thomas B. Edsall, "Christian Coalition Shrinks as Debt Grows," *Washington Post*, April 10, 2006, Al.

53. The Church of the Nazarene is associated with the Third Great Awakening, which saw the beginnings of American fundamentalist Christianity. Its roots can be traced to the holiness movement, which sought to renew the teachings of John Wesley (1703–1791) and Methodism on the meaning of perfection in the sanctified Christian life—a life in which believers know they are corrupted by sin but nevertheless try to live lives without consciously being sinful. The Nazarene Church was born in a small town called Pilot Point, Texas, in 1908, and in its centennial year of 2008 had more than 1.7 million members (21,000 congregations) in 151 countries. Its headquarters are now in Kansas City, Missouri. See the Church of the Nazarene Web site, www.nazarene.org/ministries/administration/visitorcenter/about/display.aspx.

54. Dobson's first book (other than a manual on mental deficiency in children) was *Dare to Discipline* (Wheaton, IL: Tyndale, 1970), a diatribe against permissive parenting. He had produced four others by 1980—all on topics related to marital relations and child rearing.

55. The FRC built a new headquarters in downtown Washington—financed by two conservative family-owned corporate enterprises in Michigan—and had 120 staffers and a $14 million budget when Bauer resigned as executive director in 1999 to seek a presidential bid during the Republican Party primaries in 2000. Apparently he had tried but failed to convince Dobson to be a candidate. Like Robertson before him, Bauer failed to win the nomination. The FRC at the end of the decade was virtually unrivaled as a religious lobby group "in terms of budget, profile, and influence." Gilgoff, *The Jesus Machine*, 118.

56. Dobson, along with Wildmon, and others were leaders in the long-running evangelical campaign against gay marriage rights. More than 20 "pro-family" groups were members of the Arlington Group by 2006. See "Arlington Group," *SourceWatch*, Center for Media and Democracy, undated, www.sourcewatch.org/index.php?title=Arlington_Group.

57. See, for example, Mary Jo Weaver and R. Scott Appleby, eds., *Being Right: Conservative Catholics in America* (Bloomington: Indiana University Press, 1995).

58. See Bill Berkowitz, "Bush's Campaign Courting Catholics," *Alter-Net*, April 7, 2001, www.alternet.org/story/11291; and "The Mission of Catholic Alliance," Political Responsibility Center, Priests for Life, www.priestsforlife.org/government/cathalliance.htm.

59. Gustav Niebuhr, "Ray Flynn to Head Catholic Group with Conservative Roots," *New York Times*, March 13, 1999, A7. See also "A New Movement Afoot: The Catholic Alliance for the Common Good," The National Institute for the Renewal of the Priesthood, October 4, 2005, www.jknirp.com/allian.htm, and Catholics in Alliance for the Common Good, "Catholics Launch Initiative to Promote Common Good," news release, July 19, 2006, http://www.commondreams.org/news2006/0719-19.htm. Faith in Public Life, an interfaith resource center that seeks to provide an alternative to the Christian Right's "narrow and exclusive definition of what it means to be moral and faithful in America," supports Catholics in Alliance. See Faith in Public Life, www.faithinpubliclife.org, and "Faith in Public Life," news release, June 20, 2006, http://chuckcurrie.blogs.com/chuck_currie/2006/06/faith_in_public.html.

60. Thomas B. Edsall, "Grants Flow to Bush Allies on Social Issues," *Washington Post*, March 22, 2006, A1.

61. Eleven states passed amendments banning gay marriage during the 2004 elections. Gilgoff says that Issue One—the amendment banning all types of gay unions in Ohio—was a "crucial" and "perhaps the deciding" factor in the Republican victory in Ohio, which won Bush the presidency. Gilgoff, *Jesus Machine*, 182, 195.

62. Pew Forum on Religion & Public Life, "More Americans Question Religion's Role in Politics," Pew Research Center, Washington, DC, August 21, 2008, http://pewforum.org/docs/?DocID=339.

63. Gilgoff, *Jesus Machine*, 221.

64. Ibid., 241 (as cited). The Christian Right's role in these judicial wars is explored in Chapter 8.

65. For rather chilling comments on the president's beliefs, see Justin A. Frank, *Bush on the Couch: Inside the Mind of the President* (New York: Regan, 2004), Chapter 4; Ron Suskind, "Without a Doubt," *New York Times Magazine*, October 17, 2004, 44–51, 64, 102, 106. Frank is a Washington, D.C.–based psychoanalyst and professor of psychiatry at George Washington University Medical School. Suskind is a journalist and author.

66. Jim Wallis, *God's Politics: Why the Right Gets It Wrong and the Left Doesn't Get It* (New York: HarperCollins, 2005), 3; See Martin, *With God on Our Side*, 385 (commenting on the need to redefine the relationship "in such a way as to maintain the pluralism that has served us so well"). See also Bruce Bawer, *Stealing Jesus: How Fundamentalism Betrays Christianity* (New York: Crown, 1997).

67. Cited by Shadia B. Drury, *Leo Strauss and the American Right* (New York: St. Martin's, 1997), 147.

68. Gilgoff, *Jesus Machine*, 264. Gilgoff explores Democratic attempts to reach out to evangelical conservatives in Chapter 9.

69. John Wilson, "God Fearing," *New York Times*, November 12, 2006, Book Review-63.

70. Christian Smith, *Christian America? What Evangelicals Really Want* (Berkeley: University of California Press, 2000), 7. Smith based his observation on a three-year study of evangelicals that began in 1995. The research, conducted by a team of 12 sociologists, included a 1996 survey of 2,591 Americans, "which asked detailed questions about faith, morality, pluralism, Christian social activism, and other issues of religion and public life" (2).

71. David D. Kirkpatrick, "The Evangelical Crackup," *New York Times Magazine*, October 28, 2007, 20–39, p. 39.

72. Frank Rich, "Rudy, the Values Slayer," *New York Times*, October 28, 2007, Week in Review-12.

73. Neela Banerjee, "Taking Their Faith, but Not Their Politics, to the People," *New York Times*, June 1, 2008, A20.

74. The fundamentalist takeover of the Southern Baptist Convention eventually provoked a split with more moderate members, who formed the Alliance of Baptists in 1989, and another splinter group, the Cooperative Baptist Fellowship, in 1990. This conflict has had a considerable impact on ecclesiastical institutions associated with the Southern Baptist Church, especially in the South.

75. Members include those who adhere to what they call Christian Reconstructionism, Kingdom Now Theology, Theocratic Dominionism, Theonomy, Dominion Theology, or simply Dominionism. These are interrelated conservative fundamentalist ideologies—and we have probably not named all of them—that apparently had their origin in an obscure Armenian-American named Rousas John Rushdoony, who founded the Chalcedon Foundation (after the Council of Chalcedon) in California in the mid-1960s. He claimed his family had provided a priest or minister to the church in every generation since the year 320. The Dominion movement was an outgrowth of efforts by Rushdoony and his future son-in-law Gary North. While they went their separate ways—North would start his own Institute for Christian Economics (in Tyler, Texas)—other groups with different identifications would soon emerge. See Sara Diamond, *Roads to Dominion: Right-Wing Movements and Political Power in the United States* (New York: Guilford, 1995); "Dominionism (A.K.A. Christian Reconstructionism, Dominion Theology, and Theonomy)," *Religious Tolerance.Org*, Ontario Consultants on Religious Tolerance, undated, www.religioustolerance.org/reconstr.htm; and "Dominion Theology," *The Biblicist*, undated, www.biblicist.org/bible/dominion.shtml.

76. See R. Marie Griffith, *God's Daughters. Evangelical Women and the Power of Submission* (Berkeley: University of California Press, 1997).

77. Andy Crouch, "The Emergent Mystique," *Christianity Today*, November 2004, 36–41, p 37. See also Brian D. McLaren, *A New Kind of*

Christian: A Tale of Two Friends on a Spiritual Journey (San Francisco: Jossey-Bass, 2001).

78. See, for example, Marcia Ford, "The Emerging Church: Ancient Faith for a Postmodern World," *explorefaith.org*, 2004.

79. Eileen W. Lindner, "Postmodern Christianity: Emergent Church and Blogs," in *Yearbook of American & Canadian*, 15–20.

80. Dennis M. Sullivan, "Defending Human Personhood: Some Insights from Natural Law," *Christian Scholar's Review* 37, no. 3 (2008): 289–302, p. 289.

81. Anthony Dancer, "The Reign of God and Human Politics," *Stimulus* 16, no. 3 (2008): 39–46, pp. 39–40.

82. Ibid., 40.

83. Bureau of Democracy, Human Rights, and Labor, "2008 Annual Report on International Religious Freedom," U.S. Department of State, Washington, DC, September 19, 2008, www.state.gov/g/drl/rls/irf/2008/index.htm.

84. Gilgoff, *Jesus Machine*, 280.

85. "What Is the Definition of Torture and Ill Treatment?," International Committee of the Red Cross, February 15, 2005, www.icrc.org/Web/Eng/siteeng0.nsf/html/69MJXC. See also High Commissioner for Human Rights, "Convention Against Torture and Other Cruel, Inhuman or Degrading Treatment or Punishment," United Nations, 1984, www2.ohchr.org/english/law/cat.htm.

86. Scripture neither condones nor condemns the use of force to make people speak against their will, "but the Old Testament does clearly teach that severe and intentional infliction of pain was willed by God not only as eternal punishment for the wicked in hell but also as humanly imposed temporal punishment for convicted malefactors." See Brian W. Harrison, "The Church and Torture," *Catholic Culture: Living the Catholic Life*, undated, www.catholicculture.org/culture/library/view.cfm?id=7390&C-FID=20514554&CFTOKEN=33707045.

87. "Tortured Logic," *The Christian Century*, April 8, 2008, 7.

88. "An Evangelical Declaration against Torture: Protecting Human Rights in an Age of Terror," Executive Summary, Evangelicals for Human Rights, undated, www.evangelicalsforhumanrights.org/index.php?options=com_content&task=view&id=145&itemid=42.

89. "Declaration of Principles for a Presidential Executive Order on Prisoner Treatment, Torture and Cruelty," the National Religious Campaign Against Torture, Evangelicals for Human Rights, and the Center for Victims of Torture, undated, www.nrcat.org/index.php?option=com_content&task=view&id=211+itemid=160.

90. White evangelical/fundamentalists have a greater concentration in the South, are generally more conservative on social issues, younger, less educated, and in lower income categories than other religious groups

(such as mainstream Protestants and Roman Catholics). But we have not found any scholarly studies that really examine the role of social class in conservative religious politics. See Wilcox, *Onward Christian Soldiers?*, 45–52.

91. Hood and Smith, "On the Prospect of Linking," 707.

92. John H. Garvey, "Introduction: Fundamentalism and Politics," in Marty and Appleby, *Fundamentalisms and the State*, 13–27, p. 16.

CHAPTER 2

Media, Religion, and Politics: Conservative Voices

The Democratic and Republican candidates for president of the United States made a pilgrimage to Saddleback Church in Lake Forest, California, on August 16, 2008. They had submitted to a request by Rick Warren, the pastor of this megachurch and the country's latest evangelical media celebrity, to be examined on their credentials to lead the most powerful nation in the world.

"We're going to look at leadership, specifically their character, their competence, their experience," Warren said. "I want to give America a better, closer look at the two candidates. I think we want to see not just their values, but their vision, their virtues." Warren interviewed Barack Obama and John McCain separately for one hour, and the interviews were then aired on ABC News. Warren refused to endorse either candidate, but the litmus test for many Christian conservatives was their "relationship to Jesus Christ," he said. "I'm going to give them a chance to explain themselves."[1]

If nothing else, the fact that Warren could summon the two presidential candidates to his church to submit to interviews—interviews that were then aired on national television—is a testament to the enduring power of Christian conservatives in American politics. The fact that the media ignore the majority of Christians and their leaders who are *not* religious conservatives speaks volumes about the standing of mainstream Christianity—as well as the standing of Americans of other faith traditions or of no faith tradition—both in the media and in the corridors of American political power. In reporting this interview, most journalists focused on which candidate "won" this war of words. Kathleen Parker, a conservative syndicated columnist, was a rare exception: "The winner, of course, was Warren, who has managed to position himself as political arbiter in a nation founded on the separation of church and state," she said. "The loser was America."[2]

This chapter explores the media's role in representing Christian conservatives in America's political culture. It is divided into six sections. Section 1 outlines two different perspectives that engage media professionals and scholars alike over the relationship between media and religion in American society. Section 2 examines some of the constraints that undermine the journalist's quest for objective news coverage of events and issues in American society. Section 3 describes media coverage of religious news in the past, and Section 4 does the same for radio and television. Section 5 discusses the interaction between media and religion today, and Section 6 offers examples of the emergence of conservative media in politics.

MEDIA AND RELIGION IN AMERICAN SOCIETY

The role the media play or should play in communicating news about religion is the topic of considerable debate—a debate that segues easily into a broader debate about the role media play in American society. There are two perspectives on media coverage of religion today, and both are conditioned by differing perspectives about the role of media in society.

Media Coverage of Religion: A Traditional View

The traditional view is based on two premises—carefully cultivated for many decades by media professionals and academics, and communicated to the general public. The first premise is that there is an "objective" or "true" reality that exists apart from its mediated representations (for instance, a news story about a speech). The role of the mass media is simply to mirror, reflect, or re-present a reality that is already there. The mediated image substitutes for the "real" or true image.

Journalists typically define objectivity, for example, as a requirement that two sides are represented in any report about the natural or human world. They tend to assume there are only two sides, a strategy most media professionals claim they employ as they try to produce marketable stories that consumers can identify with. The audience must be exposed to the image for identification to take place—then the link between the identity claim and identification is completed. If you see but cannot identify with the meaning of a mediated image, this usually means the image has no fixed meaning for you.

In analyzing the shortcomings of the news media, critics often assume they can identify distortions in news coverage by measuring the gap between the mediated images and their personal images, which they regard as truer or more accurate images. News propaganda or bias is perceived as a journalist's failure to describe an event in a way that is consistent with a *critic*'s perception of the event.

The second premise is that media and religion are separate and autonomous institutions—as in the distinction between the secular and the sacred. Each has its own protocols and standards, its own way of distinguishing social reality. Media and religion may interact and even intersect with each other at times, these critics assume, but each operates independently of the other.

Journalists are concerned with the known world, and they believe that everything newsworthy in that world can or should be known. News for journalists must happen today or tomorrow, it must be verifiable, and it must have what is called in the profession a news peg—an element(s) in a story that will provide the mechanism to turn it into a news story. Pregnancy among teenage girls is common, certainly, but it does not become *news* until a teenager tries to dispose of her baby in a dumpster. The act of disposing of the baby is the news peg.

Religion may have its peculiar ecclesiastical traditions, histories, and doctrines, but it is preoccupied with the unknown world—with matters of faith, belief, mystery, and an empirically unverifiable world. Journalists and clergy alike accept the premise that they "see" the world in different terms. In this sense, then, the religious view of the world is perceived as an unverifiable worldview. When journalists interview religious experts or use religious material in a news story, the religious angle is news only if it fits the news prism constructed by journalists.

Media Coverage of Religion: An Alternative View

We argue for an alternative view—both in terms of how we see the role of media in society and how we see the relationship between media and religion. Instead of assuming a distinction between a mediated and an unmediated reality, we accept the assumption that all mediated images are representations of cultural practices.[3] Of course, there is a material world outside the mediated image, but the material world *means* something to human beings only when they give meaning to it.

Media descriptions of real issues and problems are not benign or neutral. A news event cannot be separated from its mediated image. Media *represent*, as well as re-present, our world. The act of mediation itself is constitutive of the event—it enters into the event and is part of the event. Instead of assuming that the mass media simply communicate religious messages to their audiences, we suggest the mediating mechanism itself is shaping the contours of these religious images.[4]

We also accept the view that media and religion are not distinct entities in communicating the realities of the modern world. "What seems obvious now," as Stewart M. Hoover, a professor of communication and religion, notes, is "the extent to which all media, and the entire sphere of commodity culture, can be, and is, a religious sphere."[5] The religious "storyteller" today, as Claire Hoertz Badaracco, another specialist in communication and religion, suggests, is the commercial mass media, which have "had a profound influence on the styles of religious communication and on messages about hope, transcendence, endurance, triumph, and what it means to be human."[6]

We argue not only that American media have played a significant role in communicating religious narratives, but also that the media in this process have reconfigured the religious narratives themselves. If we are to understand religion's role in contemporary American culture, "we must understand it as expressed, practiced, and experienced."[7] The possibilities for manipulating and merging religious symbols and myths in painting, music, architecture, literature, science, and journalism have become virtually unlimited with the development of new, computer-driven technologies. Religious narratives are often present in secular events—in the discourse of sports, pop concerts, celebrity happenings, and in local, national, and international news. Exploiting both old and new media, traditional Christian messages have been reshaped, refined, repeated, and redirected to new audiences.

Mediated images are expressed and exchanged primarily through language (whether written, oral, or visual), and mediated messages typically are linked to power. Language is rarely simply a means of communication: it is a tool of political, social, economic, and religious power.[8] Events in and of themselves always have complex meanings: a fixed meaning does not exist for human beings until it is interpreted, until it is represented. While the meanings of words can never really be frozen forever, some meanings can be privileged over other meanings.

Power intervenes in language to fix meaning—to make that meaning the one, true meaning. The power of language to persuade an individual, group, community, or nation to accept a meaning as true, or at least "preferred," played a critical role in empowering the conservative religious community. When it became the language of everyday life, this worldview became a dominant discourse in America's political culture.

CONSTRAINTS ON OBJECTIVE NEWS COVERAGE

We argue here and in subsequent chapters that journalists today face severe constraints in the quest for objectivity. We describe three interrelated constraints in this section. Journalists have generally abandoned the principles of objectivity developed in the past: they rely on a two-dimensional understanding of objectivity that fails to capture the multidimensional realities of the world news prism. Journalists also depend on the power of binary language to express these realities, and they frame news reports in ways that reinforce a two-dimensional news agenda.

Journalists and the Principles of Objectivity

Many critics believe that objective journalism has been ignored, misused, and/or abused by journalists to such an extent that it is no longer relevant when discussing how the media might better portray the world to their audiences. We do not agree. An objective approach must be rehabilitated in an ongoing effort to reestablish and reimpose ethical standards for today's journalists. It is not viewed as a way to guarantee neutrality but as a way to compensate for the human inability to be neutral.

Journalists often cite (a) the pressure of deadlines, (b) the need to decide which of an infinite number of events and issues are important for an audience to know about, and (c) limited resources in terms of staff and access to information as examples of why objectivity in news reports is usually understood only as giving equal time or space to two sides of a story. Most journalists, however, do not appreciate the principles of objectivity as they were defined and gradually refined in the media of mass communication in the generations between the Civil War and the Cold War.

The literature on objectivity in American journalism is quite extensive, and it is linked securely to the triumph of the scientific method and the transformation of the human and natural sciences in Europe and America—especially during the nineteenth and early twentieth centuries.[9] Journalism "played a significant role in the secularization of American public life," as sociologist Richard W. Flory notes, "by spreading ideas adopted from other institutional spheres of knowledge-production to the general public [and by offering] a modern, scientific perspective, appropriate to the age."[10]

Journalism, which was jingoistic, mean, partisan, and politicized in early America, began to change from the late 1830s, as more Americans became interested in news, and editors and writers sought new ways to attract these potential readers. As the scientific method became the dominant narrative in communicating knowledge, more and more journalists began to incorporate the scientific perspective, and to emphasize factual information (as in the well-worn cliché, "opinion is free, but facts are sacred") in their own work. They aligned journalism with a less partisan and more balanced approach, which not only enhanced the credibility of journalism, but also proved to be more profitable. Journalism was redefined as a profession, standards were imposed, and the principles of objectivity in news reporting and writing were gradually implemented.

As early as 1867, for example, New York publisher Jesse Haney produced for literary and newspaper writers a book describing principles that were later seen as fundamental to an objective approach. Newspapers that strive to be profitable must not reflect political or other interests: they must report news, not opinion, the guide said. When quoting an authority, the journalist must "do so fairly, and copiously enough to do him [writers were typically men] justice." When reporting public records, the journalist should "endeavor to give news, rather than opinions," and when covering meetings the journalist should report "fairly and honestly as a matter of news, giving his personal views in another portion of his paper."[11]

The overarching goal of one who uses an objective approach is to describe as accurately as possible those realities deemed to be newsworthy. The philosophical underpinnings for objectivity are clarity, accuracy, and completeness in identifying, gathering, and reporting information, and honesty about personal preferences and idiosyncrasies.

Journalists should demonstrate a willingness to find and consider new evidence and alternative explanations and show a healthy skepticism toward authority, the powerful, and the self-righteous. They must take the initiative in finding answers and solutions to problems, find ways to expose lies and deception, and bring imagination, creativity, and logical consistency to news coverage. They should project impartiality, fairness, and disinterest in reporting and refuse to serve any political, social, religious, cultural, or scientific agenda. They should verify findings in subsequent reports and share their findings when applicable with others in the profession.

None of this excludes analysis and interpretation in information collection and writing, as some critics charge. Early admonitions like keeping one's opinion out of the story referred to personal opinion unsupported by evidence. They did not refer to evidence-based analysis and interpretation that could be used to guide story selection, information collection, writing, and editing.

The standards of an objective approach apply to commentary as well as to news. This does not mean commentary must not contain opinion. It does mean those opinions must be clearly labeled and well supported by compelling evidence. The opinions expressed certainly should not be based on faulty or incomplete information that could ultimately lead to poor decision making.[12]

Ethical journalists honor the principles of objectivity—whether they call it pragmatic objectivity, epistemological objectivity, good journalism, or something else—because their output will be transparent, rational, coherent, logical, and factual. "Objectivity is part of our culture's attempt to say what knowledge is and how to pursue truth in the many domains of inquiry," as media ethicist Stephen J. A. Ward and others have argued. "Objectivity, properly understood, is a bulwark against authoritarianism in belief and practice." It provides "a defence against an obscurantism that allows the clever to manipulate the naïve or vulnerable." Journalism professor Richard Streckfuss also notes that objective journalism provides "an antidote to the emotionalism and jingoism of the conservative American press" and is "a demanding, intellectually rigorous procedure holding the best hope for social change."[13]

Few journalists today, however, honor or practice the historic, objective approach to journalism. This is one reason why journalists are so often used by unscrupulous sources, who want to manipulate the language of news coverage. An objective approach is the standard against which we judge journalistic practice in this book.

Expressing Reality in Binary Language

Journalists do assign meaning to words (or they allow their sources to assign meaning to words), and this also constrains news objectivity. Two aspects of an argument originally articulated by the Swiss-French scholar Ferdinand de Saussure (1857–1913)—the founding father, as it were, of structural linguistics—seem particularly compelling in seeking to understand the power of language to interpret the Christian conservative impact on American society today.[14]

- Language is not a spontaneous act: language is given meaning by human beings, who comprise in the first instance a language community. Words are meaningless unless the language community assigns them values.
- Words typically are assigned meaning in terms of their opposition to other words. The widespread use of dichotomies in language, along with the apparent need to see the world in terms of these kinds of oppositions, suggest that they fulfill a deeply felt social need.

Binary language is used to express one's experiences: these are conceptual maps of meaning that help human beings make sense of the world. The development of modern industrial culture in the West was constructed out of binary signs. Where these dichotomies are widely accepted, they can become dominant ideological discourses in democratic as well as nondemocratic societies.

An example illustrating the use of binary language in framing reality as two distinct and opposing worldviews is shown in Table 2.1. The words are derived from a short list we compiled of negative statements assigned by various commercial and religious media outlets to Muslims in the months between September 11, 2001, and the invasion of Iraq in March 2003. The positive virtues of Christians in opposition to these Muslim statements are assumed virtues.

Interwoven into the fabric of explanations for terrorism even before the 9/11 attacks was the idea that Islamic culture is responsible for a clash of civilizations,[15] and modern secular lifestyles are being challenged by premodern (pre-Enlightenment) Muslim fundamentalists bent on destroying Western culture.[16] As we shall see in Chapter 8, the media's war frame intensified the stereotyping of persons perceived to be Muslim or of Arab descent.[17] Public paranoia after 9/11 reached a point at which Muslim Americans had to be careful about what they said and did at school, at university, in travel and recreational pursuits, at work, and even at worship.

The argument that the mediated world is best expressed in binary language is being challenged as America's economy and society moves inexorably toward a postmodern epoch, but it remains an integral part of how many people perceive social reality. The world of binary signs reemerges again and again during periods of real or imagined crisis to dominate the discourse of the cultural, especially the political, order.

The power of mass media lies precisely in the ability to confer meaning (or to enable others to confer meaning) on personalities, events, and issues in the public sphere. Mass-mediated news generates primarily a dichotomous discourse that presumes a certain stability of language. The production of news is by definition a process that seeks to secure a fixed or preferred reading of the text, essentially an unambiguous reading, and news opinion polls and surveys function mainly to determine whether these readings are understood and accepted by news audiences.

Expressing Reality in News Frames

A third constraint on news objectivity lies in the news frames journalists use to structure their stories. Information in and of itself has

Table 2.1.   Binary Language Describing Muslims and Christians

Negative Statements (assigned) Muslim	Positive Virtues (assumed) Christian
uncivilized behavior	civilized behavior
non-Western values (authoritarian, socialist, led by dictators, etc.)	Western values (democratic, capitalist, personal freedom, individualism, etc.)
premodern (regressive)	modern (progressive)
evil/bad (sin, impure, unsaved)	good (grace, pure, saved)
dogmatic	rational
insane (barbaric, abnormal)	sane (normal)
radical (emotional, extremist)	measured (detached, seeks consensus)
intolerant (backward, bigoted)	tolerant
closed societies (exclusive)	open societies (inclusive)
terrorists (criminals, thugs, etc.)	patriots (peace loving, etc.)
lack of respect for human life (inhuman)	respect for human life

no intrinsic meaning until journalists weave these facts and opinions into a coherent story. As sociologist William A. Gamson puts it, "They take on their meaning by being embedded in a frame or story line that organizes them and gives them coherence."[18] The mechanism employed to create news stories is called in the profession a media frame.

Media frames are "interpretive structures that set particular events within their broader context." They are story lines constructed "to arrange the narrative, to make sense of the facts, to focus the headline, and to define events as newsworthy."[19] News that seems to be relevant, interesting, important, and acceptable within a society's norms and values is woven into a conceptual frame in ways that journalists trust will be believable and compelling. As media critic Todd Gitlin once said, "*Media* frames, largely unspoken and unacknowledged, organize the world both for journalists who report it and, in some important degree, for us who rely on their reports" (italics in the original).[20]

Media frames function to define problems and issues, determine causes, offer judgments, and suggest solutions. A frame maker selects bits of information (while ignoring many other bits) and incorporates them in story frames, "which are manifested by the presence or absence of certain keywords, stock phrases, stereotyped images, sources of information, and sentences that provide thematically reinforcing clusters of facts or judgments."[21]

There are thousands of journalists, and virtually all of them frame news stories in similar ways. War, for example, may be framed as sanitized theater;[22] Arabs may be framed as uncivilized, violent, and ignorant;[23] motorcycle gangs may be framed as outlaws;[24] animal-rights activists may be framed as "domestic terrorists."[25] Media frames seldom permit alternatives, but they are contested whenever they appear to depict realities deemed unacceptable to those depicted in those frames.

Media news frames are influenced by the rhetorical strategies of governmental, ideological, and political elites.[26] News is an important site of contention in the political process because anxious readers, listeners, and viewers look to the news media when they need help making sense of the senseless, finding answers to complex and agonizing questions, and deciding what behavior is appropriate or inappropriate in difficult situations. A narrative frame repeated over and over again in the news media is the frame that will have persuasive power over its audience.[27]

Media news frames incorporate binary language widely approved and used by media professionals, politicians, social critics, and ordinary people. The conservative-liberal divide, as we outlined in Chapter 1, has been a mantra of many Christian conservatives since the early twentieth century as they seek through fixed language a more exclusive identity to distinguish themselves from more inclusive Christians, and it has been the mantra in conservative politics since the 1960s.

Religious and nonreligious conservatives became partners in hammering out a political-cum-social agenda that gave new meaning and a new authority to the terms "conservative" and "liberal" as employed in public discourse. Conservatives were linked inextricably with the Republican Party—just as liberals were linked inextricably with the Democratic Party. Conservatives constructed for themselves an alternative media in contrast to the mainstream press and network television, which they claimed was dominated by liberals. Conservative religious operatives were characterized—again, in contrast to liberals— by the intensity both of their religious beliefs and of their patriotism. These two attributes were framed as one for political purposes in conservative media and assigned to the Republican Party.

Conservatives have been extraordinarily successful in convincing the American public that the mass media are *liberal* and that *liberal* is a dirty word. This is a tactic they use to ensure (a) that the media are and will remain fundamentally conservative and (b) that they will represent the world in dichotomous, liberal-conservative terms. Media scholars Kathleen Hall Jamieson and Joseph N. Cappella demonstrate the power of these media to frame political realities as a party-driven, conservative-liberal divide. They argue that this is a positive phenomenon in the sense that it provides an alternative perspective and adds "an element of accountability to the [mass media] system."[28]

They note historical antecedents, cite the "advantages to consistently framed, ideologically coherent argument," and provide a detailed, survey-based analysis of how the conservative media's one-sided, partisan politics works. Strategies are examined to show how conservative frames can reinforce conservative perspectives even when audiences are exposed "to conflicting points of view...by watching mainstream media." They also detail the disadvantages of this dichotomous mindset when mainstream media are identified as biased, untrustworthy, and prone to use a double standard in political news coverage of Democrats and Republicans. The Democrats are "the enemy party" from the conservative perspective, "morally defective, disloyal to the country's principles, menacing basic values." Two-party politics has become polarized to such an extent that there is "no point in attempting to deliberate across ideological lines."[29]

Jamieson and Cappella, however, do not critically examine the framing of conservatism and liberalism in America's contemporary political culture. They have not taken into account the broader drift toward conservatism that has transformed *mainstream media* in the past generation. Nor have they considered the cumulative impact that conservative *religious* media have had on America's political culture. Above all, they accept as given the binary language used to frame this conservative-liberal political divide.

The four national television networks (American Broadcasting Company, ABC; National Broadcasting Company, NBC, Columbia Broadcasting System, CBS; and Fox Broadcasting Company, Fox)—and their counterparts in the mainstream press—are all components of international, multi-industry corporate conglomerates that are hardly liberal in their political and business practices. ABC is owned by The Walt Disney Company, NBC by General Electric Company, and CBS by Westinghouse Electric Corporation (1995), before it was bought by Viacom (2000) and then split into two parts (2005). Ownership and control of the dominant mass media shrank from 50 separate media corporations in 1983 to 5 by 2004. The big five at that time were Time Warner Inc., Disney, Australian Rupert Murdoch's news empire (which includes Fox), Viacom, Inc., and Bertelsmann AG (Germany).[30]

No evidence supports the frequently stated claim of a liberal Democratic bias in media news coverage. Not even National Public Radio (NPR)—one of the few broadcast outlets in America believed by a wide spectrum of listeners to be politically liberal—is all that liberal. Fairness & Accuracy in Reporting, a national media watchdog group based in New York City, examined stories in NPR's major news programs, for example, in 1993 (during the Clinton administration) and again in 2003 (during the Bush II administration). "Elite sources dominated NPR's guest list," according to the report. "These sources—including government officials, professional experts, and corporate representatives—accounted for 64 percent of all sources." Conservative think tanks, conservative commentators, and Republican-based sources far outweighed Democratic-based sources in both years surveyed. "That NPR harbors a liberal bias is an article of faith among many conservatives," the report noted, "[but] little evidence has ever been presented for a left bias at NPR."[31]

Media critics such as Robert McChesney, Eric Alterman, and Douglas Kellner demonstrate that the mass media in the last generation if anything became more conservative in response to the impact of conservatism on America's political culture.[32] "The heart of the problem," syndicated columnist Arianna Huffington argues, is not conservative voices on right-wing radio and television. It is "mainstream media that have completely internalized how the right frames all political debate. The right-wing message has become a part of the news media's DNA."[33]

The recent appearance "of a liberal media echo chamber with no pretense of balance" to challenge the conservative media establishment at its own game was "all but inevitable," Jamieson and Cappella say. They point as examples to mainstream cable-television networks that have sought to engage the programs of rival Fox News with programs such as MSNBC's *Countdown with Keith Olbermann* and *Hardball with Chris Matthews*, and to Air America Radio[34] in the scramble by the Left as well as the Right for a greater share of the limited audiences watching this form of political entertainment.[35]

For the moment, however, conservative media own the rights to this news frame. While the guests and the issues might change, the political and religious landscape is framed almost exclusively in binary conservative and liberal terms. The preferred metaphorical option is one of military engagement between two opposing forces—only one of which can win.

THE PRESS AND RELIGION IN THE PAST

The relationship between the mass media and religion in the United States is multifaceted but historically one of interdependence. Religion news until relatively recently meant news about Christianity, and Christianity for much of its mediated history in America meant Protestant Christianity. Christians have always exploited the technologies of the day to gain strong urban as well as rural constituencies, from the regional fringes to the mainstreams of American society. Christians of all theological leanings—whether they were later labeled as liberal or conservative—have long used and even depended on mainstream news media (a) to communicate their messages to larger, secular audiences and (b) to portray Christian values and norms positively and in what activists perceive as appropriate contexts.

Religion as News in the Secular Press

Religion has been covered by the mass media in the United States since the eighteenth century, but it was James Gordon Bennett Sr. (1795–1872) and his newspaper, the *New York Herald*, who first treated religion as news. The *Herald* (founded in 1835) was the first mass circulation daily in the United States, and religious events were treated like any other news event of the day. Bennett's interest in religion— he was a Roman Catholic brought up in Presbyterian Scotland— extended to the yearly meetings (they were called "anniversaries") of the major denominations and groups allied with antislavery, temperance, and other social causes of this period.

Religious leaders, politicians, and the business elite did not welcome Bennett's often-critical religion coverage, but he won a showdown in 1840 (it was described at the time as a "Moral War"). In later years, Bennett even provided regular coverage of Sunday sermons, and his treatment of religion news as "human interest" news was the journalistic standard, as religion professor Mark Silk says, for competing newspapermen such as Bennett's rival, Horace Greeley (1811–1872) of the *New York Tribune* (founded in 1841). In subsequent decades, the clergy were also given considerable space to air their views "on questions of faith, morals, and public policy."[36]

General-circulation religious publications could not compete with daily-circulation commercial newspapers, and it was already clear that Christian perspectives were dependent on the secular press if they wished to reach the masses. Newspapers were happy to oblige. Leading social reformers (such as Congregational minister Henry Ward Beecher [1813–1887] and lawyer Wendell Phillips [1811–1884], in the nineteenth century) and leading preachers and evangelists (such as Dwight L. Moody [1837–1899] and Charles Finney [1792–1875] in the nineteenth century and William "Billy" Sunday [1862–1935] in the early twentieth century)—together with a host of other national, regional, and local figures—were given wide coverage.

Religion news for much of this period was good for business, and religious leaders were aware of the benefits of this publicity—despite misgivings about the role the "impious," mass-circulation newspapers had assumed in the advancement of Christianity. Daily press coverage of that peculiarly American phenomenon, the Revival, for example, was so detailed that researchers today use these newspapers as a primary source of information. Revivals, awakenings, and crusades—the terms used varied according to time and place—were regular events throughout the country during this era. In the same manner, the popular press gave widespread coverage to the activities of those involved in the social gospel movement and later to the muckrakers, many of them openly professing traditional Christian moral values as the inspiration for their social crusades.

News agencies were getting involved in the organization and distribution of religion news beginning in the 1930s. The National Conference of Christians and Jews (founded in 1928 to combat antisemitism) launched its Religious News Service (RNS) in 1934. The title of RNS was changed to "Religion" News Service to reflect a more interfaith, ecumenical orientation only in 1994, when RNS became a unit of Newhouse News Service and claimed it was the "only secular newswire focused exclusively on religion and ethics."[37]

The Associated Press and United Press wire services in the early 1950s named religion beat reporters to provide regular news stories and yearly features during religious holidays. A small group of committed religion reporters formed the Religious Newswriters Association in 1949 (also later changed to "Religion" in 1971) and were instrumental in slowly upgrading and refining professional standards in the reporting and writing of religion news. White Christian males, however, dominated the association.[38]

Decline of Religion News in the Secular Press

Despite these developments, religion journalism in the secular press was actually declining both in terms of quality and quantity from at least the 1920s. Scholars have cited a number of reasons for this decline, but two seem crucial—the emergence in the twentieth century of journalism as a profession and a transformation in religious consciousness.

Journalism as a Profession

The first reason involves the emergence of journalism as a profession, like medicine or law, during the course of the twentieth century. As the scientific method became the dominant narrative in other professions, more and more journalists began to incorporate the scientific perspective in their own work. Vocational courses for journalists in higher education stressed the importance of a rational and detached mindset. Stories were broken down into component parts (as in the who, what, where, when, why, and how of journalistic practice); news was compartmentalized; and the better journalists received further training as specialists in politics, sport, or some other designated activity of the profession. Techniques were gradually devised to ferret out overt or covert bias and to separate news from comment and opinion, and "hard" news from "soft" or entertainment news.

As journalism became increasingly professionalized, religion news became one of many news compartments in the newspaper. It was written in conformity with standardized journalistic practices and competed with other news categories for placement in the newspaper. A few dailies had been sequestering religion news in separate pages for decades, but with the advent of the so-called Saturday church page virtually all daily newspapers were restricting religion news to one page by the 1920s and 1930s.

Religion reports consisted of Sunday worship services, announcements of meetings, and soft, devotional-oriented features. Churches were happy to advertise their services on a single page in the mainstream press—most news copy, as religion editors in a 1952 survey acknowledged, actually was based on church press releases. In this "realm of sacred space . . . no one's faith or denominational identity would henceforth be put to the challenge."[39]

The religion page became a "ghetto" for journalists with little or no hope of advancement, and ignorance in matters of religion became almost a virtue for those assigned to the job. Religion news was to be as bland and noncontroversial as possible—editors often refused even to publish letters from readers on the topic.[40] The advertising-crammed Saturday church page "symbolized the relationship between newspapers and religion as service provider and client," as Stewart M. Hoover puts it, "rather than journalist and object of scrutiny."[41]

In the generation after World War II, of course, press coverage of religious events was not always restricted to the Saturday religion page. The widespread conviction that Jewish and Christian communities needed to find common cause in fighting communism during the Cold War brought many religious agencies together. One example was a campaign to provide advertising inserts in hundreds of American newspapers to promote Religion in American Life: sponsors claimed press support helped raise church attendance considerably during the 1950s.

Extensive press coverage was provided for events such as Vatican II and such issues as religious support for the civil rights movement and religious involvement in anti-Vietnam War protests, causes that many mainstream Christians of this generation supported. But the religion angle was news only if it was deemed to be newsworthy by journalists, and those who were mainly responsible for providing the religious perspective on these events and issues were few in number. One study claimed that "religious America" in secular media at the beginning of the 1980s was depicted mainly in the work of "about 12 to 15 persons."[42]

Transformation in Religious Consciousness

The second reason for the decline in religion news coverage is linked to a transformation in religious consciousness, a transformation that became much more pronounced from the 1970s. Religious hierarchies and denominations—a hallmark of the Protestant establishment and of the Roman Catholic Church in the United States especially before Vatican II—were being perceived with widespread suspicion, if not alienation. As we noted in Chapter 1, virtually all mainstream-Protestant denominations experienced a dramatic decline in numbers in the last third of the twentieth century, while the Catholic population remained more or less stable only because many new immigrants, especially from Latin America, identified with this faith tradition. Religious meaning became more personal and private, and it was deemed by many to be the preserve of the individual rather than the institution.

The dominance of the Protestant establishment in religion news coverage for more than a century was finally broken. These denominations were identified historically with a print-based culture, which coincided with the decline in power and influence of print media. The shift to a worldwide, electronic-based culture coincided with the explosive growth in non- or interdenominational churches and evangelical fundamentalist denominations outside the Protestant establishment.[43]

RELIGION ON RADIO AND TELEVISION IN THE PAST

While Christian conservatives as a constituent body were not yet a distinct force in America's political culture, the theological and social underpinnings that framed so much of this political narrative were communicated by new media of mass communication, first in radio and then in television, from the 1920s. Conservative broadcasters dominated the religious agenda on secular radio airwaves almost from the beginning of the first commercial wireless stations.

Evangelist Aimee Semple McPherson, for example, began broadcasting on commercial radio in the early 1920s. She was the first woman to preach a sermon on radio and the first given a broadcast license (in 1924) by the Federal Radio Commission (the name was changed to the Federal Communications Commission in 1934). McPherson (1890–1944) was also among the first religious personalities in the electronic media to define a political agenda for Christian conservatives: she defended Prohibition (the 18th Amendment banning alcohol was passed in 1919) and campaigned against the teaching of evolution in schools. Most significantly, she linked faith with patriotism as an inseparable Christian doctrine. Like her successors, McPherson warned her listeners that the anti-Christ—it would be communism for the next two generations—was bent on destroying America's religious heritage (meaning conservative Protestant heritage). Patriotic Americans had to return to the "old-time" religion if they were to save America.[44]

Other conservative Protestant radio evangelists such as the Baptist preacher Charles E. Fuller (1887–1968) were more circumspect in communicating their political (although not their social) views. Fuller's *The Old-Fashioned Revival Hour*—the program aired from 1937 until his death in 1968 from studios in Hollywood and Long Beach, California—was not only "the most popular religious radio program" at the time, according to sociologist of religion Nancy T. Ammerman, but also "perhaps the most popular radio program of any kind" during this era.[45] Fuller also was one of the founders of Fuller Theological Seminary in 1947, and it is still one of the major training seminaries for conservative Protestant clergy.

The Canadian-born firebrand Charles E. Coughlin (1891–1979), a Roman Catholic priest, was among the first religious commentators to use the new medium as a platform for extremist political propaganda. He started with a weekly radio program at a local station in his hometown of Detroit in 1926, and it was being broadcast on CBS's national network by 1930. A fervent anti-communist, his radio broadcasts and periodicals such as *Social Justice Weekly* attracted a huge audience in the 1930s.

"Father Coughlin," as he was called, became one of the most powerful political-cum-religious figures in the media, but his ultraconservative views were increasingly inflammatory. Coughlin became a spokesman for the isolationist movement and supported Hitler's regime on the grounds that it was anti-communist. His anti-semitic and anti–African-American racist rhetoric, his vehement attacks against Franklin Delano Roosevelt, and his opposition to America entering the war highlighted Coughlin's radio and print commentaries in the late 1930s and early 1940s. The National Association of Broadcasters finally silenced Coughlin's radio broadcasts when America joined the Allies in World War II, the United States Post Office Department banned him from using the mail for distributing *Social Justice Weekly*, and the Roman Catholic clerical hierarchy ordered him to cease all political activities in 1942.[46]

Fulton J. Sheen (1895–1979) was another Catholic media personality of this period, but he reached out to a broader spectrum of Christians than Coughlin and focused more on Christian family values. He began *The Catholic Hour* in 1930, which reached 4 million weekly listeners over a 22-year run. His *Life Is Worth Living* television series, launched in 1951, reached an estimated 30 million Catholic and non-Catholic viewers every week. The series aired first on the DuMont Television Network and later on ABC until 1957. *The Fulton Sheen Program*, aired later in syndication, ran for most of the 1960s. He also produced more than 70 books and wrote two syndicated newspaper columns.

The Emmy Award–winning Sheen spoke to the camera on *Life Is Worth Living* as he discussed moral issues and current events, a format that probably would not work in today's visual world. Sheen proselytized for Catholicism and, like other media clergy of his day, was politically as well as socially conservative. A fervent anti-communist, he supported fascist Francisco Franco against the communists during the Spanish Civil War; he also opposed Freudian psychoanalysis (he recommended that people go to confession) and birth control. He supported compulsory religious activities and corporal punishment in schools, but toward the end of his media career he argued against racism and the War in Vietnam.[47]

Controlling Religion News in Broadcast Media

The political commentaries of Coughlin and others like him[48] alarmed the major national radio networks at the time (CBS, NBC, and the Mutual Broadcasting System [MBS]). Radio stations were obliged by the Federal Communications Commission (FCC) to provide "public interest" programming, and the stations assumed that selling or providing free broadcast time to selected religious speakers would help fulfill this requirement. MBS—launched in 1934, it survived the classic era of radio and was finally closed down only in 1999—had been the only radio network to offer commercial time slots to religious broadcasters without restrictions. Nevertheless, all the networks had imposed restrictions on religious programming by the mid-1940s.

The networks decided to provide free airtime only to broadcasters affiliated to religious bodies deemed to be most representative of America's religious groups. The three designated bodies were the Conference (originally Council) of Catholic Bishops, the Federal Council of Churches, and a coalition of three national Jewish organizations. The radio and television networks (when commercial television became more widely available) employed the FCC's new policy in the late 1940s and early 1950s. Programs were limited in duration to 30-minute broadcasts on Sunday mornings, and broadcasters were forbidden to solicit funds on air.[49]

Many conservative Protestant groups, however, felt they were excluded from the Federal Communications Commission's arrangement, which clearly favored the mainstream Protestant churches. The National Association of Evangelicals (NAE) was founded in 1942 in large part because these Christians felt threatened by the control the Federal Council of Churches (renamed the National Council of Churches in 1950) had over Protestant religious broadcasting. They launched in 1944 the National Religious Broadcasters, the oldest conservative religious broadcasting network in the nation, and embarked on a long campaign to persuade the FCC to reverse its policy.[50]

The Federal Communications Commission did not exclude those who belonged to larger, more conservative denominations—such as the Southern Baptists and Mormons, who were not members of the NAE—and especially other Christian conservative groups that were able to buy airtime on radio and non-network television stations. The first television evangelists were more often leaders of nondenominational churches with a conservative social agenda but not a partisan political agenda.

Rex Humbard (1919–2007) and Granville Oral Roberts, for example, were among the first to build ministries that incorporated radio and television broadcasting in the 1950s. Humbard, with his megachurch ministry, and Roberts, with his megatent ministry, were national leaders in paid religious television programming on Sundays during this decade, but audiences and stations carrying the programs of these forerunners in televangelism were still relatively limited.

Broadcast Deregulation and Emerging Conservative Voices

The Federal Communications Commission finally bowed to pressure from conservative religious groups and ruled in 1960 that local stations could sell airtime for religious programs to any religious group—not just the three designated faith groups as in the past—and get public interest credit. Conservative religious programs paid for by their constituents soon flooded the market and pushed religious programs sponsored by Protestant denominations affiliated to the National Council of Churches, for example, to the margins.

This was the case both for AM (amplitude modulation) radio, the dominant medium of broadcasting for much of the twentieth century, and for FM (frequency modulation) radio, which emerged as a viable commercial alternative in the late 1960s and 1970s. AM radio thereafter would attract mostly talk shows and news programming, while music radio and public radio, where more religious programs vied with each other for listeners, shifted mainly to FM broadcasting. While 53 percent of all religious broadcasting was paid time in 1959 (before the ruling), 92 percent of all religious programming was paid-time broadcasting by 1977. Conservative religious commentators controlled most of these programs.[51]

The Federal Communications Commission was weakened to the point that it had very little control over radio and television programming under the administration of Ronald Reagan in the 1980s. The numbers of FCC commissioners were reduced to five from seven members, and a chairman was appointed who felt only the marketplace should determine public policy. Television, he said, "was no different from a toaster."[52] The FCC's budget was cut, and all programming was commercialized. Religious programming—like news, sports, or weather programming—was treated and sold like any other commodity. The Reagan administration virtually deregulated all electronic media, and among other things it became much easier for power to be centralized in a relatively few, multinational, multimedia corporations.

Conservative political and religious dominance of commercial radio became a fact of life when the Federal Communications Commission finally revoked the so-called Fairness Doctrine, after a lengthy congressional and court battle, in 1987. The Fairness Doctrine, created in 1949 in the early stages of the Cold War, was applied on a case-by-case basis until it was incorporated into FCC regulations in 1967. The Doctrine had essentially curtailed partisan news and commentary on radio by requiring that stations provide free airtime for listeners to respond to any controversial opinions that were broadcast. The end of the Fairness Doctrine meant that the partisan, talk-show format—in which conservative pundits excelled—became common in the industry.

The Electronic Church—or the Electric Church, as evangelical fundamentalists use the term—also spread its wings in the wake of the Reagan administration's deregulation policies. Christian conservatives based either in denominations or in mega nondenominational churches dominated the funding of religious programming on radio, television, cable, and satellite in the next generation. Christian conservatives today control the vast majority of religious radio and cable television stations and "blanket the nation." The diversity in religious programming that in theory should be enforced by the FCC has been abandoned. As religion media scholar William Fore puts it, "The religious right has become so strong . . . that it would be political suicide for any politician to challenge these stations."[53]

Christian conservatives were among the first to exploit, in the 1960s and 1970s, new technological innovations that provided an alternative to dependence on the three major television networks at the time (ABC, NBC, and CBS). As religious conservatives bought their way onto the airwaves, the invention of videotape, for example, helped them gain access to more and more stations. Programs no longer had to be filmed—a process that often took months to plan and then send via mail from station to station. Now they were mass produced to fit a calendar deadline (especially useful for religious holidays) and sent to stations immediately. In the same way, conservative evangelicals took advantage of cable television when it became cheaper to buy and more widely available to consumers in the 1970s. Aided by other developments, such as paid cable-television programming (started in 1972) and satellite technology (which became commercially viable in the 1980s), the Electronic Church became almost exclusively an Electronic Christian Conservative Church.

The Electronic Church was most visible in the programs of televangelists on cable television. About 9 or 10 televangelists—all of them evangelical Protestants—had a virtual monopoly on the national religious television audience, for example, in the 1980s.[54] Most of the these religious leaders—which included Robert H. Schuller, Jimmy Swaggart, Marvin Gorman, Oral Roberts, Rex Humbard (1919–2007), Jerry Falwell, Jim and Tammy Bakker (1942–2007), Pat Robertson, and James Robison—had expanded their television programs overseas and launched nonprofit agencies that enhanced the power of their ministries, especially in religious training, relief work, and Christian higher education. Several founded full-fledged universities (such as Roberts, Falwell, and Robertson), and the most powerful among them became partisan political activists.[55]

American Christianity in the mass media was increasingly viewed through the lens of an ever-expanding horizon of conservative political, social, and religious concerns in the closing decades of the twentieth century. The phenomenon of the Electronic Church was rightly regarded as instrumental in providing religious conservatives with a public voice not only in America but also in many other parts of the world. The Christian conservative experience in America had become a global phenomenon.[56]

MEDIA AND RELIGION TODAY

Journalists in the secular mainstream media today still cover religion in much the same way it was covered during the twentieth century. Religion news falls into two categories. Sectarian religious stories are treated as soft news, and coverage emphasizes features and stories mainly about noncontroversial events and issues. They are still found typically on the Saturday church page in the press and on specific Sunday service program slots aired on network television, but they now include a wider range of Christian and non-Christian religious activities. Religious stories are treated as hard news, and placed in the news departments of print and electronic media, when they are components of secular news stories or are deemed to be newsworthy on their own merits.

Billy Graham, a Special Case

Partisan religious views rarely have been framed as news reports in the mainstream press since World War II. Although ABC, CBS, and NBC occasionally provide non-Sunday programming for special events sponsored by recognized, mainstream Protestant, Roman Catholic, and Jewish religious bodies, with few exceptions the national television networks will not allow sectarian religious programs to be aired in primetime weeknight slots.

The one significant exception was that public icon of American evangelism, William Franklin Graham Jr., known throughout the world as Billy Graham. He first gained national prominence during an eight-week crusade in Los Angeles in 1949—in part because newspaper mogul William Randolph Hearst (1863–1951) admired him and ensured that the crusade would get priority news exposure in Hearst publications. Henry Luce (1898–1967) placed Graham on the cover of *Time* magazine in 1954 (and again in 1993 and in 1996 with his son and successor, Franklin Graham). While Graham turned down lucrative offers from networks such as NBC to host his own televangelism show, he was a pioneer in using the media to communicate an ambitious religious program. His crusades remain after more than 50 years fixtures on network prime-time television.[57]

Graham remained a conservative Protestant evangelist—a successor in his organization, methods, and style of preaching to the great revivalists of the nineteenth century such as Finney and Moody. In his early years as a Christian crusader, Graham made partisan-political statements that in retrospect were objectionable—such as his expression of admiration for Joseph McCarthy, his bashing of the Left in the 1960s, and the antisemitic remarks he made to President Richard Nixon in 1972—but he also refused to segregate his crusades in the 1950s, supported Martin Luther King Jr. and the civil rights movement in the 1960s, and in his later years preached world peace, a rapprochement with Russia and China, and dialogue with believers in all faith traditions.

Graham in his later years also sought to be a prophet who stood apart from political partisanship—rejecting the tactics of the Religious Right in the 1980s and 1990s. His understanding of evangelical Christianity generally avoided doctrine and denomination. Thus, mainstream and alternative conservative media provided space not only for Graham but also for conservative affiliates deemed to be non-controversial such as Campus Crusade for Christ.[58] While Graham was disengaged from the poor, his "passionate center," as literary critic Harold Bloom said in a favorable retrospective some years ago, was soul saving. A counselor to almost every American president since World War II, Graham ministered "to a particular American need: the public testimony of faith."[59]

Religion News Coverage in the Mass Media

The coverage of religion in the mass media should be a complex, multifaceted process, but there has been a discernible shift in the use of framing devices that journalists employ to reflect religious realities. Religion news, like political news, is a two-dimensional discourse that comes distressingly close at times to being framed as celebrity and spectacle. In essence, religion news has become entertainment news.

Most controversial religious personalities, events, and issues are typically found piggybacked to hard news stories in the secular press and broadcast networks, and in the religion sections of newsmagazines such as *Time* and *Newsweek*. Religion news, like other news, is still usually about conflict. Religion stories are typically about violence, scandal, dying churches, exotic rituals, homophobia, and bizarre cults (as in the 1978 Peoples Temple mass suicides in "Jonestown," Guyana, the 1997 Heaven's Gate tragedy in California, polygamous activities in various renegade Mormon sects, or the fascination with Scientology and celebrity Scientologists). Journalists also tend to view newsworthy religion news as stories about personalities in trouble—as in the Episcopalian (also Methodist and Presbyterian) furor over the ordination of gay clergy or pedophile Roman Catholic priests.

Religious perspectives typically are either liberal or conservative, in part because the journalist "tends to see the world through a political prism in which there are often only two sides, conservative and liberal" to every story. Krista Tippett, founder of National Public Radio's *Speaking of Faith*, points out that this is the "political divide that religious people have squeezed themselves into, and they have gotten smaller for it. And our public life is diminished for it."[60] As with gay marriage, abortion, and other religion debates, every issue is reduced to a two-sided argument. "We only care *whether* Catholics are for or against abortion, but not *why* they are [italics in the original]. . . . What do we miss when journalism fails to grasp religion? The full spectrum of the evangelical movement, for one."[61]

Secular news reports about the Christian religion also tend to be framed in the context of news about Christian evangelical fundamentalists. Christian perspectives that deviate from these conservative messages have relatively no presence in America's mass media networks. In a particularly trenchant critique of Mel Gibson's *The Passion of The Christ* in 2004, for example, Frank Rich, film critic at the time for the *New York Times*, cited Debra Haffner, a Unitarian Universalist minister, as "one of the rare progressive [Christian] religious voices to get any TV time." Haffner says the mass media have an "understanding ... that religion 'is one voice—fundamentalist.' " Rich suggested this exposure had little to do with the religious views of television power brokers or even the fundamentalists themselves: it had everything to do with the widespread belief that Christian conservatives triumphed with George W. Bush's election, and the combative stance of fundamentalists had much greater entertainment value than the views of other Christians.[62]

America's mainstream journalists began to provide more coverage of religion in the 1970s and early 1980s, but it was largely in response to the activities of conservative evangelical political and social activists. They treated conservative religious leaders initially with the same skepticism they typically brought to their interactions with politicians and other partisan sources, and Christian conservatives were not happy with what they regarded as unfair coverage of their activities.

As Christian conservatives expanded their political and social agendas in the 1980s and 1990s, they came under more critical scrutiny from mainstream media. Media researchers Peter A. Kerr and Patricia Moy examined 2,696 stories, culled from newspapers between 1980 and 2000, featuring specifically fundamentalist Christians. They acknowledged the tremendous power mass media could have "in shaping public perceptions of fundamentalist Christianity," and they found that coverage of these activities was mixed. The number of articles about this topic increased consistently, and there was a "relatively mild but constant level of antipathy" toward fundamentalists.[63] A study by Peter A. Kerr of the framing of fundamentalist Christians on network television news during the same period reached a similar conclusion.[64]

A journalistic bias against conservative religious activities, however, was contested both by Kerr and by other studies that suggested there was no liberal bias against Christian conservatives, against Christianity, or against religion in general. While advocates on either side could always find liberal or conservative bias in religion coverage, as journalist-writer Katie H. Porterfield said in a summary of research findings on this topic, Christian conservatives were the most sensitive to charges of bias. Roman Catholic clergy also complained about critical media coverage of sexual abuse by priests, but Porterfield concluded that in both cases the stories were highlighted because they exhibited conflict, controversy, and other news values that would generate public interest as news stories.[65]

Surveys in the 1990s also suggested that journalists in the secular press were not as indifferent or antagonistic toward religion as conservatives asserted. Indeed, they were not different from the general public as far as personal religious belief was concerned. Communication scholars Doug Underwood and Keith Stamm, for example, found in a nationwide survey of American and Canadian journalists in 1998 that a majority had a "strong general religious orientation." Seventy-two percent of respondents said religion was "important or very important" to them. The term Christian, moreover, was defined in exclusivist terms that would appeal directly to conservatives. Even journalists who had no religious affiliations "responded strongly to fundamental calls for moral action as long as they were framed as part of a journalistic, rather than a religious, mission."[66]

The number of reporters actively engaged in religion reporting and writing gradually increased during the 1980s. Religion news broadcasters were admitted to the Religion Newswriters Association (RNA) at the end of the decade, and membership in the RNA increased rapidly to more than 250 by the end of the century. It seems to have become more culturally diverse (in terms of religious preference, race, and gender), but estimates vary on the actual number of religion journalists working in the secular press today.[67]

Some major newspapers—such as the *Dallas Morning News*, the *Atlanta Journal-Constitution*, and the *Washington Post*—assigned several reporters to the religion beat and coverage of religion news rose dramatically. National Public Radio assigned a full-time reporter to the religion beat, ABC became the first national television network to hire a full-time religion reporter, and there was a noticeable increase in the number of religion-oriented stories on other networks in the 1990s. On the whole, however, very few religion journalists in the secular press had any formal seminary training, and many were ill-informed in religion studies. The incompetence of journalists on the religion beat— as compared, for example, with political or sports reporters or even fashion or gardening writers—remained a constant refrain.[68]

Televangelism and the Cult of the Self

Scholars in religion and media studies began to examine critically the role of religion in the news only in the early 1990s,[69] and it was initially in response to the impact conservative Protestant televangelists were having on popular culture. Televangelism's obvious religiosity—in terms of packaging, content, and programming—was reaching people far beyond the target audience of like-minded Christians, but few studies considered what these broadcasts meant to those who were not members of this audience. Critics focused negatively on the televangelists—highlighting (a) financial and religious scandals (especially in the late 1980s) and (b) the more sobering argument that they were secularizing the gospel message to the point that Christ was just another commodity in the marketplace.

The last point resonated far beyond academia and continues to resonate with critics of American religious practices today. The age of the contemporary televangelists, beginning in the 1970s, was not unlike their radio evangelist contemporaries—indeed, sometimes they were the same people.

They sold Jesus as the gospel of prosperity that believers could trust to provide them with respect, contentment, and status, and they offered biblical texts to suggest that financial success had a biblical foundation. Their theology, moreover, was driven increasingly by the medium used to proclaim the gospel message. As television costs increased and the number of outside ministries funded by televangelists increased, fund-raising became an integral component of these sermons, targeting the appeal mainly to the personal needs of the viewer or listener. As Billy Graham biographer Marshall Frady put it, "Crusades now existed for their televised reproductions; the television event now existed to produce more television events."[70]

These radio and television evangelists were also tapping into a deep-seated well, the American preoccupation with the self. The quest to eliminate negativity and promote a positive sense of well-being—of self-confidence, self-esteem, self-support, and self-generated happiness—has a long history in American popular culture. The televangelists of this generation were not that far removed in spirit from religious and nonreligious predecessors, who also offered guides to happiness, peace, and success in one's personal life. They also relied on the media of the day—press and radio, and later television, and usually a seminal book—to support their self-improvement programs.

Some were preachers in the conservative Protestant tradition—such as Norman Vincent Peale (his most successful book, *The Power of Positive Thinking*, 1952), who got involved in partisan politics with his anti-Catholic stance during the 1960 presidential election. Some had no public religious affiliation at all but were simply business entrepreneurs—such as Dale Carnegie (his most successful book, *How to Win Friends and Influence People*, 1936). The Dale Carnegie public-speaking guide on achieving self-confidence and financial success was a template for business professionals, especially after the Great Depression.

Most newspaper and magazine columnists and radio and television talk-show hosts in the personal-growth business after World War II have not been partisan political activists. Only a few have partisan agendas—such as the conservative marriage and family therapist Laura Schlessinger (her radio call-in show, *Dr. Laura*, is syndicated nationally). And a few are interfaith or beyond faith—self-help stars such as Deepak Chopra and Eckhart Tolle—who sell their own versions of wellness.[71]

Religious spokespersons in the self-help industry today tend to be conservative Protestant leaders of nondenominational, multimedia ministries such as Joel Olsteen, Rick Warren, Creflo Dollar, and T. D. Jakes—all of whom claim they are not involved in partisan politics. Olsteen's Lakewood Church in Houston, Texas, for example, is reputedly the largest in the country (with 47,000 members), and Lakewood's multimedia worship services are now broadcast in more than 100 countries. Olsteen claims he uses the pulpit to promote "democracy" and not to endorse political parties or politicians.[72]

A decline in televangelism's political and fund-raising capacities did seem evident to some observers at the turn of the century. While many of the same faces were still on the screen, according to one nationwide survey (reported in the evangelical Christian magazine *Christianity Today*) televangelists devoted "almost no airtime to politics" and "only a small amount for fundraising and promotion."[73]

Religion on the Internet

Media and religion also interface on the Internet—the most democratic medium of mass communication currently available to the public. Here the cult of the self remains supreme, for there is room for virtually every individual to express his or her point of view. Most Roman Catholic parishes and Protestant churches have their own Web sites and their own online directories: whereas 35 percent of Protestant churches had Web sites in 2000, for example, almost 60 percent did in 2006. In addition, religious Web sites represent virtually every belief system today. Favored ones, such as the progressive www.beliefnet.com, are nonpartisan in the sense that they are geared especially to the seeker who is not committed to a particular faith.[74]

Web sites provide source material for noncanonical and canonical Christian texts (such as www.earlychristianwritings.com and www.blueletterbible.org), where users can compare more than 10 versions of a verse on one screen, read commentaries, and view the Greek or Hebrew text. The Yale University Divinity School (www.library.yale.edu/div/electext.htm) maintains a list of the "Best Free Online Resources for the Study of Christianity," and Believers Church in Tulsa, Oklahoma (www.believers.org/otherc.htm #URL10) lists Christian conservative Web sites maintained by missions, universities, churches and ministries, media, and pro-life groups.

There are directories of religious blogs (personal Web sites) (such as www.blogs4god.com), retreat directories (such as www.findthe devine.com), hymn sites (such as www.cyberhymnal.org), and religious sites for persons and communities in need (such as www.disaster news.net, www.churchworldservice.org, and www.healingenviron ments.org). Every Christian denomination and every major non-Christian faith tradition have their own official Web sites (such as www.muslimgateway.com and www.Buddhism.about.com). There is even a Web site (www.catholic-church.org) that creates free Web sites for Catholic organizations throughout the world. There are Web sites for ex-Christians, atheists, and agnostics—the list is virtually endless.

In the politics of religion, conservative voices on the Internet must operate in this context. A major study published in 2003, for example, found "the more religious an individual is, the less likely he or she will use the Internet." And in general the Internet is not "used by individuals to interact on a communitywide level." But the researchers agreed, "religiosity is a determinant of overall Internet use." There could well be a "reciprocal relationship between religiosity and Internet use"—including the possibility that personal religious beliefs are affected by the ways in which these beliefs are communicated on the Internet.[75]

"Ideological polemics," says Virginia Heffernan in writing about the popular video-exchange site YouTube among youth, "are what really engage the online faithful." While Tangle.com (formerly God-Tube), the Web site for Christian conservatives, might be "the fastest-growing website in the United States" in 2007, Jewish youth could access numerous Web sites, such as the International B'nai B'rith Youth Organization (bbyo.org/aza), and various youth sites created for Orthodox, Conservative, and Reform Jewish believers. Muslim youth could access sites such as those sponsored by the Islamic Broadcasting Network (youth.ibn.net) or sites linked to the major Muslim Internet site (muslim.com).[76]

The Christian brand today is a multinational industry publicized and advertised in a variety of cultural formats, and Christian conservatives are undoubtedly seeking to be the dominant force in this market.[77] They have their own Internet Evangelism Coalition, for example, offering advice on how to use iPods, smartphones, and BlackBerries; cell phones and MP3 players; and video clips, electronic mail, and Internet sites to spread the Gospel. They were among the pioneers in digitizing religion—of using high-tech alternatives to promote evangelism through such innovations as worship Web sites and discussion chat rooms—but numerous other faith traditions now use this format.[78]

A wide spectrum of religious commentary can be found in personal and family blogs and in sites set up for youth of all religious faiths. And the Internet itself is merely one component of a bewildering array of media venues—including personalized audio and video tapes, CDs and DVDs, popular songs and performance art, T-shirts, wristbands, car stickers, and other souvenirs—competing in the marketplace of belief today.

CONSERVATIVE MEDIA IN POLITICS[79]

Conservative religious perspectives diffused into a broader conservative political discourse between the 1960s and the 1990s. The conservative political agenda, like the conservative religious agenda, was framed in binary language based on what it meant to be a conservative and a liberal in America's two-party political culture. Critics of a conservative bias in news coverage, however, have paid little or no attention to those media structures and practices that have provided a public platform for the conservative voice. This lack of engagement on the part of mainstream secular *and* religious media has paid enormous dividends for the conservative voice in the ongoing battle to define the political, social, economic, and religious agendas for ordinary Americans.

An alternative conservative political-cum-religious media—an amalgam of direct-mail advertising, newsletters, books, pamphlets, talk-radio and cable television programs, and Internet Web sites— played a crucial role in framing a political agenda for believers and nonbelievers alike. Perceiving themselves as an aggrieved, beleaguered minority, conservative politicians and operatives, religious leaders, businessmen and women, and their allies in the media maintained that news coverage in mainstream media was biased and prejudiced against conservative perspectives.

Media Evangelists and Partisan Politics

The extent to which media evangelists are involved in partisan politics remains a matter of debate. First, most of these evangelists favor a conservative social agenda on issues such as limiting if not banning women's reproductive rights and prohibiting gay marriage and family rights. They favor activities such as posting biblical sayings on government buildings and conducting sex-abstinence (as opposed to sex-education) courses, Bible-centered Christian courses, and prayers in the schools that are indistinguishable from the Christian conservative political agenda.

Second, most of these evangelists remain politically conservative. For example, *Time* magazine's list of the 25 "most influential evangelicals in America" in 2005—all of whom use various media (including print, radio, and cable television) to communicate their ideas—suggests that the majority are partisan, conservative Republicans. Conservative religious television networks today, such as Trinity Broadcasting Network and Daystar, all have programs that feature evangelical preachers with partisan political agendas.[80]

Third, the most prominent figures in conservative religious politics between the 1980s and the early 2000s—Jerry Falwell, Pat Robertson, and James Dobson—had their own media of mass communication, while also having access to other conservative religious and secular outlets. As we noted in Chapter 1, the link between conservative politics, patriotism, and religion was cemented both in the public mind and in the mass media with the rise to national prominence of these Protestant evangelical fundamentalist leaders.

Falwell had established a diverse multimedia organization by the beginning of the 1980s. It consisted of books (he wrote about 20 in his lifetime), tapes, videos, and cassettes of speeches and sermons, television specials, and his weekly radio-television show, the *Old Time Gospel Hour* (syndicated nationally until 2004)—to service his many religious, social, and political concerns. Falwell's Moral Majority provided a forum and a focus for conservative religious interests, but in its heyday the organization spoke primarily to and on behalf of evangelical fundamentalists like Falwell himself.

Robertson's Christian Coalition expanded the Republican Party's conservative religious support base in part because he was a master of modern religious programming. The Christian Broadcasting Network was launched in 1961, and its flagship program, *The 700 Club*, was on the air starting in 1966 and can now be viewed in 97 percent of America's television markets. Robertson's power in religious broadcasting was secured when he started the first cable television network—CBN Cable—in 1977. Having control over a network, Robertson's *700 Club* pioneered the use of religion in a political news talk-show format—based on the news and current-affairs style created by the CBS program *60 Minutes*. The Christian Broadcasting Network itself eventually became one of the largest multimedia religious ministries in the world.[81]

Dobson and the various Focus on the Family enterprises churned out audio and film dramas, published a magazine and newsletter, and had its own Web site. A prolific writer, Dobson authored or co-authored more than 30 books in 30 years. *Monthly Focus* alerts were even inserted into Sunday worship service bulletins in many conservative Protestant churches. Dobson's nationally syndicated radio show *Focus on the Family* attracts between 5 and 10 million listeners a week, and it is carried by about 2,000 stations nationwide. Books, pamphlets, films, videos, and taped broadcasts are sold throughout the nation and beyond, and Dobson had created another multimedia religious empire with a worldwide audience by the beginning of the twenty-first century.[82]

Pioneers of Conservative Political Media

Many scholars trace the roots of the contemporary conservative force in the media to the 1950s and the Cold War—beginning with small anti-communist journals such as the weekly newsletter (later a tabloid) *Human Events* (1944) and the libertarian journal *Freeman* (1950). The chief spokespersons for the conservative cause were people such as Russell Kirk (1918–1994) and William F. Buckley Jr. (1925–2008), who sought to bring coherency and a sense of cohesion to conservative programs and policies. Buckley, a Roman Catholic, was the best known of the intellectual mediators and his magazine, the *National Review* (1955), was the best-known conservative publication of the day. Buckley and his colleagues on the *Review* have been credited with providing a forum for resurrecting the two primary themes in conservative political activism—patriotism and religion—and for helping to (a) articulate the philosophical tensions within the conservative movement at the time, (b) eliminate or contain extremists, and (c) promote a consensus on conservative cultural values and political goals.[83]

Book Publishing

Regnery Publishing Company (1947) produced many of their books—beginning with such classics as Buckley's *God and Man at Yale* (1951) and Kirk's *The Conservative Mind* (1953). The authors in Henry Regnery's stable were virtually a who's who of conservative activists in America during the 1950s and 1960s. They ranged from journalists such as James J. Kilpatrick and the Catholic writer Leo Brent Bozell Jr. (1926–1997), Buckley's brother-in-law, to rabid anti-communists such as Whittaker Chambers (1901–1961) and Robert W. Welch Jr. (1899–1985), founder of the John Birch Society in 1958. Regnery Publishing maintained its status as the leading publisher of conservative literature in the 1980s, 1990s, and into the new century with such authors as Haley Barbour, Barbara Olson, Newt Gingrich, and Ann Coulter. This was the company that published *Unfit for Command*, John E. O'Neill and Jerome R. Corsi's 2004 book attacking John Kerry's war record during the 2004 election.[84]

Religious publishing also became big business, and books by Christian conservatives seem to have established a corner on this market. Some evangelical authors—such as Warren (*The Purpose Driven Church*, 1995, and *The Purpose Driven Life*, 2002), Olsteen (*Your Best Life Now*, 2004, and *Become a Better You*, 2007), and Bruce Wilkinson (*The Prayer of Jabez*, 2000)—were on virtually every best-seller list in the past decade or so.[85] While they may or may not have had a political agenda, others did.

The enormously successful *Left Behind* books by conservative Protestant leaders Tim LaHaye and Jerry B. Jenkins, all published by Tyndale House Publishers, offer a prime example of conservative Christianity's impact on partisan politics. The authors spin a modern-day rapture in which believers are spirited off to heaven, leaving everyone else behind to face famine, plague, war, and other calamities. They cite selected passages of scripture as proof the story is based on the Bible. Muslims, Jews, Buddhists, Hindus—and Christians who do not adhere to the conservative interpretation of Christianity—do not have seats on heaven's bus. The first *Left Behind* book was published in 1995, and there are now about 16 in the series. Estimates of the number of copies sold ranged between 42 and 65 million by 2005—not counting spin-offs such as greeting cards, books for children and teens, CDs, videos and an audio series, two movies, and a television series. The *Left Behind* books today are marketed worldwide in many languages.[86]

The success of books produced by Regnery and conservative religious firms such as Tyndale House and Multnomah Publishers (its stable included Dobson and Wilkinson) had a major impact on the mainstream publishing world. The biggest firms now have their own conservative book imprints—such as Random House (with Crown Publishing Group), Penguin Group (with Sentinel), and Simon & Schuster (with Threshold Editions). They also have subsidiaries that are tapping into the burgeoning evangelical Christian book market. Doubleday, a subsidiary of Random House (which in turn is a subsidiary of the German media giant Bertelsmann), for example, created WaterBrook Press in 1996, which bought Multnomah Publishers in 2006. Rupert Murdoch's ownership of HarperCollins and the hiring of more conservative editorial staffers also suggest that the marketing of conservative political and religious books is big business today.

Conservatives are kept informed of this literature through conservative book clubs such as American Compass that operate nationwide. Access to a broader audience (at relatively cheap prices) is obtained by marketing conservative books through corporate chain bookstores (such as Barnes & Noble and Borders), multipurpose retail and wholesale giants (such as Wal-Mart Stores and Costco), and through the Internet (using sites such as Amazon.com and the conservative news Web site WorldNetDaily).

Conservative Think Tanks

Conservative intellectuals have scholarly think tanks such as the American Enterprise Institute (1943) and the libertarian Cato Institute (1977), but conservative ideas moved out of the realm of academic discussion and into the mass marketplace of ideas primarily through the activities of The Heritage Foundation (1973). Headquartered in Washington, D.C., Heritage was envisaged as a conservative counterpart to the Brookings Institution, another public policy research agency in the capital. Republican Party strategist Paul Weyrich was one of the founders and its first president, while initial funding came from Joseph Coors, founder of the Coors Corporation, and Richard Mellon Scaife, a billionaire newspaper publisher and heir of the Mellon financial, oil, and aluminum empire.

Heritage is a major research facility with state-of-the-art, radio-broadcast studios and a media visitor's center. As the leading conservative research and training institution inside the Washington Beltway, Heritage's researchers and resident scholars provide a continuing supply of news releases, information reports, and professional expertise to mainstream as well as conservative media outlets throughout the country.

They are joined by a plethora of special-interest groups seeking to influence public policy. As noted in Chapter 1, some are Christian family-value groups like Dobson's Focus on the Family and Beverly LaHaye's Concerned Women for America. Others have more overt political agendas, such as the Free Congress Research and Education Foundation or simply Free Congress Foundation (1974), a training ground for young political activists, and the affiliated Committee for the Survival of a Free Congress, which was founded initially to counterbalance what conservatives saw as liberal, labor-based influences in Congress. The Survival committee produced several spin-offs such as the Free Congress Political Action Committee and the Coalitions for America, which actively endorsed and funded conservative family-values candidates and members of Congress. The organizing guru behind these groups was the GOP (Grand Old Party) lobbyist Weyrich, who had helped found the Heritage Foundation.

Educational Activities

Education and the training of young conservatives was another focus of conservative intellectuals in Buckley's generation. The first national student organization for conservatives in higher education was called the Intercollegiate Society of Individualists (ISI) (1953)—now known as the Intercollegiate Studies Institute—and it was founded by Frank Chodorov (1887–1966), a libertarian academic and initially one of Buckley's philosophical mentors. ISI increased rapidly in size and influence—organizing programs, monitoring the political and social attitudes of teachers, scrutinizing media coverage of campus activities, and providing financial and technical support for conservative student media. The best-known ISI publication is *Intercollegiate Review* (1965). Through the *Review* and other outlets, the Institute issues reports and publishes surveys and even books (through ISI Books) on a range of topics—from the teaching of American history and politics on American campuses to the best and worst nonfiction books of the twentieth century.[87]

The Intercollegiate Studies Institute provides a significant educational thrust to the conservative movement, but it is not the only one. Morton C. Blackwell, a GOP operative who first entered national politics in the early 1960s, has spent a career as the high-profile leader in the training of youth activists. His Leadership Institute (1979) receives lavish funding to train students in the art of election organizing and communication skills—such as public speaking and debate, how to elect conservatives to student government on college campuses, and how to communicate conservative ideas in college publications. M. Stanton Evans, journalist and author (among other publications, a biography of Senator Joseph McCarthy), founded the National Journalism Center in 1977—offering 6- to 12-week training courses in the profession. Based in Washington, D.C., the Center "has given birth to a number of alumni who, through their engagement in public policy journalism and activism, have proven extremely effective in promoting conservative ideas."[88]

Senator Barry Goldwater of Arizona was the politician generally credited with bringing the conservative political agenda to national attention when he ran for president as the Republican Party candidate in 1964. In the war of words during the election, conservative media at the time were no match for the media machine created by Lyndon B. Johnson and the Democrats. Nevertheless, Goldwater's campaign highlighted a then-new fund-raising strategy based on small donations and the use of alternative print outlets such as local and regional newsletters and opinion journals, self-published political tracts, and networks of citizen activists—mobilizing thousands of younger voters (like Backwell), who remained active in galvanizing grassroots political, social, and religious support for conservative causes.

The Cold War journals continued to provide publicity to fledgling conservative groups and the issues that concerned them inside the Washington Beltway, but there were few outlets for contemporary conservative views in the mainstream press before the 1970s. The *Reader's Digest* was regarded as a conservative journal, and there were editorial staffers on several dailies in the South and the Midwest who provided conservative voices in regional newspapers. Conservative voices in print, however, were heard mainly in smaller, community newspapers such as William Loeb's (1905–1981) *Manchester Union-Leader* (New Hampshire) and especially chains such as Raymond C. Hoiles's (1878–1970) Freedom Newspapers (now known as Freedom Communications and based in Santa Ana, California, home of its flagship newspaper, the *Orange County Register*).

Direct Mail and the Single Issue Campaign

Direct mail was perhaps the most pervasive medium used in the making of a conservative voting constituency in the aftermath of Goldwater's campaign. Richard Viguerie, the pioneer in direct mail political advertising, claimed this was the primary tool used to communicate the conservative message. It was self-funding advertising: the message was communicated to and paid for by consumers who received the message. Direct mail provided key lists of potential conservative activists for fund-raising and promoting the conservative agenda. Direct mail informed and updated them on the key issues and advised them on how they could help the conservative cause. Viguerie argues that direct-mail advertising helped "to create the conservative mass movement" between 1964 and 1980.[89]

Direct mail also provided an alternative to politics as dictated either by the party hierarchy or by large corporations. By appealing directly to conservative constituents, it helped democratize the political process for conservatives. Ordinary citizens could focus on "the conservative agenda rather than the Republican [Party] agenda," which were not always the same. Anticipating the Internet by decades, direct mail made it possible for activists to promote and finance political activity—bypassing what conservatives saw as mainstream liberal media to get their message to individuals, and bypassing corporate America to raise funds at the grass roots. Viguerie claimed that direct advertising was the least expensive type of fund-raising before the 1980 presidential election, which meant that religious and social conservatives could promote their own causes and support their own candidates independent of the GOP hierarchy's choices.[90]

Viguerie's company spawned media such as the *Conservative Digest* (1975), a monthly that claimed the largest national circulation for a political journal at the time.[91] The focus in terms of content both in the *Digest* and in direct-mail newsletters was increasingly on single issues—especially social issues such as abortion, pornography, and prayer in schools—in the belief that single-issue appeals could swing votes toward conservatives in most modern elections in which the difference between a win or a loss was 5 percentage points or less.

Single-Issue Campaigns

While direct-mail politics may not have been as decisive in fueling the modern conservative movement as Viguerie says, single-issue appeals cloaked in religion and politics became the vogue of conservative media activists. The timing of single-issue campaigns, moreover, was shortened dramatically with new media technologies. Whereas it might take weeks to mount a campaign through direct mail (which got a boost first with the use of computers and second with the widespread marketing of fax machines), it was a matter of days with radio or even hours with cable television, and potentially a matter of minutes with the Internet. Single-issue campaigns have remained the preferred strategy of conservatives in media to this day.

The classic example in the 1970s was Phyllis Schlafly, a Roman Catholic housewife with a law degree who gained national prominence when the Goldwater campaign distributed thousands of copies of her first book, *A Choice Not an Echo* (1964), which was a diatribe against the Republican establishment. Schlafly's political newsletter, the *Phyllis Schlafly Report* (1967) and the *Eagle Forum Newsletter*—voice of the Eagle Forum, the antifeminist advocacy group she founded in 1975—were primary modes of communication used in a sustained effort to halt passage of the 1972 Equal Rights Amendment (ERA). Although 35 of the 38 states needed to pass the amendment voted in favor, Schlafly's grassroots "Stop the ERA" campaign attracted a broad political and religious spectrum of ordinary citizens and almost single-handedly caused the measure to be defeated in 1982.[92]

Single-issue campaigns—employing the rhetoric of personal derision, confrontation, and character assassination—became the *cause célèbre* of conservative media in the 1980s and 1990s. The health-care reform initiative under the leadership of Hillary Clinton, to take another example, was the centerpiece of President Bill Clinton's legislative reform measures in 1993–1994. A host of actors contributed to the defeat of health-care reform, and the Clinton administration provided them with plenty of ammunition. But what amounted to a conservative-mediated blitz against any Clinton-inspired health-care reform was a significant factor in turning public opinion against the plan.[93] It also divided the Democratic Party and provided Newt Gingrich and his allies in Congress with a key issue for the Republicans to use in gaining control of the House and the Senate in the 1994 congressional elections.[94]

President Clinton's sexual escapades provided conservative media with another trump card to use in the political wars waged during the Clinton era—the most infamous being coverage of the Monica Lewinsky affair, a campaign that almost ended in the president's conviction on impeachment charges in 1998.[95] The most bizarre single-issue campaign in recent years was probably the attempt by conservative lobby groups to prolong the life of Theresa "Terri" Schiavo (1963–2005), who had been on life support in a vegetative state since 1990. Conservative advocacy through direct mail, talk radio, and cable television helped immeasurably to keep this campaign alive for seven long years, and innumerable legal, medical, and congressional battles, until Schiavo finally died. Some critics cite the public reaction to this saga as a contributing factor in the Democratic takeover of the Republican-controlled Congress in the 2006 midterm elections.

The fusion of individual faith, politics, patriotism, and social commitment in conservative media outlets in the past 25 years or so has been extraordinary. Mainstream daily newspapers (even though the long-term decline in readership was well under way), weekly magazines, and network television had been the preferred source of news for most consumers whatever their political leanings before the 1980s. The preferred source of news for most consumers since then has been an array of other media outlets, where conservative voices have often held sway.

Radio and Cable-Satellite Television

Conservative news and opinion at present are communicated primarily through radio and cable or satellite television—supplemented by direct mail, film,[96] and increasingly by the Internet. Evangelical Christian conservatives in 2005, according to journalist Mariah Blake, controlled nearly all of the roughly 2,000 radio stations in the United States and at least six national cable television networks—many of which have their own news operations. The world's Christian television networks formed their own cooperative news service at the National

Religious Broadcasters' convention that year. "Many Christian broadcasters attribute the success of their news operations," as Blake puts it, "to the biblical perspective that underpins their reporting in a world made wobbly by terrorist threats and moral relativism."[97]

Many Christian-based, conservative radio networks offer a potpourri of news and commentary, music, and drama. Among the pioneers was Crawford Broadcasting (founded by evangelist Percy B. Crawford in 1959), which remains a family-owned business. USA Radio Network (1985), based in Dallas, offers a national Christian news service (USA merged with Information Radio Network in 2008). Salem Radio Network—a satellite radio network based in Irving, Texas—is probably the largest of the national networks and "the only Christian-focused news organization," according to its Web site, "with fully-equipped broadcast facilities at the U.S. House, Senate, and White House manned by full-time correspondents." American Family Radio (1991), based in Tupelo, Mississippi, is perhaps the most prominent of the fast-growing regional networks.[98]

Their audiences were primarily Protestant Christians, but conservative Roman Catholics were also active on talk radio with such networks as the Ave Maria Radio Network, launched by Domino's Pizza magnate Tom Monaghan from Ave Maria College, the college he built and financed in Florida.[99] Although the audience base for Christian radio is difficult to estimate, the strength of these religious broadcasters was and is in their appeal to Christian conservatives across the spectrum of political parties.[100]

Conservative Religion on Commercial Radio

Most commercial broadcast news was given over to conservative news and opinion with the revocation of the Fairness Doctrine in 1987. The demise of the Fairness Doctrine was followed in the 1990s by more legislation benefiting the conservative voice. Congress relaxed radio ownership rules in 1992, for example, by allowing companies to have more than two radio stations in a given radio market.

The controversial Telecommunications Act of 1996—an attempt to overhaul its predecessor, enacted in 1934—effectively deregulated the entire media industry. Promoters claimed the legislation would stimulate competition and more cultural diversity, encourage investment in new media technologies, provide more jobs, pass on savings to consumers, and open public access to new media. Critics foresaw that the legislation would open the door to even more acquisitions and mergers, less diversity, and higher prices. Media consolidation became a reality, and among the chief beneficiaries in the radio industry were the burgeoning conservative media conglomerates.[101]

Clear Channel Communications, a family-owned company launched in San Antonio in 1972, best expressed the power of the conservative voice in commercial radio in the aftermath of this legislation. Since there was no longer any limit on the number of radio stations one company could own, Clear Channel gobbled up radio stations—the conglomerate grew from 43 to more than 1,200 radio stations between 1995 and 2001. It became the largest owner of radio stations in the United States—in terms of both the number of stations owned and the revenue generated by these stations—branched into television, and established a network of radio and advertising-related operations overseas.

Clear Channel effectively destroyed the independence and idiosyncratic style of an older commercial radio tradition that kept listeners entertained and updated on breaking news of the day. The management's cost-cutting measures—including less local news, homogenized play lists, and "the practice of importing voice-tracked disc jockeys cross-country . . . aided by a cheat sheet of local reference information"—became a common theme in the industry. Aided by investigative journalism exposés in online political outlets such as *Salon* and by inquiries from the U.S. Securities and Exchange Commission, however, Clear Channel's shares plummeted in the early 2000s. The conglomerate was forced to sell some of its nonradio operations and in 2005 was split into three separate companies, the radio broadcasting company being Clear Channel Communications. Two private equity firms bought Clear Channel in 2006 and announced plans to privatize the company in 2008.[102]

Conservative Talk Shows

The leading conservative talk-show host since the Fairness Doctrine was revoked is Rush Limbaugh. His radio program—*The Rush Limbaugh Show*, first aired in 1988—is now syndicated by Premiere Radio Networks, which is owned by Clear Channel Communications. Limbaugh is credited with reviving the flagging fortunes of AM radio and developing the now standard news format for talk-show radio hosts. Limbaugh today has many imitators—conservatives with radio shows of their own (and, in several cases, television shows) such as Sean Hannity, Michael Medved, Michael Savage (real name, Michael Alan Weiner), Bill O'Reilly, and Tony Snow (who was the Bush While House press secretary before he died in 2008)—but Limbaugh's radio show remains the leader in every radio rating category. It is aired on more broadcast stations and has more listeners than any other radio talk show in America, and even Limbaugh's many detractors acknowledge his role in making conservative rhetoric both attractive and entertaining to millions of ordinary Americans.[103]

The conservative-liberal political debates on secular radio and cable-satellite television are as one-sided as the religious debates. The conservative push to gain control of the television talk-show format was initiated when print journalists and syndicated columnists—such as George F. Will, Robert Novak, Cal Thomas, Mona Charen, Pat Buchanan, and William Safire—began appearing in the medium. Buckley's program, *Firing Line*, was a very visible conservative voice on PBS (Public Broadcasting Service) in the 1960s and 1970s, and it was followed by John McLaughlin's long-running weekly public television program, *The McLaughlin Group*, launched in 1982.

The legendary rise of Fox News Channel as a cable-satellite network, however, was really the catalyst that gave legitimacy and urgency to the modern conservative agenda to viewers in America and overseas. Fox News, launched by Rupert Murdoch in 1996, provided for conservatives an alternative to CNN (Cable News Network, founded in 1980) and MSNBC (founded in 1996), the two mainstream cable-satellite networks.

Programs with formats that framed political dialogue as a choice between "Right" (conservative) or "Left" (liberal) have become the *modus operandi* on cable television, and McLaughlin—a former Catholic priest and the Washington, D.C., editor of Buckley's *National Review*—was one of the early hosts of these programs. Viewers could choose from a range of talk shows—beginning with the popular *Crossfire* program that aired on CNN from 1982 to 2005. During this span, media pundits from the Right featured Buchanan (the original creator of the show along with Thomas Braden, the designated Left), McLaughlin, Novak, John Sununu, Snow, Lynn Cheney, Mary Matlan, and Tucker Carlson. The popularity of this show led to others such as Fox News Channel's *Hannity & Colmes*, featuring hosts Sean Hannity and Alan Colmes (the "liberal"). Other conservative news shows departed from the two-host format—such as Fox News Channel's *The O'Reilly Factor* featuring host Bill O'Reilly.

Jamieson and Cappella's study of the *Wall Street Journal* editorial and opinion pages, Limbaugh's radio show, and selected Fox News talk-show hosts (especially Sean Hannity, Brit Hume, and Carl Cameron) clearly show how conservative media hosts employ common language in which each host legitimizes the others with "similar lines of argument, shared evidence, and common tactical approaches in their defense of conservatism and their attack on its opponents." They represent different media of mass communication and different constituencies,[104] but together they provide a master narrative of the world for their audiences, a world remarkable for its simplicity and single-mindedness.

A biblical metaphor for conservative-liberal politics as mediated by conservatives might depict David in combat with Goliath, where the conservative David is seen as the vulnerable innocent who is unbiased, reliable, and straight-talking in his news coverage and the liberal Goliath is seen as biased, untrustworthy, and deceitful. The conservative-liberal dichotomy is vital for conservatives, because it has helped target divisive issues, undermine mainstream media credibility, and promote "cohesion within the conservative audience."[105]

The conservative litmus test is always that version of conservatism embodied by Ronald Reagan and his administration in the 1980s. Reaganism has been elevated to god-like status as the personified answer to every political, economic, or social issue America faces. Reagan's conservative policies "succeeded where Franklin Roosevelt's liberalism failed." Reagan's political philosophy is the unifying theme in the conservative media's construction of a coherent ideology. These core arguments are employed to attack the liberal media—which, conservative media claim, aggressively distort Reagan's conservative ideology—and to vet GOP candidates seeking the party's nominations.[106]

The conservative political, social, and religious agenda was a major factor in the shift that occurred in news viewing habits during the 1990s. Cable television and radio news and commentary supplanted network television broadcast news for a majority of the television audience. Viguerie and his collaborator, David Franke, for example, offer data gleaned from Nielsen Media Research and Pew Research Center ratings between 1993 and 2003 that showed an overall rise in audiences seeking their national and international news and opinion from the three news cable networks—Fox News, CNN, and MSNBC—and an overall decline in those watching the three television broadcast news networks—ABC, CBS, and NBC. And in each of the three presidential campaigns before 2008 (1996, 2000, 2004), cable television news gained market share over network television news.[107]

The Internet

The latest vehicle for communicating conservative values is the Internet. As we noted earlier, however, the distinction between liberal and conservative in America's contemporary political culture is difficult to maintain in this medium. Important sources of information and opinion can be found in a myriad of commercial and nonprofit group Web sites, but they offer a wide spectrum of views on issues of importance to these enterprises. The mainstream press and television networks—both international (such as BBC News and Xinhua News Agency, China's official news agency) and national (such as ABC News, CNN, the *New York Times*, and the *Los Angeles Times*)—are among the leaders in terms of online readership.

The first conservative Internet newspaper, *WorldNetDaily*, was launched in 1997. When media mogul Rupert Murdoch bought the *Wall Street Journal* (*WSJ*) in 2007 (and also acquired Dow Jones, the stock market company index), readers in early 2008 were allowed free access to videotaped interviews and the ultraconservative editorial and opinion pages of the hitherto subscription-only *WSJ* Web site.[108]

Most people, however, use the Internet for reasons other than seeking political news and opinion. The main exception is during election campaigns—a trend first noticed between the 1996 and 2004 presidential elections—when that percentage of the population using the Internet showed a discernible increase.[109] While liberal and conservative news sites expanded dramatically during these years, they could no longer be defined narrowly as "liberal" or "conservative." Dissenting voices could be found everywhere along the political spectrum. In Internet politics, there was little identification with party politics, the classic example being the campaigns conducted on the Internet for and against the Iraq war.

Partisan political commentary, like partisan religious commentary, is confined largely to personal blogs, and political candidates and lobby groups as well as other kinds of advocacy groups have adopted this strategy as the best way to communicate their interests and concerns to the Internet audience and beyond.[110] The Internet became a fierce and often personal battleground in the anti-Clinton campaigns of the late 1990s and in the anti-Bush campaigns virtually throughout the years of his presidency. By this point, Democrats and Republicans, and third-party candidates as well, were using the Internet as an effective organizing, recruiting, and fund-raising tool in election politics.[111]

Conservative voices—and for the most part these remain Christian conservative voices—have had an enormous and cumulative impact on American political attitudes for almost two generations. Conservative media overlook no issue in news or entertainment in communicating their messages, and they have worked hard to ensure that these messages also reach the mainstream press and network television. The result is a powerful media machine that at least in the public sphere can persuade individuals, groups, communities, and at times even the nation to accept the conservative perspective on political, social, and religious values as the true or the preferred perspective. Conservatives truly have a media establishment of their own today.

NOTES

1. Jake Tapper, "Purpose Driven Candidates: Obama, McCain Seek Warren's Blessing," *ABC News*, August 15, 2008 (citing Warren on the *Good Morning America* talk show publicizing the forthcoming event), http://abcnews.go.com/GMA/Politics/Story?id=5586670&page=1.

2. Kathleen Parker, "Candidates' Pastoral Screening Was Supremely Wrong," *Houston Chronicle*, August 21, 2008, B9.

3. The role that critical-cultural paradigms can play in teaching journalism is discussed in Les Switzer, John McNamara, and Michael Ryan, "Critical-Cultural Studies in Research and Instruction," *Journalism & Mass Communication Educator* 54, no. 3 (1999): 23–42.

4. See Stuart Hall, ed., *Representation: Cultural Representations and Signifying Practices* (London: Thousand Oaks, CA: Sage, 1997), Chapter 1.

5. Stewart M. Hoover, "Media and the Construction of the Religious Public Sphere," in *Rethinking Media, Religion, and Culture*, ed. Stewart M. Hoover and Knut Lundby (Thousand Oaks, CA: Sage, 1997), 283–297, p. 295. Lundby and Hoover argue that the traditional view "of mediated religion as religious messages *transported by mass media to people*" has been replaced "with a cultural interpretation of religious or sacred symbolism *as shaped by the mediation itself* (italics in the original)." See Knut Lundby and Stewart M. Hoover, "Summary Remarks: Mediated Religion," in *Rethinking Media, Religion*, 298–309, p. 298.

6. Claire Hoertz Badaracco, *Quoting God: How Media Shape Ideas about Religion and Culture* (Waco, TX: Baylor University Press, 2005), 3. See also Stewart M. Hoover and Shalini S. Venturelli, "The Category of the

Religious: The Blindspot of Contemporary Media Theory?," *Critical Studies in Mass Communication* 13, no. 3 (1996): 251–265.

7. Stewart M. Hoover, "The Culturalist Turn in Scholarship on Media and Religion," *Journal of Media and Religion* 1, no. 1 (2002): 25–36, p. 27.

8. The concept that language is power is very old. On the power of the English language, see Seth Lerer, *Inventing English: A Portable History of the Language* (New York: Columbia University Press, 2007).

9. For recent studies, see David T. Z. Mindich, *Just the Facts: How "Objectivity" Came to Define American Journalism* (New York: New York University Press, 1998); Richard W. Flory, "Promoting a Secular Standard: Secularization and Modern Journalism, 1870–1930," in *The Secular Revolution: Power, Interests, and Conflict in the Secularization of American Public Life*, ed. Christian Smith (Berkeley: University of California Press, 2003), 395–433; and Stephen J. A. Ward, *The Invention of Journalism Ethics: The Path to Objectivity and Beyond* (Montreal: McGill-Queen's University Press, 2004). Early works include *Haney's Guide to Authorship: Intended as an Aid to All Who Desire to Engage in Literary Pursuits for Pleasure or Profit* (New York: Haney, 1867); and Charles G. Ross, *The Writing of News: A Handbook* (New York: Henry Holt, 1911).

10. Flory, "Promoting a Secular Standard," 397.

11. *Haney's Guide to Authorship*, 44, 85, 92.

12. Michael Ryan, "Journalistic Ethics, Objectivity, Existential Journalism, Standpoint Epistemology, and Public Journalism," *Journal of Mass Media Ethics* 16, no. 1 (2001): 3–22.

13. Ward, *Invention of Journalism Ethics*, 318; Richard Streckfuss, "Objectivity in Journalism: A Search and a Reassessment," *Journalism Quarterly* 67, no. 4 (1990): 973–983, p. 973.

14. De Saussure's ideas were developed and revised by various scholars—such as Claude Lèvi-Strauss (anthropology), Jacques Lacan (psychology/psychiatry), and Roland Barthes (linguistics/semiology). De Saussure's influence has been felt throughout the human sciences—including mass communication. Ferdinand de Saussure, *Course in General Linguistics*, ed. Charles Bally and Albert Reidlinger, trans. Wade Baskin (New York: Philosophical Library, 1959).

15. This thesis has had a long shelf life. Samuel Huntington first used the contemporary phrase "clash of civilizations"—an updated version of an old theme among academic critics, who see Western civilization at risk, under threat, or in decline. Samuel P. Huntington, *The Clash of Civilizations and the Remaking of World Order* (New York: Touchstone, 1997). For a recent refinement, see Anthony Pagden, *Worlds at War. The 2,500-Year Struggle between East and West* (New York: Random House, 2008).

16. One spirited attack against this pre-9/11 frame-making mindset insists terrorism is an outgrowth of America's Cold War foreign policy. Mahmood Mamdani, *Good Muslim, Bad Muslim: America, the Cold War, and the Roots of Terror* (New York: Pantheon, 2004).

17. See, for example, Mona Eltahawy, "What *Should* a U.S. Muslim Look Like?," *Houston Chronicle*, April 7, 2002, C1, C5.

18. William A. Gamson, "News as Framing: Comments on Graber," *American Behavioral Scientist* 33, no. 2 (1989): 157–161, p. 157.

19. Pippa Norris, "Introduction," in *Women, Media, and Politics*, ed. Pippa Norris (New York: Oxford University Press, 1997) 1–18, p. 2.

20. Todd Gitlin, *The Whole World Is Watching: Mass Media in the Making & Unmaking of the New Left* (Berkeley: University of California Press, 1980), 7.

21. Robert M. Entman, "Framing: Toward Clarification of a Fractured Paradigm," *Journal of Communication* 43, no. 4 (1993): 51–58, p. 52.

22. Cynthia Carter and C. Kay Weaver, *Violence and the Media* (Buckingham, UK: Open University Press, 2003); Will Barton Catmur, "Theatre of War: High Culture and Popular Entertainment in the Spectacle of Kosovo," *Javnost: The Public* 7, no. 3 (2000): 67–76; Sandra B. Hrvatin and Martina Trampuz, "Enjoy Your Enemy or How the Kosovo (Media) War Broke Out," *Javnost: The Public* 7, no. 3 (2000): 77–86.

23. The negative stereotyping of "those who hold different political, cultural and religious values" has a long pedigree in the entertainment industry—especially in film. See Jack G. Shaheen, *Reel Bad Arabs: How Hollywood Vilifies a People* (New York: Olive Branch, 2001).

24. Ross Stuart Fuglsang, "Framing the Motorcycle Outlaw," in *Framing Public Life: Perspectives on Media and Our Understanding of the Social World*, ed. Stephen D. Reese, Oscar H. Gandy Jr., and August E. Grant (Mahwah, NJ: Erlbaum, 2001), 185–194.

25. Frankie Trull, "Animal-Rights Extremists a Menace to Human Progress," *Houston Chronicle*, August 24, 2008, E6.

26. Dhavan V. Shah, David Domke, and Daniel B. Wachman, "The Effects of Value-Framing on Political Judgment and Reasoning," in *Framing Public Life*, ed. Reese, Gandy, and Grant, 227–243. See also William A. Gamson, *Talking Politics* (Cambridge: Cambridge University Press, 1992).

27. S. Elizabeth Bird and Robert W. Dardenne, "Myth, Chronicle, and Story: Exploring the Narrative Qualities of News," in *Media, Myths, and Narratives: Television and the Press*, ed. James W. Carey (Newbury Park, CA: Sage, 1988), 67–86.

28. Kathleen Hall Jamieson and Joseph N. Cappella, *Echo Chamber: Rush Limbaugh and the Conservative Media Establishment* (New York: Oxford University Press, 2008), 244.

29. Conservative media both "protect" and "insulate" their audiences from "opposing messages" and "increase the likelihood that the audience will try to persuade others." Any information "hospitable to opposing views" will be contested. Conservative pundits will seek to generate "moral outrage," because "emotional involvement invites action and engagement rather than distancing and lethargy." They use various strategies that (a) build a strong informational base for conservative rhetoric in opposition to the

informational base for "liberal" rhetoric, (b) "balkanize" news content through a process that selectively exposes audiences to "knowledge, interpretations of current events, and rationalizations about election outcomes," and (c) refer continually to "liberal" double standards, personally denigrate the opposition, and frame "the political world as one unburdened by either ambiguity or common ground across the ideological divide." All media messages in harmony with conservative values are perceived as values of the larger, conservative community—not as values held by nonconservatives in the population. The building of a conservative community with a "worldview" provides conservatives with a wider support base, creates space for differences in public policy specifics, and minimizes "the likelihood of defection." Jamieson and Cappella summarize the advantages and disadvantages in Ibid., Chapter 14.

30. Ben Bagdikian has documented the dangers of media consolidation and control for many years. The latest rendition in this series is Ben H. Bagdikian, *The New Media Monopoly* (Boston: Beacon, 2004).

31. NPR is funded partially by the federal government and partially by public subscriptions. The network reaches about 22 million listeners each week on 750 affiliated stations, and it claims to provide a diverse and inclusive approach to news reporting. Steve Rendall and Daniel Butterworth, "How Public Is Public Radio? A Study of NPR's Guest List," *FAIR* (Fairness and Accuracy in Reporting), May/June 2004, www.fair.org/index.php?page–1180.

32. The notion that there is "a 'left-wing' bias" in the mainstream press and television networks "is a peculiar myth," according to McChesney, which "has little to do with the intellectual strength of the arguments and a great deal to do with the right-wing political muscle behind them, including conservative power within the mainstream media." Robert W. McChesney, *The Problem of the Media: U.S. Communication Politics in the Twenty-First Century* (New York: Monthly Review Press, 2004), 9 (and especially Chapter 3). See also Eric Alterman, *What Liberal Media? The Truth about Bias and the News* (New York: Basic Books, 2003). "The mainstream corporate media are largely subservient to corporate interests," as Douglas Kellner puts it in a book about media and politics during the Bush II years. "[They] follow the sensation of the moment, and rarely engage in the sort of investigative journalism that was once the ideal." Journalists "are easily intimidated when the right-wing army e-mails, calls, writes, and harasses any corporate media source" critical of Bush's policies. Douglas Kellner, *Media Spectacle and the Crisis of Democracy: Terrorism, War, and Election Battles* (Boulder, CO: Paradigm, 2005), xi.

33. Arianna Huffington, "Why Are Media Heavies Hiring Right's Blowhards?" *Houston Chronicle*, April 28, 2008, B7.

34. Rush Limbaugh's "liberal" counterpart was the comedian Al Franken—the apparent winner of Minnesota's Senate race in 2008—who

was the host of Air America Radio's flagship news talk-show program. Air America was created in 2004 and filed for bankruptcy in 2006 but survived when it was purchased by Green Family Media—a corporation owned by Stephen and Mark Green, two New York real estate investors—in 2007.

35. Jamieson and Cappella, *Echo Chamber*, 248. The idea that voters seem to rely on words and images that appeal to emotions rather than reason in political decision making has been gaining ground among Democrats, who are tired of losing to Republicans. For a recent book that focuses on this prescription, see Drew Westen, *The Political Brain: The Role of Emotion in Deciding the Fare of the Nation* (New York: PublicAffairs, 2007). In a critical review, conservative commentator David Brooks writes, "It's not necessary to dumb things down to appeal to emotions . . . . The best way to win votes . . . is to offer people an accurate view of the world and a set of policies that seem likely to produce good results. This is how you make voters happy." Brooks, "Stop Making Sense," *New York Times*, August 26, 2007, Book Review-13.

36. Mark Silk, *Unsecular Media: Making News of Religion in America* (Urbana: University of Illinois Press, 1995), 18, 20.

37. Religion News Service, www.religionnews.com.

38. The Religion Newswriters Association, for example, had 100 members in 1980: about one-third were women, and there were a token number of African Americans and Jews. John Dart, "The Religion Beat," *The Reporting of Religion in the Media* (New York: Rockefeller Foundation, August 1981), 19–26, pp. 20–21.

39. Silk, *Unsecular Media*, 25.

40. Ibid., 26.

41. Stewart M. Hoover, *Religion in the News: Faith and Journalism in American Public Discourse* (Thousand Oaks, CA: Sage, 1998), 23.

42. Dart, "Religion Beat," 24.

43. These parallels in print-based and electronic-based religious cultures have not really been explored by media and religion scholars, but see Peter G. Horsfield, *Religious Television: The American Experience* (New York: Longman, 1984), 15–19; and Michele Rosenthal, " 'Turn It Off!': TV Criticism in the *Christian Century* Magazine: 1946–1960," in *Practicing Religion in the Age of the Media: Explorations in Media, Religion, and Culture*, ed. Stewart M. Hoover and Lynn Schofield Clark (New York: Columbia University Press, 2002), 138–162.

44. Matthew Avery Sutton, *Aimee Semple McPherson and the Resurrection of Christian America* (Cambridge, MA: Harvard University Press, 2007). See also Daniel Mark Epstein, *Sister Aimee: The Life of Aimee Semple McPherson* (New York: Harcourt Brace, Jovanovich, 1993). McPherson exploited all the media of her day—print, film, radio, and photography—when conducting her crusades. She was also one of the first itinerant preachers to exploit the automobile—in her "gospel car," originally a 1912 Packard

touring car—for cross-country, tent-revival evangelism. The new Protestant denomination she started——the International Church of the Four-Square Gospel (now called the Foursquare Church)—claimed more than 5 million members in about 30,000 congregations worldwide in 2000.

45. Nancy T. Ammerman, "North American Protestant Fundamentalism," in *Media, Culture, and the Religious Right*, ed. Linda Kintz and Julia Lesage (Minneapolis: University of Minnesota Press, 1998), 55–114, p. 87.

46. See Alan Brinkley, *Voices of Protest: Huey Long, Father Coughlin and the Great Depression* (New York: Knopf, 1982), Chapters 4–5, 11, and Epilogue.

47. Kathleen L. Riley, *Fulton J. Sheen: An American Catholic Response to the Twentieth Century* (New York: Alba House, 2004).

48. Methodist pastor and radio evangelist Robert "Fightin Bob" Shuler (1880–1965), the Prohibition Party candidate for a U.S. Senate seat in California in 1932, also lost his radio license for intemperate social and political remarks.

49. The networks paid for the television productions and in exchange were given public interest credit by the FCC. Each designated faith tradition (Protestant, Roman Catholic, and Jewish) had its own Sunday TV slot before 1960. Information on radio-television regulations is based mainly on Jeffrey K. Hadden and Anson Shupe, "Televangelism in America," Electronic Text Center, University of Virginia Library, 2003, http://etext.virginia.edu/ etcbin/toccer-new2?id=HadTelr.xml&images=images/modeng&data=/ texts/english/modeng/parsed&tag=public&part=all; and William F. Fore, "The Unknown History of Televangelism," World Association of Christian Communication (WACC), undated, http://archive.waccglobal.org/wacc/ publications/media_development/2007 1/the_unknown_history_of _televangelism. The WACC is a mainstream Christian organization affiliated with the World Council of Churches, and Fore is a former president of WACC.

50. The National Religious Broadcasters—an international association of Christian conservative communicators that represented more than 1,400 member organizations by 2006—"succeeded in strengthening the power of the Religious Right by legitimizing, legalizing, and protecting the rights of an array of fundamentalist media groups." Christine J. Russo, "National Religious Broadcasters," *Afterimage* (February–March 1995): 6.

51. Hadden and Shupe, "Televangelism in America," Section 1, 65 (citing a report by the communications committee of the United States Conference of Catholic Bishops to the FCC).

52. Cited by Fore, "Unknown History of Televangelism."

53. Ibid. Fore, an ordained Methodist clergyman, argues that the theological message of evangelical fundamentalism on the airwaves resonates with "the values and worldview of secular America" and enables religious conservatives to play a major role in the corridors of political power in contemporary America.

54. Estimates of the size of audiences watching televangelists are notoriously unreliable—with so many prejudicial stockholders—but one conducted in 1985 by Nielsen Media Research for televangelist Pat Robertson's Christian Broadcasting Network has been cited as a kind of measuring yardstick. The study of Robertson's television program, *The 700 Club*, found that 4.4 million viewers watched the show on any given day. Hadden and Shupe, "Televangelism in America," Section 3, 70–71.

55. See Steve Bruce, *Pray TV: Televangelism in America* (London: Routledge, 1990), Chapters 8–9, which deal specifically with televangelists in politics.

56. See, for example, Peter Horsfield, "American Religious Programs in Australia," 313–328, and Eric Shegog, "Religion and Media Imperialism: A European Perspective," 329–351, in *Religious Television: Controversies and Conclusions*, ed. Robert Ableman and Stewart M. Hoover (Norwood, NJ: Ablex, 1990).

57. The weekly radio show *Hour of Decision* also remains on the air after more than 50 years. The Billy Graham Evangelistic Association produces a long-running newspaper column ("My Answer") and its official publication, *Decision* magazine. Other enterprises launched by Graham and his associates include a film company (World Wide Pictures) and the leading highbrow evangelical journal *Christianity Today*, which Graham founded in 1956 as an alternative to the "liberal" *The Christian Century*.

58. Campus Crusade, launched in 1951 by evangelists Bill and Vonette Bright as a service to college students, has morphed into a worldwide organization with more than 1,400 ministries that include high school students, athletes, families, and adults. Campus Crusade for Christ International has offices in Washington, D.C., and the United Nations and operated in 91 countries in 2000—the largest single evangelical organization of its kind in the United States. See Campus Crusade for Christ, www.campuscrusade forchrist.com.

59. Although Harry S. Truman was lukewarm to Graham's ministry, every president from Dwight D. Eisenhower to George W. Bush was obliged to seek his advice and counsel. Graham was never tainted with personal or professional, sexual or financial scandal. If American evangelical Christianity, as Bloom put it, "is an indigenous American religion—and I think [it] is, quite distinct from European Protestantism—then Graham remains its prime emblem." Harold Bloom, "The Preacher: Billy Graham," in *"Time 100: Who Should be the Person of the Century?,"* *Time*, June 14, 1999, 194–197, p. 197.

60. Gal Beckerman, "Across the Great Divide FAITH," *Columbia Journalism Review*, May/June 2004, 26–30, p. 29.

61. Ibid., 29, 30. Beckerman was assistant editor of *Columbia Journalism Review* at the time she wrote this article.

62. Frank Rich, "2004: The Year of 'The Passion,' " *New York Times*, December 19, 2004, Arts-1, 7. Another recent example: The United Church of Christ (UCC) caused a brief furor when the major national networks (and their affiliate cable-satellite stations) and later Viacom rejected the denomination's attempts to place paid advertisements in 2005–2006 promoting a message of inclusion—especially its "open and affirming" stance on Gays. The UCC noted a study (by *Media Matters*, a "liberal" TV watchdog agency) showing clergy from the Religious Right provided virtually all the guests over a period of nine years on Sunday morning talk shows discussing gay rights and other social issues of interest to faith communities. Mainline Protestant churches such as the UCC, United Methodist Church, Presbyterian Church (U.S.A.), Evangelical Lutheran Church in America, Christian Church (Disciples of Christ), American Baptists, and the African Methodist Episcopal Church—members of the National Council of Churches—were excluded. J. Bennett Guess, "Amplifying the Mainline," *United Church News*, June–July 2006, 8–9.

63. Peter A. Kerr and Patricia Moy, "Newspaper Coverage of Fundamentalist Christians, 1980–2000," *Journalism & Mass Communication Quarterly* 79, no. 1 (2002): 54–72.

64. Newscasts involving fundamentalists were usually about politics, according to Kerr, and these stories "are reported in a consistent, mildly negative manner." Peter A. Kerr, "The Framing of Fundamentalist Christians: Network Television News, 1980–2000," *Journal of Media & Religion* 2, no. 4 (2003): 203–235.

65. Katie H. Porterfield, "Religion," in *Media Bias: Finding It, Fixing It*, eds. Wm. David Sloan and Jenn Burleson Mackay (Jefferson, NC: McFarland, 2007), 50–64, pp. 60–61.

66. The questionnaire was in two parts. Part 1 was concerned with religious belief, and the meaning of the term "Christian" was defined in thoroughly orthodox terms. Part 2 framed the moral obligation to seek peace and social justice in Judeo-Christian terms. Doug Underwood and Keith Stamm, "Are Journalists Really Irreligious? A Multidimensional Analysis," *Journalism & Mass Communication Quarterly* 78, no. 4 (2001): 771–786.

67. Thomas Kunkel, dean of the Philip Merrill College of Journalism at the University of Maryland, cited an estimate by the RNA that 400–500 reporters in the print media were spending a "significant" amount of time on religion news, and virtually all newspapers with circulations above 100,000 had newsmen and women covering religion issues. See Kunkel, "Have a Little Faith: At Last, the Mainstream Media Get Religion," *American Journalism Review*, June/July 2006, 4. Gal Beckerman, however, claimed that "religion writers remained a tiny minority in the newsroom"—perhaps 200 in the secular press today. Beckerman, "Across the Great Divide," 28.

68. See Christian Smith, "Religiously Ignorant Journalists," *Christianity Today*, January 1, 2004, http://www.christianitytoday.com/bc/2004/janfeb/

2.06.html; John Dart, "Covering Conventional and Unconventional Religion: A Reporter's View," *Review of Religious Research* 39, no. 2 (1997): 144–152. John Dart, now news editor of *Christian Century*, and Jimmy Allen conducted a benchmark study into newsroom religious attitudes for the Freedom Forum. The report found "little overt antireligious bias … but that ignorance about religion, and discomfort with religious symbols and lesser known practices led to inaccuracies and unfair characterizations." Dart and Allen, "Bridging the Gap," Freedom Forum First Amendment Center at Vanderbilt University, Nashville, Tennessee, 1993.

69. See Lynn S. Clark and Stewart M. Hoover, "At the Intersection of Media, Culture, and Religion: A Bibliographic Essay," in *Rethinking Media, Religion, and Culture*, ed. Stewart M. Hoover and Knut Lundby (Thousand Oaks, CA: Sage, 1997), 15–35.

70. Marshall Frady, *Billy Graham: A Parable of American Righteousness* (Boston: Little, Brown, 1979), 314.

71. Jesse McKinley, "The Wisdom of the Ages, For Now Anyway," *New York Times*, March 23, 2008, SundayStyles-1, 12.

72. Lakewood Church, Houston, www.lakewood.cc/Pages/index.aspx. Olsteen's assertion was downloaded in May 2008. It has since been dropped from that location.

73. Stephen Winzenburg, "Televangelist Report Card," *Christianity Today*, October 22, 2001, 88–91, p. 91. He monitored 150 broadcasts of 22 different television ministries from September to November 2000.

74. Steven Waldman, co-founder and chairman of Beliefnet, has made this kind of comment several times in talking to journalists. See *Beliefnet*, http://www.beliefnet.com.

75. Greg G. Armfield and R. Lance Holbert, "The Relationship Between Religiosity and Internet Use," *Journal of Media and Religion* 2, no. 3 (2003): 129–144.

76. Some of these sites are listed in Virginia Heffernan, "God and Man on YouTube," *New York Times Magazine*, November 4, 2007, 22, 24.

77. Strawberry Saroyan, "Christianity, the Brand," *New York Times Magazine*, April 16, 2006, 46–51.

78. Stephanie Simon, "Digitizing Religion," *Houston Chronicle*, June 3, 2006, F1, F4.

79. The literature that focuses specifically on the role of conservative media in America's political culture is surprisingly thin, but three books in particular have informed this section. The standard guide to periodicals is found in the second of an exhaustive two-volume work, Ronald Lora and William Henry Longton, eds., *The Conservative Press in Twentieth-Century America* (Westport, CT: Greenwood, 1999), Parts 6–10. The conservative perspective is detailed in Richard A. Viguerie and David Franke, *America's Right Turn: How Conservatives Used New and Alternative Media to Take Power* (Chicago: Basic Books, 2004). The most recent scholarly study is Jamieson

and Cappella's *Echo Chamber*. The axis of the conservative establishment for these authors is the editorial and opinion pages of the *Wall Street Journal* (second in circulation only to *USA Today* among metropolitan newspapers in the United States), the Rush Limbaugh radio show (the highest-rated talk show in terms of listeners and number of stations in the United States), and political pundits on the "most-watched cable network" Fox News television (ix). These conservative voices are examined mainly in the context of Democratic and Republican politics during congressional and presidential election cycles.

80. David Van Biema, "The 25 Most Influential Evangelicals in America," *Time*, February 7, 2005, 35–39, 41–43, 45. Not included were several megachurch televangelists—like John Hagee, pastor of the 19,000+-member Cornerstone Church in San Antonio, and Rod Parsley, pastor of the World Harvest Church, a Pentecostal megachurch of more than 12,000 members in Columbus, Ohio—who were probably not on the national political radar screen until the Democratic and Republican election primaries in 2008.

81. CBN, according to its Web site, was providing programming by cable, broadcast, and satellite in 71 languages to about 200 countries by 2008. Christian Broadcasting Network, www.cbn.com.

82. Dobson's media-related activities are detailed in Dan Gilgoff, *The Jesus Machine: How James Dobson, Focus on the Family, and Evangelical America Are Winning the Culture War* (New York: St. Martin's, 2007).

83. *Human Events*, probably the best known of the anti-communist journals, and *Freeman*, the longest lived of the libertarian journals, reflected the philosophical tensions between the two major groups within the conservative movement at the time, the "Libertarians" and the "Traditionalists." These tensions were also present in top "Traditionalist" journals such as *National Review*, *Modern Age* (1957), and *University Bookman* (1960). Buckley and his colleagues are credited with being a primary force in eradicating right-wing extremists—such as the antireligious Ayn Rand and her disciples, and the John Birch Society—from the ranks of the modern conservative movement. Lora and Longton, *Conservative Press*, 512–514, and especially *National Review* entry, 515–530.

84. Regnery Publishing is now owned by Eagle Publishing, which also publishes the weekly political *Human Events*. Eagle Publishing was founded by Thomas L. Phillips, a pioneer marketer of conservative literature. Eagle was accused in a lawsuit of virtually giving away its books through outlets such as book clubs that it also owned. The suit was later dismissed. See Motoko Rich, "Authors Suit Dismissed," *New York Times*, February 2, 2008, B8.

85. Religious books by top-selling Protestant evangelists dominate the Christian book market today. Others include John Eldredge, the author of several bestsellers who formed his own Ransomed Heart Ministries in 2000,

and Bruce Max Lucado, author of 50 books that "have sold close to 40 million copies." Rachel Donadio, "Faith-Based Publishing," *New York Times*, November 28, 2004, Book Review-35.

86. Tim LaHaye and Jerry B. Jenkins, *Left Behind: A Novel of the Earth's Last Days* (Wheaton, IL: Tyndale, 1995). Although classified as fiction and targeted initially at youth, the *Left Behind* books have been read by countless numbers of adults and seriously examined in seminary courses, on cable TV, and in conservative religious journals such as *Christianity Today*. *Time* magazine, in its special February 7, 2005, feature on evangelical leaders, noted that the *Left Behind* books have "set the image that many people—believers and non-believers alike—now have about how the world will end." Biema, "The 25 Most Influential."

87. The Intercollegiate Studies Institute, Action Foundation for Entrepreneurial Excellence, www.isi.org; Lora and Longton, *The Conservative Press*, 559–571 (*Intercollegiate Review*).

88. "National Journalism Center," *Sourcewatch Encyclopedia*, http://www.sourcewatch.org/index.php?title=National_Journalism_Center.

89. Viguerie and Franke, *America's Right Turn*, 91. "Even today, conservatives may get most of their political *news* through talk radio, cable television, and the Internet, ... but most activist communication between individual conservatives and their organizations and causes and candidates takes place through the U.S. mail" (108).

90. Ibid., 113. Viguerie's firm was sending "perhaps 70 million letters a year" to its conservative constituents by 1978, but he acknowledged that "liberal" colleagues were also exploiting the use of direct-mail politics. In the aftermath of Ronald Reagan's victory in the 1980 election—the highpoint, according to Viguerie, in the conservative monopoly of direct-mail political advertising—"[liberals] probably even *surpassed* conservatives in the effective use of direct mail" (italics in the original) (134, 145).

91. Ibid., 125.

92. The Eagle Forum had numerous spin-off programs in future decades—including an Eagle Forum Education and Legal Defense Fund (1981) as well as youth-oriented and continuing education programs. Schlafly was primarily interested in abortion and other family issues of concern to religious conservatives, but the extremist theocratic rhetoric of later years marginalized her influence in national politics. For Schlafly's impact on America's political culture, see Donald T. Critchlow, *Phyllis Schlafly and Grassroots Conservatism. A Woman's Crusade* (Princeton, NJ: Princeton University Press, 2005).

93. Health-care reform at the time was linked in conservative media with various mediated scandals involving the Clinton family—especially the so-called Whitewater affair (the investigation into the Clintons' financial activities when the president was governor of Arkansas). Hillary Rodham Clinton herself said on several occasions that conservative media turned the

tide of public opinion against the health-care plan, and there is considerable evidence to support this claim. The conservative voice on this issue was communicated in direct mail, in the daily press—from the *Wall Street Journal* to the *Washington Times* (launched in 1982 by Unification Church founder Sun Myung Moon and his disciples)—in right-wing opinion journals such as the Jewish-oriented *Commentary* and the more acerbic *American Spectator*, and on talk radio and talk cable television.

94. Gingrich (who had won a Republican seat as a House representative from Georgia in 1978) and his colleagues exploited C-SPAN (Cable-Satellite Public Affairs Network, started in 1979) to discuss the conservative political and social agenda—using a rule allowing any legislator to bring up an item at the end of the day (when very few legislators were present). Gingrich's "Contract with America" was released first over C-SPAN during the GOP election campaign in 1994. Viguerie and Franke, *America's Right Turn*, 214–217.

95. For an indictment of the media's role in promoting the impeachment event, see Sidney Blumenthal, *The Clinton Wars* (New York: Farrar, Straus, and Giroux, 2003).

96. The film industry has had a proven record of financial success with biblical epics. Although there was a public outcry among religious conservatives over Martin Scorsese's *The Last Temptation of Christ* (1988), Gibson's *The Passion of The Christ* (2004) augured well for filmmakers aiming at the expanding conservative religious market. The Christian multimedia company Good News Holdings, for example, under the leadership of David Kirkpatrick, a former mainline film studio executive, has "an ambitious range of media endeavors," according to journalist Michael Gross, "financed and supported by some of the most prominent and politically connected conservative Christian groups in the United States." The chair of Holdings is conservative pollster George Barna, "who contends that deploying the power of the mass media to help save children's and teenagers' souls is a critical cultural battle that Christians must fight." Kirkpatrick, Barna, and their associates view the present dispensation in apocalyptic terms—"a worldview that interprets human thoughts and actions as the product of unseen battles between angels and demons." Their agenda ranges from producing horror films for teenagers to "inspirational cell-phone ring tones" and Internet sites for "Christian dating." Michael Joseph Gross, "A Once-Feared Kingmaker Called to a Different Battle," *New York Times*, December 10, 2006, Arts and Leisure-13, 25.

97. Mariah Blake, "Stations of the Cross," *Columbia Journalism Review*, May–June 2005, 32–39, p. 35. Blake was an assistant editor at *CJR*.

98. Crawford Broadcasting Company, www.crawfordbroadcasting .com; USA Radio Network, www.usaradio.com; Salem Radio Network, www.srnnews.com; and American Family Radio, www.afr.net/newafr/ default.asp.

99. Ave Maria Radio network, www.avemariaradio.net.

100. Religious programming on radio today is popularly referred to as "salt radio"—a reference to Jesus's description of believers as "the salt of the earth" (Matthew 5:13). Based on data supplied by Arbitron, the national radio ratings service, one study done in 1980, for example, noted that 20.4 million people listened to Arbitron's 66 syndicated religious programs and 14.9 million of these listened to the top-10 programs. The size of these audiences was much smaller than claims radio ministries were making about their audiences. Hadden and Shupe, "Televangelism in America," Section 2. *CJR's* Blake says that Christian radio stations have on average today "about 5 percent market share," which is one-third the audience of news-talk radio stations. Conservatives, however, dominate both media venues. Blake, "Stations of the Cross," 35.

101. The Telecommunications Act also contained so-called indecency provisions—prohibiting the transmission of material deemed to be indecent or obscene if it was likely to be viewed by minors and requiring broadcasters to devise a rating system for programs—that critics claimed would violate First Amendment rights of free speech. See "U.S. Policy: Telecommunications Act of 1996," Museum of Broadcast Communications, undated, www.museum.tv/archives/etv/U/htmlU/uspolicyt/uspolicyt.htm, and Common Cause, "The Fallout from the Telecommunications Act of 1996: Unintended Consequences and Lessons Learned," Common Cause Education Fund, Washington, DC, May 9, 2005.

102. For a recent history of Clear Channel Communications, see Alec Foege, *Right of the Dial: The Rise of Clear Channel and the Fall of Commercial Radio* (New York: Faber and Faber, 2008). The San Antonio–based Mays family, which still operates Clear Channel, refused to cooperate with the author.

103. Limbaugh for many conservatives is the voice of conservatism in broadcast media today, but he remains as controversial as ever. Limbaugh's impact is detailed in Jamieson and Cappella, *Echo Chamber*.

104. Limbaugh and the political pundits on Fox News have a "mass appeal" audience consisting mainly of "disproportionately white [males], of above average income, older, churchgoing, and southern." The *Wall Street Journal* audience consists mainly of white businessmen who are "upper-class fiscal conservatives." Ibid., xii, 76–77, 91. See Chapter 6 for the audience analysis.

105. Ibid., xi.

106. Ibid., xii. See Chapter 4 for the "Reagan Narrative."

107. Viguerie and Franke, *America's Right Turn*, 222–229, 326, 332–333.

108. Mark Sweney, "Wall Street Journal Website Lifts Some Pay Barriers," *Guardian* (Manchester), January 10, 2008, www.guardian.co.uk/media/2008/jan/10/wallstreetjournal.newscorporation?gusrc=rss&feed=media.

109. Viguerie and Franke, *America's Right Turn*, Chapter 13. The data they used are based on rankings of Web sites by Alexa.com, a division of Amazon.com, the Pew Internet and American Life Project ("Counting on the Internet," completed in December 2002), and reports from the Pew Research Center. Those using the Internet for information during election campaigns rose to 13 percent of the American population in 2004 from 9 percent in 2000.

110. The Internet is dominated by personal and family blogs, but only a few of these are overtly political in terms of content. An early political blogger was Matt Drudge (*The Drudge Report*), who became famous with his Monica Lewinsky *exposé* and other anti-Clinton stories in the late 1990s.

111. Classic cases in recent election cycles of prodigious online fundraising and volunteer recruitment campaigns include Howard Dean and Moveon.com during the 2004 Democratic primaries, and Barack Obama and social networking sites such as MySpace, Twitter, and YouTube during the 2008 Democratic primaries. Many others—from Jesse Ventura (Minnesota) to Jerry Brown and Arnold Schwarzenegger (California)—have also employed the Internet for these purposes. "The Right has been better at utilizing the Internet as a news and opinion medium," Viguerie and Franke claim, "while the Left has been better at utilizing it as a medium for political organization." Viguerie and Franke, *America's Right Turn*, 286; Noam Cohen, "The Wiki-Way to the Nomination," *New York Times*, June 8, 2008, Week in Review-4.

CHAPTER 3

American Conservatism: "A Jungle of Twisted Thoughts"

Conservatism is one of those terms that journalists, scholars, and others often throw around without having a clear idea what they mean by it or how their listeners interpret it.[1] They evidently assume that (a) nobody will notice they cannot define what they are talking about; (b) everyone knows what they are talking about and no definition is required; or (c) it is just too hard to define the term because conservatism is, as former Richard Nixon aide John W. Dean says, "a jungle of twisted thoughts and strange growths."[2]

The many branches of contemporary conservative thought grew out of a common tradition. Historically, political conservatism, like religious conservatism, was a reaction against a host of social, scientific, political, religious, cultural, and economic innovations envisaged in the eighteenth century and gradually implemented in the nineteenth and twentieth centuries. Demands for new kinds of government and economic systems, for human equality, for new approaches to understanding the Christian faith, and for new ways of viewing and measuring the natural world percolated through the literate classes.

Edmund Burke (1729–1797), a spokesman for Britain's propertied class and a staunch supporter of inherited monarchy, was frightened enough by some of the new ideas—and by the French Revolution in 1789—to define conservatism as a struggle against innovation. Russell Kirk (1918–1994), the acknowledged intellectual pioneer of contemporary American conservatism, credited Burke, a British statesman and writer, as the founder of modern conservatism.

Burke's extraordinary prophecy about the dangers of innovation and the need to respect laws that he thought were eternal has been central to most definitions of conservatism for more than two centuries. For Burke, Britain had achieved reasonable constitutional change by preserving what was best in the customs and practices of government. It was an understanding of the "natural order" based essentially on government by precedent. Burke identified the main pillars of modern conservative thought—fear of change, divine intent, and acceptance of inequality—in his most famous work, *Reflections on the Revolution in France*, published originally in 1790. Innovation was dangerous, he said, because it challenged moral law, which for Burke was immutable, preexisting, and universal.[3]

Burke and his conservative successors would be dismayed if they could see that the changes envisaged in the eighteenth and early nineteenth centuries became realities in the last half of the nineteenth and early twentieth centuries. They might feel especially threatened by (a) the inroads that biblical criticism, the social gospel, and the modern ecumenical movement made in the seminaries, in Christian literature, and in many Christian congregations and by (b) Darwinism and the new scientific revolution in the so-called Newtonian Age, which pitted those who embraced a sacred science against those who embraced secular science.[4]

Our aim in this chapter is not to produce a universal, unassailable definition of contemporary conservatism, for that is beyond the scope of this book. We attempt instead to describe some major components of contemporary conservatism and to identify some of the ideas that unite conservatives and some of the tensions that divide them. This chapter is divided into four sections. Section 1 explores the major pillars of conservative thought—divine intent, resistance to change, and an entrenched belief in inequality. Section 2 examines the psychological dimensions of conservative thought. Section 3 is an overview of traditionalist conservative, neoconservative, and Christian conservative thought. Section 4 outlines some of the tensions that have threatened the unity of the conservative coalition in recent years.

THREE PILLARS OF CONSERVATIVE THOUGHT

Conservative scholars such as Russell Kirk and Francis Graham Wilson (1901–1976) argued that conservatism has no specific agenda for resolving social issues and problems and is less an ideology than a state of mind.[5] Other scholars—like Willmoore Kendall (1909–1968)—saw conservatism in opposition to liberalism, with the key difference centering on reforms designed to help the disadvantaged. He contrasted the pessimism of conservatives, who assume reforms will not work, with the optimism of liberals, who assume they will.[6]

Many other observers, however, support the view that conservative and liberal perspectives are ideological perspectives.[7] Conservative ideology is defined by political scientists Charles W. Dunn and J. David Woodard "as a defense of the political, economic, religious, and social *status quo* from the forces of abrupt change ... based on a belief that established customs, laws and traditions provide continuity and stability in the guidance of society."[8] This definition incorporates ideas that have long been the foundation for conservative political thought.

Divine Intent

God, or some divine intent, was central to most definitions of early conservative thought and to many definitions of contemporary conservatism. Dunn and Woodard's definition does not mention God explicitly, but "divine intent" often is assumed under "customs, laws and traditions." Other definitions are much more explicit about divine intent. Libertarian philosopher Frank S. Meyer (1909–1972), for example, says, "The Christian understanding of the nature and destiny of man is always and everywhere what Conservatives strive to conserve."[9] And comments in the *National Review* suggest that "the conservative believes ours is a God-centered, and therefore an ordered, universe [and] that man's purpose is to shape his life to the patterns of order proceeding from the Divine center of life."[10]

Russell Kirk acknowledged that divine intent was one of the canons of early conservative thought in the political arena: conservatives believe "a divine intent rules society as well as conscience, forging an eternal chain of right and duty which links great and obscure, living and dead. Political problems, at bottom, are religious and moral problems."[11] Conservatives of all types—but not all conservatives—are comforted by the view that a divine intent rules society and that one need only read the Bible to learn what is "right" (and what is "wrong").

It is not surprising that divine intent would be considered a major pillar of contemporary American conservative thought. As we saw in Chapter 1, most Americans claim they are Christian, almost two-thirds of the population attend church at least once a month, and religion in general is "very important" in their lives.[12] The difficulty arises as Americans try to decide how their religious convictions should manifest themselves in their political actions. Here are four possibilities:

- Private citizens may say that religious values inform their political actions, such as voting, conversing with friends, or commenting in media outlets (writing letters to editors, for example). These actions reflect their understanding of God's will, but they do not try to impose their religious values on others. A religious conservative, for example, may see scientific evolution as inconsistent with biblical teaching but may speak against the teaching of intelligent design in high school biology classes.

- Private citizens may try to impose their understandings of God's will on others through political action groups.[13] The Catholic League, for instance, urged parents in 2007 to boycott *The Golden Compass*, not because the film was offensive, but because it might encourage children to read the book, which the League claims contains anti-Christian themes. Several Christian groups have demanded that the book be removed from school and public libraries.[14]

- Public officials may try to follow their consciences—based on their understandings of the Bible or other religious or moral teachings—as they make their daily decisions, but they try not to impose their religious views on others. A candidate for president, for instance, may argue that he (or she) will not put religious doctrine above the constitutional duties of the office, as presidential candidate John F. Kennedy promised in the 1960 election campaign.

- Public officials may feel compelled to impose their personal views on everyone else based on their perceptions of God's will. Chris Comer, science director for the Texas Education Agency (TEA), for example, says she was forced to resign from the job she held for nine years because a TEA staff member claimed she appeared biased against the teaching of intelligent design in Texas public schools. Comer was suspended for 30 days in October 2007 after she announced an upcoming speech by a critic of intelligent design to an online community.[15] She resigned in November 2007.

There is considerable ambiguity in these positions, for the actions of public officials and political activists nearly always affect someone. If these decisions are based on religious values, critics may charge that the public official or activist is trying to impose personal views in the public square. Much was made of Mitt Romney's attempt in 2008 to clarify the role, for him, of religion in politics. Romney mainly wanted to convince evangelical Christians that his Mormon faith was not unlike their own, but he also said he would not let his faith drive his policies, even as he said he believes in his Mormon faith and tries to live by it.[16] Nothing could be more confusing.

Resistance to Change

Resistance to change, a foundation for conservative thought for centuries, remains so in the twenty-first century. For historian Clinton Rossiter (1917–1970), conservatism "is an attitude of opposition to disruptive change in the social, economic, legal, religious, political, or cultural order .... The distinguishing mark of this conservatism," he said, "is the fear of change, which becomes transformed in the political arena into the fear of radicalism."[17] Research suggests that conservative resistance to change and liberal acceptance of change is the main factor separating the two groups when individuals describe themselves as liberals or conservatives.[18]

Contemporary conservatives fear the consequences of changes that occurred even decades ago. Many still have not accepted the reality of scientific evolution, for example, outlined in the 1850s and supported in thousands of studies since then. They also fear recent technological and medical advances, such as the vaccine to protect girls and women against cervical cancer, which many religious conservatives believe will make young people more promiscuous.[19]

Conservative P. J. O'Rourke, a *Weekly Standard* correspondent and Mencken Research Fellow at the Cato Institute, a libertarian think tank, describes in humorous, but telling, terms why he fears change:

> I became a conservative at 11:59 p.m. on December 4, 1997, the way many people become conservatives. My wife gave birth. Suddenly all the ideal went out of any idealism for change .... Things that once were a matter of indifference become ominous threats—refrigerator magnets and gay marriage. I used to consider erotic preferences a matter of laissez faire. Then I realized, if my children think homosexuality is acceptable, it could lead them to think something really troubling—that sex is acceptable.
>
> Conservatives want things to remain exactly the way they are, not because these things are good but because these things are there. If I have to deal with them I know where they live. Conservatives are opposed to change not because change is bad but because change is new. It's modern and confusing. I don't know how to work the remote. And I can't find the off button.[20]

Politicians frequently play on the fear of change to gain political advantage. John Dean notes that members of the Bush II administration "add a fear factor to every course of action they pursue, whether it is their radical foreign policy of preemptive war, their call for tax cuts, their desire to privatize social security, or their implementation of a radical new health care scheme."[21] Many conservative politicians clearly use the term liberalism as a conservative code word for change to instill fear in the electorate.

Fear of change drives many conservative politicians to campaign for the return of the *status quo*—by which they mean to cede present and future decision-making authority to those who exercised power in the past. They often want to return to an earlier *status quo*, one in which conservatism dominated over what they regard as radicalism. Many white evangelical Protestants, for example, yearn for a time— the 1950s is often perceived as an idyllic decade—when laws prohibited the teaching of evolution in many public schools (particularly in the South), gay and lesbian communities did not have a public face, women understood that they were primarily homemakers and caregivers, and black people did not attend the University of Alabama.

Inequality

Conservatives typically view society as inevitably hierarchical and unequal.[22] The conservative suspicion, or even rejection, of equality is rooted in the conservative resistance to change in general. Many conservatives, for example, objected strenuously to aspects of Lyndon B. Johnson's Great Society program of the 1960s because many Democrats wanted to use public funds to reduce inequality by building social and economic safety nets for the poor and disadvantaged. This opposition dates from at least the Constitutional Convention, when conservatives were asked to support a document that guaranteed freedom and liberty for all, which they supported, and equality for all, which they did not.[23]

Liberty, freedom, and equality often are seen as interchangeable terms, but for the conservative they are not. A society that wants to ensure its citizens share wealth and power equally must take money, land, and possessions from the rich and give them to the poor. Many conservatives see nothing wrong with a society in which some can accumulate great power and wealth within a system that creates inequality.

The taking of money, land, and possessions from the rich infringes, conservatives argue, on the liberty or freedom of those whose wealth and power are taken. Conservatives argue that (a) government "does not have to be enlarged to the extent of becoming oppressive as the enforcer of equality," (b) citizens no longer wish to excel when liberty is less important than equality, and (c) "material equality is not nearly as important as moral equality under God." Many conservatives argue that people "are entitled to equality of opportunity and suffrage; beyond this the conservative is unwilling to go."[24]

In the conservative view, equality was privileged over liberty during much of the twentieth century (starting with the New Deal of the 1930s). Presidential and congressional actions and accompanying rhetoric in recent decades suggest that conservatives intend to restore the balance. For example, the huge Republican tax cuts for the wealthy in the George W. Bush administration, conservatives would argue, simply returned to the rich the material wealth taken from them in earlier decades. The importance of freedom and liberty in contemporary conservative ideology also is reflected in presidential rhetoric about the war in Iraq: President Bush consistently argued that the United States will bring freedom and liberty, but not necessarily equality, to the people of Iraq.

PSYCHOLOGICAL DIMENSIONS OF MODERN CONSERVATISM

Hundreds of studies have explored some of the psychological dimensions of conservative and liberal political thought since the early 1950s.[25] University professors John T. Jost, Jack Glaser, Arie W. Kruglanski, and Frank J. Sulloway analyzed this body of literature under the rubric *motivated social cognition*. This approach "integrates theories of personality (authoritarianism, dogmatism-intolerance of ambiguity), epistemic and existential needs (for closure, regulatory focus, terror management), and ideological rationalization (social dominance, system justification)."[26]

A number of social-cognitive motives influence an individual's tendency toward political conservatism, the studies suggest. Two components of these theories are (a) authoritarianism and (b) dogmatism or intolerance of ambiguity, and the need for closure.

Authoritarianism

Speculation about the relationship of political conservatism to authoritarianism is not new. Contemporary conservatives generally prefer not to be associated with him, but Joseph de Maistre (1753–1821), with Burke, was one of the first to begin articulating a conservative worldview. De Maistre—author of *On the Pope* (1819) and *An Examination of the Philosophy of Bacon* (1836), and a Roman Catholic—argued that the pope had supreme authority in political and religious matters. He also advocated a return to a hereditary monarchy in France. Only those European governments founded on Christian principles, he said, could avoid a violent revolution, such as that which toppled the French monarchy in 1789. De Maistre railed against the new ideas about government and equality, which he said destroyed established authority.[27] His call for unquestioning obedience to legitimate authority remains a central idea in any definition of authoritarianism.

Scholars began to study the authoritarian strain of political conservative thought in a systematic way with the publication of *The Authoritarian Personality* (1950), a groundbreaking study by the musicologist and social theorist T. W. Adorno (1903–1969) and several colleagues. They cited evidence to suggest that authoritarian personality traits are linked mainly to conservative political attitudes and not to liberal attitudes.[28]

Authoritarian conservatism "begins with basic conservative beliefs—order, distrust of change, belief in traditional values—and branches in the direction of favoring state power to protect these beliefs."[29] Psychologist Robert A. Altemeyer found that conservative authoritarianism is characterized by "a high degree of submission to the authorities who are perceived to be established and legitimate; a general aggressiveness, directed against various persons, which is perceived to be sanctioned by established authorities; and a high degree of adherence to the social conventions which are perceived to be endorsed by society."[30] Conservatives often direct their antipathy toward public officials, such as the judges they frequently describe as bleeding hearts.

John Dean goes further in his book *Conservatives without Conscience*. For Dean, the malfeasance, misfeasance, and nonfeasance he found since the mid-1990s in Washington political circles could be accounted for by a growing conservative authoritarianism:

> Authoritarianism is not well understood and seldom discussed in the context of American government and politics, yet it now constitutes the prevailing thinking and behavior among conservatives.... [A]uthoritarians are frequently enemies of freedom, antidemocratic,

antiequality, highly prejudiced, mean-spirited, power hungry, Machiavellian, and amoral. They are also often conservatives without conscience who are capable of plunging this nation into disasters the likes of which we have never known.[31]

Considerable empirical research supports Dean's observation. Scholars, for instance, have documented a strong relationship between right-wing authoritarianism and racism[32] and prejudice against gays and lesbians. Research also suggests a strong relationship between religious fundamentalism and authoritarianism,[33] between religious fundamentalism and homophobic prejudice, but an inverse relationship between racism and religious fundamentalism. Brian Laythe and his colleagues suggest that religious fundamentalism is inversely related to racism because "modern Christianity explicitly proscribes racism, [but] it does not necessarily proscribe prejudice against gays and lesbians."[34]

The twenty-first century push by the Bush administration for government intrusion into private lives and for the denial of due process for detainees reflects the nondemocratic, authoritarian mentality that is condemned by civil libertarians. Law professor Robert C. Vaughn suggests "authoritarian governments are identified by ready government access to information about the activities of citizens and by extensive limitations on the ability of citizens to obtain information about the government."[35]

Dogmatism, Intolerance of Ambiguity, and the Need for Closure

Psychologist Else Frenkel-Brunswik (1908–1958) was a pioneer in the study of intolerance of ambiguity, which she described as a generalized personality trait related to prejudice. Personal traits such as "aggression toward authority, fear, weakness, or elements of the opposite sex in oneself," she said, are "projected onto others," which also engenders "a narrowness of rigidity of consciousness."[36] Later research suggested that intolerance of ambiguity can lead to

> the early selection and maintenance of one solution in a perceptually ambiguous situation, inability to allow for the possibility of good and bad traits in the same person, acceptance of attitude statements representing a rigid, black-white view of life, seeking for certainty, a rigid dichotomizing into fixed categories, premature closure, and remaining closed to familiar characteristics of stimuli.[37]

Those who have a low tolerance for ambiguity tend to see ambiguous situations as threatening and to jump at quick solutions, as many Americans did when George W. Bush defined the 9/11 attacks as a war demanding a military response—as opposed to a mass murder demanding a legal and law enforcement response. Bush repeatedly raised the specter of a terrorist massacre and created a new worldview for many Americans that a traditional war is the best response to terrorism. As we shall see in Chapter 8, Bush forcefully resolved any ambiguity about what the terrorist attacks meant and what the U.S. response should be.

The attempt by social psychologist Milton Rokeach (1918–1988) to measure dogmatism, often referred to as mental rigidity or closed-mindedness, was a reaction to critics who said the efforts to measure tendencies to fascism were flawed because they failed to measure authoritarianism among liberals. Rokeach correlated responses to measures of three theoretical constructs: (a) opinionation, a measure of general authoritarianism and intolerance that assessed traits such as the denial of contradictions in respondents' own beliefs, willingness to consider contradictory beliefs, and orientations toward authority and the future; (b) dogmatism, generally defined as a closed cognitive system; and (c) liberalism and conservatism. Results "stubbornly suggest that people to the right of center are somewhat more prone to authoritarianism and intolerance than people to the left of center." Rokeach also reported positive, but slight, correlations between dogmatism and conservatism. Furthermore, "the dogmatism scores correlate more highly with right than with left opinionation."[38]

Knowledge can be acquired in a number of ways, but the process often leads to cognitive closure, or to a decision. The need for cognitive closure is greater among conservatives than among others, researchers suggest. Results are particularly compelling because they have been reported in Germany, Italy, Finland, Belgium, and the United States.[39] The need for closure, moreover, is (a) positively related to religiosity, anti-immigration attitudes, nationalism, and demands for law and order and autocratic, centralized leadership and (b) negatively related to pluralism, egalitarianism, and multiculturalism.[40]

A number of factors may motivate an individual to seek closure. "These have to do with the perceived benefits and costs of possessing (or lacking) closure," Jost and his colleagues argue, "and may vary as a function of the person, the immediate situation, and the culture."[41] An individual's disposition or circumstances can help determine whether he or she is motivated to be open or closed to additional knowledge. An individual who is motivated to be closed is likely to seize on whatever knowledge is available and to rush to a decision. An autocratic leader will almost certainly prefer a strong need for closure among his or her followers, for that would "assure faster decisions [and] reduce discussions and hesitations."[42] The perceived authority of the Bush II administration was exploited in the rush to close debate and push the nation to war with Iraq, as we shall see in Chapter 9.

Regulatory systems theory also is used to explore the nature of the authoritarian mindset. This theory focuses on the goal of prevention (which includes security, responsibilities, and safety) and promotion (which includes growth, advancement, and aspirations). A regulatory system typically tries to meet both goals: individuals will opt for change over stability when growth and advancement require change, but they will opt for stability over change when they believe their safety and security are threatened.

Individuals who are more open to accomplishment and advancement tend to be more open to change than those who are more open to safety and security. Political conservatism that is motivated in part by the need to avoid change and to desire stability and safety might well induce "a prevention-oriented regulatory focus [and] a conservative shift in the general population."[43] Conservative attacks against efforts by gays and lesbians to marry, as we shall see in Chapter 6 are motivated by a fear that the institution of marriage might somehow change and that Americans will be less safe and secure.

Terror Management

The need to manage terror, or fear, is yet another characteristic of the authoritarian mindset. It suggests that societies create and maintain worldviews that protect individuals from the terrors that can arise when they contemplate their own deaths.[44] "The cornerstone of this position is that awareness of mortality, when combined with an instinct for self-preservation, creates in humans the capacity to be virtually paralyzed with fear. Fear of death, in turn, engenders a defense of one's cultural worldview." As they are confronted with their own mortality, individuals "appear to behave more conservatively by shunning and even punishing outsiders and those who threaten the status of cherished worldviews."[45]

Conservatives fear not only death, of course. A 2008 study from Northwestern University supports previous research suggesting that conservatives fear unrestricted or uncontrolled human behavior that challenges the *status quo*. Authors Dan P. McAdams and Michelle

Albaugh asked 128 individuals the question, "What if there were no God?" Respondents lived in the Chicago area, were quite devout, attended church regularly, and were active politically. They expressed fear of chaos and social disorder, which could result from the break-down of institutions such as the family and the government.[46]

Ideological theories concerned with social dominance and system justification help clarify the relationship between political conserva-tism and sexism, racism, and intolerance. Conservatives who have a social dominance orientation love to lead and to have power over others. They tend to be ruthless, unfeeling, amoral, manipulative, and tough. The authoritarian/leader's worldview is somewhat differ-ent from that of the authoritarian/follower. "Authoritarian leaders see the world as a competitive jungle in which the fittest survive," as Dean puts it: "authoritarian followers see the world as dangerous and threatening."[47]

The social dominators try to minimize conflict and tension within their supportive groups by "developing ideological belief systems that justify the hegemony of some groups over others," according to John Jost and his colleagues.

> This is achieved through the promulgation of various "legitimizing myths," such as the following: (a) "paternalistic myths," which assert that dominant groups are needed to lead and take care of subordinate groups, who are incapable of leading and taking care of themselves; (b) "reciprocal myths," which claim that a symbiotic relationship exists between dominant and subordinate groups and that both groups help each other; and (c) "sacred myths," which allege that positions of domi-nance and subordination are determined by God or some other divine right. Ideological devices such as these are inherently conservative in content because they seek to preserve existing hierarchies of status, power, and wealth and to prevent qualitative social change.[48]

Social dominators do not support movements to expand equality, and they do not perceive themselves to be subject to moral restraint. They tend to agree with such statements as, "There really is no such thing as 'right' and 'wrong'; it all boils down to what you can get away with."[49] They tend to disagree that people should do unto others as they would have others do unto them and that people should never do unfair things to others. Social dominators understand that authori-tarian followers trust leaders who tell them what they want to hear, and they are quite adept at making their followers trust them. As social psychologist Stanley Milgram (1933–1984) said, "Ordinary people, simply doing their jobs, without any particular hostility on their part, can become agents in a terrible destructive process."[50]

The term "system justification," according to Jost and his colleagues, refers to the tendency of individuals to "perceive existing social arrangements as fair, legitimate, justifiable, and rational, and perhaps even natural and inevitable."[51] Since the powerless—the poor and the marginalized—also tend to support the *status quo*, political conservatism pervades all social classes, and inequality is maintained. They hypothesize that "situations of crisis or instability in society will, generally speaking, precipitate conservative, system-justifying shifts to the political right, but only as long as the crisis situation falls short of toppling the existing regime and establishing a new *status quo* to justify and rationalize."[52] The triumph of the conservative mindset in America's political culture is inextricably linked to the crisis mode that has characterized society in the United States since the 9/11 attacks.

STRANDS OF CONTEMPORARY CONSERVATIVE THOUGHT

The three pillars of historical conservatism divine will, resistance to change, and a belief in inequality—have framed the political views of many Americans throughout the nation's history. Although not articulated in a detailed, comprehensive worldview, the precursor to contemporary strands of conservative thought did call for limited government, freedom and liberty (but not equality) for all, and adherence to universal Christian values in the public sphere.

This worldview, however, increasingly came under assault early in the twentieth century. Poor working conditions and pay for men, women, and children who toiled in the fields of the South and the factories of the North were exposed at the turn of the century and demands for reform became increasingly strident. The Great Depression, two world wars, and calls for an increased U.S. presence in world affairs could not be ignored. Conservatives could only watch as government expanded and raised taxes in response to the enhanced role of the United States in international affairs, to renewed calls for help for the disadvantaged, and to demands for the increased regulation of business. Fissures began to appear in historical conservative thought during this period.

As we first noted in the Introduction, three major strands of thought emerged: traditionalist conservatism, neoconservatism, and

Christian conservatism.[53] Traditionalist conservatives are securely
rooted in the eighteenth and nineteenth centuries, when writers such
as John Stuart Mill (1806–1873), John Locke (1632–1704), Adam
Smith (1723–1790), and Edmund Burke began to argue for free markets, small government, individual freedom and liberty, and a strong
military to protect vital national interests. The traditionalist
conservative view began to be articulated more completely after the
Great Depression, largely in response to Franklin Delano Roosevelt's
New Deal. In foreign affairs it was first given voice by George
F. Kennan (1904–2005), a key presidential adviser during the later
1940s and early 1950s, who was the principal architect of the policy
of *Realpolitik*, with specific reference to containment in response to
the Soviet Union during the Cold War, and the chief spokesperson
for this policy as a critic of American foreign policy in later years.[54]

Neoconservatism is rooted in the turbulent 1930s and 1940s, when
a number of intellectuals warned against the threat of international
communism and were horrified by the results of Nazi fascism. This
movement gathered more and more followers after World War II as
the perceived communist threat increased. Neoconservatives today
argue that the United States must use military force if necessary to
make the world safe, particularly for their brand of democracy.

The roots of Christian conservatism, as we outlined in Chapter 1,
lay in the history of the evangelical fundamentalist Protestant movement in the first half of the twentieth century. The Christian
conservative political coalition pieced together in the 1970s and
1980s embraced a social, economic, and religious agenda that in its
essentials was in harmony with both the traditionalist and neoconservative political agenda.

None of the strands was new, and none is as simplistic or mutually
exclusive as these brief definitions suggest. They simply had not been
widely perceived as separate, partly because each had some roots in
historical conservatism. As each began to define itself more clearly,
differences began to emerge to influence contemporary conservative
political discourse, particularly that of the Republican Party, with
which they tended to associate. We describe these strands more completely in the following section.

Traditionalist Conservatism

Traditionalist conservatives—known by some as secular conservatives, libertarians, or simply as conservatives—can be distinguished from

religious conservatives primarily by their view of religion's role in politics. Most hold religious convictions and many are deeply devout. They avoid making decisions that contradict their moral values, but religious concerns are not their prime motivation for political decision making.

Traditionalist conservatives became increasingly uncomfortable in the second half of the twentieth century with the idea that government decision making should be driven by God's will. During a period of increased secularization of government and society, many conservatives considered it inappropriate to invoke God's law, natural law, or church law in public affairs. These conservatives restricted their understanding of "laws" to those statutes and court decisions created by states, nations, and other governments.

Andrew Sullivan, a political commentator from England who regards himself as a libertarian conservative, argues from an even more extreme position that Christian activists have had a negative influence on traditionalist conservative politics. He views Christian conservatives as religious fundamentalists who have driven the idea of doubt out of their vocabulary. He says they threaten traditionalist conservatism because doubt is "the defining characteristic of the conservative." The conservative "begins with the assumption that the human mind is fallible, that it can delude itself, make mistakes, or see only so far ahead. And this, the conservative avers, is what it means to be human."[55] The core of religious fundamentalism "is not the individual conscience, but God himself, and the decision of the individual to surrender himself to God entirely is the premise of every action he commits and every decision he makes."[56] A religious fundamentalist, as well as many other Christian conservatives, knows the truth. "The fundamentalist doesn't guess or argue or wonder or question. He doesn't have to. He *knows*" (italics in the original).[57]

Barry Goldwater (1909–1998), whose conservative supporters gained control of the Republican Party in 1964 and nominated him for president, argued that solutions to the problems conservatives faced in the America of the 1960s may be found in the values of the past,[58] especially the "economic, social, and political practices based on the successes of the past."[59] Goldwater protégé John Dean notes that "any thought of the government's imposing its own morality, or anyone else's, on society" was absent from Goldwater's definition. "In other words, the values of today's social, or cultural, conservatism had no place in the senator's philosophy."[60]

Goldwater's conservative philosophy rested on two primary values— economic freedom and political liberty.[61] He traced conservatism's economic roots to Adam Smith, the founding father of laissez-faire capitalism: Smith argued that in any economic exchange participants on each side must benefit, and the beneficiaries must be free of government constraints.[62] Goldwater's political liberties were based on (a) the strict separation of legislative, executive, and judicial power as outlined in the Constitution; (b) the idea that political decision making must be at local levels where ordinary citizens can participate; and (c) the notion that the rule of law must be respected and enforced.

After Lyndon Johnson defeated Goldwater in the 1964 presidential election, many political observers concluded that traditionalist conservatism and the Republican Party had sustained a terrible blow. Journalist and historian Robert J. Donovan (1912–2003), for example, wrote, "The Democrats have all but crowded the Republicans off the main positions of the day.... The challenge [Republicans] face in returning to the eminent position they once occupied, however, is an appallingly difficult one."[63]

That "appallingly difficult" challenge was met less than a decade later when Richard Nixon won the White House. When he ran for president in 1968, Nixon, a Quaker, represented himself as (a) a master of foreign relations who would end the war in Vietnam and as (b) a staunch anti-communist. Nixon had cultivated his reputation as an anti-communist when, as a member of the U.S. House Un-American Activities Committee in the late 1940s and early 1950s, he insisted on a trial for Alger Hiss (1904–1996), an official with the Department of State who was denounced as a communist.[64]

Nixon ran in 1968 as a traditionalist conservative, a law-and-order candidate who would stop inner city riots, unite a divided nation, shelve at least part of the civil rights and social legislation passed under Lyndon Johnson, and control a federal government that had poured too much money into social programs. Conservatives rallied around Nixon to give him the presidency in 1968 and 1972.[65]

Many traditionalist conservatives were disappointed that Nixon did not reduce the size of government, that he was supposedly responsible for the most serious economic crisis in decades, that the federal budget soared, and that his mishandling of the Watergate fiasco led to his resignation and the assumption by Gerald Ford of the presidency. Ford, the caretaker president, was defeated by Jimmy Carter in 1976, dealing another blow to Republican conservative politics.

The party recovered once again nationally when Ronald Reagan defeated Jimmy Carter in the 1980 presidential election. Reagan— a master of simple, dichotomous language—emphasized family values and limited government, and thereby employed both Christian and traditionalist conservative discourse to advance his policies. A rejuvenated Christian conservative political agenda (particularly in the South and the West), along with a more rigorous defense of conservative values in the media, in academic circles, and in the proliferation of conservative think tanks such as the Heritage Foundation and the Cato Institute gave Reagan and conservative ideas legitimacy and made them appear innovative.

Traditionalist conservatives were not altogether disappointed by Reagan. They got their tax cuts and welfare reforms (although spending on welfare programs increased between 1981 and 1989), and they were able to attribute the breakup of the Soviet Union to Reagan's military buildup. They seemed unconcerned that the 1981 and 1986 tax cuts, which helped increase the wealth of the wealthy, and the massive defense spending during Reagan's administration contributed to the largest federal deficits in history at that time. Ironically, negotiation and dialogue did more to end the Cold War than the military buildup.[66]

But they did not get other reforms dear to their hearts. Reagan, who accepted the view that the state is a threat to society and who argued for a smaller, leaner government, "didn't abolish a single major federal agency," as journalist Jacob Heilbrunn put it: "he strengthened Social Security by approving a payroll tax hike and he added $1.4 trillion to the national debt."[67] Reagan also approved the deregulation policies that led to "the looting of the Department of Housing and Urban Development" and to a savings and loan crisis that cost taxpayers billions.[68]

Christian conservatives supported Reagan, but they did not benefit much from the Reagan presidency. "On the social and cultural issues dear to the religious right—from abortion to prayer in public schools—the administration delivered mainly lip service."[69] Reagan in fact was not particularly religious. As historian John Diggins points out, Reagan "subscribed to a Jeffersonian belief in religion because it enabled the mind to resist political tyranny—and not, as some Christian fundamentalists wish, because he wanted to impose it as a pledge of allegiance."[70]

Reagan became something of a mythical icon for conservatives after he left office—and especially after his death. Mike Huckabee, a Christian conservative candidate for the Republican presidential nomination in 2008, said, "It's important to remember that what Ronald Reagan did was to give us a vision for this country, a morning in America, a city on a hill." John McCain, the traditionalist conservative who won the nomination and lost the election, said, "Ronald Reagan used to say we spend money like a drunken sailor" and called for a return to a Reaganesque austerity.[71]

George H. W. Bush won a term as president with support from traditionalist conservatives, neoconservatives, and religious conservatives, all of whom perceived that Bush was one of them. He lost the support of many traditionalist conservatives when he promised tax cuts (many still recall his "read my lips, no new taxes" pledge) and then raised them. He lost neoconservative support by embracing the policy of containment in the 1991 Gulf War and by refusing to intervene in the 1992 Bosnian civil war.[72] And he lost the support of religious conservatives by essentially ignoring them.

George W. Bush—a born-again Christian whose religious beliefs did guide his public policy decisions—benefited mightily from the support of his conservative religious backers. And as we have seen, they benefited from the Bush presidency in the form of appointments to key federal offices and access to federal dollars for religious purposes. Bush promised to uphold the principles of fiscal conservatism, but his regressive tax policies contributed to huge deficits. His indifference to government oversight of markets, moreover, pushed the country to the brink of depression in 2008, while the invasion of Iraq decimated the military and contributed to massive budget deficits. His mishandling of the Hurricane Katrina disaster also is cited as evidence of the government's inability to cope with domestic crisis.[73]

Many traditionalist conservatives charged that George W. Bush was not really a conservative because he did not uphold the Constitution, tried to disenfranchise minority voters, allowed the budget deficit to soar and government to expand, equated dissent with treason, and launched a war against a nation, Iraq, that was not a threat. Conservative media icons such as George Will and Robert Novak, for example, refused from the beginning to back the war in Iraq because they did not perceive that Iraq threatened American interests.

Neoconservatism

Many neoconservatives advocate free markets and small government, and many would like the nation (and the world) to embrace the values they believe dominated U.S. society before the 1960s. But neoconservatives are defined primarily by their views of the role they think the United States should play in international affairs.

Their priority is to ensure that the United States has an active, or dominant, role in international relations. It is the responsibility of the United States to maintain world peace, because they do not trust multilateral institutions to do the job. "An American empire is a perfectly plausible scenario for neoconservatives; containment is a policy they believe is outmoded."[74] Most would impose American values and traditions on the peoples of other nations—through military force, if necessary—and they are not uncomfortable with the idea of perpetual war to ensure U.S. domination in international affairs.[75]

Neoconservative thought is rooted in the 1930s and 1940s, when Jewish, Christian, and secular intellectuals—many from working-class families in New York City—debated the fascism and socialism of that era. Many were influenced by Leon Trotsky's warnings about the dangers of Nazi fascism and its threat to the Jews, and his condemnation of Josef Stalin's order to German communists to fight Germany's Social Democrats and not the Nazis.[76] Activists such as Irving Kristol and Max Schachtman (1904–1972), for example, failed at first to grasp the dangers posed by Hitler—particularly his impact on the Jewish community—and refused initially to support a war against Germany.

These intellectuals ultimately did support the war and many were drawn to Marx's call for class consciousness during a period in which many, particularly the Jewish intellectuals, had firsthand experience with discrimination in America.[77] The infatuation with communism began to ebb in the 1940s as details of Stalin's atrocities in Russia and later Mao Zedong's atrocities in China "convinced neoconservatives of the non-negotiable importance of morality."[78]

By the end of World War II, most of the future neoconservative lobby had become profoundly anti-communist. Many, such as Lionel Trilling (1905–1975) and Sidney Hook (1902–1989), viewed Russia as a "degenerated workers' state."[79] James Burnham (1905–1987) warned in the *Partisan Review* soon after the war ended in 1945 that Soviet expansion plans were a threat to the entire world and that Stalin was an effective and dangerous leader who must be stopped.[80] Some future neoconservatives even joined liberals in supporting the nonpartisan Americans for Democratic Action, an anti-communist political lobby group formed in 1947 by leading activists in the Democratic Party.[81]

These forerunners of the neoconservative movement gained a higher political profile in the 1960s as they attacked what they perceived was the government's soft stance on the Soviet Union, on Israel's beleaguered position as a nation in the Middle East, and on the threat of antisemitic violence in the United States. Leo Strauss (1899–1973), one of the founding fathers of neoconservatism, fretted about "a liberal failure of nerve in confronting the Soviet Union and in defending Israel . . . . Were the United States to allow Israel to collapse, it would signal a fatal weakness in the larger struggle against Soviet totalitarianism."[82]

Many future neoconservatives voted for Lyndon Johnson in 1964 and supported social programs such as Medicare and civil rights legislation designed to ensure that all Americans are equal under the law. They moved to the Right when they observed the marches against the war in Vietnam, free speech demonstrations, and protests against discrimination on the basis of gender and sexuality. Many saw these events "as contributing to the degradation of tradition and authority, cultural relativism, and ultimately a kind of moral void and insecurities that would undermine cherished institutions and national stability."[83] These reactions, of course, were not unlike those of many GOP (Grand Old Party) conservative traditionalists and Christian conservatives.

Many proto-neoconservatives voted for Richard Nixon in 1968 because he was vehemently anti-communist and because he promised a return to traditional values. However, one of Nixon's most vaunted foreign policy achievements—the opening to China—alienated many of the so-called hawks of the day. These men and women, who by 1973 were known as neoconservatives,[84] also complained about the attempt to achieve détente with the Soviet Union, which many said was "nothing more than a Soviet ploy in the Cold War and did more to undermine than benefit U.S. national security."[85] Many also were critical of the administration's failure to pursue what they called a winning policy in Vietnam.

Some future neoconservatives during Nixon's terms retained their anti-communist views, but many aligned themselves with hawkish Democrats because they could not support what they saw as the Nixon-Kissinger policy of appeasement toward the communist world. Future neoconservatives such as Richard Pearle, Paul Wolfowitz, and Douglas Feith aligned themselves with Washington Senator Henry Jackson (1912–1983), who was an untiring supporter of the defense industry, a vocal opponent of any reapproachment with the Soviet Union, and a proponent of a military victory in Vietnam.

Neoconservatives who had supported Lyndon Johnson and Democratic proposals to extend civil rights to all and to create safety nets for the disadvantaged finally broke with their intellectual counterparts in the Democratic Party, in part because they opposed "liberal" initiatives such as affirmative action, appeasement toward communism, and the feminist movement.[86] They became conservative Republicans, in part as a reaction against Democrat Jimmy Carter's continuation of the Nixon administration's policy of détente with the Soviet Union.

Ronald Reagan was a primary beneficiary of this new allegiance.[87] Neoconservatives who were not Republicans before Reagan was elected switched after he took office. They displayed their anti-communist credentials, "rebuffed Fidel Castro . . . , claimed the Soviet Union was permanently unalterable, and then took credit for its collapse while hailing America's triumph in the cold war."[88]

Neoconservatives were put off by George H. W. Bush's lack of commitment to nation building and foreign interventions, but they found an ally in George W. Bush. Although he also decried nation building and military intervention for humanitarian reasons during the 2000 presidential campaign, he stocked his administration with neoconservatives whose views he endorsed. Vice President Dick Cheney, the neocon in chief, together with his major ally, Defense Secretary Donald Rumsfeld, treated as enemies those in the Bush administration who disagreed with their neoconservative policies. Cheney staffed the White House with as many cronies who shared his views as he could, and he sometimes worked behind Bush's back to achieve his goals.[89]

The 9/11 attacks enabled Bush and the neoconservatives to launch their project to remake the Middle East. They used 9/11 "to justify a new nationalism and a new reliance on militarism," as political scientist Stephen Eric Bonner points out. "Constriction of civil liberties and a preoccupation with national loyalty, combined with a staggering increase in funds for 'security' and 'defense,' helped fuel the imperialist experiments with 'regime change' in Afghanistan and Iraq."[90]

Neither Afghanistan nor Iraq posed a military threat, but neoconservatives claimed it was morally appropriate to launch preventive wars against unspecified *future threats*. A report of the neoconservative Project for the New American Century argues, for instance, that "American military preeminence will continue to rest in significant part on the ability to maintain sufficient land forces to achieve political goals such as removing a dangerous and hostile regime when necessary."[91] Neoconservatives argue that nations giving safe harbor to terrorists may be attacked under international law: terrorists constitute an imminent threat and must be stopped, even if innocents in a nation suffer.[92]

For neoconservatives—religious studies professor Ira Chernus argues—the war against terrorism is not altogether about reducing the terrorist threat against the United States. "The main goal is to give Americans a global arena where they can show their moral strength, their allegiance to permanent moral values, and their ability to hold back the whirlwind of change. To prove all that, Americans need to be fighting against sin, evil, and moral weakness; they need monsters to destroy. So the point of the war is not to win. It is, on the contrary, to keep on fighting monsters forever."[93] Given this worldview, neoconservatives could argue years later—even after it became clear that neither Iraq nor Afghanistan constituted threats—that America should launch another war against Iran because they believed it constituted a threat.

Neoconservatives are not focused entirely on one issue. Many share with many Christian conservatives the view that U.S. culture has not recovered from the turbulence of the 1960s—that values changed for the worse and that conservative values remain under attack. Many take the elitist position: "Since the average American has become too weak to accept traditional rules voluntarily, those rules have to be imposed externally, by law."[94]

They share with social and religious conservatives a desire to maintain the traditional, male-dominated, heterosexual institution of marriage. This alliance helped make the neoconservative ascendancy possible. Many support and rely upon the traditional patriarchal model "to reverse the progress of feminism and lesbian/gay rights," as political theorist R. Claire Snyder puts it.[95]

Many neoconservatives also share with many Christian conservatives a belief in the inherent worth of the individual human being. This belief that each of us has inalienable privileges and rights is at the core of the "fear that technology commodifies and alienates man from himself."[96] Biotechnology, for example, is giving scientists and doctors increasing power over the reproductive process. Adam Wolfson, editor of the conservative political and cultural journal *The Public Interest*, argues that this power would make "human procreation . . . take on the semblance of manufacture, and parents would come to think of themselves as 'smart shoppers.' "[97] Moral values for these neoconservatives must be imposed on a sinful world—through force if necessary.

Christian Conservatism

We merely summarize the Christian conservative political worldview here, as we have already discussed that mindset in detail in earlier chapters. Divine intent is central to the Christian conservative world-view. Government action must be consistent with their vision of God's will, as expressed in the authority of scripture, ecclesiastical tradition, rational decision making, and the personal experiences of the conservative believer. Government decisions should be made within this framework of Christian thought.

Christian conservatives typically share with neoconservatives and traditionalist conservatives a fear of change, an intolerance of ambiguity, an authoritarian mindset, a need for closure, and an acceptance of inequality. But they do not always agree about precisely *how* Christian thought should affect public policy. Sociologist Christian Smith, who has written much about the evangelical movement, suggests that conservative Protestantism, for example, "comprises a conglomeration of varied subgroups that differ on many issues and sometimes clash significantly."[98] This comment could apply to the entire conservative religious community.

Evangelical Protestants comprise the largest faction in the conservative religious coalition. They became more vociferous political activists when the U.S. Supreme Court ruled in *Engel v. Vitale* (1962, 1963) against voluntary or involuntary prayer in public schools,[99] and in *Epperson v. Arkansas* (1968) that school boards had no constitutional right to ban the teaching of scientific evolution in public schools. Conservative Catholics joined them when the Supreme Court ruled in *Roe v. Wade* (1973) that women had a constitutional right to abortion. As we noted in Chapter 1, the civil rights movement, the anti-Vietnam war movement, feminism, and the so-called sexual revolution were perceived to be threatening the social order and were catalysts, with the Supreme Court decisions, for conservative religious activism in the 1970s and 1980s.

Many Christian conservatives share with traditionalist conservatives the view that government's primary duty is to ensure markets are free to function without government interference, to enforce law and order, and to guarantee political liberty. And many share with neoconservatives the view that the United States must establish order in the world and make the planet safe for America's version of democracy.

ENDURING TENSIONS

Political and media analysts of conservative coalition politics have shown for at least a generation a surprising lack of interest in the historical context or in the complexity of issues relating to the conservative partnership. Few even recognized a conservative coalition—which first began to emerge nationally during the 1964 presidential election cycle—as a political force until Ronald Reagan's election, even though the coalition had helped elect candidates in many local and state elections for many years prior to 1980.

Some analysts noted the presence of the conservative coalition during the Reagan years, and some even predicted a national political realignment that would favor conservatives in the future. Few, however, recognized or reported historic tensions within this coalition that would inevitably reemerge to threaten this vision in the twenty-first century.

The dominant role of conservatives in America's political culture in the past 30 years or so obscured another reality that different partners in the coalition have played greater or lesser roles in the control over conservative discourse. Conservative politics within the GOP seemed to be driven in some election cycles by traditionalist conservatives, in others by neoconservatives, and in still others by religious conservatives. Alliances were continually shifting as new tensions arose and old tensions resurfaced to challenge the unity of the coalition.

The Glory Years

One could well argue that the Clinton presidential era during the 1990s constituted a high point in the political solidarity of the conservative coalition. The communist menace—the threat that had united conservatives for decades—was over. The new enemy—terrorism—was in the future. In the interim, there were "the Clintons."

Conservatives, as we noted in Chapter 2, rallied and railed to defeat Hillary Clinton's universal health-care plan, which was introduced during the first years of the Clinton administration. The health-care proposal was tainted with the label of "socialism" and dubbed "Hillarycare" from the beginning. Any legislative compromise was made impossible in the midst of the chorus of voices raised in conservative media against the plan.

The alliance of unlikely partners at the time included conservative religious activists (from the Christian Coalition to Focus on the Family), prominent neoconservatives (such as William Kristol), and powerful conservative lobby groups (from the Health Insurance Association of America—with its "Harry and Louise" attack advertisements—to the National Federation of Independent Business and the National

Association of Manufacturers). The plan divided the Democratic Party and opened the door to a Republican takeover of the House of Representatives in the 1994 Congressional elections for the first time in 40 years. House Speaker Newt Gingrich (1995–1999), the "Hammer" Tom Delay (R-Sugar Land, Texas), and their allies were leaders in what was called the Republican Revolution in Congress during the Clinton years.

Christian conservatives had become *primus inter pares* (first among equals) in relation to their traditionalist conservative and neoconservative partners on any issue relating to cultural affairs, as the Clintons would soon realize. Pat Robertson's Christian Coalition was at its height in the mid-late 1990s, and the pervasive conservative religious moral presence at local and state levels—in the schools, in censorship boards of all kinds, in laws and statutes being passed by city councils and state legislatures, and in scores of political and social action committees—was seemingly an act of divine will.

Conservatives and the conservative media establishment (substantially in place by the late 1990s) orchestrated the scandals that dogged the Clinton administration throughout the 1990s. While the conservative coalition managed to impeach the president (but not secure a conviction in the Senate) over his "affair" with Monica Lewinsky, this story supplanted virtually all others in the news media and turned the 2000 presidential election, as *New York Times* journalist Sam Tanenhaus put it, "into a referendum on Mr. Clinton's character."[100]

Cracks in the Coalition

No one will argue that George W. Bush's victory in the 2000 elections, while legitimately disputed, came about in large part because the conservative coalition was well organized, well funded, and very determined. The alliance between Christian conservatives, traditionalist conservatives, and neoconservatives was cemented during the Bush II administration. The cement had not dried, however, before cracks began to appear.

Tensions in the Conservative Coalition since 9/11

The 9/11 attacks and the subsequent moral panic, some would say hysteria, that gripped the American public provided a historic opportunity for neoconservatives to use the military to remake the troublesome Middle East. It also allowed "neoconservatives and evangelicals," as Tanenhaus argues, to find "common cause in their shared belief in American exceptionalism and in the idea that the country's values could be exported abroad."[101] Their ally, of course, was the new Republican president, George W. Bush.

Bush and the neoconservatives, with the acceptance of a broad spectrum of Christian and other religious conservatives, began to open up "free" markets worldwide under the rubric of fighting the war against terrorism. Traditionalist conservative notions of economic freedom and political liberty were abandoned as the administration invaded Iraq to establish a free-market economy, one that could benefit U.S. corporations and extend U.S. dominance in the oil-rich region. Other governments followed suit.[102]

The war in Iraq placed a mighty strain on the conservative coalition and ignited a sometimes-heated debate about the meaning of conservatism in party politics. "A chorus from the right has been noisily distinguishing between conservative and Republican," as *New York Times* journalists David D. Kirkpatrick and Jason DeParle suggest, "blaming deviation from conservative principles for the election losses."[103] Dimitri K. Simes, co-publisher of the *National Interest* and president of the Nixon Center, argued from the traditionalist conservative perspective: "Acquiring additional burdens by engaging in new wars of liberation is the last thing the United States needs .... The principal problem is the mistaken belief that democracy is a talisman for all the world's ills, including terrorism, and that the United States has a responsibility to promote democratic government wherever in the world it is lacking."[104]

Failing Markets and Big Government

Many traditionalist conservatives, relatively minor partners in George W. Bush's White House, and some Christian conservatives watched in horror as "disaster capitalism," a term coined by journalist Naomi Klein, was embraced by the Bush administration. They were concerned about spending for the wars in Iraq and Afghanistan, and about domestic spending, which soared under Republican leadership. Pork-barrel projects reached an all-time high in the Republican-controlled Congress. The year before Republicans gained control in 1995, for example, roughly 1,300 earmarked items (for a total of $7.8 billion) were added to the budget, compared to roughly 14,000 (for a total of $27.3 billion) earmarked items in 2005.[105]

Many traditionalist conservatives were also concerned about the lack of progress in reducing the size of government and about the failure of the financial markets, which Republicans had helped to deregulate. Many were aghast as they watched the unfolding credit crisis on Wall Street and the slide into recession in late 2008. They were deeply divided over government interference in the market as they watched the Bush administration and Congress fund bailouts of banks and other financial institutions to rescue the credit industry.[106]

The stress caused by the growth of government, the expanding deficit, and the market crises in the Bush administration put particular strains on the conservative coalition. Big Government conservatives, as conservative guru Richard A. Viguerie calls them, believe in, well, big government, and traditionalist conservatives do not. Viguerie fired this broadside at the so-called Big Government conservatives—in reality, the neoconscrvatives:

> Ronald Reagan won his first election as president with 51% of the popular vote, a ten-point margin over the incumbent. He carried 44 states. When he ran for reelection, he won 59% of the vote and carried 49 states.... Big Government "conservative" George W. Bush won his first election by five Electoral College votes and actually finished second in the popular vote, with 48%. Running for reelection, he won 50.76% of the vote against some of the most pitiful opposition in recent political history.... As a political force, I'll take conservatism over "Big Government conservatism" any day of the week.[107]

Conservative *New York Times* columnist David Brooks also bemoans the tendency of Republican political gurus from the mid-1990s to divide Americans into groups, "to mobilize their coalition with a form of social class warfare." The West Coast and the Northeast are largely lost to Republicans, Brooks says, and doctors, lawyers, investment bankers, and technology company officials contribute more to Democrats than to Republicans. "The party is losing the working class by sins of omission—because it has not developed policies to address economic anxiety. It has lost the educated class by sins of commission—by telling members of that class to go away."[108]

There is no single definition of conservatism that is acceptable to conservatives in America today. The vision of America espoused by Christian social conservatives and neoconservatives in George W. Bush's administration has now been widely discredited, and it was rejected by America's voters in the 2008 elections. It may be difficult to negotiate trade-offs to secure a compromise that will sustain the conservative political coalition in the foreseeable future, but conservatism and the Republican Party are by no means dead.

The Imperial Presidency

The neoconservative vision of an American "empire" intervening in nations at will to impose "democracy" and "freedom" throughout the world found a home in George W. Bush's White House.[109] The enormous growth in presidential power during this administration, for example, was fueled largely by neoconservative apparatchiks such as Vice President Cheney and his allies in Congress and in various departments controlled by the White House. Journalist Charlie Savage won a Pulitzer Prize in 2007 for detailing the use of presidential signing statements—the power to impose line-item vetoes of parts of legislation not acceptable to the president. The expansion of executive power and privilege under Bush's "imperial" presidency, as Savage puts it, would have significant ramifications in domestic politics and in American foreign policy.[110]

Traditionalist Republican conservatives found a sympathetic reception from many Democrats in rejecting the latest incarnation of the imperial presidency—the so-called "unitary executive" as espoused by George W. Bush and his neoconservative allies. The growth of presidential power has been the source of controversy from the beginning of the Republic. Since the publication of *The Imperial Presidency*, the exploration of abuses in Richard Nixon's administration by historian Arthur M. Schlesinger Jr., the power of the executive branch of the government has become a source of controversy among strict constructionists in both parties.[111]

They are united in their concern that the balance of power among the executive, judicial, and congressional branches of government has been increasingly skewed in favor of the executive branch in recent election cycles. They point to Clinton's efforts to bypass Congress by selectively vetoing parts of bills presented to him without vetoing the whole bill. The Line Item Veto Act of 1996, however, was disallowed by the U.S. Supreme Court in *Clinton v. City of New York* (1998).[112] George W. Bush continued this tradition with the "signing statement," in which he specified what parts of legislation he would actually enforce. The Bush administration invoked far more signing statements than in previous administrations, and they were broader in scope—embracing such issues as the right to torture enemy combatants and the right to spy on American citizens without issuing warrants.

The war against terror as pursued by the Bush administration was the catalyst that (a) generated support from religious and secular conservatives for an imperial presidency and (b) led not only to "the historic surrender of [congressional] authority," as journalist Jonathan Mahler puts it, but also "to question whether Congress really wants to be a full partner in America's government." More and more matters of public policy were discussed in secret in the White House, information was passed along to Congress that was often incomplete and misleading, and "unwanted disclosures" were routinely denied or effectively blocked by "invoking the formerly obscure 'state-secrets privilege.' "[113]

Congressional politics became polarized almost solely along party lines with the 1994 elections, when the GOP regained control of Congress. Led by its neoconservative wing, "party loyalty" took precedence over all other concerns—including the concerns of constituents—Mahler maintains. While "single party rule" had not inevitably "translated into a timid Congress" in the past, the "political warfare" of modern party politics is unprecedented. GOP party loyalty has been placed "ahead of institutional loyalty"—especially in the Senate[114]—and the Democrats have followed suit. In terms of the current war against terrorism, Mahler argues that Congress essentially has abrogated responsibility and "left its duty to oversee the prosecution of the war largely in the hands of a judiciary that has historically been loath to interfere with the president's war-making power."[115]

The making of an imperial presidency, of course, is a bipartisan problem. "History has shown that where you stand on executive authority," as Mahler says, "is largely a matter of where you sit." Even when the Democrats regained control of Congress in 2006, the president was able to rewrite the Foreign Intelligence Surveillance Act (originally passed in 1978), which both McCain and Obama supported during the 2008 election debates, that made "it easier for the White House to spy on American citizens" and granted "immunity to telecom companies that cooperated with the government's secret surveillance program." The "federal bailout bill" pushed through Congress in 2008 also "vested almost complete control over the economy in the Treasury secretary (who reports to the president)."

Mahler concluded his article with this sobering thought: "even if the legislative branch does reassert itself in the next administration, what exactly will that mean?"[116]

NOTES

1. Our focus is on conservative thought in the United States, which is quite different from conservative thought elsewhere, particularly in Europe. British conservative views of gay marriage, the proper response to terrorism, taxes, the meaning of Christianity and the role of religion in politics, and a host of other issues, for example, differ radically from the views of their American counterparts. For a good description of the differences between American and British conservatism, see John Micklethwait and Adrian Wooldridge, *The Right Nation: Conservative Power in America* (New York: Penguin, 2004), Chapter 14.

2. John W. Dean, *Conservatives without Conscience* (New York: Viking, 2006), xxxix.

3. Jeffrey Hart, "Burke and Radical Freedom," in *Keeping the Tablet: Modern American Conservative Thought*, ed. William F. Buckley Jr. and Charles R. Kesler (New York: Harper & Row, 1988), 45–61.

4. Eva Marie Garroutte, "The Positivist Attack on Baconian Science and Religious Knowledge in the 1870s," in *The Secular Revolution: Power, Interests, and Conflict in the Secularization of American Public Life*, ed. Christian Smith (Berkeley: University of California Press, 2003), 197–215.

5. Francis Graham Wilson, *The Case for Conservatism* (Seattle: University of Washington Press, 1951); and Russell Kirk, *The Conservative Mind: From Burke to Eliot*, 7th ed. (Chicago: Regnery, 1986).

6. Kendall brings the argument full circle, however, suggesting that there might be little difference between liberals and conservatives. Since conservatives "differ in the degree of their pessimism, and liberals differ in the degree of their optimism . . . the line between them is occupied simultaneously by the most optimistic of the pessimists, and the most pessimistic of the optimists—both of whom, one gathers, might very well, and with strict accuracy, be called *either* a 'conservative' or 'liberal' " (italics in the original). Willmoore Kendall, *The Conservative Affirmation* (Chicago: Henry Regnery, 1963), 4, 5 (citing Clinton Rossiter).

7. Robert Nisbet, for example, says conservatism is an ideology, which he defines as "any reasonably coherent body of moral, economic, social and cultural ideas that has a solid and well known reference to politics and political power." See Robert Nisbet, *Conservatism: Dream and Reality* (Minneapolis: University of Minnesota Press, 1986), vii.

8. Charles W. Dunn and J. David Woodard, *The Conservative Tradition in America* (Lanham, MD: Rowman & Littlefield, 1996), 30.

9. Frank S. Meyer, *In Defense of Freedom: A Conservative Credo* (Chicago: Regnery, 1962).

10. M. Stanton Evans, "Techniques and Circumstances" in M. Morton Auerbach, "Do-It-Yourself Conservatism," *National Review*, January 30, 1962, 57–59, p. 58.

11. Russell Kirk, "The Idea of Conservatism," in Buckley and Kesler, *Keeping the Tablet*, 42–45, p. 43.

12. "Faith-Based Funding Backed, But Church-State Doubts Abound," The Pew Research Center for the People & the Press, April 10, 2001, at http://people-press.org/reports/display.php3?PageID=111.

13. Political activism frequently grows out of charitable or educational ministries. While few clergy use their churches for overt political activism (in part because it might threaten their tax-exempt status), lay members, ministers, and priests often organize political action through the church. "In the 1950s and 1960s, the civil rights movement was based in African American churches, leaving a legacy of church-centered political mobilization that continues today." Anti-abortion and anti-gay movements, for instance, frequently are based in churches. Robert Booth Fowler, Allen D. Hertzke, Laura R. Olson, and Kevin R. Den Dulk, *Religion and Politics in America: Faith, Culture, and Strategic Choices* (Boulder, CO: Westview, 2004), 34.

14. Conservatives have a long history of demanding that certain books be banned for the public good. The controversy about *The Golden Compass* is somewhat different in that critics are split. The Catholic League wants moviegoers to boycott the film, while the United States Conference of Catholic Bishops' Office for Film and Broadcasting reviewed the film positively. Sarah Viren, "Does Film *Compass* Steer Kids in Wrong Direction?" *Houston Chronicle*, December 7, 2007, A1, A8.

15. Comer had announced an upcoming lecture by Barbara Forrest, author of *Inside Creationism's Trojan Horse* and a critic of intelligent design, to an online community. Lizzette Reynolds, an advisor to George Bush when he was governor of Texas and a staffer in the U.S. Department of Education, called for Comer to be fired. Rick Casey, "Why Science Needs History," *Houston Chronicle*, December 5, 2007, B1, B4.

16. Romney, who worked hard in the 2007 campaign to portray himself as a social conservative, was viewed with suspicion by social conservatives from other religious faith groups. Many of these critics were not concerned that George W. Bush wore his religion on his sleeve and that he often did, in fact, let religious doctrine guide his political decisions. Alan Bernstein, "Romney: Faith Personal, Not Political," *Houston Chronicle*, December 7, 2007, A22.

17. Clinton Rossiter, "Conservatism," in *International Encyclopedia of the Social Sciences*, vol. 3, ed. David L. Sills (New York: Macmillan, 1968), 290–295, p. 291. See also Clinton Rossiter, *Conservatism in America*, 2nd ed. (New York: Knopf, 1962).

18. Pamela Johnston Conover and Stanley Feldman, "The Origins and Meaning of Liberal/Conservative Self-Identifications," *American Journal of Political Science* 25, no. 4 (1981): 617–645.

19. On the other hand, they will embrace technology when it supports their agenda—such as medical advances that prolong "life" and thus complicate immeasurably the meaning of "death"—as in the Terri Schiavo affair.

20. P. J. O'Rourke, "The Unthinking Man's Guide to Conservatism," in *Why I Turned Right: Leading Baby Boom Conservatives Chronicle Their Political Journeys*, ed. Mary Eberstadt (New York: Threshold Editions, 2007), 23–41, pp. 37, 39.

21. Dean, *Conservatives without Conscience*, 172.

22. Anthony Giddens, *The Third Way: The Renewal of Social Democracy* (Cambridge, UK: Polity, 1998), 40–42.

23. Frank S. Ravitch, *Masters of Illusion: The Supreme Court and the Religion Clauses* (New York: New York University Press, 2007), Chapter 5.

24. Dunn and Woodard, *Conservative Tradition*, 57.

25. We must limit our discussion of these studies mainly to those dealing with a predominantly conservative mindset, although some have focused on liberal mindsets as well.

26. John T. Jost, Jack Glaser, Arie W. Kruglanski, and Frank J. Sulloway, "Political Conservatism as Motivated Social Cognition," *Psychological Bulletin* 129, no. 3 (2003): 339–375, p. 339. Much of this discussion is based on the meta-analysis of 88 different samples "that used direct measures of political identification, conservative ideological opinion, resistance to social and political change, and/or preference for social and economic inequality" (344).

27. Richard Lebrun, *Joseph de Maistre: An Intellectual Militant* (Kingston, ON: McGill-Queen's University Press, 1988).

28. T. W. Adorno, Else Frenkel-Brunswik, Daniel J. Levinson, and R. Nevitt Sanford, *The Authoritarian Personality* (New York: Harper, 1950). Some scholars argue that conservatism is a component of authoritarianism, while others suggest that authoritarianism is a component of conservatism, the larger construct. See Glenn D. Wilson, "A Dynamic Theory of Conservatism," in *The Psychology of Conservatism*, ed. Glenn D. Wilson (London: Academic Press, 1973), 257–266.

29. Dunn and Woodard, *Conservative Tradition*, 89–90.

30. Robert A. Altemeyer, *Right-Wing Authoritarianism* (Winnipeg: University of Manitoba Press, 1981), 148.

31. Dean, *Conservatives without Conscience*, xii.

32. A real-world example of this racism is the song *Barack the Magic Negro*, a parody making the rounds among conservatives such as talk-show host Rush Limbaugh to the Republican National Committee. Sung to the tune of *Puff the Magic Dragon* by someone intended to be the Reverend Al Sharpton, the song includes these lines: "Barack the Magic Negro/Made

guilty whites feel good/They'll vote for him and not for me/Cause he's not from the 'hood.' " Jason DeParle, "Republicans Receive an Obama Parody to Mixed Reviews," *New York Times*, December 28, 2008, A19.

33. Bob Altemeyer and Bruce Hunsberger, "Authoritarianism, Religious Fundamentalism, Quest, and Prejudice," *International Journal of the Psychology of Religion* 2, no. 2 (1992): 113–133.

34. Brian Laythe, Deborah G. Finkel, Robert G. Bringle, and Lee A. Kirkpatrick, "Religious Fundamentalism as a Predictor of Prejudice: A Two-Component Model," *Journal for the Scientific Study of Religion* 41, no. 4 (2002): 623–635, p. 625. See also C. Daniel Batson, Patricia Schoenrade, and W. Larry Ventis, *Religion and the Individual: A Social-Psychological Perspective* (New York: Oxford University Press, 1993).

35. Robert C. Vaughn, "Transparency—The Mechanisms: Open Government and Accountability," *Issues of Democracy* 5, no. 2, August 2000, electronic journal, U.S. Department of State, http://www.usembassy.it/policy/ejournals/Files/3-de.asp.

36. Else Frenkel-Brunswik, "Intolerance of Ambiguity as an Emotional and Perceptual Personality Variable," *Journal of Personality* 18, no. 1 (1949): 108–143, p. 141.

37. Adrian Furnham and Tracy Ribchester, "Tolerance of Ambiguity: A Review of the Concept, Its Measurement and Applications," *Current Psychology* 14, no. 3 (1995): 179–200, p. 180.

38. Milton Rokeach, *The Open and Closed Mind* (New York: Basic Books, 1960), 126.

39. See, for example, Markus Kemmelmeier, "Need for Closure and Political Orientation among German University Students," *Journal of Social Psychology* 137, no. 6 (1997): 787–789; Antonio Chirumbolo, Alessandra Areni, and Gilda Sensales, "Need for Cognitive Closure and Politics: Voting, Political Attitudes and Attributional Style," *International Journal of Psychology* 39, no. 4 (2004): 245–253; Malgorzata Kossowska and Alan Van Hiel, "The Relationship between Need for Closure and Conservative Beliefs in Western and Eastern Europe," *Political Psychology* 24, no. 3 (2003): 501–518; and Jost et al., "Political Conservatism."

40. Chirumbolo, Areni, and Sensales, "Need for Cognitive Closure," 250.

41. Jost et al., "Political Conservatism," 348.

42. Arie W. Kruglanski, "A Motivated Gatekeeper of Our Minds: Need-for-Closure Effects on Interpersonal and Group Processes," in *Handbook of Motivation and Cognition: Foundations of Social Behavior*, Vol. 3, ed. E. Tory Higgins and Richard M. Sorrentino (New York: Guilford, 1996), 465–496.

43. Jost et al., "Political Conservatism," 349.

44. Jeff Greenberg, Jonathan Porteus, Linda Simon, and Tom Pyszczynski, "Evidence of a Terror Management Function of Cultural Icons: The Effects of Mortality Salience on the Inappropriate Use of Cherished

Cultural Symbols," *Personality and Social Psychology Bulletin* 21, no. 11 (1995): 1221–1228.

45. Jost et al., "Politcal Conservatism," 349.

46. Dan P. McAdams and Michelle Albaugh, "What If There Were No God? Politically Conservative and Liberal Chrisitian Imagine Their Lives without Faith," *Journal of Research in Personality* 42, no. 6 (2008): 1668–1672. McAdams and Albaugh also report that liberals fear emptiness and lack of feeling in a world without God.

47. Dean, *Conservatives without Conscience*, 57.

48. Jost et al., "Political Conservatism," 349.

49. Bob Altemeyer, *The Authoritarian Specter* (Cambridge, MA: Harvard University Press, 1996).

50. Stanley Milgram, *Obedience to Authority: An Experimental View* (New York: Harper, 1974), 6.

51. Jost et al., "Political Conservatism," 350.

52. Ibid., 351.

53. Godfrey Hodgson cleverly likened conservatism in the 1950s to a narrow stream. "Its transformation into a broad river, sweeping through wide stretches of the nation's political and social life, came about because powerful tributaries poured in from different directions. Three, in particular, brought water from distant watersheds, deep in half-forgotten hinterlands of American history." Hodgson's three tributaries correspond to the three types of conservatives described in this book: neoconservatives, traditionalist conservatives, and social, Christian, conservatives. Godfrey Hodgson, *The World Turned Right Side Up: A History of the Conservative Ascendancy in America* (Boston: Houghton Mifflin, 1996), 158.

54. See John Lukacs, *George Kennan: A Study of Character* (Binghamton, NY: Vail-Ballou, 2007).

55. This view, of course, is in opposition to other definitions of conservatism, even to definitions of traditionalist conservatism. Sullivan points out that the philosophy of doubt is distinct from relativism or nihilism, both of which are vigorously rejected by most conservatives. See Andrew Sullivan, *The Conservative Soul: How We Lost It, How to Get It Back* (New York: Harper-Collins, 2006), 173.

56. Ibid., 29.

57. Ibid., 23.

58. Barry Goldwater, *The Conscience of a Majority* (Englewood Cliffs, NJ: Prentice-Hall, 1970), Chapter 1.

59. Barry M. Goldwater (with Jack Casserly), *Goldwater* (New York: Doubleday, 1988), 121.

60. Dean, *Conservatives without Conscience*, 18.

61. Historian Donald T. Critchlow makes a case that Goldwater, along with Ronald Reagan, represented a new conservatism and that they buried the traditional, moderate Republican Party. See Donald Critchlow,

The Conservative Ascendancy: How the GOP Right Made Political History (Cambridge, MA: Harvard University Press, 2007).

62. Stephen Mihm illustrates the perils of economic freedom, for example, in the 2007–2008 meltdown of the housing market. He says the free-market credit system that supported this market was nothing new. The U.S. credit system "has often been, in effect, a confidence game writ large, relying heavily on shaky paper promises, shell games and other trickery." The U.S. economy depends on credit, and "it is by credit alone that she . . . can continue to flourish." Mihm, "Counterfeit Nation: America's Reliance on Dubious Credit Goes All the Way Back to the Country's Founding," *New York Times Magazine*, August 19, 2007, 15–16, p. 15.

63. Robert J. Donovan, *The Future of the Republican Party* (New York: New American Library, 1964), 139.

64. Robert Dallek, *Nixon and Kissinger: Partners in Power* (New York: HarperCollins, 2007), Chapter 1.

65. Ibid., Chapter 3.

66. John Patrick Diggins, "The Misunderstood Champion: Ronald Reagan's Real Legacy," *Chronicle of Higher Education*, February 2, 2007, B10–B11.

67. Jacob Heilbrunn, "Why They Fight: Two Critiques of the Bush Presidency, from the Right and from the Left," *New York Times Book Review*, March 4, 2007, 18.

68. Sean Wilentz, "Sunset in America: The End of the Age of Reagan," *The New Republic*, May 7, 2008, 24–26, p. 25.

69. Ibid., 25.

70. Diggins, "Misunderstood Champion," B11.

71. Wilentz, "Sunset in America," 24.

72. Bush, with Secretary of State James Baker, declined to intervene in Bosnia because the war did not threaten the U.S. strategic interests, "which in the conventional view meant vital resources, or strategic geography, or the safety of allies." Joshua Muravchik, "The Neoconservative Cabal," *Commentary*, September 2003, 26–33, p. 32.

73. Wilentz, "Sunset in America," 26.

74. Dean, *Conservatives without Conscience*, 78.

75. Disillusioned conservative Philip Gold has described neoconservatives as "people who fall in love with their own grandiose notions concerning America's ability to redeem the world, then get mad (or start tap dancing) when reality doesn't conform." Philip Gold, *Take Back the Right: How the Neocons and the Religious Right Have Betrayed the Conservative Movement* (New York: Carroll & Graf, 2004), 238.

76. Jacob Heilbrunn, "The Neoconservative Journey," in *Varieties of Conservatism in America*, ed. Peter Berkowitz (Stanford, CA: Hoover Institution Press, 2004), 105–128, pp. 112–113. See also Joseph Nedava, *Trotsky and the Jews* (Philadelphia: Jewish Publication Society of America, 1972).

77. Kristen L. Buras and Michael W. Apple, "Radical Disenchantments: Neoconservatives and the Disciplining of Desire in an Anti-Utopian Era," *Comparative Education* 44, No. 3 (2008): 291–304.

78. Jonathan D. Moreno and Sam Berger, "Biotechnology and the New Right: Neoconservatism's Red Menace," *The American Journal of Bioethics* 7, no. 10 (2007): 7–13.

79. Heilbrunn, "Neoconservative Journey," 111.

80. James Burnham, "Lenin's Heir," *Partisan Review* 12, no. 1 (1945): 61–72, pp. 66–67.

81. Some neoconservatives at the time, however, still believed liberals were too soft on communism. Irving Kristol wrote, "There is one thing that the American people know about Senator McCarthy: he, like them, is unequivocally anti-communist. About the spokesmen for American liberalism, they feel they know no such thing. And with some justification." Irving Kristol, " 'Civil Liberties,' 1952—A Study in Confusion," *Commentary*, March 1952, 228–236, p. 229.

82. Cited by Heilbrunn, "Neoconservative Journey," 120.

83. Buras and Apple, "Radical Disenchantments," 295. See also Ira Chernus, *Monsters to Destroy: The Neoconservative War on Terror and Sin* (Boulder, CO: Paradigm, 2006), 20–22.

84. Democratic socialist Michael Harrington used the term neoconservative in 1973 in an article in *Dissent* magazine, and the term became a rallying cry for the neoconservative agenda in later years.

85. Dallek, *Nixon and Kissinger*, xi. Dallek argues that Henry Kissinger was as responsible as Nixon for these decisions.

86. Joshua Muravchik describes the parting of ways this way: "We neocons were a small group of political thinkers who broke with fellow liberals during the war in Vietnam. Most liberals came to believe that the United States got into Vietnam because of what President Jimmy Carter later called an 'inordinate fear of communism.' By contrast, neocons held to the conviction that communism was a monstrous evil and a potent danger. For our obstinacy, we were drummed out of the liberal camp and dubbed 'neoconservatives.' " Joshua Muravchik, "The Neocons Will Ride Again," *Morning Herald* (Sydney, Australia), November 28, 2006, www.smh.com.au/news/opinion/the-neocons-will-ride-again/2006/11/27/1164476133735.html.

87. John W. Dean, *Worse than Watergate: The Secret Presidency of George W. Bush* (New York: Little Brown, 2004), 132–136.

88. Diggins, "Misunderstood Champion," B11.

89. Barton Gellman, *Angler: The Cheney Vice Presidency* (New York: Penguin, 2008).

90. Stephen Eric Bonner, "Resisting the Right: Challenging the Neoconservative Agenda," in *Confronting the New Conservatism: The Rise of the Right in America*, ed. Michael J. Thompson (New York: New York University Press, 2007), 269–283, pp. 270–271.

91. "Rebuilding America's Defenses: Strategies, Forces and Resources for a New Century" (Washington, DC: Project for the New American Century, September 2000), 61. For a more moderate view, see Anatol Lieven and John Hulsman, *Ethical Realism: A Vision for America's Role in the World* (New York: Vintage, 2006).

92. For a critique of the Bush administration's use of the preemptive strike, see Norman K. Swazo, "Primacy or World Order? The New Pax Americana," *International Journal on World Peace* 21, no. 1 (2004): 15–37.

93. Chernus, *Monsters to Destroy*, x.

94. Ibid., 26.

95. R. Claire Snyder, "Paradox or Contradiction: The Marriage Mythos in Neoconservative Ideology," in *Confronting the New Conservatism: The Rise of the Right in America*, ed. Michael J. Thompson (New York: New York University Press, 2007), 144–163, pp. 144–145.

96. Jonathan D. Moreno and Sam Berger, "Biotechnology and the New Right: Neoconservatism's Red Menace," *The American Journal of Bioethics* 7, no. 10 (2007): 7–13, p. 8.

97. Adam Wolfson, "Why Conservatives Care about Biotechnology," *New Atlantis*, Summer 2003, 55–64, p. 59.

98. Christian Smith, *Christian America? What Evangelicals Really Want* (Berkeley: University of California Press, 2000), 13.

99. The Court went against public opinion with its *Engel* rulings. A 1964 survey by the National Opinion Research Center-General Social Surveys "showed that 83 percent of the respondents favored allowing prayers to be said in public schools." See Mariana Servín-González and Oscar Torres Reyna, "The Polls-Trends: Religion and Politics," *Public Opinion Quarterly* 63, no. 4 (1999): 592–621, p. 598.

100. Sam Tanenhaus, "Down, But Maybe Not Out," *New York Times*, May 20, 2007, Week in Review-1, 14, p. 14.

101. Ibid., 14.

102. Naomi Klein, *The Shock Doctrine: The Rise of Disaster Capitalism* (New York: Metropolitan, 2007).

103. David D. Kirkpatrick and Jason DeParle, "For Conservatives, It's Back to Basics," *New York Times*, Week in Review-1, 4, p. 1.

104. Dimitri K. Simes, "America's Imperial Dilemma," *Foreign Affairs*, November/December 2003, 91–96, 97–102, pp. 97, 100.

105. Jeff Flake, "GOP Must Show Courage on Earmark Reform," *Human Events*, June 23, 2008, 11, 14.

106. See comments by Eric Cantor (R-Virginia) and Jeb Hensarling (R-Texas) in George F. Will, "Rejecting Bailout Was Easy, But Not Necessarily Wrong," *Houston Chronicle*, October 2, 2008, B11.

107. Richard A. Viguerie, *Conservatives Betrayed: How George W. Bush and Other Big Government Republicans Hijacked the Conservative Cause* (Los Angeles: Bonus Books, 2006), xx.

108. David Brooks, "Why Modern Conservatism Is Now a Thing of the Past," *Houston Chronicle*, October 11, 2008, B9.

109. The New American Empire has generated a small library of publications. Some are supportive—such as Robert Kagan's *Of Paradise and Power: America and Europe in the New World Order* (New York: Knopf, 2003). Many more—such as Chalmers Johnson's *The Sorrows of Empire: Militarism, Secrecy, and the End of the Republic* (New York: Metropolitan, 2004)—are not. Like the New World Order in postcolonial studies, the New American Empire tends to foreshadow studies of earlier empires, such as John Darwin, *After Tamerlane. The Global History of Empire since 1405* (London: Bloomsbury, 2008).

110. Charlie Savage, *Takeover: The Return of the Imperial Presidency and the Subversion of American Democracy* (New York: Little, Brown, 2007). On presidential executive power, see also Frederick A. O. Schwarz Jr. and Aziz Z. Huq, *Unchecked and Unbalanced: Presidential Power in a Time of Terror* (New York: New Press, 2007).

111. Arthur M. Schlesinger Jr.'s *The Imperial Presidency* (Boston: Houghton Mifflin, 1973) went through new editions in 1989, 1998, and 2004 to cover new presidential administrations. See also Michael A. Genovese, *The Power of the American Presidency 1789–2000* (Oxford, UK: Oxford University Press, 2001); Bert A. Rockman and Richard W. Waterman, eds., *Presidential Leadership: The Vortex of Power* (New York: Oxford University Press, 2008). For a history of presidential power from the traditionalist conservative perspective, see John V. Denson, *Reassessing the Presidency: The Rise of the Executive State and the Decline of Freedom* (Auburn, AL: Mises Institute, 2001).

112. *Clinton v. City of New York*, 524 U.S. 417 (1998).

113. The story is detailed in Jonathan Mahler, "After the Imperial Presidency," *New York Times Magazine*, November 9, 2008, 42–49, 58, 60, 62, p. 45.

114. This has meant that GOP traditionalist conservatives—Mahler cites among others John Warner, Arlen Specter, and John McCain—who sought to maintain an independent stance on some policies promoted by the Bush administration were forced to vote for the neoconservative agenda or remain silent to maintain party unity. Collegial relationships between senators within the same party and between parties have also suffered because (a) they can no longer afford to relocate their families near the capital and (b) they spend about four out of seven days of the week in fund-raising activities (or with their families) in their home states. Andrew J. Bacevich—a retired army officer whom Robert Kaiser calls a "self-described" Catholic conservative "with a reputation as one of the leading intellectuals in our armed services"—arrives at the same point with regard to Congress. "No one today seriously believes that the actions of the legislative branch are informed by a collective determination to promote the common good," Bacevish says. "The chief . . . function of Congress is to ensure the re-election of its members." See Robert G. Kaiser,

"American Hubris," *Houston Chronicle*, September 7, 2008, reviewing Bacevich's *The Limits of Power: The End of American Exceptionalism* (New York: Metropolitan, 2008), Book Reviews-13, 16, p. 13.

115. Mahler, "After the Imperial Presidency," 60.

116. Ibid., 62.

CHAPTER 4

The Constitution and Civil Religion: Obstacles to Christian Conservatives

Pope Urban II launched in 1095 the first of eight major crusades to free Christians in the Holy Land from Muslim rule and to help Byzantine emperor Alexios I Komnenos save his empire from the Seljuk Turks. Urban's political actions, taken during an era in which church and state typically were inseparable, resulted in the eastward migration of thousands of European peasants and knights, who murdered and raped the local inhabitants who got in their way. These Western crusaders—most of whom joined the crusade for religious reasons and did not accumulate great wealth—seized lands and created new states as they marched toward Jerusalem, which they captured in 1099.[1]

It almost certainly did not occur to Pope Urban (1042–1099) to question whether a powerful religious/political leader should use his position to effect political, social, and religious change—change that resulted in considerable misery and injustice—for that was the norm in premodern Christian Europe. Church and state officials sometimes formed uneasy alliances to govern, and individuals sometimes filled church and public offices simultaneously. State policy typically reflected religious beliefs, and religious principles sometimes were "adjusted" to support state policy.

Church/state relations began to change in early-modern Christian Europe as philosophers such as John Locke challenged the unity of government and religion. Locke, writing in the seventeenth century, argued that power should be limited and shared, and those who held power should be able to relinquish it peacefully and without fear of retaliation: "In order to escape the destructive passions of messianic faith, political theology centered on God was replaced by political philosophy centered on man. This was the Great Separation," as Mark Lilla, humanities professor at Columbia University, put it.[2] This separation led inevitably to questions about the proper functions of formal religious denominations and governments and to the rise of what some scholars call an informal "civil religion"—a phrase first used by Jean-Jacques Rousseau in *The Social Contract* (1762).[3]

Civil religion has been debated for centuries, sometimes under that name and sometimes not. It has been called folk religion, public religion, public philosophy, religious nationalism, public theology, civic piety, political religion, transcendent universal religion, civic faith, and democratic faith.[4] Civil religion in America often was portrayed by the mid-1960s as a set of myths, beliefs, historical narratives, symbols, rituals—the classic example being the Pledge of Allegiance—and some idea of a moral order in which everyone participates and that unites individuals within a political group and helps stabilize and legitimize the group and its leadership.[5]

American civil religion today typically is deemed neither Christian nor sectarian, but it does reflect the shared values of society—and the view in America that groups and individuals are charged with carrying out the will of a transcendent authority.[6] Civil religion serves society by imposing moral obligations on its citizens and by providing "a religious sanction for the political order and a divine justification of and support for civic society and a nation's practices."[7] Civil religion was debated with new urgency during the administration of George W. Bush, who reportedly claimed he is a messenger of God. Bush, aided by a legion of conservative followers, tried to manipulate civil religion to achieve his political/religious goals—even as some of his actions were constrained by civil religion.

The forces that ultimately led to the separation of powers between civil authorities (first monarchs and then elected leaders) and religious authorities produced a revolutionary change in the rule of law. Democratic societies invested in civil authorities—typically in a judicial branch separate from executive and legislative branches—the power to make and interpret law and to adjudicate legal disputes. The ultimate legal authority in the United States today is the U.S. Supreme Court, a body that occasionally thwarts the aspirations of civil and religious leaders alike.

Pope Urban did not have to contend with a court that could order him to change a policy or to worry that violating the tenets of a civil religion could help galvanize critics to oppose his actions. But twenty-first century religious and government leaders in America must act in an environment filled with pressures that may keep them from attaining their goals, particularly when decisions have religious overtones. This chapter describes two sources of pressure—civil religion in Section 1 and the U.S. Supreme Court in Section 2—that can make it difficult for religious and political conservatives to implement their agendas. Some of the obstacles that thwart efforts by the conservative leadership to reform the system are described in Section 3.

AMERICAN CIVIL RELIGION

Three European writers—British philosopher John Locke (1632–1704), French philosopher Jean-Jacque Rousseau (1712–1778), and French sociologist Emile Durkheim (1858–1917)—were among the first of many to question the relationship between church and state and to propose alternatives to the unified church/state model.[8] They and others laid the foundation for what came to be known as American civil religion. Locke argued that church and state should be separate, Rousseau was the first to use the term "civil religion" in describing what he saw as the proper relationship between church and state, and Durkheim argued that religion was changing and that religious attitudes were reflected in society's ceremonies.

Locke on Separation of Church and State

Teachers of U.S. government invariably introduce their students to the political theories of John Locke, whose work had a profound influence on the framers of the Constitution.[9] Locke's views often are portrayed as secular or even atheistic, modern terms that do not apply well to seventeenth-century ideas, but he was a devout Christian whose writings reflected his religious beliefs. Locke, a severe critic of Protestant and Catholic leaders and practices, initially argued that only a state church had the power to bring order to the chaos of his day. However, he later "challenged the traditions, customs, and hierarchies of the churches, as well as the right of rulers to make laws with respect to ecclesiastical matters."[10]

Locke, who ultimately advocated the separation of church and state, owed much to philosopher Thomas Hobbes (1588–1679), who suggested "it might be possible to build legitimate political institutions without grounding them on divine revelation."[11] But Locke's tolerance was limited. It did not extend to atheists because he believed their lack of belief threatened the bonds of society and undermined religion. Furthermore, atheists could not be good citizens because their views were antithetical to his belief that government's role is simply to make it possible for men and women to find God.[12]

Locke's views were not tolerated because he rejected the assumption of the powerful that *they* could and should interpret and impose God's will as they saw fit. He argued, for example, that leaders of any church must show proof that Christ himself imposed a given law (or edict) on the church. "And let not any think me impertinent, if, in a thing of this consequence, I require that the terms of that edict be very express and positive. For the promise that he [Christ] has made us, that 'wheresoever two or three are gathered together in his name, he will be in the midst of them' (Matthew 18:20) seems to imply the contrary."[13]

Locke argued that it is each individual's duty to act according to his or her own conscience without being coerced by church or state[14] and that the individual is more likely than civil or religious officials to know what pleases God and what does not.[15] The individual is more likely to know the will of God because "church and state often are motivated by factors other than the care of souls. Each wishes to increase its stature and power and, thus, the one serves to corrupt the other in the performance of its duties to its constituents."[16] It is no surprise that Locke rejected orthodoxies and creeds that prescribed only one path to salvation.

Locke helped establish the foundation for one definition of what later would be called civil religion, a definition that is reflected in large part in the U.S. Constitution.[17] Natural law (derived from God) demands that all men and women must be equal and free, he said, and it is the duty of government to ensure that all men and women enjoy liberty and that they do not interfere with the liberty of others. Freedom of religion is central to this view of liberty. "Accordingly, rather than civil authorities using coercive power to enforce religious *doctrine*, they are to use their power to preserve the greater probability of authentic religious *conviction*" (italics in the original), Locke argued. "They are to ensure each individual's maximum chance to find his or her way to God by keeping individual conscience free."[18]

Locke would exclude coercion, but not persuasion, as individuals try to steer others along the path to salvation.[19] Civil authorities should guarantee tolerance for all views, but religious leaders should have no authority over government. In fact, "ecclesiastical authority over the salvation of souls extends only to the enforcement of church rules in its own congregation," Barbara A. McGraw, professor of social ethics and law, writes. "Its only legitimate instrument of punishment is excommunication: and this extends only to removing the violator of such rules from the group. It cannot result in the loss of any civil rights."[20]

Rousseau on Government-Imposed Religion

Jean-Jacques Rousseau argued that the separation of state and church—and he meant Christianity—weakened the nation-state.[21] This separation instilled in Christians a dual allegiance: one to God and one to the state. It "brought about the internal divisions which have never ceased to trouble Christian peoples. This double power and conflict of jurisdiction have made all good polity impossible in Christian States," Rousseau argued, "and men have never succeeded in finding out whether they were bound to obey the master or the priest."[22]

Rousseau hit upon civil religion as a way around this conundrum, but his definition of civil religion was quite different from that of most subsequent moral and political philosophers. "No state has ever been founded without a religious basis," Rousseau said. A commitment to moral principles, not force, legitimizes the state, and social stability must be achieved through adherence to a civic creed. This civic creed must reflect the will of the people, Rousseau said. It must be developed and imposed by the state, not as religious dogma, but as "social sentiments without which a man cannot be a good citizen or a faithful subject."[23] Like Locke, Rousseau was convinced that everyone must believe in God, for a belief that good is rewarded and evil is punished contributes to the common good.[24]

Rousseau also argued that the state and its citizens must tolerate all religions that tolerate other religions, "so long as their dogmas contain nothing contrary to the duties of citizenship. But whoever dares to say, 'Outside the Church is no salvation,' ought to be driven from the State [or killed], unless the State is the Church, and the prince the pontiff. Such a dogma is good only in a theocratic government; in any other, it is fatal." The public creed

ought to be few, simple, and exactly worded, without explanation or commentary. The existence of a mighty, intelligent, and beneficent Divinity, possessed of foresight and providence, the life to come, the happiness of the just, the punishment of the wicked, the sanctity of the social contract and the laws: these are its positive dogmas. Its negative dogmas I would confine to one, intolerance, which is a part of the cults we have rejected.[25]

Rousseau's argument that the state must impose a civil religion, and drive out or kill those who disagree with its sentiments, has generally been ignored by subsequent writers. Indeed, this aspect of his civil religion has been called "a source of embarrassment for those who otherwise admire Rousseau."[26] Nevertheless, Rousseau's other points—that a widespread belief in religion can help assure social stability and that a civil religion can help ensure widespread belief—have been influential.

Durkheim on Ceremonies of Affirmation

Emile Durkheim often is cited by those who write about civil religion, but he never used the term. Durkheim argued, with Locke and Rousseau, that religion, a critical force for social integration, ensures the preeminence of values and beliefs that ensure social stability and solidarity.[27] Individuals who form a group or society will have a common faith or religion to unite them, and they will periodically profess their faith together. Indeed, he said, there "can be no society that does not experience the need at regular intervals to maintain and strengthen the collective feelings and ideas that provide its coherence and its distinct individuality."[28]

Locke and Rousseau saw religion as (a) a permanent part of the social fabric of any society, (b) critical to the integration, stabilization, and preservation of a society, and (c) essentially unchanging. Durkheim agreed that religion is permanent and critical to maintaining social order, but he did not see religion as unchanging. Sacred rites in premodern and modern societies perform the same functions, to maintain order by uniting individuals around common values. "What basic difference is there," Durkheim asked, "between Christians' celebrating the principal dates of Christ's life, Jews' celebrating the exodus from Egypt or . . . a citizens' meeting commemorating the advent of a new moral charter or some other great event of national life?"[29]

Perceptions of the sacred change, however, as societies lose continuity with the past and the sense of community, a societal phase that Durkheim called moral mediocrity. Modern men and women celebrate together and become "conscious of their moral unity," just as premodern men and women did,[30] but their sacred attachments might be quite different, as sociologist Robert Wuthnow argues. For a modern woman, a sense of the sacred might be attached to a flag, a monument, or a song. For a premodern man, this sense might be attached to a rock or an animal.[31] The sense of the sacred endures, however, even as memories of specific religious icons, values, attitudes, and practices fade.

Durkheim seemed to agree with John Locke, and to an extent with Jean-Jacques Rousseau, that religious ideals, or a sense of the sacred, are matters best left to the individual, although Durkheim even more than the others would not coerce belief. Civil religion is not imposed by the state, as Rousseau would have it, but is a social force that acts on each individual. "Civil religion springs from society itself and is carried on every time the group meets and celebrates together. Social representations, values, beliefs, ingrained in the collective mind, are carried from generation to generation."[32] For Durkheim, civil religion seemed to be one of self-definition—there was no overarching definition of the term.

Bellah on Civil Religion

The existence and possible role of civil religion were debated, sometimes heatedly, following publication of ideas such as those of Locke, Rousseau, and Durkheim. But the debate was neither intense nor focused in America until sociologist Robert Bellah defined the term in his 1967 article, "Civil Religion in America." Bellah argued that individual religious worship and belief are private, but that "there are, at the same time, certain common elements of religious orientation that the great majority of Americans share." These elements have been critical to the nation's development and they "provide a religious dimension for the whole fabric of American life, including the political sphere."[33]

Bellah cited speeches and writings of the founding fathers and of presidents John F. Kennedy and Lyndon B. Johnson to demonstrate the existence and importance of civil religion. Bellah argues that the following excerpts from Kennedy's inaugural address—the first sentences and the last—reflect American civil religion:

We observe today not a victory of party but a celebration of freedom—symbolizing an end as well as a beginning—signifying renewal as well as change. For I have sworn to you and Almighty God the same solemn oath our forebears prescribed nearly a century and three quarters ago . . . .

> With a good conscience our only sure reward, with history the final judge of our deeds, let us go forth to lead the land we love, asking His blessing and His help, but knowing that here on earth God's work must truly be our own.[34]

Kennedy's address suggests he recognized that religion in public life "not only provides a grounding for the rights of man which makes any form of political absolutism illegitimate, it also provides a transcendent goal for the political process." The complete address, Bellah argues, can be understood as the "statement of a theme that lies very deep in the American tradition, namely the obligation, both collective and individual, to carry out God's will on earth."[35]

Subsequent research—such as that of Cynthia Toolin, an expert in dogmatic and moral theology—has provided further evidence of an American civil religion. Toolin's analysis of inaugural addresses from 1789 to 1981 suggested that most messages referred to a deity of some sort, cited such virtues as freedom and duty, and contained religious content, "not only in the form of a Judeo-Christian tradition but also in a unique American tradition that recalls the Constitution, the Revolution, and George Washington as parts of a mighty past or golden age."[36]

A president, by invoking God and other elements of civil religion in inaugural addresses and other messages, serves as "the nation's principal preacher and chief pastor," as Gary Scott Smith—author of *Faith and the Presidency* (2006)—puts it. Presidents long "have employed civil religion to unite Americans and to frame and win support for specific policies."[37]

Civil religion is reflected in much more than presidential addresses, however. Katherine Meizel, an expert in ethnomusicology, argues that two patriotic songs—Lee Greenwood's "God Bless the U.S.A." and Irving Berlin's "God Bless America"—reflect "a relentless need to define Americanness in civil-religious terms."[38] During the week following 9/11, "God Bless the U.S.A." was "played 7,800 percent more frequently on the radio than it had been the preceding week," and "God Bless America" became the number one anthem in the days after 9/11.[39] The two songs "celebrate in civil-religious language the defense of [the American] dream, from the early years of its presence in the national consciousness through its growing worldwide distribution."[40] American civil religion also is apparent in cultural activities such as baseball.[41]

Advocates typically claim that civil religion (a) reflects the beliefs and values of the whole of society, not simply those of a single group, (b) gives Americans a shared sense of "who we are," and unites diverse groups and individuals as they decide which national objectives to achieve and how best to achieve them, (c) legitimizes government and the social order, and (d) springs spontaneously from the people and is not imposed from above by government. Most definitions of civil religion today consist of three primary principles:

- Neither the federal nor state governments are absolute unto themselves, but are subject to a transcendent authority, which Bellah calls God. "In American political theory," he said, "sovereignty rests, of course, with the people, but implicitly, and often explicitly, the ultimate sovereignty has been attributed to God."[42] This God is a bit "on the austere side, much more related to order, law, and right than to salvation and love."[43] American civil religion assumes a life after death, that "bad" will be punished and "good" will be rewarded, and that religious intolerance is intolerable.

- Americans have been blessed by this transcendent authority, making them a special people who will prosper if they are virtuous. The definition of "virtuous," however, is contested terrain. Many Americans reject the idea that this nation is unique in God's eyes, but they do believe that Americans should work for international peace and justice, and against poverty and hunger. Many Christian conservatives argue that the United States is an instrument of God in evangelizing the world, while still others argue that Americans are God's instrument in spreading democracy and the principles of capitalism. All these views are linked in some way or another to a darker theme in American history—the theme of manifest destiny, "which has been used to legitimate several adventures in imperialism since the early-nineteenth century."[44]

- American civil religion also is reflected in numerous ceremonies and symbols that have been handed down over the generations. The flag and the Declaration of Independence are two of the most compelling symbols of American civil religion. Well-known ceremonies include pledging allegiance to the flag, the inauguration or funeral of a president, and the observance of Memorial Day. Such ceremonies help to unite societies around common values and goals, to maintain order and stability, and to reaffirm a collective identity.[45] Some of the symbols of national solidarity are shown in Table 4.1.

Christianity and Civil Religion

Civil religion, as defined by Bellah, is not antithetical to Christianity, but it is not sectarian and it is not Christian. Civil religion in theory is independent of any formal church, in part because its "conception of God

Table 4.1.   Some Symbols of National Solidarity

Ceremonies	Holidays
Funeral for a head of state	*Martin Luther King Day (1986)*
Inauguration of a head of state	*Flag Day (1916)*
Pledge of Allegiance (1892, first recited in public schools) "Under God" inserted (1954)	*Decoration Day (1868) Memorial Day replaced Decoration Day (1967)*
Voting	*Independence Day (1776)*
Legislative prayers	*Christmas (federal holiday 1879)*
U.S. Supreme Court prayer	*Thanksgiving (1621)* .
Documents	*Easter*
Constitution	*Presidents' Day (created in 1880 to honor George Washington)*
Declaration of Independence	
Gettysburg Address	Locations
Bill of Rights	*White House*
Songs	*Arlington National Cemetery*
"God Bless America"	*Supreme Court Building*
"God Bless the U.S.A."	*U.S. Capitol*
"America the Beautiful"	*Lincoln, Jefferson Memorials*
"Star-Spangled Banner"	*War memorials*
"Battle Hymn of the Republic"	*Washington Monument*
	Independence Hall
	Gettysburg National Military Park

is unique and does not follow the doctrine of any particular religious group." Civil religion today is not concerned with the elements of a traditional religion: "Civil religion has no theology of the person, no view of creation, no eschatology, no ecclesiology, no single creed."[46]

Civil religion and formal Christianity, in fact, serve different functions. A primary function of civil religion is to "generate powerful symbols of national solidarity and to encourage Americans to achieve national aspirations and goals."[47] This means in practice that civil religion theoretically overrides the conflicting values and beliefs one finds in a modern, multicultural society with many faith traditions.

Civil religion, though firmly embedded in the American psyche, is not wholly *static*, for civil religion may condone a practice in one period but not in another. Bellah cites the Civil War, one of the bloodiest of the nineteenth century, as one of two watersheds in the evolution of civil religion.[48] Prior to the Civil War, only white Americans were unique in God's world. African Americans and other minorities, particularly in the South, were excluded from this vision. In the years leading up to the Civil War, powerful forces—including religious and secular groups, and the state—began contesting the fundamental assumption of civil religion that nonwhites could be excluded from the American dream.

Abraham Lincoln was bound to preserve the union, but he also was determined to abolish slavery. An important step was to change the meaning of American civil religion, which had tolerated, or even condoned, slavery. Protestant churches played key roles in this changing discourse, because in 1860 America was an overwhelmingly Protestant Christian nation, and most of its church bodies originated as denominations in Britain.[49] Philadelphia Quakers, who were among the first to challenge publicly the widespread acceptance of slavery, were widely criticized by secular and religious groups when they sent to the first Congress a petition demanding abolition. But abolition ultimately became a divisive issue in other denominations, and many split along pro- and antislavery lines. The schisms were to last until well into the twentieth century.[50]

Most white churches and leaders in the Southern Baptist Convention, the dominant church of the South, condoned slavery before the Civil War, citing the Bible in defense of the practice. Many had earlier converted black slaves to Christianity and used scripture to educate them. "But the enormous conversion of slaves and former slaves to Christianity did not prevent Southern religious leaders from defending that inhuman institution in religious terms." They combined their defense of Southern state's rights with a defense of "Southern culture and religious faith."[51]

Most of the Southern Baptist Convention's black churches and leaders opposed the Convention's stance. Frederick Douglass (1818–1895), Henry Highland Garnet (1815–1882), Theodore N. Wright (1797–1847), Samuel E. Cornish (1795–1858), and many other black ministers had participated in the National Negro Convention Movement, begun in 1831. "[I]t was within those ranks that competing tactics for achieving liberation were debated, embraced, or rejected," as sociologist Mary R. Sawyer put it. "Moral persuasion endured as a trademark of the Black Church, but increasingly enfranchisement was embraced as the true road to freedom, a posture that was forcefully argued in theological terms."[52]

Americans in the North largely accepted civil religion's new position on slavery following the Civil War. They recognized and accepted the Declaration of Independence's promise of the American right to life, liberty, and the pursuit of happiness. Many Southerners, however, refused to recognize these rights and they created in the 1870s and 1880s a racist, exclusivist culture that dominated Southern civil religion for nearly 100 years. African Americans who were freed by the Emancipation Proclamation continued to serve as "a lower-caste group working under explicit or implicit Jim Crow policies, with little opportunity to gain educational or financial resources."[53]

Many Southerners tried to mobilize the population to reject this racism. Whites such as William J. Northen (1835–1913) and E. G. Murphy of Georgia fought lynching along with the Association of Southern Women for the Prevention of Lynching, a largely Methodist group. African Americans agitated for racial equality through organizations such as the Women's Auxiliary of the National Baptist Convention, the Highlander Folk School, the Commission on Interracial Cooperation, the Fellowship of Southern Churchmen, and the Southern Conference for Human Welfare.[54]

Black and white civil rights leaders joined the fight for equality following World War II.[55] One of the biggest victories in the battle was passage of the Voting Rights Act of 1965, which Bellah cites as but one example of the way in which civil religion can be used to mobilize Americans to achieve national goals.[56] President Lyndon B. Johnson appealed for a fundamental change in American civil religion when he asked Congress to pass the measure: "God will not favor everything that we do. It is rather our duty to divine His will. But I cannot help believing that He truly understands and that He really favors the undertaking that we begin here tonight."[57]

Criticism of American Civil Religion

The evidence that a civil religion even exists is inconsistent and contradictory, critics argue, and it is difficult to demonstrate the ways in which civil religion is reflected in contemporary life. An example of the difficulty lies in the analyses of the religious views of the founding fathers and, more important, what they thought the proper relationship should be between government and religion. Those who argue that the founders believed religion and government should be forever separated note that religion is mentioned in only two places in the

Constitution, and these provisions seem to mandate a separation between church and state affairs.

Many of the same founding fathers, however, supported measures—both before and after the Constitutional Convention—that merged religious customs and practices with civil affairs. Many voted for Congress and the Continental Army to have official chaplains and services, for example, and called in June 1775 for a day of fasting and prayer, urging Americans to take the day off from work and to engage in public worship. "In observance of this fast day, Congress attended an Anglican service in the morning and a Presbyterian service in the afternoon."[58]

They passed in 1787 the Northwest Ordinance, which provided for the governance of the lands beyond the Ohio River, in part "to advance 'religion and morality.'" President George Washington signed in 1789 a proclamation creating a day of Thanksgiving and prayer, a day that has been celebrated for more than 200 years. The proclamation was a response to a resolution passed by the House of Representatives, which stated, among other things: "We acknowledge with grateful hearts the many signal favors of Almighty God, especially by affording them an opportunity peacefully to establish a constitutional government for their safety and happiness."[59]

Because so little is known about the founders' intentions, all sorts of ideas and motives are attributed to them. Scholars know, for instance, that Thomas Jefferson apparently thought government must be conducted according to moral precepts, but "religious and political disputes are a sign of faulty thinking and should therefore be mostly ignored."[60] This sentiment was expressed in the 2007–2008 primary debates in which Republican and Democratic candidates claimed their faith influenced their views, but "their religious views would not be imposed on anyone."[61]

Part of the contradiction may be traced to the value civil religion places on dissent, even against its own principles. Scholars have lamented the changing nature and difficulty of defining American civil religion, but this is because civil religion tends to reflect the changing nature of American cultural norms: it is always contested terrain, because some part of civil religion "will be objectionable to one group or another."[62]

Sociologists Stephen A. Kent and James V. Spickard even suggest the possibility of competing or alternative civil religions. Their example is the "other" civil religion of non-predestinarian Quakerism, which was "a civil religion that questioned the role of educational, social, and political institutions and their leaders in carrying out God's purposes. Its civil calling emphasized spontaneous charity and a gloom about any lasting good that institutions by themselves can bring."[63]

The meaning of American civil religion has long been contested. Some religious conservatives, for example, have attempted to position the traditional heterosexual family unit as the starting point for a good society and to sell the idea that individual freedom depends on the individual's ability to generate capital in a free-market economy. This view is contested by many Americans, including those Roman Catholics who are "suspicious of an unregulated economy" and "would not look at the human person in terms of capital accumulation and free exchange."[64]

A different view, popularized by some mainstream Protestants and Catholics, embraces the "prophetic voice" of all faith traditions "and others of good will," who believe any concept of civil society must include ideals of social justice and dialogue among competing groups. This view is also contested by those who regard a dialogue with religious fundamentalists—on the assumption that "theological divisions can be pragmatically dissolved in order that social justice can be achieved"—as naïve.[65]

A recurring criticism of American civil religion is that it does not always take a noble form. Communication and government scholar Roderick P. Hart, for example, noted a generation ago that "a type of ideological imperialism, a demand for a set of public symbols which will suffice for all Americans," is implicit in Bellah's civil religion.[66] Furthermore, says religion professor Conrad Cherry, "civil religion, like any religion which enjoys the fruits of its culture, is always more than a little inclined to sanction blindly dominant cultural values and cover national vices with a pious façade."[67]

One of the dominant values that civil religion seemingly has sanctioned blindly is American moralism and exceptionalism. The view that Americans are exceptional (or better than non-Americans) is grounded in several traits, including individualism, populism, antielitism, lack of respect for authority, concern for civil liberties and the rights of the accused, patriotism, the need to achieve, and intense religious fervor. Political sociologist Seymour Martin Lipset (1922–2006) describes the negative implications of these traits, which are reflected to a greater or lesser degree in American civil religion:

> The lack of respect for authority, anti-elitism, and populism contribute
> to higher crime rates, school indiscipline, and low electoral turnouts.

The emphasis on achievement, on meritocracy, is also tied to higher levels of deviant behavior and less support for the underprivileged. Intense religiosity is linked to less reliance on contraception in premarital sexual relationships by young people . . . . The stress on individualism both weakens social control mechanisms, which rely on strong ties to groups, and facilitates diverse forms of deviant behavior.[68]

Some critics question whether civil religion can serve as an integrative force. Civil religion's "values and its ritual manifestations may be meaningful only to certain segments of the population, or they may benefit certain groups at the expense of others."[69] Worse, some leaders may try to use civil religion to generate support for or opposition to potential decisions and actions. It is weakened when "the state itself departs from the standards of civil religion, while continuing to invoke its symbols," leaving individuals "caught in a 'double-bind' between dissent and disloyalty."[70] Civil religion loses its power to integrate, and its symbols are tarnished, when the state uses those symbols to mask political and economic excesses.

Those who supported slavery before the Civil War, for example, ultimately were forced to reject the principle of equality embedded in the Declaration of Independence and the Constitution—two of the most enduring symbols of American civil religion. More recently, as Bellah suggested, "an American-Legion type of ideology that fuses God, country, and flag has been used to attack non-conformist and liberal ideas and groups of all kinds."[71]

Scholars have given this aspect of American civil religion too little attention, sociologist Marcela Cristi argues. They always mention Rousseau because he first used the term civil religion, but they have largely ignored the dark side of his argument: that civil religion should be independent of organized religion and articulated and controlled by the state: "the Rousseauan version is fundamental to an understanding of why civil religion may be consciously used in democratic societies for political ends." Cristi worries that civil religion can be manipulated—that it can become an *imposed*, rather than a *spontaneous*, force in society, and that it can evolve from a civil to a political religion.[72]

The trend toward globalization makes it increasingly feasible for government and corporations to impose on other cultures the values reflected in American civil religion, particularly in light of the "increasing consolidation of the international entertainment industry and the supremacy of a very few, very powerful corporations,"

Katherine Meizel observes. Shows such as *American Idol*, with their patriotic themes and representations of American values, help create a desire to participate in the American Dream among peoples who live far beyond America's shores.[73]

We assume in this book the existence of an American civil religion—defined as the historical narratives, symbols, values, myths, beliefs, and rituals (religious and secular) that loosely bind Americans and that help society maintain stability. American civil religion obviously is not static. Historic shifts are apparent in American understandings of national identity, of what is virtuous and what is not, and of what institutions or policies are legitimate and what are not. Civil religion is subjected to all the stresses and strains one might expect in a multicultural, ethnically and religiously diverse, and even chaotic society. It is one of three primary forces—the others being government (including the courts) and formal faith groups—that compete in the public square to shape the body politic.

Government and/or religious leaders may try to use civil religion for their own ends. They may try to manipulate civil religion to benefit one group at the expense of others, to legitimize questionable actions or policies in times of crisis, to coerce actions or beliefs that Americans are reluctant to accept, or to impose their own beliefs on the body politic. Civil religion is contested ground, but those who would challenge the symbols of civil religion often are thwarted by contravening forces. We are particularly interested in the primary symbol of civil religion—the Constitution—and the one force assigned to interpret its meaning for America's religious and nonreligious communities today—the Supreme Court.

RELIGION AND THE U.S. CONSTITUTION

Many contemporary American Christians, like many of the original colonists, condemn America's founders for failing to establish a thoroughly Christian state. The founding fathers sought instead to establish a government in which matters of church and state are largely separated and the individual's right to worship (or not) as he or she pleases is guaranteed. They did not create official mechanisms to facilitate the exercise of religious influence. Nor did they make it impossible to exert influence through unofficial channels, such as the mass media, demonstrations, personal and professional friendships, political action committees, and partisan publications. Indeed, they sought to protect Americans' right to exert informal influence through the First Amendment's free speech and free press guarantees.

Delegates at the Constitutional Convention in Philadelphia faced two choices concerning religion, according to constitutional historian Frank Lambert. One choice was the Massachusetts model, which would "ensure that all citizens received public religious and moral instruction deemed by many to be the cornerstone of a peaceful, law-abiding society." The second choice was the Virginia model, which refused "to grant any power whatever to the federal government concerning religion, thereby leaving religion as a voluntary pursuit of individuals and their churches."[74]

It may seem odd that the delegates even considered the Virginia model, since America was essentially a theocracy from 1630 to 1787. As Father Robert F. Drinan (1920–2007), a Catholic scholar and human rights activist, noted,

> Adherence to a religion was expected of everybody and was, in fact, even coerced. Tax exemption was granted to all religious entities, chaplains in legislatures were taken for granted, and the Protestant religion was, without hesitation, taught in the schools. In addition, the clergy were expected to have a principal role in the formation of public morality.[75]

The delegates rejected the unified church-state model, which was privileged by the civil religion of the day, in favor of the Virginia model, in part because they did not want a tyrant gaining power "by giving a popular religious group a position of favor in the eyes of the state" or future religious leaders trying "to promise political support to the regime that would grant them privileges."[76] They approved a Constitution that addresses religion only in Article VI, Clause 3, which holds that "no religious Test shall ever be required as a Qualification to any Office or public Trust under the United States." The ban was "calculated to secure religious liberty, deter religious persecution, ensure sect equality before the law, and promote institutional independence of civil government from ecclesiastical domination and interference at the federal level."[77]

The founding fathers' failure to give greater prominence to God and religion was challenged from the beginning. "Regret at the omission of any direct recognition of God or of the Christian religion in the Federal Constitution was expressed in at least five of the state conventions called to ratify the document."[78] Representatives of the Associated (Presbyterian) Church and the Reformed Presbyterian Church, for example, abstained from voting until the Constitution was amended to recognize God's sovereignty.

The Constitution was amended, although perhaps not in the way the dissenters hoped, with passage of the First Amendment, which reads in part, "Congress shall make no law respecting an establishment of religion, or prohibiting the free exercise thereof."[79] The First Amendment created (a) the establishment clause, which enjoins Congress from creating a national church or from favoring any religion, and (b) the free exercise clause, which allows citizens who do not subscribe to the views of a dominant religious group to be let alone, for "government preference accorded to religion in the public sphere is, in many other ways, unfair to minority religions and to unbelievers."[80] Both of these principles are embedded, to a greater or lesser extent, in most definitions of contemporary civil religion.

The Constitution and the First Amendment seemed to institutionalize the view that "religion was a matter best left to individual citizens and the respective state governments,"[81] in part because the founding fathers wanted to keep the federal government from interfering in state affairs. However, provisions of the Bill of Rights, including the religion guarantees, were applied to the states with passage in 1868 of the Fourteenth Amendment, section 1 of which reads in part: "No State shall make or enforce any law which shall abridge the privileges or immunities of citizens of the United States; nor shall any State deprive any person of life, liberty, or property, without due process of law; nor deny to any person within its jurisdiction the equal protection of the laws."[82] This was adopted mainly to ensure that states did not deny to former slaves the rights enjoyed by all other citizens, and "to substantially reduce state sovereignty, so that there would be no recurrence of a Southern secession from the Union."[83]

The language of the First Amendment's religion clauses pitted, from the very beginning, "separationists" against "accommodationists." It generated two critical questions that have not been resolved. "Does this mean that religion must be entirely private and free of state influence, even supportive state influence? Or does it mean that government can promote religion—but must not prefer one religion to another?"[84]

Separationists such as legal scholar John Hart Ely argue for a strict constructionist approach. They believe "judges deciding constitutional issues should confine themselves to enforcing norms that are stated or clearly implicit in the written Constitution."[85]

Accommodationists such as the late Supreme Court Justice William J. Brennan (1906–1997) believe the amended Constitution is "the lodestar for our aspirations," that the Constitution's "majestic generalities and ennobling pronouncements are both luminous and obscure. This ambiguity of course calls for interpretation, the interpretation of reader and text."[86] Furthermore, "[i]n interpreting the Constitution, one should not approach the intent of the framers as being so fixed as to prevent some measure of freedom in determining the meaning of the text."[87]

Members of the National Reform Association (NRA), organized in 1863, were among the most committed accommodationists. The NRA proposed a Constitutional amendment that would correct the founding fathers' failure to recognize the proper place of God in the government. Its manifesto follows:

> The objects of this society shall be to maintain existing Christian features in the American government; to promote needed reforms in the action of the government touching the Sabbath, the institution of the family, the religious element in education, the oath, and public morality, as affected by the liquor traffic and other kindred evils; and to secure such an amendment to the Constitution of the United States as will declare the nation's allegiance to Jesus Christ, and its acceptance of the morals of the Christian religion, and to indicate that this is a Christian nation, and place all the Christian laws, institutions, and usages of our government on an undeniable legal basis in the fundamental law of the land.[88]

Though supported by a committed and vocal minority, neither the NRA's proposal nor similar proposals gained sufficient support in Congress or in the White House to gain approval. These setbacks, however, did not mean that accommodationists would withdraw from the struggle to unite church and state.

The Supreme Court and the Religion Guarantees

The U.S. Supreme Court began trying in 1878 to clarify ambiguities raised by the First Amendment's obscure language about the church-state relationship. The Court, which seemed to view the free exercise and establishment clauses as a cohesive unit until roughly the mid-twentieth century, sought to preserve individual religious freedom by maintaining the separation of church and state. "It set up a regime in which religious exercise and religious institutions were on their own," as First Amendment scholar Randall P. Bezanson put it, "unable to seek government financial or other assistance."[89] Religious denominations, of course, were then free to develop as they would without federal government influence or interference.

Faith groups did face state influence, regulation, or interference until the Supreme Court made it clear in a series of rulings beginning in 1925 that the states were bound by the First Amendment. Justices heard the case of New York socialist Benjamin Gitlow, who was indicted for printing a pamphlet calling for government overthrow. The court ruled in *Gitlow v. New York* (1925) that the right to free speech and free press is protected from state regulation under the due process clause of the Fourteenth Amendment.[90]

The Court extended the First Amendment's religion protections to citizens in each of the 50 states in *Cantwell v. Connecticut* (1940).[91] Newton Cantwell, a Jehovah's Witness, ran afoul of a Connecticut law forcing religious groups to get a license before launching door-to-door fund-raisers. Newton and his sons were convicted for pros-elytizing without a license in a Catholic neighborhood in New Haven.[92] The court found in *Cantwell* that the Connecticut statute, "as construed and applied to the appellants, deprives them of their liberty without due process of law in contravention of the Fourteenth Amendment." Justice Owen J. Roberts (1875–1955), writing for the Court, noted that (a) the First Amendment enjoins Congress from making laws "respecting an establishment of religion or prohibiting the free exercise thereof" and (b) the Fourteenth Amendment extended the prohibition to state legislatures.[93]

The Court interpreted the separation of church and state guarantee strictly until roughly the 1950s, when it began to permit greater latitude. This was because, according to Bezanson,

> [I]n cases involving exemption of the Old Order Amish Children from compulsory education laws, state aid in the form of textbooks, equipment, and special education services for children in religious schools—as well as cases challenging school prayer, property tax exemptions for churches, the teaching of evolution in public schools—the separationists had to defend results that appeared increasingly mean-spirited and hostile to religion and the exercise of religious liberty by individuals. To avoid such results, the "wall of separation" between church and state was made increasingly porous, ultimately riddled with exceptions that began to undermine the basic premises and principles of separation.[94]

Those who wrote dissenting opinions began to propose new views of national and Constitutional history, new definitions and interpretations of unclear words and provisions in the Constitution, and new ideas about the Constitution's religion guarantees. A thorough analysis of U.S. court decisions in religion-based cases is well beyond the scope of this book, but we offer a summary of several key cases (a) to illustrate how the Supreme Court has interpreted the religion guarantees, (b) to show how and why the Constitution's religion guarantees have become such contested ground, and (c) to suggest some implications of Supreme Court decisions for definitions of civil religion.

The Establishment Clause

The Court addressed the establishment clause in *Everson v. Board of Education* (1947), which was the first in a long series of cases that explored the relationship of religion to public education. The case was presented to the Court in 1941, when New Jersey lawmakers decided that nonprofit schools, including religion schools, could be reimbursed for the costs of hiring public buses to transport students. Ewing Township's Board of Education decided in 1942 to reimburse the parents of students riding public buses to and from public and Catholic schools. As Jesuit priest and activist Robert Drinan said, "[M]any Protestants and nonbelievers felt that even the incidental benefits of bus rides for children of church-related schools was a government benefit that violated the Establishment Clause of the First Amendment."[95]

A vice president of the New Jersey Taxpayers' Association sued the board of education, arguing the payments were unconstitutional under the First Amendment. Justice Hugo Black (1886–1971), writing for the majority, attempted to define in clear terms the meaning of the establishment clause:

> Neither a state nor the Federal Government can set up a church. Neither can pass laws which aid one religion, aid all religions, or prefer one religion over another. Neither can force nor influence a person to go to or to remain away from church against his will or force him to profess a belief or disbelief in any religion. No person can be punished for entertaining or professing religious beliefs or disbeliefs, for church attendance or non-attendance.... Neither a state nor the Federal Government can, openly or secretly, participate in the affairs of any religion organizations or groups and vice versa. In the words of Jefferson, the clause against establishment of religion by law was intended to erect "a wall of separation between Church and State."[96]

The Court ruled 5–4 that the board of education's decision did not violate the establishment clause, however, for two reasons. First, denying parochial school students reimbursement for their bus transportation could constitute discrimination based on their religious beliefs. The state, Black wrote, "cannot exclude individual Catholics ... or the members of any other faith, because of their faith, or lack of it, from receiving the benefits of public welfare legislation."[97] Second, "[t]he tax was not, in short, expenditure in support of religion or a religion, but was instead in support of student safety."[98]

Dissenting justices argued that the Court should find the reimbursement program unconstitutional because it violated the separation of church and state. The majority opinion certainly suggested that the strict separation of church and state was not as strict as earlier Court decisions had suggested.[99]

The Supreme Court's decision in *Engel v. Vitale* (1962) banning prayer in public schools created a storm of controversy that persists to this day. The case originated in public schools in New York's Nassau County, where the day began with a voluntary prayer: "Almighty God, we acknowledge our dependence on Thee, and we beg Thy blessings upon us, our parents, our teachers and our country."[100] Five parents, including Steven Engel, challenged the constitutionality of the daily prayer in a suit against the New Hyde Park School Board. The trial court did not find the prayers violated the establishment clause, and the New York appellate courts concurred.

The Supreme Court ultimately found that "by using its public school system to encourage recitation of the Regents' prayer, the State of New York has adopted a practice wholly inconsistent with the Establishment Clause."[101] It went further in subsequent cases—*Lee v. Weisman* (1992) and *Santa Fe Independent School District v. Doe* (2000)—and banned school-sponsored prayers at football games, graduation ceremonies, and other extracurricular events.[102] As legal scholar Randall P. Bezanson suggests, *Engel v. Vitale* turned out to be "the opening salvo in a series of legal challenges to other practices," such as

> moments of silence in school, prayer at the beginning of legislative sessions, religious symbols in school and in public displays during the holidays, the teaching of creation science, the posting of the Ten Commandments in courthouses, and Congress's addition in the mid-1950s ... of the phrase "under God" in the Pledge of Allegiance.[103]

The notorious Scopes Monkey Trial of 1925 had ignited a flurry of legal maneuvers intended to establish the power of a state to prohibit the teaching of scientific evolution in public schools. The Scopes case was inconclusive because it did not make it to the Supreme Court for technical reasons. Other cases did, one of which was *Epperson v. Arkansas* (1968). Susan Epperson, a biology teacher at Little Rock's Central High School, taught scientific evolution in violation of an Arkansas law that prohibited the teaching of any theory suggesting that humans ascended from lower animal forms. As we shall see in Chapter 7, Epperson, who agreed to be the test case, filed a brief challenging the law, which was largely ignored by the state's teachers.

Epperson won in the lower court but lost in the Arkansas Supreme Court, which upheld the law. The Supreme Court, in a unanimous decision written by Justice Abe Fortas (1910–1980), struck down the Arkansas law. "There is and can be no doubt that the First Amendment does not permit the State to require that teaching and learning must be tailored to the principles or prohibitions of any religious sect or dogma," Fortas wrote. The decision was widely applauded, but the opinion was also criticized, primarily because it left open the possibility that schools could teach "creation science" or, more recently, "intelligent design," so long as they were neutral and did not have a religious purpose for doing so.[104] The teaching of evolution was banned in Arkansas "precisely because, and only because, the theory contradicts certain religious views."[105]

The student government at the University of Virginia in the early 1990s did not know its decision to deny student funds to Wide Awake Productions—publisher of *Wide Awake*, a Christian evangelical, proselytizing student magazine—would lead to a Supreme Court decision. But it did.

The student government denied the $5,800 grant Wide Awake Productions sought to pay for printing costs, noting that Wide Awake was a religious group that said it "promotes or manifests" a belief in an ultimate deity or reality.[106] "Under university guidelines, such groups could not receive funding from student activities fees because such funding would violate the separation of church and state mandated by the establishment clause."[107]

Wide Awake sued, arguing that the university had denied its free speech rights. The federal district and appeals courts upheld the university's decision on grounds that the establishment clause justified the refusal to fund religious activities. The Supreme Court split 5–4.

The majority argued that *Rosenberger v. University of Virginia* (1995) was a free speech case and that the university violated Wide Awake's rights under the free speech clause. Justice Anthony Kennedy, writing for the majority, said, "The governmental program here is neutral toward religion. There is no suggestion that the University created it to advance religion or adopted some ingenious device with the purpose of aiding a religious cause."[108]

The minority opinion was written by Justice David Souter, who said, "Using public funds for the direct subsidization of preaching the word is categorically forbidden under the Establishment Clause, and if the Clause was meant to accomplish nothing else, it was meant to bar this use of public money."[109] The Court's decision did little to clarify the meaning of the establishment clause.

Free Exercise Clause

The Supreme Court's first application of the free exercise clause came in *Reynolds v. United States* (1878), in which the Court considered the case of George Reynolds, a polygamist and member of the Church of Jesus Christ of Latter-day Saints.[110] Reynolds, a Mormon convicted for bigamy, argued that his conviction should be overturned because the free exercise clause guaranteed he could practice his religion, which endorsed polygamy, as he saw fit. Writing for the Court, Chief Justice Morrison Waite (1816–1888) asked,

> Suppose one believed that human sacrifices were a necessary part of religious worship, would it be seriously contended that the civil government under which he lived could not interfere to prevent a sacrifice? Or if a wife religiously believed it was her duty to burn herself upon the funeral pile of her dead husband, would it be beyond the power of the civil government to prevent her carrying her belief into practice?[111]

The Court, citing Thomas Jefferson, ruled that "Congress was deprived of all legislative power over mere opinion, but was left free to reach [religious] actions which were in violation of social duties or subversive of good order."[112] The Court had declared that religious duty was not an acceptable defense against a criminal indictment and established the important distinction between belief (which cannot be regulated) and action (which may be).

Conscientious objectors have relied frequently on the free exercise clause in seeking exemptions from military service. "During the

1920s and 1930s, the court indicated clearly in dicta that whether to grant any exemption to objectors was a matter of legislative judgment, that the Free Exercise Clause accords no right to an exemption."[113] The Court later ruled in *United States v. Seeger* (1965) that one does not necessarily have to believe in a Supreme Being to gain conscientious objector status,[114] and it ruled in *Welsh v. United States* (1970) that one does not have to prove he has had religious training and belief to earn conscientious objector status. Religious belief was not seen as a prerequisite for granting conscientious objector status. Indeed, to protect objectors with religious beliefs and not objectors with secular beliefs would be unconstitutional.

The Court had to address in *Wisconsin v. Yoder* (1972) the potential conflict between the establishment clause and the free exercise clause, in part by defining what the Constitution meant by religious exercise.[115] The case began in 1964, when Old Order Amish families moved to Wisconsin to escape Iowa's compulsory education laws. Iowa requires education, public or private, until age 18. The Amish children typically leave school after the eighth grade, when they focus on learning Amish values or attend Amish schools in which teachers are educated only through the eighth grade. Attendance beyond the eighth grade, Amish parents believe, would jeopardize their own salvation and that of their children.[116]

As in Iowa, the Amish clashed with local officials about compulsory attendance rules, dress in gym classes, and modern curricula in higher grades. Three Amish fathers were found guilty in lower Wisconsin courts of failing to send their children to school, a decision the Wisconsin Supreme Court reversed on grounds that it violated the free exercise clause. The Supreme Court affirmed the constitutional right of the Amish to withdraw their children after eighth grade, noting that "enforcement of the State's requirement of compulsory formal education after the eighth grade would gravely endanger if not destroy the free exercise of respondents' religious beliefs."[117]

The Native American Church has long endorsed the use of peyote, a hallucinogen, as part of its religious practices. Consumption of the drug is prohibited under the Federal Controlled Substances Act of 1970, and Oregon state law prohibits the consumption of illegal drugs, even for religious purposes.

Alfred Smith ingested peyote in 1984 as part of a Native American Church religious ceremony and was fired from his job as a counselor for a private drug and alcohol treatment center in Douglas County, Oregon. Unemployment benefits for Smith and Galen Black, who was discharged for the same reason, ultimately were denied because they had been fired for misconduct. Oregon appellate courts reversed the decision on grounds that refusal to pay benefits violated the free exercise clause.[118]

The state appealed the decision to the U.S. Supreme Court. Justice Antonin Scalia, writing for the majority, noted in *Employment Division v. Smith* (1990) that Smith and Black "contend that their religious motivation for using peyote places them beyond the reach of a criminal law that is not specifically directed at their religious practice, and that is concededly constitutional as applied to those who use the drug for other reasons."[119] Smith and Black were seeking to extend the free exercise clause "one large step further," Scalia wrote. The Court reversed the Oregon appellate courts, saying the law prohibiting peyote use was constitutional. Critics claimed the decision gave the states power to regulate religious activities and rendered the free exercise clause meaningless.[120] That was not the case, as courts began to ask simply whether laws were "neutral and generally applicable," with no exceptions for religious activities.[121]

The Court essentially reaffirmed *Smith* in *Locke v. Davey* (2004). The case centered on Washington State's Promise Scholarships, which were designed to encourage talented Washingtonians to attend in-state colleges. The scholarships were available to all college students *except* those who wanted to study for the ministry. Students could use the scholarships at accredited colleges, including religious colleges, in the state, and they could use the money to pay for devotional theology courses, which are preclergy classes. However, state law required that "students may not use such a scholarship to pursue a devotional theology degree."[122]

Joshua Davey challenged the law because he wanted to use the scholarship to study for the clergy. Davey lost in the U.S. district court, but the Ninth Circuit Court of Appeals agreed that denial of the scholarship infringed on Davey's right to free exercise of religion.

The Supreme Court reversed the decision—using the neutrality test developed in *Smith*—and upheld the Washington law prohibiting the use of state money to help pay for a degree in theology. Writing for the seven justices in the majority, Chief Justice William Rehnquist (1924–2005) noted that many states, in trying to prohibit the establishment of a religion, had "placed in their constitutions formal prohibitions against using tax funds to support the ministry." But the court found no evidence of hostility toward religion in the Locke case, as the Promise Scholarship program "goes a long way toward including religion in its benefits."[123]

The opinion was regarded by legal scholars such as Bezanson as "a bit inconsistent, uncertain, and disappointing"—lacking "consistent principle" and raising more questions than answers.[124] Writing in dissent, Justice Antonin Scalia argued, "[W]hen the State withholds [any] benefit from some individuals solely on the basis of religion, it violates the Free Exercise Clause no less than if it had imposed a special tax."[125]

The Supreme Court Conundrum

The Constitution is largely silent on religion questions and religious liberty, primarily because its framers believed that the states should resolve such questions. Indeed, by the time of the Constitutional Convention, the 13 colonies already had constitutions or charters in place that dealt with religion questions. This reluctance to address religion issues has led to a good deal of confusion. A few of the issues are particularly troubling:

- The Supreme Court's view of the establishment clause is unclear, as the establishment cases summarized here suggest. Leonard W. Levy, a constitutional historian, was right when he said the Supreme Court "has managed to unite those who stand at polar opposites on the results that the Court reaches; a strict separationist and a zealous accommodationist are likely to agree that the Supreme Court would not recognize an establishment of religion if it took life and bit the Justices."[126] John Witte Jr., a specialist in religious liberty and legal history, concurs: "Few areas of law today are so riven with wild generalizations and hair-splitting distinctions, so given to grand statements of principle and petty applications of precept, so rife with selective readings of history and inventive renderings of precedent."[127]

- The free exercise clause generates somewhat less controversy than the establishment clause, but recent interpretations seem to take the Court away from the framers' intent. The Court's thinking in the early part of the twenty-first century is particularly murky in the *Smith* and *Davey* cases. The Court seems to reject the founding fathers' view (accepted by the justices in *Cantwell*) that free expression deserves special protection. The founding fathers "incorporated within this free exercise clause the principles of liberty of conscience, freedom of religious expression, religious equality and pluralism, and separation of church from the state."[128]

  The justices in *Davey* seemingly ignored these principles and "made a pragmatic judgment that the harms from discriminatory subsidy programs were unlikely to be sufficiently great to justify the costs of judicial intervention, except when the state acted on the basis of hostility to religion (or to particular religions)."[129] Critics such as John Witte argue that the Court should reconsider or overturn *Smith*.

- The definition of "religion" is central to all debates about the religion guarantees, and yet agreement about the definition has been elusive. The Court observed in *Davis v. Beason* (1890), for example, that religion "has reference to one's views of his relations to his Creator, and to the obligations they impose of reverence for his being and character, and of obedience to his will."[130] But the Court held nearly 80 years later that the religion guarantees did not necessarily apply only when a Supreme Creator is cited. The Court ruled in *United States v. Seeger* (1965) that atheists could be granted a religious conscientious objector exemption because atheism reflected an ultimate commitment that was like a religion.[131]

  This leads to questions like those posed by Julia K. Stronks, an expert on the relationship between public policy and faith: "So, does religion involve concepts like God, salvation, sin, prayer and so forth? Or, is religion any ultimate value about humanity that functions as a faith commitment (including secularism)? The difference is important because it forms the foundation of the debates that make up modern-day religious freedom disputes."[132]

- The Supreme Court has done little to reconcile competing visions of the First Amendment guarantees. In considering religion guarantee cases, the Supreme Court must grapple with some of the toughest issues in law, for the guarantees reflect "fundamentally conflicting visions: one focusing on the institutions of religion (church versus state), the other focusing on the individual (freedom of conscience in religious belief and exercise)."[133]

ENDURING TENSIONS

Many religious conservatives are outraged when the Supreme Court renders a decision that tends to thwart their social and political agendas (such as outlawing abortion and reinstating prayer in public schools). These conservatives have been thwarted so frequently, in their opinion, they consider themselves "to be in exile from the Constitution" and they view "the task of conserving the Founders' political achievement to be, in important part, a task of recovery."[134] The task is complicated by legal precedents, which are quite difficult to overcome.

Many religious conservatives work hard to help elect public officials who share their worldview and who will appoint judges who will interpret the Constitution as they think it should be interpreted. And they try to find ways to circumvent Constitutional restrictions. One way is through congressional earmarks, the process that allows lawmakers to put money into the federal budget for personal projects. Money has been earmarked for programs such as Teen Challenge, an effort by Christian conservatives to "help young people overcome substance abuse through 'the life-changing message of salvation through Jesus Christ.' "[135]

Religious conservatives may also be perplexed by some contemporary definitions of civil religion. They do not understand, for example, the opposition of so many Americans to the invasion of Iraq. War opponents argue that American civil religion precludes preventive wars of any kind, but some Christian conservatives will argue that civil religion does countenance preventive war. Others argue that civil religion may not have countenanced preventive war in the past, but new circumstances call for a redefinition: they work to change the meaning of civil religion so it will encompass a view of moral issues that is more to their liking. And they try to manipulate civil religion, as scholars such as Marcela Cristi have argued, to impose their own views on others.[136]

Some of the tensions created when the Constitution, civil religion, and Christian conservative activists intersect are addressed in this section.

Civil Religion, the Constitution, and the Pledge of Allegiance

The controversy about one of the most prominent symbols of American civil religion, the Pledge of Allegiance, illustrates the conflict that characterizes the relationship of civil religion and the Constitution to religious conservatives. The Pledge—composed in 1892 by Francis Bellamy, a Christian socialist and Baptist minister, for *The Youth's Companion*—did not mention God. Congress added the phrase "under God" in 1954.

Nearly 50 years later, a three-judge panel of the U.S. Court of Appeals for the Ninth Circuit ruled—in response to Michael Newdow's challenge against Elk Grove Unified School District's policy that a teacher must lead the class in the Pledge—that the addition of "one nation under God" violated the establishment clause. The U.S. Senate and House—responding to outraged constituents who thought the phrase was crucial to the definition of "Americanness"—voted the next day to affirm the language, including "under God," in the Pledge.[137] The circuit court's decision was appealed to the

U.S. Supreme Court in *Elk Grove Unified School District v. Newdow* (2004). The Court dodged the issue by ruling that Newdow, who brought the suit on behalf of his minor daughter, was a noncustodial parent who, therefore, had no standing before the court.[138]

To complicate matters further, a three-judge panel of the U.S. Court of Appeals for the Fourth Circuit ruled in *Myers v. Loudoun County Public Schools* (2005) that "a Virginia statute providing for daily recitation of the Pledge of Allegiance does not violate the Establishment Clause, because the addition of 'under God,' although religiously significant, does not alter the nature of the Pledge as a patriotic activity."[139] The Supreme Court ultimately will be called on to settle the matter since two circuit courts have rendered conflicting decisions, which seem based on different views of how one should view God and the Pledge:

- One view is that the addition of "under God" to the pledge makes it a religious proclamation. Justice Clarence Thomas agreed with the Ninth Circuit Court that the amended Pledge is a religious proclamation that is coercive and that violates the establishment clause.
- Another view sees the Pledge as a secular ritual that has little religious import. Ted Olson, the Bush administration's solicitor general, argued that "one nation under God" is a descriptive, not a normative, statement. The words merely acknowledge the historical fact that the nation was founded by men who believed in God.
- Still another view is that the amended Pledge falls into the category of ceremonial deism. Former Justice Sandra Day O'Connor said references to God on coins, in the national motto and song, and in the words used to open Supreme Court and legislative sessions, fall into the category of ceremonial deism and, therefore, do not violate the establishment clause.[140]

The controversy surrounding the Pledge of Allegiance suggests that continued challenges to the interpretations of religion clauses in the Constitution, coupled with a continued drift by the Supreme Court, could lead to

increased scrutiny for other forms and rituals of civil religion, such as the National Motto inscribed on our coins, the employment of legislative and military chaplains, the opening of legislative sessions with prayer, prayers at presidential inaugurations, displays of the Ten Commandments on public property, the use of the phrase 'God save the United States and this Honorable Court' at the opening of Supreme Court proceedings, the singing of certain patriotic songs in public settings, and certain national holidays (e.g. Christmas and Thanksgiving).[141]

Preservationists, Pluralists, Priests, and Prophets

Tensions also arise as individuals with differing views debate the meaning of civil religion. Those who have a "preservationist" understanding of civil religion argue that traditional symbols of civil religion must be preserved to maintain stability and cultural coherence, and to preserve Americans' sense of national identity. Preservationists, such as the late political scientist Samuel P. Huntington (1927–2008), argue that Americans must have the right to refuse "to engage in any religiously tainted practice" they dislike, but that they must accept mainstream hegemony or resign themselves to perpetual alienation.[142] "[P]reservationists are not just waxing nostalgic for a 'golden age' of unified national identity. They are also willing to use such a vision to exclude or marginalize whomever is currently regarded as the religious or cultural *Other*" (italics in the original).[143]

Americans who hold "pluralist" views reject the idea that anyone must accept a permanent state of alienation and embrace the idea of an evolving civil religion that can celebrate tolerance and respect. For Martha C. Nussbaum—a law, ethics, and religion expert—"We need a poetry of the love of free citizens, and of their noisy, chaotic, sometimes shockingly diverse lives, constructing emotions that provide essential undergirding for good laws and institutions."[144] However, if the goal of civil religion is to help retain a singular sense of purpose and identity, as it is for the preservationists, "it would be very difficult for a self-consciously pluralist civil religion to achieve such ends."[145]

Civil religion also serves what some call "priestly and prophetic functions." The priestly function of American civil religion helps to legitimize the state, its policies, and institutions by "infusing its rituals with religious rhetoric and deploying theological symbols and warrants in support of the regnant political order," religion scholars Grace Y. Kao and Jerome E. Copulsky argue. "In the specific case of the Pledge of Allegiance, then, the phrase 'under God' could be understood to mean that 'God is on our side.'" The prophetic function, however, also calls on the nation to be responsible to a higher authority, to acknowledge that the nation is not absolute. In this interpretation, "civil religion neither automatically celebrates, nor uncritically accepts, whatever the nation does, but actually makes possible quite radical political self-criticism."[146]

Civil Religion and Coalition Politics

Not all conservatives and not even all Christian conservatives adhere to a definition of civil religion that "grants America a special place in the divine order, sees the nation as God's instrument to evangelize the world, gives biblical legitimacy to capitalism, and understands the American form of government to enjoy lasting legitimacy because it was created by founding fathers ... who were deeply influenced by Judeo-Christian values."[147] Not all religious or secular conservatives in the conservative coalition support the struggle to return prayer to the public schools, to use public funds to support some religious activities, or to ensure that government actions conform to religious teachings. Many condemn these struggles as irrelevant or even harmful to the conservative movement, and some over the years have moved toward more moderate pluralist positions. Instead of seeing Americans as a chosen people, they stress human rights, peace, justice, poverty, and international interdependence.

Robert Wuthnow, a sociologist of religion, cautions against making too much of liberal/conservative religious divides. Differences often are depicted by the media as a cultural war characterized by considerable conflict and polarization, but as we saw in Chapter 2 this can be a false division that stereotypes the role of both religion and politics in American culture. According to Wuthnow,

> Religious conservatives *are* more likely than liberals to say they value their relationship with God, try to obey God, try to follow the Bible, and are guided by moral principles. But the two do not differ on the full range of values and moral orientations that are prominent in U.S. culture. Both conservatives and liberals are guided by self-interest and by what feels good, both are oriented toward their work and families, and both are deeply wedded to making money and living a comfortable life (italics in the original).[148]

Debates about constitutional guarantees of religious freedom and the meaning of civil religion in America will undoubtedly continue into the foreseeable future. The essential conflict is captured by Randall Bezanson, who asks, "Is the separation of the secular and the religious, of the realms of reason and faith, of church and state, the primary of the two religion guarantees? ... Or is the individual's liberty to exercise his or her religion the primary of the two guarantees?"[149]

NOTES

1. Thomas Asbridge, *The First Crusade: A New History* (New York: Oxford University Press, 2004).

2. Mark Lilla, "The Politics of God," *New York Times Magazine*, August 19, 2007, 28–35, 50, 54, 55, p. 33.

3. Robert N. Belah, "Civil Religion in America," *Daedalus* 96, no. 1 (1967): 1–21, p. 5.

4. Russell E. Richey and Donald G. Jones, eds., *American Civil Religion* (New York: Harper & Row, 1974), 14–18; and Marcela Cristi, *From Civil to Political Religion: The Intersection of Culture, Religion and Politics* (Waterloo, ON: Wilfrid Laurier University Press, 2001), 3.

5. Mark Lilla uses the term political theology, but it seems to refer to what he sees as a struggle by Christians, Muslims, and persons of other faith groups "to bring the whole of human life under God's authority." This is quite different from what most scholars mean by civil religion. Lilla, "The Politics of God," 30.

6. Our discussion is limited to *American* civil religion, although some scholars have tried to identify civil religion in other cultures and countries with mixed results (such as Japan, Italy, and Mexico). Western scholars do not always recognize that other cultures have political and religious values and beliefs that are unlike those in the West. Coleman, for example, suggests "in America we find almost a unique case of civil religion differentiated from both church and state." See John A. Coleman, "Civil Religion," *Sociological Analysis* 31 (1970), 67–77; Robert N. Bellah and Phillip E. Hammon, *Varieties of Civil Religion* (San Francisco: Harper & Row, 1980).

7. Gary Scott Smith, "Civil Religion in America," *Christian History & Biography*, August 8, 2008, http://www.christianitytoday.com/ch/2008/issue99/12.4.html, 3.

8. These were not the only early philosophers to discuss civil religion and the relationship of church and state. See Ronald Beiner "Machiavelli, Hobbes, and Rousseau on Civil Religion," *The Review of Politics* 55, no. 4 (1993): 617–638.

9. For example, Jerome Huyler, *Locke in America: The Moral Philosophy of the Founding Era* (Lawrence: University of Kansas Press, 1995).

10. Barbara A. McGraw, *Rediscovering America's Sacred Ground: Public Religion and Pursuit of the Good in a Pluralistic America* (Albany: State University of New York Press, 2003), 24. Locke's views were so controversial that he wrote anonymously and went into exile in Holland for six years.

11. Hobbes argued that "the new political thinking would no longer concern itself with God's politics; it would concentrate on men as believers in God and try to keep them from harming one another." Lilla, "Politics of God," 33. Hobbes' major work was *Leviathan* (1651).

12. See John Locke, *Four Letters on Toleration*, 7th reprint ed. (London: Alexander Murray, 1870) and *Political Writings of John Locke*, ed. David Wootton (London: Mentor, 1993), 426.

13. Locke, *Four Letters*, 8.

14. See John Locke, *The Reasonableness of Christianity*, ed. George W. Ewing (Washington, DC: Regnery Gateway, 1965), 155.

15. Locke wrote, for example, that "no man can so far abandon the care of his own salvation as blindly to leave it to the choice of any other, whether prince or subject, to prescribe to him what faith or worship he shall embrace. For no man can, if he would, conform his faith to the dictates of another." John Locke, *A Letter Concerning Toleration*, trans. William Popple (Raleigh, NC: Alex Catalogue, n.d.), 4 (e-book).

16. McGraw, *Rediscovering America's Sacred Ground*, 31.

17. John Locke did not use the term civil religion, although that is in fact what he was writing about in *Letter Concerning Toleration* and other writings.

18. McGraw, *Rediscovering America's Sacred Ground*, 36.

19. "Any one may employ as many exhortations and arguments as he pleases, towards the promoting of another man's salvation. But all force and compulsion are to be forborn. Nothing is to be done imperiously. No body is obliged in that matter to yield obedience unto the admonitions or injunctions of another, farther than he himself is persuaded." Locke, *Four Letters*, 27.

20. McGraw, *Rediscovering America's Sacred Ground*, 45. Locke wrote, "Excommunication neither does nor can deprive the excommunicated person of any of those civil goods that he formerly possessed. All those things belong to the civil government, and are under the magistrate's protection." Locke, *Four Letters*, 10.

21. Cristi, *From Civil to Political Religion*, 17.

22. Jean Jacques Rousseau, *The Social Contract and Discourses*, trans. G. D. H. Cole (New York: E. P. Dutton, 1950), 131–132.

23. Ibid., 133, 139.

24. Cristi, *From Civil to Political Religion*, 24.

25. Rousseau, *Social Contract*, 139, 140.

26. John B. Noone Jr., *Rousseau's Social Contract: A Conceptual Analysis* (Athens: University of Georgia Press, 1980), 6. See also *The Political Writings of Jean-Jacques Rousseau*, 2 vols, ed. Charles E. Vaughan, (Oxford, UK: Blackwell, 1962); and Alfred Cobban, *Rousseau and the Modern State*, 2nd ed. (Hamden, CT: Archon. 1964).

27. Cristi, *From Civil to Political Religion*, 32.

28. Emile Durkheim, *The Elementary Forms of Religious Life*, trans. Karen E. Fields (New York: Free Press, 1995), 429.

29. Ibid., 429.

30. Ibid., 391.

31. Robert Wuthnow, *Producing the Sacred: An Essay on Public Religion* (Urbana: University of Illinois Press, 1994), Chapter 6.

32. Cristi, *From Civil to Political Religion*, 40. See also N. J. Demerath III and Rhys H. Williams, "Civil Religion in an Uncivil Society," *Annals of the American Academy of Political and Social Science* 480, no. 1 (1985): 154–166.

33. Bellah, "American Civil Religion," 3, 4.

34. Cited in Bellah, "American Civil Religion," 21, 22.

35. Bellah, "American Civil Religion," 4, 5.

36. Cynthia Toolin, "American Civil Religion from 1789 to 1981: A Content Analysis of Presidential Inaugural Addresses," *Review of Religious Research* 25, no. 1 (1983): 39–48, p. 46.

37. Smith, "Civil Religion in America," 3–4. See also Smith's *Faith and the Presidency: From George Washington to George W. Bush* (Oxford, UK: Oxford University Press, 2006).

38. Katherine Meizel, "A Singing Citizenry: Popular Music and Civil Religion in America," *Journal for the Scientific Study of Religion* 45, no. 4 (2006): 497–503, p. 497.

39. Ibid., 500.

40. Ibid., 502.

41. Joshua Fleer, "The Church of Baseball and the U. S. Presidency," *NINE* 16, no. 1 (2007): 51–61.

42. Robert Bellah, *Beyond Belief: Essays on Religion in a Post-Traditional World* (New York: Harper & Row, 1970), 171.

43. Bellah, "American Civil Religion," 7.

44. Ibid., 14.

45. See Horst Mewes, "Religion and Politics in American Democracy," in *The Secular and the Sacred: Nation, Religion and Politics*, ed. William Safran (London: Frank Cass, 2003), 13–31.

46. Derek H. Davis, "Civil Religion as a Judicial Doctrine," *Journal of Church and State* 40, no. 1 (1998): 7–23, p. 16.

47. Cristi, *From Civil to Political Religion*, 2.

48. The other watershed was the American Revolution, "which was seen as the final act of the Exodus from the old lands across the waters. The Declaration of Independence and the Constitution were sacred scriptures and Washington the divinely appointed Moses who led his people out of the hands of tyranny." American civil religion was focused on the Revolution until the Civil War. Bellah, "American Civil Religion," 9.

49. Of the 55,000 places of worship identified in the 1860 census, only 2,550 (less than 5 percent) were Catholic and only 77 were Jewish. No Native American, Hindu, Eastern Orthodox, Buddhist, Muslim, or any other places of worship were identified. Seventy-five percent of organized religious bodies represented "the major British-origin churches: Methodist, Baptist,

Presbyterian, and Congregational." See Mark A. Knoll, "Nineteenth-Century Religion in World Context," *OAH* (Organization of American Historians) *Magazine of History*, July 2007, 51–56, p. 51.

50. Benjamin Franklin was president of the Society for Promoting the Abolition of Slavery, the name of the group under which the Quakers organized. Presbyterians split along North-South lines in 1837, Methodists in 1845, and Baptists in 1845. See Mewes, "Religion and Politics," 18.

51. Ibid., 18.

52. Mary R. Sawyer. "The Black Church and Black Politics: Models of Ministerial Activism," *Journal of Religious Thought* 52/53, nos. 2/1 (1995–96): 45–62, p. 47.

53. Seymour Martin Lipset, *American Exceptionalism: A Double-Edged Sword* (New York: W. W. Norton, 1996), 115.

54. Paul Harvey, *Freedom's Coming: Religious Culture and the Shaping of the South from the Civil War Through the Civil Rights Era* (Chapel Hill: University of North Carolina Press, 2005).

55. The list of activists included Ralph Abernathy, James Lowery, John Lewis, James Lawson, Andrew Young, Martin Luther King Jr., Jesse Jackson, and many other prominent civil rights leaders who were Christian ministers. The Southern Christian Leadership Conference sponsored rallies and marches, collected funds, distributed information—and offered prayers—in its quest to help expand the civil liberties of all Americans. Sawyer, "Black Church," 48–51.

56. Bellah, "American Civil Religion," 14.

57. Lyndon B. Johnson, "Special Message to the Congress: The American Promise," Lyndon Baines Johnson Library and Museum, University of Texas, Austin, Texas, March 15, 1965, www.lbjlib.utexas.edu/johnson/archives.hom/speeches.hom/650315.asp.

58. M. Stanton Evans, "The Custom of the Country," *The American Spectator*, March 2007, 20–24, p. 23.

59. Ibid., 24.

60. See Davis, "Civil Religion as a Judicial," p. 12. Because Jefferson stated that an individual's primary duty was to God and not to the state, some conservative critics argue that the founders did not really intend to create a wall between church and state.

61. Matt Malone, "God and Politics," *America*, December 17, 2007, 9–14, p. 14.

62. Grace Y. Kao and Jerome E. Copulsky, "The Pledge of Allegiance and the Meanings and Limits of Civil Religion," *Journal of the American Academy of Religion* 75, no. 1 (2007), 121–149, p. 141.

63. Stephen A. Kent and James V. Spickard, "The 'Other' Civil Religion and the Tradition of Radical Quaker Politics," *Journal of Church and State* 36, no. 2 (1994): 373–387, p. 381.

64. Joseph M. Palacios, "Reconfiguring American Civil Religion: The Triumph of Values," *Contemporary Sociology* 35, no. 4 (2006): 351–354,

p. 351. Palacios, a Roman Catholic sociologist, cites two books as examples of an ongoing conversation between and among theologians, scholars, and religious activists in mainstream Catholic and Protestant circles about American civil religion. Palacios contrasts the views of Rick Santorum, a conservative Catholic and former GOP senator from Pennsylvania (the author of *It Takes a Family*, published in 2005) with official Catholic social positions that take a dim view of those Catholics who would link individual personhood with a preferred economic perspective—such as unregulated capitalism. See also footnote 65.

65. Palacios also criticizes Jim Wallis, an evangelical Protestant (the author of *God's Politics*, published in 2005), who "has tacked Catholic social teaching, biblical science, and liberal social ethics onto evangelicalism without understanding how difficult or impossible it is for many evangelicals and fundamentalists to organize and analyze social issues in a systematic framework given their Bible-only intellectual world." Palacios, "Reconfiguring American Civil Religion," 353.

66. Roderick P. Hart, *The Political Pulpit* (West Lafayette, IN: Purdue University Press, 1977), 106.

67. Conrad Cherry, "American Sacred Ceremonies," in *American Mosaic: Social Patterns of Religion in the United States*, ed. Phillip E. Hammond and Benton Johnson (New York: Random House, 1970), 303–316, p. 314. Cherry argued, however, that these are not the *only* functions of American civil religion and that it performs other, positive functions.

68. Lipset, *American Exceptionalism*, 290.

69. Cristi, *From Civil to Political Religion*, 9. See also Michael W. Hughey, *Civil Religion and Moral Order: Theoretical and Historical Dimensions* (Westport, CT: Greenwood, 1983).

70. Richard K. Fenn, *Toward a Theory of Secularization* (Storrs, CT: Society for the Scientific Study of Religion, 1978), 41.

71. Bellah, "American Civil Religion," 14.

72. Cristi, *From Civil to Political Religion*, 7.

73. Meizel, "A Singing Citizenry," 502.

74. Frank Lambert, *The Founding Fathers and the Place of Religion in America* (Princeton, NJ: Princeton University Press, 2003), 249, 250.

75. Robert F. Drinan, "The Advocacy Role of Religion in American Politics," in *The Role of Religion in the Making of Public Policy*, ed. James E. Wood Jr. and Derek Davis (Waco, TX: J. M. Dawson Institute of Church-State Studies, 1991), 221–235, pp. 221–222.

76. Lambert, *Founding Fathers*, 264.

77. Daniel L. Dreisbach, "The Constitution's Forgotten Religion Clause: Reflections on the Article VI Religious Test Ban," *Journal of Church and State* 38, no. 2 (1996): 261–295, p. 262.

78. Anson Phelps Stokes, *Church and State in the United States*, Vol. 3 (New York: Harper & Brothers, 1950), 583.

79. This language was based on a draft proposed on June 8, 1789, by James Madison: "The civil rights of none shall be abridged on account of religious belief or worship, nor shall any national religion be established, nor shall the full and equal rights of conscience be in any manner, or any pretext infringed." See John Witte Jr., *Religion and the American Constitutional Experiment*, 2nd ed. (Boulder, CO: Westview, 2005), 81.

80. Davis, "Civil Religion as a Judicial."

81. Dreisbach, "The Constitution's Forgotten," 294.

82. Some constitutional scholars and historians question whether those who wrote the First Amendment and those who drafted the Fourteenth Amendment viewed the free exercise clause in the same way. Some "have contended that the framers of the Fourteenth Amendment intended that its adoption should transform all the specific limitations on federal power found in the Bill of Rights into rigid limitations on state authority." That would mean that no state could make a law after 1868 "respecting an establishment of religion, or prohibiting the exercise thereof," an interpretation Court majorities have rejected. See Mark de Wolfe Howe, "The Constitutional Question," in *Church and State in American History: Key Documents, Decisions, and Commentary from the Past Three Centuries*, 3rd ed., ed. John F. Wilson and Donald L. Drakeman (Cambridge, MA: Westview, 2003), 213–218, p. 215.

83. Derek H. Davis, "Completing the Constitution: Enforcement of the Religion Clauses Against the States under the Fourteenth Amendment," *Journal of Church and State* 42, no. 3 (2000): 433–442, p. 438.

84. See Randall P. Bezanson, *How Free Can Religion Be?* (Urbana: University of Illinois Press, 2006), 9.

85. John Hart Ely, *Democracy and Distrust: A Theory of Judicial Review* (Cambridge, MA: Harvard University Press, 1980), 1.

86. William J. Brennan, "The Great Debate: Interpreting Our Written Constitution," speech, Text and Teaching Symposium, Georgetown University, Washington, DC, October 12, 1985, www.fed-soc.org/resources/id.50/default.asp.

87. Davis, "Completing the Constitution," 437.

88. Stokes, *Church and State*, 584.

89. Bezanson, *How Free Can Religion Be?*, 4.

90. The due process clause reads as follows: "No state shall make or enforce any law which shall abridge the privileges and immunities of citizens of the United States; nor shall any State deprive any person of life, liberty, or property, without due process of law; nor deny to any person within its jurisdiction the equal protection of the laws."

91. Barbara Yarnold notes that the U.S. Supreme Court consistently upheld the First Amendment's religion clauses between 1970 and 1990, although some appellate courts did not. She attributes this not to sincere constitutional interpretation but to pressures from "anti-religion forces" and to judicial activism. See Barbara M. Yarnold, "The U.S. Supreme Court

in Religious Freedom Cases, 1970–1990: Champion to the Anti-Religion Forces," *Journal of Church and State* 40, no. 3 (1998): 661–673.

92. Wilson and Drakeman, *Church and State*, 191–193.

93. *Cantwell v. Connecticut*, 310 U.S. 296 (1940).

94. Bezanson, *How Free Can Religion Be?*, 4–5.

95. Drinan, "Advocacy Role of Religion," 224.

96. *Everson v. Board of Education*, 330 U.S. 1 (1947).

97. Ibid.

98. Bezanson, *How Free Can Religion Be?*, 37.

99. Frank S. Ravitch, *Masters of Illusion: The Supreme Court and the Religion Clauses* (New York: New York University Press, 2007), 72–74.

100. Cited in Bezanson, *How Free Can Religion Be?*, 104.

101. *Engel v. Vitale*, 370 U.S. 421 (1962).

102. *Lee v. Weisman*, 505 U.S. 577 (1992) and *Santa Fe Independent School District v. Doe*, 530 U.S. 290 (2000).

103. Bezanson, *How Free Can Religion Be?*, 106.

104. *Epperson v. Arkansas*, 393 U.S. 97 (1968). Bezanson notes that the Arkansas law could not be "defended as an act of religious neutrality.... What is important about the Court's statement ... is that it implies that if the law were 'neutral,' the constitutional questions would be different and the law might be constitutional." Bezanson, *How Free Can Religion Be?*, 101.

105. Christopher L. Eisgruber and Lawrence G. Sager, *Religious Freedom and the Constitution* (Cambridge, MA: Harvard University Press, 2007), 190.

106. *Rosenberger v. University of Virginia*, 515 U.S. 819 (1995).

107. Bezanson, *How Free Can Religion Be?*, 188.

108. *Rosenberger v. University of Virginia*, 515 U.S. 819 (1995).

109. Ibid. (Justices Stevens, Ginsburg, and Breyer joined Souter in dissent.)

110. The Court cited religious liberty in an 1871 case that did not turn on the free exercise clause. The Court found unconstitutional a Kentucky common law that pitted proslavery and antislavery members of a Presbyterian church. Kentucky courts had ruled that church property could be held in trust only if the church had departed from fundamental church doctrine. The Supreme Court found that courts must not resolve disputes about church content. *Watson v. Jones*, 80 U.S. (13 Wall.) 679 (1871).

111. *Reynolds v. United States*, 98 U.S. 145 (1878).

112. Ibid.

113. Kent Greenawalt, *Religion and the Constitution: Volume 1; Free Exercise and Fairness* (Princeton, NJ: Princeton University Press, 2006), 59. See, for example, *Hamilton v. Regents*, 293 U.S. 245 (1934).

114. *United States v. Seeger*, 380 U.S. 163 (1965).

115. *Wisconsin v. Yoder*, 406 U.S. 205 (1972).

116. The Amish believe education should be limited to the basics of reading, mathematics, and writing. "They reject the teaching of modern subjects based on modern culture, values, and styles of living, such as psychology, history, art, literature, and sociology." See Bezanson, *How Free Can Religion Be?*, 52.

117. *Wisconsin v. Yoder*, 406 U.S. 205 (1972).

118. Bezanson, *How Free Can Religion Be?*, 151–186.

119. *Employment Division v. Smith*, 494 U.S. 872 (1990).

120. Religious and civil rights groups were so outraged by the *Employment Division* decision they pressured Congress to pass the Religious Freedom Restoration Act of 1993, which was intended to restore religious freedom guarantees that supposedly were lost. The Supreme Court found the law unconstitutional in *Boerne v. Flores*, 521 U.S. 507 (1997).

121. Eisgruber and Sager, *Religious Freedom and the Constitution*, 45.

122. *Locke v. Davey*, 540 U.S. 712 (2004).

123. Ibid.

124. Bezanson, *How Free Can Religion Be?*, 272.

125. *Locke v. Davey*, 540 U.S. 712 (2004) (Justice Thomas joined Scalia in dissent.)

126. Leonard W. Levy, *The Establishment Clause: Religion and the First Amendment* (New York: Macmillan, 1986), 163.

127. John Witte Jr., *Religion and the American Constitutional Experiment*, 2nd ed. (Boulder, CO: Westview), 225.

128. Ibid., 177.

129. Eisgruber and Sager, *Religious Freedom and the Constitution*, 227.

130. *Davis v. Beason*, 133 U.S. 333, 342 (1890).

131. *United States v. Seeger*, 380 U.S. 163 (1965).

132. Julia K. Stronks, *Law, Religion, and Public Policy: A Commentary on First Amendment Jurisprudence* (Lanham, MD: Lexington, 2002), 3.

133. Bezanson, *How Free Can Religion Be?*, 274.

134. Ramesh Ponnuru, "Constitution Cons: That Which Unites Conservatives," *National Review*, December 19, 2005, 50–51, p. 51.

135. Rob Boston, "Egregious Earmarks?" *Church & State*, April 2008, 7–9, p. 7. Groups such as Americans United for Separation of Church and State frequently challenge public funding for religious groups and state laws such as the "moment of silence" in Texas public schools. The group, with the American Civil Liberties Union, has challenged a 2003 amendment that added "pray" to the list of things students could do during the moment. See "Americans United Opposes Amended Texas 'Moment of Silence' Statute," *Church & State*, July/August 2008, 20.

136. Cristi, *From Civil to Political Religion*, 6–13.

137. Kao and Copulsky, "Pledge of Allegiance," 123.

138. *Elk Grove Unified School District v. Newdow*, 542 U.S. 1 (2004).

139. Kao and Copulsky, "The Pledge of Allegiance," 123, n. 4. See *Myers v. Loudoun County Public Schools*, 418 F.3d 395 (4th Cir 2005).

140. Witte, *Religion and the American*, 258, n. 11.

141. Kao and Copulsky, "Pledge of Allegiance," 142.

142. Samuel P. Huntington, *Who Are We? The Challenges to American National Identity* (New York: Simon & Schuster, 2004), 82.

143. Kao and Copulsky, "Pledge of Allegiance," 134.

144. Martha C. Nussbaum, "Radical Evil in the Lockean State: The Neglect of the Political Emotions," *Journal of Moral Philosophy* 3, no. 2 (2006): 159–178, p. 178.

145. Kao and Copulsky, "Pledge of Allegiance," 138.

146. Ibid.

147. Derek H. Davis, *Religion and the Continental Congress, 1774–1789: Contributions to Original Intent* (Oxford, UK: Oxford University Press, 2000), 221.

148. Robert Wuthnow, "Restructuring of American Religion: Further Evidence," *Sociological Inquiry* 66, no. 3 (1996), 303–329, p. 326.

149. Bezanson, *How Free Can Religion Be?*, 273–274.

CHAPTER 5

Sex, Gender, and Religion: The Contraception and Abortion Conundrum

Texas Governor Rick Perry, a devout Methodist and normally a champion of social and religious conservatives, issued on February 2, 2007, an executive order mandating that girls in public schools get vaccinated against the virus that causes cervical cancer. Perry thought he was bypassing opposition to the order from conservative legislators, religious conservatives, parents who like to make their daughters' medical decisions, fiscal conservatives who thought the price for the program would be too high, and critics who thought Perry was favoring the pharmaceutical industry. Perry ordered that girls in sixth grade must be inoculated with the new vaccine that protects against most strains of human papillomavirus.

Perry's end run failed. The Texas House of Representatives moved to overturn the executive order and 26 of 31 Texas senators asked Perry to rescind the order. Conservative groups across the state mobilized their followers to tell the governor to withdraw the order and let the legislature decide whether vaccinations should be mandatory. Kelly Shackelford, president of the Free Market Foundation in Plano, Texas, said, "I haven't seen this kind of explosion in the grass roots in a number of years."[1] Much of the opposition came from Christian conservatives who thought the program would encourage girls to engage in sexual activities. Perry soon withdrew the order.

The Texas dustup illustrates the depth of feeling about human sexuality and gender, issues that have driven conservative religious, social, and political agendas for more than a generation. The Christian conservative stance on these issues is anchored in the belief that biblical texts supplemented by church tradition constitutes the primary authority for belief and behavior. Most believe that Christian attitudes toward the sexual and social rights of women and gays today are based on sexual and social mores that prevailed in the biblical past.

The debate over women's rights and gay rights—like other debates in the so-called cultural wars being waged on so many fronts in contemporary America—is grounded in premodern, patriarchal perceptions of sex, gender, and religion. We establish a framework for discussing these rights in this chapter and explore the controversy about birth control and abortion. We explore the controversy about gay marriage and family rights in Chapter 6.

Section 1 describes the power of patriarchy and religion in the construction of two sex and gender models—past and present. Section 2 offers a critique of the contemporary patriarchal sex and gender model—focusing on the feminist critique. Section 3 explores linkages between women's reproductive rights, particularly birth control and abortion, the media, and religion in light of the contemporary two-sex model. Section 4 outlines birth control and abortion debates since the seminal *Roe v. Wade* (1973) ruling, and Section 5 examines several ongoing tensions that frame these debates today.

PATRIARCHY, RELIGION, AND SEX-GENDER MODELS

For most of us, our sex is known from birth. Sexual identity, however, refers not only to one's anatomy, but also to one's sexual orientation and understanding of intimacy, eroticism, pleasure, and even of the reproductive process. "Sexuality is experienced and expressed in thoughts, fantasies, desires, beliefs, attitudes, values, behaviours, practices, roles and relationships," as the World Health Organization report puts it. A person's sexual orientation "is influenced by the interaction of biological, psychological, social, economic, political, cultural, ethical, legal, historical, religious and spiritual factors."[2]

The perceived lines between one's sexuality and one's gender are so fluid in the real world that it is often difficult to distinguish between the two terms. Most people are typically perceived to be either of the male or of the female gender, but the gendering of our bodies can be a lifelong process. Gender identity refers to how we perceive of ourselves in terms of gender and how we represent ourselves to others in terms of the clothes we wear, for example, the way we style our hair, behave in company with others, select our toys (Barbie versus Ken;

Porsche versus Saturn), or profess opinions that reflect our perceived gender identities. One's gender also is not fixed: males and females can and do adopt traits traditionally deemed to be characteristic of the other gender. Gender identities are public—what a particular society considers to be conduct appropriate for men and women—as well as private, and the two images may be and often are contradictory. In the social construction of gender, these public and private images are hopelessly intertwined and continually shifting.

Power is another central element in perceptions of human sexuality and gender. Indeed, no discussion can begin without a discussion of power—the power to determine and control the meaning of sexuality and of gendered relationships. Power is the dynamic in desires, practices, fantasies—all those elements that make us human—and it reflects a particular understanding of the complexities of sexuality and gender. The power to define and describe the meaning of sexuality and gender was and is grounded in a system of patriarchy. Power in this sense has had a profound impact on the ways in which we perceive sexual and gendered differences in society.

Premodern Patriarchy, Religion, and the One-Sex Model

Patriarchy is a very old social system that characterized most pre modern societies throughout the world. Indeed, some link its origins to the invention of the alphabet and the advent of literacy—in which men came to be dominant over women in all categories of life. Patriarchy is the power to determine what constitutes the difference between males and females at home, on the job, in church, synagogue, or mosque, in politics, at war, and in the pursuit of pleasure. Patriarchy is the power to determine the material or economic relationships between genders—the power to produce, manage, and distribute human and natural resources within a small social group or a complex society.

Custodians of Tradition

The patriarchal view of sexuality and gender in Western society is anchored in the biblical record, but the binary language religious conservatives employ today to defend a patriarchal culture was simply not in fashion in antiquity. This was a world in which there were no distinctions between the secular and the sacred. The divine presence was perceived to be an active agent in human affairs, and only by participating in the divine life could men be truly human. The Hebrew and Greek texts themselves were made authoritative because of the traditions that informed these texts. The canon in both the Hebrew Bible and the Christian Bible is essentially a compilation and interpretation of these traditions.[3]

Political and religious leaders, rhetoricians, and writers were the custodians of tradition in all premodern cultures, and they shared with their audiences an understanding of these traditions—of interpretations of the past, the present, and the future that were radically different from our understandings today. They used any number of sources—oral and written accounts, sayings, parables, and miracle stories—but these sources were not subjected to linguistic, literary, historical, or scientific investigation. There were no rules for validating or testing evidence presented in these sources. There was little interest in distinguishing "fact" from "fiction" or "myth" from "reality." These modern concepts had little meaning in most premodern societies. The custodians of the "truth" assumed that if the sources did not betray the traditions, they did not betray the truth.

The custodians of tradition in antiquity shared a worldview based on a one-sex patriarchal model, a model of women as subordinated to men for religious conservatives today.[4] The model is reflected in the story of Adam and Eve in Genesis, in which Eve is fashioned from Adam's rib (2:22–23) and causes Adam to eat of the forbidden fruit in the Garden of Eden (3:6, 12). Woman is therefore subordinated to the man ("he shall rule over you" in 3:16).

Women were imperfect versions of men in the one-sex model. Women's genitalia were believed to be copies of men's genitalia, but a woman's genitals were inside the body and therefore could not penetrate a man's body. Sex in biblical times was between dominant and submissive partners, but a man could not by virtue of his understanding of sexuality—an understanding prescribed by the values, traditions, roles, and practices of the day—play the role of a submissive partner.[5]

The one-sex model, however, did not assign gender to either males or females in biblical antiquity—masculinity and femininity were attributes of each human being. Biological differences were not seen as gendered differences. The social status of men and women was grounded in a patriarchal hierarchy that was determined by cultural tradition. Males and females who ranked higher in social status had more control over their bodies than those who ranked lower in social status. Slavery in these premodern cultures, for example, typically was based not on what one could see but on one's social status within these hierarchies. A person's status—hence control over one's life—was not determined by factors such as one's physical attributes or sexual preferences, ethnicity, or skin color, as it would be in the two-sex model.

Emerging Sexual Mores

Hebrew sexual mores that emerged from the premodern culture in which the Hebrew Bible (Old Testament) was written were in many ways no different from the sexual mores that emerged in other premodern, patriarchal cultures. Men in these cultures were under tremendous pressure to marry and procreate. Hebrew law and custom proscribed any activity that interfered with, or did not promote, reproduction.[6]

Marriage was supposed to be an exclusive act between Hebrews within the 12 tribes of Israel. Laws demanded female (not male) virginity but proscribed male as well as female adultery for married couples; the Torah also did not proscribe unmarried members of either gender from having sexual relations with married members of the opposite gender. If Jewish law and custom were followed, God would reward a person (meaning a man) with a long life and many children. Most ancient Hebrews believed a person could live on after death through a man's children.[7]

Female prostitution (as long as women were not virgins at the outset) was considered normal and necessary to safeguard the virginity of unmarried females and to protect the property rights of males. Men in the Hebrew Bible practiced polygamy (many wives) and had concubines (a woman living with a man to whom she was not married), and these practices were not condemned. Jesus, a Jew living within this cultural context, did not condemn polygamy or levirate marriage (the ancient custom whereby a childless widow was required to marry her late husband's oldest brother in the hope of producing a male heir).[8]

Modern Patriarchy, Religion, and the Two-Sex Model

Patriarchy in modern Western culture begins not with the premodern, one-sex model but with the modern, dichotomous two-sex model. Sexual preference based on this model is associated with the transformation in the economies and societies of Europe between roughly the sixteenth and ninteenth centuries—what we now refer to as the beginnings of the modern capitalist era. Patriarchy was still the norm, but women in some societies were no longer simply the property of men. Heterosexual relationships were beginning to be characterized by romantic love and monogamous conduct, and women were relatively privileged in the Western patriarchal two-sex model.

Binary Language and Gender Stereotyping

The binary language employed to arrange our gender order today is embedded in the eighteenth century—another by-product of the Enlightenment. The two-sex model was not only a sexual hierarchy, but also an economic, social, and racial or ethnic hierarchy until relatively recently. It was a monogamous family model linked inextricably to the emergence of industrial capitalism and to the rise of what was then identified as the middling classes—and indemnified especially in Victorian Europe during the nineteenth century. It was a model created and sustained by most white males (and supported, defended, and reinforced by most of their white female counterparts) in what today we would identify as the upper-middle and upper strata of society.[9]

The heterosexual model of marriage and family life in patriarchal America is also a product of the last 150 years or so and is not at all like the model that was dominant in patriarchal antiquity or in premodern Europe. "The ideal of the male provider/female homemaker marriage," as marriage and family historian Stephanie Coontz notes, became a "doctrine" in the nineteenth century that embraced all social classes and assumed "men and women had innately different natures and occupied separate spheres of life."[10]

The gendered messages of male and female characteristics projected in the two-sex model prevailed within and between all social classes and geographical localities, and in all ethnic groups that we still designate primarily by skin color as white, brown, or black. Those who did not conform to these stereotypes risked societal censure at best and criminal action at worst. In the process, same-sex relationships were distinguished from heterosexual relationships. They were no longer part of the whole but now had their own separate, minority category.[11] The term "homosexual" as a category that expresses one's "identity," however, "was unknown until the early twentieth century."[12]

Most Americans assume that biological differences between men and women are observable—after all, men have penises and women have vaginas—and therefore human populations can be categorized as either male or female. The two-sex marriage and family model continues to frame debates over sexuality and gender for many people—especially religious conservatives—today (see Table 5.1).

Modern science provides additional ways to distinguish males from females. These distinctions are based not only on what is observed—such as sex organs—but also on chromosomal and, to a lesser degree, hormonal structures. Binary language creates two and only two sexual options. Biological categories are then fused with social categories in this two-sex model of sex and gender that is then used to structure male dominance from birth.

A Religious and Social Conservative View

The construction of gender identity for some religious and social conservatives is a "natural" consequence of these biological distinctions. The man may be perceived as the physically stronger, active, dominant sex, while the woman may be perceived as the physically weaker, passive, recipient of sex. Men may be perceived to have bigger brains than women and thus be more intelligent. Men may be perceived to be more rational (hence they can be political and corporate leaders), whereas women may be perceived as more emotional

Table 5.1. The Two-Sex Marriage and Family Model

If this:		
Sex Category	*Female*	*Male*
Then this:		
Gender	*Feminine (Woman)*	*Masculine (Man)*
And this:		
Sexual Orientation	*Desires Men*	*Desires Women*
And this:	Wife/Mother	Husband/Father
Desired Role	*Homemaker/Caregiver*	*Provider/"Breadwinner"*

Source: This table is based on one profiled in Sara L. Crawley, Lara J. Foley, and Constance L. Shehan, *Gendering Bodies* (Lanham, MD: Rowman & Littlefield, 2008), 16 (Figure 1.1). The boxes have been extended to include the subcategory "Desired Role."

(hence they should not enter politics or seek corporate leadership). Men may be perceived to be the providers, so their primary task will be in the workplace. "Male activities" (such as holding down a job) will almost always be privileged over "female activities" (such as homemaking or child rearing).

Religious and social conservatives who believe "a woman's place is in the home," however, may give equal weight to homemaking (for which there is little or no remuneration) and to working outside the home. They may profess admiration for those who are caregivers for their children and the caretakers of their homes (even though they are not paid). Although most married women in America now also work outside the home, they endure inequality in terms of salaries, advancement, and career opportunities. Many men have assumed some of the tasks of homemaking and caregiving, but most women still bear the heavier workload at home. As the French feminist writer Simone de Beauvoir put it almost 60 years ago: "One is not born, but rather becomes, a woman." And in the two-sex model, a man "becomes a man."[13]

Many religious and social conservatives exploit what they see as a fixed biological distinction between men and women. In turn, they project these normative social values back onto everyone else in a kind of "gender feedback loop" that requires everyone to believe and behave in ways that conform to these distinctions.[14] Virtually all societies, past and present, create a gendered world in which "the ideas of 'man' and 'woman' are cultural constructs"[15] that must be maintained and protected. Religious and social conservatives in modern America make it their business to ensure these constructs never change.

For many religious conservatives, these sexual and gendered distinctions are inherited from the supposed biblical past and reenacted from infancy—beginning with the family. They are reinforced in religious, educational, and media practices. And perhaps most of all, these gender divisions are reified in personal interactions with peers and outsiders in everyday life. Critical-cultural theorist Michel Foucault (1926–1984) observed that (a) individuals were and are under continual public surveillance and (b) have internalized these normative rules and disciplined themselves to conform to them. This observation applies to the customary protocols and rituals that have affected relations between the sexes since antiquity.[16]

The nature-nurture debate today, from the perspective of many religious and social conservatives, begins with the naturalness of biological distinctions and morphs easily into a nurturing environment that ideally naturalizes the meaning of masculinity and femininity for all the population. The language of little boxes defines our bodies and our lives. This sex-gender model remains the dominant discourse for many of these conservatives, and they insist that sex role differences continue to exist because they promote what they understand as cultural stability. It is part of what they mean by America's social order.

CRITIQUES OF THE PATRIARCHAL, TWO-SEX MODEL

The perceived biological differences between males and females—a critical distinction in the conservative religious view of what it means to be masculine and feminine—is a good place to start any critique of the two-sex model. Feminist social *and* natural scientists have criticized the two-sex model, because they believe it is politically and culturally biased.

They point to the range of chromosomal structures that may be present in the human population and criticize studies that distinguish between male and female hormones. Those who argue that male and female hormonal changes are more alike than different also suggest that the assignment of physical and social attributes to males and females has had a profound impact on how males and females see themselves and are seen in America.

The two-sex model is no longer fixed as a biological or social definition of sexuality in Western culture. "Female and male bodies operate as symbols creating differential access to the social world," as women's studies scholars Sara L. Crawley, Lara J. Foley, and Constance L. Shehan report. "Our beliefs are based on fitting into the social process of what we believe to be 'normal,'" but "*there is no specific, distinct measure that will consistently determine maleness or femaleness for all persons*" (italics in the original).[17]

The medical profession today has the technology to manipulate genetic structures—the so-called XY (male) and XX (female) chromosomes—even before conception to determine sex. Surgical and/or hormonal tools can be utilized to initiate sex changes at almost any point in one's life. The human body is now perceived "as a template," as syndicated columnist Ellen Goodman puts it, "to be altered as we please."[18] Men and women, and persons of all ages, continually pursue various surgical enhancement strategies to improve the image they (and hopefully others) have of themselves.

Prenatal tests can now determine a wide range of abnormalities in fetuses—fetuses with various diminished physical and mental capacities, such as cystic fibrosis, Down syndrome, muscular dystrophy, and premature Alzheimer's disease—and potentially terminate pregnancies. Procedures associated with *in vitro* fertilization allow "fertile couples . . . to gain greater control over the genetic makeup of their children," as journalist Amy Harmon reported in a *New York Times* article about genetic testing. Medical specialists can prescreen embryos not only for sexual preference and for numerous inherited diseases, but also for traits such as intelligence, athletic ability, and beauty, and potentially "implant only embryos with the desired genetic makeup."[19] Genetic engineering, reproductive technologies, and advances in cybernetics make the two-sex model as the biological determinate of sexual identification increasingly obsolete in today's world.

Feminists and the Two-Sex Model

The feminist movement—which has always included male and female voices—is the most powerful force in the social deconstruction of patriarchal sex and gender models in the modern era. Feminist scholars usually divide the history of the movement in America into three "waves." The first wave is associated with the suffragettes of the nineteenth and early twentieth centuries—the period of political activity that triumphed when women were given the right to vote in the United States in 1920. The second wave is associated with the battle to secure equal rights for women that began in the 1960s and effectively ended with the failure to pass the Equal Rights Amendment in 1982. The third wave is associated with continued efforts to pass this amendment, internal shifts within the movement over women's differing experiences and responses to patriarchy and inequality, a renewed emphasis on *symbolic* as well as material discrimination, and sexual harassment in *domestic life* as well as the workplace outside the home.[20]

Working outside the Home

Public debates about perceived conflicts between women as homemakers and job seekers took place following World War I and became more intense after World War II, when many women who had worked outside the home to support the war effort wanted to keep working. The modern feminist movement reemerged in part as an organized political response to issues created as more and more women entered the workplace. Media coverage increased as women demanded the right to work, and a new generation of feminists gave voice and coherency to women's interests and needs.

Many scholars believe the modern feminist movement was most influential in the so-called second wave between roughly the mid-late 1960s and the early 1980s. Feminists began working with other groups—anti-Vietnam War groups, gay and lesbian groups, and African-American and other ethnic minority groups—who were also fighting for change in America's social order. These were the years when the "war between the sexes"—a favorite media conflict frame—was coupled with human-interest personality stories depicting activists such as Betty Friedan (1921–2006) as the "mother," and activists such as Gloria Steinem, Germaine Greer, and Kate Millett as the "spokespersons" for the movement. Friedan's influential work, *The Feminine Mystique*, was published in 1963, and Greer's seminal work, *The Female Eunuch*, was published in 1970.

These were also the years when feminist activists adapted the strategies employed in the African-American civil rights movement—especially with the triumph of the Civil Rights Act of 1964.[21] This potential "master frame" was "based on legal equality and individual rights as a citizen," as political scientists Anne N. Costain, Richard Braunstein, and Heidi Berggren suggest, and it "resonates strongly in a culture with a cherished Constitution and historic commitment to a policy-setting system of courts."[22]

A symbol of the women's struggle for equal rights at the time was the Equal Rights Amendment (ERA), which was first introduced at a women's conference in New York in 1923. The ERA was refined in 1943 to say that equal rights for women "under the law shall not be denied or abridged by the United States or by any state on account of sex."[23] Congress finally adopted the amendment in 1972 after all the stakeholders (including organized labor) had accepted its provisions.

The proposed Twenty-Seventh Amendment was then presented to the states to be ratified, and the feminist movement spent the next 10 years with rallies, marches, petitions, picketing (among other venues, the White House), fund-raisers, intense lobbying, and even civil disobedience to get the amendment ratified. Congress extended the deadline for ratification in 1979 to 1982, but America's political culture had already shifted to the right. The number of states voting for ratification declined dramatically in the mid-late 1970s—Indiana being the 35th and last state to ratify the ERA Amendment in 1977.

The triumph of the Reagan Republicans in the 1980 elections, coupled with the efforts of anti-ERA activists such as Phyllis Schlafly, crippled the pro-ERA campaign. Thirty-eight states were needed to secure approval, and the amendment effectively died when the new deadline in June 1982 was not met.

While new strategies were developed to keep ERA hopes alive, the feminist movement itself underwent a transformation that began in the late 1970s. The female critique of patriarchal models in the first two waves had been largely a white middle-class vision—a vision that had not really considered the widely differing experiences of women in other social, ethnic, and cultural settings.[24]

Emerging Hierarchies of Gender

"Hierarchies" of gender—a term employed by the feminist scholar Mary Holmes—began to emerge within the feminist movement in the last decades of the twentieth century to demonstrate how gender inequality intersected with other kinds of inequalities. These ranged from ethnic origin and social class—such as the kinds of inequalities experienced by working-class Latina or African-American women or white working-class versus white middle- and upper-class women— to inequalities experienced by women in different religious communities or geographical regions, by women in different age groups or suffering from physical or mental disabilities, or by women working in different sectors of the economy. These hierarchies drove home a simple reality—the less privileged women were, the less free they were "to 'do' gender in any way that takes our fancy."[25]

Feminists began to broaden their understandings of patriarchy, as they became more concerned with symbolic and material forces that perpetuate systemic inequality. But many women continued to endure social and economic disadvantages and to be vulnerable to physical and emotional abuse from some men. For most postmodernist feminist scholars and activists, "women's identity," as Holmes puts it, must still "be understood as constructed in relation to what it [has] meant to be a man."[26] It was the one common denominator that had solidified more than a century of feminist political activity, and it is still a unifying battle cry.

Opponents of gender discrimination have continued to challenge the most obvious economic and social inequalities—as in political, educational, religious, work-related, and recreational pursuits in the public sphere—but they have broadened the challenge to encompass discrimination that is often more subtle and more difficult for many women and men to discern or appreciate. Challenges to patriarchy, for example, have also shifted somewhat from the marketplace to the domestic sphere, where the family until relatively recently was not subjected to much public scrutiny. Patriarchy (in terms of women's, men's, and children's desired roles) remains a force in domestic life, marriage and family, and women's reproductive rights, and it takes on new meanings in today's gendered world.

Media Framing of the Feminist Critique

Behaviors based on perceived gender and sexual differences are learned behaviors that are repetitive, performance driven, and influenced by all sorts of personal interactions—including those among family and friends, in religious settings, in schools, and in the places where we work. One of the most significant in our opinion is the consumer's interaction with mass media—newspapers and magazines, radio and television, and the Internet—as well as cell phones, Black-Berries, iPhones, and personal Internet blogs that package individual desires and needs.

The mass media both *reflect* what they identify as the "real" world and *represent* the realities that people talk about, as we explained in Chapter 2. In the process, media profoundly influence the ways in which people *frame* the news agenda and perceive issues and problems—in this case, news about sex and gender roles. This is why individuals and groups— such as feminists—typically contest media frames that contrast them negatively with others—such as nonfeminists.

The Demonization of Feminists

Communication scholars Rebecca Ann Lind and Colleen Salo found in their study of electronic media content aired in 2002 that feminists rarely appeared in news stories and when they did they were "often demonized." Echoing earlier research, they found stories in public affairs and news programs framed "women" and "feminists" as separate categories. Feminists were not regarded as "regular women" and were "less often associated with day-to-day work/leisure activities of regular women." On the other hand, feminists were depicted as having more control over their destinies, were less often depicted as "victims" in stories, and were more often involved in public affairs than nonfeminists.[27]

Feminists, for example, were contrasted negatively with men in media coverage of the Promise Keepers, the Christian men's group that reached the high point of its influence in 1997 at an open-air gathering in Washington, D.C., called "Stand in the Gap: A Sacred Assembly of Men." Estimates of the number of those who attended ranged from 500,000 to 1 million people—this was the largest religious rally ever recorded at the time in the nation's capital.

Feminists launched a countercampaign before the rally was held, arguing that the Promise Keepers comprised what they believed to be "an ultra-conservative political group that only used religious rhetoric to disguise its true [patriarchal] goals," according to communication scholar Jennifer Young Abbott. An analysis of television news coverage of the rally in the months before, during, and after the event showed how the rhetoric of the Promise Keepers was "endorsed" by the networks for its "sincerity and sentimentality," while the rhetoric of the feminists was "dismissed . . . as paranoid and self-serving."[28]

Popular culture in the 1990s had legitimized the feminine-sensitive male hero, and this was reenacted in media coverage of the Promise Keepers, whose members were "allowed . . . to perform femininity and still remain masculine." The feminists, on the other hand, were framed negatively as "masculine" women, who did not support the healthy, heterosexual family model celebrated by the Promise Keepers.[29]

Abbot's study also demonstrated that the ways in which the media frame a religious event such as this one can have unpredictable ramifications. The feminist critique was a critical factor in highlighting the rally for the public, but media coverage declined dramatically when the feminists lost interest in the Promise Keepers. Attendance at future rallies sponsored by the Promise Keepers dwindled, and the sponsors never succeeded in regenerating public interest in the organization.

Framing in Patriarchal Terms

Many feminists argue that media "construct hegemonic definitions" of acceptable realities that are framed in patriarchal terms. The "ideology" of America's patriarchal system, as media scholars Cynthia Carter and Linda Steiner put it, "is being actively made to appear as 'non-ideological,' 'objective,' 'neutral,' and 'non-gendered.' " Hence "hegemonic realities must be continuously renegotiated, contested, reconstructed, and renaturalized."[30]

The so-called gender gap, to take another example, was initially identified in the 1982 congressional elections by the National Organization of Women to publicize the significance of the female vote in local and national elections. Mainstream media framed the 1992 elections as the "Year of the Woman," when the number of women elected to the House and Senate rose to 47 from 29 in the previous election. Women remained then—as they remain today—a small minority in Congress, and the vast majority of these are members of the Democratic Party. The Grand Old Party (GOP) landslide in the 1994 congressional elections was framed in similarly unrealistic terms as the "Year of the Angry White Male." These media frames proved to be momentary sound bites exploiting the binary gender gap in election results, and they had little positive impact in the ongoing feminist struggle against mediated gender frames.[31]

Media frames, as political scientist Pippa Norris suggests, "may be positive, negative, or neutral for women, depending upon the broader political context."[32] These frames changed as more women were employed as reporters and editors in print and broadcast media. Women journalists enriched media coverage of stories on a range of issues of importance to women—including childcare, sexual harassment, domestic violence, women's politics, and controversial topics such as birth control and abortion. But the glass ceiling still deterred women seeking higher levels of decision making as managers, executives, and media owners, which translated into persistent negative or unrealistic portraits of feminists, women in politics, and women activists who have become public figures.[33]

Women's voices remain relatively underrepresented in almost every category of journalism. One study contrasting medium size and larger newspapers in the Midwest examined not only content but also the perceptions of the journalists and their audiences to this content. The researchers found that the newspapers studied "reflect the masculine cultural hegemony that prevails in U.S. culture" and "sustain gender stereotypes" of men and women. Differences in perceptions between male and female staffers could be seen on the question of equal representation in all sections of the newspaper—especially in the news and sports sections. Newspaper readers interviewed felt that women were less represented than men in every story category in this study.[34]

Television journalist and researcher Ginger Miller Loggins noted that the "dearth of female voices" in the media today has had a negative impact on the feminist movement. In examining conservative claims that media were biased in favor of "liberal" feminism, she noted that research has documented a broader antifeminist bias than profeminist bias in the media. This bias, however, was attributed not to media bias against women, but to the media's reflection of *society's* bias against women.[35]

WOMEN'S REPRODUCTIVE RIGHTS, THE MEDIA, AND RELIGION

Binary language is particularly abusive in a single-issue debate such as that over women's contraception and abortion rights. The protagonists in the women's reproductive rights debate, for example, label themselves "pro-life" and "pro-choice." Pro-choice activists argue that they also are pro-life in terms of the child, but they lobby primarily for the rights of motherhood. Pro-life activists argue that they also are pro-choice in terms of the mother, but they lobby primarily for the rights of the unborn child.

Media for the most part employ the term "abortion" to frame women's reproductive rights today, but this word has legal implications because it "implies intent or purpose," as university librarian Mark Y. Herring puts it. "Only rarely does a definition of abortion include references to viability or period of gestation."[36] Journalists and scholars cannot agree on the terminology to be used. William Saletan, for example, says that the terms "anti-abortion rights" and "pro-right-to-life" add bias to the abortion debate, and that the "least biased solution is to let each side choose its name."[37] Stephen E. Stewart uses pro-choice in referring to the pro-choice lobby, because it "does not judge the morality of abortion." But he uses "anti-abortion" in referring to the anti-abortion lobby, because he claims it "does not say whether an abortion destroys a human life."[38]

We argue that the *contexts* of the debate are concerns over human (including civil) rights for women and unborn fetuses, whereas the *texts* of the debate are opposing claims between pro- and anti-abortion groups. While we agree that the meaning of abortion carries all sorts of positive and negative connotations, depending on one's point of view, it is the one term now used by ordinary people to identify a person's position in these debates. We use the term pro-abortion to identify those activists on the pro-choice side of the debate and anti-abortion to identify those activists on the pro-life side of the debate. Both sides together generate on average "more than $1 billion annually" from individual donations alone to support their causes. As might be expected, the pro-abortion forces are strongest in the eastern and western seaboard states, and the anti-abortion forces are strongest in the South and the Midwest.[39]

Patriarchal Sex-Gender Models and the Bible[40]

Religious conservatives in monotheistic faith traditions have had the most intense and pervasive hostility to women who fight for reproductive rights, and to women and men who want the right to define their own sexuality. The conservatives generally derive divine inspiration from a single, written source—whether it is the Hebrew Bible, the Christian Bible, or the Qur'an. And they believe that their worldviews are grounded in these sacred texts.

Many, perhaps a majority, of those who are members of these faith traditions would not accept that recognizing women's sexual and reproductive rights would contradict their religious beliefs. Our concern here, however, is with Christian conservatives and their religious, political, and social allies in America who hold this view and have the political, economic, religious, and social clout to enforce their personal and collective views on the nation.

Christian conservatives cannot look to the Bible for passages promoting monogamous, heterosexual marriage or condemning women's reproductive rights. Such passages are not there because women were regarded as male property and, therefore, had no reproductive rights. Marriage in the premodern and early-modern past, as historian John Boswell points out, was a world "where heterosexual matrimony tended to be viewed as a dynastic or business arrangement, and love in such relationships, where it occurred, arose *following* the coupling" (italics in the original).[41]

Terms such as "birth control" or abortion cannot be found in biblical texts. The only penalties that could be imposed in cases of abortion were those in which men's property rights were in jeopardy. One biblical reference, for example, refers to the loss of a fetus that might occur in the following circumstance: "When men fight, and one of them pushes a pregnant woman and a miscarriage results, but no other damage ensues, the one responsible shall be fined according as the woman's husband may exact from him" (Exodus 21:22).

Life, of course, is sacrosanct in the biblical record. The breath of the Creator was discerned at every stage of the birth (and death) process. Mothers with children, and the children themselves, were blessings from Yahweh. It would be surprising indeed if life for the Israelites—although not for their enemies—were *not* sacrosanct in the biblical record. Procreation was both a sacred demand and an economic necessity for all premodern cultures. It was a matter of survival.

Birth control and abortion practices, however, were widespread in all premodern cultures—including ancient Israel.[42] Egyptian, Greek, and Roman texts from antiquity provide ample evidence that herbal remedies, primitive intrauterine devices, and male condoms were used—along with a variety of less-conventional methods (by contemporary standards) of inducing abortion (including physical violence). Graco-Roman legal authorities accepted abortion as a matter of property law—providing the husband consented to the abortion.

Even for anti-abortion advocates, the New Testament is silent on the issue of abortion. The idea that contraception and abortion were sinful acts emerged from the writings of early church fathers, and in some church councils and encyclicals, although even here there were exceptions. The absence of voices from early church mothers on these issues, of course, speaks volumes about the dangers of projecting current biases against women's reproductive rights onto these ancient texts.[43]

The most important question for many ancient authorities centered on when conception actually occurred. A fetus was a life only when a pregnant woman felt the movements of her unborn child. The process was called "quickening" in early modern Europe, but it was the traditional sign of life for all prescientific cultures. In a one-sex model, moreover, the male fetus was believed to form earlier than a female fetus—adherents claimed this speeded up the quickening process and gave hope to pregnant mothers that the unborn child would be a male.

The quickening process in today's terminology would have been in the fourth or fifth month of pregnancy—well into the second trimester. Christian theologians adopted this perspective of delayed ensoulment—that moment when the soul entered the fetus and the unborn child was declared to be human—and it was also a legal definition in many countries (including England and the United States) up to the modern era. The Roman Catholic Church, for example, "implicitly accepted early abortions prior to ensoulment" and did not condemn the practice until 1869.[44]

Women's Reproductive Rights before *Roe v. Wade*

The debate over reproductive freedom for married and unmarried women had its origins in and is inextricably tied to (a) the economic, scientific, and social transformation associated with the beginnings of modernity and (b) the emergence of monogamous marital relationships associated with the nuclear heterosexual family. The dominant role of the male in this two-sex family model framed the debate in its early stages, but some women moved out of cloistered domesticity and into public life to alter the course of the debate.

Feminists framed women's reproductive rights in its early stages as a modern response to protecting a more egalitarian, monogomous two-sex family model. It was solidified in American popular culture during the nineteenth century. Campaigns to control sexual behavior—to criminalize contraception, abortion, and polygamy; to restrict or ban alcohol consumption and gambling; to stop prostitution; to ban pornographic or obscene materials; and to stop other vice-related acts—were components in a broader crusade to banish any sexual or social activity that threatened what now had become the modern two-sex patriarchal family. Women's rights activists mounted these "purity" campaigns after the Civil War in the belief that "any expression of sexuality outside the home [was] a threat to marriage and decency."[45]

Women's reproductive rights, however, threatened the male "power structure," as Alexander Sanger, a leader in the contemporary Planned Parenthood movement, puts it, "in nineteenth century America."[46] Physicians sought a legal monopoly over the practice of medicine—shifting control over reproductive rights from the home to the office and hospital. Midwives and self-styled doctors who lacked the necessary educational qualifications (set by the medical profession) were prevented from dispensing drugs and offering their services to the public.

Many white Protestants believed birth control as practiced by the Protestant majority threatened the dominance of the Protestant establishment as white Roman Catholic immigrants were producing more babies per family. Led by the American Medical Association (formed in 1847), the campaign to criminalize abortion gathered strength, and the Comstock Act—named after Anthony Comstock (1844–1915), leader of a YMCA (Young Men's Christian Organization) vice squad in New York City—was passed in 1873. The act effectively prohibited distribution through the U.S. mail of any material that could be deemed "obscene" or that provided information about birth control or abortion. Misdemeanor charges (which could result in a fine of $100–$5,000 and/or a prison sentence of 1–10 years) would be laid against any individual who broke this law.

The states quickly followed with their own laws, so that both birth control and abortion in any form were now criminalized at state and federal levels. These services did not go away—they simply went underground in a black market that thrived in the aftermath of the Comstock Act. The rich continued to practice birth control (and abortion) because they could afford to do so, and the overall birth rate continued to decline in the last quarter of the nineteenth century. The powerless—the poor, uneducated, and disenfranchised—were most affected by the Comstock Act, because they were the most vulnerable.

The medical profession, faith organizations, and the courts—the societal groups that had served anti-abortion forces so well in the nineteenth century—began to lose power over sexual issues in the early twentieth century. The backlash against the forces that would control sexuality was probably inevitable in the changing culture of modernity that many Americans were embracing. Margaret Sanger (1879–1966), Alexander's grandmother, is credited with being the primary inspiration behind the birth-control movement in this country in the first half of the twentieth century.[47]

Margaret Sanger was able to reinterpret the restrictions associated with the Comstock Act so that they were rendered "toothless"— largely because she made reproductive rights a moral crusade for safeguarding monogamy and motherhood in the two-sex family model. Thus "the ability of a woman to control and limit her childbearing was good for the woman, her children, and the rest of her family, but was also good for the public health, society, and the economy." Family planning rhetoric was used to highlight the power of doctors as caregivers who could provide birth-control services. As a trained nurse, Margaret was in a good position to offer sex education in her work, in a column she wrote (entitled, "What Every Girl Should Know"), in a newspaper she launched (entitled, *The Woman Rebel*), and in America's first birth-control clinic, which she opened in New York in October 1916. She was perhaps the first person to proclaim in public that a woman owned her own body and had the right to choose motherhood or not.[48]

Two court decisions that helped dismantle the Comstock law— *People v. Sanger* (1918)[49] and *United States v. One Package of Japanese*

Pessaries (1936)[50]—moved birth control from being illegal, to being legal in preventing sexually transmitted diseases, to being permitted either to prevent an undesirable pregnancy or to promote the patient's well-being. Margaret's "victory over Comstrock," as Sanger puts it, "was sealed when she convinced physicians to switch sides from opposing birth control to supporting it under their control." Public opinion by the 1960s had shifted in favor of birth control, and court decisions would gradually endorse Margaret's argument "that reproductive freedom was a biological and social necessity for women, men, and children."[51]

Birth Control and the Right to Privacy

Pro-abortion activists argued that the campaign to promote birth control was founded on a fundamental human and constitutional right—the right to privacy. Thus the strategies used to overturn the Comstock law were employed largely through the courts on issues relating to individual privacy. The Supreme Court ruled 7–2 in *Griswold v. Connecticut* (1965) that states could not prohibit married couples from getting birth control information, counseling, and medical treatment (or the Planned Parenthood League of Connecticut and other groups from giving advice). The justices used the First, Third, Fourth, and Ninth amendments to the Bill of Rights to create a constitutional right to privacy in marital relationships.[52]

Contested Government Role

Previous court rulings reflected an assumption that government had a constitutional right to regulate the private lives of individuals. The *Griswold* decision sought to limit government interference in matters of privacy by maintaining that the right to practice birth control was a constitutional right between married couples—a right that was extended to unmarried couples in *Eisenstadt v. Baird* (1972).[53]

These decisions reflected public opinion on issues relating to birth control. New birth-control technologies were made more widely available from the 1960s. The birth-control pill for women (approved by the U.S. Food and Drug Administration, FDA, in 1960) was limited initially to married women and single women over 21, but the age of consent was lowered to 18 when the twenty-sixth Amendment was ratified in 1971 lowering the voting age to 18. Medical researchers had begun to unravel the reproductive process inside the womb in the nineteenth century, and the various stages in fetal development were more or less mapped out by the 1960s—although this remains an ongoing issue in medical research.

A better understanding of the reproductive process in the last decades of the twentieth century resulted in other forms of contraception. These included more sophisticated male condoms, female diaphragms and sponges, hormonal injections, birth-control pills, more elaborate intrauterine devices, and a more precise calibration of the reproductive cycle that might influence the timing of intercourse.

Birth-control rights and the claim that the government should not interfere in a private decision between consenting adults became much more contentious after the *Griswold* case. The distinction between contraception and abortion, moreover, was not always honored in these politicized debates. This can be illustrated in the controversy about Plan B, the emergency contraceptive whose approval was delayed because of opposition from religious conservatives in George W. Bush's administration.

Plan B was intended as an emergency contraceptive to be used when preventative measures either failed or were not taken during intercourse. Plan B prevents "ovulation or fertilization," and it actually consists of two pills—one taken "within 72 hours of unprotected sex and the second 12 hours later."[54] While other versions of this emergency contraceptive had been used in Europe for decades, the FDA approved of Plan B only by prescription in 1999. Barr Laboratories, the manufacturer of the drug in the United States, sought to get the FDA to approve over-the-counter sales of Plan B in 2004—and immediately encountered resistance from religious conservatives in the Bush administration.

The FDA's nonprescription drugs advisory committee and the reproductive health drugs advisory committee approved Barr's request, but some members of the joint committee, including the chair, objected. Although two outside panels and three FDA offices studied the safety and effectiveness of Plan B and recommended the contraceptive be sold without a prescription, the request was not approved.

The FDA's rejection was unusual in many respects, according to an investigation by the Government Accountability Office. Evidence suggests that (a) high-level managers (political appointees) were more involved than is usual in such an application; (b) FDA officials who would typically sign a rejection letter did not agree with the decision and did not sign; (c) the decision to reject Barr's request was made even before FDA scientists had completed their evaluations of Plan B, although accounts differ on this point; and (d) the rejection apparently was based on novel, nonscientific considerations.

The nonscientific considerations were implied by Steven Galson, acting director of the Center for Drug Evaluation and Research, who wrote that the application could not be approved unless the company could show that "Plan B can be used safely by women under 16 years of age without the professional supervision of a practitioner licensed by law to administer the drug." Galson was primarily concerned that Plan B sold over the counter to "younger adolescents" would encourage them "to engage in unsafe sexual behaviors because of their lack of cognitive maturity compared to older adolescents." Galson "acknowledged" that the rationale for using the "cognitive development" of adolescents to reject the application "was unprecedented."[55]

The political appointees apparently believed, or bowed to pressure from a coalition of Christian conservative activists who believed, that Plan B would lead to sexual promiscuity, particularly among teenagers. Research showed that Plan B did not lead to increased sexual activity, but its critics did not concede the point. Other critics claimed Plan B was an abortion pill, which of course it was not. After almost 25 years of debate, one of the more controversial issues in the history of the Food and Drug Administration was finally settled when Plan B was approved in 2006 for over-the-counter sale without a prescription to women 18 and older.[56]

As the Plan B controversy illustrates, birth-prevention issues were hopelessly mired in the rhetoric over sexual morality and abortion issues.[57] Women's abortion rights in reality would be the all-consuming topic for both sides in debates over women's reproductive rights after *Roe v. Wade*.

THE ABORTION WARS: *ROE V. WADE* AND BEYOND

The U.S. Supreme Court decision in *Roe v. Wade* (1973) established the parameters of the abortion rights debate for the foreseeable future. Pro-abortion forces had campaigned vigorously for many years—with success in such cases as California's *People v. Belous* (1969)[58] and

United States v. Vuitch (1971)[59]—but *Roe* was the decision that finally legalized a woman's right to have an abortion.[60]

Women's Reproductive Rights and the Courts

The justices in *Roe* ruled 7–2 that the right of privacy introduced in the *Griswold* and *Eisenstadt* decisions included a woman's right to choose whether or not to end a pregnancy. But this was a "qualified right," as Justice Harry Blackmun (1908–1999) noted. This right would be based on the "trimester" system. The government could not interfere during the first trimester of pregnancy—abortion decisions should be a matter between the pregnant woman and her doctor. Government interference in the second trimester should be limited to regulations "that are reasonably related to maternal health." In practice, these regulations simply covered who could perform an abortion and where it could take place. The court presumed that the "viability" of the fetus was achieved only in the third trimester, when the government could regulate and even ban abortion procedures.[61]

The companion case was *Doe v. Bolton* (1973), in which the justices in yet another 7–2 decision effectively struck down all restrictions relating to abortion in a Georgia law—which required, among other things, Georgia residency and approval of three doctors and a hospital committee before an abortion could be performed. The "viability" of a pregnant woman's health, the Court said, should be determined by a licensed physician, and the decision should encompass "all factors—physical, emotional, psychological, familial, and the woman's age—relevant to the well-being of the patient," Justice Blackmun wrote. The decision to abort, which could now include economic and emotional considerations, theoretically could be made at any point up to the act of birth itself. The two decisions together affected all states with anti-abortion laws and statutes, because in effect this was interpreted as abortion on demand.[62]

Other Favorable Decisions

The 1970s witnessed more court cases that favored women's reproductive rights. In *Planned Parenthood of Missouri v. Danforth* (1976), for example, the justices ruled 6–3 that states could not force a married woman to obtain the consent of her husband if she wished to terminate a pregnancy; nor could the state "impose a blanket parental consent requirement . . . as a condition for an unmarried minor's abortion during the first 12 weeks of her pregnancy." A state cannot give a third party an absolute, and potentially arbitrary, veto over a patient's and her physician's decision to terminate a pregnancy, Justice Harry Blackmun wrote for the Court.[63]

The right of a minor to have an abortion without parental consent was reaffirmed in *Bellotti v. Baird* (1979), in which the justices judged the constitutionality of a Massachusetts law requiring a minor to have parental consent before having an abortion. The minor could obtain authorization from a superior court judge without parental consent if she could show "she is mature enough and well enough informed to make her abortion decision" or "even if she is not able to make this decision independently, the desired abortion would be in her best interests." Justice Lewis F. Powell Jr. (1907–1998), writing for the Court, said that a state that requires parental consent also "must provide an alternative procedure whereby authorization for the abortion can be obtained." While accepting the desirability of parental consent, the justices (by an 8-1 vote) found the Massachusetts law unconstitutional because it allowed judicial authorization to be withheld from a "mature and competent" minor and because it required parental notification in all cases.[64]

These decisions invalidated most state anti-abortion laws and sparked a dramatic increase in the numbers of abortion clinics in various parts of the country. The presence of these clinics made abortions safer; they reduced the number of backstreet, illegal abortions; and they contributed to an increase in the numbers of abortions. The overall abortion rate doubled, according to Mark Herring, in the seven years following *Roe*, but abortion rates seemed to peak in 1990 and gradually declined thereafter.[65]

There were about 1.2 million abortions in 2005, which is slightly higher than the recorded abortion rate in 1976. Explanations for this decline and whether it is now moving upward again were hotly disputed, but there can be no doubt that the initial increase after *Roe* ignited the anti-abortion lobby and helped set the stage for the surge in pro-family political activism beginning in the 1980s and 1990s.

A Mixed Decision

The Supreme Court heard more than 20 cases involving abortion issues in the 1970s and 1980s, but the first major challenge to

Roe came in *Planned Parenthood of Southeast Pennsylvania v. Casey* (1992). The case centered on a Pennsylvania law requiring five conditions for an abortion: (a) a woman must give her informed consent before an abortion, and she must be given information about abortion at least 24 hours before the procedure; (b) a minor contemplating abortion must have permission of at least one parent, with a "judicial bypass procedure" in place if parents refuse; (c) a married woman contemplating abortion must sign a statement that she has notified her husband of her intention; (d) a woman facing a "medical emergency" is excused from these requirements; and (e) facilities supplying abortion services must file reports (for example, patients' ages, abortion procedures, and dates of abortions) to the state.[66]

The Supreme Court upheld most of the provisions of the Pennsylvania law, and it created a new criterion for judging state laws that would restrict abortions: courts must determine whether an abortion law imposes an "undue burden" on or imposes a "substantial obstacle" in the path of a woman seeking an abortion. The Court did not uphold provisions requiring a woman to (a) notify her husband of her intention to have an abortion and to (b) report to the state why she did not notify her husband, because each provision "constitutes an undue burden" on a woman's right to abortion.[67]

The Court also substituted the term "viability" for the more specific "trimester" as a legal guide in determining when a fetus could be considered a viable human being. "[A] state may not prohibit any woman from making the ultimate decision to terminate her pregnancy before viability," the majority said, while acknowledging that advances in reproductive technology had lowered the threshold of viability from 28 weeks (at the time of *Roe*) to 23 or 24 weeks or perhaps "even slightly earlier." The decision—written by Justices Sandra Day O'Connor, David H. Souter, and Anthony Kennedy—seemed to open the door for states to pass legislation restricting abortion rights after redefining viability (which cannot be fixed, even today).[68]

Fighting Funding for Abortion

The abortion wars in the wake of *Roe v. Wade* gained intensity and were fought on multiple fronts. Opponents discovered early on that they might not be able to make abortions illegal, but they might be able to stop the use of public money to fund them. If they were successful, they would reduce the numbers of abortions for the people most likely to seek them, poor women. A portent of the future was legislation introduced in Congress in the late 1970s. Senator Henry Hyde (R-Illinois) sponsored the so-called Hyde Amendment in 1976, a continual rider to the yearly Medicaid appropriations bill, which for the first time essentially prohibited Medicaid funding for abortions to low-income women.

Only 17 of 50 states—most of them mandated by the courts— provided such funding through Medicaid as of 2004. The Hyde Amendment eventually denied federal funding for abortions to federally funded overseas agencies (mainly through the U.S. Agency for International Development)[69] and to all women funded by the federal government in the United States, including "Native Americans, federal employees and their dependents, Peace Corps volunteers, low-income residents of Washington, DC, federal prisoners, military personnel and their dependents, and disabled women who rely on Medicare." The only exceptions—and these came about largely through protests from pro-abortion groups—were in cases of rape or incest, or when the mother's life was in danger.[70]

The effort to cut off public funding for abortion was also fought in the courts—especially the federal district courts and the U.S. Supreme Court—where decisions favoring anti-abortion advocates gradually gained ground. The Supreme Court, for example, ruled 6-3 in *Beal v. Doe* (1977) that Title XIX funds requiring states to participate in the Medicaid program did not have to be used for "nontherapeutic abortions"—abortions that had no bearing on the health of the mother. Medicaid, however, could be used to fund prenatal care for women wishing to continue their pregnancies.[71] In *Rust v. Sullivan* (1991), justices in a more conservative Supreme Court ruled 5-4 in favor of a section of the Public Health Service Act that prohibited federal funds from being "used in programs where abortion is a method of family planning." In essence, the Court said it was appropriate for the U.S. Department of Health and Human Services to issue "regulations limiting the ability of Title X fund recipients to engage in abortion-related activities."[72]

Abortion and Religious Communities

The abortion wars after the 1970s were also fought inside religious communities, where conservatives generally endorsed the anti-abortionist agenda. The Roman Catholics and Southern Baptists[73]—the two largest Christian denominations in America—probably attracted a majority of the anti-abortion religious activists.

Pope Paul VI's (1897–1978) controversial *Humanae Vitae* (1969) and later Pope John Paul II's (1920–2005) encyclical letter *Evangelium Vitae* (1995) provided a firm ecclesiastical condemnation of contraceptives and all forms of abortion for Roman Catholics.[74] Pope Benedict XVI, a formidable intellect in defense of traditional doctrine and morality, reiterated this position when he became pope in 2005. Conservative Catholic theologians equated the anti-abortion crusade as part of a broader struggle—from "euthanasia" and "capital punishment" to "nuclear war and life-threatening poverty." In the battle "to protect the rights of the unborn," Catholic conservatives were joined by evangelical Protestants and Orthodox Jews.[75]

Catholic bishops in America, however, are divided over whether to grant communion to Catholic politicians who are pro-abortion. One group feels the issue is a private matter and no action should be taken. Another group feels it is wrong to grant communion to pro-abortion candidates but will not refuse communion to those who ask for it. Two groups—and they seem to constitute the majority of bishops in America—refuse to grant communion to politicians—the last group going so far as to refuse to grant communion to ordinary congregants who vote for pro-abortion politicians. Catholic theologians such as Daniel Maguire, however, regard abortion as a holy and sacred decision. As sociologist Anne Hendershott puts it, "the question of Catholic teaching" on abortion, remains "contested terrain."[76]

The conservative Protestant stance on this issue was perhaps most visible in religious radio and televangelism, and in the actions of the Moral Majority, the Christian Coalition, and James Dobson's Focus on the Family and Family Research Council—especially from the 1980s. "Evangelicals," as sociologists John P. Hoffmann and Sherrie Mills Johnson noted in an article on the attitudes of devout Americans toward abortion, "comprise much of the pro-life movement in the U.S.," and they "increasingly sense that the prevalence of all types of abortions is detrimental to the nation's moral fabric."[77]

Church leaders were enlisted in the 2008 election, for example, to defy the Internal Revenue Service (IRS) and promote Republican candidates John McCain and Sarah Palin from the pulpit. Ministers from 22 states challenged the law, and most of those who participated were "pro-life pastors." Wiley S. Drake of the First Southern Baptist Church of Buena Park, California, was typical in proclaiming to his members that Christians who adhere to the Bible on issues such as abortion could not vote for Barack Obama. The Alliance Defense Fund, initiated by a legal group in Arizona that claims the tax code discriminates against the clergy's First Amendment rights, urged church leaders to break the tax rules and participate in what they called Pulpit Freedom Sunday, an event they hoped church leaders would use to urge their congregations to vote for the GOP ticket. So far the IRS does not seem to have responded to the challenge.[78]

The pro-abortionists could count on Protestant members of many mainstream denominations, Jewish members of many Conservative and Reform denominations, and progressives who regarded themselves as spiritual, but had no formal links to ecclesiastical bodies, or who were agnostics or atheists. But it seems the pro-abortion lobby also had the support of some liberal Catholics. Public opinion polls suggested in 2008 that 49 percent of Roman Catholics and 49 percent of Protestants (but only 33 percent of white evangelical Protestants) support a right to abortion in all or most cases.[79] The abortion rate for Protestant women—Protestants comprised about 54 percent of the population—was 37 percent, whereas the abortion rate for Roman Catholic women—Roman Catholics comprised 31 percent of the population—was 31 percent.[80]

Abortion, the Media, and Public Opinion

The abortion wars after the 1970s were also fought in the corridors of public opinion—especially in the media.[81] Publicity surrounding *The Silent Scream* (1984), a short documentary film purporting to depict the reaction of an 11-week-old fetus being aborted and its grief-stricken mother, for example, was shown to President Ronald Reagan at a White House screening and was used by anti-abortion politicians to their advantage in congressional campaigns during the 1980s.

Best-selling evangelical authors such as Francis A. Schaeffer (1912–1984) helped make abortion a voting issue for religious conservatives. Schaeffer co-authored a book in 1983 with C. Everett Koop, the future surgeon-general, entitled, *Whatever Happened to the Human Race?* They decried the deaths of the unborn and warned of looming struggles against euthanasia and infanticide. Videotapes of this and other books (especially *How Should We Then Live? The Rise and Decline of Western Thought and Culture,* first published in 1976) were shown to thousands of evangelical congregations across the nation.

Violence in the Anti-Abortion War

One of Schaeffer's books, *A Christian Manifesto* (1981), had a decided impact on extremists such as Randall Terry and his group, Operation Rescue, which espoused violent tactics. Operation Rescue "at one time wielded the single-largest measure of pro-life power of any organization in North America," Herring argues. But killing medical professionals and blowing up abortion clinics were eventually seen as counterproductive even for Christian conservatives— most of whom had abandoned Operation Rescue by the end of the 1990s.[82]

In retrospect, Operation Rescue was only a temporary public relations disaster for anti-abortion activists. The new century ushered in a Republican president who was more sympathetic to the anti-abortion cause than any previous president in the modern era. The rhetoric of abortion—as articulated by NARAL Pro-Choice America, NOW (National Organization of Women), and Planned Parenthood, the major abortion-rights groups—was losing out to the rhetoric of Concerned Women for America and numerous other anti-abortion coalition groups.

Although a landmark study by David Shaw (1943–2005) of the *Los Angeles Times* in 1990 had concluded that the media were biased in favor of the pro-abortion lobby,[83] the largely anecdotal evidence since then has been more ambiguous. Journalists might be "predisposed to favor choice," as the journalist Stephen Stewart suggests, which probably was reinforced through "interaction with fellow journalists,"[84] but more and more voters apparently were shifting toward the anti-abortion banner.

Pro-abortion activists themselves claimed they were "under siege." The "language" used and "topics" chosen by journalists, Planned Parenthood leader Gloria Feldt argues, "shape and define the way people think about issues." She accused the news media of adopting the "inflammatory and misleading" language of anti-abortion activists to frame the contemporary abortion debate for press, radio, and television consumers. Such words as "liberal" or "feminist," she argued, were "demonized" by journalists and rendered politically incorrect in the corridors of power. She noted a "favorite" tactic of the anti-abortion lobby was to castigate mainstream media as "too liberal and pro-choice, causing reporters and editors to bend over backward to prove that they are not."[85]

Abortion and the Disadvantaged

While both sides used abortion statistics selectively to support their positions, more attention was now being paid to one reality—abortion was primarily the option for ethnic minorities. More than 75 percent of all abortion clinics were positioned next to or within minority communities. More than 35 percent of all abortions were performed on African Americans, although they constituted only 12 percent of the population. Hispanic-American and Native-American women, along with poor white women, were also more likely candidates for abortion.

Some studies, moreover, suggested a link between abortion rates and lower crime rates—angering minority activists and undoubtedly strengthening the anti-abortion lobby within these communities. The pro-abortion lobby seemed unwilling to counter this argument, even though a major rationale for women's reproductive rights was based on the perception that poor woman with the least access to resources were most in need of abortion services.[86]

Abortion rights traditionally were championed by the feminist movement, but increasingly some feminists were muddying the pro-abortion/anti-abortion debate by questioning the idea that reproductive freedom and abortion rights were synonymous. Like religious conservatives, they framed abortion as a "moral" issue and not only an issue of women's rights. The "long and arduous movement towards inclusion," as political theorist Jean Bethke Elshtain put it, placed the "unborn child . . . within the boundary of the moral community rather than outside it." They cited studies to suggest the "negative" impact of abortion "on women themselves." Claiming that abortion rights had degenerated into "sexual irresponsibility and cultural degradation," they called for abortion decisions to be "returned to the state legislatures."[87]

Anti-abortion coalitions had also succeeded, sociologist Susan Markens argues, in co-opting feminist reproductive rhetoric. Dramatic developments in "biomedical and genetic technologies" had revolutionized the concept of motherhood. "Test-tube" babies were first conceived in 1978, but the procedure remained "largely unregulated in the United States." The anti-abortion lobby's focus on the morality of traditional families—a topic that was also highlighted in debates about gay civil rights—fed on public fears of commoditizing motherhood and parenthood. Markens says, "[T]he politics of reproduction ... is bound up with social conflicts about gender, particularly the role of motherhood in women's lives." Fears about the future of the nuclear heterosexual family were fused with fears about "the significance of motherhood for women's identity" and "the seeming decoupling of motherhood from marriage." Hence, pro-abortion feminists, she says, would have limited "effectiveness ... in shaping the legislative agenda."[88]

Anti-abortion forces have won the abortion war, *Slate* national correspondent Saletan proclaimed in a 2003 study. He claimed pro-abortion activists had sought an unholy alliance with a broader conservative constituency by framing "abortion restrictions as an encroachment by big government on tradition, family, and property." The pro-abortion lobby, he said, had gradually shifted attention "away from women's particular moral experiences, away from their collective welfare and moral competence, and toward the simpler and less challenging message that the government should leave abortion decisions to families."[89]

Anti-Abortion Strategies during the Bush Administration

The decades-long war of attrition fought primarily through the federal courts, Congress, state legislatures, the media, and the court of public opinion continued during the administration of George W. Bush. Anti-abortion activists, however, tried a new strategy, one that called for fine-tuning the viability of life issue in accord with definitions emerging from the courts (recall *Planned Parenthood of Southeast Pennsylvania v. Casey*) as well as from medical research.

Anti-abortion forces also continued to focus on protecting the mother and the unborn child from the "violent" actions of late-term abortions. The new mantra was to ban so-called partial-birth abortions—a medical technique (called intact dilation and extraction or evacuation) perfected only in the early 1990s and designed to minimize the risk of late-term abortions. A doctor using this procedure—usually conducted in the second trimester—typically pulls the body from the womb and pierces or crushes the skull so it will pass through the cervix.

Public opinion polls suggested that Americans accepted abortions in the first trimester but did not favor late-term abortions. According to one poll in 2005, for example, 72 percent were against abortion in the second trimester and 86 percent in the third trimester.[90] Two pieces of abortion legislation passed by the Republican-dominated Congress in the Bush presidency, moreover, did not evoke much debate.

The Born-Alive Infants Protection Act (2002) ensured that every baby born alive, including those who might survive an attempted abortion but be left to die, "is to be legally considered a person . . . . Killing a born-alive infant would be considered murder." Almost all members of Congress could and did accept this legislation. The Unborn Victims of Violence Act (2004) prescribed penalties for injuring or killing an unborn child during the commission of crimes. The law applied only to those crimes in which the federal government had jurisdiction—to scores of federal laws dealing with crimes of violence. State laws applied to these types of crimes where the states had jurisdiction. Although criticized by pro-abortion groups such as Planned Parenthood and the American Civil Liberties Union, both houses of Congress passed the legislation by large majorities.[91]

The Partial Birth Abortion Ban Act—two earlier versions had been vetoed by President Bill Clinton—was also finally signed into law in 2003. In harmony with "at least 27 states" that had already banned the practice, the legislators claimed this type of abortion was "a disfavored procedure" in the medical community, was not "medically necessary," posed "serious risks to the health of a woman undergoing the procedure," and "could ultimately result in maternal death."[92] The National Right to Life Committee cited public opinion polls showing overwhelming support for the legislation.

The phrase "partial birth"—instead of "late-term abortion" as used by clinicians—reflected the political rhetoric of the day. Partial birth abortion was not usually defined, but was instead depicted in graphic, gruesome terms—often with accompanying photographs. The legislation claimed to "draw a bright line that clearly distinguishes abortion and infanticide, that preserves the integrity of the medical profession, and promotes respect for human life."[93]

The U.S. Supreme Court upheld the legislation 5-4 in *Gonzales v. Carhart* (2007). Justice Samuel Alito and Chief Justice John Roberts—both appointed to the Court by President Bush—joined the majority in declaring that the act did not impose an unnecessary burden for a woman seeking an abortion, and that it was not unconstitutional simply because it lacked an exception to protect the woman's health. Justice Ruth Bader Ginsburg called the decision "alarming" in her dissenting opinion. "It tolerates, indeed applauds, federal intervention to ban nationwide a procedure found necessary and proper in certain cases by the American College of Obstetricians and Gynecologists

(ACOG) . . . . And, for the first time since Roe, the Court blesses a prohibition with no exception safeguarding a woman's health."[94]

Other campaigns to get anti-abortion legislation through Congress during the Bush years failed, however. Probably the most significant of this legislation was the Unborn Child Pain Awareness Act of 2007, which would have required doctors to tell a pregnant mother (a) that the unborn fetus was experiencing "excruciating pain" (an unborn child being defined as a fetus as early as 20 weeks) and (b) that the mother could request "anesthesia" for the fetus during the course of the abortion. The legislation failed in the House of Representatives in December 2006—one month before the Democrats took over as the majority party in Congress.[95] The essential provisions on abortion rights in *Roe v. Wade* remained intact at the end of the Bush administration.

ENDURING TENSIONS

Public opinion is deeply divided over birth control and abortion rights. The polls that suggest the public still believes in a woman's *right* to abort also suggest disapproval of the decision to *have* an abortion. The polls that suggest the public is *against* government getting involved in legislating against abortion also suggest the public *approves* of the steps government is taking "to reduce abortions." These ambiguities undoubtedly reflect (a) the cumulative impact of more than a generation of acrimonious debate over abortion rights and (b) the fact that the majority of adult Americans under 40 years of age have never experienced life in a country that did not allow abortion. While the numbers of abortions are declining, at least 35 percent of women in America will still choose abortion at some point during their lives.[96]

This lack of consensus suggests that tensions within the Christian community and between that community and other secular and religious communities about a host of gender and sexuality issues—from abortion, to contraception, to reproductive rights, to prostitution, to gender roles and identities—may well escalate over the next several years. For one thing, Republican George W. Bush has left office and Democrat Barack Obama has assumed power at a critical stage in the culture wars. Obama, unlike Bush, favors reproductive choice. He would trust women to make their own decisions, and he can be expected to support free choice under *Roe v. Wade;* he favors the teaching of abstinence *and* contraception in the public schools; and he favors funding for and access to contraception.[97]

The number of appointments of social and religious conservatives to federal offices almost certainly will not reach the levels seen under Bush. And they are less likely to be appointed to federal judgeships. Obama appointments to the court could ultimately change the balance of power in the judiciary and have a profound impact on a wide range of decisions that affect sexuality and gender issues.

The U.S. Supreme Court now has five Catholic justices (John Roberts, Anthony Kennedy, Antonin Scalia, Clarence Thomas, and Samuel Alito), two Jewish justices (Stephen Breyer and Ruth Bader Ginsburg), and two Protestant justices (David H. Souter, who announced his retirement in May 2009, and John Paul Stevens). Tensions most certainly will increase if a challenge to *Roe v. Wade* makes its way to the Court in the future.

Pro-abortion forces paint a dark picture, indeed, of America if *Roe* is overturned. They note that legal abortions today are a "safer" procedure "than childbirth."[98] An abortion ban will not affect the rich, who will continue to get abortions because they can afford them. The poor and otherwise marginalized, however, will again be forced to get abortions illegally in whatever ways they can. The numbers of illegal abortions will soar (and they will not appear in official statistics), and women's reproductive options will revert to what they had been at the beginning of the twentieth century.

Feminist scholar Cristina Page claims that one-third of the doctors now willing to perform abortions live in states where abortions will no longer be legal in this post-*Roe* scenario. Family planning services will wither away, and doctors aiding women seeking care after an abortion will again be subject to criminal penalties. Women will be encouraged not to delay marriage and childbearing, which might well discourage them from entering the workforce.[99]

George W. Bush worked to the very end of his presidency to ensure that this scenario would become a reality. He continued to impose the so-called "global gag rule," which prohibits federal funds from being used to support any United Nations or other international family-planning agency involved in overseas birth control and abortion activities. He also sought to muddy the waters further by expanding the concept of freedom of conscience to include the right *not* to perform services on a range of health-care-related activities.[100]

We argue that women's reproductive rights and gay civil rights became more and more polarized the closer debates got to deconstructing the two-sex marriage and family model. Perhaps this has always been the case with women's reproductive rights, but recent developments in contraception and reproduction technology have given new credence to conservative forces that would exercise total control over a woman's right to her own body. We conclude by citing a few of the tensions we think will generate debate in coming years.

Resisting and Enforcing Gender Stereotypes

The two-sex model historically was most closely associated with the values and norms of modernizing white, middle-upper-class males in American society. They had the economic and cultural capital—the money, the status, and the social and political networks—to explain and demonstrate how the two-sex model should be applied among all ethnic groups and social classes in everyday life.

The two-sex model, however, was never as pervasive in the lower-middle and lower strata of society. Poorer white, Hispanic, and African-American heterosexual households in the United States have always exhibited a greater variety of personal lifestyles than would be countenanced in the traditional two-sex model. Nevertheless, feminists argue that even in the midst of today's racial and cultural diversity a majority of the dominant heterosexual community adheres to the generic, patriarchal two-sex model.

Many men and women will continue to resist stereotypes about sexuality and gender, even as many social and religious conservatives will continue the campaign to preserve traditional cultural restraints based on the two-sex model. Men who are sensitive to feminist perspectives, however, often have difficulty in finding a nonauthoritative and fluid model of masculinity that provides a viable alternative to the traditional model. Individuals may wish to shape their own lives, but the lives they shape will be organized, structured, and constrained to an enormous degree by the dominant heterosexual discourses they encounter every day of their lives.

The challenge in gender relations turns in part on whether authentic female and male voices can be represented throughout society apart from the dominant Male Voice. Can a female sexuality emerge from a dominant model of male sexuality? Can a male sexuality emerge unburdened by the dominant model of male sexuality? Is it possible to live in a world without gender dichotomies? If these questions are too daunting, how about a list of subsidiary questions such as these: What exactly is the relationship between our biological bodies and our gender? Why does being a woman still mean to be less well rewarded and recognized in public life? How free are people to express gender in everyday life?[101]

Late-Term Abortions

Some critics claim that there is at least one area of the abortion debate about which the opposing forces seem to agree: late-term abortions. Even most pro-abortion activists would agree with most Americans that abortions should not be permitted—except in special cases (such as incest or rape)—beyond 24 weeks. They would see the right to abort as both a moral and legal choice that is made at some point in the continuum between conception and birth. Abortion in the later stages of pregnancy is not only less legal but also less moral.

"We make a distinction between a few cells that haven't yet been implanted in a woman's uterus," as Page puts it, "and a six-month-old fetus that might live outside the womb. In abortion, earlier is better."[102] The reckoning by some *Christian* pro-abortion activists that abortions should *not* be permitted beyond 24 weeks approaches the *medieval* view of the moment of quickening, about 20 weeks, when the Church in premodern Europe believed the fetus contained a "soul" and was therefore a human being.

Even this potential consensus is fleeting, however, because the anti-abortion lobby has increasingly fused medical technology with fundamentalist theology to determine "life" in the mother's womb. The three limited anti-abortion laws passed during the George W. Bush administration, the blocking of federal funding to support family-planning projects overseas, and the blocking of embryonic stem-cell research inside the country, for example, are not enough. Anti-abortion activists would enact laws that protect all stages of fetal development from conception (as some states now do)—including a fertilized egg artificially inseminated before insertion into a womb—to birth. Personhood would be endowed on fetuses at all stages of development.

Birth Control and Privacy Rights

The legality of contraception has been grounded in privacy rights guaranteed by the Constitution—rights that also have been compromised with federal interference. Pro-abortion activists point to the many years of campaigning to get Plan B finally approved for over-the-counter sale to adults. They point to the ban on federal funding for contraception programs overseas and the failure of abstinence-only sex-education programs directed at middle- and high-school students.[103] And they point to studies—such as one by the *Journal of Adolescent Health* in 2008—suggesting that a comprehensive sex-education program has the best success rate in preventing teenage pregnancies—America has the highest rate of teenage pregnancies in the so-called developed world.[104]

Planned Parenthood's Alexander Sanger argues that all attempts by government in the past to prohibit, promote, regulate, or otherwise control the birth rate have been ineffective. Government is expected to prohibit incest, rape, bigamy, and polygamy and "validly protect the institution of marriage and the marriage contract, especially where there are children involved." Government is also expected to allow abortions in cases of incest or rape, when a serious birth defect has been found in the fetus, or when the pregnancy endangers the health of the woman. Future developments in cloning and genetic engineering may also call for government restrictions, but society should interfere "only when reproductive freedom causes health or other damage to society."[105]

Sanger counters the anti-abortion claim that abortions must be prevented to preserve life with the argument that *life* means allowing "a couple to carry out their reproductive strategies to have healthy children that they can invest in so that the children in turn will survive to reproduce and invest in turn in their progeny." Science suggests that human evolutionary history is not based on the preservation of life—however one defines this term—but on continuing reproduction. This "reproductive freedom" respects the right of women to determine when to become mothers. "Assigning an absolute right to life is as biologically and morally meaningless as saying that life consists of DNA and nothing more."[106]

The same questions being debated today are the questions debated in the 1970s and undoubtedly they will be the questions debated in the future. When should contraceptives be made available to women? Should age, marital status, poverty, and other social and/or economic considerations be a factor in abortion decisions? Should federal funding be provided for family planning, abortion, prenatal care, genetic screening, and other childbearing services? Should abortion decisions be based on the trimester system (as in *Roe*) or after fetal viability (as in *Casey*)?

We give Sanger the last word here, because he argues that men have framed all abortion-rights issues. Men and women have different "strategies," he suggests, in the struggle for reproductive survival:

"The battle of the sexes is over the control of reproduction" (italics in the original). Men make the laws, and the laws reflect a society that—echoing the journalist Ginger Loggins—"does not trust women."[107] Only when we change the conditions giving rise to these debates will we begin to understand the meaning of motherhood—and fatherhood—as a lifetime commitment to preparing our children for this struggle.

NOTES

1. Cited by Robert T. Garrett, "Opposition Mounts to Perry's HPV Order: Senate Majority Wants Directive Dropped; He Defends Shots for Girls," *Dallas Morning News*, February 7, 2007, B29.

2. "Sexual Health," World Health Organization, United Nations, undated, www.who.int/reproductive-health/gender/sexualhealth.html#2. This is not an official definition of the World Health Organization.

3. The canon of the Hebrew Bible (Old Testament) as we know it was actually not completed until 140 CE. The orthodox canon of the Christian Bible (New Testament) as we know it (27 books) was first considered canonical by that venerated orthodox apologist Athanasius, the bishop of Alexandria, in a letter to the churches in Egypt in 367 CE. The Christian canon, however, was never actually subjected to a formal vote until the Roman Catholics legitimized their canon—in response to Protestant reformers—at the Council of Trent (1545–1563).

4. This section is based on public lectures Les Switzer has given on biblical notions of patriarchy and sexuality and on studies of the one-sex model. See, for example, Mary Holmes, *What is Gender? Sociological Approaches* (Los Angeles: Sage, 2007), 22–25; John Shelby Spong, *Living in Sin? A Bishop Rethinks Human Sexuality* (New York: Harper & Row, 1988); Paul Veyne, *Did The Greeks Believe in Their Myths? An Essay on the Constitutive Imagination*, trans. Paula Wissing (Chicago: University of Chicago Press, 1988); Leonard Shlain, *The Alphabet Versus the Goddess: The Conflict Between Word and Image* (New York: Viking, 1998).

5. The second century Greek physician Galen, for example, concluded that women's genitals were an inverted, invisible version of men's visible genitals. In essence, women's sex organs were "less perfect" copies of men's sex organs. Thomas Laqueur, *Making Sex: Body and Gender from the Greeks to Freud* (Cambridge, MA: Harvard University Press, 1990), 4–5. Galen is the crowning figure in the classical Greek medical tradition that began with Hippocrates six centuries earlier, and his views on the human anatomy would prevail in medieval Europe for more than a millennium. See "Galen," Claude Moore Health Sciences Library, University of Virginia Health System, undated, www.hsl.virginia.edu/historical/artifacts/antiqua/galen.cfm.

6. Celibacy in any form was abnormal—single, unmarried adults were not acceptable. Sexual intercourse during a woman's menstrual period, for example, was forbidden—as was semen excreted on the ground (i.e., masturbation). The menstrual cycle was involuntary and masturbation was voluntary, but neither one aided the reproductive process and were regarded as "unclean." Intercourse itself was regarded as "unclean" until sundown.

7. Ancient Hebrew traditions apparently accepted that this was the only life one would ever have, but one's deeds on the earth as well as one's children could extend one's life through its influence on future generations. Jewish understanding of an afterlife evolved to the point that it was a majority consensus probably by the time the Maccabees (the Hasmoneans) revolted against the Seleucid Empire in the second century BCE. See Wayne A Meeks, ed., *HarperCollins Study Bible: New Revised Standard Version* (New York: HarperCollins, 1993), 1716–1717. This reference is to 2 Maccabees, Chapter 12:38–45. The explanatory note for verse 43 reads in part: "The author of 2 Maccabees took it [a sin offering for the dead] as applying to the dead and thus proof of Judas's belief [Judas Maccabeus was a leader of the Maccabeean revolt at this point] in the *resurrection*" (italics in the original). See also Daniel 12:1–3. Vestiges of the older tradition, however, were still present for those who identified with the Sadducees during Jesus's ministry in the early first century CE. The Sadducees—unlike two other known groups at the time, the Pharisees and the Essenes—did not believe in the immortality of the soul. See New Testament texts such as Mark 12:18 and Acts 23:8 (on the Saduccees).

8. While the Law of Moses allowed for divorce, Jesus goes further and actually condemns the practice—the only custom from which he seems to have deviated from other Jewish sages (such as Rabbi Hillel) of his day (see Mark 10:1–10; Matthew 5:31–32, 19:1–10).

9. The link between patriarchy, capitalism, the heterosexual family, and the emergence of modernity in the West remains a topic of heated debate—ever since Marxist scholars first reexamined these relationships in the 1970s. See Roberta Hamilton, *The Liberation of Women: A Study of Patriarchy and Capitalism* (London: Allen & Unwin, 1978); Nicholas Abercrombie and John Urry, *Capital, Labour, and the Middle Classes* (London: Allen & Unwin, 1983); Pavla Miller, *Transformations of Patriarchy in the West, 1500–1900* (Bloomington: Indiana University Press, 1998).

10. Stephanie Coontz, *Marriage, A History: From Obedience to Intimacy or How Love Conquered Marriage* (New York: Viking, 2005), 175, 176. The literature analyzing the origins of the two-sex heterosexual model is growing. See also Steven Mintz and Susan Kellogg, *Domestic Revolutions: A Social History of American Family Life* (New York: Free Press, 1988).

11. Historian and cultural critic Michel Foucault traces the "repression" of sexuality from the seventeenth century. Michel Foucault, *The History of Sexuality*, trans. Robert Hurley (New York: Vintage, 1990).

12. "Homosexuality," entry by Philip Culbertson in Edward Kessler and Neil Wenborn, eds., *A Dictionary of Jewish-Christian Relations* (Cambridge: Cambridge University Press, 2005), 197.

13. Holmes, *What is Gender?*, 4 (for Beauvoir citation), 90 (for male citation). Simone de Beauvoir's *The Second Sex* was originally published in French in 1949.

14. The argument for a societal gender feedback loop is detailed in Sara L. Crawley, Lara J. Foley, and Constance L. Shehan, *Gendering Bodies* (Lanham, MD: Rowman & Littlefield, 2008), 29–32.

15. Timothy F. Taylor, "The Origins of Human Sexual Culture: Sex, Gender and Social Control," *Journal of Psychology & Human Sexuality* 18, nos. 2/3 (2006): 69–105, p. 96.

16. Discussed in Holmes, *What Is Gender?*, Chapter 5.

17. Crawley, Foley, and Shehan, *Gendering Bodies*, 28–29.

18. Ellen Goodman, "The Mother (or Is It the Father?) of All Childbirth Stories," *Houston Chronicle*, July 13, 2008, E4.

19. Amy Harmon, "Genetic Testing + Abortion = ???" *New York Times*, May 13, 2007, Week in Review-1, 4, p. 4.

20. The history of the modern feminist movement in America, of course, remains contested terrain. Two recent books offer useful insights. See Ruth Rosen, *The World Split Open: How The Modern Women's Movement Changed America* (New York: Viking, 2000); and Winifred Breines, *Trouble Between Us: An Uneasy History of White and Black Women in the Feminist Movement* (Oxford, UK: Oxford University Press, 2006).

21. Title VII of this act had a list prohibiting discrimination in employment and preemployment practices based on "race, color, religion, sex, or national origin." The category "sex"—inserted by hard-liners in an attempt to kill the act—instead opened the door for feminists to pursue a civil-rights strategy in the quest for equal rights. See "Title VII of the Civil Rights Act of 1964," U.S. Equal Employment Opportunity Commission, Washington, DC, January 15, 1997, www.eeoc.gov/policy/vii.html. On the importance of this provision in the Civil Rights Act for the women's movement, see Nancy MacLean, "Gender Is Powerful: The Long Reach of Feminism," *OAH* (Organization of American Historians) *Magazine of History*, October 2006, 19–23, p. 20: "Women used it not only to enter good jobs of all kinds long closed to them but also to end pregnancy discrimination and fight sexual harassment. Indeed they [women interpreting Title VII] raised foundational questions about gender and power with reverberations in every area of American life."

22. Anne N. Costain, Richard Braunstein, and Heidi Berggren, "Framing the Women's Movement," in *Women, Media, and Politics*, ed. Pippa Norris (New York: Oxford University Press, 1997), 205–220, p. 208.

23. Roberta W. Francis, "The History behind the Equal Rights Amendment," *The Equal Rights Amendment*, Alice Paul Institute and the

ERA Task Force of the National Organization of Women's Organizations, www.equalrightsamendment.org/era.htm. Francis is co-chair of the ERA Task Force.

24. There were also generational divisions between feminists over strategies to promote women's rights. Many alienated women left the feminist movement after 1920 because "the elite, white National Women's Party [NWP] made that label anathema to women working for wider social justice." They objected to the NWP's single-minded pursuit of an Equal Rights Amendment, "a gender-blind approach that threatened hard-won, gender-conscious reforms like protective legislation" that had been advocated by the first wave of feminists. MacLean, "Gender Is Powerful," 20.

25. Holmes, *What Is Gender?*, 181.

26. Ibid., 124.

27. Rebecca Ann Lind and Colleen Salo, "The Framing of Feminists and Feminism in News and Public Affairs Programs in U.S. Electronic Media," *Journal of Communication* 52, no. 1 (2002): 211–228, p. 211. The researchers conducted a content analysis of 35,000 hours of news and public affairs content in ABC, CNN, PBS, and NPR (National Public Radio) programs between May 1993 and January 1996. See also Leonie Huddy, "Feminists and Feminism in the News," in Norris, *Women, Media, and Politics*, 183–204.

28. Jennifer Young Abbott, "Religion and Gender in the News: The Case of Promise Keepers, Feminists, and the 'Stand in the Gap' Rally," *Journal of Communication and Religion* 29, no. 2 (2006): 224–261, pp. 225–226. The author conducted a rhetorical analysis of news about the rally on ABC, CBS, NBC, and CNN between 1996 and 1998.

29. Ibid., 249.

30. Cynthia Carter and Linda Steiner, eds., *Critical Readings: Media and Gender* (Maidenhead, UK: Open University Press, 2004), 2–3.

31. Pippa Norris, "Introduction," 1–18, and Everett Carll Ladd, "Media Framing of the Gender Gap," 113–128, in Norris, *Women, Media, and Politics*.

32. Norris, "Introduction," 9.

33. This remains a hotly debated topic that resists facile characterization, but see Kay Mills, "What Difference Do Women Journalists Make?," 41–56; Shanto Iyengar, Nicholas A. Valentino, Stephen Ansolabehere, and Adam F. Simon, "Running as a Woman: Gender Stereotyping in Women's Campaigns," 77–98; and Betty Houchin Winfield, "The First Lady, Political Power, and the Media: Who Elected Her Anyway," 166–180, in Norris, *Women, Media, and Politics*.

34. María E. Len-Ríos, Shelly Rodgers, Esther Thorson, and Doyle Yoon, "Representation of Women in News and Photos: Comparing Content to Perceptions," *Journal of Communication* 55, no. 1 (2005): 152–168. The study compared a sample of medium-sized (cir. about 200,000) and larger (cir. about

475,000) Midwestern newspapers from February 1998 to March 1999. Cultural attitudes in the newsroom "may change," the researchers suggested hopefully, with the new generation of younger journalists.

35. Ginger Miller Loggins, "Gender," in *Media Bias: Finding It, Fixing It*, ed. Wm. David Sloan and Jean Burleson Mackay (Jefferson, NC: McFarland, 2007), 90–104, p. 91 (italics not in the original).

36. Mark Y. Herring, *The Pro-Life/Choice Debate* (Westport, CT: Greenwood, 2003), xvii (citing a source published in 1992).

37. William Saletan, *Bearing Right: How Conservatives Won the Abortion War* (Berkeley: University of California Press, 2003), 3–4.

38. Stephen E. Stewart, "Abortion," Sloan and Mackay, *Media Bias*, 65–80, p. 66.

39. Herring, *The Pro-Life/Choice Debate*, 192.

40. This section is also based largely on public lectures Les Switzer has given on biblical notions of sexual identity. For additional sources, see Thomas C. Caramagno, *Irreconcilable Differences? Intellectual Stalemate in the Gay Rights Debate* (Westport, CT: Praeger, 2002), Chapters 4–6; William Countryman, *Dirt, Greed and Sex: Sexual Ethics in the New Testament and Their Implications for Today*, rev. ed. (Minneapolis, MN: Fortress, 2007).

41. John Boswell, *Same-Sex Unions in Premodern Europe* (New York: Vintage, 1995), 280.

42. See Konstantinos Kapparis, *Abortion in the Ancient World* (London: Duckworth, 2002). He traces abortion debates essentially in the Greco-Roman classical era—ca. 400 BCE to 400 CE. Abortion decisions were "inextricably linked to personal, emotional, religious, cultural, political, social and economic circumstances." Konstaninos argues, "[I]n the end . . . it all came down to one simple fact: if the woman *from her perspective and in her own mind* thought that continuing with the pregnancy under existing circumstances would make her life unbearable, then she would not be deterred either by law, or religion, or even the real threat against her own life" (italics in the original) (195–196).

43. The male authorities of the church would periodically condemn contraception or abortion especially in times of crisis—the most significant being the Black Death in the mid-fourteenth century, which killed between one-third and one-half of Europe's population in four years.

44. Leslie J. Reagan, *When Abortion Was a Crime: Women, Medicine, and the Law in the United States, 1867–1973* (Berkeley: University of California Press, 1997), 7. Interpretations of the historical record on these issues, of course, are matters of dispute. Anti-abortionists tend to base their arguments on readings of selected texts taken from the Bible, writings of the early church fathers, and the decisions made by ecclesiastical bodies. Pro-abortionists tend to base their arguments on more critical readings of these texts and decisions and situate them in broader historical and cultural contexts. Mark Herring, a university librarian who tries unsuccessfully to claim

a neutral position in these debates, concludes that "two immediately recognizable trends" can be discerned in this literature before "the close of the eighteenth century." While "abortion and infanticide were both practiced," he says, "history presents an almost unbroken record of condemning or . . . stringently discouraging abortion, and, yes, even contraception." Herring, *Pro-Life/Choice Debate*, 18. Alexander Sanger, head of the American regional office of the International Planned Parenthood Federation, points to theological concepts eventually enshrined in secular law "delaying the declaration of a pregnancy and thus of human life until the woman could confirm she was pregnant . . . . Before quickening, termination of the 'pregnancy' was not prohibited because the woman was not deemed under the law to be pregnant." Alexander Sanger, *Beyond Choice: Reproductive Freedom in the 21st Century* (New York: Public Affairs, 2004), 22–23.

45. Sanger, *Beyond Choice*, 29.

46. Ibid.

47. Margaret Sanger was only one among many pro-abortion voices during this period. Herring, for example, cites a number of other early feminists—from the French physician Madeleine Pelletier (1874–1939) and the English women's suffrage leader Emmeline Pankhurst (1858–1928), to Emma Goldman (1869–1940), Mary Coffin Ware Dennett (1872–1947), Ruth Barnett (who operated an abortion clinic in Oregon from 1918 to 1969), and Betty Friedan (1921–2006)—as pioneers in birth control and abortion rights. Herring, *Pro-Life/Choice Debate*, Chapter 3.

48. Sanger, *Beyond Choice*, 30.

49. *People v. Sanger*, 222 NY 192 (1918). The New York Supreme Court turned down Margaret Sanger's attempt to overturn a misdemeanor conviction for breaking a section of the penal code that proscribed advertising and/or selling birth-control paraphernalia. The justices, however, noted that physicians were already protected from this provision: they could give birth-control "help and advice" to married persons "to cure or prevent disease," and this right "would also extend to the druggist, or vendor, acting upon the physician's prescription or order."

50. *United States v. One Package of Japanese Pessaries*, 86 F.2d 737 (2nd Cir. 1936). The U.S. Court of Appeals for the Second Circuit ruled that the Comstock Act—which prohibited obscene matter, including contraceptives or information about contraceptives, from being shipped through the mail service—could not be used to seize shipments ordered by a physician.

51. Sanger, *Beyond Choice*, 38–39. Herring argues that "the pro-life side" had the unqualified support of the doctors, the clergy, and "the entire legal system" in the nineteenth century. Margaret Sanger and others began "chipping away the arguments, one by one, until the majority in the legal, medical, and clerical professions became divided on the question." Americans were "lost in a fog of conflicting rights and constitutional protections" as the debate essentially shifted in favor of the pro-abortion side in the first

half of the twentieth century. Herring, *Pro-Life/Choice Debate*, 77. A modified version of the Comstock Act, however, is still in force.

52. *Griswold v. Connecticut*, 381 U.S. 479 (1965).

53. *Eisenstadt v. Baird*, 405 U.S. 438 (1972).

54. Gardiner Harris, "F.D.A. Approves Broader Access to Next-Day Pill," *New York Times*, August 25, 2006, A1, A18, p. A18.

55. Government Accountability Office, "Decision Process to Deny Initial Application for Over-the-Counter Marketing of the Emergency Contraceptive Drug Plan B Was Unusual," Report to Congressional Requesters, Washington, DC, www.gao.gov/new.items/d06109.pdf, 5, 39 (from not-approvable letter to Barr Research).

56. For a history of the controversy about Plan B before FDA approval in 2006, see Cristina Page, *How the Pro-Choice Movement Saved America: Freedom, Politics, and the War on Sex* (New York: Basic Books, 2006), Chapter 5.

57. The blurring of the boundary between birth control and abortion is also illustrated by the long-running controversy over RU-486, which was manufactured initially by a French company and marketed for decades in Europe. It was also initially misnamed a "morning after pill" when in fact it was a drug to induce medical abortions in women: if taken at any time during the first 63 days of pregnancy, the drug effectively terminates about 92 percent of pregnancies. Fearful of an anti-abortion backlash, the RU-486 was marketed by prescription only by an American company under the brand name *Mifeprex*. Although finally approved by the FDA in 2000, the anti-abortion campaign against all forms of medical abortion has cast a long shadow over the future status of this drug. The latest legislation, the proposed RU-486 Suspension and Review Act, would have the FDA review its findings and suspend marketing and sale of the drug. The bill is still pending in Congress as of 2008. RU-486 was distributed in more than 29 countries worldwide as of 2005. Page, *How the Pro-Choice*, 62–64. See also "H.R. 63: RU-486 Suspension and Review Act of 2007," *govtrack.us*, 110th Congress, 2007–2008, www.govtrack.us/congress/bill.xpd?bill=h110-63.

58. *People v. Belous*, 458 P.2d 194 (Cal. 1969).

59. *United States v. Vuitch*, 402 U.S. 62 (1971).

60. The long history of anti-abortion and pro-abortion campaigns in America before *Roe* is detailed in Reagan, *When Abortion Was a Crime*. The California Supreme Court ruled 4-3 in *Belous* (with two judges not participating) that the state's abortion laws were unconstitutional. The *Vuitch* case involved a ruling by the district court in the District of Columbia over the constitutionality of a D.C. law admitting abortions only by licensed doctors and only in cases where "a mother's life or health" was in jeopardy. On appeal, the U.S. Supreme Court ruled 5-4 that the meaning of "health" was mental as well as physical, and the law was valid. This case opened up the possibility that abortions could be performed whenever the emotional or psychological well being of the pregnant mother was

deemed to be at risk. See "Further Readings," *JRank Law Library—American Law and Legal Information*, http://law.jrank.org/pages/13295/United-States-v-Vuitch.html.

61. *Roe v. Wade*, 410 U.S. 113 (1973).

62. *Doe v. Bolton*, 410 U.S. 179 (1973). The law also limited abortions to Georgia residents only and permitted abortions only in cases of rape, severe deformity, or danger to the mother. Blackmun delivered the majority opinion in *Roe* and in *Doe*.

63. *Planned Parenthood of Missouri v. Danforth*, 428 U.S. 52 (1976).

64. *Hunerwadel v. Baird* was consolidated with *Bellotti v. Baird*, 443 U.S. 622 (1979).

65. Herring, *Pro-Life/Choice Debate*, 89. Melody Rose, *Safe, Legal, and Unavailable? Abortion Politics in the United States* (Washington, DC: CY Press, 2007), 29–31. Statistics for abortion rates are complex (when broken down, for example, by socioeconomic status, ethnicity, geography, and age) and incomplete. The statistics are based on legal abortions only—illegal abortions undoubtedly increased as more states banned late-term abortions. Between four and six states, moreover, do not provide abortion reports. This includes California, the most populous state, where only federally funded programs such as Medi-Cal have figures available to researchers. Most publications cite abortion-rate figures compiled by the Alan Guttmacher Institute, a nonprofit research agency based in New York that has been tracking abortion rates since 1974. These figures show that abortion rates moved up and down for several years in the 1980s before reaching a high point of 1.6 million in 1990. Abortions overall have been in decline since the 1990s, although medical abortions (by pill and by surgery) actually may have increased in the last few years. The latest available figures are for 2005, which showed abortion rates had fallen to 1.2 million—the lowest level since 1976. See "Abortion in the United States: Statistics and Trends," National Right to Life, October 20, 2004, www.nrlc.org/ABORTION/facts/abortionstats .html (citing figures from the Guttmacher Institute, 1973–2005, and the Centers for Disease Control and Prevention); and Rebecca Wind, "U.S. Abortion Rate Continues Long-Term Decline . . . ," Guttmacher Institute, news release, January 17, 2008, www.guttmacher.org/media/nr/2008/01/17/index.html.

66. *Planned Parenthood of Southeastern Pennsylvania v. Casey*, 505 U.S. 833 (1992).

67. Ibid.

68. Ibid.

69. Abortion is the cause of about 50 percent of maternal deaths worldwide, and virtually all of these deaths occur in the so-called developing world. Most women, according to one study, turn to abortion as a "last resort to prevent an unwanted birth." Süsheela Singh, Stanley K. Henshaw, and Kathleen Berentsen, "Abortion: A Worldwide Overview," in *The Sociocultural and*

Political Aspects of Abortion: Global Perspectives, ed. Alaka Malwade Basu (Westport, CT: Praeger, 2003), 15–47. America has stopped funding the United Nations Population Fund (formerly the U.N. Fund for Population Activities)—the major world body funding population control programs—every year of the Bush administration beginning in 2002—despite money being allocated for this purpose by Congress. The United States also stopped funding all related agencies involved in any way with birth control overseas. Page, *How the Pro-Choice Movement*, Chapter 6.

70. "Public Funding for Abortion: What Is the Hyde Amendment?" American Civil Liberties Union, July 21, 2004, www.aclu.org/reproductive-rights/lowincome/16393res20040721.html; Jessica Arons, "The Hyde Amendment: 30 Years Is Enough," Center for American Progress, October 5, 2006, www.americanprogress.org/issues/2006/10/hyde_intro.html.

71. *Beal v. Doe*, 432 U.S. 438 (1977).

72. *Rust v. Sullivan*, 500 U.S. 173 (1991).

73. See, for example, Francis J. Beckwith, *Defending Life: A Moral and Legal Case Against Abortion Choice* (Cambridge: Cambridge University Press, 2007). Beckwith is a professor at Baylor University, a private university in Waco, Texas, affiliated to the Southern Baptist church. He employs moral and legal arguments to defend the anti-abortion stance.

74. Pope Paul's *Humanae Vitae*, which even some Catholic priests called "the pope's clinger," was not well received by moderate Catholics who were counting on a change in the church's position on contraception. The pope's message, coming at "the very height of the questioning of traditional sexual morality and the position of women in the secular society, flatly reaffirmed the church's traditional teaching on contraception and the family. The consequences can be tracked unmistakably in the statistics for [falling] church attendance." Godfrey Hodgson, *The World Turned Right Side Up: A History of the Conservative Ascendancy in America* (Boston: Houghton Mifflin, 1996), 165.

75. Eugene J. Fisher, "Abortion" in *A Dictionary of Jewish-Christian Relations*, ed. Edward Kessler and Neil Weinborn (Cambridge: Cambridge University Press, 2005).

76. Anne Hendershott, *The Politics of Abortion* (New York: Encounter, 2006), 95 (citing a report published in *Catholic Insight*). Daniel McGuire's most famous book—*Sacred Choices: The Right to Contraception and Abortion in Ten World Religions* (Minneapolis, MN: Fortress, 2001)—has had a decided impact on pro-abortion arguments in religious circles.

77. "The pro-life movement's consistent rhetoric condemning all types of abortions has become so generalized in the community of younger Evangelicals that abortion is perceived by many as a monolithic issue." John P. Hoffmann and Sherrie Mills Johnson, "Attitudes Toward Abortion among Religious Traditions in the United States: Change or Continuity?," *Sociology of Religion* 66, no. 2 (2005): 162–182, p. 179. This longitudinal study examined data from nationwide General Social Surveys between 1972 and

2002, restricting their analysis to respondents claiming they attended religious services at least once a month.

78. Duke Helfand, "Pastors Plan to Defy IRS on Politics: Ministers Will Intentionally Violate Ban on Campaigning by Nonprofits in Hopes of Generating Test Case," *Los Angeles Times*, September 25, 2008, B1; Starita Smith, "Putting Politics in Church Must Carry Consequences," *Houston Chronicle*, October 12, 2008, E6. See also *Tax Guide for Churches and Religious Organizations: Benefits and Responsibilities under the Federal Tax Law*, Internal Revenue Service, *USA.gov*, undated, www.usa.gov/Business/Nonprofit .shtml. A religious organization may not devote "a substantial part of its activities" to lobbying, which includes trying to influence Congress, legislatures, city councils, or votes in public referenda, ballot initiatives, and other initiatives (5).

79. Gregory Smith, "Slight but Steady Majority Favors Keeping Abortion Legal," Pew Forum on Religion & Public Life, Pew Research Center, Washington, DC, September 16, 2008, http://pewforum.org/docs/? DocID=350.

80. Hendershott, *The Politics of Abortion*, 102 (citing Alan Guttmacher Institute report for 1995). The governing bodies of numerous Protestant denominations have "official statements in support of reproductive choice as a matter of conscience," including the Unitarian Universalists, the United Church of Christ, the Episcopal, Presbyterian, and United Methodist churches, and Reformed Judaism (84).

81. The abortion wars were also debated in higher education. See Ibid., Chapter 8.

82. Herring, *The Pro-Life/Choice Debate*, 117.

83. David Shaw's four-part series, "Abortion and the Media," appeared in the *Los Angeles Times*, July 1–4, 1990.

84. Stewart, "Abortion," 76.

85. Gloria Feldt, *The War on Choice: The Right-Wing Attack on Women's Rights and How to Fight Back* (New York: Bantam, 2004), 173, 189.

86. The abortion lobby's reluctance to get involved in arguments linking high abortion rates in minority communities with a decline in crime rates stems in part from the past. The eugenics movement with its selective breeding campaigns in the late nineteenth and early twentieth centuries had a disastrous influence both on government policy and on the fledgling anti-abortionist movement. Laws requiring sterilization for women deemed to be "unfit"—in practice, mostly nonwhite, minority women—had been enacted in 30 states by the early 1900s. Anti-abortionist leaders such as Margaret Sanger "had supported some eugenic goals and this support continues to haunt the pro-choice movement today." It was reinforced when eugenics became a mantra for the Nazis in the Holocaust. Sanger, *Beyond Choice*, 57. See also Angela Franks, *Margaret Sanger's Eugenic Legacy:*

The Control of Female Fertility (Jefferson, NC: McFarland, 2005). On "race" and abortion politics, see Hendershott, *The Politics of Abortion*, Chapter 2.

87. Jean Bethke Elshtain, "Preface," vii–x; Candace C. Crandall, "Three Decades of Empty Promises," 14–21; and Paige Comstock Cunningham, "The Supreme Court and the Creation of the Two-Dimensional Woman," 103–121, in *The Cost of "Choice": Women Evaluate the Impact of Abortion*, ed. Erika Bachiochi (San Francisco: Encounter Books, 2004).

88. Susan Markens, *Surrogate Motherhood and the Politics of Reproduction* (Berkeley: University of California Press, 2007), 172, 179, 180. Markens focuses on the role of surrogate mothers in reproduction politics. Just as fears of a declining birth rate in an earlier century were predicated primarily on a declining white birth rate, so recent issues like "delayed marriage and childbearing," "increased infertility," and "lack of 'adoptable' babies" are fears "clearly focused on the reproduction of white, middle-class families" (171).

89. Saletan, *Bearing Right*, 2, 75.

90. Hendershott, *The Politics of Abortion*, 140 (citing 2005 Harris Poll).

91. The Born-Alive Infants Protection Act of 2002, http://frwebgate .access.gpo.gov/cgi-bin/getdoc.cgi?dbname=107_cong_public_laws&docid =f:publ207.107. The Unborn Victims of Violence Act of 2004, *FindLaw*, http://news.findlaw.com/hdocs/docs/abortion/unbornbill32504.html.

92. This description is drawn from the Partial Birth Abortion Ban Act of 2003, *FindLaw*, http://news.findlaw.com/hdocs/docs/abortion/2003s3.html.

93. Ibid.

94. Two cases initiated by the Center for Reproductive Rights and Planned Parenthood had challenged the legality of the 2003 Act. See *Gonzales v. Carhart*, 550 U.S. 124 (2007). (Justices Stevens, Souter, and Breyer joined Ginsburg in dissent.)

95. S. 356: Child Pain Awareness Act of 2007, *GovTrack.us*, undated, http://www.govtrack.us/congress/bill.xpd?bill=s110-356. Another significant piece of legislation was the Child Interstate Abortion Notification Act, first introduced in 2005, which would have subjected pregnant teenage girls seeking the services of a pro-abortion state to be legally bound (along with consenting doctors and other "responsible" adults) to the anti-abortion laws of their home states. See Child Interstate Abortion Notification Act, *GovTrack.us*, September 27, 2006, www.govtrack.us/congress/record.xpd? id=109-s20060927-64.

96. Sanger cites nationwide Gallop Polls in 1975 and 2002 that suggest a relative consistency in respondent views for almost 30 years. At the extremes, about 20–25 percent of Americans "support each position." The other 50–55 percent of Americans feel that abortion should be allowed "under certain circumstances." But he cites other polls—a *New York Times/ CBS News* poll in 1998 and a Zogby International poll in 2002—that suggest

"a declining support for abortion rights in recent years." Sanger, *Beyond Choice*, 10–13, 274.

97. "Barack Obama on Abortion," *On the Issues*, undated, www.ontheissues.org/Social/Barack_Obama_Abortion.htm.

98. Sanger, *Beyond Choice*, 78.

99. Page, *How the Pro-Choice Movement*, Chapter 7. "The anti-working-woman climate of the eighties," Page notes, "included constant media coverage of what was made to seem like widespread satanic, ritualistic sex abuse in day-care centers" (43). These and other stories—especially stories about the negative impact of so-called "latch-key kids" on society—connected with deep-seated fears of children being raised by themselves or by strangers outside the family. Page also cites the Family and Medical Leave Act, which among other things provided that working mothers could take off 12 working days each year to care for newly born or sick children. Even though the Act covers only about 60 percent of workers, the votes against this legislation (which President Clinton signed into law in 1993) were mainly from congressmen who supported the anti-abortion lobby (45).

100. One of the last of "a flurry of federal regulations" that the Bush administration implemented just before the president left office gave health-care workers the right to "refuse to provide services that they believe violate their personal, moral or religious beliefs." Government officials could stop federal funding of any health-care facility—and more than 584,000 would be affected by the regulation—that refused to allow their employees to exercise this right of refusal. This right included any request having to do with women's reproductive rights—even from rape victims. It is by no means clear that this regulation, and others like it, can be repealed easily and effectively in Obama's administration, although bills were already introduced in Congress to do so. See "Rule Shields the 'Right of Conscience,' " *Houston Chronicle*, December 19, 2008, A6.

101. Some of these questions are posed by Holmes, *What is Gender?*, 180.

102. Page, *How the Pro-Choice Movement*, 62.

103. One study sponsored by the General Accountability Office in 2004 "found little evidence that [these programs] succeed in preventing teen pregnancy." Another study also in 2004, released by Congressman Henry Waxman (D-California), "found that over 80 percent of abstinence-only curricula . . . contained false, misleading, or distorted information about abortion, contraception, and gender roles, and routinely presented religious beliefs as scientific fact." Heidi Bruggink, "Miseducation: The Lowdown on Abstinence-Only Sex-Ed Programs," *The Humanist*, January–February 2007, 4–6. The southern states, with the highest rates of sexually transmitted diseases and the highest numbers of teenage mothers, have the most abstinence-only programs, but most states still accept federal funding for this purpose.

104. Pamela K. Kohler, Lisa E. Manhart, and William E. Lafferty, "Abstinence-Only and Comprehensive Sex Education and the Initiation of Sexual Activity and Teen Pregnancy," in *Journal of Adolescent Health* 42, no. 4 (2008): 344–351. The researchers concluded as follows: "Adolescents who received comprehensive sex education were significantly less likely to report teen pregnancy than those who received no formal sex education . . . . Abstinence-only education did not reduce the likelihood of engaging in vaginal intercourse." The federal government did not fund comprehensive sex-education programs in schools as of 2007. Tremayne Gibson and Rusty Mason, "Abstaining from Comprehensive Sex Education," *Harvard Political Review*, April 10, 2007, http://hprsite.squarespace.com/abstain-sex-education-042007.

105. Sanger, *Beyond Choice*, 263, 270.

106. Ibid., 264.

107. Ibid., 147, 295. Reproductive strategies for both sexes are outlined in Chapters 4 and 5. The dangers of new reproductive technologies for both men and women are outlined in Chapter 6.

CHAPTER 6

Sex, Gender, and Religion: The Gay Marriage and Family Conundrum

Thomas Beatie gave birth to a daughter on Sunday, June 29, 2008, at a hospital in Bend, Oregon. The bearded 34-year-old man was born a girl in Hawaii and given the name, Tracy Lagondino. He underwent what is now called gender reassignment surgery to become a man, but he kept his female reproductive organs. Beatie met and married Nancy, and the couple decided to have a child together. Because Nancy already had a hysterectomy—she has two grown children—Beatie stopped his hormone therapy to have the baby. They purchased anonymous donor sperm from a sperm bank, and Beatie was inseminated at home when the couple could not get a doctor to do it.

Beatie says he is "transgender, legally male, and legally married." While technically there may be "nothing remarkable" in his actions, as Mara Kiesling, director of the National Center for Transgender Equality in Washington, D.C., puts it, Beatie is the first "transman" (shorthand for a transgender or bisexual person who undergoes a female-to-male sex change) "to go public" with the decision to have a child.[1] Beatie follows in the footsteps of predecessors such as Christine Jorgensen, who underwent America's first known male-to-female sex change (the operation was actually performed in Sweden) in 1951.[2] Beatie has told his story on Oprah Winfrey's television talk show (which showed a film clip of Beatie undergoing an ultrasound test), the tabloid press, and the Internet—and eventually on to mainstream print and electronic media. He was first profiled in *The Advocate*, a gay publication, in which he posed shirtless in advanced pregnancy—recalling the very pregnant actress Demi Moore in a similar pose for *Vanity Fair* in 1991.

Beatie is not reticent about telling the world how doctors and other health-care professionals, friends, and even family in the heterosexual community have shunned both him and his wife. His case, however, illustrates the reality that gender boundaries are being increasingly redrawn in America's changing cultural mores.

Our focus in this chapter is on gay civil rights—we prefer to use the term gay rather than homosexual[3]—especially gay marriage and family rights. Section 1 briefly outlines the gay community's response to sex and gender stereotypes and summarizes the main biblical texts used by religious conservatives to defend a homophobic stance against gays. Section 2 recounts the struggle for gay civil rights in the public arena in the aftermath of the so-called Stonewall Riots. Section 3 offers a snapshot of contemporary gay politics and the battles with religious conservatives over gay ordination, gay marriage, and family rights. Section 4 details some of the enduring tensions that promise to characterize the battles for extending gay civil rights to include marriage and family rights in future.

SEX, GENDER, AND THE GLBT (GAY, LESBIAN, BISEXUAL, AND TRANSGENDER) COMMUNITY

The two-sex model—like the use of binary language in general to sustain a patriarchal understanding of sexuality and gender—has been unraveling at an accelerating pace, as we saw in Chapter 5. The ways in which we arrange our sexual and social worlds today are conditioned by the possibility that we can live meaningful lives in a world without dichotomies. For many Americans, one's sexual organs no longer determine what it means to be a man or a woman. As gender studies scholar Eve Kosofsky Sedgwick puts it, "People experience gender very differently and some have really individual and imaginative uses to make of it. That's an important thing for people to wrap their minds around."[4]

Marginalized Communities

Four marginalized communities have become increasingly vociferous in demanding that their sexual and gender identities be recognized and legitimized in the public sphere. Bisexuals are defined as those persons with an ambiguous sexual identity, who are attracted to both sexes. Transgendered persons are identified as those who do not fit comfortably into either sexual category. Transsexuals—defined as those who are undergoing or have undergone surgery to change or alter their gender—are usually identified as one distinct component within the transgendered community. The most significant politically are gays and lesbians—those who are sexually active with members of their own sex. These communities together now form a not inconsiderable constituency in American political, social, and economic life.

These communities argue that the two-sex model is not fixed as a social or even a biological definition of sexuality in Western culture. As we noted in the previous chapter, medicine can now alter one's sexual organs at virtually every point in the life cycle. Some people, for example, are born neither male nor female while others have a penis or a vagina that does not fall within the "normal" range of sizes and shapes and is therefore designated "abnormal." In premodern cultures, individuals born with mixed genitalia were often privileged members of the community. Since there was no recognized sexual identity outside the two-sex model in modern, Western cultures, the only medical remedy for these "mistakes" of nature was surgery to make the newborn conform to one or the other sex—a procedure perfected gradually only in the last half of the twentieth century. The medical profession did not begin to alter its position on these perceived "deficiencies" until about 10 years ago.

The social construction of sex and gender has become increasingly blurred as males and females defy gender stereotypes in expressing their own sexuality. Sexual identity for many men and women does not always correlate with gender identity: they may feel trapped in a sexual body that does not represent their gender needs. In addition, the meaning of masculinity and femininity depicted in the two-sex model does not always conform to gender practices as they are, or have been, in other, non-Western cultures.

Individuals of all ages, ethnic groups, and social classes may embrace sexual desires or needs that are not sanctioned by the dominant culture. Gender identities, for example, are often challenged by junior or middle and high school students—many of them members of organized teen lobby groups—across the nation today.[5]

Many religious conservatives seem to think that any sexual encounter between members of the same sex makes the relationship a "homosexual" relationship: they do not accept the idea that it is not the sexual act that determines one's sexuality but one's sexual orientation. A person, for example, can be gay without being sexually active.

Indeed, gays and lesbians themselves argue that their sexual orientation is at the center of their sexual identification and not simply a preference for a same-sex sexual partner. The fluidity of biological and
social permutations seems to be as marked between men and between
women as it appears to be between men and women in America
today.[6]

The gay voting bloc in the 2000 general elections was roughly
equivalent to the Hispanic-American bloc and about one-half of the
African-American bloc. Although tensions exist between the gay-
lesbian and African-American communities[7]—both arguably subjugated minorities in the dominant, white, heterosexual model—they
are overwhelmingly Democratic in their voting habits. "In a close
election, gay votes can make the difference between victory and
defeat," says Sean Cahill, director of the National Gay and Lesbian
Task Force Policy Institute.[8]

The gay community as a whole is a considerable force in American
culture, and consequently it is framed much more positively in the
mass media than it was in the past. Mainstream news media perspectives on the topic of homosexuality began to change when gay activists
organized and framed their own arguments in terms of gay civil rights.
As the GLBT community gained power in America's political culture,
its image in the media began to change.

Mainstream media now emphasized "positive and proactive
aspects," as journalism professor Dave Cassidy notes, and "rarely
sought to report information that would reflect negatively on the
[gay civil rights] groups." Consequently, "homosexuality" was "no
longer" framed "as an illness, a reversible life choice, or a crime
against nature. Mainstream publications . . . no longer refer to it as
abhorrent, criminal, depraved, deviant, or perverted." Instead,
"homosexuality" was often portrayed "as biologically determined
and influenced by genetics"—journalists used science, as it were, to
move gay identities beyond the boundaries of public debate. Media
critics could point with some justification to the absence of gay bashing in the media, although there was no evidence that journalists were
celebrating, much less promoting, gay lifestyles.[9]

The plea of the contemporary GLBT community is to make gender
a fluid rather than a fixed biological and social choice for adults—a
choice without religious, legal, political, or legislative restrictions.
In the end, the patriarchal "naturalness of femininity and masculinity"
are "powerful illusions," as feminist scholar Mary Holmes suggests, a
"set of scripts, that we perform, with slight variations."[10] The feeling

among many constituencies inside and outside the GLBT community today is that as Americans we can alter these scripts—scripts that consign gays to the category of an object, the "other" who is different and therefore must be subjugated. We have an unprecedented opportunity to remake sexual and gendered identities that are indeed more fluid and more authentic because they are our own scripts.

"Homosexuality," the Bible, and the Premodern World

Christian conservative activists typically seek biblical authority for their homophobic positions, but they also use many of the same arguments now that their predecessors used against women's political rights (such as voting), women's social rights (from initiating legal contracts to being in public, especially at night, unaccompanied by children or a male adult), and women's economic rights (especially in employment) in the nineteenth and twentieth centuries. The same arguments were also used against African Americans and other ethnic groups who had sex with or married whites—contravening the whites-only version of the two-sex model.[11]

Sexual Diversity in Antiquity

The stigma of homosexuality remains an anti-gay and anti-lesbian mantra among Christian conservatives. GLBT communities must not have civil rights equal to those of heterosexual communities, they argue. Gay unions of any kind must be legally prohibited, and they must not be given family rights because they do not conform to the heterosexual model. Today's negative stereotypes of homosexuality are not in harmony with the historical record even in early Christian Europe.

Sexual relations between younger and older males, and between adult males (and probably females), apparently were common in all premodern cultures. Same-sex bonding also seems to have played a role in preparing for manhood. No clear picture emerges from case studies that have attempted to determine whether same-sex relationships were completely accepted in the past, although practices that many today would call deviant—same-sex, bi-sex, and transgender relationships—seem to have been widespread across both Western and non-Western cultures and were present even in cave paintings dating to 17,000 BCE.

Tolerance for sexual diversity can be found in cultures as diverse as the pre-Christian communities of North, Central, and South America and Africa (including ancient Egypt and other civilizations in North Africa), and in pre-Christian Polynesia, China, India, Japan, Southeast Asia, and Australasia. Sexual diversity was also common in ancient Greece, Rome, and the Middle East, although in the cradle of Western civilization some scholars have suggested that images of human sexuality were more complex—especially in matters of same-sex marriage. In Greece, however, the model for "truest love," as historian Stephanie Coontz notes, was "the association of an adult man with a much younger male."[12]

The concept of sexual orientation was not part of the religious mindset in antiquity, and the authors of the Bible did not write about it. Stories in the Hebrew Bible occasionally celebrate bonding relationships between males and between females—such as David and Jonathan, Ruth and Naomi, and Daniel and Ashpenaz—but no biblical passage suggests that any of these relationships were sexually active relationships. Premodern Jewish and Christian writers assumed everyone was heterosexual. Monogamous relationships between a man and woman were sanctified under God in numerous biblical passages, and there are proscriptions in rabbinical tradition, for example, against both men and women having sex outside marriage. Nevertheless, it is reasonable to assume that gay and lesbian relationships did exist in biblical times.

Biblical Proof Texts

The biblical proof texts used by religious conservatives to defend current biases against same-sex unions emerged from premodern cultures that had no terms referring to homosexual *or* heterosexual orientation. The English bibles we use, moreover, are at least two languages away from the original sources—in the case of the Christian Bible (New Testament), from Aramaic (the language Jesus presumably spoke) and from Koinë Greek (the "common" Greek of the texts).

Translators were and are agents of their culture(s) and hardly the neutral or unbiased observers who merely translate the message, as Christian conservatives would like to believe. Many English versions of the Bible are filtered by the theological beliefs and cultural (including sexual) biases of modern translators. As we noted in the

Introduction, moreover, the ancient manuscripts have so many variations that it is impossible to recreate an original text for any book in
the New Testament.

Nevertheless, five or six passages have emerged as major proof texts
for the Christian conservative position on same-sex issues.[13] Three are
in the Hebrew Bible (hereafter the Old Testament)—Genesis 19:1–20
(the story of Sodom and Gomorrah), Leviticus 18:22, and 20:13
(Holiness Code prescriptions against male-male sex). Three are in
the Christian Bible (hereafter the New Testament)—1 Corinthians
6:9–10/11 (Pauline prescriptions against "male prostitutes"), 1 Timothy 1:8–11 (concerning the legitimate use of Jewish law), and Romans
1:24–27 or 18–32 (more Pauline prescriptions against "unnatural"
passions).

Four words or terms—two Hebrew and two Greek—play a crucial
role in interpreting the meaning of these texts, and they are mistrans-
lated in many English versions of the Bible. The Hebrew words found
in the Old Testament are *qadesh* (also spelled *kadesh* or *k'deshah*) and
to'ebah:

- *qadesh* means a male who engaged in ritual sex in a religious temple. The
  female word is *qadeshah*. It is frequently misread as "sodomite,"
  "whore," or "prostitute." A *qadesh* and a *qadeshah* were not simply prostitutes. They had a specific role to play in the temple. They represented
  a god or goddess, and they engaged in ritual sexual intercourse in that
  capacity with members of the temple. Thus the Jews were proscribed
  from participating in these cultic practices, as in Deuteronomy 23:18.
  "No Israelite woman shall be a cult prostitute, nor shall any Israelite
  man be a cult prostitute."
- *to'ebah* means a condemned foreign or pagan religious or cult practice,
  and it is usually translated as "abhorrence" in the Hebrew Bible and
  "abomination" in Christian Bibles. Eating food that contains both meat
  and dairy products is *to'ebah*. A Jew eating with an Egyptian was *to'ebah*.

The context for the Genesis story is the long Jewish rite of passage
to monotheism. It seeks to set up boundaries of exclusivity—much like
the Ten Commandments. The text is really about hospitality—hospitality codes prescribed correct moral conduct. Certain Hebrew words
used in these texts, such as the word *yadah* ("to know"), have an
ambiguous sexual meaning, but the intent is clear. It is a passage about
power and submission. The sin of Sodom is primarily one of inhospi-
tality and greed, and of excess wealth and a failure to aid the poor and

needy (as interpreted by later Hebrew prophets in the Old Testament).[14]

Leviticus contains the only verses in the Torah specifically directed at male-male sexual activity.[15] They comprise a tiny section of the Holiness Code—a collection of regulations on behavior compiled as a barrier to distinguish the Jews from surrounding pagan peoples such as the Egyptians and the Canaanites. There is no specific reference to female-female sexual activity in the Torah, although the Holiness Code is presumed in rabbinical interpretations to include this activity. These verses turn on the word *to'ebah*, but this word has nothing to do with modern notions of human sexual orientation. Contemporary rabbinic interpretations—at least in Conservative, Reform, and Reconstructionist congregations—would not accept that the *to'ebah* proscription as detailed in Leviticus is applicable to gay relationships today.

Greek Words in the New Testament

The Greek words *malakoi* (singular *malakos*) and *arsenokoitai* (singular *arsenokoites*) have a similar meaning in the New Testament:

- *Malakoi(os)* can mean "soft," as when referring to clothes (e.g., Luke 7:25), or "soft" when referring to effeminate persons (e.g., Matthew 11:8) or perhaps to a generalized degenerate class of persons (as in several early English translations of the New Testament). The word as used by Paul is definitely derogatory, but there is no specific sexual connotation in the *meaning* of this word.

- *Arsenokoitai(es)* is more difficult to translate because it is rarely used, but it is a compound word translated as "man (or men) lying in bed." Even at this point, it can mean "a man who lies in the bed [with anyone]" or "one who lies with men"—depending on whether "man" is used as the subject or the object. While the intentional meaning of this Greek word remains unclear, it does *not* mean "sodomite" or "a man who has intercourse with males" as in many English translations. Even some contemporary Greek/English lexicons have translated the word to mean male homosexuality—thus perpetuating the homophobic myth.

The theme of letters from Paul to congregations in Corinth and Rome, as well as the letter purported to be from Paul to his disciple Timothy, reflects Paul's firm belief that the kingdom of God—Jesus's return to Earth—is eminent. We have a kind of laundry list of sinful social activities in 1 Corinthians and another in 1 Timothy that are unrighteous in the eyes of God. Those who participate in these activities will not enter the kingdom.

Some Christian conservatives also tend to pair words in these lists—such as "fornicators," "male prostitutes," and "sodomites" (NRSV 1 Corinthians 6:9), and "fornicators" and "sodomites" (NRSV 1 Timothy 1:10)—to emphasize New Testament references condemning homosexual practices. Other interpreters, however, see the same words as references to temple prostitutes or to forbidden sexual practices between heterosexual couples. As noted earlier, neither of the Greek words employed to describe these activities can be translated in English as homosexual activities, and in the case of *arsenokoitai(es)* there is no consensus on what the word(s) really meant in Paul's era.

The letter to the congregation in Rome contrasts the "natural" passions one should follow in worshipping the "true" God as opposed to the "unnatural" passions Paul observes in idol worship. The new Judaism—as Paul understands his mission to gentiles—encounters all sorts of false gods with their false cultic practices. They are performing all sorts of abominations—sexual and otherwise. But Paul was as much a part of his culture as we are. He supported slavery, believed in and condemned what he perceived as witchcraft and sorcery, and was a misogynist in his attitude toward women.

Paul had what one might term a patriarch-laden, heterosexual understanding of what was natural. Everything else was unnatural. To have the text refer to homosexual persons, one has to argue that homosexuality is a deviation from the normative heterosexual orientation—the perceived natural orientation. Paul's concern, however, was with the wider issue of what constitutes unrighteous behavior. The persons whom Paul condemns were not homosexual: they were heterosexual persons who had turned from their natural ways. Today we have a more inclusive understanding of human beings on issues such as slavery, the role of women in society, and sexual orientation.

Modern observers must understand that the meanings they give to biblical sexual practices that are now labeled homosexual activity must be interpreted in the specific cultural contexts in which they were proscribed. The writers of these and other texts about this topic condemned forced sexual acts (as between a slave owner and a slave), cultic sexual acts (as in pagan sexual rituals in temples), and promiscuous sexual acts (unnatural passions that undermined the integrity of the family and the community). Procreation was a sacred duty in Jewish law and custom, as we noted in Chapter 5. Any act that did not produce children was condemned.

Some Jewish conservatives—mainly but not exclusively members of Orthodox congregations—do read the Hebrew texts as literal proscriptions of all forms of homosexual relations, and Jewish rabbinical interpretations and Jewish social practices in the past have banned "all male homosexual sex, whatever its form or context." These "textualists," as Rabbi Elliot N. Dorff puts it, insist that a fixed, literal reading of biblical texts best preserves "the authority of the Torah" and hence "divine authority." Human sexuality, however, became a topic of discussion and debate only in the late nineteenth century, and conservative religious approaches to homosexuality as depicted in the biblical record are merely one of several alternative interpretations today.[16]

Other approaches, Dorff argues, also preserve divine authority without diminishing the authority of the Torah. One approach appeals to the view that monogamous, loving, gay relationships were not understood in biblical antiquity, and another approach points to biological (genetic and neurological) as well as cultural markers that determine homosexual identity. While there is merit in both perspectives, Dorff endorses a third approach that sanctifies gay unions on *moral* grounds—the same approach endorsed by many Christians, including gay Christians, and one we shall revisit in this chapter.

THE STRUGGLE FOR GAY CIVIL RIGHTS

The last half of the nineteenth century gave voice to homosexual experiences and finally crystallized into a political movement that advocated for homosexual rights in Western society—first in Europe and then in America. While Europe experienced a brief window of tolerance in the first half of the twentieth century, the United States seems to have experienced a deepening of homophobic bias. Gays were deemed deviant and abnormal by medical professionals, and they were subjected to public censure and surveillance, moral condemnation, and criminalization in communities and states throughout the nation. The twin horrors of the Nazi Holocaust and Stalin's purges effectively destroyed the gay cultural movement in Europe, while the impact of World War II and the purge against gays during the Joseph McCarthy era in the early-mid-1950s crippled whatever remained of a public gay voice in the United States.[17]

The Stonewall Riots and Their Aftermath

The contemporary gay rights movement really begins in the turbulent 1960s, and the so-called Stonewall Riots are celebrated today as the beginning of the modern era in gay resistance politics. There were confrontations in other cities (such as Los Angeles and Chicago), and in other countries (such as France) in the late 1960s, but they did not grab the American public's attention or imagination like Stonewall. Gay men and women, transvestites, drag queens, and even the homeless (or street people, as they were called at the time) fought back when the police conducted one of their routine raids on a gay bar called The Stonewall in Greenwich Village, New York City, on June 27–28, 1969. The riots lasted two days and the bar was destroyed, but this event sparked a kind of collective resistance to centuries of censorship and oppression directed against these sexual and gendered minorities.

Militant Organization and Confrontation

The history of the gay liberation movement in America during its early years is linked inextricably with broader countercultural themes that were emblematic of a nation in turmoil. The first wave, as it were, was between 1969 and 1972: the emphasis was on militant organization and confrontation, and solidarity with other organizations (such as black and other ethnic minority groups, as well as student, feminist, civil rights, and antiwar groups), which at the time were grouped under the umbrella term the New Left Movement.

This was a period of experimentation and struggle with the meaning of sexuality—in best-selling books and above-ground films,[18] in a new and defiant gay press,[19] in gay rights organizations springing up across the nation, and in a pattern of petitions, protests, demonstrations, and marches never before seen in America. "Gay liberation never thought of itself as a civil rights movement for a particular minority," as sociologist Barry Adam puts it, "but as a revolutionary struggle to free the homosexuality in everyone, challenging the conventional arrangements that confined sexuality to heterosexual, monogamous families."[20]

The Gay Liberation Front (GLF) was a term given to more than 80 gay advocacy groups—the first of which was formed in New York City in 1969. Members of GLF engaged in the tactics of nonviolent resistance—from signing protest petitions and making public speeches to conducting marches and demonstrations, sit-ins, and street theater. They also engaged in less conventional tactics such as conducting "zaps" designed to shame organizations using anti-gay language (or engaging in anti-gay hiring practices), and disrupting public events to which gays were not welcome. A favorite tactic during the 1970s and 1980s was called "outing," which was directed at secretly gay celebrities and at men who frequented gay bars, dance halls, and bathhouses, but would not come out of the closet, as it were, and say they were gay.

The GLF was committed to solidarity with other New Left groups. Early attempts to focus on concerns specific to gay rights, such as the splinter group called the Gay Activists Alliance (GAA) (1969), were not successful. Gay activists might participate in both organizations, but the gay rights movement at the time was committed to the radical transformation—as opposed to the reform—of existing social and political institutions. Autonomous gay groups representing other sexual orientations and other ethnic groups were also formed to pursue this agenda. They included groups such as the Street Transvestite Action Revolutionaries (1970), the first transgender organization, and the Third World Gay Revolution (1970), which was made up largely of African-American and Hispanic-American gays.

The GLF and its affiliates achieved some early success. After a fierce internal struggle, the American Psychiatric Association finally removed "homosexuality" as a pathological disease from its official diagnostic manual in 1973 (and reaffirmed and strengthened in 1992), although a clause remained allowing psychoanalysts to provide treatment should a client seek help in changing his or her sexual orientation. The National Association of Social Workers (which resolved that homosexuality was not a disease in 1972) also removed discriminative barriers to gay rights. The National Association for Mental Health called on states to decriminalize gay lifestyles in 1970, and several states did so beginning in 1971 (including Connecticut, Colorado, and Oregon). A federal court also ruled in 1971 that federal employees could not be fired just because they were gay.

Promoting Change from within Mainstream Culture

The radical phase of the gay rights movement ended with the demise of the New Left in the mid-1970s. Umbrella organizations in solidarity with New Left ideals such as the Gay Liberation Front and the Gay Activists Alliance faded away—the GLF essentially collapsed in 1972 and the GAA in 1974—but, as with the feminist movement, the resulting crisis generated new and revitalized groups that were more diverse and more interested in working within existing institutions to promote change. The National Gay Task Force (NGTF), formed in 1973 ("lesbian" was included in the title only in 1986), was committed to grassroots organizing, and the NGTF claimed it was the only national body working for the civil rights of all alternative sexual orientations—gay, lesbian, bisexual, and transgender orientations—at local/community and state/regional levels before the late 1980s.[21]

The academic debate over gay rights in the 1970s led to the creation of gay caucuses on many college campuses and in several disciplines, including librarianship (1970), modern languages and psychology (1973), sociology (1974), history and public health (1975), and nursing and social work (1976). The Gay Academic Union was launched in New York in 1973, and it gained more and more affiliates in subsequent decades until it was recognized as the national body representing gay rights in higher education.[22]

Gays began starting their own businesses, establishing so-called gay housing "ghettos"—districts in major cities that were known to have majority gay populations—and gradually developing a specifically gay lifestyle. Gay bars, restaurants, discos, hotels, gay salons and gay hairdressers, gay festivals, and later yearly Pride Parades sprouted up everywhere in what has been called the "capitalization of homosexuality" that began in the early 1970s. Lawyers and doctors, real estate and insurance agents, credit lenders, and stockbrokers provided social services geared for a gay clientele.

The new gay subculture at this time was mainly a gay, white, male subculture with a patriarchal stance that sometimes alienated lesbian and other groups within the gay community. Gay male liberation at this stage also generated a public display of sexual eroticism or "fast-food sex" that seemed far removed from the homosexual and the heterosexual ideal type—a nonexploitive, consensual, and monogamous loving relationship. The marketing of "gay male sexuality" alienated many gay men and women and provided ammunition for the conservative backlash against gay human rights—a backlash that seemed providential to many religious conservatives when the AIDS pandemic shocked America 10 years later.[23]

Bisexual, Transgender, and Lesbian Voices

The overall picture that emerges in the struggle for gay civil rights in the last 30 years is one of reforming and eventually transforming, rather than trying to revolutionize, the existing system of power and privilege. Perhaps the most noticeable component of reform within the homosexual community during these decades was the emergence of revitalized and autonomous gay voices other than gay male voices—bisexual, transgender, and especially lesbian voices—that reflected different experiences and represented different perspectives about the meaning of diversity.

Bisexual and Transgender Voices

Bisexual and transgender communities have probably experienced the most discrimination. They were not really accepted even within the established gay community until relatively recently. New York and San Francisco launched the earliest and longest-lasting bisexual networks. The first student groups were formed in the mid-1960s in New York and the first bisexual networks with specifically bisexual publications were based in New York and San Francisco from the early-mid-1970s—the oldest being the New York–based National Bisexual Liberation Group and its newsletter, *The Bisexual Expression* (1972). The oldest surviving bisexual community center first opened its doors in San Francisco in 1976.

Grassroots bisexual organizations—initially made up mainly of male activists—spread rapidly in numerous cities in the Midwest and along the western and eastern seaboards in the 1980s. The first female bisexual network with its newsletter *BI Women* was formed in Boston in 1983—the same year that BiPOL, a specifically bisexual political activist group, was launched in San Francisco. Grassroots organizing and the involvement of bisexual groups in local and regional politics became much more visible across the nation from the latter 1980s. *Bisexuality: News, Views, and Networking*, the first national bisexual newsletter, was launched in 1988, and *Anything That Moves: Beyond the Myths of Bisexuality*, the first and only national bisexual magazine, was launched in 1991. Bisexual activists began expanding from regional to national and international networks only during the 1990s.

Representatives from 20 states and five countries attended the first national bisexual conference in San Francisco in 1990, where the national organization, the North American Multicultural Bisexual Network, was created.[24] National bisexual conferences are now held every two years, and they are probably the main public forum for addressing and communicating issues of concern to the bisexual community nationwide. As more local and regional bisexual networks were formed, the literature on bisexuality expanded, academic courses on bisexuality were created, sympathetic treatment of bisexual issues in the media became more widespread (*Bisexual Network*, the first TV series by and for the bisexual community, was produced in 1993), and a bisexual voice within the GLBT community on civil rights topics ranging from family law to employment became more pronounced.[25]

Although transgender persons have always been with us, this community is undoubtedly the least understood and the most marginalized of America's mosaic of sexual orientations today. The term "transgender" is a product of the early 1980s: the definition embraces lifestyles that are on a continuum—from transsexuals, cross-dressers and transvestites, drag kings and queens, to adults with ambiguous sexual organs, who live as transgendered people. Not all persons in these "transgendered" categories would regard themselves as members of the transgender community—indeed, some persons reject all gender identities—but the term is meant to include persons who do not and/or cannot relate either to the binary heterosexual or to the homosexual sex/gender models.

The transgender community did not become a national force in gay politics until the 1990s. The first national forum to educate and advocate on behalf of this constituency was the Intersex Society of North America, which was created in 1993.[26] Bisexuals began to address issues of concern to the transgender community at their national conferences only at the beginning of the twenty-first century. While many state and local municipalities have enacted laws and statutes seeking to protect transgender persons, they continue to be discriminated against in areas such as family law, public health, and employment. Although this constituency has gained public visibility in the last decade or so and is now a legitimate force within the homosexual community, transgender rights have yet to be understood or accepted in the heterosexual community.[27]

Independent Lesbian Voices

The lesbian voice as a force in feminist politics and in the GLBT community (or as lesbians would put it, the LGBT community) was initially an uneven and at times even a subordinated voice in the broader struggle for equal rights. Feminists did not really accept lesbian perspectives in the movement until the beginning of the 1970s, and gay organizations at the time were concerned primarily with gay male issues.

The development of an autonomous Lesbian Voice was a product of the 1970s and 1980s. Lesbians launched their own publications, started lesbian businesses catering to lesbian women, and created recreational spaces where lesbian women could meet and socialize. For a few years many activists withdrew from gay men's politics. They concerned themselves with issues that concerned all women—protesting against male violence and fighting for financial independence, demanding equal rights and opportunities in employment, and challenging female heterosexual stereotypes about the meaning of motherhood and domesticity. Thus the construction of a distinctly lesbian identity *also* meant a temporary withdrawal from feminist politics for many members of the lesbian community.

The lesbian reintegration into gay and feminist mainstream politics was driven in part by forces beyond their control in the 1980s and 1990s—especially the AIDS epidemic and the triumph of all things conservative in American political culture. But lesbians had arrived at that stage in identity politics in which they could now help to revitalize both heterosexual feminists and male gay rights activists as equal partners in forging new and creative ways to address the challenges posed by the opposition. They would be joined in these efforts by bisexual and transgender constituencies in an alliance that would reach out to sympathetic heterosexual communities in the continuing struggle for gay civil rights in the twenty-first century.

Christian Conservatives and Gay Civil Rights

The anti-gay crusades took many forms, but the conservative religious assault on human rights for those who did not fit into the patriarchal, two-sex model of human development looms large in any assessment of the gay civil rights struggle in the past three decades. Anti-gay religious activists such as Phyllis Schlafly and Anita Bryant were household names in the 1970s and early 1980s during what has been called the first wave of homophobia in national politics.

Religious leaders such as Jerry Falwell and Pat Robertson orchestrated a new wave of homophobic campaigns in the 1980s and 1990s. They were joined by a host of other religious-cum-political conservatives, who sought to repeal whatever gains had been made in gay rights legislation. Although they largely failed at the national level, they did succeed in repealing legislation favoring gay rights in several local communities and states—and they were buoyed by a U.S. Supreme Court ruling in *Bowers v. Hardwick* (1986). The 5-4 decision upheld a Georgia sodomy law criminalizing anal and oral sex between consenting adults in private. The so-called Sodomy Act would remain in force for another 17 years.[28]

The Private Domestic Battleground

Debates about gay civil rights have a trajectory that is similar in many respects to debates about women's reproductive rights. The guardians of the two-sex family and marriage model, however, brought more pressure to bear on gay and lesbian couples after gay activists started demanding in the 1980s and 1990s the right to be ordained; to marry in a church, synagogue, temple, or mosque, or alternatively to have a civil marriage with full legal rights; and to enjoy the same family rights as non-gays. Many Christians at the time were troubled by what they saw as new threats to the traditional two-sex model.

Gay couples were applying for marriage licenses or seeking alternative routes to secure legally bonded relationships, while many wanted religious commitment ceremonies if they could not obtain full civil marriage rights. Gay partners were becoming surrogate parents—through sperm donation or *en vitro* insemination or by adopting children either through adoption agencies or through foster-care placement. Some children were biological offspring from prior marriages or relationships with heterosexual partners. This became a particularly thorny legal and religious issue when men and women with children decided to change gender while continuing to live with their spouses and children. Family services in many municipalities were facing parental and custody issues as early as the 1980s: social service networks were "unprepared" and lacked "knowledge and understanding" to deal with these blended families.[29]

Religious conservatives launched a new round of anti-gay campaigns targeted specifically at attempts being made to extend marriage and family rights beyond the heterosexual community. The conservative "family values" movement led by people such as James Dobson (Focus on the Family), Gary Bauer (Family Research Council), Louis Sheldon (Traditional Values Coalition), and Ralph Reed (Christian Coalition) fought vigorously to get local and state governments to pass discriminatory measures against same-sex unions and families. In the rhetoric of homophobia, the voices of prominent, white, Protestant conservatives were indistinguishable from those of prominent black, Protestant conservatives, Roman Catholic conservatives, religious separatists such as Nation of Islam leader Louis Farrakhan, or extremist Christians linked to the Dominion/Reconstructionist movement.

The family-values coalition also grouped gay marriage and family issues in a much broader conservative agenda that ranged from opposition to affirmative action, immigration, and medical benefits for legal migrants to abortion rights, pornography, and the Equal Rights Amendment. These groups were outspending the gay lobby by at least four to one by the early 2000s. As Sean Cahill notes, gay relationships were attacked harshly during the last two decades of the twentieth century and the first decade of the twenty-first century and gay rights issues "remain a defining fault line in American politics."[30] Religious conservatives had considerable success in the 1980s and 1990s in urging voters to return to what they called America's "traditional morality."[31]

The moral offensive launched by the Religious Right during the presidency of George W. Bush at the beginning of the twenty-first century threatened to derail the gay community's crusade to win approval for the right to marry and raise a family. Conservative opposition at heart was centered on the premise that same-sex marriages and blended families violated the sacred two-sex model. As law professor Daniel R. Pinello argued, "[S]ame-sex couples' biological inability to procreate permeates the American political debate over civil marriage for lesbians and gay men."[32]

RELIGION, POLITICS, AND GAY CIVIL RIGHTS TODAY

The nexus between Christian conservative opposition politics and gay activist politics has become increasingly apparent in recent decades. The ever-changing political agendas that seem to structure public debate about gay issues have been forged mainly in the war of words waged between gay activists and the conservative religious opposition. They vie with each other in organizing grassroots pro- and anti-gay campaigns, and in establishing beachheads in the media and in the courts to voice their views—however unequal these contests may seem from the perspective of gay lobbyists. They are, indeed, the "perfect enemies."[33]

The gay civil rights movement in the late twentieth century was a political force with enough clout in the public sphere to make a differ- ence when it opposed what gay activists saw as repressive legislation or championed policies to protect their rights. But while the gay voting bloc had reached a "critical mass," as social scientists Ellen D. B. Riggle and Barry L. Tadlock put it, it also "ignited political con- flict."[34] When concerns about gay and lesbian civil rights expanded to include marriage and family rights, there was a discernible shift not only in conservative strategy but also in public opinion—a shift that separated gay civil rights from gay marriage and family rights.[35]

Many religious conservatives in gay rights debates conceded that gays should be given civil rights like other groups in society, and they sometimes accepted laws to protect gays and lesbians (although more rarely for bisexual/transgender persons). They defined gay civil rights, however, in ways that excluded the ordination of gay clergy, the reli- gious blessing of same-sex unions, and the granting of civil or reli- gious marriage and family rights to gay couples.

A New Emphasis on Grassroots Organizing

While a few militant groups such as Queer Nation (1990) sought to inject the revolutionary spirit of the New Left into the gay rights movement, the GLBT community by and large has remained com- mitted to compromise rather than confrontation in the struggle for gay rights. The major political focus in the gay civil rights movement in the past generation has been on grassroots organizing.

Grassroots Organizing

Grassroots organizing at the national level involved several old and new groups—such as the Human Rights Campaign (1980), the National Gay and Lesbian Task Force, and the National Black Les- bian and Gay Leadership Forum (1988)—that sought to provide educational platforms and networks of political lobbyists to communicate gay and lesbian concerns to the electorate. The Democratic-oriented Gay and Lesbian Victory Fund (1991) and its Republican counterpart, Log Cabin Republicans (1993), sought to promote and support the election of openly gay and lesbian activists to political office at all levels of government. Activists also mobilized in conventional ways—such as Gay Men's Health Crisis (1981) and AIDS Action Council (1984)—and in less conventional ways—such as ACT UP (AIDS Coalition to Unleash Power, 1987)—to confront secular and religious indifference or overt opposition to finding solutions to the AIDS crisis.

Gays also crusaded to have sexual orientation rights inserted into human rights codes at local community and state levels as well as the national level. This effort got a massive boost when the U.S. Supreme Court overturned *Bowers v. Hardwick* (1986), a ruling that in effect invalidated all state laws that criminalized private sexual acts between consenting adults. The court in *Lawrence and Garner v. Texas* (2003) essentially guaranteed the right of privacy to all groups regardless of sexual orientation. This 6–3 decision immediately affected the 14 states that still had sodomy laws. A majority of American cities with populations in excess of 250,000, however, had already enacted statutes prohibiting discrimination based on sexual orientation, and this trend continued.[36]

Several pieces of legislation that stalled in Congress during the Bush administration would advance gay civil liberties even further if they are passed under the new Democratic president and Democratic Congress. These include the latest version of the nationwide Hate Crimes Act—named after Matthew Shepard, a 21-year-old college student murdered in an anti-gay hate crime in Wyoming in October 1998—and an extension to the Employment Non-Discrimination Act to incorporate members of the GLBT community.

Many gays also are integrated into mainstream, heterosexual society. The gains have been pronounced in areas such as higher education and the professions, in business and employment practices, in housing, in civil rights law, and in a variety of state and federal services.[37] Some aspects of what mainstreamers consider gay lifestyles—from home or interior designs and fashion designs to hairstyles, food tastes, and recreational choices—have also had a decided impact on heterosexual cultural practices. And organizations such as the National Gay and Lesbian Task Force have had considerable success in having sexual orientation inserted into hate crimes legislation in many states. More and more openly gay and lesbian candidates have stood for and won city and statewide elections in recent years.

The AIDS Pandemic

The AIDS pandemic was perhaps the one single issue in the last two decades of the twentieth century that brought organizational solidarity to the GLBT community and mobilized support from the heterosexual community both in the United States and overseas. The initial view—morphed into a moral panic by conservative media—was that AIDS was confined only to the homosexual community. But attempts to restrict research funding, limit health-care services, and generally force gays back into the closet failed. As the AIDS crisis began to affect the heterosexual population in America, funding increased for research on a variety of medical, pharmaceutical, and therapeutic approaches. By the 1990s, the battle against AIDS had enlisted support from a wide range of otherwise diverse groups in a common cause that bridged age, ethnicity, geography, conservative and liberal political labels, as well as people of all sexual and gender orientations.

In the end, the ongoing battle against AIDS has had a positive impact (a) in bringing public legitimacy to gay-friendly volunteers, educators, and caregivers, (b) in bringing public recognition to gay-friendly organizations and services, and (c) in focusing public awareness on a complex, worldwide heterosexual and homosexual issue. Above all, it helped stimulate public discussion and debate about the complexities of human sexuality, which perhaps more than any other issue has led to the gradual inclusion of gays in America's cultural mosaic.

The experiences of the GLBT community in fighting AIDS and discrimination in America, moreover, were shared with GLBT communities fighting AIDS and discrimination around the world. The International Lesbian and Gay Association, the "only worldwide federation," as it claims on its Web site, "fighting for lesbian, gay, bisexual, transgender and intersex rights," celebrated its 30th anniversary in 2008.[38]

The trend suggests increasing tolerance for gay civil rights. It was manifested in the Pew Forum public opinion surveys between 1992 and 2008 on religious attitudes toward gays cited in the Introduction. A nationwide survey conducted by the Pew Forum on Religion and Public Life in August 2008, moreover, suggested that voters ranked

gay marriage (along with abortion) at the bottom of their list of election priorities: gay marriage was regarded as "very important" by
only 28 percent of the respondents (as opposed to 32 percent in the
October 2004 survey).

More than half (54 percent) supported same-sex civil unions "with
many of the same legal rights as married couples," but only 39 percent
supported same-sex marriage. This division was also present when
respondents were questioned about allowing gays and lesbians to adopt
children. While 46 percent were in favor, 48 percent were opposed—
a statistical tie. As was the case with same-sex civil unions versus same-
sex marriage, those in favor of allowing gays to adopt children tended
to be women, the college educated, those under 30 years of age, and
those religiously unaffiliated. More whites (48 percent) supported gay
adoption than blacks (35 percent), and more Democrats (54 percent)
than Republicans (31 percent). Religious groups most adamantly
opposed to gay adoption were white and black evangelical Protestants,
and Hispanic Catholics.[39]

The public discourse about human sexuality has now shifted to
debates about the meaning of human rights, and from the 1990s most
international organizations removed offensive language (such as the
World Health Organization, which dropped "homosexuality" as a
classified "disease" in 1993), prohibited sexual discrimination in any
form, and allowed GLBT communities to air human rights grievances
before the United Nations.[40]

A Conflicted Religious Community

The ordination of gay clergy, gay marriage, and family rights—
along with female abortion rights—have been long-simmering issues
within individual congregations and within denominations—both
Protestant (including Episcopalian, Methodist, Presbyterian, and
Lutheran) and Roman Catholic. While those Christian conservatives
who loudly oppose gay rights get most of the media attention, many
mainstream religious communities are deeply divided over these
issues.[41]

Many Protestants, for example, would agree with many Roman
Catholics that a distinction should be made between gay civil rights
and gay marriage rights. While the United States Conference of
Catholic Bishops opposed same-sex marriage in a 1996 statement,
the bishops also said that "individuals and society must respect the

basic human dignity of all persons, including those with a homosexual orientation." Members of the gay community "have a right to and deserve our respect, compassion, understanding, and defense against prejudice, attacks and abuse."[42]

Congregations within these denominations are just as divided on the gay ordination issue as they were divided on the ordination of women clergy a generation or so ago—and as many Protestant denominations (such as the Southern Baptists and Missouri-Synod Lutherans) and Roman Catholics still are today. Only a few mainstream Christian denominations—such as the United Church of Christ and the Unitarian Universalist church—have officially adopted inclusive positions in all categories of gay religious rights.[43] Consequently, members of the GLBT formed their own Christian fellowship in the Metropolitan Community Church (the first congregation was launched in Los Angeles in 1968), which has congregations in about 23 countries.[44]

Christians typically endorse the teachings of their faith groups.[45] Members of a conservative congregation will likely be taught that homosexual behavior is abnormal, unnatural, and condemned by God. A minister in such a congregation will not bless gay marriages or other kinds of unions, and the conservative congregation will not accept them—or endorse gay and lesbian couples having children or family rights. Individuals choose this lifestyle, but it can and must be changed. *It is something that a person does.*

Members of some moderate congregations may be taught that homosexual behavior is abnormal and unnatural, but that some aspects of this lifestyle may be accepted. Some ministers as well as members may opt for a more tolerant response—based essentially on the "don't ask, don't tell" option—and accept chaste, lifelong gay relationships, discourage the ordination of gays but bless gay unions privately, or perhaps even publicly, on a case-by-case basis. But ministers as well as members may also believe gays should have limited civil marriage and family rights, and they may share with more conservative Christians the view that this lifestyle can be changed because it is a lifestyle *that a person does.*

Ministers and members of other moderate and most if not all progressive congregations may well view homosexuality as a natural, unchangeable sexual orientation for a minority of human beings. They may accept genetic and/or hormonal markers that suggest there is a biological disposition to being gay, even though the evidence also suggests that many other factors, including developmental and cultural factors, play significant roles in this nature/nurture debate. They may believe that this natural condition is accepted by God and that gay relationships and gay unions should have the same political, legal, and religious rights, and the same marriage and family rights, as heterosexual relationships and unions. They may also support the ordination of homosexual men and women and assert that attempts to reorient the homosexual orientation are both immoral and unjust. *It is something that a person is.*

The Courts as Battleground

Religious conservatives and gay rights advocates have taken their fight to the courts and the legislatures of America as more and more gay and lesbian couples engage in religious commitment ceremonies and, where possible, civil unions or domestic partnerships (which grant some legal rights and benefits to partners).

America's courts had recognized only traditional heterosexual marriage rights until 1993, when the Hawaii Supreme Court ruled in *Baehr v. Lewin* that the state's law against same-sex marriages *might be* illegal under the state's Equal Rights Amendment.[46] Those who opposed gay marriage worried that other states would have to honor a marriage in Hawaii, including one between gays or lesbians.[47] The justices remanded the case to a lower court to determine whether the state could show it had a "compelling" interest in denying same-sex marriage. The case languished in the courts until 1998, when Hawaii's voters adopted a constitutional amendment giving the legislature power to ban same-sex marriages.

Congress, in response to *Baehr* and other challenges, passed the Defense of Marriage Act in 1996.[48] This measure, enacted during the Clinton administration, denied federal benefits to couples in same-sex marriages and was specifically designed to maintain the marriage contract as the exclusive preserve of heterosexual couples. The act also was designed to prevent the application of the full faith and credit clause to gay marriages; that is, no state is required to honor a gay marriage contract from another state.

Vermont became the first state to legalize same-sex civil unions as an alternative to civil marriages in a law passed in 2000. The law was mandated by the Vermont Supreme Court in *Baker v. Vermont* (1999), which ordered the legislature to find a way to grant to homosexual couples the same rights and privileges enjoyed by heterosexual couples. The legislature authorized town clerks to issue licenses to homosexual couples for civil unions. These couples enjoy the same benefits and rights of couples in heterosexual marriages, but the law applies only in Vermont.[49]

Massachusetts became the first state to legalize gay marriage after the Massachusetts Supreme Judicial Court ruled in 2003 that a ban on same-sex marriage violated the Massachusetts constitution. The ruling prompted the legislature to pass a law legalizing same-sex marriage in the state.[50] The law, effective in 2004, meant gay and lesbian couples living in Massachusetts or intending to move to the state would enjoy the same legal rights and privileges accorded by the state to heterosexual couples.

California—five years after Massachusetts—became the second state to grant marriage licenses to same-sex couples in 2008 following a 4-3 high court ruling. Ronald George, chief justice of the California Supreme Court and a Republican, wrote for the majority: the court had "relied heavily" on an "equally historic" decision by the same court in 1948 that outlawed the state's "ban on interracial marriage."[51] Connecticut became the third state to authorize same-sex marriages following a 4-3 high court ruling later in the same year, and Iowa, in 2009, became the first state in America's "heartland" to allow gay unions when the Iowa Supreme Court unanimously declared unconstitutional a state law defining civil marriage as a union between a man and a woman. The law, the court said, violated the equal protection clause of the Iowa Constitution.[52]

Californians in the 2008 general election, however, approved Proposition 8, which overturned the California Supreme Court ruling on gay marriage rights, and this proposition was upheld by the court in May 2009. A campaign supported mainly by religious groups—especially the Mormons, African-American and white evangelicals, and Roman Catholics—played perhaps the pivotal role in this decision. Churches were politicized as bishops and priests, ministers, and lay preachers used the pulpit to get their message across to their congregations.[53] Gay civil unions, however, are still legal in California, and anti–Proposition 8 forces will challenge the legality of the measure in the future.

An avalanche of state laws and statutes specifically prohibiting same-sex marriages followed the Massachusetts decision. The following year, 11 states passed constitutional amendments banning same-sex marriage, which increased to 26 states as of 2008, and 43 states have statutes limiting marriage to heterosexual couples. Nevertheless, six states—Connecticut, Iowa, Maine, Massachusetts, New Hampshire, and Vermont—have legalized same-sex marriage. Several states—for example, California, Colorado, Hawaii, Maryland, Nevada, New Jersey, Oregon, Washington, and the District of Columbia—have legalized gay civil unions and/or domestic partnerships with varying degrees of legal rights. Gay couples in states with gay marriage, gay civil union, and/or gay domestic partnership laws, however, are still denied more than 1,000 federal rights and benefits under the Defense of Marriage Act.[54]

Gay partners with families continue to pose all sorts of challenges both for states that have and for states that do not have laws in place protecting the marriage/partnership and/or family rights of same-sex couples. According to the 2000 census, while 46 percent of married heterosexual couples had at least one child under the age of 18 living at home, 34 percent of lesbian couples and 22 percent of gay male couples had minor children at home—a continuing trend that challenges the claim often made about parenting as an exclusively heterosexual activity.

"The vast majority of children's advocacy organizations," as Sean Cahill notes, "recognize that gay and lesbian parents are just as good as heterosexual parents, and that children thrive in gay- and lesbian-headed families." Research on this topic suggests that gays and lesbians are much less likely than heterosexuals to abuse their children. Statements made by conservative political and religious activists (and often communicated as truisms in an uncritical media) that gays are "more likely to abuse their children" and "more likely to be pedophiles" ignore overwhelming evidence contradicting these claims. A groundbreaking study by the American Medical Association in 1998 found that 95 percent of pedophiles in the United States were heterosexual (and 90 percent were men).[55]

The American Civil Liberties Union regularly updates a handbook detailing the civil rights of the GLBT community in a wide variety of areas, including immigration rights, public and private sector employment rights, and housing and loan rights. One of the most interesting sections deals with the legal rights of same-sex parents, the legal environment of same-sex parenting, and the legal rights of children and youths from same-sex family structures in school. It is apparent from this reading that blended, same-sex family structures—such as gay marriages—remain just as much a legal frontier as they are a religious frontier in America's gender wars today.[56]

ENDURING TENSIONS

The most pressing goals for the gay and lesbian community today are (a) to attain for same-sex couples the marital and family rights that heterosexual couples enjoy under civil law and (b) to gain recognition— for those who yearn for a religious affirmation—for marriages performed in churches, synagogues, and other religious venues, and the same rights to ordination that heterosexuals enjoy.

Conservative religious opposition has solidified and tensions have intensified as gays have sought to extend gay civil rights to the private, domestic sphere. The politics of liberation has remained as a kind of subtext in the activities of groups such as Queer Nation, but the thrust since the mid-1970s has been assimilation into mainstream culture.[57] For the GLBT community, gay civil rights *includes* heterosexual marriage and family rights.

A Heterosexual Implosion

Conservative political-cum-religious leaders have framed current debates over gay marriage rights to suggest that gay marriage threatens the foundation of heterosexual domestic rights. The opposition is expressed in municipal statutes, in state laws, in the courtroom, in social services, and perhaps most important of all, in the court of heterosexual public opinion.

Gay rights activists attempt to demonstrate that these issues are much more complex than conservative religious and political pundits claim. They point out that the two-sex family model has no biblical foundation, and the nuclear heterosexual family really has its origins in the nineteenth century. Same-sex unions, as we have noted, were widespread in antiquity, and gay marriage ceremonies were performed even in medieval Christian Europe.[58]

The gay community often is blamed by religious and social conservatives for problems—such as high divorce rates and the increased numbers of single-parent households—that afflict heterosexual families today. The evidence suggests, however, that the implosion of marriage and family structures has been a problem primarily for heterosexuals over the past four decades or so, and that heterosexual couples themselves have been responsible for changing attitudes toward the traditional two-sex family model.

Heterosexuals initiated the high divorce rate (depending on the source, approximately 40 percent of first marriages now end in divorce). Married, heterosexual couples in the 2000 census constituted no more than half of U.S. households and represented less than 25 percent of households with children.[59] More than 30 percent of heterosexual families in this country comprised "either single-parents or two unmarried, cohabiting parents." Gays and lesbians represented perhaps 5 percent of the American population—a hotly disputed figure—but 60–66 percent claimed they were in "partnered relationships," which translates into at least 3 million same-sex households in America.[60]

Heterosexual men and women first began adopting children as single parents and opted to live alone if a suitable marriage partner could not be found. Heterosexuals pioneered the reproductive revolution that changed relationships between sex and marriage, and transformed conception, childbirth, and parenting practices. Heterosexuals embraced new gender relations that challenged the traditional marriage model. As marriage and family historian Stephanie Coontz notes, "[G]ay and lesbian marriage is not at all a cause of the changes in married life. It's a result of the revolution that heterosexuals have made in how marriage is organized."[61]

Gay attempts to seek societal approval of gay marriage and family relationships will require a strong moral stance to challenge the frayed moral stance of religious and political conservatives, who maintain that marriage and family rights should be extended only to those whose relationships conform to the dominant heterosexual model. "To be human has too often been equated with the kinds of characteristics, interests, and priorities associated with being male, white, and heterosexual," Carlos A. Ball argues. "The better choice is to present and defend a more convincing and nonoppressive conception of what it means to be human and to lead a fully human life." Ball says that America's commitment to religious inclusiveness and cultural diversity provide the gay community with a unique opportunity to argue persuasively on moral grounds for state and federal support and official recognition of gay marriage and family rights.[62]

The Question of Morality

Gay strategists from the mid-1970s framed their arguments in terms of human rights (the right to life, liberty, and the pursuit of happiness) and in terms of civil rights (the right to have their human rights protected by civil authorities). They focused on (a) legislation that would indemnify private, sexual acts of individuals from criminal action and (b) equal wage and employment opportunities, equal access to housing and public accommodation, and equal rights in the use of public services. And they sought protection from the same governing authorities—local and state authorities and ultimately federal authorities—who traditionally had denied them protection.

Gay ghettoes continue to exist in most major cities, and the results of a generation of efforts (a) to decriminalize sexual codes and (b) to halt intimidation, harassment, and violence by police and judicial officials nationwide have been mixed. But the overall trend has been toward more tolerance and the elimination of discrimination against gays in the public arena.

Although the guardians of heterosexual tradition, particularly in some of the early battles over gay civil rights, argued that homosexual acts were immoral and must be sanctioned by the state, gay activists refrained from entering into these debates. They took the position that the morality of individual homosexual acts was irrelevant. The long struggle to secure equality with heterosexuals in public sphere activities was a matter of civil rights, but it was only partly successful—discrimination in employment, marriage, family, government benefits, religious ordination, and access to public services and benefits continued to exist.

Gay organizations, especially since the 2004 elections, are recognizing the value of treating gay marriage as both a moral issue, as Ball suggested, and a civil rights issue. The framing of same-sex marriage as a moral issue by conservative opponents, according to Barry L. Tadlock and C. Ann Gordon of Ohio University and Elizabeth Popp of the University of Illinois, was "the single best predictor" in garnering public support against same-sex marriage and civil unions. And, as other scholars have pointed out, it was a factor in Republican congressional victories and George W. Bush's presidential victory in the 2004 elections.[63]

Gays began using much the same language that had been used in earlier crusades defending interracial marriage as they sought to convince the heterosexual community that homosexual unions should be given the same rights as heterosexual unions. Same-sex marriage mattered because marriage itself mattered. It was the foundation for all lifelong commitments—whether heterosexual or homosexual. As journalist Lisa Miller expressed it in a *Newsweek* cover story, marriage is both a civil and a religious institution in America. Gay civil rights advocates embrace both. The legal civil ceremony provides "practical benefits to both partners," but the religious ceremony "offers something else: a commitment of both partners before God to love, honor and cherish each other . . . . In a religious marriage, two people promise to take care of each other, profoundly, the way they believe God cares for them."[64]

Democratic President Barack Obama—whose views on gay civil rights are not the same as those of his predecessor, George W. Bush—may well typify the majority public opinion in the heterosexual community at present. Obama (like his opponent, John McCain) opposed a federal constitutional amendment banning same-sex marriage and made a distinction between same-sex civil unions with full legal rights, which he supported, and same-sex marriage unions, which he opposed.[65]

Obama's election comes at a time when homosexuals are demanding the same civil rights that heterosexuals enjoy—a campaign that has unified gay communities around the world. Gay marriage and family rights are now recognized in all Canadian provinces. Same-sex civil unions (and in some cases same-sex marriages) with most or all of the same rights as heterosexual unions—child custody and family rights, welfare benefits, immigration advantages, property, inheritance, tax, and other financial rights—have become the norm in most of Europe, Australia and New Zealand, Israel, and South Africa. South America—led by Brazil—seems to be moving in the same direction. The international "trend toward protecting the committed relationships of same-sex couples"[66] may be irreversible.

NOTES

1. See Guy Trebay, "He's Pregnant. You're Speechless," *New York Times*, June 22, 2008, SundayStyles-1, 12; and James Bone, " 'Pregnant Man' Thomas Beatie Gives Birth to Baby Girl," *TimesOnline*, London, July 4, 2008, www.timesonline.co.uk/tol/news/world/us_and_americas/article4265368.ece.

2. Christine was born George Jorgensen Jr. in New York. The surgical procedure was nothing new—sex-change operations, for example, had been performed in Germany—but the story was given wide publicity in America. Christine became perhaps an unwitting poster child, as it were, for the transsexual community.

3. "Homosexual" is now a rather outdated and somewhat pejorative term. We retain it only on those occasions where "homosexual" seems appropriate in specific historical or religious contexts, in contrasting "homosexual" with "heterosexual" political identities, and when it is used in direct quotation. We prefer the term "gay" with reference to gay men, but we shall also use "gay" interchangeably with "GLBT"—a generic acronym referring to gay, lesbian, bisexual, and transgender communities. In keeping with common usage, then, "gay" and "GLBT" are used interchangeably when referring to all groups whose sexual orientations deviate from the dominant heterosexual population, but "gay" is also used in preference to "homosexual" when referring specifically to men. In a similar vein, we shall use the contemporary term "same-sex marriage" rather than "homosexual marriage" to refer to gay male and female unions.

4. Cited by Trebay, "He's Pregnant," 12.

5. More than 3,500 teen groups in 40 local chapters are now allied to the Gay, Lesbian and Straight Education Network, a national organization founded in 1990. It was originally called the Gay and Lesbian Independent School Teachers Network. See John Cloud, "The Battle over Gay Teens: What Happens When You Come Out as a Kid? How Gay Youths Are Challenging the Right—and the Left," *Time*, October 10, 2005, 42–48, 51; and Maggie Galehouse, "A Better Reception to Being 'Out,'" *Houston Chronicle*, June 23, 2008, A1, A5. Youths are now known to "experience same-sex attraction" even before 11 years of age, and the attitudes of parents or guardians "profoundly influences the child's mental health as an adult," according to one recent study. Lisa Leff, "How Family Reacts to Gays Is Key to Health as Adults," *Houston Chronicle*, December 29, 2008, A4 (citing a study published in the *Journal of the American Academy of Pediatrics*).

6. "I am hardwired as a heterosexual woman," as science writer Deborah Rudacille puts it, but "the range of gender expression *within* the categories 'man' and 'woman' seems to vary nearly as much as it does between them . . . . I no longer view my sexual orientation and gender identity as 'normal,' generic, or 'regular' " (italics in the original). Deborah Rudacille, *The Riddle of Gender: Science, Activism, and Transgender Rights* (New York: Pantheon, 2005), 291.

7. These tensions are discussed in Eric Brandt, ed., *Dangerous Liaisons: Blacks, Gays, and the Struggle for Equality* (New York: New Press, 1999).

8. Sean Cahill, *Same-Sex Marriage in the United States: Focus on the Facts* (Lanham, MA: Lexington, 2004), 77.

9. Dave Cassady, "Homosexuality," in *Media Bias: Finding It, Fixing It*, ed. Wm. David Sloan and Jenn Burleson Mackay (Jefferson, NC: McFarland, 2007), 81–89, p. 81.

10. Mary Holmes, *What is Gender? Sociological Approaches* (Los Angeles: Sage, 2007), 61, 180.

11. Sean Cahill, for example, shows a "clear parallel" in the tactics used by conservative groups opposing same-sex marriage from the 1990s and the tactics used by conservative groups opposing interracial marriage before the 1970s. "Almighty God," as a court judgment put it in a 1967 case, "separated the races" because "He did not intend for the races to mix." At the time of this court decision, "72% of Americans opposed interracial marriage, and 48% believed it should be a crime." Cahill, *Same-Sex Marriage*, 13.

12. Stephanie Coontz, *Marriage, A History: From Obedience to Intimacy or How Love Conquered Marriage* (New York: Viking, 2005), 77. For brief sketches of same-sex gender relations between antiquity and America before the 1960s, see Barry D. Adam, *The Rise of a Gay and Lesbian Movement*, rev. ed. (New York: Twayne, 1995), Chapters 1–4; Thomas C. Caramagno, *Irreconcilable Differences? Intellectual Stalemate in the Gay Rights Debate* (Westport, CT: Praeger, 2002), Chapter 3.

13. This section again was based initially on public lectures Les Switzer has given on biblical notions of homosexuality and on S. Michael Pater, "Homosexuality and the Bible," May 8, 2004, workshop given at First Congregational Church in Houston, Texas (Rev. Pater at the time was associate minister of this church). See also "The Bible and Homosexuality," Ontario Center for Religious Tolerance, undated, www.worldpolicy.org /projects/globalrights/sexorient/bible-gay.html; and Walter Wink, ed., *Homosexuality and Christian Faith: Questions of Conscience for the Churches* (Minneapolis, MN: Fortress, 1999). Samuel Karff, rabbi emeritus of a Reform congregation in Houston, Shaul Osadchey, rabbi of a Conservative congregation in Houston, and his wife Bobbie, a classmate of Switzer in a Christian seminary in Houston, provided an ongoing critique that was especially helpful in revising this section for publication.

14. See Ezekiel 16:49: "Only this was the sin of your sister Sodom: arrogance! She and her daughters had plenty of bread and untroubled tranquility; yet she did not support the poor and the needy."

15. Leviticus 18:22: "Do not lie with a male as one lies with a woman; it is an abhorrence." Leviticus 20:13: "If a man lies with a male as one lies with a woman, the two of them have done an abhorrent thing; they shall be put to death—their bloodguilt is upon them."

16. This paragraph and what follows is based on Elliot N. Dorff, *Matters of Life and Death: A Jewish Approach to Modern Medical Ethics* (Philadelphia & Jerusalem: Jewish Publication Society, 1998), 139–151. Dorff is a rabbi in the Conservative tradition and a specialist in Jewish ethics.

17. The literature on gay life in America before Stonewall (see the following section) is growing. See, for example, *Before Stonewall: The Making of a Gay and Lesbian Community*, Emmy-winning Public Broadcasting Service documentary, 1985, available on DVD; Vern L. Bullough, ed., *Before Stonewall: Activists for Gay and Lesbian Rights in Historical Context* (Binghamton, NY: Harrington Park, 2002); Patrick Moore, *Beyond Shame: Reclaiming the*

Abandoned History of Radical Gay Sexuality (Boston: Beacon, 2004), Section 1; and Michael S. Sherry, *Gay Artists in Modern American Culture: An Imagined Conspiracy* (Chapel Hill: University of North Carolina Press, 2007).

18. They included reprintings and sometimes new editions of books such as Herbert Marcuse's *Eros and Civilization* (1955), James Baldwin's *Giovanni's Room* (1956), Alan Ginsberg's epic poem, *Howl* (1956), and the works of other members of the Beat Generation such as Jack Kerouac's *On the Road* (1957) and William S. Burrough's *Naked Lunch* (1959). The many strands of the gay liberation movement at the time were woven together by Carl Wittman in San Francisco. His *Gay Manifesto* was first published in 1970. This decade also saw an outpouring of commercial films with explicitly gay themes or gay characters for heterosexual audiences such as *Staircase* (1969), *Little Big Man* (1970), *Myra Breckinridge* (1970), *The Boys in the Band* (1970), *Cabaret* (1972), *The Rocky Horror Picture Show* (1975), *Dog Day Afternoon* (1975), and the French film *La Cage aux Folles* (1978), which led to two sequels and a Broadway musical in the 1980s, and Hollywood remakes (*The Bird Cage*) in the 1990s.

19. They included pioneers of gay activist journalism such as Harry Hay (the subject of the 2002 documentary film *Hope Along the Wind: The Life of Harry Hay*), W. Dorr Legg, and Jim Kepner and pioneering national gay publications that have survived such as *The Advocate*. See, for example, Jim Kepner, *Rough News, Daring Views: 1950s' Pioneer Gay Press Journalism* (New York: Haworth, 1998); Chris Bull, ed., *Witness to Revolution. The Advocate Reports on Gay and Lesbian Politics, 1967–1999* (Los Angeles: Alyson, 1999); and Bullough, *Before Stonewall*. Kepner not only helped found several newspapers (including *The Advocate*), but he also launched what became the International Gay and Lesbian Archives (1956). See Larry P. Gross, *Up From Invisibility: Lesbians, Gay Men, and the Media in America* (New York: Columbia University Press, 2001).

20. Adam, *The Rise of a Gay*, 84.

21. National Gay and Lesbian Task Force, www.thetaskforce.org.

22. Gay Academic Union, www.rainbowhistory.org/gau.htm.

23. Adam, *The Rise of a Gay*, 106–108.

24. The International Conference on Bisexuality—a periodic worldwide gathering of bisexual activists—held its first convention in Amsterdam in 1991.

25. For the history of and information about the bisexual movement in America, see *BiNet USA*, www.binetusa.org.

26. Intersex Society of North America, www.isna.org.

27. The literature on transgender studies—and in depictions of transgendered people in parallel media such as television and film—has expanded dramatically in the past 10 years or so. In terms of the typology of the transgender category, see David Valentine, *Imagining Transgender: An Ethnography of a Category* (Durham, NC: Duke University Press, 2007). In terms of

legal status, see Paisley Currah, Richard M. Juang, and Shannon Price Minter, eds., *Transgender Rights* (Minneapolis: University of Minnesota Press, 2006). The tragic history of the transgendered community in America is detailed by Rudacille, *The Riddle of Gender*.

28. *Bowers v. Hardwick*, 478 U.S. 186 (1986).

29. See, for example, Norman L. Wyers, "Homosexuality in the Family: Lesbian and Gay Spouses," *Social Work*, March–April 1987, 143–148. Wyers was a professor of social work in Portland, Oregon, and presented these findings originally to the Annual Program Meeting, Council on Social Work Education, Detroit, March 1984. Gay couples had applied for marriage licenses from the 1970s—the earliest recorded was in May 1970—but all attempts in the 1970s and 1980s to legitimize same-sex marriage failed. See also Daniel R. Pinello, *America's Struggle for Same-Sex Marriage* (Cambridge: Cambridge University Press, 2006), 22–23.

30. See Cahill, *Same-Sex Marriage*, 101.

31. Stephanie L. Witt and Suzanne McCorkle, eds., *Anti-Gay Right: Assessing Voter Initiatives* (Westport, CT: Praeger, 1997), 11. See also Clyde Wilcox, *Onward Christian Soldiers? The Religious Right in American Politics* (Boulder, CO: Westview, 1996), Chapters 3 and 4; Sean Cahill, "The Anti-Gay Marriage Movement," in *The Politics of Same-Sex Marriage*, ed. Craig A. Rimmerman and Clyde Wilcox (Chicago: University of Chicago Press, 2007), 155–191.

32. Pinello, *America's Struggle*, 157. See also Rudacille, *The Riddle of Gender*, 287 (on the "biological reality" of women as child bearers and "primary caregivers"). Recent court decisions against same-sex marriage suggest a tendency in the same direction. When the New York Supreme Court upheld a legislative ban against same-sex marriage in 2006, the majority noted that "the vast majority of procreation still occurs as a result of sexual intercourse between a male and a female." Quoting a lower court decision, it also said the state could reasonably assume that children raised by "opposite-sex couples" would "have better opportunities to be nurtured and raised by two parents within long-term, committed relationships, which society has traditionally viewed as advantageous for children." See *Samuels v. New York State Department of Health*, 2006 NY Slip Op 01213.

33. The phrase comes from a book written by journalists John Gallaher and Chris Bull, *Perfect Enemies: The Religious Right, the Gay Movement, and the Politics of the 1990s* (New York: Crown, 1996). See also Craig A. Rimmerman, *From Identity to Politics: The Lesbian and Gay Movements in the United States* (Philadelphia: Temple University Press, 2002), Chapter 5; Caramagno, *Irreconcilable Differences?*, Chapters 10–11.

34. Ellen D. B. Riggle and Barry L. Tadlock, "Gays and Lesbians in the Democratic Process: Past, Present, and Future," in *Gays and Lesbians in the Democratic Process: Public Policy, Public Opinion, and Political Representation,*

ed. Ellen D. B. Riggle and Barry L. Tadlock (New York: Columbia University Press, 1999), 1–21, p. 17.

35. See, for example, Katie Lofton and Donald P. Haider-Markel, "The Politics of Same-Sex Marriage versus the Politics of Gay Civil Rights: A Comparison of Public Opinion and State Voting Patterns," in Rimmerman and Wilcox, *Politics of Same-Sex*, 313–340.

36. *Bowers v. Hardwick*, 478 U.S. 186 (1986) and *Lawrence and Garner v. Texas*, 539 U.S. 558 (2003).

37. A good recent example is gays in America's armed forces, where public opinion and the opinion of military personnel concur—separate polls suggest more than 70 percent are in favor of gays in the military. Those surveyed apparently did not make a distinction between the "don't ask, don't tell" policy currently in place in the United States and the openly gay policies practiced by the military in 24 other nations—virtually all of whom are America's allies. Nathaniel Frank, "What Does It Mean to be Moral?," *Houston Chronicle*, March 18, 2007, E1, E5 (citing a Gallup poll on public opinion and a Zogby poll on military opinion in 2006).

38. International Lesbian and Gay Association (ILGA), www.ilga.org. "ILGA is ... the only international non-profit and non-governmental *community-based* federation focused on presenting discrimination on grounds of sexual orientation as a global issue" (italics in the original). It has more than 600 member organizations in 90 countries, including America's National Gay and Lesbian Task Force.

39. Pew Forum on Religion & Public Life, "More Americans Question Religion's Role in Politics," Pew Research Center, Washington, DC, August 21, 2008, http://pewforum.org/docs/?DocID=339.

40. There is now a considerable literature on gay politics outside America, from its origins in Berlin, Germany, in 1897, to the worldwide GLBT communities of today. For a useful overview in English, see Barry D. Adam, Jan Willem Duyvendak, and André Krouwel, eds., *The Global Emergence of Gay and Lesbian Politics: National Imprints of a Worldwide Movement* (Philadelphia: Temple University Press, 1999).

41. A delegate to the United Methodist Church's yearly national conference in 2008, for example, said gay marriage and abortion issues have "roiled the denomination for more than 30 years." Richard Vara, "No Consensus Expected," *Houston Chronicle*, April 19, 2008, F2. Since American Methodists, like most other American denominations, are usually components of worldwide church bodies, a high percentage of delegates (30 percent at this conference) are non-Americans and are often more conservative on these issues than their American counterparts.

42. Committee on Marriage and Family Life, "Statement on Same-Sex Marriage," United States Conference of Catholic Bishops, July 1996, www.usccb.org/laity/marriage/samesexstmt.shtml. See also John J. DiIulio Jr.,

"The Catholic Voter: A Description with Recommendations," *Commonweal*, March 24, 2006, 10–12.

43. In other words, these denominations welcome gays and integrate them into the life of the congregational community, ordain gay clergy, bless gay unions and marry gays, and endorse gay families. Individual congregations within the United Church of Christ, however, have complete autonomy, and therefore not all congregations adhere to the official position of the church.

44. Metropolitan Community Churches, http://mcchurch.org/AM/Template.cfm?Section=Home.

45. The range of theological perspectives on same-sex marriage and family life is large and varies between and within denominations. The following paragraphs are based on Patricia Beattie Jung and Ralph F. Smith, *Heterosexism: An Ethical Challenge* (Albany: State University of New York Press, 1993), 22–31, especially Table 1.1. See also Kenneth D. Wald and Graham B. Glover, "Theological Perspectives on Gay Unions: The Uneasy Marriage of Religion and Politics," 105–129; and David C. Campbell and Carin Robinson, "Religious Coalitions for and against Gay Marriage: The Culture War Rages On," 131–154, both in Rimmerman and Wilcox, *The Politics of Same-Sex*.

46. *Baehr v. Lewin*, 74 Haw. 645, 852 P.2d 44 (1993).

47. The clause is in Article IV, Section 1. States are required to honor legal actions such as marriage and divorce in other states.

48. The 1996 Defense of Marriage Act was "largely in response" to the Hawaiian court decision. The Hawaiian legislature consequently amended its own constitution in 1998 to limit marriage rights to heterosexual couples. Donald J. Cantor, Elizabeth Cantor, James C. Black, and Campbell D. Barrett, *Same-Sex Marriage: The Legal and Psychological Evolution in America* (Middletown, CT: Wesleyan University Press, 2006), 120–122.

49. *Baker v. Vermont*, Sup. Crt. 98, 032 (1999). On the Vermont decision and its ramifications, see Michael Mello, *Legalizing Gay Marriage* (Philadelphia, PA: Temple University Press, 2004). Mello at the time was a professor of law at the Vermont Law School.

50. *Goodridge v. Massachusetts Department of Public Health*, 440 Mass. 309, 798 NE2d 941 (2003).

51. The California Supreme Court ruled against the state law prohibiting mixed marriages in *Perez v Sharp*, 32 Cal.2d 711, 198 P.2d 17 (1948). The 4-3 decision in this case came at a time when "29 other states had laws barring interracial marriage." Adam Liptak, "Gay Marriage through a Black-White Prism," *New York Times*, October 29, 2006, Week in Review-3. The U.S. Supreme Court waited 19 years before outlawing state laws banning sexual activities between ethnic groups. They were not finally declared illegal until *Loving v. Virginia*, 388 U.S. 1 (1967). See also Howard Mintz, "Gay Ruling to Define Judge's Legacy," *Houston Chronicle*, June 1, 2008,

A30; and "Same Sex Marriage, Civil Unions and Domestic Partnerships," National Conference of State Legislatures, November 2008, www.ncsl.org/programs/cyf/samesex.htm.

52. See *Kerrigan v. Commissioner of Public Health*, 289 Conn. 135, 957 A.2d 407 (2008) and *Varnum v. Brien*, No. 07-1499 Iowa SCt (2009). The voters of Iowa could overturn the court decision only through a constitutional amendment, a process that could take three years.

53. Arizona and Florida also passed measures banning same-sex marriage in the 2008 general election, while Arkansas passed a measure banning unmarried couples from serving as adoptive or foster parents.

54. "Massachusetts Court Rules Ban on Gay Marriage Unconstitutional," CNN, February 4, 2004. The specific Web site that displayed the original story has been removed, but links to this information can be obtained through the CNN general Web site, www.cnn.com.

55. Cahill, *Same-Sex Marriage*, 34–35. Cahill says the American Academy of Pediatrics, the National Association of Social Workers, and the American Psychological Association are among the organizations that reject the idea that gay and lesbian parents are not as good as their heterosexual counterparts. See also William C. Holmes and Gail B. Slap, "Sexual Abuse of Boys: Definitions, Prevalence, Correlates, Sequelae and Management," *Journal of the American Medical Association* 280, no. 21 (1998): 1855–1862.

56. Nan D. Hunter, Courtney G. Joslin, and Sharon M. McGowan, *The Rights of Lesbians, Gay Men, Bisexuals, and Transgender People: The Authoritative ACLU Guide to a Lesbian, Gay, Bisexual, or Transgender Person's Rights*, 4th ed. (Carbondale: Southern Illinois University Press, 2004).

57. Of course, some members in the gay community would argue that they should remain separate from the majority and enjoy the freedom to do what they please. Those who advocate the right to maintain a Queer political and social stance face the same sorts of questions faced by members of other newly liberated minorities who wish to be exclusive in America today. Here are two: Will gays who do not want assimilation into mainstream, heterosexual society confront new levels of social stigma and discrimination if they opt to remain exclusive within their community? What about the freedom of gays who do not want to live in committed, monogamous sexual relationships but want to express their sexual orientations serially and freely in public—if it is consensual and does not harm others?

58. In Eastern Orthodox churches, where clergy performed marriage ceremonies, "in all known cases priests performed the same-sex union." In Roman Catholic churches, ordained clergy did not actually perform the ceremony: "the two parties *marry each other*; the priest merely acts as a witness" (italics in the original). Hence same-sex unions also occurred. John Boswell, *Same-Sex Unions in Pre-Modern Europe* (New York: Vintage, 1994), 281.

59. Married couples counted for "less than half of U.S. households" by 2006. Leah Ward Sears, "We Judges Can Help in Saving Marriage," *Houston Chronicle*, November 5, 2006, E1, E4. Sears at the time was chief justice of the Georgia Supreme Court. See also "Divorce Rates," Americans for Divorce Reform, Arlington, Virginia, undated, www.divorcereform.org/rates.html.

60. See Cahill, *Same-Sex Marriages*, 43–45 (citing figures based on the 2000 census). The GLBT community as a percentage of the total population in America is a topic of considerable debate. Anti-gay lobbyists will cite studies that are near 1–2 percent, while pro-gay lobbyists will cite studies nearer 10 percent. Those who identify themselves as gay will be fewer in number than those who are gay but refuse to identify themselves as gay. The number of individuals who have had a same-sex experience once or twice during their lives, moreover, is far greater than the number of self-identified gay people.

61. Monica Mehta, "The Myth of Marriage," *AlterNet*, July 21, 2005, www.alternet.org/story/23400, interviewing Stephanie Coontz about her book, *Marriage, a History: from Obedience to Intimacy, or How Love Conquered Marriage* (New York: Viking, 2005).

62. Carlos A. Ball, *The Morality of Gay Rights: An Exploration in Political Philosophy* (New York: Routledge, 2003), 10. Ball examines the views of various political and legal theorists—including John Rawls, Ronald Dworkin, Richard Rorty, Martha Nussbaum, Michael Sandel, and Michel Foucault—in the context of his discussion on the morality of same-sex marriage and family issues.

63. See Barry L. Tadlock, C. Ann Gordon, and Elizabeth Popp, "Framing the Issue of Same-Sex Marriage: Traditional Values versus Equal Rights," 193–214, p. 211; and DeWayne L. Lucas, "Same-Sex Marriage in the 2004 Election," 243–271, both in Rimmerman and Wilcox, *The Politics of Same-Sex*.

64. Lisa Miller, "Our Mutual Joy: Opponents of Gay Marriage Often Cite Scripture; But What the Bible Teaches about Love Argues for the Other Side," *Newsweek*, December 15, 2008, 28. Same-sex marriage has drawn criticism from some gay feminists and nationalists, but this is very much the minority view in the gay community. These arguments are outlined in Rimmerman, *From Identity to Politics*, 72–74. One of the leading gay-marriage lobbyists is Evan Wolfson, a gay-rights lawyer, who founded the national gay-marriage organization, Freedom to Marry. He was named one of the "100 most influential people in the world" by *Time* magazine in 2004. See Evan Wolfson, *Why Marriage Matters: America, Equality, and Gay People's Right to Marry* (New York: Simon & Schuster, 2004).

65. Hillary Clinton, who lost to Obama as the Democratic choice for president, held the same views as Obama on this issue. For candidate views on gay marriage rights in the 2008 election, see "LGBT Issues," CNN

Election Center, November 2008, www.cnn.com/ELECTION/2008/issues/issues.samesexmarriage.html.

66. Cahill, *Same-Sex Marriage*, 110. On the issue of gay rights, George W. Bush continued almost to the last day of his administration to reject any attempt by the United Nations or any other overseas agency to decriminalize this lifestyle. The United Nations in December 2008, for example, garnered the support of 66 members (mainly from Europe and Latin America) in the 192-member general assembly for an "unprecedented declaration" condemning "human rights violations based on homophobia, saying such measures run counter to the universal declaration of human rights." At present, "homosexuality is banned in nearly 80 countries and subject to the death penalty in at least six." The United States was joined in its negative response by the Roman Catholic Church and members of the Organization of the Islamic Conference—the same groups that condemn UN-sponsored birth control and abortion measures—along with Russia and China. Neil Macfarquhar, "In a First, Gay Rights Are Pressed at the U.N.," *New York Times*, December 18, 2008, A22.

CHAPTER 7

Science, Theology, and Charles Darwin's Legacy

Galileo Galilei and Maffeo Barberini were good friends. Barberini wrote a poem commending Galileo for studies in which he used one of those newfangled telescopes. And he once wrote to Galileo, "[Y]ou will find in me a very ready disposition to serve you out of respect for what you so merit and for the gratitude I owe you."[1] These friends eventually became key players in what is often portrayed as one of the early wars between science and religion.

Galileo (1564–1642) was deeply influenced by Nicolaus Copernicus's theory that a heliocentric model of planetary movement could explain planetary orbits better than Ptolemy's geocentric model. This geocentric model placed the earth and human beings at the center of the universe, which theologians in the sixteenth century still agreed was the earth's proper position—more than a millennium after Ptolemy's death. The heliocentric model placed the sun at the universe's center with the earth orbiting the sun, an assertion both Protestant Reformation and Roman Catholic ecclesiastical authorities believed contradicted scripture.

Copernicus (1473–1543) was convinced "the planets are arranged in space, from innermost to outermost, according to their increasing periods of revolution about the Sun"—an argument detailed in his classic work, *On the Revolutions of the Celestial Orbs* (1543). Copernicus's ideas were widely enough known to attract the attention of Martin Luther (1483–1546) and other sixteenth century Protestant and Roman Catholic theologians. They claimed the Bible stated clearly that the sun moved around the earth, and they cited three biblical passages to support their assertions: (1) Ecclesiastes 1:5, which reads:

"The sun rises and the sun sets—and glides back to where it rises";
(2) Psalm 93:1, which reads in part: "The Lord is king . . . . The world
stands firm; it cannot be shaken"; and Joshua 10:12–13, which reads
in part: "On that occasion, when the Lord routed the Amorites before
the Israelites, Joshua addressed the Lord; he said in the presence of the
Israelites: 'Stand still, O sun, at Gibeon, O moon, in the Valley of
Aijalon!' And the sun stood still And the moon halted, While a nation
wreaked judgment on its foes." As any believer in the geocentric model
and Holy Scripture would expect, the sun apparently was in motion
when Joshua commanded it to stop.[2]

Luther attacked Copernicus, who studied canon law at the University of Bologna, for questioning this interpretation of the Bible.
"Whoever wants to be clever must agree with nothing that others
esteem. He must do something of his own. This is what that fellow
does who wishes to turn astrology upside down. Even in these things
that are thrown into disorder I believe the Holy Scripture, for Joshua
commanded the sun to stand still and not the earth."[3] Protestants
John Calvin (1509–1564) and Philip Melanchthon (1497–1560) were
just as enthusiastic in their condemnations of Copernicus.[4]

Copernicus escaped much of the controversy that later engulfed
Galileo, partly because he did not have the tools he needed to confirm
the accuracy of his mathematical computations and partly because his
mathematical concepts were so difficult to grasp. If best-seller lists had
been compiled in the sixteenth century, *On the Revolutions of the
Celestial Orbs* would have been near the bottom, for it was filled with
complex computations that were meaningful only to a small number
of astronomers and cosmologists.

GALILEO AND THE TELESCOPE

Galileo, a follower of Copernicus, was destined for trouble when he
started using a telescope, invented in 1608, to study the planets. His
studies, published in *Starry Messenger* (1610) and *Letters on Sunspots*
(1613), convinced him that the heliocentric theory was correct.
Although he could not prove the theory, his observations did contradict some of the objections astronomers raised against the heliocentric
model.[5] Galileo's nontechnical books drew the attention of the highest Roman Catholic officials, who also believed that acceptance of
the heliocentric model meant rejection of scripture.

It was Galileo's bad luck that the Catholic Church had experienced the Protestant Reformation—splitting Western Europe's religious map into two parts, Protestant and Catholic—early in the sixteenth century. One of the most divisive issues centered on who should interpret God's will: ordinary people reading with open hearts, as most Protestants believed, or authoritative fathers of the Church, as the Roman Catholic hierarchy believed.[6] Catholic officials revived the Inquisition, tightened their already authoritarian bureaucracy, and sought to prevent deviations from approved beliefs. According to a decree issued at the Council of Trent (1545–1563), scripture was to be interpreted only by Church fathers:

> [T]he Council decrees that, in matters of faith and morals . . . , no one, relying on his own judgment and distorting the Sacred Scriptures according to his own conceptions, shall dare to interpret them contrary to that sense which Holy Mother Church, to whom it belongs to judge their true sense and meaning, has held and does hold, or even contrary to the unanimous agreement of the Fathers, even though such interpretations shall never at any time be published.[7]

The Church did not welcome heliocentric theory and the enthusiasm with which Galileo promoted it. The Inquisition censured in 1616 the theory that the earth revolves around the sun and placed Copernicus's *On the Revolutions of the Celestial Orbs* on the Index of Prohibited Books. Historian of science David C. Lindberg argues that the real issue was not whether the heliocentric model contradicts scripture. "The larger issue that lay behind this question was that of epistemological authority: are cosmological truth-claims dependent on science or on theology—on conclusions drawn from reason and sense experience or on the content of biblical revelation as interpreted by the fathers of the church?"[8]

Galileo's luck seemed to change in 1623 when his friend Maffeo Barberini was elevated to pope. Barberini, or Pope Urban VIII (1568–1644), granted Galileo permission to write about heliocentric theory, although (a) he did not find the theory credible, (b) he told Galileo he must not portray the theory as true, and (c) he said Galileo must describe the views of Ptolemaic astronomers. Galileo violated the agreement, however, when he defended heliocentric theory in *Dialogue Concerning the Two Chief World Systems* (1632).

Not only did he violate the agreement, Galileo seemingly tried to make Urban look foolish. One argument in support of heliocentric theory centers on the motions of the tides. Galileo claimed "the only adequate explanation of the tides was to see them as the sloshing of water in the great sea basins owing to the double motion of the earth (annual about the Sun and daily on its axis)."[9] One of the characters in the *Dialogue* is Simplicio, a not-too-bright defender of the geocentric model. Galileo had Simplicio use words similar to those spoken by Urban to Galileo years earlier as Galileo sought permission to publish his book. Simplicio (see Figure 7.1) is refuting the argument that tidal motion supports heliocentric theory.

An angry Pope Urban convened a commission to look into the matter, and Galileo was tried in 1633 for disobedience. Galileo "clarified" his book's purpose in court:

> I freely confess that it [*Dialogue Concerning the Two Chief World Systems*] seemed to me composed in such a way that a reader ignorant of my real purpose might have reason to think that the arguments presented for

Figure 7.1.   Pope Urban VIII and Simplicio Defending Scripture

Pope Urban in Conversation with Galileo (1624)	**Simplicio in *Dialogue Concerning the Two Chief World Systems***
Let us grant you that all of your demonstrations are sound and that it is entirely possible for things to stand as you say. But now tell us, do you really maintain that God could not have wished or known how to move the heavens and the stars in some other way? Then you will have to concede to us that God can, conceivably, have arranged things in an entirely different manner, while yet bringing about the effects that we see. And if this possibility exists, which might still preserve in their literal truth the sayings of Scripture, it is not for us mortals to try to force those holy words to mean what to us, from here, may appear to be the situation.	I confess that your idea seems to me much more ingenious than any others I have heard, but I do not thereby regard it as true and convincing . . . . I know what you would answer if . . . you are asked whether God with His infinite power and wisdom could give to the element water the back and forth motion we see in it by some means other than by moving the containing basin; I say you will answer that He would have the power and the knowledge to do this in many ways, some of them even inconceivable by our intellect. Thus, I immediately conclude that in view of this it would be excessively bold if someone should want to limit and compel divine power and wisdom to a particular fancy of his.

Source (above left): Giiorgio de Santillana, *The Crime of Galileo* (New York: Time, 1962), 166; (above right): Maurice A. Finocchiaro, *Galileo on the World Systems: A New Abridged Translation and Guide* (Berkeley: University of California Press, 1997), 306–307.

the false side [the heliocentric model], which I really intended to refute, were expressed in such a way as to . . . compel conviction.[10]

When this clarification was judged insufficient, Galileo recanted his position saying, "I still hold, as very true and undoubted Ptolemy's opinion, namely the stability of the earth and the motion of the sun."[11] Galileo was sentenced to imprisonment, but he spent the rest of his life under house arrest.

Religion and Science at "War"

The story of Galileo, heliocentric theory, and the response of Roman Catholic and Protestant church leaders is important in understanding the contemporary relationship between science and religion. For one thing, framing the story as a magnificent war between science and religion, as writers such as Andrew Dickson White (1832–1918) have done, encouraged the idea common in the West that science was at war with religion. Viewed through a different lens, however, one can understand that the "battle" was far more complex.

For his part, Galileo acknowledged the Bible's authority, accepted that the heavens were created by God, and assumed that scientists and theologians could examine the cosmos without conflict.[12] Furthermore, heliocentric theory—the idea that the sun and not the earth is at the center of our solar system—was not widely supported by Galileo's fellow astronomers and cosmologists, many of whom considered him arrogant and wrong. The clergy were also divided. "Among the clergy, differences of opinion regarding principles of biblical interpretation were tolerated," as Lindberg points out, "and some clergy, adopting Galileo's exegetical principles, counted themselves among his vocal supporters." Therefore, he argues, "conflict was located as much *within* the church (between opposing theories of biblical interpretation) and *within* science (between alternative cosmologies) as *between* science and the church" (italics in the original).[13]

The Galileo affair had important ramifications. Pope Urban did not forbid Galileo to write about heliocentric theory, as he had the power to do; he simply told him not to present the theory as true. Had Galileo not deceived and ridiculed Urban, things might have evolved quite differently. As Lindberg suggests, "[I]t seems clear that had he played his cards differently, with more attention to diplomacy, Galileo might well have carried out a significant campaign on behalf of heliocentrism without condemnation."[14]

The Galileo affair clearly did not resolve the central question of epistemological authority. Are questions about the natural order of things, in this case the orbits of the planets, resolved by reading sacred scripture or by scientific research? Is one authority preeminent, or can questions, especially in areas of overlap, be resolved through collaboration?

This chapter focuses on the relationships among contemporary science, religion, and government. It is divided into four sections: Section 1 explores briefly the complex relationship between science and religion in the West. Section 2 examines the attempts by some Christian conservatives, particularly Protestant evangelical fundamentalist activists, to ban the teaching of scientific evolution in public schools or to ensure that creationism or intelligent design is taught alongside evolution. Section 3 offers a snapshot of what can develop into an adversary relationship with science when Christian biblical literalists enjoy government support—as happened during the George W. Bush administration. Section 4 examines some of the enduring tensions that characterize relationships between science and religion today.

SCIENCE AND RELIGION IN WESTERN CULTURE

Traditional views of "science" and "scientists" were being challenged not only in Italy at roughly the time of the Galileo-Urban affair but also in skirmishes in other parts of Europe. The skirmishes, according to sociologist of religion Eva Marie Garroutte, pitted two approaches to the study of the natural world. "One . . . imagined a fundamentally *sacred science*, sustained by contributions from diverse practitioners. The other, which I will call positivism, assumed a strictly *secular science*, nurtured and presided over by a bounded set of professionals" (italics in the original).[15]

Practitioners of sacred science "justified their right to comment upon scientific activity by reference to the Christian scriptures," but advocates of secular science insisted that observers of the natural world use a systematic method (later called the scientific method) without regard for supernatural explanations.[16] Many shared the view of mathematician Isaac Newton (1642–1727), who discovered the significance of gravity and who insisted that knowledge about the natural world must be based on observation and experimentation.

They professed belief in God, but argued that God intended human beings to discover the secrets of the natural world.[17]

Controlling the Intellectual Terrain

Secular scientists ultimately gained control of the scientific terrain in the nineteenth century and excluded supernatural explanations from scientific study. As modern science expanded in all directions and its objective methodologies were more widely practiced both in the natural and human sciences, most religious leaders came to accept its fundamental assumptions and conditions. The relationship between science and religion, however, continued to be framed as one of conflict—a war of words in which military metaphors were used by both sides in the ongoing struggle to win in the court of public opinion.

In the nineteenth century, British scientist Thomas H. Huxley (1825–1895) and Irish physicist John Tyndall (1820–1893) alienated theologians and scientists alike when they argued that the only way to gather knowledge about human beings and nature was through scientific research methods. Tyndall told the British Association for the Advancement of Science in 1874 that scientists must "wrest from theology, the entire domain of cosmological theory . . . . Acting otherwise proved always disastrous in the past, and it is simply fatuous today."[10]

John William Draper (1811–1882)[19] and Andrew D. White[20] charged that conflict between science and religion was inevitable because "religion was wedded to traditional dogma while science offered a new route to the truth that inevitably exposed the inadequacies of past ideas. This was a war that science was bound to win because it was the only reliable source of information."[21]

In the twentieth century, people such as Woodbridge Riley, religion scholar and son of a Presbyterian minister, argued that science revolutionized human worldviews—primarily by overcoming ignorance and the fear that stems from it. In *From Myth to Reason* (1926), Riley (1869–1933) identified sources of knowledge in five ages: the Age of Myth, in which mythical explanations (such as creationism) of the natural world predominated; the Age of Magic, in which magical explanations (such as alchemy and astrology) predominated; the Age of Discovery, in which empirical observations (by people such as Copernicus and Newton) of the natural world began to appear; the Age of Mechanics, in which individuals developed or improved machines (such as clocks and mechanical fountains), and scientists (such as French mathematician-philosopher René Descartes) began speculating about machine intelligence and the role of human beings in a machine world; and the Age of Evolution, in which Charles Darwin and others "showed that man is no more the favorite child of nature than he is the darling of the gods."[22] Riley described religious opposition to the scientific ideas expressed during the last three ages, but he concludes that "conceited and complacent views of man's place in nature" will give way to the advance of learning.[23]

Later scholars expressed similar views. Chemist Peter W. Atkins describes science as "omnicompetent" and refers to the "limitless power of science."[24] Richard Dawkins, the Oxford don who says the existence of God is improbable, argues that religion has retarded the advancement of reason and science by promoting supernatural explanations and pitting scientists against theologians.[25] Biologist Edward O. Wilson says that "the reasons why I consider the scientific ethos superior to religion [are]: its repeated triumphs in explaining and controlling the physical world; its self-correcting nature open to all competent to devise and conduct the tests; its readiness to examine all subjects sacred and profane."[26]

Foregrounding Theology in Research

Pouring gasoline on the blaze are people such as Alvin Plantinga, philosophy professor at Notre Dame, who argue for a kind of theistic science, in which scholars foreground Christian teachings in their research. "[T]he Christian [scientific] community ought to think about the subject matter of the various sciences—again, in particular the human sciences, but also to some degree the so-called natural sciences—from an explicitly theistic or Christian point of view," he said.[27] Iranian theoretical physicist and philosopher Mehdi Golshani argues that it is naïve to think that science has no ideological basis and that " 'Islamic Science,' or for that matter, 'religious science,' has no relevance at . . . the theoretical level and the practical level."[28]

Scientific materialism (or naturalism), a term seldom used by scientists, often is employed to suggest that scientists, particularly during the modern era, wanted people to believe that "truth and meaning were to be found only in that which could be known objectively and with the kind of narrow exactness that we find in mathematics," as philosopher of religion James P. Danaher points out. "That was the great metanarrative of modernity to which everyone was forced to conform if they wished to be considered rational."[29] Critics who see science as a threat to their religion-based worldviews frequently attribute this attitude to scientists as part of their attack against the perceived threat of objective scientific research.

More nuanced analyses of the relationship between science and religion tend to acknowledge conflict, defined in a number of ways, but they identify other possibilities as well. Ian G. Barbour, a frequently cited writer concerned with religion and science, proposed four ways in which religion and science might relate: (a) conflict, in which proponents of science and religion openly clash; (b) independence, in which science and religion share no methods, findings, or theories and have little contact; (c) dialogue, in which there is a sharing of views among theologians and scientists whose assumptions and methodologies may be similar; and (d) integration, which involves "a greater conceptual unity between the fields, often by a more systematic and extensive reformulation of traditional theological concepts."[30]

These categories have been criticized and altered by other scholars. Geoffrey Cantor and Chris Kenny, who study the history and philosophy of science, criticize the Barbour taxonomy as analytically unhelpful, primarily because scholars have not produced a universally accepted definition of science and because of what they see as too much emphasis on conflict,[31] Barbour himself acknowledges that conflict is problematic "because it groups together two views at opposite ends of the theological spectrum: biblical literalism and scientific materialism."[32]

While scientists today are not swayed by supernatural explanations of natural events, some (a) acknowledge the important role of religion in bringing communities together and in helping the faithful find meaning in their lives[33] and (b) agree with Galileo, Sir Francis Bacon (1561–1626), and others that God created the natural world for human beings to discover. This seems an argument for independence, dialogue, or integration. While conflict is apparent in many situations, conflict need not be the only, or even the most important, dimension of the religion-science relationship.

The Age of the Earth

Disagreement about the age of the earth, which has simmered for centuries, often is portrayed as an example of the war between science and religion. Early Western estimates of the earth's age were based on scripture. Theophilus of Antioch (died about 184), Julius Africanus (died about 240), and Isadore of Seville (died in 636) calculated that the earth was roughly 6,000 years old.[34] Archbishop of Armagh James Ussher (1581–1656) gave the most authoritative answer to the question in the mid-seventeenth century. Based on his understanding of ancient historical chronology and a selective, literal reading of the Bible, Ussher pinpointed the date of creation as October 23, 4004 BCE.[35] That date was published in the English-language Authorized King James Version of the Bible in 1701 and was not removed for more than 100 years.[36]

Public challenges to Ussher's date came from French naturalist Georges-Louis Buffon (1707–1788) and Scottish geologist James Hutton (1726–1797).[37] Buffon, basing his estimate on observations of the cooling rates of metal, said the earth was more than 200,000 years old, a time frame that seemingly did not fit at all with a literal reading of the story of Genesis.[38] The Sorbonne's theological faculty made Buffon deny his work, *L'Histoire Naturelle* (1749). "I declare that I had no intention to contradict the text of Scripture," he said. "I abandon everything in my book respecting the formation of the earth, and generally all which may be contrary to the narrative of Moses."[39]

Hutton proposed a theory of gradual change based on studies of fossils (particularly of marine animals), minerals, and rock formations. Hutton argued for three geological time periods, each of undetermined length. In proposing that the geological record has no beginning and no end, he suggested that the earth is eternal. He did not deny the possibility of a beginning and an end, but this did not satisfy some of his critics.[40] Sir Charles Lyell (1797–1875), writing in the nineteenth century, endorsed Hutton's theory of gradualism. Lyell, a geologist, said the earth's mountains and valleys and other features were not caused by the Great Flood, and he placed the age of the earth at 240 million years.[41]

Past disagreements among biblical literalists and scientists about the age of the earth, however, often were tempered by new ways of interpreting the Bible. Some Christians began as early as the Protestant Reformation to read and interpret the Bible in nonliteral terms. "Increasingly, the literal reading of the Bible (what the words say)," as historian Mott T. Greene puts it, "was separated from the figurative reading of the Bible (how the words form a connected and prophetic history)." Many Christians in the nineteenth century were debating how to read the Bible. Religious authority was eroding "with the emancipation of Catholicism [a reference to church officials' diminishing authority over ordinary Catholics], the repeal of the tests of religious orthodoxy as a condition of government employment, and the explosive growth of dissenting and nonconformist Protestant sects, especially evangelicals."[42] Furthermore, the scientific community was not particularly inclined toward public conflict because geology was a young, developing discipline that needed public support.

The age of the earth controversy lost much of its remaining momentum in the late nineteenth century, in part because critics found other issues to address when Charles Darwin's (1809–1882) *On the Origin of Species by Means of Natural Selection* was published in 1859. Biologists and geologists, however, continued to seek an accurate estimate of the earth's age.

The discovery of radioactivity and the mechanical calculator made it possible for geoscientist Arthur Holmes (1890–1965)—who by the mid-1940s was using lead isotopes from the geological strata—to estimate the earth's age at 3,350 million years. When the innovative scientist Claire Patterson (1922–1995) found that the earth's rock samples did not contain primordial lead, he calibrated the lead system using meteorites. He estimated in 1956 that the earth is 4,550 million years old (give or take 70 million years).[43] Scientists today estimate the earth's age at roughly 4.6 billion years, based on several factors, including the movement of liquefied rock beneath the earth's mantle and the movement of the earth's tectonic plates.[44]

Contemporary conservative religious insistence that the earth is no more than a few thousand years old gathered momentum in the second half of the twentieth century. Many found evidence in a 1961 book by creationist theologian John C. Whitcomb Jr. and hydraulic engineer Henry M. Morris—who argued that Noah's flood, described in Genesis 6:17 and 7:24,[45] caused rapid geological changes.[46] "For months afterward, the planet convulsed with earthquakes, tsunamis and volcanoes. After a brief ice age, the earth became the ecosystem we know today. Continents shifted; the water receded; the animals left the ark and spread over the earth."[47] Belief in a catastrophic event such as Noah's flood that accelerated geological change is central to the contemporary argument that the earth is only a few thousand years old.

John Baumgardner, a Christian fundamentalist and a scientist with the U.S. Department of Energy's Los Alamos National Laboratory, also believes the earth is only a few thousand years old. He created a computer program called Terra—which the National Laboratory uses to study earthquakes, volcanoes, and the movement of continental plates—that he says "proves" the truth of Genesis 7:18: "The waters swelled and increased greatly upon the earth, and the ark drifted upon the face of the waters." Terra also "proves," he says, the earth is less than 10,000 years old.

Geologists disagree. They note that the Terra computer data produce a more accurate estimate of the earth's age when more realistic assumptions are used.[48] The disagreement about the age of the earth is but one illustration of the contemporary conflict between science and some religious conservatives.

CHRISTIAN CONSERVATIVES, EVOLUTION, AND INTELLIGENT DESIGN

Charles Darwin changed the relationship between science and theology when he demonstrated that his theory of descent with modification (evolution) occurs without direction or purpose, that natural selection drives this evolution, and that species survive through adaptation. Mutations or recombinations that occur by random chance during reproduction change the genetic makeup of new generations. "These tiny changes, and their differential expression during stages of embryonic development, lead to the endless variation of life." Some species inherit traits that help them survive and others do not. Still others inherit traits that reduce their chances of survival.[49]

Darwin's theory of natural selection—which holds that individuals who inherit critical traits will have a better chance for survival than those who do not—explains why "some 99.9 per cent of all species that ever existed are now extinct," as Australian physiologist-pharmacologist Geoffrey P. Dobson says. "That is, it explains why, of the total 30 *billion* species of animals and plants believed to have existed over the past 3.5–3.8 billion years, only 15–30 *million* are around today" (italics in the original).[50]

Naturalists and Literalists

Darwin did not intend to challenge literalist interpretations of scripture, particularly Genesis 1:26–28,[51] or the existence of a supreme being, and he did not initially discuss the origin of the human species. Still, Darwin's findings were challenged and defended in dichotomous terms that usually managed to pit scientific naturalists against biblical literalists. Thomas H. Huxley portrayed evolution as "another step in science's advance toward the truth, another nail in the coffin of religious dogma."[52] Huxley wrote in his review of Darwin's book: "Extinguished theologians lie about the cradle of every science as the strangled snakes beside that of Hercules."[53] Huxley was not reluctant, as Darwin was, to apply scientific evolution to human beings. His *Evidence as to Man's Place in Nature* (1863) generated a great deal of consternation and debate.

The Rationalist Press Association (RPA) in Britain (founded in 1899) also joined the debate: "[I]t stressed the need for a rational approach to the study of nature as a means of undermining belief in the supernatural," as biology historian Peter J. Bowler puts it. "By popularizing the philosophy of scientific naturalism, they would convince ordinary people that the churches should be swept away, and with them the old social hierarchy."[54] The RPA is alive and well today, publishing books opposing doctrinaire religious approaches to science.[55]

Some religionists offered the counterclaim that an intelligent force in nature drives humanity to achieve moral goals and that life exists apart from the body. "These theories invoked what the rationalists had dismissed as the supernatural," as Bowler notes, "and they were regarded as the key to a new philosophy in which nature was directed by the nonphysical agents of life and mind." Biblical literalists and their academic supporters also claimed that the theory of the ether (rather than an atomistic theory) "would sweep away the foundations of materialism by showing that the whole universe was a harmonious cosmos."[56] The theory of ether—the substance that facilitated the movement of electromagnetic waves—was disproved in the late 1880s.

Other religionists, and some scientists, simply could not accept that human beings and apes had descended from a common ancestor. Alfred Russel Wallace (1823–1913), for example, who sent Darwin a paper in 1858 describing a theory of natural selection that was very similar to Darwin's and who presented a co-authored paper with Darwin about natural selection, refused to exclude divine intervention as an explanation for the origin of the human species. Wallace agreed initially with Darwin that human minds and bodies evolved over time, but he later claimed that a large brain that could make moral distinctions could not have evolved without intervention. Wallace argued: "[A] superior intelligence has guided the development of man in a definite direction, and for a special purpose, just as man guides the development of many animal and vegetable forms."[57]

Circumstances changed somewhat during the course of the twenti-eth century. A new professional class of scientists was more enchanted by the empirical search for nature's fundamental laws than by biblical interpretations of the natural world. They were better educated. Some were members of faith groups with their own stories of creation that differed from those in Genesis, and others argued that they were exploring a natural world created by a supreme being whose methods could not be comprehended by human beings.

Many Christians were reading the Bible as a metaphorical descrip-tion of human events and the natural world. As philosopher of religion James P. Danaher has written, "Christianity will always be a personal relationship with the risen Christ, and never an explanation of how things are for everyone everywhere."[58] Many Christians would not accept that meaning and truth could be found only in objective sci-ence, but they saw no particular conflict between science's accounts of creation and those reported in Genesis. For them, the science-religion relationship could be characterized by greater conceptual unity (integration), a continuing exchange of views by theologians and scientists (dialogue), and/or separation (independence).

Resistance to Science

Some conservative religious activists, particularly in the United States, were not (and are not) prepared to concede what they see as defeat in their struggle against modern science. For them, the Bible contains universal truths that apply to all individuals and communities in all situations. As we noted in Chapter 1, they equate God's laws with natural law, and they share a nostalgic, premodernist view of the world. They yearn for an imagined past in which they are not isolated, alien-ated, or challenged by modernity's focus on rationality and objectivity.

Scientific evolution is a lightening rod for this criticism, for these Christian conservatives fear that evolution undermines the biblical view of creation and challenges the uniqueness of human beings. "For two millennia, Western civilization has imagined people as cat-egorically different from and vastly superior to other animals," David Sloan Wilson, a professor of biology and anthropology, says. "The list of supposedly unique human attributes has been almost end-less, encompassing language, tool use, intelligence, morals and aesthetics."[59] Charles Darwin and his disciples challenged this anthropomorphic vision of the past.

Protestant conservatives in particular tried with some success in the early decades of the twentieth century to convince state legislatures and school boards, especially in the South, to ban the teaching of evolution and to ban textbooks that mentioned Charles Darwin. The first major hiccup came in 1925 in what Edward J. Larson, a Pulitzer Prize–winning historian, called perhaps "the most famous encounter between science and religion to have occurred on American soil."[60]

The encounter, of course, was the trial in Dayton, Tennessee, of John T. Scopes, a teacher who violated a new state law that banned the teaching of evolution in public schools. Scopes (1900–1970) accepted the request of the American Civil Liberties Union (ACLU) to challenge the law in court. The case, called "the trial of the century" by the press, drew considerable attention because the law violated the First Amendment's establishment clause and because much of America's cultural elite—including the Protestant hierarchy—now refused to privilege a literal reading of the Bible's creation story over scientific evolution. All reputable scientists employed in the United States now relied on the scientific method, but "the enactment of the Tennessee statute suggested that significant political support existed for accepting religion over science on a matter central to modern biology."[61]

The trial pitted William Jennings Bryan (1860–1925), a conservative Presbyterian who held some liberal political views, against Clarence Darrow (1857–1938), one of America's best-known and most successful trial lawyers. "The prospect of the two renowned orators Bryan and Darrow actually litigating the profound issues of science versus religion and academic freedom versus popular control over public education turned the trial into a media sensation then [at the time of the trial] and then the stuff of legend thereafter."[62] The trial looked more like a circus than it might have because the judge permitted journalists to take telegraph tickers, cameras, and microphones into the courtroom.

The trial lasted eight days and the jury took nine minutes to decide Scopes was guilty of violating the Tennessee statute. He was ordered to pay a fine of $100. Darrow appealed the decision to the Supreme Court of Tennessee, which upheld the trial court decision. The case could not be appealed to the U.S. Supreme Court because of a technicality.

Despite the verdict, as we noted in Chapter 1, the case was really a defeat for the creationists. Tennessee won its case, but only two other southern states—Mississippi and Arkansas—subsequently enacted laws prohibiting the teaching of evolution in public schools. Northern states such as Rhode Island and Minnesota defeated such laws.

The trial "inspired thousands of ordinary white Protestants to attach themselves to the fundamentalist crusade,"[63] but other Protestant Christians in the South as well as the North were embarrassed or dispirited by the trial and withdrew from the political arena. Christians such as Shelton Hale Bishop, curate of St. Philip's Episcopal Church in Harlem, New York, expressed the view of many at the time when he said that both perspectives "contain immortal and everlasting truths"—there was no contradiction between scientific evolution and the Bible.[64]

The Mississippi, Tennessee, and Arkansas bans and those by local school boards were to remain on the books for another 43 years. Challenges to the constitutionality of bans against the teaching of evolution in public schools did not reach the U.S. Supreme Court until the late 1960s, when the Court ruled in *Epperson v. Arkansas* (1968) that such bans were unconstitutional.[65]

Christian conservative activists fought back by offering creation science as a "scientific" explanation for the world's origins. Advocates of creation science attempted to prove that (a) scientific discoveries about evolution, the earth's history, biology, and cosmology were wrong, (b) floodwaters at one time covered the earth, and (c) the biblical account of creation was correct. They pressured local school boards to ban the teaching of evolution from science classes and to require the teaching of creation science. If that did not work, they demanded that school officials require both creation science and evolution be taught.

They suffered a minor setback when a U.S. District Court in Arkansas ruled in *McLean v. Arkansas Board of Education* (1982) that the state's attempt to balance the treatment of evolution and creation science in its public schools violated the establishment clause.[66] Judge William R. Overton set down five criteria that must be met before creationism (or other theories) could be deemed a science: its principles and conclusions must be (a) based in natural law, (b) explained by reference to natural law, (c) testable by empirical methods, (d) tentative, or not the final word, and (e) falsifiable. Creation science could meet none of these criteria, but creationism continued to be taught because the ruling applied only to the eastern district of Arkansas.

All U.S. schools were affected, however, when the U.S. Supreme Court, in *Edwards v. Aguillard* (1987), declared unconstitutional a Louisiana law requiring that creation science be taught when scientific evolution is taught. "The Act impermissibly endorses religion by advancing the religious belief that a supernatural being created humankind," the Court held in finding the law violated the establishment clause. "The Act's primary purpose was to change the public school science curriculum to provide persuasive advantage to a particular religious doctrine that rejects the factual basis of evolution in its entirety."[67]

Intelligent Design

Religious conservatives, and they were primarily Protestant evangelical fundamentalists, came back from the drawing board with intelligent design, proponents of which assume that a superior intelligence designed the natural world. Intelligent design was not a new idea. Thomas Chalmers, a Scottish leader of the Free Church of Scotland and a mathematician, advocated divine design in the nineteenth century.[68]

Chalmers (1780–1847) was one of many scientists and theologians who believed that an object that serves a specific purpose must have been designed by a superior intelligence. "If the solar system looked as if it were not the result of necessity or of accident, if it appeared to have been made with a special end in mind, then it must have had a designer, namely God." Enthusiasm for divine design waned as it became increasingly clear that evidence of design by a superior intelligence would not be forthcoming, and as more and more natural phenomena, such as the earth itself and the solar system, were seen "as products of natural law rather than divine miracle." Defenders of divine design focused increasingly on "the origin of the laws that had proved capable of such wondrous things. Many Christians concluded that these laws had been instituted by God and were evidence of His existence and wisdom."[69]

Pope John Paul II reflected the religious views of most contemporary scientists when he finally said in a 1996 message to the Pontifical Academy of Sciences that "new knowledge has led to the recognition of the theory of evolution as more than a hypothesis." Scientific evolution has been accepted widely "following a series of discoveries in various fields of knowledge. The convergence ... of the results of work that was conducted independently is in itself a significant argument in favor of the theory."[70] The pope did not denigrate the importance of God in the creation of human beings; he suggested that evolution can be seen as part of God's plan, a view that is consistent with traditional Roman Catholic teachings.

Intelligent Design, Journalists, and "Irreducible Complexity"

Biochemist Michael J. Behe of Lehigh University helped resurrect intelligent design near the end of the twentieth century.[71] Behe, a Roman Catholic, argues that evolution cannot work when a system is "irreducibly complex," meaning a complex system such as the eye cannot be created through gradual change. "[A]ny precursor to an irreducibly complex system that is missing a part is by definition non-functional," Behe says. "Irreducible complexity is just a fancy phrase I use to mean a single system which is composed of several interacting parts, and where the removal of any one of the parts causes the system to cease functioning."[72]

Behe and others argue, for example, that a bird's wing—or an animal's eye, blood clotting mechanism, or genetic makeup—could not have evolved gradually; "it would have to arise as an integrated unit, in one fell swoop, for natural selection to have anything to act on." Their conclusion is that an intelligent agent, not necessarily God, created complex systems such as eyes and wings "in one fell swoop." Intelligent design does not explain everything, and it "does not mean that any of the other factors [for example, natural selection, population size, migration, and common descent] are not operative, common, or important."[73] This argument is not unlike that of Alfred Wallace, who asserted that it strained credibility to assume that the human being's large skull and ability to make moral decisions evolved over time without intervention by a superior intelligence.

What is different about the contemporary version of intelligent design offered by Behe and others is the assertion that it is based in science and not theology. If they could show that intelligent design is based in science, proponents argue, they might be able to satisfy the U.S. Supreme Court, which has shown no inclination to permit the teaching of nonscientific alternatives to evolution. Furthermore, proponents of intelligent design are careful to attribute complex designs to a "superior intelligence" and not to God, for the Supreme Court has not looked with favor on those who would introduce God into a biology class.

School Board Controversies

The Kansas Board of Education—which dropped most references to evolution in new science guidelines in 1999, only to reinstate evolution two years later when voters replaced three conservative members—

was an early adopter of the new approach. A new board approved in November 2005 standards "recommending that schools teach specific points that doubters of evolution use to undermine its primacy in science education." The standards also specified that teachers "would not be explicitly limited to natural explanations," a recommendation that opened the door to the teaching of intelligent design.[74] That decision was reversed in 2007 when the board adopted standards that are consistent with mainstream science.[75]

The new strategy also was tried in Dover, Pennsylvania, but that school board's action became the subject of yet another high-profile trial. This one began in October 2005, in a case that tested the constitutionality of teaching intelligent design in public schools. The case, *Kitzmiller v. Dover Area School District* (2005), was filed by the ACLU on behalf of concerned parents after the local school board voted 6–3 to endorse the following change to the biology curriculum: "Students will be made aware of gaps/problems in Darwin's theory and of other theories of evolution including, but not limited to, intelligent design."[76]

U.S. District Judge John E. Jones III, however, dealt the intelligent design advocates a severe blow when he ruled that Dover schools could not require teachers to disparage evolution or to refer to intelligent design. The Dover policy, Jones ruled, violated the Constitution's establishment clause. The judge left no doubt about his view of the Dover policy when he wrote the following:

Those who disagree with our holding will likely mark it as the product of an activist judge. If so, they will have erred as this is manifestly not an activist Court. Rather, this case came to us as the result of the activism of an ill-informed faction on a school board, aided by a national public interest law firm eager to find a constitutional test case on ID [intelligent design], who in combination drove the Board to adopt an imprudent and ultimately unconstitutional policy. The breathtaking inanity of the Board's decision is evident when considered against the factual backdrop which has now been fully revealed through this trial. The students, parents, and teachers of the Dover Area School District deserved better than to be dragged into this legal maelstrom, with its resulting utter waste of monetary and personal resources.[77]

Framing Evolution and Intelligent Design

Some journalists covering the original board decision or the subsequent trial evidently did not recognize, as Judge Jones did, the "breathtaking inanity of the Board's decision," for they framed intelligent design as a serious alternative to scientific evolution. One example is Michael Powell's story in the *Washington Post* about the 2004 decision to have teachers poke holes in evolution and to teach intelligent design. Powell writes:

> DOVER, Pa.—"God Or Darwin?"
>
> Lark Myers, a blond, 45-year-old gift shop owner, frames the question and answers it. "I *definitely* would prefer to believe that God created me than that I'm 50th cousin to a silverback ape," she said. "What's wrong with wanting our children to hear about all the holes in the theory of evolution?" (italics in the original).

And in the fifth paragraph of this story: " 'The school board has taken the measured step of making students aware that there are other viewpoints on the evolution of species,' said Richard Thompson, of the [conservative, nonprofit] Thomas More Law Center, which represents the board and describes its overall mission as defending 'the religious freedom of Christians.' "[78]

Powell frames the story with quotations from an opponent of evolution, a person who (a) states erroneously that evolution is full of holes, (b) pits God against evolution, and (c) expresses opposition in the most inflammatory terms (that human beings evolved from apes). He then cites a source who implies incorrectly that there are other scientific views of evolution. Powell has given proponents of intelligent design a soapbox from which to attack evolution, has heightened the perceived conflict in the situation, and has represented intelligent design as a serious scientific alternative to evolution, which it is not.

Powell's story is not unique. Evolution and intelligent design often are covered by political reporters who focus on the false "controversy" between evolution and intelligent design and not by science writers who know the scientific case favors evolution overwhelmingly. According to journalist Chris Mooney and science and media expert Matthew C. Nisbet,

> [S]cience writers generally characterize evolution in terms that accurately reflect its firm acceptance in the scientific community. Political reporters, generalists, and TV news reporters and anchors, however, rarely provide their audiences with any real context about basic evolutionary science. Worse, they often provide a springboard for anti-evolutionist criticism of that science, allotting ample quotes and sound bites to Darwin's critics in a quest to achieve "balance."[79]

By treating intelligent design and evolution as scientific equals, the news media confer on intelligent design a credibility it does not deserve, for there is no evidence of an "intelligent agent's" hand in the shaping of the universe. As Mooney and Nisbet note, "The pairing of competing claims plays directly into the hands of intelligent-design proponents who have cleverly argued that they're mounting a *scientific* attack on evolution rather than a religiously driven one, and who paint themselves as maverick outsiders warring against a dogmatic scientific establishment" (italics in the original).[80]

Journalists should be able to find (a) knowledgeable sources who can speak with authority and (b) sources who would not use journalists for their own purposes. These are two arguments for an objective approach, as we argued in Chapter 2. Scientist and religion critic Richard Dawkins is one such expert in the intelligent design fracas. He argues that the "self-evident truth" of Behe's "irreducible complexity" is, in fact, not self-evident at all.

"A cataract patient with the lens of her eye surgically removed can't see clear images without glasses, but can see enough not to bump into a tree or fall over a cliff," Dawkins says. Similarly, a partial wing (one not completely evolved) might save a life. "Half a wing could save your life by easing your fall from a tree of a certain height. And 51 per cent of a wing could save you if you fall from a slightly taller tree." Science offers no evidence that complex systems such as wings or eyes could not evolve gradually. Dawkins warns that one should not declare systems to be irreducibly complex: "the chances are that you haven't looked carefully enough at the details, or thought carefully enough about them."[81]

The Discovery Institute

One of the primary backers of intelligent design is Seattle's Discovery Institute, a public policy think tank that supports research through its Center for Science & Culture. The center (a) challenges scientific evolution, (b) supports intelligent design, and (c) explores "the impact of scientific materialism on culture." It also encourages schools to teach students about the weaknesses and strengths of scientific evolution.[82] A media-savvy organization, the Institute gets its messages out through public debates and conferences, books and articles, mass media, legislative testimony, and reports. It also operates a sophisticated Web site and publishing arm. Michael Behe is one of the Institute's senior fellows.

Intellectual Dishonesty

The Center for Science & Culture has been widely criticized for bias, inaccuracy, and poor scientific methodology. The statement on its main Web page that it supports research by scientists who challenge evolution is a clear indication of bias or, at the very least, poor science. Legitimate scientists and other scholars are committed to finding truth, whatever that truth may turn out to be, which means they do not decide in advance what they want to "prove" and then seek data to support their preconceptions.[83] The Center is asking scholars to work backward to generate approved results.

When the Discovery Institute was preparing to raise funds for the Center for Science & Culture, one of its fund-raising proposals declared the following:

> Yet a little over a century ago, this cardinal idea [human beings are created in God's image] came under wholesale attack by intellectuals drawing on the discoveries of modern science. Debunking the traditional conceptions of both God and man, thinkers such as Charles Darwin, Karl Marx, and Sigmund Freud portrayed humans not as moral and spiritual beings, but as animals or machines, who inhabited a universe ruled by purely impersonal forces and whose behavior and very thoughts were dictated by the unbending forces of biology, chemistry, and environment.[84]

This masterful propaganda probably raised gobs of money for the Center, but it is an inaccurate description of events of the last 100 years and is intellectually dishonest. The document is inaccurate because none of these three men portrayed human beings as animals or machines and because the idea that human beings were created in God's image was never under wholesale attack by scientists. The document is intellectually dishonest because the writer unfairly associates the Discovery Institute's primary villain, Charles Darwin, with Sigmund Freud (1856–1939) and Karl Marx (1818–1883). Freud and Marx, whose ideas about the existence of a supreme being were quite complex, often are described simplistically as the most visible atheists in the nineteenth and early twentieth centuries.[85]

The Institute's document also ignores the views of many scientists and religionists at that time. Darwin, for example, actually believed in God, whom he credited with creating the natural world. And astronomer John F. W. Herschel (1792–1871)—who penned an extraordinary analysis and defense of the method of science—argued, and many scientists agreed, that science must "stop short of those truths which it is the object of revelation to make known," and that scientific discovery "places the existence and principal attributes of a Deity on such grounds as to render doubt absurd and atheism ridiculous."[86] Furthermore, many theologians shared the view of Benjamin B. Warfield (1851–1921), a leading proponent of biblical inerrancy and a professor at the Princeton Theological Seminary, that there was no "general statement in the Bible or any part of the account of creation . . . that need be opposed to evolution."[87]

Advocates of intelligent design have resorted to the two-pronged strategy the tobacco, asbestos, and energy industries have used in opposing scientific inquiry or results they see as threatening: they use their own "science" to fight science. "The scientific 'expert' or 'professional' is a powerful cultural symbol," as Kathleen E. Jenkins, a sociologist of religion, argues. "The ID movement presents their centers and researchers as part of a professional scientific conversation." They try to legitimize their ideas and theories by portraying scientists in professional conferences, classrooms, and research settings. These images and ideas appear in documentaries, publications, and Web sites such as those produced and maintained by the Discovery Institute. "Active promotion of ID publications and assertive public relations efforts," as Jenkins puts it, "strengthen ID's subcultural impact."[88]

An inconvenient truth is that the science of intelligent design is not scientific and its researchers are not taken seriously. Intelligent design "miraculously intervenes just in the places where science has yet to offer a comprehensive explanation for a particular phenomenon," according to science historian Michael Shermer. God once controlled the weather, for instance, "but now that we understand it, He has moved on to more difficult problems, such as the origins of DNA and cellular life. Once these problems are mastered, then [God or intelligent design] will no doubt find even more intractable conundrums."[89]

Advocates of intelligent design use an ingenious strategy to skirt such criticism: they claim they are on the cutting edge of a knowledge revolution and that they are persecuted by establishment science. William A. Dembski, a senior fellow at the Center for Science & Culture, declares that he takes "all declarations about the next big revolution in science with a stiff shot of skepticism. . . . Despite this, I grow progressively more convinced that intelligent design will revolutionize science and our conception of the world."[90]

A persecution complex also is common among intelligent design advocates. Michael Behe frequently is portrayed as intelligent design's bravest martyr. When you read the criticisms of Behe's work, Dembski asserts, "you'll think he's a crank, a fraud and a knave. His work, we are told, has been 'thoroughly discredited,' 'completely demolished' and 'utterly destroyed.' "[91] For intelligent designers, he is a misunderstood visionary who is merely trying to persuade mainstream science to consider a reasonable alternative to evolution.

In fact, the claim that Behe and others are persecuted visionaries is a sophisticated propaganda tactic. The movie *Expelled: No Intelligence Allowed* (2008), an effort by the Discovery Institute to promote intelligent design, suggests that this persecution is an attack against academic freedom. It is part of the new mantra of intelligent design activists, echoing philosophers such as Notre Dame's Alvin Plantinga, who say they are denied their right to conduct research as they see fit.

The movie has been shown to lawmakers in at least two states, and several (including Louisiana, Alabama, Michigan, Missouri, and Texas) have introduced or are contemplating legislation to "protect public-school educators," who critique scientific evolution or offer "alternative" perspectives. The purpose of the movie is to foster "what might be described as the public's right to remain ignorant regarding science," according to journalist Lauri Lebo, who covered the Dover, Pennsylvania, school board trial. "But it also involves something more. It uses fear to attack curiosity. And wonderment."[92]

Generating Conflict

Another tactic is to seize any opportunity to create conflict. In one of its more unusual actions, the Institute accused public broadcasting station WGBH in Boston of violating the Constitution by introducing religion into the classroom. WGBH had produced an educational documentary, one segment of which says: "Q: Can you accept evolution and still believe in religion? A: Yes. The common view that evolution is inherently anti-religious is simply false." The Institute charges that the documentary encourages practices that are unconstitutional. "According to Casey Luskin, an attorney with the Discovery Institute, this answer favours one religious viewpoint.... 'We're afraid that teachers might get sued [if they show the documentary],' he says."[93]

This would be the same Discovery Institute that would put biology teachers in legal jeopardy by having them teach intelligent design.

The Discovery Institute is not the only organization that attacks scientific findings that seem to contradict biblical teachings and create research that supports their points of view. Answers in Genesis, a creationist group in Petersburg, Kentucky, opened its Creation Museum in 2007 to convince visitors that the Genesis account of creation is correct. "With its wide-open spaces and interactive exhibits, the place feels like a slick museum of natural history, updated for the Hollywood age."[94] A depiction of Noah's ark, dinosaurs, and models of Adam and Eve all reinforce the central message that the Bible is right and science is wrong.

Religious conservatives—again led by Protestant evangelical fundamentalists—also have created institutes such as the Medical Institute for Sexual Health, based in Texas and Washington, D.C., and the National Association for the Research & Therapy of Homosexuality, based in Encino, California, to push their scientific agendas. The Institute for Youth Development in Washington, D.C., has even started a "peer-reviewed" journal whose "referees" must pass a Christian conservative-oriented religious test. The journal is a response to charges that intelligent design research is never peer-reviewed. "Researchers" now argue that, because of this journal, their work is peer reviewed and therefore is credible.

RELIGION, SCIENCE, AND GOVERNMENT IN CONFLICT

The relationship between science and religion was marked increasingly by conflict in the new century as Christian conservatives demanded that the Republicans they helped elect to public office give them a substantive voice in governing. Many evangelical politicians and bureaucrats embedded in governments across the country, including the administration of George W. Bush, were in positions to impose their religious views on their fellow citizens. This religion-government coalition, rare in the history of science and religion, did little to improve the science-religion relationship in the United States.

Politicizing Science

George Deutsch is an example of the new politicized bureaucrat. Deutsch was 24 when he landed a job with the National Aeronautics

& Space Administration's (NASA) public affairs office. He had no science background, but he had written columns favorable to the Bush administration for the *Battalion*, the student newspaper at Texas A&M University. He had also worked for the Bush reelection campaign in 2004, and he allowed people to think he had earned a journalism degree at A&M.

Deutsch, a proponent of intelligent design, told a contractor developing a Web site featuring Albert Einstein that he could use "Big Bang" only when the phrase was followed by the word "theory." For Deutsch and millions of Christians like him, the idea that the universe began with a Big Bang contradicts biblical accounts of creation. "It is not NASA's place, nor should it be to make a declaration such as this about the existence of the universe that discounts intelligent design by a creator," Deutsch told the contractor in an electronic mail message. "This is more than a science issue, it is a religious issue. And I would hate to think that young people would only be getting one-half of this debate from NASA." NASA fired Deutsch, not because he imposed his religious views, but because he did not have a degree from Texas A&M.[95]

Hundreds of other bureaucrats and political activists are still in place, however, trying to impose personal religious views on others. For example, Grand Canyon National Park's bookstore, like all things under the jurisdiction of the U.S. National Park Service, is mandated by Congress to promote scientific literacy. Its chief of interpretation approved in 2003 the sale in the bookstore of *Grand Canyon: A Different View*, a coffee-table book edited by creationist Tom Vail, "who leads 'Christ-centered' tours through the canyon."[96] The book contains articles by several creationists and argues the canyon was created only a few thousand years ago by Noah's flood.

The book contradicts legitimate geological evidence showing the Grand Canyon is roughly 17 million years old. The most recent estimate was made in 2008 by geologists who dated mineral deposits in caves from nine sites throughout the canyon. The geologists, from the University of New Mexico, say there were actually two canyons, one in the west and one in the east that met as a single canyon roughly 6 million years ago. The rate of erosion in the eastern canyon was faster than that in the western canyon.[97]

The heads of seven geological organizations sent a letter to park superintendent Joseph Alston warning, "The National Park Service should be extremely careful about giving the impression that it approves of the anti-science movement known as young Earth creationism or endorses the advancement of religious tenets as science." The head of the U.S. Department of Interior's Geologic Resources Division said the book repudiates legitimate science and promotes creation science. "Its sale in the park bookstores directly conflicts with the Service's statutory mandate to promote the use of sound science in all its programs." Conservative evangelical fundamentalists mobilized to support the book, which was sold in the bookstores and marketed on the Grand Canyon's Web site. The book was subsequently moved from the natural science to the inspirational books section.[98]

Scientists were so concerned about the politicization of science during the Bush years that 20 Nobel Prize winners signed a letter expressing outrage about political interference in scientific affairs:

> When scientific knowledge has been found to be in conflict with [the Bush administration's] political goals, the administration has often manipulated the process through which science enters into its decisions. This has been done by placing people who are professionally unqualified or who have clear conflicts of interest in official posts and on scientific advisory committees; by disbanding existing advisory committees; by censoring and suppressing reports by the government's own scientists; and by simply not seeking independent scientific advice .... Furthermore, in advocating policies that are not scientifically sound, the administration has sometimes misrepresented scientific knowledge and misled the public about the implications of its policies.[99]

The scientists' concern seems justified. "From global warming to lead poisoning, from AIDS research to pregnancy prevention," as journalist and community activist Esther Kaplan put it, "the Bush administration has chosen to sacrifice science whenever it conflicts with the needs of Bush's corporate patrons or his evangelical base."[100]

Those who criticize and manipulate science enjoy some success in part because absolute answers, particularly for science at the cutting edge, are rare. As Geoffrey Dobson says, "[S]cience's conceptual schemes and laws are valid only in relation to the methods and assumptions used to derive them." In social, natural, and physical sciences, "each problem begins and ends with a question. Thus the very essence of science does not lie in its permanence, but in its development toward greater learning and understanding."[101]

Scientists identify problems to study by looking for questions raised in research by other scientists. Their research points still other researchers to fruitful questions. Because scientists produce knowledge about what was previously unknown, "uncertainty is a normal and necessary

characteristic of scientific work."[102] Disagreements ultimately are settled after new research techniques or tools are developed, a process that
can take years or decades, or after a preponderance of research supports a
finding, thus "proving," to the extent that a natural phenomenon can be
proved, historical and natural events. When that happens, one can continue struggling against all evidence or one can reinterpret scripture in
accordance with new knowledge, rather than interpret scientific findings
in accordance with scripture.[103]

The Bush administration's frequent efforts to politicize or ignore science or to interpret scientific discoveries in accord with scripture will
likely be reversed in the administration of Democrat Barack Obama.
When he announced his first appointments to scientific positions,
Obama said, "Whether it's the science to slow global warming; the
technology to protect our troops and confront bioterror and weapons
of mass destruction; the research to find life-saving cures; or the innovations to remake our industries and create twenty-first century jobs—
today more than ever, science holds the key to our survival as a planet
and our security and prosperity as a nation." He followed up by
appointing two Nobel Prize winners to key positions and at least three
of five initial appointees favored government limits on greenhouse gas
emissions, which the Bush administration opposed.[104]

ENDURING TENSIONS

The relationship between science and religion in the late twentieth
and early twenty-first centuries is marked by considerable agreement
as most Americans, including most Christians, seem to support the
scientific enterprise.[105] But that agreement is largely overshadowed
by high-profile conflict—reported and distorted by many in the mainstream media—between and within political and religious
conservative constituencies and the scientific community. The types
of tensions described in this section will continue to have an impact
on the Christian community and will potentially impede progress in
science and technology. It also threatens the conservative coalition's
thrust for a new, national, political realignment in the future.

Religion and Science

Questions about the earth's position in the solar system have been
settled. As Copernicus and Galileo suggested, the earth is not the

center of the solar system—an idea that contradicts the ancient three-layered view of the world in which "heaven and hell could be thought of as literal places or spaces, one above the clouds, the other below ground."[106] Most would agree with Swiss theologian Hans Küng's notions of heaven: "the naïve and anthropomorphic notion of a heaven above the clouds is now impossible for us." His answer is to recognize that "the heaven of faith is not a place but a mode of being."[107]

Even the Roman Catholic Church's official position on the views of Copernicus and Galileo, which were rejected for centuries, now takes a stance that goes beyond mere acceptance of the heliocentric model. Pope John Paul II (1920–2005) summarized the church's position in 1992:

> From the Galileo affair, we can learn a lesson that remains valid in relation to similar situations that occur today and that may occur in the future.... There exists two realms of knowledge, one that has its source in revelation and one that reason can discover by its own power. To the latter belong especially the experimental sciences and philosophy. The distinction between the two realms of knowledge ought not to be understood as opposition. The two realms are not altogether foreign to each other; they have points of contact. The methodologies proper to each make it possible to bring out different aspects of reality.[108]

Pope Benedict XVI reinforced John Paul's teaching during Christmas 2008 when he said Galileo Galilei had helped the faithful comprehend and "contemplate with gratitude the Lord's works."[109]

The question of epistemological authority, however, remains unanswered for many Christian conservatives. Their efforts to cast doubt on scientific research that conflicts with biblical accounts of the natural world and the origins of humanity—efforts that frequently cause conflict within the conservative coalition and within the Christian community—find some success. Many Americans remain woefully ignorant about science, even as most express support for science and technology. A study by the National Science Board, for example, showed that 83 percent of respondents agree the federal government should support science that advances knowledge "even if it brings no immediate benefits." Less than half, however, accept scientific evolution, and most have never heard of nanotechnology, know little about genetically modified foods, and cannot answer simple questions about science.[110]

The Authority of Science in the Schools

While Christian conservatives have temporarily given up on the effort to have scientific evolution dropped from high school biology classes, some continue to pressure school boards to expand curricula to include intelligent design. Many other Christians actively oppose the movement to have intelligent design taught in public schools, as the following examples suggest.

- The Campaign to Defend the Constitution—a nonprofit, online organization created in 2005 by the San Francisco–based Tides Center to maintain separation of church and state—sent a letter to all 50 governors asking them to "protect science and to oppose inclusion of intelligent design in science curricula." The letter was signed by 100 scientists and 100 clergy. "The battle of intelligent design is not between those who believe in God and those who believe in science but over what is best for the education of our children," said pastor James Forbes of the Protestant mainstream Riverside Church in New York City. "Our children should learn established science in science class and take other opportunities in the school day to discuss the meaning, origins and wonder of life."[111]
- More than 11,000 members of the Christian clergy have joined the Clergy Letter Project, which was initiated in 2004 by biology professor Michael Zimmerman of Butler University in Indianapolis, "to let the public know that numerous clergy from most denominations have tremendous respect for evolutionary theory and have embraced it as a core component of human knowledge, fully harmonious with religious faith."[112] The letter opposes the false dichotomy between religion and science and argues that those who claim individuals must choose between science and religion do not speak for most religious leaders. Science and religion "should be seen as complementary rather than confrontational." The two-paragraph letter calls for teaching evolution in public schools.[113]

Religion and the Environment

Most Americans, whether religious or not, held a rather anthropocentric view of nature before publication of Rachel Carson's *Silent Spring* in 1962: human beings are special and the natural world was created to "fuel human industry."[114] Nearly 50 years later, many religious conservatives still reject the environmental movement because they perceive that it privileges animals and plants above human beings.

Protestant evangelical fundamentalists, for example, have provided a religious stamp of approval on Republican environmental policies for years. A Brookings Institution study in 1996 concluded that white evangelicals "were by far the most anti-environment religious group in the nation."[115] Many Christians of all denominations bought into the stance of the Bush II White House that human needs took precedence over endangered species and other environmental needs.[116] Genesis 1 creation stories were interpreted to mean "nature was designed for human use," and religious conservatives were far more willing than religious moderates and progressives to accept arguments against global warming.[117]

Numerous books and articles "dismiss population pressure, global warming, and ozone depletion . . . and belittle specific actions such as recycling or wilderness preservation." Even the religiously progressive Sojourners Community and Evangelicals for Social Action, "until recently, tended to regard the environmental movement as a luxury of the comfortably developed northern nations and an excuse to ignore the deep human needs of the poor."[118]

Protestant conservatives were a driving force behind the "Cornwall Declaration on Environmental Stewardship," the product of a group called the Interfaith Council for Environmental Stewardship. The 1999 document seemed to support secular and religious initiatives to preserve the environment, but it affirmed the primacy of human beings and noted, "We aspire to a world in which widespread economic freedom—which is integral to private, market economies—makes sound ecological stewardship available to ever greater numbers."[119] Some prominent Catholics signed the declaration because it "flagged several core issues for environmentalists, including global warming, overpopulation, and rampant species loss, as 'unfounded or undue concerns.' "[120]

Peter Illyn—director and founder of Restoring Eden, a Christian environmental stewardship group—claimed the "Cornwall Declaration" was "free market environmentalism" based on the belief "that unrestrained capitalism is God's chosen economic system and unfettered capitalism will end up creating the best environmental effect." Calvin Beisner, a professor at Knox Theological Seminary in Florida, an evangelical institution associated with a conservative Presbyterian group, says those who signed the declaration do not believe empirical studies that document an environmental crisis. While many environmentalists are concerned with overpopulation, for example, many conservative evangelicals believe "man is fundamentally a producer and a redeemer, a reconstructer of things." Thus the more people there are, the better it will be for the environment.[121]

Christian conservatives who oppose the environmental movement find support among many GOP traditionalist conservatives and neoconservatives who oppose the movement for different reasons: it costs too much, harms business and industry, weakens the United States in world affairs, and simply is not necessary because the earth can absorb any human-generated pollution.

However, many other Christians now support environmental regulations to protect the earth for future generations. Stronger regulation, for example, was favored by 55 percent of all American respondents—52 percent of evangelical Protestants, 61 percent of mainline Protestants, and 60 percent of Catholics—in a 2004 Pew Forum on Religion & Public Life survey.[122]

An important pillar of the environmental movement for many Protestants and Catholics is sustainability—the idea that human beings are at the center of ecological concerns and must preserve the environment for future generations. This view, expressed in various religious and nonreligious venues over many years,[123] was endorsed in a United States Conference of Catholic Bishops' statement in 2001 entitled "Global Climate Change: A Plea for Dialogue, Prudence and the Common Good." Preserving the environment, the bishops said, "is about our human stewardship of God's creation and our responsibility to those who come after us," not about gaining partisan advantage.[124]

Many Christian conservatives who have joined the effort to address issues relating to the environment cite the principles developed in a breakthrough document called the "Chicago Declaration of Evangelical Social Concern," produced in 1973 by Evangelicals for Social Action. The declaration "spans the divide between evangelism and social action" and calls for evangelical action on numerous other issues, including racism and the oppression of women. Christian evangelicals were asked "to demonstrate repentance in a Christian discipleship that confronts the social and political injustice of our nation."[125]

This attitude parallels a 1987 United Church of Christ (UCC) report entitled "Toxic Wastes and Race in the United States," where the phrase "environmental justice" first was used "in a religious context." The UCC, along with African-American faith groups, "conferred legitimacy on the effort" to expand the environmental movement to address "the common patterns of environmental harm suffered by inner-city African Americans, Native Americans on reservations, and rural Mexican Americans (especially farmworkers)."[126]

This attitude also is reflected in the "Evangelical Climate Initiative"—a document condemning global warming drafted initially by National Association of Evangelicals (NAE) lobbyist Richard Cizik in 2005–2006. He referred to the initiative as Creation Care—citing the biblical injunction in Genesis 2:15: "The Lord God took the man, and placed him into the garden of Eden, to till it and tend it." More than 85 evangelical leaders signed the "Evangelical Climate Initiative" because of a "commitment to Jesus Christ and concern for His Creation."[127] The first major signatory to the petition was multimedia evangelical icon Rick Warren, one of the nation's more influential contemporary Protestant leaders. Others included David Neff (editor of *Christianity Today*), Todd Bassett (head of the Salvation Army), and the presidents of 30 evangelical colleges.[128] Even televangelist Pat Robertson said on his *700 Club* television show that evangelicals needed to stop the burning of fossil fuels to save the planet.[129]

Cizik was pressured to withdraw his name from the Climate Initiative when the NAE refused to sign the document—together with the leaders of the Southern Baptist Convention (SBC), Focus on the Family, and various other groups associated with James Dobson and his close associate, Don Wildmon of the American Family Association.

Some younger Southern Baptists, however, began speaking out against their denomination's "too timid" stance on the environment, declaring Baptists had "a biblical duty to stop global warming." A 25-year-old seminarian—a former GOP precinct chair in Georgia and the son of a former SBC president—initiated another document in 2008 entitled "A Southern Baptist Declaration on the Environment and Climate Change." He was eventually able to get the SBC president and several past presidents to sign the petition.[130] Even the National Association of Evangelicals reversed course and announced in 2007 that it would join prominent scientists in demanding "urgent changes in values, lifestyles and public policies to avert disastrous changes in climate."[131]

Many Catholic theologians cite the papal encyclical *Rerum Novarum* of 1891 as a foundation for engaging in environmental activism. Although he did not mention the environment, "Pope Leo XIII [1810–1903] placed the social and economic concerns of that day firmly on the agenda of the Catholic church."[132] Pope John Paul II heightened Catholic awareness of environmental issues roughly 100 years later. He designated St. Francis of Assisi, for example, as the patron saint of those who would protect the environment, and he called for environmental stewardship in his message "The Ecological Crisis: A Common Responsibility" in 1990.

Catholic scholars then began to address seriously the Catholic responsibility to the environment. The United States Conference of Catholic Bishops issued its own "pastoral letter" entitled "Renewing the Earth: An Invitation to Reflection and Action on Environment in Light of Catholic Social Teaching," which set forth "a Catholic environmental ethic for their American flock."[133] Most important, perhaps, was the bishops' attempt to link concern for God's creation to efforts to protect the disadvantaged and to seek justice.[134]

Objectivity, Media Frames, and Conflict News

Christian conservative activists—whether they are labeled creationists or spokespersons for intelligent design—are quite skilled at manipulating the media. They badger, coerce, and flatter journalists until writers treat nonscientific ideas as science and uninformed sources as experts. These ongoing science wars demonstrate journalism's failure to employ an objective approach in the treatment of science news. Michael Powell's 2004 story about the Dover school board's decision to inject intelligent design into the curriculum and to have teachers punch holes in scientific evolution, for example, is not a model of objective reporting. Powell framed the story so that (a) intelligent design had essentially the same credibility as evolution, a view that is rejected by almost all reputable scientists; (b) conflict was maximized by citing a source who cast the controversy in dichotomous terms and focused on the most inflammatory aspect of evolution—that human beings descended from apes; and (c) a clearly uninformed source was given maximum exposure in the lead paragraphs. This sort of framing, which is quite common, perpetuates the view that intelligent design has a place in a biology classroom, and it encourages those who work so hard to ensure that it is there.

Powell's story is in direct contrast to that of Amy Harmon, who wrote for the *New York Times* a story about the clash of faith and science over evolution and the difficulty of teaching evolution in high school. Her focus was on David Campbell, a Jacksonville, Florida, science teacher who struggled to meet the state's new requirement that schools must teach scientific evolution. "Some [students] come armed with 'Ten questions to ask your biology teacher about evolution,' a document circulated on the Internet that highlights supposed weaknesses in evolutionary theory. Others scrawl their opposition on homework assignments. Many just tune out."[135] By focusing on the student-teacher relationship and the difficulty with teaching evolution, Harmon avoided much of the conflict that characterizes stories about evolution in public schools, and she relied on sources—teachers and students—who may be more knowledgeable than anyone about the issues.

Darwinian science is now actually "obsolete," as plant physiologist Lewis Ziska has observed, and mainstream media coverage of science has helped make it so. The irony of evolution as viewed through the lens of Victorians such as Charles Darwin and Alfred Wallace was that these were models of a natural process "independent of human interference"—a critical variable in all evolutional science models today. From this perspective, the pollution of science by creationist/intelligent design advocates is yet another human variable, however unanticipated, in the evolutionary equation.[136]

NOTES

1. David C. Lindberg, "Galileo, the Church, and the Cosmos," in *When Science & Christianity Meet*, ed. David C. Lindberg and Ronald L. Numbers (Chicago: The University of Chicago Press, 2003), 33–60, p. 50.

2. Ibid., 38, 48.

3. *Luther's Works, Vol. 54: Table Talk*, ed. Theodore G. Tappert (Philadelphia: Fortress, 1955), 359.

4. Geoffrey P. Dobson, *A Chaos of Delight: Science, Religion and Myth and the Shaping of Western Thought* (London: Equinox, 2005), 269.

5. Lindberg, "Galileo, the Church," 42.

6. Mott T. Greene, "Genesis and Geology Revisited: The Order of Nature and the Nature of Order in Nineteenth-Century Britain," in Lindberg and Numbers, *When Science & Christianity Meet*, 139–159.

7. The Council of Trent, the nineteenth Ecumenical Council of the Roman Catholic Church, was the church's response to the Protestant Reformation. It met in three lengthy sessions—1545–1547, 1551–1552, and 1562–1563—and approved the Tridentine Mass as the standard liturgy. The council also (a) clarified doctrines relating to salvation, the biblical canon, and the sacraments; (b) called for a revised *Vulgate*, a fifth century version of the Bible; (c) approved the breviary, which contained public Psalms, readings, hymns, and prayers; and (d) called for a revised missal, which contains texts and directions for celebrating the Mass. "Decrees of the Council of Trent Session IV," April 8, 1546, in Richard J. Blackwell, *Galileo, Bellarmine, and*

the Bible (Notre Dame, IN: University of Notre Dame Press, 1991), 181–184, p. 183.

8. Lindberg, "Galileo, the Church," 47–48.

9. Ibid., 52.

10. Cited in Jerome J. Langford, *Galileo, Science and the Church*, rev. ed. (Ann Arbor: University of Michigan Press, 1966), 144.

11. *The Galileo Affair: A Documentary History*, ed. and trans. Maurice A. Finocchiaro (Berkeley: University of California Press, 1989), 286.

12. Peter Machamer, ed., *The Cambridge Companion to Galileo* (Cambridge: Cambridge University Press, 1998).

13. Lindberg, "Galileo, the Church," 58.

14. Ibid., 57.

15. Eva Marie Garroutte, "The Positivist Attack on Baconian Science and Religious Knowledge in the 1870s," in *The Secular Revolution: Power, Interests, and Conflict in the Secularization of American Public Life*, ed. Christian Smith (Berkeley: University of California Press, 2003), 197–215, p. 197.

16. Ibid., 212.

17. Ronald L. Numbers, "Science Without God: Natural Laws and Christian Beliefs," in Lindberg and Numbers, *When Science & Christianity Meet*, 265–285, pp. 268–269.

18. Ibid., 281.

19. John William Draper, *History of the Conflict Between Religion and Science*, 5th ed. (New York: D. Appleton, 1875).

20. Andrew D. White, *A History of the Warfare of Science with Theology in Christendom* (New York: George Braziller, 1955). Originally published in 1896.

21. Peter J. Bowler, *Reconciling Science and Religion: The Debate in Early-Twentieth-Century Britain* (Chicago: The University of Chicago Press, 2001), 10.

22. Woodbridge Riley, *From Myth to Reason: The Story of the March of Mind in the Interpretation of Nature* (New York: D. Appleton, 1926), 5.

23. Ibid., 7.

24. P. W. Atkins, "The Limitless Power of Science," in *Nature's Imagination: The Frontiers of Scientific Vision*, ed. John Cornwell (Oxford, UK: Oxford University Press, 1995), 122–132.

25. Richard Dawkins, *The God Delusion* (Boston: Houghton Mifflin, 2006). See also Richard Dawkins, *The Selfish Gene*, 2nd ed. (New York: Oxford University Press, 1989).

26. Edward O. Wilson, *On Human Nature* (Cambridge, MA: Harvard University Press, 1978), 201.

27. Alvin Plantinga, "Science: Augustinian or Duhemian?" *Faith and Philosophy* 13, no. 3 (1996): 368–394, p. 369.

28. Mehdi Golshani, "How to Make Sense of 'Islamic Science,'?" *American Journal of Islamic Social Sciences* 17, no. 3 (2000): 1–21, p. 1.

29. James P. Danaher, "The Postmodern Gospel," *Evangelical Review of Theology* 29, no. 4 (2005): 292–295, p. 295.

30. Ian G. Barbour, "Response: Ian Barbour on Typologies," *Zygon* 37, no. 2 (2002): 345–359, p. 350.

31. In defining science, they ask, "Do we include economics and psychoanalysis within science? Should science be limited to its theories, or does it encompass the scientific methods, laboratory practices, and even the social structure of scientific communities?" See Geoffrey Cantor and Chris Kenny, "Barbour's Fourfold Way: Problems with His Taxonomy of Science-Religion Relationships," *Zygon* 36, no. 4 (2001): 765–781, p. 777.

32. Barbour, "Response," 349.

33. Willem B. Drees, *Religion, Science, and Naturalism* (Cambridge: Cambridge University Press, 1996). While Drees does make a strong case for the scientific method, he does not reject the possibility of an overarching intelligence.

34. One of the best descriptions of the dating problem prior to the nineteenth century is Dennis R. Dean, "The Age of the Earth Controversy: Beginnings to Hutton," *Annals of Science* 38, no. 4 (1981), 435–456. See also Cherry L. E. Lewis and Simon J. Knell, eds., *The Age of the Earth: From 4004 BC to AD 2002* (London: Geological Society of London, 2001).

35. Ussher also calculated that Adam and Eve were expelled from the Garden of Eden on November 10, 4004 BCE, and Noah's Ark landed on Mount Ararat on May 5, 2348 BCE. From James Ussher, *The Annals of the World: Deduced from the Origin of Time* (London: E. Tyler, 1658).

36. Dobson, *A Chaos of Delight*, 341.

37. James Hutton, *Theory of the Earth: with Proofs and Illustrations* (New York: Stechert-Hafner Service, 1972). Early estimates based on biblical texts had long been criticized by those who had studied the written histories of non-Western societies. Pharonic history, for example, was estimated to have extended more than 18,000 years. "Similarly, Christian historians had long confronted Chinese and Indian chronological traditions that both antedated and ignored the Flood, although China and India had supposedly been founded by the sons of Noah." See Dean, "Age of the Earth," 445.

38. Many of the early estimates of the earth's age assumed that one day in God's time was 1,000 years in human time. Buffon knew his estimate of the earth's age would not be well received. He "shoehorned the immense geological time period into six grand epochs corresponding to the six biblical days—each of around 35,000 years—plus another epochal day extending to the present." Rather than make his estimate more palatable, the ploy instead ignited debate about earth's official start date. See Dobson, *A Chaos of Delight*, 340.

39. Cited by White, *A History of the Warfare*, 9.

40. Dean, "Age of the Earth," 453–454.

41. Charles Lyell, *Principles of Geology; or, The Modern Changes of the Earth and Its Inhabitants Considered as Illustrative of Geology*, 3 vols. (London: J. Murray, 1850).

42. Greene, "Genesis and Geology Revisited," 148, 150.

43. Cherry Lewis, *The Dating Game: One Man's Search for the Age of the Earth* (Cambridge: Cambridge University Press, 2000).

44. Chandler Burr, "The Geophysics of God," *U.S. News & World Report*, June 16, 1997, 55–58.

45. Genesis 6:17: "God said, 'For My part, I am going to bring the Flood—waters upon the earth—to destroy all flesh under the sky in which there is breath of life; everything on earth shall perish.'" Genesis 7:24: "And when the waters had swelled on the earth one hundred and fifty days."

46. John C. Whitcomb Jr. and Henry M. Morris, *The Genesis Flood: The Biblical Record and Its Scientific Implications* (Grand Rapids, MI: Baker Book House, 1962).

47. Summarized by Hanna Rosin, "Rock of Ages, Ages of Rock," *New York Times Magazine*, November 25, 2007, 30, 32, 34, 36, 38, p. 32.

48. Geologists assume, for example, that the "liquidlike flow" of rock within the earth has been consistent over the millennia, and they use today's value to determine the viscosity of the earth's mantle. They also assume that one of the mantle's deformation cycles is completed every 100 million years. Baumgardner rejects the views that geological change is consistent and is not changed by a catastrophe such as Noah's flood. Burr, "The Geophysics of God."

49. See Dobson, *A Chaos of Delight*, 321. Darwin addressed only biological evolution. In chemical evolution, "inorganic substances self-associate to form more complex molecules and compounds. Over many millions of years and almost infinite opportunities, these products of chemical evolution in turn combined to form independent cells capable of self-regulation, growth and reproduction" (321).

50. Ibid., 342.

51. Genesis 1:26–28: "And God said, 'Let us make man in our image, after our likeness. They shall rule the fish of the sea, the birds of the sky, the cattle, the whole earth, and all the creeping things that creep on earth.' And God created man in His image, in the image of God He created him; male and female He created them. God blessed them and God said to them, 'Be fertile and increase, fill the earth and master it; and rule the fish of the sea, the birds of the sky, and all the living things that creep on earth.'"

52. Bowler, *Reconciling Science and Religion*, 15.

53. Thomas H. Huxley, *Darwiniana: Essays* (New York: Appleton, 1886), 52.

54. Bowler, *Reconciling Science and Religion*, 17.

55. See Bill Cooke, *The Gathering of Infidels: A Hundred Years of the Rationalist Press Association* (Amherst, NY: Prometheus, 2004).

56. Bowler, *Reconciling Science and Religion*, 19.

57. Alfred Russel Wallace, *Contributions to the Theory of Natural Selection: A Series of Essays* (London: Macmillan, 1870), 359. See also Timothy Shanahan, *The Evolution of Darwinism: Selection, Adaptation, and Progress in Evolutionary Biology* (Cambridge: Cambridge University Press, 2004), 250–253.

58. James P. Danaher, "The Postmodern Gospel," *Evangelical Review of Theology* 29, no. 4 (2005): 292–295, p. 294.

59. David Sloan Wilson, *Darwin's Cathedral: Evolution, Religion, and the Nature of Society* (Chicago: University of Chicago Press, 2002), 225.

60. Edward J. Larson, "The Scopes Trial in History and Legend," in Lindberg and Numbers, *When Science & Christianity Meet*, 245–264, p. 245.

61. Ibid., 246.

62. Ibid., 255.

63. Jeffrey P. Moran, "The Scopes Trial and Southern Fundamentalism in Black and White: Race, Region, and Religion," *The Journal of Southern History* 70, no. 1 (2004): 95–120, p. 118.

64. Ibid., 111.

65. *Epperson v. Arkansas*, 393 U.S. 97 (1968).

66. *McLean v. Arkansas Board of Education*, 529 F. Supp. 1255, 1258–1264 (E.D. Ark. 1982).

67. *Edwards v. Aguillard*, 482 U.S. 578 (1987).

68. Thomas Chalmers, *On the Power, Wisdom and Goodness of God as Manifested in the Adaptation of External Nature to the Moral and Intellectual Constitution of Man*, Vol. 1 (London: William Pickering, 1834), 30–31.

69. Numbers, "Science Without God," 274–275.

70. "Truth Cannot Contradict Truth," address of Pope John Paul II to the Pontifical Academy of Sciences, *New Advent*, October 22, 1996, www.newadvent.org/library/docs_jp02tc.htm.

71. See Michael J. Behe, *Darwin's Black Box: The Biochemical Challenge to Evolution* (New York: Free Press, 1996).

72. Michael J. Behe, "Evidence for Intelligent Design from Biochemistry," speech to God and Culture Conference, Discovery Institute, Seattle, WA, August 10, 1996, www.arn.org/docs/behe/mb_idfrombiochemistry.htm.

73. Ibid.

74. Jodi Wilgoren, "Kansas Board Approves Challenges to Evolution," *New York Times*, November 9, 2005, A14.

75. Suzanne Goldenberg, "Creationists Defeated in Kansas School Vote on Science Teaching," *Guardian* (Manchester), February 15, 2007, www.guardian.co.uk/science/2007/feb/15/schoolsworldwide.religion.

76. *Kitzmiller v. Dover Area School District*, 400 F. Supp. 2d 707 (M.D. Pa 2005).

77. Ibid.

78. Michael Powell, "Evolution Shares a Desk With 'Intelligent Design,'" *Washington Post*, December 26, 2004, A1, A20, p. A1.

79. Chris Mooney and Matthew C. Nisbet, "Undoing Darwin: When the Coverage of Evolution Shifts to the Political and Opinion Pages, the Scientific Context Falls Away, *Columbia Journalism Review*, September/October 2005, 30–39, p. 32.

80. Ibid., 34.

81. Dawkins, *God Delusion*, 123–124.

82. Center for Science & Culture, Discovery Institute, Seattle, WA, www.discovery.org/csc/aboutCSC.php.

83. Michael Ryan, "Ethical Issues in Communication Research," in *Research Methods in Communication*, ed. Wm. David Sloan and Shuhua Zhou (Northport, AL: Vision, 2009), 39–54.

84. The Institute created this document, posted on the Internet in 1999, in 1996. The Institute affirmed this point in July 2005. "The 'Wedge Document': How Darwinist Paranoia Fueled an Urban Legend," Truth Sheet #03–05, Discovery Institute, Seattle, WA, July 2005, www.discovery.org/scripts/viewDB/index.php?command=view&id=2735&program=News&callingPag.

85. Marx, for example, "was interested in faith not in terms of right and wrong but because of what it told him about the human condition," as *Los Angeles Times* columnist Gregory Rodriguez says. Marx recognized "religion as a source of solace that should be abolished only until the source of people's pain—an unfair economic system—had been eradicated." Marx may have been wrong in thinking that one's material conditions alone dictate belief, but surveys suggest that faith prevails in America in large part because believers fear the "incessant conflict and chaos" of a godless world. For Marx, to ask people to give up their religious beliefs "is to call on them to give up a condition that requires illusions. The criticism of religion is . . . the criticism of that vale of tears of which religion is the halo." Rodriguez points out that most people cite Marx's famous line, "religion is the opium of the people," out of context. "Religious suffering," as Marx put it, "is, at one and the same time, the expression of real suffering and a protest against real suffering. Religion is the sigh of the oppressed creature, the heart of a heartless world and the soul of soulless conditions. It is the opium of the people" (citing Marx's *Critique of Hegel's Philosophy of Right*, published originally in 1843). See Gregory Rodriguez, "Finally Getting to the Heart of What Marx Really Meant," *Houston Chronicle*, October 13, 2008, B9.

86. John F. W. Herschel, *Preliminary Discourse on the Study of Natural Philosophy* (London: Longman, Rees, Orme, Brown, Green, and John Taylor, 1830), 7.

87. David N. Livingstone and Mark A. Noll, "B. B. Warfield (1851–1921): A Biblical Inerrantist as Evolutionist," *Isis* 91, no. 2 (2001): 283–304, pp. 293, 296.

88. Kathleen E. Jenkins, "Genetics and Faith: Religious Enchantment through Creative Engagement with Molecular Biology," *Social Forces* 85,

no. 4 (2007): 1693–1712, pp. 1701–1702. See also Michael Ryan, "Science Literacy and Risk Analysis: Relationship to the Postmodernist Critique, Conservative Christian Activists, and Professional Obfuscators," in *Handbook of Risk and Crisis Communication*, eds., Robert L. Heath and H. Dan O'Hair (New York: Routledge, 2009), 247–267.

89. Michael Shermer, "The Gradual Illumination of the Mind," *Scientific American*, February 2002, 35.

90. William A. Dembski, *The Design Revolution: Answering the Toughest Questions about Intelligent Design* (Downers Grove, IL: InterVarsity, 2004), 19.

91. Ibid., 291.

92. Lauri Lebo, "Using Academic Freedom to Keep God in the Science Classroom," *Washington Spectator*, June 1, 2008, 1–3. The editor of the *Spectator* is Lou Dubose, a celebrated Texas writer and critic of the Bush White House.

93. "Evolution Wars Take a Bizarre Twist," *New Scientist*, November 17, 2007, 7.

94. Rosin, "Rock of Ages," 32.

95. Rick Casey, "An Aggie's Big Bang at NASA," *Houston Chronicle*, February 10, 2006, B1, B4, p. B1.

96. Esther Kaplan, *With God on Their Side: How Christian Fundamentalists Trampled Science, Policy, and Democracy in George W. Bush's White House* (New York: New Press, 2004), 91.

97. Victor Polyak, Carol Hill, and Vemane Asmerom, "Age and Evolution of the Grand Canyon Revealed by U-Pb Dating of Water Table-Type Speleothems," *Science*, March 7, 2008, 1377–1380.

98. Kaplan, *With God on Their Side*, 93–94.

99. "Restoring Scientific Integrity in Policy Making," Union of Concerned Scientists, Center for American Progress, February 19, 2004, www.americanprogress.org/issues/kfiles/b33731.html.

100. Kaplan, *With God on Their Side*, 95.

101. Dobson, *Chaos of Delight*, 17, 18.

102. Stephen C. Zehr, "Scientists' Representations of Uncertainty," in *Communicating Uncertainty: Media Coverage of New and Controversial Science*, ed. Sharon M. Friedman, Sharon Dunwoody, and Carol L. Rogers (Mahway, NJ: Erlbaum, 1999), 3–21, p. 3.

103. Michael Shermer, founding publisher of *Skeptic* magazine, addresses the relationship between scripture and science in his *How We Believe: The Search for God in an Age of Science* (New York: W. H. Freeman, 2000).

104. Gardiner Harris, "Choice of Science Advisers Hints at Obama Priorities," *Houston Chronicle*, December 21, 2008, A4.

105. Americans supported scientific inquiry, even as it was under attack by those who have argued for "a science that is infused with or guided by

values, ideology, or religion." See Mikael Stenmark, "A Religiously Partisan Science? Islamic and Christian Perspectives," *Theology and Science* 3, no. 1 (2005): 23–38, p. 23.

106. Douglas F. Ottati, "Theological Musings: The News from Mars," *Network News*, Winter 2004, 20–21, p. 20.

107. Hans Küng, *Credo: The Apostles' Creed Explained for Today* (New York: Doubleday, 1992), 161, 162.

108. Richard Blackwell, "Could There Be Another Galileo Case?" in *The Cambridge Companion to Galileo*, ed. Peter Machamer (Cambridge: Cambridge University Press, 1998), 348–366, p. 350.

109. Nicole Winfield, "Vatican Confesses Its Error in Galileo Trial," *Houston Chronicle*, December 24, 2008, A10.

110. National Science Board, *Science and Engineering Indicators 2006* (Washington, DC: Division of Science Resources Statistics, National Science Foundation, 2006), Chapter 7. The report is a compilation of data from many statistical sources having varying margins of error. All American studies had margins of error of at least plus or minus 3.5 percentage points.

111. "Campaign Opposes 'Intelligent Design,'" *Christian Century*, November 1, 2005, 14.

112. Michael Zimmerman, "Evolution Weekend: The Clergy Letter Project," undated, www.butler.edu/clergyproject/Backgd_info.htm.

113. Michael Zimmerman, "At Long Last, a Meeting of the Minds on Evolution? Clergy Letter Gives Hope of Common Ground on the Topic," *Houston Chronicle*, January 28, 2008, B7. The list of clergy who signed the letter is available at www.butler.edu/clergyproject/Christian_Clergy/chr_C-D .htm#D.

114. Loren Wilkinson, "How Christian Is the Green Agenda?" *Christianity Today*, January 11, 1993, 16–20, p. 18.

115. Dan Gilgoff, *The Jesus Machine. How James Dobson, Focus on the Family, and Evangelical America Are Winning the Culture War* (New York: St. Martin's, 2007), 269 (citing a Brookings Institution report).

116. William A. Galston, "Catholics, Jews & Stem Cells: When Believers Beg to Differ," *Commonweal*, May 20, 2005, 13–17, p. 15.

117. Numerous texts are taken from the first chapter of Genesis. "When God began to create heaven and earth—the earth being unformed and void. ..." (1:1–2); "And God said, 'Let us make man in our image, after our likeness. They shall rule the fish of the sea, the birds of the sky, the cattle, the whole earth, and all the creeping things that creep on earth'" (1:26); "God blessed them and God said to them, 'Be fertile and increase, fill the earth and master it; and rule the fish of the sea, the birds of the sky, and all the living things that creep on earth'" (1:28).

118. Wilkinson, "How Christian Is the Green?" 16, 18.

119. The document was drawn up in West Cornwall, Connecticut. Melissa Jones, "Evangelicals and 'Creation Care,'" *National Catholic Reporter*, June 17, 2005, A4, A5, A8, p. A5.

120. John L. Allen Jr., "Ecology: A New Frontier; The Environment Is Emerging as a Catholic Concern," *National Catholic Reporter*, March 16, 2007, 15, 18, p. 15.

121. Jones, "Evangelicals and 'Creation Care,'" A5.

122. Pew Forum on Religion & Public Life, "Religion and the Environment: Polls Show Strong Backing for Environmental Protection Across Religious Groups" (Pew Research Center, Washington, DC, 2004), www .pewforum.org/docs/index.php?DocID=121. The margin of error is plus or minus 3.5 percentage points.

123. Sustainability was discussed in 1987, for example, during the influential U.S. Earth Summit in Rio de Janeiro. See Gro H. Brundtland, ed., *Our Common Future: The World Commission on Environment and Development* (Oxford, UK: Oxford University Press, 1987). The report urged nations to encourage economic development in a way that protected the environment.

124. *Global Climate Change: A Plea for Dialogue, Prudence, and the Common Good* (Washington, DC: United States Conference of Catholic Bishops, 2001).

125. Allan Effa, "The Greening of Mission," *International Bulletin of Missionary Research* 32, no. 4 (October 2008): 171–176, p. 173.

126. Keith Douglass Warner, "The Greening of American Catholicism: Identity, Conversion, and Continuity," *Religion and American Culture* 18, no. 1 (2008): 113–142, p. 122.

127. Eric Berger, "Faith, Science Find Common Ground on Planet Earth," *Houston Chronicle*, October 16, 2006, A1, A6.

128. The "Evangelical Climate Initiative" is discussed in Gilgoff, *Jesus Machine*, 268–274.

129. This is the same man who warned Dover voters—who ousted the school board members who voted to have intelligent design taught in their schools—that they voted God out of their schools. And he said God might not help them should some disaster strike. See "Robertson Warns Dover's Anti-ID Voters not to Expect Protection from God," *Church & State*, January 2006, 17.

130. Neela Banerjee, "Taking Their Faith, But not Their Politics, to the People," *New York Times*, June 1, 2008, A17; Rachel Zoll, "Southern Baptist Leaders Urge Fight against Warming," *Houston Chronicle*, March 10, 2008, A3. This petition is not binding on congregations affiliated to the SBC. Like congregations in the United Church of Christ and some other Protestant denominations, they are autonomous and make their own decisions on issues presented to them.

131. "Evangelicals, Scientists Join on Warming," Associated Press, January 18, 2007, www.highbeam.com/doc/1Y1-102252934.html.

132. Warner, "Greening of American Catholicism," 115.

133. Ibid., 114. The work of Roman Catholic theologian Pierre Teil-hard de Chardin (1881–1955) is the foundation for much of the current thinking about social justice, sustainability, and the environment. Though many of his ideas were condemned at the time, Teilhard, a Jesuit priest, is often cited for his views about the sacredness of the world and the human presence in it. His best-known book is *The Phenomenon of Man* (New York: Harper, 1976).

134. Effa, "Greening of Mission."

135. Amy Harmon, "A Teacher on the Front Line as Faith and Science Clash," *New York Times*, August 24, 2008, A1, A18, A19, p. A1.

136. Lewis Ziska is quoted by Tom Christopher, "Can Weeds Help Solve the Climate Crisis?" *New York Times Magazine*, June 29, 2008, 42–47.

CHAPTER 8

Terrorism, Media, and Religion: From 9/11 to Afghanistan

Christian communities in America were celebrating World Communion Day on Sunday, October 7, 2001, when the United States started bombing Afghanistan.[1] The religious significance of this political event was not lost on some Americans—on the day when Christians throughout the world take communion in a symbolic act of unity and peace.

Years later, Americans are fighting two traditional wars as part of its war against terrorism, a war that is not going well because the traditional wars in Afghanistan and Iraq have (a) helped create conditions favorable to terrorism and (b) diverted attention from other actions that would enhance U.S. security. Even U.S. Department of State officials have acknowledged that the wars in Afghanistan and Iraq have produced the opposite of what they were intended to prevent: the terrorists have set the agenda for the war against terrorism.[2]

Countless numbers of Muslims have died at American hands in these wars, which have also contributed to the continuing violence between Jew and Muslim in the Israeli/Palestinian heartland. The fragile balance of power in the Middle East has been destabilized—probably for the foreseeable future—and in the process terrorism has become a global threat.

Civil liberties and constitutional rights have been undermined in the United States, supposedly to protect national security; immigrant groups have been demonized in ways not seen in decades; and the conservative coalition that twice helped put George Bush in the White House and that helped give the Republican Party control of the House and the Senate has been fragmenting. While the traditional wars are draining money, personnel, and morale at alarming rates, the nontraditional war has fostered a climate of public paranoia—generated by a web of secrecy and surveillance, and punctuated by periodic terror alerts.

How did America get to this point? Is there something in our "collective psyche," as global financier and philanthropist George Soros put it a few years ago, that makes us a "fearful giant" lashing out at "unseen enemies," inciting cycles of violence that seemingly place America and the rest of the world on the verge of "a permanent state of war"?[3] Politicians like to cast the United States as "a peaceful nation," as George W. Bush did when he announced the bombing of Afghanistan.[4] But did a military option have to be part of the response to the 9/11 attacks?

This chapter—which explores the relationships among the media, religion, and terrorism, particularly since 9/11—is divided into four sections. Section 1 explores terrorism as a concept and outlines the goals of political terrorism. Section 2 examines the language of terrorism with specific reference to the ways in which mass media have framed terrorism. Section 3 describes the situation immediately after September 11, 2001, leading up to the invasion of Afghanistan. Section 4 outlines some of the enduring tensions generated by the threat of terrorism in the wake of the 9/11 attacks.

THE MEANING OF TERRORISM

Political terrorism is by design chaotic, irrational, ferocious, inhumane, and unpredictable. There seem to be no rational explanations, except to terrorists, for events such as suicide bombings in Israel, the 2003 bombings of United Nations (UN) and International Red Cross headquarters in Baghdad, the attacks against many mosques in the United States, the deaths of at least four individuals who "looked like" Arabs or Muslims in the weeks following 9/11, the bombings and burnings of black churches, the 1995 bombing of the Alfred P. Murrah Federal Building in Oklahoma City by homegrown terrorists, the murder of a doctor who performed abortions, and the vandalism of sport utility vehicles in America.

The story of modern political terrorism, which historian Michael Burleigh traces in a recent survey to the mid-nineteenth century, has been recorded in virtually every geographical region of the world.[5] Other kinds of terrorism—such as sexual terrorism[6] and other forms of abuse;[7] racial terrorism and hate crimes;[8] electronic terrorism, or cyberstalking;[9] criminal violence;[10] and the battle to protect the earth's resources by "environmental" or "ecological" terrorists[11]—are more ambiguous, often hidden, and sometimes controversial.

A common theme can be found in the actions of many terrorists. They use violence and threats that seem irrational to others precisely because they cannot win military, legal, cultural, personal, environmental, or electoral victories. Thus, terrorism is often associated with the tactics of the powerless against those who wield power. Acts of terrorism are often committed because terrorists perceive they have no other choices, terrorism being the last resort of the powerless.

Difficulties in Defining Terrorism

"Terrorism" has become a formulaic term of abuse that discourages, if not deadens, any rational discussion or debate and encourages what has been called (often by the powerless) state-sponsored terrorism.[12] International attorney John V. Whitbeck argues that the word terrorism itself "is dangerous because many people apply it to whatever they hate as a way of avoiding and discouraging rational discussion and, frequently, excusing their own illegal and immoral behavior."[13]

Many in the international community perceived that the United States applied terrorism arbitrarily following 9/11 and would not be criticized "for doing whatever it deems necessary in its war on terrorism." No one, therefore, "should criticize whatever they [other governments] now do to suppress their own terrorists."[14] Governments did enjoy greater freedom to track down and kill terrorists following the 9/11 attacks, because any nation, challenged by separatists or insurgents within its borders, could label its opponents terrorists.

Terrorism is a term used to demonize anyone who defies the *status quo*—meaning the social order—imposed and defined by governments throughout the world. The targets of the various wars against contemporary terrorism, moreover, are overwhelmingly Muslim.[15] The United States, for example, listed 33 groups as "foreign terrorist organizations" in 2002, and almost all were Islamic groups based in the Middle East.[16]

Scholars have identified several *kinds* of terrorism, but there is no universally accepted definition of terrorism because it is a term of abuse. The Organization of the Islamic Conference, a 57-member grouping that sought to counter a perceived defamation campaign against Muslim religion and culture following the 9/11 attacks, could not produce a definition. The world's largest Islamic body reiterated that Islam rejects aggression and values respect, peace, and tolerance, but it left the job of defining terrorism to the United Nations. The UN had not, as late as 2008, produced an internationally accepted definition.[17]

Not surprisingly, the international community has not been able to provide a definition that pleases most parties, largely because "everyone tries to include one's adversaries in the definition while keeping one's allies and one's own (actual or potential) activities outside it."[18] Jarna Petman, an expert in global governance, however, thinks it would be better if the international community, and not an individual power, identified and then opposed acts of terrorism:

> [I]f some violent action should be condemned as "terrorism" because of the exceptional danger to the [international] community that it entails, then it is the task of the community—instead of some hegemonic actor within it—to take action to oppose it. That such action would be governed by law, and not by moral or theological impulse, would affirm its contingent nature and its amenability to control and critique within the community.[19]

Goals of Terrorism

Regardless of whether it can be defined or identified, terrorism in all its forms typically has similar goals. As a government task force put it in 1990—long before the 9/11 attacks: "Terrorism is a tactic or technique by means of which a violent act or the threat thereof is used for the prime purpose of creating overwhelming fear for coercive purposes."[20]

Terrorists try to generate fear among large numbers of ordinary citizens in hopes these citizens will change the ways they live or accept, or even demand, repressive measures. As terrorist-inspired fear increases, for instance, pregnant women may avoid abortion clinics, UN personnel may leave a country in which they feel they are not safe, consumers may stop buying or building homes in the "wrong" places, and government may impose repressive measures that deny some individuals their civil rights.[21] Terrorists typically hope:

- To convey the propaganda of the deed and to create extreme fear among their target group

- To mobilize wider support among the general population and international opinion by emphasizing such themes as the righteousness of their cause and the inevitability of their victory
- To frustrate and disrupt the response of the government and security forces, for example, by suggesting that all their practical anti-terrorist measures are inherently tyrannical and counterproductive or an unnecessary overreaction
- To mobilize, incite, and boost their constituency of actual and potential supporters and in so doing to increase recruitment, raise more funds, and inspire further attacks.[22]

MEDIA FRAMES AND THE LANGUAGE OF TERRORISM

Terrorism and terrorist events have extraordinary impact in the mediated world in which we live, because terrorism helps create a world marked by fragmentation, instability, and disorientation. As French cultural theorist Jean Baudrillard (1929–2007) and his many interpreters argue, the mediated world is a flat, one-dimensional world—a world of endless repetitions or simulations, a world of endless copies without originals. Media play a critical role in communicating a kind of "hyper-reality," as Baudrillard said, a simulated reality that is more real than real. In the hyper-reality of mediated terrorism, meaning is blurred in an endless series of images repeated endlessly that have changed the way we see and understand the world.[23]

The binary world typically described by the media generates a hyper-real world, a world of celebrity and spectacle, as we described in Chapter 2. Many journalists argue that the process of dividing and classifying information into opposing categories and groups—omitting some information and excluding other information—gives readers, viewers, and listeners a sense of social continuity. But as communication professor Frank D. Durham argues, "[T]he same power [modernist journalism] that forces the present to 'make sense' [to the audience] leaves its representation of society incomplete."[24]

Framing Terrorism

The framing of terrorism is a hyper-real frame that is "more real" than the reality it depicts, and it stereotypes both parties being portrayed. Terrorism is always framed by anti-terrorists in binary, law-and-order terms that threaten the social order: "The major focus of this frame is the need to respond to a *threat* being posed by some upstart," as political scientist Gadi Wolfsfeld says, "and the justification for using force to stop that threat and maintain order" (italics in the original). The pro-terrorist, of course, is the weaker antagonist, who will typically employ a counter frame also characterized by binary language. This frame will highlight "a particular grievance against a more powerful antagonist and includes a call for the oppressed to confront the more powerful enemy."[25]

The American mass media employed language, narrative, and image to demonize Saddam Hussein (1937–2006)—a former ally—in the 1991 Persian Gulf War and to frame the military effort as a *defensive* response to *aggression* by Iraq. As Cynthia Carter and C. Kay Weaver, experts in media coverage of violence, put it:

> It was a story told within the limits of a good versus evil dynamic, as Kuwait was rescued from an evil dictator and "democracy" restored in the region. Violence was safely packaged in formats that were palatable to home audiences, thereby shielding them from the harsh realities of death and destruction which might have encouraged awkward questions to be asked about the factors behind the conflict.[26]

The Danish newspaper, *Politiken*, analyzed the British press's war coverage and concluded that journalists had essentially declared war in the Persian Gulf by using the kind of binary language shown in Figure 8.1 to frame stories.

The binary view of social reality is most apparent when groups compete to create a dominant frame. "They do this by talking across each other, not by dialogue. Dialogue means that when one side raises a subject, the other side addresses it. When there is true dialogue, stakeholders bring facts to each other's attention and debate the value of these facts."[27] Controversies in a binary world are not resolved because combatants are unwilling to move away from their partisan positions, and the ways in which they frame problems and issues reflect these positions.

The Spectacle of Terrorism

Terrorists perceive their acts as persuasive "essays," in which they try to convince others that their grievances are real and their proposed solutions are workable. The ways in which these acts are framed

Figure 8.1. Binary Signs in Framing the 1991 Gulf War

The Allies have	The Iraqis have
Army, navy, and air force	*A war machine*
Guidelines for journalists	*Censorship*
Briefings to the press	*Propaganda*
The Allies	**The Iraqis**
Eliminate	*Kill*
Neutralize	*Kill*
Hold on	*Bury themselves in holes*
Conduct precision bombings	*Fire wildly at anything*
The Allied soldiers are	**The Iraqi soldiers are**
Professional	*Brainwashed*
Cautious	*Cowardly*
Full of courage	*Cannon fodder*
Loyal	*Blindly obeying*
Brave	*Fanatic*
The Allied missiles	**The Iraqi missiles**
Do extensive damage	*Cause civilian casualties*
George Bush [senior] is	**Saddam Hussein is**
Resolute	*Intractable*
Balanced	*Mad*

Source: "War of Words," *In These Times,* February 13–19, 1991, 5 (citing a study by the Danish newspaper *Politken*).

ultimately determine how others perceive such incidents. Terrorists understand that the media must frame their violence as persuasive, rhetorical statements, for this frame helps them gain maximum exposure for and recognition of their goals.[28] Terrorists know they cannot succeed if the media do not frame violence in ways that maximize feelings of foreboding and spectacle and if the media do not report their violence widely and continuously.[29]

It is difficult for terrorists to achieve their goals when their violence is framed consistently, and *only*, as crimes against human decency, and their grievances are ignored. Terrorism "achieves its goal not through its acts but through the response to its acts."[30] Terrorists seldom "win" in societies in which the media do not report terrorist actions (because they are not allowed to or because they choose not to).[31]

"Terrorism wins only if you respond to it in the way that the terrorists want you to . . . . If you choose not to respond at all, or else to respond in a way different from that which they desire, they will fail to achieve their objectives. The important point is that the choice is yours. That is the ultimate weakness of terrorism as a strategy."[32] The weakness is apparent, however, only when the media refuse to play the game.

The news media in the United States *do* play the game. They *do* give meaning to violent attacks and threats. Knowledgeable terrorists know American journalists value conflict, timeliness, oddity, proximity, prominence, and consequence. The violent acts and threats of terrorists typically reflect most of these values. Their statements even contain the element of prominence when they manage to murder a UN official, Spanish ambassador, Red Cross worker, or U.S. colonel. "Terrorists engage in recurrent rhetorical forms that force the media to provide the access without which terrorism could not fulfill its objectives."[33] Some are so sophisticated they have been described as "choreographers" of terror:

> These new transnational gunmen are, in fact, television producers constructing a package so spectacular, so violent, so compelling that the networks, acting as executives, supplying the cameramen and the audience, cannot refuse the offer. Given a script with an uncertain ending, live actors—the terrorists, the victims, the security forces, the innocent bystanders—and a skilled director who choreographs the unfolding incident for maximum impact, television is helpless.[34]

Forensic psychiatrist Park Dietz suggests that terrorists manipulate the news media and make them a kind of advertising agency, "recruiting them into providing intense coverage to increase the societal impact of an attack. Terrorists use sensational and innovative methods of attack, select high-profile targets, submit prepared messages directly to news organizations, and even attack the news organizations themselves to boost coverage."[35]

Despite criticism that the commercial news media, especially television, are used by terrorists, the media continue to report violent threats and acts. As political scientist Brigitte L. Nacos notes, "[W]hen more blood is spilled in instances of political violence, more printer's ink and air time are devoted to those events by the mass media." Terrorist stories even before 9/11 could push every other news story to the margins or even off the page. Terrorism in 2000, for example, was discussed more often on radio and television news shows than were poverty, Social Security, health insurance, and Medicare.[36]

The news media report terrorist threats and actions not only because Americans are interested but also because of the government position on terrorism. As Central Intelligence Agency (CIA) veteran Paul R. Pillar notes, "Combating international terrorism is—now, as at times in the past—a major objective of the United States. There is broad support for this effort within different branches of government, across the political spectrum, and among the American public."[37]

Indeed, the media, typically reflecting the views of U.S. political and military leaders, cast potential responses to threats as "battles" (or "epic struggles") that must be won. "This pattern has been most apparent with U.S. policies toward state sponsors of terrorism, in which unyielding hard lines have sometimes been favored over strategies of engagement that—although they might be better suited to elicit further improvements in behavior from the states involved— are avoided as being soft on terrorism."[38]

Media organizations may also cover terrorist threats and acts extensively to increase circulation or audience share or to be perceived as being on the "right" side. Certainly, the label "war against terrorism" is catchy, and, when it is repeated over and over again, it helps a news medium claim it has aligned itself with public opinion. It is not profitable to raise uncomfortable questions when public opinion seems to be resolute in favor of vengeance.

"The irony is that in seeking to grab the attention of audiences," as British television critic Greg Philo puts it, "programme makers are actually fostering very negative attitudes towards the developing world and other international issues and in the long run will reduce audience interest."[39] When broadcast journalism is driven by audience ratings, most reporting "is reduced to a simplistic version of often complex realities, a process that is compounded by the absence of any credible and comparable alternative global news service."[40]

Both U.S. government planners and al-Qaida marketed the 9/11 attacks as a media event. This "PR-ized warfare model" favored the media-savvy Americans over the terrorists, at least in the short term.[41] U.S. media were already well versed in the news value of international terrorism. In their analysis of a RAND Corporation study of terrorist acts between 1968 and 1980, Gabriel Weimann and Hans-Bernd Brosius found that "deviance" was the most compelling factor in defining the significance of these events. Their research supports the allegation

that American media—especially network television—played a significant role in the diffusion of international terrorism prior to 9/11.[42]

The media typically can cover only one conflict at a time, and they
generally focus on only the violent phases of that single conflict.
"[T]he media are largely responsible for the absence of these [other]
conflicts from the public agenda or the policy agenda, and major conflicts (and the massive amount of human suffering that they entail) will
be ignored."[43] The media thus help "to shift focus and funds from
more cost-effective, long-term efforts directed at preventing violent
conflict and rebuilding war-torn societies to short-term emergency
relief."[44] Still, the media do have options in framing the potential
responses to terrorist attacks and to the threat of terror, if they choose
to exercise them:

- At one extreme, a frame may exclude all information about a terrorist
  attack—there is simply no narrative, or story, because there is no frame
  on which to hang the narrative.
- At the other extreme, a frame may include essentially all details about a
  terrorist attack, and the narrative elevates the act to spectacle. One example occurred in the summer of 2000, when armed terrorists held hostages
  on the island of Jolo in the Southern Philippines. International journalists
  beamed to audiences around the world images of suffering hostages. "The
  hostage drama on Jolo was not reality television of the *Survivor* variety, but
  brutal real life drama." Very little was excluded from the frame, and "the
  lines between news and entertainment were often blurred."[45]

AFGHANISTAN AND THE RESPONSE TO 9/11

The context within which government and religious leaders and the
media responded to the political violence of September 11, 2001, was
not unknown to those who launched the attacks. Political terrorism
was common around the world long before 9/11. The news media
were inclined to report extensively about terrorist activities, frequently
elevating them to the level of spectacle, and the American people generally supported counterterrorism measures. "This consensus for
counterterrorism is made possible by the nature and clarity of the
counterterrorist mission, which involves the prevention of malicious
and sometimes lethal harm against innocent and unsuspecting
people." As the CIA's Pillar notes, "Saving innocent lives is about as
noncontroversial as issues of public policy ever get."[46]

Five kinds of responses to terrorism had been identified by the time of the 9/11 attacks, and the nation's leaders could have argued for any or all of them: (a) to use political and diplomatic pressure, including censure, travel restrictions, and the breaking off of diplomatic relations; (b) to employ economic pressure, including trade embargoes, reduced investments, withdrawal of aid, and seizure of assets; (c) to use military strikes; (d) to launch covert operations against the terrorists; and (e) to engage law enforcement personnel to pursue terrorists. These options, of course, are not mutually exclusive.

The military option had not been used often in the more than 2,400 terrorist actions aimed at American citizens and interests from 1983 to 1998.[47] In almost every case, the preferred counterterrorism response was law enforcement. The government used military force in only three incidents: "the 1986 Libyan bombing of a West German discotheque; the 1993 Iraqi attempt to assassinate former President Bush in Kuwait; and the 1998 bombing of two US embassies in East Africa by [Osama] bin Laden operatives."[48]

This section describes the main steps taken to ensure that the military option would be used in Afghanistan. These steps included establishing the proper frame for persuading the public the military response was appropriate, casting the debate in religious terms, identifying and assigning groups and individuals to "sides," marginalizing dissent, and demanding immediate action.

Establishing the Frame

During the initial eight hours following the 9/11 attacks, the broadcast media apparently adhered to the first step in framing. They tried to help define the problem by serving primarily as information sources: "[M]ore than 76% of the stories were identified as presentation[s] of facts, whereas 19% of stories were primarily analytical." The media also emphasized political or economic factors more than human-interest factors: "Only 4% of the stories were framed from a human interest perspective."[49]

What television coverage of 9/11 did *not* emphasize during the first eight hours also is important: "Patriotism was not a visible theme in the coverage. There was no demonstrated patriotism in 96% of the news stories, some patriotism in 3% of the stories, and high patriotism in less than 1% .... American values demonstrated through the use of specific words and expressions were not a frequent occurrence in the news coverage. Only 3% of the stories emphasized freedom/liberty."[50]

Media scholar Carolyn Kitch, in a study of U.S. newsmagazines after the 9/11 attacks, also noted the following: "Bearing witness and giving testimony were key to the first stage of coverage, which corresponded with what anthropologists call 'separation'—the first stage of the funeral, which is the loss of the dead and the resulting tear in the social fabric."[51] The newsmagazines' coverage initially expressed disbelief and shock.

A Military Option

The frame makers in government, religion, and the media went to work on the second day. No evidence suggests that everyone met the second day to craft a master plan that would guarantee public support for the military option. However, such a plan did evolve in the days following the attacks.

The decision to use the military option perhaps was inevitable, given the long U.S. history of militarism and its leadership at the time. The government was led by a president who had little experience in foreign affairs, who was trying to cope with the job and get his administration organized, who surrounded himself with neoconservatives who would not shrink from using military force to extend U.S. influence throughout the world, and whose primary constituency consisted of ultraconservative voters.[52] One such follower, political commentator Ann Coulter, said of the U.S. response, "We should invade their countries, kill their leaders and convert them to Christianity."[53] While the president may not have endorsed such an extreme position, much of his constituency did.

The neoconservatives, who at the time wielded much greater power than their numbers in the Republican Party would suggest, struck early to shape the response to the 9/11 attacks. Forty-one men and women, representing much of the neoconservative establishment,[54] said in an open letter to Bush that "policy must aim not only at finding the people responsible for this incident, but also target those 'other groups out there that mean us no good.' "[55] They urged military action in Afghanistan; support for anti-Saddam Hussein factions in Iraq, including U.S. military forces if necessary; retaliation against Iran and Syria if they refuse to stop supporting Hezbollah; and denial of assistance to the Palestinian Authority until it stops terrorism in territories under its control.

The Bush administration—well-stocked with Christian conservatives who saw the 9/11 attacks as part of a holy war between Islam and Christianity[56] and with neoconservatives who were keen on extending U.S. power around the world—was able to field an army of official and unofficial war advocates within days following the attacks. They manipulated language to shape the "debate" about possible responses to the terrorist threat. They stifled dissent against the use of military strikes in the "war" against terrorism, and they instilled such fear in the populace that it would support nearly any measure proposed to defeat terrorism.[57] A *Washington Post-ABC News* poll in September 2001 showed, for example, that 77 percent of Americans backed the military option in Afghanistan even if innocent people were killed.[58]

Compliant Journalists

Under ordinary circumstances, skeptical journalists would not have allowed themselves to be used as part of the administration's attempt to impose its war frame on the debate. During 2001, 2002, and much of 2003, however, the media failed to bring an appropriate skepticism to their reporting of Bush's pronouncements. "The understandable attempt to make sense of these disruptive events," as media policy expert Bernhard Debatin put it, "rapidly led to a simplifying and mainstreaming narrative centered on a desire for retaliation in the 'monumental struggle of good versus evil,' as President Bush proclaimed and the media echoed."[59]

The news media assumed from the start that military strikes would be part of the U.S. response. The *New York Times*, for example, "constructed and celebrated heroes and bolstered leaders as they responded to the crisis. It mobilized for war and warned of a foreboding future, of suffering and sacrifice to come."[60] Other mainstream media networks were even more extreme in supporting the war option against terrorism, as research by Brigitte Nacos suggests: "ABC News broadcast eighty-six stories that contained the terms 'war' and 'terrorism,' CBS News aired ninety-six such segments, NBC News broadcast 133, CNN televised 316, and National Public Radio aired 166."[61]

Nacos's results parallel those of research by Michael Ryan showing that editorial writers for the 10 largest newspapers in the United States "created—during perhaps the most critical month in the war against terrorism—a singular symbolic narrative about possible military strikes in that 'new kind of war.' " The editorials were published between September 12, 2001, and October 8, 2001, in the *Wall Street Journal*, *USA Today*, the *New York Times*, the *Los Angeles Times*, the *Washington Post*, the *New York Daily News*, the *Chicago Tribune*, *Newsday*, the *Houston Chronicle*, and the *Dallas Morning News*.[62]

None of the 104 editorials published argued against or suggested alternatives to military intervention, although two did *refute* arguments against a military response. Twelve editorials counseled caution, Ryan found, but few detailed potential risks of military intervention. Ninety-five of the 104 editorials failed to mention potential Afghan casualties. The nine editorials that did address the issue were published primarily after September 30, when military strikes were imminent. The editorials said any civilian casualties must be minimized, but they neither suggested a strategy for keeping civilians safe nor demanded that the administration disclose such a strategy.

The justification for military strikes was assumed by 76 editorials, while 10 noted the terrorists attacked U.S. civilians; nine said the terrorists declared war; and seven said strikes would be legitimate acts of self-defense. The *New York Daily News* stated yet another justification: "Make no mistake. The enemy will use all means to obtain those weapons [of mass destruction] and will use those weapons against us. Unless we destroy the enemy first."[63]

That this frame was a work in progress is suggested by these editorials, which Ryan divided into three time periods: September 12–20, September 21–29, and September 30–October 8. Twenty-seven editorials demanded after September 20 that someone must "get" Osama bin Laden; this was after evidence linked him to the terrorist attacks. Similarly, most of the 14 demands to depose the Taliban came after September 29, after the Taliban had rejected Bush's demand to "turn over" bin Laden. The Taliban and bin Laden were essentially outside the frame before September 21.

Forty-one editorials (primarily before September 21) said an objective should be to make governments stop sheltering terrorists. Editorials mentioned this objective less frequently after it was clear the administration would need at least some of those countries to contribute to the war against terrorism.

The mass media generally did not examine seriously the difficulty associated with declaring an untraditional war against terrorism:

> Unlike most wars, [counterterrorism] has neither a fixed set of enemies nor the prospect of coming to closure, be it through a "win" or some other kind of denouement. Like the cold war, it requires long, patient, persistent effort, but unlike it, it will never conclude with the internal collapse of an opponent. There will be victories and defeats, but not big, tide-turning victories. Counterterrorism is a fight and a struggle, but it is not a campaign with a beginning and an end.[64]

Missing during this crucial period was the knowledge and understanding that would have helped Americans know their enemy. People based decisions solely on images that may or may not have been accurate.[65]

Casting Debate in Religious Terms

The debate about the proper response to the 9/11 attacks—and particularly the potential role of the U.S. military in that response—frequently was cast in religious terms. In what some saw as a grand irony, many Christian conservatives agreed with neoconservatives that a military response was required after the attacks to establish peace in the world. Their response to events following 9/11 mirrored the official governmental response—endorsing a crusade ethic that used similar language and imagery. Just as the word "terrorist" is a synonym for anyone who questions the social order, "non-terrorist" is a synonym for anyone who supports that order.

This was hardly the first time that some Christians had argued for military intervention or that religion had become inextricably intertwined with one's patriotic duty to wage war. Christianity has been used to justify America's wars since the British first began to colonize what is now the United States.[66] The current link between religion and patriotism was demonstrated when Christian conservatives joined their political allies in seeking to secure fixed, singular readings of written, oral, and visual signs to wage the war against terrorism. The broader message was clear from the beginning: America is pursuing absolute, noble, and unlimited goals in the pursuit of freedom and liberty, and the American way of life is right for the rest of the world.

Justifying Violence in Religious Terms

It was inevitable, perhaps, that George W. Bush would lead the effort to justify violence in religious terms. As an evangelical Christian, he was, as media scholar David Domke said, "already inclined to see the hand of God in most happenings." Like-minded members of Bush's constituency were also "likely to view their present station in life as a God-ordained 'calling,' an outlook that imbues—in their eyes, at least—subsequent policies and actions with a magnitude of moral certainty."[67]

Bush frequently framed the potential war as a great battle to preserve "freedom" and "liberty," which "are deeply ensconced in a religious fundamentalist worldview, critically intertwined with goals regarding the protection and spread of the faith." The president portrayed freedom and liberty, as *he* defined the terms, as universal, God-given rights that must be preserved.

After 9/11, Bush "became more likely to present these values both as universal norms and God's desire for all peoples and cultures."[68] The number of references to freedom and liberty in his speeches nearly doubled—to roughly one in every eight paragraphs—after the attacks. The president made frequent comments like this one: "We face a continuing threat of terrorist networks that hate the very thought of people being able to live in freedom. They hate the thought of the fact that in this great country, we can worship the Almighty God the way we see fit."[69]

One of Bush's favorite dichotomies was good versus evil. He was constantly "attacking the 'evil' of the terrorists, using the word five times in his first statement on the September 11 terror assaults," as media critic Douglas Kellner noted, "and repeatedly portraying the conflict as a war between good and evil in which the United States was going to 'eradicate evil from the world' and 'smoke out and pursue . . . evil doers, those barbaric people.' "[70] Casting the war against terrorism as a struggle between good and evil was sound strategy for a president who wanted to use military force beyond Afghanistan, and it satisfied his conservative constituents, particularly Christian conservatives and neoconservatives.

As a political term, evil typically is defined as "inflicting intentional personal harm," but the definition excludes a laundry list of other harms—such as unintentional or accidental harm, failed attempts to inflict harm, necessary harm (as when a surgeon inflicts pain during a medical procedure), structural harm (as in state-sponsored violence), and harm by reason of insanity.[71] More important, "If all of your enemies are Satan's puppets, there's no point in drawing fine distinctions among them. No need to figure out which ones are irredeemable and which can be bought off. They're all bad to the bone, so just fight them at every pass, bear any burden, and so on."[72]

This frame certainly stops debate, at least in the United States. As Tony Lang of the Carnegie Council of Ethics and International Affairs said, "[T]he very concept of evil is problematic. When it becomes used as part of political rhetoric it silences conversation. That's the real problem. Once you've defined something that way, the only policy option is to destroy the evil."[73] One difficulty is that labeling someone or something as evil is almost always self-serving and simplistic, as journalist Robert Wright suggested. "What if some terrorists will settle for nothing less than the United States' destruction, whereas others just want a nationalist enclave in Chechnya or Mindanao? And what if treating all terrorists the same—as all having equally illegitimate goals—makes them more the same, more uniformly anti-American, more zealous?"[74]

Token Religious Dissent

The Christian community as a whole was either silent, urged caution, or supported a war option in response to the attacks. Very few Christians dared to stand up and declare that the war option, as Pillar put it, "is not necessarily inevitable. That we don't need another American 'crusade for freedom.' That we don't need to express our symbolic solidarity yet again with public prayers and yellow ribbons/flowers in the pulpit or on the altar."[75]

During a White House meeting with the president on September 20, 2001, interfaith ministers expressed concern that the United States must seek justice rather than revenge and that Americans must not view the coming invasion as a religious war.[76] Southern Baptist evangelical leader Billy Graham praised the president's handling of the crisis before the invasion and urged Christians to pray for their enemies. He did not address the proposed war option.[77]

The National Council of Churches prepared an interfaith statement—signed by 3,500 Jews, Christians, Muslims, and members of other faith groups—that said in part, "But we must not, out of anger and vengeance, indiscriminately retaliate in ways that bring on even more loss of innocent life. We pray that President Bush and members of Congress will seek the wisdom of God as they decide upon the appropriate response."[78] Most members of the Religious Society of Friends urged restraint in the march to war, but even some Quakers said the United States should use the military option. "I feel less Quakerly," said one. "I believe in general that the military . . . should be a means of last resort. But I feel very much that we have reached that last resort."[79]

Pope John Paul II (1920–2005) said during a visit to Kazakhstan, "We must not let what happened lead to a deepening of divisions. Religion must never be used as a reason for conflict."[80] The Vatican later clarified the pontiff's statement, saying he did not intend to preclude the use of force.[81] The United States Conference of Catholic Bishops said America had a right to self-defense, but that military action must reflect "sound moral principles."[82]

Conservative evangelical fundamentalists, who are continually on the lookout for the New Age when Christ returns, demanded immediate military action. Anything that would hasten this millennial event was to be welcomed:

> Such a conception engenders a constant awareness of how one spends one's time, since all of one's thoughts and behaviors are considered potentially to have eternal consequences . . . . This omnipresent awareness of the importance of how individuals spend their time impels action. This is thought to be in accordance with the instructions of Jesus in the biblical book of Mark that believers should "keep on the alert; for you do not know when the appointed time [of Christ's return] may come" (brackets in the original).

Many of these Christians shared the president's view: "We can also be confident in the ways of providence, even when they are far from our understanding. Events aren't moved by blind change and chance. Behind all of life and all of history, there's a dedication and purpose, set by the hand of a just and faithful God."[83]

Those who shared this view also tended to share the view that (a) action, preferably immediate action, was imperative and (b) a God-inspired decision to act must be enduring. "[T]hese time fixations," Domke says, were evident "throughout the administration's discourse and news coverage." The time fixations enabled the Bush administration to press simultaneously "for immediate action on specific 'war on terrorism' policies and to justify this desire as a requisite step in a long-term, God-ordained process. Further, the implication—sometimes made explicit—was clear: to not act quickly or to not endure in the campaign against terrorism was to risk another September 11."[84] No Christian leader as far as we could determine argued publicly at this time against the military option, asked the president how civilian casualties might realistically be avoided, or explored possible alternatives.

Choosing Sides

A critical, early order of business in any war is the choosing of sides. The government and news media determined early on that the coming conflict was between "us" (the United States) and "them" (pretty much the rest of the world). They framed the terrorist attacks largely as an assault only against the United States, a frame one might expect of those who view Americans as God's chosen people: "It precluded other sorts of framing such as 'an attack on the West' which might have appeared had we seen the spontaneous street demonstrations of shocked and saddened people in Berlin, Copenhagen, Paris, London, and other parts of the world. The 'world' part of the WTC [World Trade Center] accounted for over 1000 now missing 'foreigners,' and the functions of many of the businesses within it were emphatically global. But ours was an American story."[85]

Print and electronic media reinforced the binary view, using slogans such as "War on America" and "America's New War" across the United States, suggesting this was a U.S. problem.[86] Editorial writers for the 10 largest U.S. newspapers also used binary terms to draw the lines between us and them. Eighteen asserted that "you're either with us or with the terrorists"—with 10 of the editorials citing Bush as their reference.[87]

Media scholars Bonnie Brennen and Margaret Duffy analyzed the rhetorical strategies the *New York Times* used in editorials, news reports, advertisements, and columns to frame Muslims and Arab Americans in the four months following the 9/11 attacks. Muslims and Arab Americans were framed as "different" from other Americans, they found, and they speculated that frames of Muslims and Arab Americans as "the 'Other' encourage the emergence of a specific ideological vision in the news coverage which has cultivated a climate of fear in United States citizens."[88]

This is a world in which everyday discourse about the "war against terrorism" can easily segue into us (civilized American Christians) versus them (foreign, and therefore uncivilized, Muslim terrorists)—in newspapers, on talk radio, on television, and even in the pulpit—as we noted in Chapter 2. The propaganda war intensified the stereotyping of persons perceived to be Muslim or Arab. Police/military/civilian agencies profiled, and homegrown terrorists waged war against, people who "looked" Middle Eastern or Arab. The mainstream media largely ignored local reports of harassment, beatings, property damage, and even the murder of so-called "Muslims."

War advocates, who eventually realized they would need the help of some Muslim governments to launch a war in Afghanistan, tried to show the upcoming struggle was not a religious war pitting Muslims against Christians. Editorial writers for the 10 largest American newspapers eventually tried to isolate the "good" Muslims from the "bad" ones—to suggest that there are a few bad dates in every batch of dates and the vast majority of Muslims had no real grievances against the people of the United States. Twenty-six writers said Muslims were not the enemy, and 13 asserted that the Afghan people were not the enemy.

USA Today used President Bush's visit to an Islamic center to make the point: "President Bush took time out of his day Monday to meet with Islamic leaders on their sacred ground. At a mosque two miles from the White House, Bush excoriated those who would intimidate and harass American Muslims, saying they 'represent the worst of humankind.' "[89] Nevertheless, Muslims—especially those deemed to be of "Middle Eastern" origin—continued to be isolated and targeted for persecution as a group.[90]

As the religious, media, and political elites dehumanized the opposition, they praised and made heroes of U.S. victims, survivors, and rescue workers. "This shift of focus from victims to heroes helped to effect a transition from death to life, and it coincided with the rhetorical shift from shock to sorrow to patriotism."[91] Political leaders also were portrayed as heroes—to their benefit. "The construction of political leaders as heroes ... can legitimize the actions of those leaders and buttress their authority at critical times. The [New York] *Times'* portrayal of President Bush as 'a leader whom the nation could follow' offered implicit (and politically important) support for the administration's response to September 11."[92]

Editorial writers treated Bush most favorably, Ryan found. The president was mentioned in 81 of 104 editorials, and none suggested he was wrong about any aspect of the war against terrorism—31 said he was right in his approach and decisions, and 23 tacitly endorsed his views by citing them without comment. Editorials applied 34 positive descriptors (for example, *able* and *bold*) to the president.

Marginalizing Dissent

President Bush was the most visible user of binary oppositions to support state-sponsored military violence. For him, and for the war advocates who uncritically endorsed his remarks, there was no middle ground. The term *terrorist* was used to demonize all international and domestic opposition, and much of the media mirrored that usage. Bush got the ball rolling when he proclaimed, "If you are not with us [supporting every action "we" take], you are with the terrorists."[93] But the merchants of war first had to ensure that the word terrorist was defined in simplistic theological or moral terms. The complexity that they wanted to avoid was captured by Nacos, who says the problem of definition is

> rooted in the evaluation of one and the same terrorist act as either a despicable or a justifiable means to political ends, as either the evil deed of ruthless terrorists or the justifiable act of freedom fighters and/or warriors of god. The slogan that "one person's terrorist is another person's freedom fighter" captures these contrasting value judgments.[94]

Demonizing Terrorists

Those favoring the war option got around the definitional problem by peddling an essentially meaningless "common sense" definition of terrorism that assigned the worst possible values to the word following the 9/11 attacks. One study analyzed 1,070 editorial cartoons published between September 11 and October 8, 2001, and found 317 representations of "the enemy." Researchers found that 220 of the 242 cartoons (91 percent) that depicted Osama bin Laden, the Taliban, or al-Qaida dehumanized the enemy. They used 11 dehumanizing categories— enemy as animal (29 percent), aggressor (21 percent), abstraction (12 percent), barbarian (8 percent), enemy of God (6 percent), faceless (5 percent), desecrator of women and children (4 percent), criminal (4 percent), and death (2 percent). "In the case of the current war, no longer are al-Qaida human beings, who might have a rationale for their behavior, but insects and rodents to be exterminated .... Dissenting views were noticeably absent in the cartoons analyzed in the present study."[95]

Brigitte Nacos found that bin Laden was mentioned in 2,538 stories—all negative—disseminated by ABC, NBC, CBS, CNN, NPR (National Public Radio), the *New York Times*, and the *Washington Post*, compared to 2,446 mentions for President Bush in her analysis of print and electronic media between September 11 and October 6, 2001. This is a bit unusual since bin Laden was unavailable for comment and Bush "went public at a breathtaking rate. In the twenty-six days from September 11th to October 6th, President Bush made more than fifty public statements."[96]

Bin Laden was demonized further in 71 editorials published in the 10 largest U.S. newspapers as corrupt, murderous, ruthless, cowardly, and hated, Michael Ryan reports. Such codes as cowardly, vicious, jealous, and extremist also were used to describe everyone who had not boarded the anti-terrorism train. Bin Laden also was demonized in reader letters, columns, and photographs published by U.S. news-magazines. *Time* and *Newsweek* "used head shots of Bin Laden in which either he was in a red light or the photo was digitally changed to make him appear red, like a devil; *Newsweek* used the image, closely cropped, as its cover." Bin Laden appeared in the crosshairs of a rifle-scope to illustrate a *U.S. News & World Report* cover story.[97]

"Terrorists" were *not* defined as the powerless attacking the power-ful, who may have wronged them. They were *not* defined as individuals who committed violent acts because they believed they had no other choices. They were *not* defined as individuals who were foreigners to the communities in which they were embedded. They were *not* defined as individuals who had legitimate grievances. In the context of the war against terrorism, they *were* defined as Muslim.

The climate for acceptance of this definition of terrorist could not have been better. The media have for decades negatively stereotyped Arab and Muslim peoples who held political, cultural, social, and reli-gious values that were perceived as different from those of the major-ity white Anglo population. The events following 9/11 merely intensified and validated the stereotyping.[98]

The administration and its supporters suppressed dissent (a) by pre-senting a unified message about war and thereby limiting chances for rebuttal and (b) by asking others to unite behind administration poli-cies and punishing those who would not. The president's Christian rhetoric, which dovetailed nicely with the neoconservative pro-war rhetoric, was echoed consistently by the media. The goal was to close "off a substantive societal—and international—conversation," as David Domke put it, "through a set of politically calculated, religiously grounded communication strategies." Rather than permit a democratic debate, "Bush's rhetoric hijacked the discussion about the significance and implications of September 11, thereby denying to U.S. citizens important opportunities for national self-examination and wide public hearing of diverse viewpoints—and also shutting out the world, much of which was extending unprecedented sympathy for U.S. citizens and the nation."[99]

The war's cheerleaders, both official and unofficial, rushed to attack dissenting voices on those rare occasions when the media published or aired them. Robert Jenson, a journalism professor at the University of Texas, received roughly 2,500 electronic mail messages attacking his commentary, published in the *Houston Chronicle*, stating that the United States had committed atrocities that were as bad as the 9/11 attacks.[100] The conservative American Council of Trustees and Alumni published a list of 117 "anti-American statements" that were made on U.S. college campuses. Joel Beinin, a historian at Stanford University, was condemned for saying, "If Osama bin Laden is confirmed to be behind the attacks, the United States should bring him before an international tribunal on charges of crimes against humanity."[101]

Official Intimidation Attempts

Government officials tried to intimidate dissenters privately. Robert Dallek, a historian at Boston University, criticized Bush for not returning immediately to Washington following the 9/11 attacks, telling *USA Today*, "The president's place is back in Washington." Karl Rove, on the day the quotation was published, "took time out from his other pressing duties to call Dallek, whom he'd never met, to tell him that Bush did not return home right away because of threats to the White House and Air Force One."[102] Dick Cheney and Rove repeated the claim, but there was no such threat.

Media personality Bill Maher felt the administration's public pressure from Ari Fleischer, the former White House spokesman. Fleischer responded to remarks by Maher, who joked that the United States was cowardly for launching cruise missiles from 2,000 miles away during U.S. attacks against suspected terrorist hideouts during the Clinton administration, but that terrorists who stayed in the airplanes when they hit the World Trade Center were not cowards. "Americans need to watch what they say, what they do, and this is not the time for remarks like that; there never is," Fleischer said.[103]

The labels "terrorist" and "terrorist sympathizer" were used to smear anyone, including dissenters in the United States, who questioned any aspect of the war against terrorism.[104] The effort to link anti-war protestors to terrorists is typified in comments such as those of military historian Mackubin Thomas Owens, who denounced "the lunatic ravings of those who hide behind the Constitution while trying to destroy it, and whose perspective is not that different from the pathological hatred and fanaticism that motivates Osama bin Laden."[105]

Localized teach-ins, socials, peace walks, petitions, rallies, and public protests across the country seeking to focus public attention on the injustice of bombing Afghanistan were essentially ignored by the mass media or rendered ineffective and counterproductive in the crusade against terrorism. The media mandated patriotic support for the military option for months. Virtually all other alternatives were ridiculed, ignored, or otherwise marginalized—opening the window of opportunity for the Bush administration in its ongoing effort to market the military option.[106]

The mainstream media and government leaders also, as Douglas Kellner put it, "privileged the 'clash of civilizations' model, established a binary dualism between Islamic terrorism and civilization, and largely circulated war fever and retaliatory feelings and discourses that called for and supported a form of military intervention."[107] Some journalists allowed themselves to be used by those who wanted to stifle dissent about the military strikes, as Nacos notes:

> As laudable as the we-are-all-in-this-together contributions of the media were in many respects, by dwelling endlessly on the outburst of patriotism and the idea of national unity without paying attention to other important matters in the political realm, the media helped to create an atmosphere in which criticism of the various crisis-related policy initiatives in Washington was mostly absent from the mass-mediated public debate. When people like Attorney General John Ashcroft questioned the patriotism of those on the right and left of the political spectrum who were critical of some aspects of his anti- and counterterrorist policy proposals, there was not a massive outcry in the media on behalf of civil liberties—most of all freedom of expression.[108]

War advocates said they were not trying to stifle dissent, but that is precisely what they were trying to do. As we argued in Chapter 3, the strategy was successful in part because intolerance of dissent is linked to the authoritarian behavior characteristic of conservatives, whether or not they were religious.

ENDURING TENSIONS

The use of overwhelming military might against Afghanistan was probably inevitable given the psychological need of most Americans to seek revenge for lives lost and property destroyed on September 11. Events moved so quickly, many gave little thought to the tensions the war against terrorism would create.

Christian Conservative War Rhetoric

Two prominent Protestant evangelical fundamentalist leaders—televangelist Jerry Falwell, founder of the Moral Majority, and televangelist Pat Robertson, founder of the Christian Coalition—were heavily criticized when they blamed the 9/11 attacks on secularism and liberal American attitudes. "I really believe," Falwell (1933–2007) said on *The 700 Club*, "that the pagans, and the abortionists, and the feminists, and the gays and the lesbians who are actively trying to make that an alternative lifestyle, the ACLU, People for the American Way, all of them who have tried to secularize America. I point the finger in their face and say 'you helped this happen.' "[109]

Falwell viewed the attacks as punishment for "throwing God out of the public square, out of the schools. The abortionists have got to bear some burden for this because God will not be mocked."[110] Robertson, host of *The 700 Club*, apparently agreed, saying, "We have sinned against Almighty God, at the highest level of our government, we've stuck our finger in your eye." Falwell later apologized for his remarks and assigned full blame for the attacks to the terrorists.[111]

Many Christians were embarrassed and appalled by the positions taken by Falwell and Robertson, in part because many Americans "assumed [the comments] to be an accurate reflection of conservative religious sentiment in the wake of the attack."[112]

The war against terrorism was a lens through which some Protestant conservatives believed they could help Israel against its Muslim enemies, since nearly all terrorist organizations were deemed by the United States to be Muslims in the Middle East. After all, "the first Zionists to settle in Palestine were in fact American Protestants, who planted successive, ill-fated colonies aimed at 'restoring' the Holy Land to the Jews, so that their subsequent conversion to Christianity would speed the Second Coming."[113]

The Bush administration's efforts to recruit oppressive governments to help in the war against terrorism did meet resistance from Protestant evangelical groups addressing the persecution of Christians in foreign countries. Neoconservatives and traditional conservatives did not want a holy war as they worked to create an international coalition to invade Afghanistan and to frame the coming fight against terrorism. But policies embracing non-Christian governments that oppressed their own Christian minorities exacerbated tensions between some conservative religious groups and their political allies in the Bush administration after 9/11.

Some groups were loosely affiliated with an international, interdenominational Christian human-rights organization dubbed Christian Solidarity Worldwide. This movement attempts to defend Christian minorities against abuse in non-Christian nations such as Pakistan, China, Sudan, Uzbekistan, Burma, and Saudi Arabia.

Steven Snyder of International Christian Concern—a human-rights group that helps Christians who are oppressed in foreign countries— wrote of the 9/11 attacks: "America is witnessing what Christians in other parts of the world have been enduring for some time. We are at war with an unseen enemy that has demonstrated its resolve to launch a 'jihad' (holy war) on Americans, Christians, and Jews—and will show no mercy for innocent lives." They were outraged when the administration "allied itself with some of the world's most dangerous regimes, including Sudan and Syria, which the Department of State classifies as 'state sponsors of terrorism.' "[114]

Conservative religious activists from many groups worked for years to mobilize American politicians to penalize foreign governments that persecuted their Christian minorities. As we noted in Chapter 1, they achieved a symbolic victory with passage of the International Religious Freedom Act of 1998, which was intended to promote religious freedom as part of U.S. foreign policy. Now some felt these efforts were being undermined by the Republican administration they served.

Christians and the Killing of Innocents

The conservative coalition faced further strains when Christians of all political persuasions began to realize the Bush administration could not or would not spare innocent Afghans—and later, innocent Iraqis—in the war against terrorism. Some of the early calls for peace after the bombing in Afghanistan began came from the international Christian community.

Leaders of the Canadian Council of Churches—which included Anglican, Mennonite, Lutheran, and Catholic leaders—urged an end to the war only a few weeks after it began. "The essential goal of preventing further terrorist attacks," they said, "will not be accomplished through military attacks on Afghanistan." The World Council of Churches in Geneva said, "We do not believe that war, particularly in today's highly technologized world, can ever be regarded as an effective response to the equally abhorrent sin of terrorism."[115]

In the United States, the church and society board of the United Methodist Church—George W. Bush and Dick Cheney's home church—recommended that the UN assume responsibility for responding to terrorism. "It is our firm belief," the board said, "that military actions will not end terrorism. As people called to be a visible sign of God's ever-present love, we know that violence will not bring God's grace .... We continue to say no to war and encourage our leaders to respond cautiously."[116] The executive council of the Episcopal Church, deliberating after the bombings began, commended the president's leadership, but said, " 'the United States need not be at war while pursuing the full force of justice' against those responsible for the Sept. 11 terrorist attacks."[117] And James M. Wall, former editor and president of the Christian Century Foundation, said, "[I]t is essential to oppose this new war," and criticized President Bush because he "said he was not interested in negotiating, which meant that he wanted revenge more than he wanted justice."[118]

Shutting the Window of Opportunity

The window of opportunity for exploring a nonviolent response to 9/11 was open for nearly four weeks—between September 11 and October 8. Anyone who wanted to explore the ground between the binary extremes could have looked seriously at the terrorists—where they came from, what their grievances were, and why they considered political violence their final option. "Understanding the enemy is very crucial because only then can we prepare creative, reasonable, and just responses," as Sam Keen, who studies ways in which the enemy is dehumanized, put it. "But I think that as long as you have an image of the enemy, you can't make a distinction between reaction and responding. We *do* have to respond, and we *do* have to seek justice, but a reaction is not a response—it's unthinking" (italics in the original).[119]

Journalists, government officials, and religious leaders are quite capable of exploring semantic space between extreme positions, but they failed in the case of the war against terrorism. They did not explore or allow others to explore the complexities of a military option as they rushed to war. Less than a month after the 9/11 attacks, America declared an open-ended, violent, worldwide war against terrorism: "In the nearly four weeks since the terror attacks of September 11th, the war metaphor had been invoked so often by media organizations and by public officials that the American public was hardly surprised when President Bush revealed the start of the military phase."[120]

The war frame was unassailable—whether the source was government or the mass media, or other educational, social, cultural, religious, and political institutions in civil society. All spoke with one, monologic voice. Those individuals or groups that endorsed and supported alternatives to the war frame were at best ignored and at worst attacked.

Individuals in all faith traditions and individuals of no faith who opposed the invasion of Afghanistan were swamped by the volume, stubbornness, and shear nastiness of those who favored the indiscriminate use of force against the innocent as well as the guilty in the war against terrorism. Journalists were instrumental in selling the military option.

The war proponents skillfully used xenophobia, religious fervor, fear, and patriotism to market, primarily through the mainstream media, a "total war" to ensure the American way of life would be the way of righteousness for the rest of the world. As the late political scientist Murray Edelman (1919–2001) noted,

> The connections among misleading language, public opinion, and public policy are powerful, though subtle. Language itself does not create errors in belief and in governmental action. But it can play powerfully on established prejudices, spread biases to a wider population, and make

them compelling elements in formulating public policy. It does so all the more effectively because the role of language as itself a form of political action is not readily recognized.[121]

The media narrative was all about evil, and America's crusade stance was certainly understood by the majority of Americans in the aftermath of 9/11. Americans were increasingly performing an unintended role in the war against terrorism—from liberators to oppressors, from being victims themselves to victimizing others—fighting terror with terror.

As we shall see in Chapter 9, tensions within the conservative coalition heightened as the United States moved toward an invasion of Iraq. More and more Christians of all political persuasions became disenchanted with the military option as they realized that (a) the genie (violence) is extraordinarily difficult to put back into the bottle after it is released, (b) innocents were continuing to die in the war in Afghanistan, contrary to prewar assurances by the administration, (c) U.S. policy had done little to protect Americans from terrorism, and (d) much of the goodwill the world showered on Americans following 9/11 was being squandered in the continued stance on terrorism.

The Christian conservative coalition initially began to fragment as disputes emerged within conservative religious congregations about whether or not to support the Bush administration's goal of overthrowing Saddam Hussein. These tensions, traceable to events that occurred during the September 11–October 8, 2001, period, continued to heighten through the invasion of Iraq, the trial of Saddam Hussein, the bloody battles between the militias and American troops, and the talk of invading Iran to stop its alleged nuclear weapons program.

NOTES

1. The bombs fell in Afghanistan on Monday, October 8, but in the continental United States the date was Sunday, October 7, 2001.

2. Richard Norton-Taylor, "Thinktank: Invasion Aided al-Qaida," *Guardian* (Manchester), October 20, 2004, www.guardian.co.uk/world/2004/oct/20/alqaida.thinktanks. Osama bin Laden's network of al-Qaida operatives had "more than 18,000 potential terrorists in 60 countries" sympathetic to its cause, according to the International Institute for Strategic Studies, and it is often acting in concert with local allies in these countries.

3. George Soros, "The War on Terror: Victims Turning Perpetrators," commencement address to the Columbia School of International and Public

Affairs, *BuzzFlash*, May 17, 2004, www.buzzflash.com/contributors/04/05/con04221.html.

4. George Bush, "Bush's Remarks on U.S. Military Strikes in Afghanistan," *New York Times*, October 8, 2001, B6.

5. Michael Burleigh, *Blood and Rage. A Cultural History of Terrorism* (London: HarperPress, 2008).

6. Marsha Houston and Cheris Kramarae, "Speaking from Silence: Methods of Silencing and of Resistance," *Discourse & Society* 2, no. 4 (1991): 387–399; Elizabeth Arveda Kissling, "Street Harassment: The Language of Sexual Terrorism," *Discourse & Society* 2, no. 4 (1991): 451–460.

7. Christopher R. Goddard and Janet R. Stanley, "Viewing the Abusive Parent and the Abused Child as Captor and Hostage: The Application of Hostage Theory to the Effects of Child Abuse," *Journal of Interpersonal Violence* 9, no. 2 (1994): 258–269; and Nicola Graham-Kevan and John Archer, "Intimate Terrorism and Common Couple Violence: A Test of Johnson's Predictions in Four British Samples," *Journal of Interpersonal Violence* 18, no. 11 (2003): 1247–1270.

8. L. Paul Husselbee and Larry Elliott, "Looking Beyond Hate: How National and Regional Newspapers Framed Hate Crimes in Jaspar, Texas, and Laramie, Wyoming," *Journalism & Mass Communication Quarterly* 79, no. 4 (2002): 833–852; and Carolyn Petrosino, "Connecting the Past to the Future: Hate Crime in America," *Journal of Contemporary Criminal Justice* 15, no. 1 (1999): 22–47.

9. Brian H. Spitzberg and Gregory Hoobler, "Cyberstalking and the Technologies of Interpersonal Terrorism," *New Media & Society* 4, no. 2 (2002): 71–92.

10. Criminologists have noted parallels between "the dynamics of crime and the desire to punish . . . . [and] between violence associated with 'common' criminality and the [state-supported] violence of war and terrorism." This is an argument against employing binary language that positions the socially inclusive "citizen" against the criminally exclusive "underclass"—a form of terrorism. See Jock Young, "Merton with Energy, Katz with Structure: The Sociology of Vindictiveness and the Criminology of Transgression," *Theoretical Criminology* 7, no. 3 (2003): 388–414, pp. 390, 410.

11. Daniel M. Schwartz, "Environmental Terrorism: Analyzing the Concept," *Journal of Peace Research* 35, no. 4 (1998): 483–496.

12. The term "state terrorism" is difficult to categorize and is open to varied interpretations—especially from the U.S. perspective. Nevertheless, many scholars recognize state terrorism as an acute form of political terrorism. An argument can be made that America has a long history in the use of state terrorism—from extending its power across what is today the United States to the use primarily of military power to gain world hegemony. The literature on this theme is too vast even to summarize, but one set of statistics speaks to U.S. militarism. Before the war in Iraq, U.S. troops were stationed

at roughly 1,000 military bases in 156 countries throughout the world. See Jules Dufour, "Review Article: The Worldwide Network of US Military Bases; the Global Deployment of US Military Personnel," Centre for Research on Globalization, July 1, 2007, www.globalresearch.ca/index.php ?context=va&aid=5564. Another example is the U.S.-led embargo against Iraq after the 1990–1991 Persian Gulf War. An estimated 1 million Iraqis, including a half million children, died between 1991 and 2000. See "Squeezed to Death," *Guardian* (Manchester), March 4, 2000, www .guardian.co.uk/theguardian/2000/mar/04/weekend7.weekend9. What some call state terrorism, of course, is not a uniquely American phenomenon. It was present in the past—as in Islamic Asia's response to colonialism [e.g., Stephen Frederick Dale, "Religious Suicide in Islamic Asia: Anticolonial Terrorism in India, Indonesia, and the Philippines," *Journal of Conflict Resolution* 32, no. 1 (1988): 37–59] and in Stalin's Soviet Union [e.g., Peter Z. Grossman, "The Dilemma of Prisoners: Choice During Stalin's Great Terror, 1936–38," *Journal of Conflict Resolution* 38, no. 1 (1994): 43–55]. And it continues in various forms today—in countries such as El Salvador [e.g., Robert W. Taylor and Harry E. Vanden, "Defining Terrorism in El Salvador: 'La Matanza,'" *Annals*, American Academy of Political and Social Science, 463 (September 1982): 106–117] and Colombia [e.g., Patricia Bibes, "Transnational Organized Crime and Terrorism: Colombia, a Case Study," *Journal of Contemporary Criminal Justice* 17, no. 3 (2001): 243–258].

13. John V. Whitbeck, "More Danger Lurks If We Allow U.S. to Define Meaning of 'Terrorism,'" *Houston Chronicle*, March 17, 2002, C1, C5, p. C1.

14. Ibid., C1.

15. Richard W. Bulliet, "Rhetoric, Discourse, and the Future of Hope," *Annals*, American Academy of Political and Social Science, 588 (July 2003): 10–17.

16. U.S. Department of State, "State Department Adds Three Groups to Foreign Terrorist List," news release, March 27, 2002, http://www.usembassy.it/file2002_03/alia/a2032709.htm.

17. "Straight UN Facts: There Is No UN Definition of Terrorism," *Eye on the UN*, Hudson Institute, New York, February 2008, www.eyeontheun.org/facts.asp?1=1&p=61.

18. Jarna Petman, "Evil and International Law," *International Law FORUM du Droit International* 5, no. 4 (2003): 236–240, p. 237. Petman describes how one of the latest efforts—by an ad hoc committee of the United Nations—had to be abandoned because the committee could not resolve the issue of national liberation movements, which may or may not be terrorist movements.

19. Ibid., 240.

20. National Advisory Committee on Criminal Justice Standards and Goals, *Disorders and Terrorism: Report of the Task Force on Disorders and*

Terrorism (Washington, DC: Law Enforcement Assistance Administration, 1976), 3.

21. Robert Dreyfus, "Domestic Antiterrorism Measures May Endanger Civil Liberties," 109–117, and Fareed Zakariah, "Freedom vs. Security," 118–126, both in *The War on Terrorism*, ed. Mitchell Young (San Diego: Greenhaven, 2003).

22. Paul Wilkinson, "Terrorism and Propaganda," in *Terrorism & the Media: Dilemmas for Government, Journalists & the Public*, ed. Yonah Alexander and Richard Latter (Washington, DC: Brassey's, 1990), 26–33, pp. 30–31.

23. Baudrillard's ideas about the role of the media in a postmodern world have had a profound influence in critical cultural studies, but he has numerous critics as well as admirers. For two useful reviews of his work, see Douglas Kellner, ed., *Baudrillard: A Critical Reader* (Oxford, UK: Basil Blackwell, 1994); Rex Butler, *Jean Baudrillard: The Defence of the Real* (London: Sage, 1999).

24. Frank D. Durham, "Breaching Powerful Boundaries: A Postmodern Critique of Framing," in *Framing Public Life: Perspectives on Media and Our Understanding of the Social World*, ed. Stephen D. Reese, Oscar H. Gandy Jr., and August E. Grant (Mahwah, NJ: Erlbaum, 2001), 123–136, p. 135.

25. Gadi Wolfsfeld, *Media and Political Conflict: News from the Middle East* (Cambridge: Cambridge University Press, 1997), 141.

26. Cynthia Carter and C. Kay Weaver, *Violence and the Media* (Buckingham, UK: Open University Press, 2003), 26.

27. M. Mark Miller and Bonnie Parnell Riechert, "The Spiral of Opportunity and Frame Resonance: Mapping the Issue Cycle in News and Public Discourse," in Reese, Gandy, and Grant, *Framing Public Life*, 107–121, pp. 110–111.

28. Ralph E. Dowling, "Terrorism and the Media: A Rhetorical Genre," *Journal of Communication* 36, no. 1 (1986): 12–24.

29. Jack Lule, "Myth and Terror on the Editorial Page: The *New York Times* Responds to September 11, 2001," *Journalism & Mass Communication Quarterly* 79, no. 2 (2002): 275–293; J. Bowyer Bell, "Terrorist Scripts and Live-Action Spectaculars," *Columbia Journalism Review*, May–June 1978, 47–50.

30. David Fromkin, "The Strategy of Terrorism," in *Contemporary Terrorism: Selected Readings*, ed. John D. Elliot and Leslie K. Gibson (Gaithersburg, MD: International Association of Chiefs of Police, 1978), 11–24, p. 19.

31. Walter Laqueur, "Terrorism Makes a Tremendous Noise," *Across the Board*, January 1978, 57–67.

32. Fromkin, "The Strategy of Terrorism," 23.

33. Dowling, "Terrorism and the Media," 14.

34. Bell, "Terrorist Scripts and Live-Action," 50.

35. Park Dietz, "The Media and Weapons of Mass Hysteria," *Facsnet*, undated, www.facsnet.org/issues/specials/terrorism/dietz.php3.

36. Brigitte L. Nacos, *Mass-Mediated Terrorism: The Central Role of the Media in Terrorism and Counterterrorism* (Lanham, MD.: Rowman & Littlefield, 2002), 84.

37. Paul R. Pillar, *Terrorism and U.S. Foreign Policy* (Washington, DC: Brookings, 2001), 1.

38. Ibid., 6.

39. Greg Philo, "Television News and Audience Understanding of War, Conflict and Disaster," *Journalism Studies* 3, no. 2 (2002): 173–186, p. 185.

40. Daya Kishan Thussu, "Managing the Media in an Era of Round-the-Clock News: Notes from India's First Tele-War. *Journalism Studies* 3, no. 2 (2002): 203–212, pp. 211–212.

41. P. Eric Louw, "The 'War Against Terrorism': A Public Relations Challenge for the Pentagon," *Gazette* 65, no. 3 (2003): 211–230.

42. Gabriel Weimann and Hans-Bernd Brosius, "The Newsworthiness of International Terrorism," *Communication Research* 18, no. 3 (1991): 333–354.

43. Virgil Hawkins, "The Other Side of the CNN Factor: The Media and Conflict," *Journalism Studies* 3, no. 2 (2002): 225–240, p. 233.

44. Peter Viggo Jakobsen, "Focus on the CNN Effect Misses the Point: The Real Media Impact on Conflict Management Is Invisible and Indirect," *Journal of Peace Research* 37, no. 2 (2000): 131–143, p. 132.

45. Nacos, *Mass Mediated Terrorism*, 78.

46. Pillar, *Terrorism and U.S. Foreign Policy*, 1–2.

47. Michele L. Malvesti, "Explaining the United States' Decision to Strike Back at Terrorists," *Terrorism and Political Violence* 13, no. 2 (2001), 85–106.

48. Ibid., 85.

49. Kirsten Mogensen, Laura Lindsay, Xigen Li, Jay Perkins, and Mike Beardsley, "How TV News Covered the Crisis: The Content of CNN, CBS, ABC, NBC and Fox," in *Communication and Terrorism: Public and Media Responses to 9/11*, ed. Bradley S. Greenberg (Cresskill, NJ: Hampton, 2002), 101–120, p. 116.

50. Ibid., 119.

51. Carolyn Kitch, " 'Mourning in America': Ritual, Redemption, and Recovery in News Narrative after September 11," *Journalism Studies* 4, no. 2 (2003): 213–224, p. 216.

52. Douglas Kellner, "September 11, the Media, and War Fever," *Television & New Media* 3, no. 2 (2002): 143–151.

53. Ann Coulter, "This Is War: We Should Invade Their Countries," *National Review Online*, September 13, 2001, http://www.nationalreview.com/coulter/coulter.shtml.

54. Patrick J. Buchanan, "Whose War Is This?" *USA Today*, September 27, 2001, A15. Buchanan rejected the neoconservative plan: "The war . . . the neocons want, with the United States and Israel fighting all of the radical Islamic states, is the war bin Laden wants, the war his murderers hoped to ignite when they sent those airliners into the World Trade Center and the Pentagon." He urged conservatives to back Bush's plan just to capture bin Laden and topple the Taliban.

55. Open Letter to the Honorable George W. Bush, Project for the New American Century, September 20, 2001, www.newamericancentury .org/Bushletter.htm. Among the signers of the letter were Richard Perle, William J. Bennett, Jeane J. Kirkpatrick, William Kristol, Norman Podhoretz, Donald Kagan, Robert Kagan, Eliot A. Cohen, Clifford May, Midge Decter, and Francis Fukuyama. Fukuyama later changed his mind and opposed the invasion of Iraq. See Francis Fukuyama, "Why Shouldn't I Change My Mind?" *Los Angeles Times*, April 9, 2006, M1.

56. Joshua Green, "God's Foreign Policy: Why the Biggest Threat to Bush's War Strategy Isn't Coming from Muslims, But from Christians," *The Washington Monthly*, November 2001, 26–33.

57. See Michael Ryan and Les Switzer, "Using Binary Language to Sell the War in Afghanistan," in *Community Preparedness and Response to Terrorism: Communication and the Media*, ed. H. Dan O'Hair, Robert L. Heath, and Gerald R. Ledlow (New York: Praeger, 2005), 97–124.

58. Valerie Strauss, " 'Eye for an Eye' Has Its Detractors: While Most Americans Support Strike Against Terrorists, Some Decry Retaliation," *Washington Post*, September 17, 2001, B7.

59. Bernhard Debatin, " 'Plane Wreck with Spectators': Terrorism and Media Attention," in Greenberg, *Communication and Terrorism*, 163–174, p. 172.

60. Lule, "Myth and Terror," 286.

61. Nacos, *Mass-Mediated Terrorism*, 146. Nacos's search of the U.S. print press available in the Lexis-Nexis archive produced a total of 5,814 articles that mentioned the two search terms, war and terrorism. The archive was searched for the period September 12, 2001, to October 6, 2001.

62. Michael Ryan, "Framing the War Against Terrorism: US Newspaper Editorials and Military Action in Afghanistan," *Gazette* 66, no. 5 (2004): 363–382, p. 363. The editorial pages of each newspaper were searched for editorials about the war against terrorism. Each had to mention possible military strikes as part of the fight against terrorism and each had to indicate support for, opposition to, or neutrality toward a possible military option. The intercoder reliability for two coders was 98 percent.

63. "Total Barbarism Demands Total War," *New York Daily News*, September 15, 2001, Editorial-40.

64. Pillar, *Terrorism and U.S. Foreign Policy*, 217–218.

65. The media, "by dwelling endlessly on the outburst of patriotism and the idea of national unity, . . . helped to create an atmosphere in which criticism of the various crisis-related policy initiatives in Washington was mostly absent from the mass-mediated public debate." See Nacos, *Mass-Mediated Terrorism*, 195.

66. See, for example, Charles M. Segal and David C. Stineback, *Puritans, Indians, and Manifest Destiny* (New York: Putnam, 1977). The relationship between Christianity and other religions encountered in the colonial era was obviously much more complex than the theme—religion and violence—highlighted here. See, for example, Nicholas Griffiths and Fernando Cervantes, eds., *Spiritual Encounters: Interactions between Christianity and Native Religions in Colonial America* (Lincoln: University of Nebraska Press, 1999).

67. David Domke, *God Willing? Political Fundamentalism in the White House, the 'War on Terror,' and the Echoing Press* (London: Pluto, 2004), 16.

68. David Domke, Kevin Coe, and Robert Tynes, "The Gospel of Freedom and Liberty: George W. Bush, the 'War on Terror,' and an Echoing Press." Paper presented to the Religion and Media Interest Group, Association for Education in Journalism and Mass Communication annual convention, Toronto, Canada, 2004, 21.

69. The White House, "President Bush Discusses Faith-Based Initiative in Tennessee," news release, February 10, 2003, www.whitehouse.gov/news/releases/2003/02/20030210-1.html.

70. Kellner, "September 11, the Media," 144.

71. Roy F. Baumeister, *Evil: Inside Human Cruelty and Violence* (New York: Freeman, 1997), 8.

72. Robert Wright, "War on Evil," *Foreign Policy*, September/October 2004, 34–35, p. 34.

73. Cited by Joaquin Cabreas, "Behind Bush's Drive to War," *The Humanist*, November/December 2003, 20–24, p. 22. "[S]ince the war is endless, and cannot be won, those who embark on such a war turn themselves into the very ogres they are supposedly pursuing." See Shadia B. Drury, *Terror and Civilization: Christianity, Politics, and the Western Psyche* (NewYork: Palgrave, 2004), 192.

74. Wright, "War on Evil," 34. Wright asks further: "Or what if Iran, Iraq, and North Korea are actually different kinds of problems? And what if their rulers, however many bad things they've done, are still human beings who respond rationally to clear incentives? If you're truly open to this possibility, you might be cheered when a hideous dictator, under threat of invasion, allows U.N. weapons inspectors to search his country. But if you believe this dictator is not just bad but evil, you'll probably conclude that you should invade his country anyway" (34–35).

75. Pillar, *Terrorism and U.S. Foreign Policy*, 217–218.

76. Larry Witham, "Clergy Urge Restraint, Justice: President Consults Interfaith Leaders," *Washington Times*, September 21, 2001, A15.

77. Doug Hoagland, "Billy Graham Praises Bush's 'Superior' Handling of Crisis: Asks Christians to Pray that Enemies 'Change Their Ways,'" *Washington Times*, October 8, 2001, A13.

78. National Council of the Churches of Christ in the USA, "Religious Leaders Endorse Interfaith Statement Calling for a Faith-Rooted Response to Terrorism," news release, September 13, 2001, www.wcc-coe.org/wcc/behindthenews/us-us11.html.

79. Lini S. Kadaba, "Talk of Retaliation Has Some Quakers Split," *Philadelphia Inquirer*, September 24, 2001, A7.

80. Rory Carroll, "On the Brink of War: Pull Back from the Brink, Urges Pope," *Guardian* (Manchester), September 24, 2001, 7.

81. Melinda Henneberger, "The World: Politics and Piety; The Vatican on Just Wars," *New York Times*, September 30, 2001, Week in Review-3.

82. Gustav Niebuhr, "A Nation Challenged: Support from Churches; Bishops Write Bush to Back U.S. Efforts," *New York Times*, September 21, 2001, B7.

83. Cited by Domke, *God Willing?*, 62, 63.

84. Ibid., 26.

85. William Uricchio, "Television Conventions," *re:constructions*, September 16, 2001, http://web.mit.edu/cms/reconstructions/interpretations/tvconventions.html.

86. Kellner, "September 11, the Media," 147.

87. Ryan, "Framing the War."

88. Bonnie Brennan and Margaret Duffy, "'If a Problem Cannot be Solved, Enlarge It': An Ideological Critique of the 'Other' in Pearl Harbor and September 11 *New York Times* Coverage," *Journalism Studies* 4, no. 1 (2003): 3–14, p. 3. They compared the *Times*'s coverage following 9/11 with coverage of Japanese Americans in the four months following Pearl Harbor.

89. "Another Kind of War," *USA Today*, September 18, 2001, A23.

90. Criticism over the demonization of the non-Western "other" was growing long before the 9/11 attacks, especially in academic circles. A pioneering study in support of this argument was written by Edward Said, who posed dichotomous stereotypes of the "Orient" and the "Occident," both Western terms, in the nineteenth and twentieth centuries. This binary discourse positioned the Oriental as "inferior" to the Occidental in every way—from religion to behavior. Orientalism is the Westerner's *modus operandi* for maintaining power by "dominating, restructuring and having authority over the Orient." This book helped to shape the modern understanding of state terrorism in the context of the Middle East (another Western term)—long before September 11. See Edward W. Said, *Orientalism* (New York: Pantheon, 1978).

91. Kitch, "Mourning in America," 219.

92. Lule, "Myth and Terror," 284.

93. George W. Bush, "Address to a Joint Session of Congress and the America People," The White House, Washington, DC, September 20, 2001, www.whitehouse.gov/news/releases/2001/09/20010920-8.html.

94. Nacos, *Mass-Mediated Terrorism*, 16.

95. William B. Hart II and Fran Hassencahl, "Dehumanizing the Enemy in Editorial Cartoons," in Greenberg, *Communication and Terrorism*, 137–150, p. 150. Percentages are based on the total number of depictions per category (e.g., enemy as barbarian) divided by the number of dehumanizing visual metaphors used ($N = 260$).

96. Nacos, *Mass-Mediated Terrorism*, 148–149.

97. Kitch, "Mourning in America," 217–218.

98. On the stereotyping of Arabs and Muslims, see Jack G. Shaheen, *Reel Bad Arabs: How Hollywood Vilifies A People* (New York: Olive Branch, 2001); and Dana L. Cloud, "Flying while Arab: The Clash of Civilizations and the Rhetoric of Racial Profiling in the American Empire," in *Terrorism: Communication and Rhetorical Perspectives*, ed. H. Dan O'Hair, Robert L. Heath, Kevin J. Ayotte, and Gerald R. Ledlow (Cresskill, NJ: Hampton, 2008), 219–236.

99. Domke, *God Willing?*, 3.

100. Robert Jenson, "U.S. Just as Guilty of Committing Own Violent Acts," *Houston Chronicle*, September 14, 2001, A33. Les Switzer and Michael Ryan also received dozens of angry telephone calls, letters, and electronic mail messages in response to their article calling for a Christian, nonviolent response to the 9/11 attacks. They received a much smaller number of messages of support. Les Switzer and Michael Ryan, "What Christians Should Do: Reconsider Revenge," October 5, 2001, *Houston Chronicle*, A39. See also Susan Sontag, "Comment: Tuesday, and After," *The New Yorker*, September 24, 2001, 27–33, p. 32.

101. Cited by Emily Eakin, "On the Lookout for Patriotic Incorrectness," *New York Times*, November 24, 2001, A15, A17, p. A15.

102. Frank Rich, *The Greatest Story Ever Sold: The Decline and Fall of Truth from 9/11 to Katrina* (New York: Penguin, 2006), 24–25.

103. Debatin, " 'Plane Wreck with Spectators,' " 174. Maher's show was subsequently canceled.

104. For more about the stifling of public debate, see Kevin J. Ayotte and Scott D. Moore, "Terrorism, Language, and Community Dialogue," in O'Hair, Heath, Ayotte, and Ledlow, *Terrorism*, 67–92.

105. Mackubin Thomas Owens, "The Academic al-Qaida: Hypocrites Hiding Behind the Constitution," *Providence (RI) Journal*, October 26, 2001, B7.

106. Joan Konner, "Media's Patriotism Provides a Shield for Bush," *The Personal Is Political*, January 9, 2002, www.margieadam.com/action/konner.htm.

107. Kellner, "September 11, the Media," 143.

108. Nacos, *Mass-Mediated Terrorism*, 195.

109. Falwell said, "I would never blame any human being except the terrorists, and if I left that impression with gays or lesbians or anyone else, I apologize." See "Falwell Apologizes to Gays, Feminists, Lesbians," *CNN.com/US*, September 14, 2001, http://archives.cnn.com/2001/US/09/14/Falwell.apology.

110. Ibid.

111. Ibid.

112. Green, "God's Foreign Policy," 26.

113. Max Rodenbeck, "Midnight at the Oasis," *New York Times Book Review*, January 28, 2007, 12, reviewing Michael B. Oren, *Power, Faith, and Fantasy: America in the Middle East, 1776 to the Present* (New York: W. W. Norton, 2007).

114. Green, "God's Foreign Policy," 26, 27.

115. "Canada's Church Leaders Urge End to Bombing," *Christian Century*, November 7, 2001, 7–8. The Church and Nation Committee of the Church of Scotland and the General Synod of the Spanish Evangelical Church were also among non-American religious groups that condemned the bombing of Afghanistan. Duncan Hanson, "Cooling on America's War," *Christian Century*, November 21–28, 2001, 8–9.

116. "GBCS [General Board of Church and Society] Issues Statement to the Church on Terrorism," *The United Methodist* newsletter, October 19, 2001, http://64.233.169.104/search?q=cache:rV9VlbLmOVAJ:www.umph.org/images/uploads/newscope/nsoct192001.pdf+methodist+%22military+actions+will+not+end+terrorism%22&hl=en&ct=clnk&cd=6&gl=us.

117. Kevin Eckstrom, "Episcopalians Say U.S. 'Need Not Be at War,'" *beliefnet*, undated, www.beliefnet.com/story/91/story_9120.html. The council also warned against policies that could erode civil liberties by expanding government's surveillance authority.

118. James M. Wall, "Impressions: Revenge or Justice?" *Christian Century*, November 21–28, 2001, 53.

119. Sam Keen, "The New Face of the Enemy," in *From the Ashes: A Spiritual Response to the Attack on America*, ed. *beliefnet* editors (Emmaus, PA.: Rodale, 2001): 122–126, p. 125.

120. Nacos, *Mass-Mediated Terrorism*, 146.

121. Murray Edelman, "Contestable Categories and Public Opinion," *Political Communication* 10, no. 3 (1993): 231–242, p. 239.

CHAPTER 9

Militarism, Media, and Religion: From Afghanistan to Iraq

The seeds for an invasion of Iraq were sown on January 19, 2001, when George W. Bush was inaugurated as the 43rd president of the United States. Bush, who harbored ambitions of overthrowing Saddam Hussein from the beginning of his presidency, was supported by millions of Americans, who at the time also supported military intervention in the Middle East. Federal agencies—including the Pentagon, the White House, and the Department of State—were stocked with conservatives who were prepared to join Bush in pressing a war agenda should the opportunity arise.

The neoconservatives certainly were ready to roll. Men and women such as William Kristol and Ann Coulter believed passionately that the United States should use its military power to impose neoconservative values throughout the world. "An American empire is a perfectly plausible scenario for neoconservatives," Richard Nixon adviser John W. Dean has said. "[C]ontainment is a policy they believe is outmoded."[1] The prospect of even an endless war to achieve noble objectives was not daunting to neoconservatives who served in the Bush administration.[2] Bush himself said during a speech to the American Enterprise Institute, "[T]he world has a clear interest in the spread of democratic values" and a "new regime in Iraq would serve as a dramatic and inspiring example of freedom for other nations in the region."[3]

Traditionalist conservatives were divided over the Iraq war issue. Some harkened back to forbearers such as Barry Goldwater and Ronald Reagan in favoring limited government, balanced budgets, and wars only to protect America's strategic interests. They opposed the war in Iraq because they thought it would be too expensive and would not serve America's strategic interests. Others supported an invasion because they felt the United States needed to secure Iraq's vast oil reserves. Oil, long a symbol of U.S. power in the world, "has been its fuel for military might, twentieth-century manufacturing supremacy, and the latter-day SUV gas-hog culture," as political commentator Kevin Phillips put it. "Oil abundance has always been part of what America fights *for*, as well as *with*" (italics in the original).[4] Iraq's oil reserve, estimated at approximately 400 billion barrels, seemed well worth the fight.

Still other traditionalist conservatives supported the invasion because they believed it would be "an easy exercise in regime change, a swift surgical procedure, after which the Iraqis would be left to build their own democracy by spontaneous civic combustion."[5] Vice President Dick Cheney and other neoconservatives, who asserted that the Iraqi people would greet American warriors as liberators when they deposed Saddam Hussein (1937–2006), continually encouraged this naïve view.[6]

Many of Bush's Christian conservative supporters, particularly Protestant evangelical fundamentalists, pounded the war drums frantically for a variety of reasons. Some were convinced that apocalyptic images they interpreted in various biblical passages (especially in Daniel and Revelation) were about to be fulfilled—that "true" Christians would, in a dazzling, wondrous moment, join Christ in Heaven, that the antichrist would rule for seven years, and that the armies of Jesus would defeat the antichrist in a glorious battle that would usher in a millennium of prosperity and peace.[7]

They were perfectly prepared to support wars in the Middle East that would help the children of Israel drive non-Jews from the land, as the Old Testament had once commanded, and ensure the existence of a Jewish state between the Jordan River and the Mediterranean Sea.[8] They saw these actions as critical to the fulfillment of end-times prophecy.[9] "Others were influenced by reports that Saddam Hussein was rebuilding the ancient city of Babylon, where, they believed, the Antichrist would establish his reign."[10]

Millions of Christians who did not necessarily give credence to these apocalyptic pronouncements also supported the war, partly because tyranny to them was unacceptable, partly because it was easy for them to buy the argument that a war would make the United States safer, and partly because they viewed an invasion as part of a holy war that Christians needed to win.

Bush may or may not have believed in end-times prophecy, but as we have seen he was most assuredly a political poster child for evangelical fundamentalist Christianity. As journalist James O. Goldsborough put it, "Unlike most presidents, Bush wears his religion on his sleeve. He has said that God wanted him to be president, that only Christians go to heaven, that creationism as well as evolution should be taught to children, that Jesus is his favorite philosopher."[11] The president and his supporters were psychologically prepared in 2001 for war. They needed only an excuse, which they got on 9/11.

This chapter, which focuses on the run-up to the war in Iraq, is divided into four sections. Section 1 describes the faltering political and religious support for war. Section 2 examines the efforts of war proponents, supported and even aided by the mass media, to continue using the same techniques—defining the response to 9/11 in oppositional binary terms, marginalizing dissent, and demanding immediate action—they refined in building support for the war in Afghanistan. Section 3 examines two critical elements used to justify the Iraq war frame in seeking (a) to sell the war to the international community and (b) to manufacture the case that Iraq was an immediate threat to the United States. Section 4 offers a critique of religious and especially media leadership in aping the conservative coalition's rationale for justifying military intervention in Iraq. Section 5 describes some of the enduring tensions created by the war in Iraq within the Christian conservative community and the conservative coalition.

FALTERING POLITICAL AND RELIGIOUS SUPPORT

The Bush administration tried very hard during the 17 months following the invasion of Afghanistan—and particularly during the period February 21–March 20, 2003—to convince Americans and the international community of the righteousness of an invasion of Iraq. However, the conservative coalition of neoconservatives, traditionalist conservatives, and Christian conservatives, which was so successful in leading the country to war in Afghanistan, began to fragment in the run-up to the new war.

Circumstances during the days leading to the Iraq invasion were quite different from those leading to the war in Afghanistan. The passions aroused by the 9/11 attacks were cooling, American costs and casualties were mounting, innocent people were dying in the war in

Afghanistan, Osama bin Laden was still free, Saddam Hussein was permitting UN inspectors to search Iraq for weapons, and increasing numbers of Americans were questioning the use of military force in the war against terrorism.[12]

Is a War of Choice Just?

Religious support faltered in part because many mainstream Christians—conservative, moderate, and progressive—were uncomfortable with a war of choice, or what Bush and the news media called a "preemptive" war—one in which the United States, acting in what it claimed was self-defense, would respond militarily to a proven threat. The "threat" in this case, of course, was "weapons of mass destruction" that the Bush administration claimed Saddam Hussein had stockpiled in Iraq.[13]

Some political and religious leaders in the post-9/11 era revived the ancient Christian criteria for judging whether a pending war is just. The criteria have been debated and articulated in all mainstream faith traditions, including Judaism and Islam. The Christian position begins essentially with Augustine (354–430) and his reflections in *The City of God*—as reworked, refined, and expanded by subsequent generations. Proponents of the just-war position claim a middle ground between the extremes in ancient and modern perspectives on war. The crusader feels free to launch war against anyone at any time, while the pacifist rejects all war.

Most Christian scholars today accept six or seven criteria—one might view them as tests—*all* of which should be met before "justifiable coercion" is acceptable. As Christian ethicist Joseph L. Allen put it in summarizing these criteria, *how* one prepares for war must be conditioned by "respect for the worth of those to be coerced, for their victims, and for others who may be affected."[14]

- War can be waged only with "just cause," which is normally (a) to protect those who have been attacked without cause, (b) to restore rights taken away without cause, and (c) to defend or reestablish a just political order overturned without cause. Just cause does not take sides in a dispute, but it does judge the relative merits of one side over another—especially when one side attacks another side without just cause. Self-defense against an armed attack is considered a just cause.
- A "legitimate authority" at the "highest level" must make the decision to go to war. The decision makers must justify their reasons for going to

war, they are held accountable for this decision, and it must be seen to be the right decision for the countries involved and for the rest of the world.

- All peaceful alternatives to war must be tried before going war. Every imaginable strategy must be pursued in negotiating a peaceful end to conflict. War is the last resort in a just-war scenario.

- A country should make a formal declaration of war. This is not on every list of just-war criteria, but it has merit because the rationale for war and the goals to be pursued in war are made known to all the players (both one's own citizens and the enemy's citizens). It can be seen as an extension of the war-as-last-resort criterion, because it gives the enemy one last chance to come to terms before war actually begins.

- War is not justified if the consequences of going to war produce more harm than good—either for the country initiating the war or for the country being attacked. Nations must not use more force, for example, than is necessary to meet a military objective. Soldiers must discriminate between combatants and noncombatants. Civilians are not permissible targets. Civilian deaths may be justified only if they occur during an attack against a military target, but every effort must be made to avoid killing and injuring them. The "proportionality" principle (meaning the deaths, injuries, and property damages in the two countries are roughly equal) is a necessary moral exercise even though it is impossible for any country to calculate adequately the costs of going to war.

- War must have a reasonable chance of success in terms of the goals that have been outlined. Decision makers must consider whether the goals outlined can actually be attained and whether the consequences of pursuing these goals—both direct (as in soldiers killed or injured) and indirect (as in civilians killed or injured)—prohibit a reasonable chance of success.

- War can be justified only "as a means to peace," so the country seeking a just war must reveal its intentions to all concerned before embarking on war. No war can be waged out of hatred or a desire for revenge. The peace following the war must be preferable to that which might have prevailed had the war not occurred.

The just-war ethic was revived in the aftermath of 9/11 in political, legal, and religious rhetoric that centered on the concept of evil and the pervasiveness of sin in the world. Even though just-war principles do not justify preventive wars, the media's response immediately following the attacks reflected the overwhelming majority of public opinion: America's attack against Afghanistan constituted a just war because Americans believed Afghanistan was an obvious threat. Osama bin Laden, who planned the 9/11 attacks and could strike again, lived there and the Taliban government protected him.[15]

Questioning the War's Morality

The Bush administration, however, found itself preparing to launch a war in Iraq in the face of opposition from many religious leaders who publicly questioned the war's morality. They refused to endorse a new war, even though many members of their congregations did, because they felt there was no real evidence that Iraq was a threat—that Saddam Hussein had any intention or capability of attacking the United States or its allies.

The determination to speak out against the invasion is evident in published letters and resolutions from various mainstream Christian agencies, including Lutheran, United Church of Christ, and other denominations affiliated to the National Council of Churches (NCC). As NCC director Bob Edgar said, "While we may have been silent then [before the war in Afghanistan], we certainly don't think the way to get rid of terrorism is to bomb every government. Even bad governments."[16] The United States Conference of Catholic Bishops sent to Bush on September 13, 2002, a letter stating, "We respectfully urge you to step back from the brink of war and help lead the world to act together to fashion an effective global response to Iraq's threats that conforms with traditional moral limits on the use of military force."[17]

Pentecostal and Charismatic Christian leaders signed an open letter to President Bush in which they argued the following:

> The Spirit of God is what enlivens our faith, transforms our mentalities, enables, empowers and equips us to live our lives out of a new set of realities. Indeed, we no longer give into fear, but rather, we are enabled to love unconditionally, empowered to be agents of change, and equipped to exercise self-restraint, particularly in the use of force or violence of any means to bring about the peace and justice, which the world seeks .... We humbly propose American Christians, the President included, radically rethink the rules and tools of engagement with powers of darkness, whether they are individual, societal or military weapons of mass destruction. In essence, we challenge them to be filled with the Spirit of God.[18]

Bush's own denomination opposed the war, as this excerpt from the statement by General Secretary Jim Winkler of the United Methodist Church General Board of Church and Society suggests:

> United Methodists have a particular duty to speak out against an unprovoked attack. President Bush and Vice-President Cheney are members

of our denomination. Our silence now could be interpreted as tacit approval of war. Christ came to break old cycles of revenge and violence. Too often, we have said we worship and follow Jesus but have failed to change our ways. Jesus proved on the cross the failure of state-sponsored revenge. It is inconceivable that Jesus Christ, our Lord and Savior and the Prince of Peace, would support this proposed attack.[19]

Prominent traditionalist conservatives—such as Robert Novak, Patrick J. Buchanan, George F. Will, Eric Margolis, Llewellyn Rockwell, Samuel Francis, and others—also opposed the invasion of Iraq. "We charge that a cabal of polemicists and public officials [primarily neoconservatives] seek to ensnare our country in a series of wars that are not in America's interests," Buchanan wrote. "We charge that they have alienated friends and allies all over the Islamic and Western world through their arrogance, hubris, and bellicosity."[20] Margolis said, "Many Americans simply don't understand their leadership is about to plunge the nation into an open-ended, dangerous colonial war. All the propaganda about democracy, human rights and regional stability is the same kind of double-talk used by the 19th century British and French imperialists who claimed they were grabbing Africa and Asia to bring the benefits of Christian civilization to the heathens."[21]

Traditionalist conservatives warned of the enormous growth of presidential power that had been championed, as we noted in Chapter 3, by the neoconservatives during George W. Bush's administration. The neoconservatives were "relatively few in number," but as David Frum, a writer for the *National Review*, commented, "They aspire to reinvent conservative ideology: to junk the 50-year-old conservative commitment to defend American interests and values throughout the world … in favor of a fearful policy of ignoring threats and appeasing enemies."[22]

Several Jewish groups—a majority of the American Jewish population supported a war against Iraq—were also concerned that these conservative critiques would generate an antisemitic backlash. They were particularly incensed by a March 2003 article by Buchanan that claimed Jewish neoconservatives in the Bush administration were driving the march toward another war in Iraq.[23]

REPRISING A SUCCESSFUL CAMPAIGN FOR WAR

Those who demanded war against Iraq were heartened by the success they enjoyed in generating support for military intervention in

Afghanistan, an effort that created an environment in which Americans felt free to invade sovereign nations that *might* be threats or that *might* harbor individuals who could be terrorists.

The Bush administration—with the witting or unwitting collaboration of the mass media—once again employed a discourse of polar opposites to market the use of military violence in the buildup to war in Iraq.[24] The war advocates were able to build a solid new frame on the old foundation. They had already managed (a) to get Americans to accept the worst possible definition of terrorist, (b) to find effective ways to marginalize dissent, (c) to put groups into "us" versus "them" categories that made the sides clear, and (d) to make the public feel compelled to rush to war.

The administration's war agenda is reflected in our study of editorials published in the 10 largest newspapers in America between February 21 and March 20, 2003—27 days before the invasion of Iraq. The newspapers were the *Wall Street Journal*, *USA Today*, the *New York Times*, the *Los Angeles Times*, the *Washington Post*, the *New York Daily News*, the *Chicago Tribune*, *Newsday*, the *Houston Chronicle*, and the *Dallas Morning News*.[25]

Two coders searched for editorials that devoted at least two sentences to a pending invasion of Iraq. Ninety-one editorials related to the invasion, compared to the 103 editorials analyzed in Michael Ryan's study of the 27 days preceding the war in Afghanistan.[26] Coders placed each sentence into one of several categories, including position on war, reasons for going to war, views of war critics, and religious sentiments. The intercoder reliability was 91.3 percent. The analysis concluded that seven newspapers were pro-war and three were neutral. No newspaper in this study opposed a new war in Iraq.

Limiting the Options

The media in our analysis generally supported the conservative coalition view that there were only two options regarding Iraq, "use military force" or "do nothing." A few editorial writers suggested that the embargo against Iraq, weapons inspections, and diplomatic efforts were working, but most agreed with the president that "doing nothing" (defined as "anything short of invasion") was not an option. In this binary world, war was the only choice.

Seventy-nine editorials (and all 10 newspapers) simply assumed Iraq would be invaded and that no one could stop the pending war.

Forty-eight of 68 editorials published in the seven pro-war newspapers we studied called for military intervention. The seven were the *Wall Street Journal*, *Newsday*, the *Dallas Morning News*, *USA Today*, the *New York Daily News*, the *Chicago Tribune*, and the *Washington Post*.[27]

While no newspaper reflected an anti-war agenda, the *New York Times*, the *Los Angeles Times*, and the *Houston Chronicle* reflected a neutral agenda. None of the 23 editorials commenting on a potential war in Iraq joined the clamor for immediate war. All said that weapons inspectors and/or diplomats should be given more time to resolve the impasse.

All 10 newspapers failed to question whether the do nothing or use military force options were the only two available. They did not really consider other options, and they failed for the most part to challenge the assertion that those who were not "with us" were "with the terrorists." This position mirrored the Christian conservative war agenda. As religion historian Martin E. Marty said, "[T]he demonization of the enemy—an 'us and them' mentality—can inhibit self-examination and repentant action, critical components of any faith."[28]

The conservative coalition's main mouthpiece, Fox News, was decidedly pro-war and did not apologize for abandoning any semblance of an objective approach in its news reports. Its newscasts—like the newscasts of ABC, CBS, and NBC, as one critic said—were "a parade ground for military men—all well-groomed white males—saluting the ethic that war is rational, that bombing and shooting is the way to win peace and, for sure, that their uniformed pals in Iraq are there to free people, not slaughter them."[29]

A few broadcast and print journalists did challenge some of the administration's "evidence" that Saddam Hussein was an immediate threat, and our study of newspaper editorials shows that the three neutral newspapers—the *New York Times*, the *Houston Chronicle*, and the *Los Angeles Times*—seemed to share the doubts of many Americans about a war against Iraq. But they, too, supported the use force or do nothing view by failing to challenge it seriously and by publishing stories suggesting that force was indeed required. The *New York Times*, for example, supported the war agenda in its news columns during the period of our study by producing incomplete news reports, by giving poor play to stories that challenged a war agenda, and by relying primarily on sources who were inclined toward war or who had a personal stake in war.

Marginalizing Dissent

Newspaper editorials and news reports marginalized religious leaders and others who wanted to avoid war by ignoring or attacking them. None of the editorials mentioned the calls by the major Protestant denominations or by Pope John Paul II (1920–2005) for a peaceful solution. The divisions within some denominations, however, were addressed in a few news reports in these and other newspapers.[30] Articles criticizing the buildup to war were scattered across the news columns of American newspapers, but they were rare. Many more editorials and news reports attacked anti-war groups or reported attacks by others.[31]

Our study of newspaper editorials in the weeks preceding the invasion of Iraq showed that the pro-war newspapers launched far more attacks against the war's critics than did the neutral newspapers. We documented 111 editorial attacks in the pro-war press compared to 10 editorial attacks in the neutral press. France, attacked in 45 editorials, was the prime target, followed by Russia with 19, Germany with 13, and the United Nations with 8. Weapons inspectors were criticized in eight editorials.[32]

The *New York Daily News* managed to criticize just about everyone when it commented on a May 7, 2003, report by Hans Blix, the chief UN weapons inspector: "France and the other eager appeasers should stop their excuse making and do what comes naturally to them: retreat. Unfortunately, they are being handed even more excuses, courtesy of Hans Blix. The chief UN arms inspector . . . is wrapping everything in such carefully parsed language, he's playing right into the hands of the cave-in crowd."[33] The *Wall Street Journal*, whose editorials in support of the war were particularly virulent, published a harsh editorial about then-Senate Minority Leader Tom Daschle, whom the *Journal* linked to the despised French. The editorial concluded, "The next time Mr. Daschle says he wants to 'work with the President,' at least we'll know which country's President he's referring to."[34]

Six editorials (five in pro-war newspapers and one in a neutral newspaper) attacked critics because they allegedly did not suggest alternatives to war. *USA Today* observed, for example, that the "allies so quick to criticize the administration for rushing to combat aren't advancing workable substitutes that might avoid conflict, such as setting clear actions Iraq must complete under tight deadlines."[35]

The seven pro-war newspapers typically noted that critics had the right to protest, but they clearly wanted to intimidate and silence the protesters—and even those who simply would not endorse a war—often by casting them as "friends" or "dupes" of terrorists. The *New York Daily News* said that opponents of the war were "determinedly blind to the facts" or were "sadly ignorant of them." It called war opponents "peaceniks" and "peacemongers."[36] Neoconservative Max Boot said in *Newsday* that war protesters are "making war more—not less—likely."[37]

Many opinion writers followed the lead of President Bush, who said the United Nations would be "irrelevant" if it did not support the march to war. The *New York Daily News* said during one attack that "the dumb-and-dumber crowd, led by France and Germany, want to give Saddam yet more time. They floated a lily-livered proposal that would extend the futile inspections for at least another five more months."[38]

The mainstream media did not always use a heavy-handed strategy. Some of the criticism was more subtle. The *Dallas Morning News*, for instance, noted that Mexico, a member of the UN Security Council at the time, can "decide for itself whether to authorize war." However, "Having enlisted to help maintain the world's security, Mexico should demonstrate it takes that responsibility seriously by supporting the United States. Having thrust itself onto the world stage, it should act with all the courage, wisdom and foresight that its role requires." Mexico would not be acting with "courage, wisdom, and foresight," presumably, were it to vote against invading Iraq.[39]

Alternatives were advanced in 13 editorials published by the neutral newspapers and in one editorial published by a pro-war newspaper. Some of the alternatives were to continue and perhaps to strengthen the blockade against Iraq, to give UN inspectors more time to find weapons of mass destruction, and to work more aggressively to find a diplomatic solution. Some editorial pages—such as those of the *New York Times*, the *Houston Chronicle*, and the *Los Angeles Times*—expressed skepticism about the administration's rush to war in the weeks before the invasion.

Some journalists using an objective approach provided credible coverage of anti-war perspectives. Warren Strobel, Jonathan Landay, and John Walcott of Knight Ridder, for example, quoted several knowledgeable sources who challenged the administration's claim that Iraq had purchased special aluminum tubes for centrifuges to enrich uranium. Some newspapers published stories—such as Kim Campbell's in the *Christian Science Monitor*, Laurie Goodstein's in the *New York Times*, and David Gibson's in the *Sunday Star-Ledger* of Newark—about religious opposition or indifference to the potential war.

Journalists could have given more space to anti-war statements by religious agencies. They could have played more prominently the views of those who suggested alternatives to war—such as giving aggressive diplomacy and weapons inspections more time, and tightening the embargo that would have made it impossible for Hussein to ship or to use unconventional weapons even if he had them. "Administration assertions were on the front page" of the *Washington Post*, says Pentagon reporter Thomas Ricks. "Things that challenged the administration were on A18 on Sunday or A24 on Monday."[40]

One of the ironies in an era crammed with ironies is that Saddam Hussein was the truth-teller (he did not have weapons of mass destruction, and he had no part in the 9/11 attacks) and that those who were attacked for proposing that the United States do nothing were in fact suggesting valid alternatives. Hussein had already dismantled his weapons program, and he did not have weapons of mass destruction, a fact that he repeated constantly and that was verified by repeated UN inspections. The problem for Hussein was that he could not prove a negative proposition—just as a defendant at trial cannot, and is not required to, prove innocence.

Defining the Sides

The media were once again portraying the United States and its allies (defined as anyone who did not question the rush to war) as a force for good against everyone else. Neil Cavuto, a Fox News anchor, opined at one point that there is nothing wrong with taking sides during war.[41] Fox anchors and reporters frequently reinforced the "us versus them" dichotomy when referring to coalition forces as "we," "us," and "our."[42]

The seven pro-war newspapers, reflecting the language of evangelical Christians in the Bush administration, used the word "evil" liberally to reinforce the us versus them dichotomy. "Evangelicals believe that, in fact, evil does come from the depravity of the human heart, and there are evil people, and Saddam Hussein is one," as Richard Cizik of the National Association of Evangelicals put it. "And so the language which Bush has used resonates in the heart and the minds of the American evangelical."[43]

Editorials and commentaries also used emotion-charged words such as outlaw and madman, although the attacks did not reach the emotional level of those launched against Osama bin Laden during the buildup to the war in Afghanistan. Still, they defined Hussein as evil and reinforced the view that the only option was to rid the world of the evil. Writers pointed to a rogue's gallery of tyrants to link Saddam Hussein to evil. They included Idi Amin of Uganda, Alfredo Stroessner of Paraguay, Jean-Claude Duvalier of Haiti, and the alleged terrorist Khalid Sheikh Mohammed.

Neutral newspaper editorials cited in our study typically referred to Hussein without identification or as a dictator or leader, but he was also called a tyrant (3 times), murderer (2 times), and global menace, despot, and repressive (1 each). Hussein was mentioned by pro-war newspapers without identification or as a dictator (21 times); a murderer and tyrant (6 each); brutal and mad (4 each); outlaw, butcher, sadistic, and cheat (3 each); and repressive, global menace, and despot (2 each). He was also called a monster, bully, thug, megalomaniacal, torturer, aggressive, psychotic, liar, cruel, terror-monger, beastly, deceptive, dirty, and dastardly (1 each).

The media needed non-American heroes (representing *us*) to vanquish the evil villain, and they embraced Tony Blair as one of us by portraying him as a hero. Blair, like other members of the coalition of the willing (us), was lauded for standing his ground in the face of considerable political opposition from other Europeans (them).

The media also needed an American hero to stand against the evil forces. They once again focused on President Bush. Photographs published in news magazines before the invasion of Iraq supported the magazines' dominant narrative, which endorsed the administration's drive to war. Photographs of President Bush portrayed a strong, confident leader, whereas stereotypical images were used to portray the enemy as weak. Photographs of troops and military hardware created an image of a determined, powerful nation ready for war. Missing were photographs that portrayed the potential economic and human costs of war.[44]

Bush was a tarnished hero, however, because his efforts to market the war to a global audience fell short. Bush was cited in 65 editorials in our study of the 10 largest newspapers, but the editorials were not altogether positive. Prior to the war in Afghanistan, negative attributes were virtually never ascribed to the president. Thirty-one editorials published in the pro-war newspapers now said he was right about some actions, but they sometimes criticized him in the same editorials.

Only two of the neutral newspapers said he was right about the pending war. The pro-war newspapers described Bush as resolute and persuasive (2 each), and as wise, gracious, respectful, straightforward, and strong (1 each). None of the neutral newspapers used such terms.

Negative descriptors of Bush were far more common in March 2003, when Bush was trying, and largely failing, to rally international support and to secure a new UN resolution. Bush was described in these editorials as confused, unfocused, cavalier, high-handed, disingenuous, reckless, wrongheaded, inflexible, and too hasty. The main substantive concerns were that Bush's diplomatic efforts were clumsy and ineffective (14 times), that he did not explain clearly the costs and risks of war (13 times), that he did not make the reasons for war clear (9 times), that he dismissed critics' concerns about the war (8 times), and that he alienated allies (6 times). This excerpt from the *Los Angeles Times* is typical: "But Bush and his advisors also bear much responsibility for the impasse that threatens to wreck the system of collective security that emerged out of World War II. Bush's disregard for international treaties and his heavy-handed diplomacy have infuriated America's allies, turning friends into foes."[45]

Pro-war newspapers in our study were willing to ignore Bush's mistakes and inconsistencies because of larger concerns. *Newsday*, for example, wrote, "Whatever diplomatic mistakes and political missteps he made in getting there, Bush has taken a stand on Iraq from which he cannot back off without damaging his office and the credibility of the nation itself."[46]

Editorial writers cited 69 sources, other than Bush, usually only one time, and most were government or military officials in the United States, Europe, or the Middle East. Among those most frequently mentioned were chief UN weapons inspector Hans Blix (26 times), British Prime Minister Tony Blair (23 times), Secretary of State Colin Powell (17 times), and French President Jacques Chirac (13 times). Blix and Chirac typically were criticized or ridiculed, while Blair and Powell were not.

Even when they cited the same sources, pro-war and neutral newspapers often gave different interpretations to what the sources said. The *Wall Street Journal* said Vice President Cheney was right to reject any attempt to give Hussein more time to disarm,[47] while the *New York Times* chided Cheney for asserting there was nothing Hussein could do short of resigning.[48]

Demanding Immediate Action

Pro-war newspapers accepted the war-advocates' view that urgent action was required—even after March 7, 2003, when Hans Blix reported increased cooperation from Saddam Hussein. Most agreed with *USA Today* that "pretending that more time would prompt Saddam's cooperation or conjure up a strong-willed international community ignores 12 years of history. It also perpetuates the kind of wishful thinking that got the world where it now stands."[49]

Editorials in the pro-war newspapers frequently posed the question, repeated incessantly by Bush and conservative activists: How much time does this evil man need? Their frustration was captured in the president's statement, "[H]ow much time do we need to see clearly he's not disarming? As I said, this looks like a rerun of a bad movie and I'm not interested in watching it."[50] Nobody in the media seemed to notice that Hussein was complying with UN directives or that Bush kept raising the bar for peace—that Hussein must allow weapons inspectors, that he must list his weapons and "be cooperative," and finally that Hussein and his sons must leave Iraq.

Eight editorials in the pro-war newspapers counseled patience in the march to war, but only if chances were good for getting international support. According to these writers, however, they were not. The pro-war newspapers generally opposed any delay, and 26 editorials said military action was urgent.[51] The *Wall Street Journal*, for example, noted, "Every day of delay also gives [Hussein], or al Qaeda, more time to plant or mobilize agents to attack the U.S. homeland.... Another [consequence of delay] is the lesson to other thugs, such as North Korea's Kim Jong II, that they can also use the U.N. to stymie and wait out American resolve."[52]

JUSTIFYING THE WAR FRAME

War proponents, both in and out of government, added two additional elements in making the case for invading Iraq, elements that were not deemed necessary in making the case for invading Afghanistan. First, they had to show that an invasion of Iraq could be justified under international law and the principles of a just war as enshrined in Christian tradition. Second, they had to show that Iraq was an imminent threat to the United States.

War advocates, who recognized the power of fear and religion as tools for achieving political objectives in the buildup to the invasion of Afghanistan, ratcheted up the volume of this rhetoric as they encountered increasing difficulty in selling the pending war in Iraq to Americans and to the international community. Neoconservatives assumed "only the looming threat of a common enemy can unite a people into a cohesive social order,"[53] and the appeal to fear was effective when it was coupled with "useful action for reducing or eliminating the threat."[54]

Fear was the overarching element of the Bush administration's war frame.[55] The president set the tone with such statements as this one:

> Over the years, Iraq has provided a safe haven to terrorists such as Abu Nidal, whose terror organisation carried out more than ninety terrorist attacks in twenty countries that killed or injured nearly 900 people, including 12 Americans. Iraq could decide on any given day to provide a biological or chemical weapon to a terrorist group or individual terrorists. Alliances with terrorists could allow the Iraqi regime to attack America without leaving any fingerprints.[56]

The administration, the media, and other war advocates did not permit the truth to deter them from making these kinds of statements. They won the rhetorical war against those who tried to tell the public at the time that Hussein feared and despised al-Qaida and would have nothing to do with Osama bin Laden. The accuracy of their assertions was affirmed years later by the Pentagon in the study "Saddam and Terrorism: Emerging Insights from Captured Iraqi Documents."[57]

Selling War to the International Community

The Bush administration and its supporters faced a huge problem in selling their war to the international community. Bush senior, an Episcopalian, did not persuade mainstream Christian leaders that just-war principles could be used to justify the 1991 Gulf War,[58] and the argument had even less credence when his son tried to use what was called the Bush Doctrine to justify the invasion of Iraq. The Bush Doctrine "asserts that the United States must remain number one in global power, so strong that no one else would even try to match us." Among the weapons in Bush's so-called doctrine was the "preemptive war," which journalist Trudy Rubin described as "a radical doctrine that reshapes America's role in the world."[59]

Justifying an Invasion

War proponents searched almost desperately for evidence of a future threat from Iraq before finally settling on weapons of mass destruction—the one threat that would frighten most Americans. It was cited as the primary reason for war in 63 editorials published by the 10 metropolitan newspapers in our study. Self-defense was cited as the reason in another eight editorials. No editorial in any newspaper questioned whether Hussein had weapons of mass destruction—all assumed he did—and none questioned how those weapons could be used against the United States.

Critics of the proposed war at the time could not prove the Bush administration had no real evidence to support its contentions that Hussein had weapons of mass destruction or a program to develop them. The war proponents knew the critics could not prove these negatives. Bush and his conservative supporters manufactured evidence "proving" Hussein had weapons of mass destruction. They did not feel the need to prove beyond reasonable doubt that Hussein had the weapons they assumed he did.

The primary mantra of the war proponents—that Saddam was evil and America must bring "freedom" to Iraq—was dutifully communicated in a compliant media without serious challenge and without questioning how these claims could be harmonized with Christian just-war theory. The top four reasons for invading Iraq in our study of editorials in 10 metropolitan newspapers were to change the regime (21 times), to bring freedom to the Iraqis (11 times), to make the world safer (10 times), and to defend America (8 times).

Media scholars David Domke, Kevin Coe, and Robert Tynes found editorials in newspapers they studied frequently mentioned freedom and liberty after 9/11 to justify military intervention. "[T]he president and respective newspaper editorials were particularly likely to emphasize freedom and liberty, both generally and as universal norms specifically, in the period immediately surrounding military action in Iraq in 2003."[60] During the prelude to war, 35 percent of the editorials contained the words freedom or liberty, and 23 percent claimed these words represented universal norms.

The editorials we examined did address some of the potential hazards of an invasion. The most frequently mentioned was a rift among allies (10 times) followed by strengthen terrorism, antagonize moderate or Islamic states, and create a financial burden (6 each), and hurt the U.S. reputation (5 times). Only five editorials cautioned that soldiers and civilians might die. None judged these hazards serious enough to stop the invasion.

War proponents and the media also were unaware of, or at least did not cover, the impact a preemptive strike by an overwhelmingly powerful Christian state driven by a conservative Christian agenda might have on a weakened Muslim state. The *Los Angeles Times* had one of the few editorials that touched on the problem:

> Opposition to immediate war cuts across religious lines, but it is especially strong among Muslims, some of whom see an attack on Iraq as a renewal of the Christian crusades against Islam. Throughout the Middle East, a postwar occupation of Iraq would become part of the myth of an American empire come to wreak havoc on the Muslims. This refueled resentment would not make the world safer. It would not make the streets at home safer.[61]

A Legal Rationale for War

Another problem for the war advocates was finding a *legal* justification for war. Most war advocates argued initially that international support, particularly UN support, was critical and that the United States should seek an additional resolution, one that unequivocally endorsed an invasion. But as the war approached and it became clear that no new resolution would be forthcoming, most decided that a new UN resolution was not needed because prior UN resolutions gave the United States all the legal authority it needed to invade a sovereign nation.

Many war proponents cited Resolution 1441 as evidence that an invasion was legal. Resolution 1441, passed in November 2002, called for Hussein to disarm or face unspecified consequences. For decades the pro-war lobby had opposed the United Nations and argued that the United States should abandon that organization. Now some found themselves arguing that a UN resolution gave the United States the authority to invade Iraq. "The very organization that Bush had routinely disparaged as worthless now took on holy status. Saddam's sin of sins was his violation of UN resolutions."[62]

No editorial in the three neutral newspapers specifically addressed the legal rationale for war. Eleven of these editorials, however, called for international support for any preemptive strike against a sovereign nation, and four editorials called for UN support. The legal rationale was important for the seven pro-war newspapers, particularly when war seemed imminent. Four editorials argued that the treaty ending the Gulf War in 1991 was sufficient legal justification, and 14 argued that prior UN resolutions, particularly 1441, were sufficient.

The Bush administration did try to address the question about whether a preemptive strike would meet the standards of a just war. Heavy hitters—such as Thomas M. Nichols of the U.S. Naval War College and Robert P. George, professor of jurisprudence at Princeton—said the invasion would be just because, well, Hussein was no good and could be stopped no other way.[63] Jay Sekulow, chief counsel for the American Center for Law & Justice, a conservative public interest law firm founded by Pat Robertson, urged Americans to "stand by" the president: "At a time when we are engaged in a global war against terrorism, we cannot stand by and watch Iraq and Saddam Hussein continue to ignore U.N. resolutions. We encourage President Bush to take whatever action is necessary to protect the United States."[64] Richard Land of the Southern Baptist Ethics & Religious Liberty Commission also claimed Hussein was developing weapons of mass destruction as fast as he could, had broken conditions of the cease-fire following the Gulf War, and had "a direct line" to the 9/11 terrorists.[65]

Conservative Christian leader Henry Blackaby argued "the first six verses of Romans 13 give leaders the authority to invoke war and also to rescue oppressed people from evil tyrants."[66] Charles Colson, former chief counsel to President Richard Nixon and now a Christian activist in the Prison Fellowship ministry, asserted that war could even be charitable. "Out of love of neighbor, then," he said, "Christians can and should support a pre-emptive strike, if ordered by the appropriate magistrate to prevent an imminent attack."[67]

Leaders of the Southern Baptist Convention actually told Bush that his "stated policies concerning Saddam Hussein ... are prudent and fall well within the time-honored criteria of the just war theory as developed by Christian theologians in the late fourth and fifth centuries A.D."[68] None of the proponents for war, of course, explored the just-war principles enshrined in Christian tradition. If a real effort had been made to do this, they would have discovered that these principles preclude preventive wars.

Manufacturing the Case for War

Some critics have charged that the mass media were little more than extensions of the Bush administration's war propaganda machine.[69]

Journalists did not do a good job by the standards outlined in Chapter 2, but they were dealing with an administration whose public dishonesty was perhaps unprecedented.

Using Lies and Deceit

That dishonesty is clear from a report in 2004 by the Carnegie Endowment for International Peace, which documented a long list of the lies and misstatements the Bush administration told about the war in Iraq.[70] The report showed the administration lied about Iraq's weapons of mass destruction, about its missile program, about its contact with terrorists, and about UN inspectors' findings. "In the end," as John W. Dean noted, "even greater deceptions were employed to get Congress to provide legal authority for war with Iraq."[71]

Several celebrated instances of dishonesty were played prominently in the mass media during the months leading up to the Iraq invasion—most of which were not exposed as false at the time. We summarize two of those instances here:

- First, the administration's most respected member, former Secretary of State Colin Powell, was told to go to the United Nations to persuade delegates to approve a resolution authorizing military action against Iraq. In his speech on February 5, 2003, Powell promised "to share with you what the United States knows about Iraq's weapons of mass destruction as well as Iraq's involvement in terrorism . . . ." Powell implied that he could not discuss all of the evidence the United States had, but he would reveal "Saddam Hussein and his regime are concealing their efforts to produce more weapons of mass destruction." He said,

We know that Saddam's son, Qusay, ordered the removal of all prohibited weapons from Saddam's numerous palace complexes. We know that Iraqi government officials, members of the ruling Baath Party and scientists have hidden prohibited items in their homes. Other key files from military and scientific establishments have been placed in cars that are being driven around the countryside by Iraqi intelligence agents to avoid detection.[72]

Powell presented photographs purporting to show weapons of mass destruction components being moved, maintained Iraq had failed to account for all of the weapons of mass destruction it amassed in the 1990s, said Iraq had mobile facilities for making biological weapons, cited the purchase by Iraq of aluminum tubes to construct centrifuges that are used to enrich uranium, and claimed Iraq had helped Osama bin Laden and al-Qaeda acquire gases and poisons.

What the United States *knew*, however, was mostly untrue. The administration knew that some of the charges were false and that some were based on questionable evidence. Administration hawks pressured Powell—an authority figure who wielded considerable credibility inside and outside the Bush White House—to level the charges anyway, and he did.

A compliant media deemed the speech a success. Powell, *USA Today* asserted in its news columns, "forcefully laid out newly declassified evidence of Iraq's efforts to develop and conceal chemical, biological and nuclear weapons, as well as new signs that an al-Qaeda terrorist cell was set up in Baghdad last year."[73] The *Pittsburgh Post-Gazette* claimed in an editorial that Powell's speech "was far more powerful than anyone had predicted" and that "Powell did produce the proverbial 'smoking gun.' "[74] Such enthusiasm was typical. According to one poll, the number of Americans who supported the Iraq invasion jumped 11 percentage points after Powell's speech.[75]

- Second, the media dutifully reported George W. Bush's assertion during his State of the Union speech on January 28, 2003: "The British government has learned that Saddam Hussein recently sought significant quantities of uranium from Africa." The uranium, yellowcake plutonium from Niger, could be enriched to make a nuclear weapon. "Imagine those 19 hijackers with other weapons and other plans—this time armed by Saddam Hussein," Bush said. "It would take one vial, one canister, one crate slipped into this country to bring a day of horror like none we have ever known."[76]

The charge had been made publicly by others in the Bush administration, but it had been discredited months before the president's address. In fact, the Central Intelligence Agency (CIA) recommended deleting the charge in Bush's speech to the United Nations in September 2002 because the information, obtained from a single foreign official, could not be confirmed. The documents on which that charge was based were clearly forged and contained internal inconsistencies. For one thing, as journalist Seymour M. Hersh later reported, a critical letter dated October 10 was stamped as received on September 28.[77]

The Federal Bureau of Investigation later determined that two employees in the Niger Embassy had forged the documents and passed them to an Italian national for sale to contacts in the international intelligence community. Sadly, a dedicated journalist could have exposed the scam with a little legwork, just as it was exposed by diplomat Joseph Wilson, who was sent by the CIA to Niger to investigate in February 2002. Wilson reported nearly a year before the invasion of Iraq that the attempt to link Iraq to uranium purchases in Niger was a scam. It would be nearly impossible for Iraq to purchase huge quantities of plutonium from Niger, a message that evidently did not reach the inner circle of the Bush administration.[78]

Media Mea Culpas

The administration's war agenda dominated the news columns of U.S. newspapers, while information that contradicted the administration's claims was ignored or downplayed. The *New York Times*, the *Washington Post*, and other individuals and media outlets essentially acknowledged after the Iraq invasion that their coverage provided support for the war.

Editors at the *Times*, for instance, "found a number of instances of coverage that was not as rigorous as it should have been .... Looking back, we wish we had been more aggressive in re-examining the claims as new evidence emerged—or failed to emerge." Reporters relied too heavily on sources who had vested interests in going to war or who had no knowledge of what was happening in Iraq. "Complicating matters for journalists," according to the *Times*, "the accounts of these exiles were often eagerly confirmed by United States officials convinced of the need to intervene in Iraq." Official claims got prominent play, "while follow-up articles that called the original ones into question were sometimes buried. In some cases, there was no follow-up at all."[79]

A story by journalist Patrick Tyler on February 6, 2003, "all but declared a direct link between Al Qaeda and Saddam Hussein—a link still to be conclusively established, more than 15 months later," according to Daniel Okrent, public editor of the *Times*. "Other stories pushed Pentagon assertions so aggressively you could almost sense epaulets sprouting on the shoulders of editors."[80]

The *Washington Post* also gave favored treatment to pro-war news. As Howard Kurtz, media reporter for the *Post*, noted, "Some reporters who were lobbying for greater prominence for stories that questioned the administration's evidence complained to senior editors who, in the view of those reporters, were unenthusiastic about such pieces."

The *Post*'s Pentagon correspondent, Thomas Ricks, noted, "There was an attitude among editors: Look, we're going to war, why do we even worry about all this contrary stuff?"[81]

A tragic war may or may not have been avoided if the media had worried about the "contrary stuff," but the public might at least have known that the primary justification for the war—Hussein's weapons of mass destruction—was bogus. Before the war, Michael Massing of the *Columbia Journalism Review* said, "[T]he coverage was highly deferential to the White House. This was especially apparent on the issue of Iraq's weapons of mass destruction—the heart of the President's case for war. Despite abundant evidence of the administration's brazen misuse of intelligence in this matter, the press repeatedly let officials get away with it."[82]

CHRISTIAN CONSERVATIVES AND THE MEDIA: A FAILURE OF LEADERSHIP

The invasion of Iraq may have been inevitable, regardless of any actions taken by those opposed to the war. The residue from the pro-war campaign successfully launched prior to the invasion of Afghanistan helped create an environment in which it was exceptionally difficult to stop the administration's rush to a new war. Religious leaders, journalists, and ordinary Americans who wanted to avoid the violence remained mired in the war mentality they had helped create in the fall of 2001.

Religious Leadership

Many Christians, as noted earlier, did challenge the administration. They said publicly that a preemptive war against Iraq could not be considered a just war in Christian ethics. They participated in marches, wrote letters and editorials, lobbied government officials, and enlisted the aid of fellow Christians. But they failed to convince the majority of Christian churchgoers—59 percent of whom said they supported the war[83]—that the war was unjust. And they did not get their message out, in part because they were ignored by the media.

Other Christians and their leaders supported the war effort by declaring that the proposed invasion would be just. Most of the just-war declarations cited only two or three just-war principles. Most pro-war religious leaders claimed that war was a "last resort" in dealing with Saddam Hussein, that it should be waged by a legitimate authority, and that it should have a reasonable chance for success.

Most religious leaders who supported the war chose not to question the administration's assurance that everything would be done to spare innocent lives. As journalist Sarah Sewell puts it, "[T]he Department of Defense has never undertaken a systemic evaluation to determine whether its efforts to spare lives succeed or fail—or what might be done to improve them." The Pentagon has not done this because "it fears further constraints on the way it fights wars."[84] The Pentagon would not try to keep account of civilian casualties in Iraq—and has denied independent estimates of "excess deaths" due to the war that may have reached more than 1 million—for the same reason.[85]

Pro-war religious advocates missed at least two other points: that a preemptive strike against a nation that *might* be an enemy is not part of just-war theory and that the Bush administration had supplied no compelling evidence that Iraq was a threat. In the end, the war did far more harm than good—to Iraqi civilians and to their country, to Americans and to their country, to other nations in the Middle East, to the worldwide Muslim community, and to the struggle against international religious extremism. And America's decision makers have not been held accountable for the decision to go to war. Religious leaders who supported the war simply closed their eyes to these realities and accepted the administration's assurances.

Media Leadership

The bulk of the news media reflected the administration's war agenda, even though (a) a persuasive case for a preemptive war was never made, (b) a huge, modern army was poised on Iraq's borders to enforce UN sanctions, (c) there was no proof Hussein had weapons of mass destruction, (d) Hussein had allowed inspectors to go where they wanted, and (e) 12 years of a U.S.-enforced embargo had devastated Iraq's civilian population, scientific community, infrastructure, military, and economy.

Journalism and Objectivity

The failure of the mainstream news media to cover adequately the run-up to war lay primarily in the failure to observe most of the principles of traditional objective journalism. The media failed to challenge and question sources they did use, ignored or did not seek other *knowledgeable* sources, accepted and advanced the administration's war agenda, failed to report completely and accurately, showed little initiative in exposing the administration's lies and deceit, were unwilling to consider seriously new and competing evidence, and were not honest about identifying and controlling their own pro-war feelings.

The mainstream media accepted the rationale for going to war largely without questioning the evidence presented by Bush administration officials. They legitimized and assigned credibility to the administration's assertions by disseminating them without challenge and by ignoring or attacking contrary information. They simply failed to meet the information needs of the American people, and they helped lead them into a disastrous pro-war stance.

Perhaps the saddest sin of omission in the media's coverage before and during the Iraq war was the failure "to make use of what is potentially one of the most powerful weapons," as journalists Lawrence Pintak, Jeremy Ginges, and Nicholas Felton said, "in the war of ideas against terrorism." They were referring to the "demonized" Arab news media. A recent survey of Arab journalists' attitudes toward America suggested, "[M]ost Arab journalists are potential allies whose agenda broadly tracks the stated goals of United States Middle East policy and who can be a valuable conduit for explaining American policy to their audiences." While the Arab media are flawed, these "news outlets are more powerful and free today than at any time in history."[86]

While some have admitted some mistakes, the media have not acknowledged their own responsibility for helping to create and maintain an environment in which no alternative to war was seriously considered. Books have been written about failed media coverage, but individual media have not explained why they broke their moral covenant with the American people to provide complete, balanced, fair, and accurate information about the charge to war. They certainly have done little to reassure readers and viewers they will behave differently the next time a U.S. president tries to lead the people into an unjust war.[87]

It is not at all clear that many journalists understand these failures, for many react defensively in the face of calls for accountability. When Knight Ridder White House correspondent Bill Douglas, a panelist at a 2005 conference, heard someone call the press corps a mouthpiece for the administration, he said, "Do not call us mouthpieces because that pisses me off more than anything."[88] He and other panelists did what other professionals do—blame everyone else. In this case, it was Karl Rove or the Democrats.

Others twist critics' words or pretend that bad coverage does not matter. When the *Washington Post* acknowledged that some of its war coverage was not up to standard, executive editor Leonard Downie Jr. said, "People who were opposed to the war from the beginning and have been critical of the media's coverage in the period before the war have this belief that somehow the media should have crusaded against the war. They have the mistaken impression that somehow if the media's coverage had been different, there wouldn't have been a war."[89] Such responses are not helpful, particularly when the issue is as profound as war and peace.

What Journalists Should Have Done

Journalists should have taken seriously the charges that Bush administration officials cherry-picked facts supporting war, particularly those suggesting Iraq had weapons of mass destruction, and ignored or hid evidence suggesting war was not necessary. They should have made it clear to readers and viewers that these sources were wrong in the past and they might be wrong again. For example, they should have learned from the invasion of Afghanistan that the administration's assurances that every effort would be made to avoid civilian casualties were empty promises.

Journalists might have addressed competing Christian agendas or competing claims by specialists and government officials during the march to war. They might have explored the views of religious leaders who understood the pending war would not be a just war. But journalists did not demand explanations from those who said the war would be just or give much print or airtime to those who said it would be unjust. They might have tapped the expertise of scholars who knew a great deal about the goals and methods of international terrorism (including the role of the media in facilitating terrorism), having studied it in many countries over many decades. They might have interviewed Middle East specialists, who knew a great deal about Iraq and the difficulties of winning an American-style peace in this country. They might have talked sooner to ordinary Iraqis and Muslims elsewhere in this volatile region to better understand some of the problems of post-war reconstruction or why many saw merit in some reasons the terrorists gave for their actions—even though they might deplore these actions.

Journalists should not have dismissed information as unimportant, as the *Post* did, for example, when it finally learned from an International Atomic Energy Agency official that Hussein had not tried to purchase yellowcake plutonium from Niger. The newspaper said the charge was not "central to the case against Saddam Hussein, and it did not even form part of Secretary of State Colin Powell's recent presentation to the Security Council,"[90] a presentation that was criticized then as misleading and which Powell now says is a blot on his record.[91] The Niger claim was just one of many that needed to be analyzed as part of a larger pattern of deceit.

ENDURING TENSIONS

The tensions within the Christian community that surfaced during the run-up to the invasion of Afghanistan certainly did not disappear with the invasion of Iraq. The Bush administration continued to cooperate with oppressive governments in fighting the war against terrorism, a tactic that was opposed by many Christians but condoned by others in the conservative coalition.

Militarism and the Christian Community

The Christian community appeared to speak with one voice in the run-up to the invasion of Afghanistan. As we saw in Chapter 8, most Christians seemed to view the invasion as a just action of self-defense in which civilian casualties would be minimized. They either kept quiet about any reservations they might have had or they openly endorsed a military response.[92]

That was not the case during the run-up to the war in Iraq. On the one hand, thousands of Christian leaders joined with Jews, Muslims, and members of other faith groups to protest against the pending war. Messages and envoys urging a peaceful response to a perceived Iraqi threat were sent by individual pastors and preachers, representatives of various Protestant denominations and the National Council of Churches, the United States Conference of Catholic Bishops, and the pope. On the other hand, 87 percent of white evangelical Christians supported the invasion in April 2003, and many evangelical leaders—including Charles Stanley, a former president of the Southern Baptist Convention, and Franklin and Billy Graham, who saw the invasion as an opportunity to proselytize Muslims—reflected the militarism of their audiences.[93]

Differing Christian views also generated tensions between Christian leaders opposed to the war and members of their congregations who supported the war. Tensions were evident between different categories of Christians—progressive, moderate, and conservative Christians—who opposed and supported the war at the congregational level. These tensions within the Christian community were exacerbated as American support for the war plummeted.

Religious and nonreligious pacifists rejected the just-war principle, of course, from the beginning. They represented "one extreme" in debates over the Iraq war: "[P[eace activists . . . do not see any use for the traditional just war theory. They can conceive of virtually no circumstances that would justify the use of military force." The "other extreme" in these debates were "the 'enablers.' . . . For them the primary function of just war theory is to enable government to employ force in the pursuit of justice. They are skeptical, if not scornful, of applying just war norms to limit the savagery of war."[94]

While pro-war advocates might acknowledge the just-war argument, most were prepared to go to war whether it was justified or not and to bend scripture to accommodate their militarism. Religion professor Charles Marsh, who analyzed sermons of prominent evangelical preachers during the run-up to war, concluded that "many of the most respected voices in American evangelical circles" had to "recast Christian doctrine" to support the war. Many ministers tried to reconcile the criteria for a just war with their desire to support the invasion. When they could not do so, many "dismissed the theory as no longer relevant." Marsh suggests the most common theme in the sermons was "our president is a real brother in Christ, and because he has discerned that God's will is for our nation to be at war against Iraq, we shall gloriously comply."[95]

Whether the invasion was right or wrong is a question that will occupy the Christian community and the nation for decades, for the way in which the United States wages war tells much about the American people. Neither American civil religion, the Constitution, nor Christian theology condone unjust wars, but the morality of preemptive wars against nonthreatening enemies is a legacy this generation of American warriors will leave for future generations to consider.

Militarism and the Conservative Coalition

The run-up to the war in Iraq exposed fissures not only within the Christian community but also within the conservative coalition. Neoconservatives promoted the Iraq war, and many were prepared to use military force against Iran and an expanding number of other countries deemed to be within the orbit of the Bush administration's "axis of evil." But many other members of the conservative coalition—especially traditionalist conservatives—were ambivalent or opposed to the Iraq war and spoke out forcefully against using military action against Iran or anyone else.

Secular conservatives and their religious conservative allies who had actively or passively supported the war in Afghanistan were challenging the proposed invasion of Iraq. The Bush administration's public relations juggernaut,[96] coupled with a compliant news media and unofficial individuals and groups that attacked all alternative views, managed to overwhelm all dissent, but their actions created tensions within the conservative coalition that will undoubtedly affect America's political culture in the future.

NOTES

1. John W. Dean, *Conservatives without Conscience* (New York: Viking, 2006), 78.

2. Shadia B. Drury, *Terror and Civilization: Christianity, Politics, and the Western Psyche* (New York: Palgrave Macmillan, 2004), 147.

3. "President Discusses the Future of Iraq," speech to the American Enterprise Institute, February 26, 2003, The White House, www.whitehouse .gov/news/releases/2003/02/20030226-11.html.

4. Kevin Phillips, *American Theocracy: The Peril and Politics of Radical Religion, Oil, and Borrowed Money in the 21st Century* (New York: Viking, 2006), 3.

5. Frank Rich, *The Greatest Story Ever Sold: The Decline and Fall of Truth from 9/11 to Katrina* (New York: Penguin, 2006), 212.

6. This statement was made in many high-profile venues. See, for example, "Interview with Vice President Dick Cheney," *Meet the Press*, NBC, March 16, 2003, www.mtholyoke.edu/acad/intrel/bush/cheneymeetthepress.htm.

7. Believers saw the devastation caused by AIDS and other diseases, natural disasters that seemed to occur more frequently, and wars in the Middle East and around the globe as evidence that end-times had begun. The "true believers" were not particularly troubled that similar prophecies "failed in the fourth century, at the millennium in 1000, amid the tumult of the medieval Crusades, during the savage seventeenth-century European

religious wars, in pre-revolutionary New England, in the U.S. Civil War period, during World War I, and in 2000." See Phillips, *American Theocracy*, 125.

8. Martin Durham, "Evangelical Protestantism and Foreign Policy in the United States after September 11," *Patterns of Prejudice* 38, no. 2 (2004), 145–158, pp. 152–153. See also Max Rodenbeck, "Midnight at the Oasis," *New York Times Book Review*, January 28, 2007, 12, reviewing Michael B. Oren, *Power, Faith, and Fantasy: America in the Middle East, 1776 to the Present* (New York: W. W. Norton, 2007).

9. A *Newsweek* magazine poll in 1999 suggested that 40 percent of all U.S. adults believe the world will end in a battle between Jesus Christ and the antichrist. Among evangelical Protestants, 71 percent said yes and 18 percent said no; among other Protestants, 28 percent said yes and 54 percent said no; and among Catholics, 18 percent said yes and 57 percent said no. The margin of error was plus or minus 4 percentage points. See "40% of All Americans Believe the World Will End," *Newsweek*, October 24, 1999, news release, The PreteristArchive, http://www.preteristarchive.com/dEmEnTiA/1999_newsweek_poll.html. See also Kenneth L. Woodward, "The Way the World Ends," *Newsweek*, November 1, 1999, 68–70, 72–74.

10. Durham, "Evangelical Protestantism," 154–155. Tim LaHaye, co-author of the influential *Left Behind* series, suggested that the antichrist would rule the world from a New Babylon in Iraq. See Tim F. LaHaye and Jerry B. Jenkins, *Left Behind: A Novel of the Earth's Last Days* (Wheaton, IL: Tyndale, 1995).

11. James O. Goldsborough, "War, Religion and National Interests," *San Diego Union-Tribune*, May 24, 2004, B7.

12. A public opinion poll conducted several months after the war in Afghanistan, for example, showed that only 15 percent of Americans thought the war against terror in Afghanistan was a success. See Charles M. Madigan, "Poll: U.S. Public Leery of War on Iraq," *Chicago Tribune*, September 5, 2002, 10.

13. Many Americans argued that Bush was really proposing a "preventive" war in which the United States, acting as an aggressor, could launch military strikes against any sovereign nation that *might* pose an unspecified threat at some unspecified time in the future. See John W. Dean, *Worse than Watergate: The Secret Presidency of George W. Bush* (New York: Little, Brown, 2004), 132–136.

14. For a useful summary of the seven criteria that should be met, see Joseph L. Allen, *Love and Conflict: A Covenantal Model of Christian Ethics* (Nashville: Abingdon, 1984), Chapter 7; and Joseph L. Allen, *War: A Primer for Christians* (Nashville: Abingdon, 1991), Chapter 3. Allen lists six just-war criteria in *Love and Conflict* and seven (adding the formal declaration of war clause) in *War*. Augustine had six criteria. Roland H. Bainton, *Christian Attitudes toward War and Peace: A Historical Survey and Critical Re-Evaluation*

(Nashville: Abingdon Press, 1960), 95–98 (on Augustine). See also Laurie Goodstein, "Threats and Responses: Catholics; Conservative Catholics' Wrenching Debate over Whether to Back President or Pope," *New York Times*, March 6, 2003, A14.

15. Just-war declarations at the national level included a manifesto issued by the Institute for American Values, a conservative think tank based in New York: "Organized killers with global reach now threaten all of us. In the name of universal human morality, and fully conscious of the restrictions and requirements of a just war, we support our government's, and our society's, decision to use force of arms against them." The declaration was signed by dozens of prominent secular and religious academics, both liberal and conservative (including people such as Richard Mouw, president of Fuller Theological Seminary, and the late Senator Daniel Patrick Moynihan, who was then at Syracuse University), ministers, editors, and directors of the country's leading policy-making institutions. See "What We're Fighting For: A Letter from America," Institute for American Values, New York, February 2002, www.americanvalues.org/html/what_we_re_fighting_for.html.

16. David Gibson, "A Just War? Religious Leaders Have No Faith in an Offensive Against Iraq," *Newark (NJ) Sunday Star-Ledger*, October 13, 2002, section 10-1, 6.

17. "Letter to President Bush from Catholic Bishops: Bishops Express 'Serious Concern' About Iraq Invasion," United States Conference of Catholic Bishops, September 13, 2002, www.globalexchange.org/countries/iraq/367.html. See Alan Cooperman, " Roman Catholic Bishops Declare U.S. War Is Moral: But Poverty and Injustice at Root of Terrorism Should Be Addressed, Pastoral Statement Says," *Washington Post*, November 16, 2001, A37.

18. "Send Judah First: A Pentecostal Perspective on Peace," an open letter to President Bush, March 3, 2003, www.ninetyandnine.com/Archives/20030303/cover.htm.

19. Statement of General Secretary Jim Winkler of the United Methodist Church General Board of Church and Society, August 30, 2002, http://74.125.95.132/search?q=cache:jRW4uGhkLUYJ:www.archdioceseofdetroit.org/aodonline-sqlimages/PressReleaseStatements/InterfaithStatements/020111Leaders_Iraq.pdf+%22Jim+Winkler%22+UMC+Statement+on+Iraq+2002&cd=9&hl=en&ct=clnk&gl=us.

20. Patrick J. Buchanan, "Whose War?" *The American Conservative* (March 24, 2003): www.amconmag.com/2003/03_24_03/cover.html.

21. Eric Margolis, "Bush's War Is Not about Democracy," *Toronto Sun*, March 2, 2003, www.fpp.co.uk/online/03/03/Margolis030303.html.

22. David Frum, "Unpatriotic Conservatives: A War against America," *National Review Online*, April 7, 2003, www.nationalreview.com/frum/frum031903.asp.

23. Buchanan denied his article was antisemitic. See Buchanan, "Whose War?" A January 2003 poll by the American Jewish Committee showed that

59 percent of U.S. Jews supported military action against Iraq. See Alan Cooperman, "Jewish Organizations Worried about Backlash for Iraq War: Groups Are Outraged over Allegations of Warmongering," *Washington Post*, March 15, 2003, A10.

24. Many in the media endorsed during this critical period the view that not only the Taliban but also Saddam Hussein should be deposed. See, for example, "Afghanistan," *Washington Post*, September 15, 2001, A26; and A. M. Rosenthal, "Get the Taliban & Saddam, Too," *New York Daily News*, September 28, 2001, 49.

25. Michael Ryan and Les Switzer, "Mirror on a War Agenda: Conservative Christian Activists and Media Coverage of the Iraq Invasion," in *Terrorism: Communication and Rhetorical Perspectives*, ed. H. Dan O'Hair, Robert L. Heath, Kevin J. Ayotte, and Gerald R. Ledlow (Cresskill, NJ: Hampton, 2008), 299–335.

26. Michael Ryan, "Framing the War against Terrorism: US Newspaper Editorials and Military Action in Afghanistan," *Gazette* 66, no. 5 (2004): 363–382.

27. The pro-war newspapers did not enjoy the unanimous support of their readers. The *Washington Post*, for instance, published a long response to critics who complained about its "drumbeat" for war. " 'Drumbeat' on Iraq?: A Response to Readers," *Washington Post*, February 27, 2003, A26.

28. Martin E. Marty, "The Sin of Pride," *Newsweek*, March 10, 2003, 32.

29. Colman McCarthy, "Militarists Rule on TV News: The Networks Offer Ex-Brass a New Revolving Door," *National Catholic Reporter*, April 25, 2003, 20.

30. See Laurie Goodstein, "Diverse Denominations Oppose the Call to Arms," *New York Times*, March 6, 2003, A14; Jim Wallis, "Is Bush Deaf to Church Doubts on Iraq War?," *Boston Globe*, December 9, 2002, A22; and Kim Campbell, "War, Peace Collide in Sermons: Many Churches Oppose Iraq Action, and Ministers Say So," *Christian Science Monitor*, February 11, 2003, A1, A4. Many newspapers also published Jimmy Carter's opposition to a war in Iraq. See Jimmy Carter, "Just War—or a Just War?" *New York Times*, March 9, 2003, Week in Review-13.

31. Some of the attempts to marginalize dissent were more personal. Peace activist G. Simon Harak reported that a pastor at a Catholic church in New York removed a war memorial from the parish school grounds. "At one point, even one of the high-ups in Homeland Security—a 'friend of the parish'—called to ask about it. He wanted to see uniformity of support for the president and the ongoing and planned military attacks. He wanted to know why the parish was doing such antiwar, pacifist things." See G. Simon Harak, "Under Which God? U.S. Policy toward Iraq Reveals What Deity We Follow," *National Catholic Reporter*, September 6, 2002, 26.

32. The attack against France was so virulent that some pro-war newspapers published editorials designed to soften the criticism. An editorial in

the *Dallas Morning News*, for example, suggested "[Americans] should resist the temptation to reduce the country to a caricature. France and its centuries-old relationship with the United States are a lot more complicated than that." See "French Fried: Relations with Staunch Ally Will Survive This Tiff," *Dallas Morning News*, February 26, 2003, A22.

33. "Blixed Messages Comfort Coddlers," *New York Daily News*, March 8, 2003, 24. Of the same report, the *New York Times* wrote, "[T]he report of the inspectors on Friday was generally devastating to the American position. They not only argued that progress was being made, they also discounted the idea that Iraq was actively attempting to manufacture nuclear weapons." See "Saying No to War," *New York Times*, March 9, 2003, Week in Review-12.

34. "Daschle's French Accent," *Wall Street Journal*, March 19, 2003, A14.

35. "U.S. Opponents Squander Last Chance to Avoid War," *USA Today*, March 10, 2003, 10A.

36. "Peaceniks Couldn't Be More Wrong," *New York Daily News*, March 14, 2003, 34.

37. Max Boot, "Anti-War Protests Make It Worse," *Newsday*, February 28, 2003, A39.

38. "What's to Debate? Saddam Must Go," *New York Daily News*, February 25, 2003, 36.

39. "Mexican Responsibility: Iraq Becomes a Serious Issue for Our Neighbor," *Dallas Morning News*, February 22, 2003, A22.

40. Cited by Howard Kurtz, "The *Post* on WMDs: An Inside Story," *Washington Post*, August 12, 2004, A1, A20, p. A20.

41. Eric Deggans, "In TV War News, the Hits and Misses," *St. Petersburg Times*, April 14, 2003, D1, D2.

42. Paul Farhi, "The Gung-Ho Morning Gang: Cable's 'Fox & Friends' Prides Itself on Patriotic Patter," *Washington Post*, April 4, 2003, C1, C7.

43. "Profile: Silent Evangelical Support of Bush's Proposed War against Iraq," *Morning Edition*, National Public Radio News, February 26, 2003, www.npr.org/programs/morning/transcripts/2003/feb/030226.hagerty.html.

44. Michael Griffin, "Picturing America's 'War on Terrorism' in Afghanistan and Iraq: Photographic Motifs as News Frames," *Journalism* 5, no. 4 (2004): 381–402. Media also were criticized for failing to portray civilian casualties. See Tom Beaudoin, "The Iraq War and Imperial Psychology," *America* (January 17, 2005): 14–16' and Lila Guterman, "Dead Iraqis: Why an Estimate Was Ignored," *Columbia Journalism Review*, March/April 2005, 11.

45. "High-Stakes Poker at the U.N.," *Los Angeles Times*, March 7, 2003, B14.

46. "Time's Up," *Newsday*, March 9, 2003, A25, A26.

47. "Chirac's Last Chance," *Wall Street Journal*, March 17, 2003, A14.

48. "President Bush Prepares for War," *New York Times*, March 17, 2003, A22.

49. "Diplomatic Blunders Don't Nullify Arguments for War," *USA Today*, March 19, 2003, A14.

50. "Bush Says Iraq Is not Disarming as Required by the U.N.: Says He Will Lead Coalition of Willing Nations to Disarm Regime," transcript, U.S. Department of State, January 21, 2003, http://usinfo.org/wf-archive/2003/030121/epf202.htm.

51. The *Chicago Tribune* and other pro-war newspapers opposed delay in part because of weather conditions. "[Bush] can defer to those who want the inspections fiasco to drag on and on and on with no hard conclusion and no enforcement. Or he can say that as the heat and wind build in Iraq, he will not imperil his troops by asking them to fight in more dangerous weather because nations that voted for Resolution 1441 now pretend it doesn't exist." See "Resolution 1441? What's That?" *Chicago Tribune*, March 6, 2003, 22.

52. "Bush in Lilliput," *Wall Street Journal*, March 12, 2003, A18.

53. Drury, *Terror and Civilization*, 147.

54. Garth S. Jowett and Victoria O'Donnell, *Propaganda and Persuasion*, 3rd ed. (Thousand Oaks, CA: Sage, 1999), 175.

55. For a revealing description of the administration's use of fear to manipulate the public, see Rich, *The Greatest Story*, 143–149.

56. Toby Harnden, "Bush Warns of Chemical Attacks on the US," *Daily Telegraph* (London), October 8, 2002, 14.

57. Institute for Defense Analyses, "The Iraqi Perspectives Project: Saddam and Terrorism; Emerging Insights from Captured Iraqi Documents," United States Joint Forces Command, Washington, DC, March 20, 2008, www.fas.org/irp/eprint/iraqi/index.html.

58. George H. W. Bush consulted the presiding bishop of the Episcopal Church, Edmond L. Browning, on the eve of the Gulf War in October 1990 about the moral justification for going to war. The president's arguments, however, did not persuade either the Episcopalians or other mainstream church leaders at the time to lend their support to the war. Instead, Bush asked the Southern Baptist evangelist Billy Graham to be at his side "on the night he ordered bombing raids over Iraq." See, for example, Bert E. Thompson, "Bush Reveals What Guides Him in War," *Houston Chronicle*, February 16, 1991, E1, E3. See also Michael J. Schuck, "When the Shooting Stops: Missing Elements in Just War Theory," *Christian Century*, October 26, 1994, 982–984. Schuck considered the relevance of the just-war principle in the context of the 1991 Iraq War.

59. Trudy Rubin, "New Doctrine, New Dangers," *Philadelphia Inquirer*, March 18, 2003, A19.

60. David Domke, Kevin Coe, and Robert Tynes, "The Gospel of Freedom and Liberty: George W. Bush, the 'War on Terror,' and an Echoing Press," paper presented to the Religion and Media Interest Group, Association for Education in Journalism and Mass Communication annual convention, Toronto, Canada, 2004, 10.

61. "The Right Way in Iraq," *Los Angeles Times*, March 14, 2003, B14.

62. Saul Landau, "Iraq War: Worse Lies Ahead; A Policy of Christian and Jewish Fundamentalism," *CounterPunch*, April 26, 2003, www.counterpunch .org/landau04262003.html.

63. Thomas M. Nichols, "Just War, Not Prevention," *Ethics and International Affairs* 17, 1 (2003): 25–30. Robert P. George, "The Cost of Fighting . . . A Just War in Iraq," *Wall Street Journal*, December 6, 2002, A14.

64. American Center for Law & Justice, "ACLJ Applauds President Bush for His Position on Iraq," news release, September 12, 2002, http:// www.aclj.org/News/Read.aspx?ID=199.

65. Cited by "Catholic Bishops Join Opposition to War," *Christian Century*, September 25–October 8, 2002, 10–11.

66. Paul in Romans refers to the "governing authorities" as "God's servants." Allie Martin, "Esteemed Christian Teacher Casts His Vote—It's a 'Just' War," April 4, 2003, news release, AgapePress, http://headlines .agapepress.org/archive/4/42003d.asp.

67. "Of course," Colson said, "all of this [his argument that an invasion of Iraq was just] presupposes solid intelligence and the goodwill of U.S. and Western leaders. I find it hard to believe that any President, aware of the awesome consequences of his decision and of the swiftness of second-guessing in a liberal democracy, would act recklessly." See Charles Colson, "Just War in Iraq: Sometimes Going to War Is the Charitable Thing to Do," *Christianity Today*, December 9, 2002, 72.

68. Joe Feuerherd, "Opinions Clash on Just War: Christian Opposition to Attack on Iraq Is Widespread, But Not Universal," *National Catholic Reporter*, February 7, 2003, 3.

69. See, for example, Michael Ryan, "Journalists Didn't Bother Vetting Iraq War Rational: News Media Owe Public an Explanation," *Houston Chronicle*, August 29, 2005, 7B; and Michael Ryan and Les Switzer, "Propaganda and the Subversion of Objectivity: Media Coverage of the War on Terrorism in Iraq," *Critical Studies on Terrorism* 2, no. 1 (20009): 45–64.

70. Joseph Cirincione, Jessica T. Mathews, George Perkovich, and Alexis Orton, *WMD in Iraq: Evidence and Implications* (Washington, DC: Carnegie Endowment for International Peace, January 2004).

71. Dean, *Worse than Watergate*, 140.

72. "U.S. Secretary of State Colin Powell Addresses the U.N. Security Council," transcript, The White House, February 5, 2003, www.whitehouse .gov/news/releases/2003/02/20030205-1.html.

73. Bill Nichols, "Powell Shares New Evidence," *USA Today*, February 6, 2003, A1.

74. "The Gun Is Smoking," *Pittsburgh Post-Gazette*, February 9, 2003, B1.

75. A CNN/*USA Today*/Gallup poll showed that 63 percent of Americans supported invading Iraq after the speech; 52 percent had supported

invasion two weeks earlier. The margin of error was plus or minus 3 percentage points. Richard Benedetto, "More People Favor a War in Iraq," *USA Today*, February 11, 2003, A5. A Washingtonpost.com/ABC poll showed that 50 percent of respondents said Powell made a convincing case for war; 19 percent said he did not. "Washingtonpost.com-ABC News Poll: Powell's U.N. Address," Washingtonpost.com, February 6, 2003, www.washingtonpost.com/wp-srv/politics/polls/vault/stories/data020603.htm. See also Karen DeYoung, *Soldier: The Life of Colin Powell* (New York: Knopf, 2006).

76. "President Delivers 'State of the Union,'" transcript, The White House, January 28, 2003, www.whitehouse.gov/news/releases/2003/01/20030128-19.html. See also Michael R. Gordon, "President Emphasizes a Need to Act Quickly: He Cites Rising Risk of Mass Destruction," *New York Times*, January 30, 2003, A5.

77. Seymour M. Hersh, "Who Lied to Whom? Why Did the Administration Endorse a Forgery about Iraq's Nuclear Program?" *The New Yorker* (March 31, 2003): 41–43. See also Michael Isikoff and David Corn, *Hubris: The Inside Story of Spin, Scandal, and the Selling of the Iraq War* (New York: Crown, 2006), Chapter 5.

78. Wilson published an account of his Niger trip on July 6, 2003, in which he confirmed that Iraq had made no attempt to purchase uranium in Niger. The implication was that the Bush administration hid this revelation from the public during the critical period in which it was trying to generate public support for the war. Shortly after that, Karl Rove identified Wilson's wife, Valerie Plame, as a CIA operative, thus launching a scandal that simmered for years. See Joseph C. Wilson 4th, "What I Didn't Find in Africa," *New York Times*, July 6, 2003, Week in Review-9.

79. "From the Editors: The Times and Iraq," *New York Times*, May 26, 2004, A10.

80. Daniel Okrent, "Weapons of Mass Destruction? Or Mass Distraction?" *New York Times*, May 30, 2004, Week in Review-2.

81. Cited by Kurtz, "The *Post* on WMDs," A20. For more about Thomas E. Ricks's take on the war and its coverage, see Thomas E. Ricks, *Fiasco: The American Military Adventure in Iraq* (New York: Penquin, 2006).

82. Michael Massing, "Now They Tell Us," *New York Review of Books*, February 26, 2004, 43–49, p. 43.

83. Jim Remsen, "Faith and War Support Linked: The Stronger the Faith, the More a Person Backs War, a Poll Shows; Yet Many Religious Leaders Oppose War," *Philadelphia Inquirer*, March 8, 2003, A6. The Gallup Organization surveyed 1,002 Americans in February 2003. The margin of error was plus or minus 3 percentage points.

84. Sarah Sewell, "An Empty Pledge to Civilians?" *New York Times*, March 21, 2003, A19.

85. There is no official U.S. agency that keeps track of Iraqi civilian deaths. As Gen. Tommy Franks once put it, "We don't do body counts."

The *documented* Iraqi civilian deaths between the start of the invasion in March 2003 and December 2008 range from 90,291 to 98,560. The figures are taken from 17,204 database entries, but the "recording and reporting" gaps "suggest that even our highest totals to date may be missing many civilian deaths from violence." The Body Count Project's estimates are at the low end of independent surveys conducted on civilian deaths in Iraq. Some experts suggest these documented deaths underestimate the total, since deaths from aerial bombardments and internecine battles between ethnic and religious groups in the ongoing internal civil war often cannot be documented. The Project's databases do not cover the whole country, and its estimates include only certain categories of deaths defined narrowly as police and civilian deaths. See Iraqi Body Count project, www.iraqbodycount.org/database. *The Lancet*, the medical journal, published controversial surveys in 2004 and 2006 to estimate the overall death toll as a result of the ongoing war. The researchers estimated there were 654,965 "excess Iraqi deaths as a consequence of the war"—601,027 "due to violence, the most common cause being gunfire"—as of July 2006. Gilbert Burnham, Riyadh Lafta, Shannon Doocy, and Les Roberts, "Mortality after the 2003 Invasion of Iraq: A Cross-Sectional Cluster Sample Survey," *The Lancet*, published online on October 11, 2006, http://74.125.45.132/search?q=cache:wiGkc7gkzcMJ:www.brusselstribunal.org/pdf/lancet111006.pdf+%22mortality+after+the+2003+invasion+of+iraq%22&hl=en&ct=clnk&cd=2&gl=us. In a review of the major surveys conducted by various scientific, media, and political "stakeholders" serving up competing estimates of the war's impact in terms of its "human cost to the Iraqi people," the Casualty Monitor estimated that "total excess Iraqi deaths" as a result of the war ranged from 392,979 to 1,131,831 as of December 2007. Casualty Monitor, "Monitoring and Analysis of Data on Civilian and Military Casualties in Iraq and Afghanistan," *Casualtiy-Monitor.org*, December 20, 2007, www.casualty-monitor.org/2007/12/iraqi-casualty-monitor.html. Another problematic statistic is the number of civilian deaths caused by the "murderous conduct of thousands of private security contractors—our contemporary euphemism for mercenaries," who "not only shattered critical relationships between our troops and the local population but also shamed our country." See Ralph Peters, "Hired Guns: The Full Story of Mercenaries in Iraq Is Finally Revealed," *Houston Chronicle*, January 4, 2009, Zest-16, reviewing Steve Fainaru's *Big Boy Rules: American Mercenaries Fighting in Iraq* (Philadelphia: Da Capo, 2008).

86. Lawrence Pintak, Jeremy Ginges, and Nicholas Felton, "Misreading the Arab Media," *New York Times*, May 25, 2008, Opinion-12. The journalists conducted a survey of 101 Arab journalists in 13 Arab countries. Among their findings, "Though many Arab journalists dislike the United States government, more than 60 percent say they have a favorable view of the American people. They just don't believe the United States is sincere when it calls for Arab democratic reform or a Palestinian state."

87. This is the view of contemporary critics. See Isikoff and Corn, *Hubris;* Rich, *The Greatest Story;* Bob Woodward, *State of Denial* (New York: Simon & Schuster, 2006); and Ricks, *Fiasco.*

88. Isadora Vail-Castro, "Bush Barriers Bother Reporters: Press Frustrated by Lack of Access," *AEJMC Reporter,* August 12, 2005, http://aejmc .net/SAT05/?20050812.

89. Cited by Kurtz, "The Post on WMDs," A20.

90. "Are Inspections Working?" *Washington Post,* March 11, 2003, A22.

91. Powell later expressed regret for the speech. Steven R. Weisman, "Powell Calls His U.N. Speech a Lasting Blot on His Record," *New York Times,* September 9, 2005, A1.

92. The Society of Christian Ethics, a network of Christian conservative clergy, scholars, and lay professionals, claimed the bombing of al-Qaeda and Taliban forces in Afghanistan was "just" because the United States tried to avoid targeting civilians and the response was "proportional," which "requires that the goal—in this case, the security of the United States and the West—offset the cost of lost lives." A minority, however, called the Afghanistan war unjust because pacifism is integral to Christian belief. See "Christian Ethicists: Afghan War Is Just," *Christianity Today,* March 11, 2002, 23.

93. Charles Marsh, "Wayward Christian Soldiers,"*New York Times,* January 20, 2006, Opinion-2. See also Marsh, *Wayward Christian Soldiers: Freeing the Gospel from Political Captivity* (Oxford, UK: Oxford University Press, 2007).

94. Drew Christiansen, "Hawks, Doves and Pope John Paul II," *America* (August 12–19, 2002): 9–11, p. 10.

95. Marsh, *Wayward Christian Soldiers.*

96. For a detailed description of the administration's public relations apparatus, see Isikoff and Corn, *Hubris.*

CHAPTER 10

Conclusion: A Christian Life in American Politics

We live in prophetic times. The 100th anniversary of Walter Rauschenbusch's seminal work, *Christianity and the Social Crisis* (1907), was commemorated in 2008 with the publication of a sequel by a great grandson, Paul Rauschenbusch, entitled *Christianity and the Social Crisis in the 21st Century*. Rauschenbusch (1861–1918), a Baptist minister, theologian, and pastor to the urban poor, was the founding father of America's social gospel movement in the early twentieth century. He pleaded for a Christian stance that, like Jesus himself, centered on the powerless.

Among the contributors to the commemorative volume were Christians such as Jim Wallis and Cornel West, who seek to revive the tradition of social reform. Another contributor was the late philosopher Richard Rorty (1931–2007), one of Rauschenbusch's grandsons, who noted that "until roughly the 1970s" it was Rauschenbusch who "helped inspire whatever minimal welfare state the United States developed .... [T]he likelihood that religion will play a significant role in the struggle for social justice seems smaller now than at any time since *Christianity and the Social Crisis* was published."[1]

Voices that echo Rauschenbusch's Christian stance can be heard in American Christianity today, but they have been largely muted—at least for the moment—in the political arena. Jim Wallis—himself a rarity among self-identified Protestant evangelicals with progressive views—cautions that Christians must "reassert and reclaim the gospel faith," a faith he believes has been defiled by some on the Right and the Left of the political spectrum. The real gospel for Wallis and others like him "challenges the powers that be to do justice for the poor." This gospel "hates violence ... and exerts a fundamental presumption against war, instead of justifying it in God's name." This gospel proclaims the sacredness of community—a community free of "racial, class, and gender divisions," an "international community over nationalist ["God Bless America"] religion." This gospel "regards matters such as the sacredness of life and family bonds as so important that they should never be used as ideological symbols or mere political pawns in partisan warfare."[2]

These voices are muted largely because the coalition of Christian conservatives, neoconservatives, and traditionalist conservatives—long the mainstay of the Republican Party—has not been particularly concerned about the powerless, which translates in practice to concern for the poor and the sick, and marginalized racial, sexual, and gendered minorities. As we have seen in this book, the conservative coalition expanded in the later twentieth and early twenty-first centuries mainly because the Grand Old Party (GOP) supported a range of social issues and quasiscientific positions that were of concern to religious conservatives. The coalition's partnership with the GOP was so successful—particularly with the election of George W. Bush—many Republicans and media commentators began to talk seriously about a restructuring of the American political landscape. These conservative voices simply overwhelmed other moderate and progressive voices inside and outside the Christian community.

We did not set out to defend, apologize for, or criticize the American Christian community, or the Christian conservative subgroup of that community. But the suspicions we held at the beginning of this project—that the conservative coalition, of which Christian conservatives are an important part, is much more complex than some seem to think; that the mainstream media could do a much better job covering Christian communities, particularly their political activities; and that many Americans base their views of Christianity largely on media portrayals of these evangelical fundamentalist activists—were not far off the mark.

Our conclusions are reported in three sections. Section 1 shows the complexity of the conservative political and religious coalition through the eyes of six hypothetical Republican couples during the 2000–2008 election cycles. These hypothetical voting patterns reflect national election results from 2000 through 2008. Section 2 returns to the topic of political theology and the Christian Right, particularly during the George W. Bush administration. We revisit two domestic issues, women's reproductive rights and intelligent design, reassess the media's role in covering religion, and cite more examples of the literature that has been critical of Christianity in America. Section 3 is a last look at some of the ambiguities of a Christian voice, including the diversity of Christian voices, in politics. We conclude with some thoughts about what we think should guide Christian involvement in America's political culture today.

GOP COALITION PARTNERS AND CULTURAL ISSUES

We begin with a snapshot of how six hypothetical couples aligned to the Republican Party might have viewed a range of political, social, and economic issues that seem to concern so many Americans today. The views of these couples—Christian conservatives Gretchen and Nathanial Parker and Edward and Mary Smith, traditionalist conservatives Juanita and Jason Garcia and Ralph and Pauline Martin, and neoconservatives William and Nan Kelley and Anne and Lee North—vary widely, as the hypothetical profile in Figure 10.1 suggests.

A Republican Comfort Zone

Republicans were in a comfort zone when the Christian conservative couples were focused on three main issues—fetal stem cell research, abortion, and gay marriage. Euthanasia and human cloning were rather minor issues, but only because nobody was suggesting seriously that these practices should be legalized.

Abortion was for decades a salient issue for Christians like the Parkers and Smiths, for they believed, at least in regard to human embryos, in the sanctity of human life. The issue was contested ground for years as conservatives argued for an unborn child's "right to life" and the opposition argued for a "woman's right to choose." The issue was argued more intensely when (a) George W. Bush was elected president and many Christian conservatives anticipated U.S. Supreme Court appointees who would reverse *Roe v. Wade* (1973), and (b) Catholic bishops appointed by Pope John Paul II (1920–2005) began to stress life issues over all other issues.[3] Debates about the prospect of same-sex marriage and embryonic stem cell research came later, but these issues, along with abortion, radicalized many Christian conservatives.

Christian conservatives like the Parkers and Smiths voted for George W. Bush in 2000 because they believed his promise to restore what they saw as moral integrity to the presidency; they thought the

Figure 10.1. Examples of Diverse Views in the Conservative Coalition

Issues	Christian Conservatives		Traditionalist Conservatives		Neoconservatives	
	Parkers*	Smiths	Garcias	Martins	Kelleys	Norths
Balance the budget	Support	Support	Support	Support	Support	Neutral
Cut taxes	Neutral	Support	Support	Support	Neutral	Oppose
Make abortion illegal	Support	Support	Support	Neutral	Oppose	Neutral
Encourage sex education (abstinence only)	Support	Neutral	Support	Neutral	Neutral	Neutral
Encourage sex education (including birth control methods)	Oppose	Support	Oppose	Support	Support	Support
Use public funds to improve nutrition for the poor	Support	Neutral	Oppose	Neutral	Neutral	Oppose
Use public funds to improve housing and health care for the poor	Support	Neutral	Oppose	Neutral	Neutral	Oppose
Ban the use of public funds for research using fetal stem cells	Support	Support	Neutral	Oppose	Oppose	Neutral
Ban human cloning	Support	Support	Support	Support	Support	Support
Legalize same-gender marriage	Oppose	Oppose	Oppose	Neutral	Support	Neutral

Issues	Christian Conservatives		Traditionalist Conservatives		Neoconservatives	
	Parkers*	Smiths	Garcias	Martins	Kelleys	Norths
Extend civil liberties to gays and lesbians, excluding marriage	Support	Neutral	Neutral	Support	Neutral	Neutral
Allow faith groups to use federal funds for social-welfare programs	Support	Support	Oppose	Neutral	Neutral	Oppose
Use federal funds to build social service facilities at religious institutions	Support	Support	Oppose	Neutral	Oppose	Oppose
Stress right-to-life themes in U.S. foreign policy	Support	Neutral	Neutral	Neutral	Neutral	Oppose
Promote human rights in foreign policy and at home	Support	Support	Oppose	Neutral	Neutral	Oppose
Make the world safe for Americans	Neutral	Neutral	Support	Neutral	Support	Support
Use military force to ensure a free flow of natural resources from abroad	Neutral	Support	Support	Support	Support	Support

Figure 10.1 (continued)

Issues	Christian Conservatives		Traditionalist Conservatives		Neoconservatives	
	Parkers*	Smiths	Garcias	Martins	Kelleys	Norths
Build nations to spread democracy	Oppose	Oppose	Oppose	Oppose	Support	Support
Police world	Oppose	Oppose	Neutral	Oppose	Support	Support
Faith group should lose tax-exempt status if leaders support or oppose candidates for office	Oppose	Oppose	Oppose	Neutral	Neutral	Neutral

*Note: While the six couples are not real, the attitudes ascribed to them are based on data reported in this book.

Democrats were on the wrong side of many social issues; they thought Bush might appoint Supreme Court justices who would reverse *Roe v. Wade;* and they were doing well financially. Traditionalist conservatives like the Garcias and the Martins were generally in harmony with these views, and they also believed Bush's promises to cut taxes and balance the budget. Neoconservatives such as the Kelleys and the Norths were convinced Bush would rebuild the military, which they believed was weakened under President Bill Clinton, and take a more active interest in spreading American-style democracy worldwide.

These conservatives voted Republican again in the 2002 off-year elections for the same reasons and because they feared Osama bin Laden or Saddam Hussein, who was falsely linked to the 9/11 attacks, would strike the United States if America did not act forcefully. They trusted the Republican Party more than the Democratic Party to keep them safe.

The Garcias, traditionalist conservatives, voted for Bush in 2004 because they feared Democrats would raise taxes and be soft on terrorism, while the Martins did not vote because they thought the war in Iraq would lead to economic disaster. The Kelleys, the neoconservatives, voted for Bush because they saw him as the country's best chance to strengthen the military, police the world, and extend democracy (and, not coincidentally, their view of American-style capitalism) throughout the world. The Norths were concerned that Bush policies were ruining America's reputation abroad, but they voted for Bush because they were afraid John Kerry, the Democratic candidate, would adopt an isolationist foreign policy.

The Parkers and the Smiths, the Christian conservatives, held their noses in 2004 and voted for Bush because they believed he would do a better job of keeping them safe; because they feared a liberal Democratic president would appoint to the Supreme Court individuals who would reaffirm *Roe v. Wade* and work to legalize same-sex marriage; and because they thought he was the better of two weak candidates. Some of their Christian conservative friends refused to vote.

Much had changed by 2006. For Christian conservatives like the Parkers and Smiths, abortion, fetal stem cell research, and same-sex marriage were less salient; the war in Iraq, the war against terrorism, and the economy were much more salient. They were concerned that too many innocent Afghans, Iraqis, U.S. soldiers, and coalition troops were being killed and injured; that illegal immigrants were taking jobs that citizens could fill and were using resources such as schools and hospitals; and that the jobs of some of their friends were being outsourced overseas.

Neoconservatives like the Kelleys and the Norths blamed the Bush administration for the poor progress in the wars in Afghanistan and Iraq, but they did not trust the Democrats to continue using military might to make the world safe for democracy. The Garcias, the traditionalist conservatives, voted Democratic because they feared the wars and the budget deficits would lead to a recession, and they worried about their jobs. The Martins voted Republican because they thought the GOP would keep their children safe.

Life issues such as abortion and gay marriage had been pushed down the saliency scale by 2008, even for Christian conservatives like the Parkers and the Smiths, and the wars in Afghanistan and Iraq were pushed down the scale, even for neoconservatives like the Kelleys and the Norths. These issues were overwhelmed by the housing crisis, high gasoline prices, the financial crisis, and, of course, the recession of 2008. These GOP families were concerned that the Democratic candidate, Barack Obama, would raise their taxes and create new social programs for the disadvantaged. The neoconservatives feared he would pull U.S. forces from Afghanistan and Iraq too quickly; Christian conservatives were concerned that Obama was pro-abortion rights and supported civil marriage for gays; and traditionalist conservatives fretted that from their perspective he would be fiscally irresponsible and move to regulate markets. The latent racism, which rarely surfaced in the polls, was also present among some secular and religious conservatives—in the North and West as well as in the South.

In the end, the Kelleys and the Norths voted for John McCain because they were sure that he would not shrink from using military force to bring peace and democratic principles to the world and that he would be tough on terrorism. The Garcias voted for Obama because they felt he could do no worse than the Republicans, the party they blamed for bringing on the recession. The Martins voted for McCain because they thought he would retain the Bush tax cuts, work to reduce the national debt, remain tough on terrorism, and encourage free markets. Mrs. Smith voted for McCain because she thought he shared her Christian values, while Mr. Smith voted for Obama because he wanted a change in economy policy, even if that meant higher taxes. Mrs. Parker voted for Obama because she thought he offered the best hope for a revitalized economy, and Mr. Parker voted for McCain because he thought he would do a better job protecting his family against terrorists and because he liked Sarah Palin, the GOP's vice-presidential nominee.

We will not push this hypothetical analysis further because we hope we have made our point. As we saw in Chapter 3, the partners in the conservative coalition played varying roles in communicating a conservative message, and the GOP could not *always* count on all elements of the conservative coalition to follow the party line. It is difficult to achieve a major shift in the political landscape because issues that are important and salient in one election cycle may be replaced by other issues in the next cycle. Issues such as the wars in Iraq and Afghanistan, the home-mortgage crisis, unemployment, and the recession tended by 2008 to overshadow all other issues, even those such as abortion and same-sex marriage, which seemed so important in the first years of the twenty-first century.

Christian Conservatives in the 2008 Election

Public opinion polls conducted during the 2008 presidential election cycle produced no evidence of a significant realignment in Christian conservative political allegiances. An overwhelming 79 percent of evangelical Protestants and 52 percent of Catholics voted for George W. Bush in the 2004 elections, whereas only 21 percent of evangelical Protestants, and 47 percent of Catholics voted for John Kerry.[4] While 26 percent of evangelical Protestants and 54 percent of Catholics voted for Barack Obama in the 2008 elections, 73 percent of evangelical Protestants and 45 percent of Catholics voted for John McCain.

Obama campaigned heavily to attract religious voters, but exit polls recorded only a marginal shift in voting habits of the two major religious groups—evangelical Protestants and Catholics each constitute roughly 25 percent of the electorate—in the 2008 elections.[5] The shift, however, was enough to make an important difference in the election results.

The Iraq war and the economy were without question the key issues in this election. Polls showed by roughly 2005 that more than half of all Americans thought the invasion of Iraq never should have happened. The president's approval rating by 2008 was 31 percent, and it dropped within months to 28 percent, in part, because he led America into what many saw as a military, moral, and financial quagmire.[6]

Obama picked up support from all religious voters who attend a worship service *more than* once a week. Bush won 64 percent of that vote for the GOP in 2004, compared to McCain's 55 percent in 2008. Kerry won 35 percent of that vote for the Democrats in 2004, compared to Obama's 43 percent in 2008. Among those who attend services once a week, Bush won 58 percent and Kerry 41 percent in 2004, while McCain won 55 percent and Obama 43 percent in 2008. Obama also scored gains among those who never attend church. While 62 percent voted for Kerry and 36 percent for Bush in 2004, 67 percent voted for Obama and 30 percent for McCain in 2008.[7]

A majority of all Catholics voted for the pro-choice, pro-gay presidential candidate Obama—despite the urging of many of their bishops and parish priests not to support any candidate who holds these views. Nevertheless, 52 percent of white Catholics supported McCain and 47 percent supported Obama—both of whom are Protestant—in the 2008 elections—against 56 percent of white Catholics who supported Protestant George W. Bush and 43 percent who supported Catholic John Kerry in the 2004 elections.[8]

Candidate views on abortion were of paramount significance for only 29 percent of Catholics, according to a Zogby International poll conducted just before the 2008 elections. While 44 percent of Catholics polled said a "good Catholic" could not endorse a candidate who supported abortion rights, 53 percent said they could. The United States Conference of Catholic Bishops had issued a report in 2007 entitled "Forming Consciences for Faithful Citizenship," which "encouraged Catholics to consider a range of the church's social justice teachings when voting."[9] The report angered many conservative Catholics who believe Catholics are obligated to reject candidates who support gay marriage and abortion rights.

The last frontier in the gay civil rights movement, as we detailed in Chapter 6, is the recognition of full legal marriage and family rights for gays. The news from the 2008 election cycle was not particularly good. A majority of states restrict marriage to heterosexual couples, and California, Arizona, and Florida joined that list in the 2008 elections. However, gay marriage was legalized after the election in Iowa, New Hampshire, Vermont, and Maine.

POLITICAL THEOLOGY AND THE CHRISTIAN RIGHT

Religious fundamentalists of all faith traditions who try to force everyone to live by their "rules" are speaking what Columbia University humanities professor Mark Lilla calls the language of political theology, which many assumed had been in decline since the Enlightenment and the spread of modern secular democracy. Nevertheless, "countless millions still pursue the age-old quest to bring the whole of human life under God's authority," as Lilla puts it:

> The revival of political theology in the modern West is a humbling story. It reminds us that this way of thinking is not the preserve of any one culture or religion, nor does it belong solely to the past. It is an age-old habit of mind that can be reacquired by anyone who begins looking to the divine nexus of God, man and world to reveal the legitimate political order.[10]

Lilla says the U.S. Constitution is one of the few barriers to religious extremism in the United States:

> Our political rhetoric, which owes much to the Protestant sectarians of the 17th century, vibrates with messianic energy, and it is only thanks to a strong constitutional structure and various lucky breaks that political theology has never seriously challenged the basic legitimacy of our institutions. Americans have potentially explosive religious differences over abortion, prayer in schools, censorship, euthanasia, biological research and countless other issues, yet they generally settle them within the bounds of the Constitution. It's a miracle.[11]

Activists used U.S. Supreme Court decisions in *Roe v. Wade* (1973), *Engel v. Vitale* (1962), and *Epperson v. Arkansas* (1968) to help mobilize Christians to support candidates and potential civil appointees who would use their positions to reverse social policies they viewed as inconsistent with biblical teaching.[12] As we noted in Chapter 4, they have attempted to bend American civil religion so that it will encompass limitations on civil liberties and enforce conservative religious stands on issues such as gay marriage, prayer in the public schools, and birth control. And they have challenged U.S. Supreme Court decisions that thwart their goals.

George W. Bush and Christian Conservatives

George W. Bush assumed office at what may have been the peak of conservative religious activism and electoral power. He was one of many Republicans elected to public office, in part, on the strength of promises to redress Christian conservative social grievances and to implement their political-religion agenda. But Bush was different from many GOP politicians who cynically pandered to religious conservatives during election campaigns and ignored them when in office. Bush named Jesus Christ as his favorite philosopher because, he said, "When you turn your heart and your life over to Christ, when you accept Christ as the Savior, it changes your heart. It changes your life. And that's what happened to me."[13]

Bush appointed individuals who shared his views and imposed Christian conservative values as widely as possible. One of many manifestations of this effort was the president's use of religious symbolism to generate support for the invasion of Iraq—which he saw as a chance to rid the world of evildoers. The president and a legion of Christian conservative war advocates did everything they could to stifle dissent—an effort that manifested itself later even in the war zone.[14] Roughly 77 percent of evangelical Protestants and 62 percent of Catholics and mainline Protestants backed the invasion and many worked hard to generate support for the war.[15]

Women's Reproductive Rights

Many Christian conservative activists have long sought to limit a woman's right to practice birth control and to make her own decisions about having children. George W. Bush was sympathetic to conservative religious views about women's reproductive rights, and he sought to create public policy that would limit those rights. As we noted in Chapter 5, this position is linked inextricably to an ideal monogamous, heterosexual marriage and family model that came into vogue only in the nineteenth century. The model favored middle- and upper-strata white males—the power brokers in American society at the time—who were supported and indeed reinforced by many of their white female counterparts. Members of this group had access to contraceptives and abortion services that were denied to the disadvantaged and minority groups.

The gender wars waged by Christian conservatives against women's reproductive rights often conflated birth control measures with abortion measures—as in the case of attempts by the Bush administration to stop over-the-counter sales of the Plan B contraceptive, because it might promote sexual promiscuity or because it might prevent a fertilized egg from attaching to the womb. Still unresolved is the controversy over the RU-486 abortion drug. Still others were the attempts to fund faith-based, anti-birth control and anti-abortion clinics, and abstinence-only sex education courses in the schools. The administration also sought to limit fetal stem cell research into birth defects and refused to fund any birth control program sponsored by the United Nations or other international agency. "With the exception of the Vatican," as Cristina Page, a NARAL Pro-Choice America reproductive rights activist, notes, "[E]very single international campaign against contraception is based in the United States .... It is our pro-lifers who are leading the movement."[16] President Barack Obama lifted the ban shortly after taking office.

The most aggressive exploitation of the heterosexual, male-female gender model, other than gay marriage and family rights, however, has been in the wars Christian conservatives have waged in the past 35 years or so to overturn *Roe v. Wade*, to prohibit all abortions, and to define "viability" at conception. The point at which viability is achieved is crucial for conservative Christians, many of whom understand that—if they cannot have *Roe v. Wade* reversed—they must urge the courts to define viability as early as possible. Some Christian conservatives, relying on reproductive technologies when it is in their interest to do so, define that moment of viability, and therefore personhood, as the moment of fertilization—whether that occurs within the uterus or in the laboratory.

These activists are relying on male-dominated, anti-abortion courts to decide the future of abortion in their favor. It is significant that the present U.S. Supreme Court consists of eight men and one woman. As sociologist Susan Markens, a specialist on the issue of motherhood, puts it, the courts have framed reproduction politics as a genetic issue that applies "a distinctively male standard of parenthood ... to both men and women."[17]

Perpetuating an Unhealthy Climate

Religious conservatives have helped create a climate in which it is difficult even to discuss abortion rights, and which seems to encourage some extremists to use any tactic, even violence, to stop abortions. Attacks against abortion clinics "are excellent examples of perceiving a social or medical situation as something that is deified, as if God himself is right there. It obscures the division between the world of God and the world of man, as if we are living in a Biblical mandate with immediate divine judgment on whatever occurs," according to Mark Juergensmeyer, author of *Terror in the Mind of God* (2000). "They infuse worldly struggles with divine meaning and significance."[18]

Terrorists identifying themselves as Christians, for example, attacked numerous clinics and employees who supplied abortion and contraception services between 1991 and 2001. Eight people were killed and 33 were wounded during this decade, which also recorded "20 cases of arson and attempted arson, 10 bombings and attempted bombings, and multiple threats of anthrax or chemical attacks on clinics in 23 states."[19] Cristina Page says the number of doctors willing to perform abortions was reduced by 37 percent (to 1,800 doctors) between 1982 and 2000.[20]

The violence continued in George W. Bush's administration. The National Abortion Federation, to take another example, recorded six cases of bombing, arson, or attempted bombing and arson of abortion clinics between 2002 and 2004. In addition, thousands of cases were recorded of home invasions, assault and battery, trespassing, burglary, death threats, harassing telephone calls, hate mail, and picketing and blockading of individuals and institutions offering birth control and abortion services.[21]

The fanaticism in this chilling scenario is illustrated in a letter written by Clayton Lee Waagner, a self-proclaimed Christian, who is on the Federal Bureau of Investigation's Ten Most Wanted list: "So the abortionist doesn't get the wrong idea, I don't plan on talking them to death. I'm going to kill as many of them as I can. I will use every talent I have and draw on every resource I can get my hands on. I consider this a war and in war there are few rules." Since doctors are well protected, Waagner said, he was prepared to kill anyone. "It doesn't matter to me if you're a nurse, receptionist, bookkeeper, or janitor, if you work for the murderous abortionist I'm going to kill you."[22]

Intelligent Design and Darwinian Evolution

Christian conservative attempts to impose the values of biblical inerrancy on science parallel attempts to derogate women's reproductive rights and gay marriage and family rights today. As we have emphasized, none of these claims is anchored in the biblical record. And as Kevin Phillips puts it, "No leading world power in modern memory has become a captive of the sort of biblical inerrancy that dismisses modern knowledge and science."[23]

An entire industry fueled largely by Protestant evangelical fundamentalists has sprung up to push the idea that creationism-cum-intelligent design should be taken seriously—that is, discussed in what they describe as scholarly journals and books, taught in public schools, and given a popular forum (such as museums and national parks) to disseminate their views. As we described in Chapter 7, they reject scientific evolution and trivialize global warming and the need to control the growth of the global population.

Charles Darwin's birthday, ironically enough, falls on the same day as Abraham Lincoln's birthday, but Darwin (1809–1882) is more reviled than revered in many conservative religious circles today. The continued controversy over the right to teach intelligent design alongside evolution in school biology courses "reveals a lot," Charles McGrath says in a *New York Times* education essay, "about the great American tradition of anti-intellectualism, which seems to be getting stronger, not weaker, even as the country supposedly becomes better educated . . . ." The United States ranks number 33 just above Turkey at the bottom of 34 countries polled "in our acceptance of evolution and its principles." Indeed, Peter Bowler, a historian of biology, notes that "extreme biblical literalism . . . may be more widespread now [in America] than even in 1859"—the original publication date of Darwin's *The Origin of Species*. The advocates of intelligent design "see themselves in a life-and-death struggle . . . [and] the gap between religious fundamentalists and those who want to preserve the principle of free scientific inquiry may be unbridgeable."[24]

Media Paint a Misleading Picture

We have attempted in this book to challenge the widespread assumption that Christian evangelical fundamentalists, in the past and at present, represent the whole of the Christian community. This assumption is affirmed almost daily by the images of Christianity that are constructed and disseminated by the mainstream news media. Given the diversity of that community, no single person or group can speak for it. "Most of the press ignores this diversity," Gal Beckerman of the *Columbia Journalism Review* argues, "and instead caricatures a movement that encompasses millions of Americans (including Jimmy Carter, one of our most liberal presidents) as politically conservative outsiders who think modern culture is evil and believe in the Bible literally."[25]

Such writers give conservative activists who speak primarily for themselves an authority that is out of proportion to their real influence. The commercial media took seriously the threats of a few Christian conservatives to boycott the 2008 presidential election if John McCain won the Republican nomination. Many journalists also take seriously the anti-science religionists who demand that intelligent design be taught in biology classes, attack scientific evolution, argue that the earth is less than 10,000 years old, and demand that government health programs teach sex-abstinence only. This deference to the bizarre assigns credibility to baseless arguments, empowers those who make them, and subjects the entire Christian community to ridicule.

The mainstream news media tend to thrive on conflict, to frame every story and every event as a conflict between, at best, good and evil, or between good and not-so-good. In religion coverage, as we noted in Chapter 2, even the larger denominations can get space or airtime only when there is some scandal, spectacle, or odd occurrence to attract an audience. Relatively trivial events command huge amounts of space and airtime, as when Victoria Osteen, co-pastor of the conservative Lakewood Church in Houston, allegedly assaulted an airline flight attendant in 2008. The media frenzy stopped only when a jury found Osteen not guilty.

Theocracy and Religion: The Critics

Many critics frequently use the media image of American Christianity as the foundation for their criticisms of all of Christianity. We cannot even scratch the surface of this literature, but we have touched on some books and articles in previous chapters and we cite a few more examples here to indicate its enduring nature.

The "degeneration of the United States into a theocracy," as Ronnie Dugger, founding editor of *The Texas Observer* put it, gained momentum as "pressures to subordinate democratic pluralism to fundamentalist domination have converged into the presidency of George W. Bush." If this trend continues, Dugger said, "we might as well resign ourselves to the transformation of the White House into a fortified cathedral." Dugger called for "one ferocious fight for our freedoms of and from religion."[26]

Kevin Phillips also blames the Republican administration for fostering a theocratic climate and cites Bush's belief that he is a spokesperson "for the Almighty," the GOP's belief that it "represents religious true believers," the party faithful who believe "government should be guided by religion and, on top of it all, a White House that adopts agendas seemingly animated by biblical worldviews."[27]

Phillips echoes other voices, alarmed by Protestant evangelical fundamentalists who have an Armageddon agenda in mind when they welcome turmoil in the Middle East because it "actually heralds the second coming of Jesus Christ." The Bush administration's attitude on a host of issues—from Darwinian science and the climate to curbing world population growth and women's birth control and abortion rights—offers more evidence of the dangers awaiting an America that embraces this conservative religious agenda.[28]

Some argue that religion is just "dangerous." Sam Harris in his latest book, *Letter to a Christian Nation* (2006), is not particularly worried about a coming theocracy, but he argues just as forcefully that Christians demanding that scripture must be accepted as literally true and applied to everyday life have a negative impact on "civilization." These convictions make the United States appear to be "like a lumbering, bellicose, dim-witted giant. Anyone who cares about the fate of civilization would do well to recognize that the combination of great power and great stupidity is simply terrifying, even to one's friends." Nothing stands in the way of intellectual honesty and critical thinking in public discourse about issues such as "ethics, spiritual experience, and the inevitability of human suffering" as "the respect we accord religious faith." This is true, he says, because "many who claim to be transformed by Christ's love are deeply, even murderously, intolerant of criticism" and of nonbelievers.[29]

Richard Dawkins, the Oxford University scientist, echoes anti-God critics such as Harris and Christopher Hitchens[30] in arguing that children are brainwashed by religious teaching to view the world through a narrow lens and that even moderation fosters fanaticism. Children grow up and are motivated "by what they perceive to be righteousness, faithfully pursuing what their religion tells them .... They perceive their acts to be good . . . because they have been brought up, from the cradle, to have total and unquestioning *faith*" (italics in the original). But faith is evil, as Dawkins sees it, because it demands no proof and tolerates no criticism. Children who are "taught the superior virtue of faith without question" and who believe that duty to God is paramount are potential recruits for militant religious crusaders and jihadists. "And they were taught *that* lesson not necessarily by extremist fanatics but by decent, gentle, mainstream religious instructors" (italics in the original).[31]

Media scholar Clifford G. Christians, who explores the potential role of religion as a home for the study of ethics, argues that "the Judeo-Christian tradition in principle provides a notable ethics for responsible action in the United States," but its value has been diminished by the rise of conservative Protestantism in American politics. "The rise of fundamentalism makes a serious pursuit of the spiritual dimension impossible. While responsibility is demanded in its strident fundamentalist rhetoric and politics, it has not included responsibility for social welfare, the lower classes, and the public good."[32] Conservative Protestantism has undermined the authority of American religion in the international arena, Christians argues. "In a world where the fault lines increasingly follow the most basic questions humans face, deep concern for a particular religion, such as Christianity, will be typically seen as fanaticism and resented as contrary to global understanding."[33]

AMBIGUITIES OF A CHRISTIAN VOICE IN POLITICS

The rise of Protestant evangelical fundamentalism as a religious force in America's Christian culture over the past century and the emergence of a Christian conservative coalition as a political force in American politics in the past 40 years or so is without precedent in modern American history. George W. Bush's claim that his life was changed when he accepted Christ as his Savior reveals one example of what can happen when a powerful Christian conservative sets out to alter the course of America's political culture.

Nevertheless, this is not the only possibility. As we noted in the Introduction, most Christians in the United States do not adhere to the president's Christian stance, and it does not reflect the interests and concerns of a citizenry that can truthfully be said to contain numerous Christianities, numerous other faiths, and increasingly people of no faith.

Christians Divided over Religion in Politics

The Iraq war, for example, was unquestionably the most divisive policy initiative during Bush's second term, at least until the recession of 2008. While the administration received support from much of the Christian community prior to launching the invasion, there was also opposition before this war from those Christians who argued the United States was not a country that launched preventive wars—wars designed to eliminate a threat that *might* arise at some future time.

Some Christians argued, as we have noted in Chapters 8 and 9, even before the invasion of Afghanistan that a military response against a sovereign state and noncombatant civilians would not be just. This chorus of Christian voices became much louder in the prelude to the invasion of Iraq. As Marie Dennis, director of the Maryknoll Office for Global Concerns, put it,

> Waging war "with deep regret," for example, about what it does to people's lives is not acceptable. Given the reality of modern weapons and war fighting, if we want to protect civilians we cannot go to war in the first place. Ninety percent of the casualties in modern wars are civilians. At the same time, in the light of the gospel and the most fundamental precepts of the Christian faith, we have to think again about our differentiation between non-combatants and combatants. Every life is precious in the eyes of God—every life.[34]

Rather than choosing to be a global cop and "intimidating others by our military might and imposing a global economy that unrelentingly benefits the already well-off minority," Dennis argues, the United States should fight terrorism by establishing "good relations with all countries, including those struggling to overcome poverty and violence."[35]

The major cultural issues that seemed to unite Christian conservatives at the beginning of the twenty-first century (especially abortion, fetal stem cell research, and gay marriage) had moved down the salience scale by 2008. Many members of all faith groups had become uncomfortable with the venom of the attacks against gays and lesbians (even as others pressed for amendments to state constitutions barring gay marriage), and with the prohibition against using fetal stem cells in medical research. Bush lowered the volume—without changing his policies or enthusiasm for pursuing them—when, near the end of his presidency, he stopped talking so publicly about inflammatory issues and tried instead to reach out to larger communities to engender support for his final initiatives as president.[36]

The Christian community, however, remains divided over the proper role of religion in public affairs. Sociologist José Casanova, for example, argues it is unreasonable to expect religious leaders "to restrict themselves to the pastoral care of individual souls . . . . [R]eligious traditions throughout the world are refusing to accept the marginal and privatized role which theories of modernity as well as theories of secularization had reserved for them." Social movements that have arisen "are religious in nature or are challenging in the name of religion the legitimacy and autonomy of the primary secular spheres, the state and the market economy." Religions, Casanova argues, are likely to continue playing key roles in shaping the modern world.[37]

Other observers argue that Christian conservatives in America went too far when they used elective offices to impose religious values on others or tried to intimidate office holders to impose religious values. Religious leaders are not particularly effective campaign consultants or policy makers, as Frances Kissling, president of Catholics for a Free Choice (now Catholics for Choice), puts it. "They stand at the margins of power, with the powerless, seeking to change the *status quo*. Dorothy Day, Martin Luther King Jr., William Sloane Coffin and the Berrigan brothers did not have a seat at the table and did not want it."[38]

Religious leaders may lose credibility— especially the power to challenge policy and politicians—when they are part of the system. Philosopher of ethics Jean Bethke Elshtain notes, "One important task of religion is . . . to raise questions when politics overreach. You cannot do that very effectively if you are simply absorbed within the forms of politics and lose a robust 'separateness.' "[39]

Toward a Christian Stance in American Politics

Perhaps the most arresting metaphor in the faith traditions that embrace both Judaism and Christianity stems from the language used at the beginning of the book of Genesis: All human beings are constructed from the dust of the earth and in the image of God, the Creator. As the *Jewish Study Bible* guide expresses it, "In this understanding, the human being is not an amalgam of perishable body and immortal soul, but a psychophysical unity who depends on God for life itself."[40] To be human, then, is to live a mortal life dependent on God.

The people of The Way (Acts 9:2; 19:9, 23; 24:22; see Mark 10:52)—the name given to those followers of Jesus in Jewish Palestine before they were called Christians—understood that the Jesus Way would be a lifelong struggle to be wholly human, in the image of God, and they also understood that it was available to all humanity. Each person is at liberty or not to seek his or her own spiritual awareness, but as religion scholar Walter Wink reminds us, "Our picture of Jesus reflects not only Jesus, but the person portraying Jesus."[41] It will always be a reflection of who we are as social beings anchored in the values and norms of our own culture.

This is not an orthodox view of Christianity. Instead of saying the Christian must believe that God incarnated Jesus—God became a man—this Christian stance is saying that Jesus's life was spent in seeking to incarnate God in his life. If one argues for Christianity from below, as it were, rather than from above, the entire, evolving human experience becomes the narrative of life in God's image. Through Jesus's humanity, believers can glimpse the divine and therefore what it means to be fully human. The creator transcends Christianity, but for Christians the Jesus Way is the gift of Christianity to the world. It was and is not meant for Christians alone.

We agree with Alan Wolfe, director of Boston College's Boisi Center for Religion and American Public Life, who argues that—as the United States reflects on the diversity and volatility of religious beliefs in the rest of the world—"it will become increasingly difficult for leaders to rally around the flag by rallying around the faith. That may make some Americans, especially those who believe we once were, and should always be, a Christian country, unhappy. But it ought to make those who take pride in its diversity and tradition of religious freedom proud."[42]

This Christian stance validates "spiritual vitality and intellectual integrity" without proclaiming its "superiority," as religion scholar Hal Taussig puts it, and embraces all those who live outside the heterosexual model of marriage and family life. This Christian stance is especially sensitive to racial and ethnic, economic, gender, age, class, and ecological injustice both in America and elsewhere in the world. It takes seriously the need to be proactive in seeking "systemic and structural justice," along with traditional Christian values such as "charity," by developing new programs that address the environmental concerns that threaten our planet.

This Christian stance demands that every effort be made to find peaceful, nonviolent solutions to resolving disputes—refining *and* adhering to a set of just-war principles for the postmodern era: war must *really* be the last resort. Above all, this Christian stance does not abuse its position in America or in the world by imposing its values and norms on any believer or nonbeliever—inside or outside the Christian community. For the Christian community, moreover, it counters "sectarian arrogance" by offering a more tolerant and authentic alternative—an open-ended "spiritual home" to those who would seek one in America today.[43]

NOTES

1. Alan Wolfe, "Mobilizing the Religious Left," *New York Times*, October 21, 2007, Book Review-23. Wolfe in this essay recognizes that Rauschenbusch had numerous religious prejudices and was "too unwary of the dangers of blending religion and politics," but he challenged the assumption by social Darwinians of the day that inequality was inevitable. And unlike some contemporary Christian social reformers, the notion of social justice espoused by Rauschenbusch and his colleagues was anchored in a serious reading of the Bible.

2. Jim Wallis, *God's Politics: Why the Right Gets It Wrong and the Left Doesn't Get It* (New York: HarperCollins, 2005), 4. Wallis is founder/editor of *Sojourners* (1971), a popular magazine that focuses on religion, politics, and culture. He established Sojourners as a nonprofit organization, and he is also the convener of Call to Renewal, a national network of churches, faith-based groups, and individuals "working to overcome poverty in America." For a more academic perspective on God and religious pluralism in American culture, see Barbara A. McGraw and Jo Renee Formicola, eds., *Take Religious Pluralism Seriously: Spiritual Politics on America's Sacred Ground* (Waco, TX: Baylor University Press, 2006).

3. *Roe v. Wade*, 410 U.S. 113 (1973). Many bishops chose to stress life issues over social issues. One exception was Cardinal Joseph Bernardin (1928–1996) of Chicago, who opened dialogue with politicians and religious leaders from across the ideological spectrum and spoke about nuclear proliferation, economic policies, and a variety of social issues. See David O'Brien, "Public Catholicism: The Church, Judge Roberts & the Common Good," *Commonweal*, September 23, 2005, 6–7.

4. John C. Green, "Religion and the Presidential Vote: A Tale of Two Gaps," Pew Forum on Religion & Public Life, Pew Research Center, Washington, DC, August 21, 2007, http://pewresearch.org/pubs/573/religion-presidential-vote.

5. Pew Forum on Religion & Public Life, "How the Faithful Voted," Pew Research Center, Washington, DC, November 10, 2008, http://pewforum.org/docs/?DocID=367.

6. "Poll: Bush Ratings Hit New Low: Americans More Pessimistic about Economy, Country's Direction, Iraq," *CBS News*, October 6, 2005, www.cbsnews.com/stiories/2005/10.06/opinion/polls/main924487.shtml. See Frank James, "Bush's 69% Disapproval a Gallup Record," *The Swamp*, *baltimoresun.com*, April 22, 2008, http://weblogs.baltimoresun.com/news/politics/blog/2008/04/bushs_69_disapproval_a_gallup.html.

7. Michael Luo, "Catholics Turned to the Democrat," The Caucus, *New York Times*, November 5, 2008, http://thecaucus.blogs.nytimes.com/2008/11/05/catholics-turned-to-the-democrat. Those who attend services more than once a week constituted 12 percent of the voters in 2008, and those who attend weekly constituted 27 percent in 2008. Those who never attend constituted 16 percent of the electorate.

8. Pew Forum, "How the Faithful Voted."

9. Barbara Karkabi, "Abortion Not Main Issue for Catholics," *Houston Chronicle*, November 1, 2008, F1–F2. Le Moyne College/Zogby has been polling Catholic voters on their spiritual beliefs and religious practices since 2001. This poll, which was conducted October 17–20, 2008, consisted of a telephone survey of 1,000 Catholics. The margin of error was plus or minus 3.2 percentage points. See "Catholic Voters: 'Abortion Not the Only Issue,'" Le Moyne College, October 2008, www.lemoyne.edu/CENTERSOFEXCELLENCE/CATHOLICTRENDS/LATESTPOLL/tabid/548/Default.aspx.

10. Mark Lilla, "The Politics of God," *New York Times Magazine* (August 19, 2007): 28–35, 50, 54, 55, p. 50. See also Lilla, *The Stillborn God: Religion, Politics, and the Modern West* (New York: Knopf, 2007). For a different perspective about public theology, see John J. O'Brien, *George G. Higgins and the Quest for Worker Justice: The Evolution of Catholic Social Thought in America* (Lanham, MD: Rowman & Littlefield, 2005), Chapter 1.

11. Ibid.

12. The U.S. Supreme Court legalized abortion in *Roe v. Wade* (1973); outlawed prayer in public schools in *Engel v. Vitale*, 370 U.S. 421 (1962); and prohibited states from outlawing the teaching of scientific evolution in *Epperson v. Arkansas*, 393 U.S. 97 (1968).

13. Stephen Goode, "Bush Brings Faith into Full View: A New Book Traces the Evolution of George W. Bush's Faith and Illuminates the Role That Religion Plays in the President's Life, Both as a Politician and a Private Person," *Insight*, May 11–24, 2004, 33–34, p. 33. The book is David Aikman's *A Man of Faith: The Spiritual Journal of George W. Bush*.

14. Major Freddy J. Welborn, for example, shut down a meeting of free thinkers and atheists in July 2007 at Camp Speicher in Iraq and allegedly threatened those who attended. Specialist Jeremy Hall, with the help of the Military Religious Freedom Foundation, filed suit in federal court, charging his First Amendment rights had been violated. He did not finish his tour in Iraq because of threats he received from other soldiers. Hall charged in a

sworn statement that Welborn said, "People like you are not holding up the Constitution and are going against what the founding fathers, who were Christians, wanted for America!" Welborn threatened to bring charges against Hall and others like him and to prevent their reenlistment. See Neela Banerjee, "Soldier Sues Army, Saying His Atheism Led to Threats," *New York Times*, April 26, 2008, A14.

15. Pew Research Center for the People & the Press, "Different Faiths, Different Messages: Americans Hearing about Iraq from the Pulpit, But Religious Faith not Defining Opinions," Pew Research Center, Washington, DC, March 19, 2003, http://people-press.org/report/176/different-faiths -different-messages.

16. Cristina Page, *How the Pro-Choice Movement Saved America: Freedom, Politics, and the War on Sex* (New York: Basic Books, 2006), 123.

17. Susan Markens, *Surrogate Motherhood and the Politics of Reproduction* (Berkeley: University of California Press, 2007), 175.

18. Cited by Adrian Humphreys, "Radical Believers: Experts not Surprised Religious Zealotry Can Lead to Shocking Violence," *National Post* (Toronto), December 27, 2007, A1.

19. Robin Morgan, "Evangelical Violence," Letter to the Editor, *New York Times*, January 21, 2007, Book Review-5. Morgan is the author of *Fighting Words: A Toolkit for Combating the Religious Right* (New York: Nation, 2006).

20. Page, *How the Pro-Choice Movement*, 147.

21. The precise figures are detailed in *ReligiousTolerance.org*, Ontario Consultants on Religious Tolerance, "Violence & Harassment at U.S. Abortion Clinics," news release, undated, www.religioustolerance.org/abo_viol.htm. See also Indiana University, "New Study Reports on Attacks against Abortion Clinics in the United States," news release, September 28, 2006, http:// newsinfo.iu.edu/news/page/normal/3781.html. One person was executed in 2003 for murdering a Florida physician, who performed abortions, along with his driver.

22. "Clayton Waagner's Message to the United States," Part 1, Army of God, June 18, 2001, www.armyofgod.com/Claytonsmessage.html. Waagner said this letter was posted "with my name on it." He did not disclaim it.

23. Kevin Phillips, "GOP Doesn't Mean 'God's Own Party': Bush Administration's Pursuit of Religion-Driven Policies and Courting of an End-Times Electorate Are Cause for Alarm," *Houston Chronicle*, April 23, 2006, E1, E4, p. E4. See also Kevin Phillips, *American Theocracy: The Perils and Politics of Radical Religion, Oil, and Borrowed Money in the 21st Century* (New York: Viking, 2006).

24. Charles McGrath, "Four Stakes in the Heart of Intelligent Design," *New York Times*, January 4, 2009, Education/Life-34, 35. McGrath cites Peter J. Bowler's *Monkey Trials and Gorilla Sermons: Evolution and Christianity from Darwin to Intelligent Design* (Cambridge, MA: Harvard University Press,

2007). "Only in the 1950s," according to Bowler, "did strict biblical literalism become the foundation for mainstream creationism" (35).

25. Gal Beckerman, "Across the Great Divide FAITH: Why Don't Journalists Get Religion? A Tenuous Bridge to Believers," *Columbia Journalism Review*, May/June 2004, 26–30, p. 30.

26. Ronnie Dugger, "It's Time for an American Offensive against Theocracy," *Free Inquiry* 24, no. 3 (2004), 16–17.

27. Phillips, "GOP Doesn't Mean 'God's Own Party,' " E1.

28. Ibid., E4. Phillips notes that the last time a world power became a captive of biblical inerrancy was in the seventeenth century, when Pope Urban, "with the agreement of inquisitional Spain," disciplined Galileo.

29. Sam Harris, *Letter to a Christian Nation* (New York: Knopf, 2006), vii, xi, 87.

30. Christopher Hitchens, *God Is Not Great: How Religion Poisons Everything* (New York: Twelve, 2007).

31. Richard Dawkins, *The God Delusion* (Boston: Houghton Mifflin, 2006), 304, 308.

32. Clifford G. Christians, "Media Ethics in Education,"*Journalism & Communication Monographs* 9, no. 4 (2008), 180–221, pp. 193, 200, 201. Christians says, "Western philosophy is incoherent without religion," but a Christian ethical stance must embrace the ethics of "the great religions" such as Judaism, Islam, Buddhism, Hinduism, and what he calls "indigenous spiritism" if Christianity is to be relevant in today's world (199).

33. Ibid., 201.

34. Marie Dennis, "Terrorism and Catholic Theology," *Peace Review* 15, no. 3 (2003): 323–329, p. 325.

35. Ibid., 327.

36. Julie Mason, a *Houston Chronicle* political writer, quoted Mark Rozell, a specialist on the presidency and religion, as saying, "He [Bush] is at a different stage in his presidency. I don't think there is much he can do politically to grow support among evangelicals, for example." Julie Mason, "Bush's Rhetoric on Faith Has Dropped a Notch," *Houston Chronicle*, December 7, 2007, A22.

37. José Casanova, *Public Religions in the Modern World* (Chicago: University of Chicago Press, 1994), 5.

38. Frances Kissling, "Looking for Salvation in All the Wrong Places, *The Nation*, April 24, 2006, 17.

39. Jean Bethke Elshtain, "God Talk and American Political Life," in "Religion and Culture: Views of 10 Scholars," *The Chronicle of Higher Education*, October 22, 2004, B7–B13, p. 13.

40. The Jewish commentary here is a reflection on Genesis 2:7, one of several passages that explore the meaning of humanity being created in God's image. See also Genesis 1:26–28, which points to human beings as stewards over all of nature—with the proviso that this stewardship is "strictly

accountable to its true Owner." Adele Berlin and Marc Zvi Brettler, eds., and Michael Fishbane, cons. ed., *The Jewish Study Bible* (Oxford, UK: Oxford University Press, 2004), 14–15.

41. Walter Wink, *The Human Being: Jesus and the Enigma of the Son of the Man* (Minneapolis, MN: Fortress, 2002), 11.

42. Alan Wolfe, "Faith and Tolerance," *Boston Globe*, February 29, 2008, A15.

43. Hal Taussig is one of many Christians working with people of all faith traditions in the trenches, as it were, in developing a new paradigm for Christians engaged in politics and society in America. See Taussig, *A New Spiritual Home: Progressive Christianity at the Grass Roots* (Santa Rosa, CA: Polebridge, 2006).

Index

Abbott, Jennifer Young, 242
ABC (American Broadcasting
  Company), 98, 113, 130
Abolition, 40, 197
Abortion, 252–62; anti-abortion extremists, 258, 453; attitude changes over
  time, 21; Born-Alive Infants Protection Act (2002), 261; Bush
  administration on, 260–62; California
  Supreme Court cases, 273 n.60; Child
  Interstate Abortion Notification Act
  (2005), 277 n.95; Comstock Act, 247–
  49; deaths caused by, 274 n.69; delayed
  ensoulment, 246; donations to support
  debates, 245; employees' right *not* to
  perform services, 263; Hyde Amendment (1976), 255; international family
  planning agencies, 255, 263, 266, 452;
  Jews and Judaism on, 21; late-term,
  260–61, 265; media framing of debate,
  244, 257–60; minority and disadvantaged communities, 259, 263; 1960s,
  52; overview of debate, 443, 451–53;
  partial-birth abortions, 260–62; Pew
  Forum surveys on, 18, 19t–20t, 21;
  pioneers in rights, 272 n.47; Plan B
  debate, 250–51, 265, 452; post-*Roe*
  scenario, 263; in premodern cultures,
  245–46; public funding for, 254–55;
  rates, 259, 262, 274 n.65; religious

communities' role in abortion wars,
  177 n.13, 245, 255–57; rhetoric, 244–
  45, 258, 261; RU-486, 273 n.57, 452;
  The Silent Scream (film), 257; 2008
  candidates' views, 449; Unborn Child
  Pain Awareness Act (2007), 262;
  Unborn Victims of Violence Act
  (2004), 261; UN support for abortion
  services, 319 n.66; viability, defining,
  244, 252, 254, 260, 262, 265, 452. *See
  also* Reproductive rights; *Roe v. Wade*
Abramoff, Jack, 65, 82 n.51
Abu Nidal, 418
Accommodationists, 204–5
ACLU (American Civil Liberties
  Union), 226 n.135, 261, 306, 335,
  339–40
ACT UP (AIDS Coalition to Unleash
  Power), 300
Adam, Barry, 291
Adam (Genesis), 232, 357 n.35
Adams, John, ix
Addams, Jane, 40
ADL (Anti-Defamation League), 70
Adoption, 297, 302, 308
Adorno, T. W., 154
Advertising, 102
The Advocate (magazine), 281, 313 n.19
Afghanistan War, 374–75; civilian
  deaths, 391; conditions favorable to

About the Authors

MICHAEL RYAN, a professor of communication in the Jack J. Valenti School of Communication at the University of Houston (UH), has taught journalism writing and editing, communication theory and research methods, and ethics at UH, West Virginia University, and Temple University. Ryan has co-authored two previous books and published more than 100 scholarly and professional articles, monographs, and book chapters. His work has appeared in *Journalism & Mass Communication Quarterly*, *Gazette*, *Critical Studies on Terrorism*, *Journal of Communication*, and *Public Relations Review*, among others. He worked as a news reporter for the *San Angelo (TX) Standard-Times* and for the Long News Service, an Austin news service that served Texas newspapers and radio stations.

LES SWITZER is a professor emeritus in communication and history at the University of Houston. He was a journalist for about nine years in the United States and South Africa, and he has about 33 years of experience in teaching, research, and administration at university level in the United States, and in Europe and South Africa. He has produced seven books and monographs, an edited conference proceeding, and about 30 book chapters, articles, and essays on a range of topics in journalism and media studies, development studies, cultural studies, South African studies, and religious studies. Reviews of his books have appeared in academic journals representing numerous disciplines, including history, politics, sociology, communication, and African

Studies, and two books were the subjects of review essays in *The Times Literary Supplement* and *The Times Higher Education Supplement*. He has received about 35 individual grants and awards from South Africa, the United Kingdom, and the United States for research activities, and he was given a Distinguished Faculty Recognition Award from the Houston City Council in 1993. He embarked on a third career after completing an M. Div. degree in 2004 and a year as a resident chaplain-in-training at a hospital in Houston. Switzer is currently working as a hospice chaplain.